The World Today Series®

Stryker-Post Publications, Harpers Ferry, WV, USA

The Middle East and South Asia

Malcolm B. Russell

2010

44th edition
Next Edition: August 2011

Malcolm B. Russell . . .

Vice President for Academic Affairs at Union College, Lincoln, Nebraska. Columbia Union College (B.A., History); School of Advanced International Studies, the Johns Hopkins University (M.A.; Ph.D.), with emphases in Middle East Studies and International Economics. A Fulbright Fellowship allowed him research opportunities in Egypt, Syria, Jordan and Lebanon, and resulted in *The First Modern Arab State: Syria under Faysal, 1918–1920* (Minneapolis, MN: Biblioteca Islamica, 1985), as well as papers at a number of professional societies. Born in Beirut, after a childhood spent there and in Egypt, he attended high school in India and later traveled widely in the Middle East. He speaks Arabic and French.

Adapted, rewritten and revised annually from a book entitled *The Middle East and South Asia 1967*, published in 1967 and succeeding years by

Stryker–Post Publications
P.O. Drawer 1200
Harpers Ferry, WV 25425
Telephones: 1–800–995–1400 (U.S.A. and Canada)
  Other: 1–304–535–2593
  Fax: 1–304–535–6513
  www.strykerpost.com
  VISA–MASTERCARD–AMERICAN EXPRESS

Photographs used to illustrate *The World Today Series* come from many sources, a great number from friends who travel worldwide. If you have taken any which you believe would enhance the visual impact and attractiveness of our books, do let us hear from you.

International Standard Book Number: 978-1-935264-13-2

International Standard Serial Number: 0084-2311

Library of Congress Catalog Number 67-11539

Cover design by nvision graphic design

Cartography by William L. Nelson

Typography by Barton Matheson Willse & Worthington

Printed in the United States of America by United Book Press, Inc.
Baltimore, MD 21207

The World Today Series has thousands of subscribers across the U.S. and Canada. A sample list of users who annually rely on this most up-to-date material includes:

Public library systems
Universities and colleges
High schools
Federal and state agencies
All branches of the armed forces & war colleges
National Geographic Society
National Democratic Institute
Agricultural Education Foundation
Exxon Corporation
Chevron Corporation
CNN

CONTENTS

Door to the Ka'aba, the sacred shrine of the Great Mosque in Mecca

The Middle East and South Asia Today

The slice of humanity captured by this volume is large, and passionate. Its peoples take their politics, ideologies, and religions with an intensity rarely matched elsewhere, exemplified in the past year by important and successful elections in India, Israel, and Lebanon, while evident manipulation of the voting results in Iran cracked the foundation of the Islamic Republic. Unfortunately for public understanding, scholars in Western countries, including the U.S., have often descended to deep bitterness when discussing important issues of the region, often losing the public's interest and understanding.

However, the Middle East and South Asia together form a most interesting and strategically important region. Beginning where the peaks and rainforests separate Southern from East Asia, it includes the Indian sixth of humanity, and Muslim countries such as Iran and Turkey that for centuries bordered Russia and blocked its access to warm-water ports. At least four straits in the region (the Bosporus, Tiran, Bab al-Mandab and Hormuz) play pivotal roles in world commerce. Threats over each of them and the Suez Canal have raised tensions or even precipitated wars in the last century. Underneath the waters of the Gulf (variously titled as Arab or Persian) and the surrounding sands lie roughly two-thirds of the world's oil deposits. Far beyond its size or wealth, the region bears strategic value and importance to trade routes. It was more than a coincidence that the term "Middle East" was popularized by a geostrategist, Alfred Mahan.

Readers bored with conflict or economics should find much else that is of interest. The three major monotheist religions developed in the west. In the east, India provided both the birthplace of the Buddha and the intricacies of Hinduism. Modern ideas and modern heroes exist as well, from the idealism of Israel's pioneers, to the founders of non-alignment in the Cold War, and beyond that to the hopes and pacifism of Mohandas Gandhi, who earned the epithet Mahatma, "the noble hearted." Aspirations of a tougher, more brutal sort also exist, whether the chauvinism of Jewish settlers seeking to evict Arabs from their ancestral homes, or Arabs and Iranians seized by religion or nationalism to kill innocents. An Islamic revival proclaims that material possessions do not suffice as the measure of value, allowing Westerners a glimpse of the spiritual fervor that motivated their ancestors.

The consistent goal of this series of books is an appreciation of the peoples and governments largely from their own perspectives but moderated by the viewpoints of the author. In the many conflicts, I hope to show the claims and charges of each side to help the general reader understand the reasons for attitudes and actions of people and governments. Doing this risks accusations of partiality, but I firmly hope that readers will share my respect for these peoples and lands, and an understanding of, if not always sympathy for, their states and political actions.

The region is also a study of contrasts. Despite recent discoveries of natural gas, for the foreseeable future, Bangladesh will rank as one of the most hopelessly and

perpetually poor nations, while parts of the United Arab Emirates stand at the top of world per capita income. Economic systems vary equally as income, with advocates of free trade and autarchy, free enterprise and state socialism. While sharp operators abound, the hospitality of most peoples represented here is famous. The geography stretches, very simply, from the highest (Mt. Everest) to the lowest (the Dead Sea), and from the wettest (Assam in northeastern India) to regions of Arabia so dry it has not rained for years. Aesthetically impoverished cities and flat, featureless farmland contrast dramatically with the desert beauty of *Wadi Rum* in Jordan and the water and greenery of the Bosporus or the Vale of Kashmir.

Sympathy, however, ought not excuse, even in Western societies that tolerate so much. The following pages draw attention to the plight of children, bonded into labor for the parents' debts, and to women who apparently disappear before census-takers arrive. Female circumcision—really several forms of genital mutilation—sometimes kills young girls in parts of Africa, including Egypt. Moreover, though crime rates in most countries of this volume are relatively low, the treatment of suspects and political rivals can descend from public humiliation to horrifying depths of brutality. Aside from the few democracies represented in this volume, most governments can expect, should they lose office, only the worst from their political opponents. Beyond individuals and ideologies, the rivalries of communities over relatively small parcels of land involve passions that Westerners, accustomed to moving from suburb to suburb, cannot fathom.

Technicalities: A few technical comments may help the serious reader. This volume bases its GDP and population data on the spring 2010 International Monetary Fund estimates, at both market exchange rates and purchasing power parity equivalent (PPP). Magnified by both U.S. inflation and the U.S. dollar's declining international value, the latter estimates sometimes shock—does the average Egyptian really enjoy an income equivalent to $6,400, or the average Qatari $95,000? Certainly not, but countries are commonly compared by Gross Domestic Product, not national income, and there is value in recognizing that the average Qatari probably enjoys an income over ten times higher than the average Egyptian's. For smaller countries, moreover, the figures are particularly imprecise when population projections vary significantly (in one case, by more than 100%).

Another issue requires a brief comment. English speakers transliterate Arabic words by a variety of systems, and multiple spellings are common. The Egyptian leader of the 1950s was Gamal Abdul Nasser to the press, but Jamal 'Abd al-Nasir to some scholars. In general, this volume retains the common English spellings for well-known personalities but adopts specialized spellings without diacritical markings elsewhere. Thus, the late King Hussein ruled Jordan; his great-grandfather was Sharif Husayn. Outside the Arab world, the national transliteration of Muslim names applies, the founder of Bangladesh being Mujibur Rahman, not Mujib al-Rahman.

M.B.R.
Lincoln, Nebraska
July 2010

WHEN WILL THE TAPS GO DRY?

Water, like bread, comes from God
Arab Proverb

From North Africa to western India, the lands of the Middle East and South Asia receive sparse rainfall, usually far less annually than the 16–20 inches essential for cultivation. With few cloudy days and the sun blazing directly overhead most of the year, hot temperatures quickly dry the landscape even when rain has fallen. Early human settlements clustered around rivers because water was always scarce. Now, the Middle East faces a worsening crisis as individual countries attempt to claim insufficient common resources. By contrast, in the Indian subcontinent seasonal floods take hundreds of lives annually and rivers inundate productive fields, carrying their valuable silt to the sea.

For thousands of years people living in the region adapted to desert and near-desert conditions. They farmed fertile lands beside rivers, some irrigating with water from mountains hundreds or even thousands of miles away, benefiting from seasonal floods that soaked the soil and deposited nourishing silt. Less moistened lands were used to graze livestock, particularly camels, goats and sheep.

Desert societies established water rights over the scarce flow of oasis wells and springs to irrigate crops and water livestock. For transport, travelers and nomads depend on the camel, with its legendary survival without water. Their days surrounded by barren desert, nomads dreamed of rivers and greenery, even seeing them in the form of occasional mirages. Both Judaism and Islam portrayed heaven as filled with trees and water.

The modern era brought sharp changes. The technology and energy of the 20th century brought appearances of abundant water. Homes enjoyed taps and sewer connections; carefully irrigated trees lined boulevards in desert cities; and industries developed. Urban water use increased rapidly, for example, doubling in arid Saudi Arabia between 1980 and 1985. But most of all, agriculture based on irrigation fed desert nations and even provided exports of tomatoes, oranges, wheat and other irrigated crops. The desert truly seemed to bloom.

Many Middle Eastern countries literally began to run out of water by the 1990s. Some of the world's fastest-growing populations, rising standards of living, and increased agricultural production now leave Israel, Jordan, and Egypt facing difficult choices between conservation and development. Aside from Yemen, societies in Arabia already depend on non-renewable ground water and desalination. In the 21st century, water scarcity threatens bitter conflicts within and between the region's

nations. Cooperation, by contrast, offers a chance to postpone water shortages, hopefully promoting peace in a region too troubled by violent conflict.

Water Resources as Threats to Peace
"River Jordan, deep and wide"
—Gospel song

The Biblical account of Joshua's tribes crossing the dry bed of the Jordan River to attack Jericho created in Christian imagination a mighty Jordan, deep and wide, celebrated in song and symbolizing the entrance to heaven. Reality was always different, with the Jordan's flow of 320 million cubic meters hardly more than the size of a large creek. Today the Jordan is only a narrow, salty stream, and the Dead Sea, deprived of the normal flow of Jordan River water, is drying up. Israel, Jordan, Syria, and the Palestinian Authority face questions of water use so difficult that one of them may attempt to settle issues by force. Indeed, recently Israel threatened Lebanon with war because it pumped modest amounts for local irrigation from a tributary of the Jordan.

Attempts to establish national water rights began in the 1950s, when U.S. President Eisenhower sent a special ambassador to negotiate the shares of the Jordan basin countries. At the technical level, his findings established reasonable national shares, but politically his mission failed. No international agreement yet apportions the river's waters.

With dreams of making the desert bloom, in the 1960s Israel constructed the National Water Carrier, a pipeline almost 10 feet in diameter, to bring water from the Jordan's Sea of Galilee to the coastal plain and the Negev desert. The water was vital. Arab threats to the project, by attempting to divert the Jordan's headwaters in Lebanon and Syria from flowing into Israel played a major role in the crises that led to the 1967 Arab-Israeli war. Israel's conquest of the Golan Heights and the West Bank ensured its unilateral use of the Jordan River.

Almost immediately, water from the Jordan proved to be insufficient for Israel's purposes. Along the coast and in the desert, Israeli farmers used two-thirds (now about 56%) of the nation's water for farming. To supply their fields as well as thirsty homes and factories, Israel had long pumped the Mediterranean coastal aquifer, a layer of porous rock that trapped water slowly seeping toward the sea.

When the volume of water pumped out began to exceed the rainwater trickling down into the aquifer, water levels and pressures began to fall. Salty sea water started to seep into the aquifer, reducing its water quality. By 1990 about 10% of the

water pumped from this resource exceeded the national limit for chloride salt. In addition, pollution increased as nitrates from fertilizers leached into the aquifer. During the winter, the Water Authority now pumps surplus Jordan River water down into coastal wells, hoping to replenish the aquifer.

The first Israeli desalination plant, completed in 2005, produces 100 million cubic meters of fresh water annually, less than 5% of the water used.

Israel's thirst also drains the separate Yarkon/Tannim aquifer. Known as the "mountain aquifer," it collects rain falling on the hilly West Bank. A few points of the aquifer extend into the 1967 boundaries, and Israel currently pumps about 20% of its water from this source. This vastly exceeds the pumping permitted the West Bank Palestinians, whose land supplies the rainfall that annually renews this resource. In addition, the roughly 300,000 Israeli settlers in the West Bank consume about as much water as the 2.4 million Arabs, whose drilling is restricted in several ways.

The creation of a Palestinian state threatens Israel's total control of the mountain aquifer. Fears of future water shortages may influence political opinion against granting concessions. The figures themselves show few alternatives: against average rainfall of 1.7 billion cubic meters, current water use reaches 1.9 billion cubic meters. Israelis consume five times as much per capita as residents of neighboring Arab nations. Because of this, the shallow wells of dozens of Palestinian West Bank villages no longer reach water. In the Gaza Strip, the contamination of water supplies has reached critical proportions.

The recent construction of the Wahda Dam on the Yarmuk River captures the flow of the Jordan's last underused tributary. The Yarmuk flows between Syria and Jordan, joining the Jordan just below the Sea of Galilee. With water resources far smaller than Israel's or Syria's, Jordan decades ago proposed building a "Unity Dam" at Maqarin to trap winter flood waters for summer use by farms, homes and industry. Israel threatened to destroy any such dam as it benefited by capturing some of the flow in the Sea of Galilee. However, its 1994 peace treaty with Jordan removed that threat.

Jordan eventually gained Syrian approval for a combined-purpose dam to provide water to Jordan and electricity to Syria, and the foundation stone was laid in 2003. However, rainfall in the Yarmuk basin falls mostly in Syria, and that country favors smaller, upstream projects within its boundaries. Such projects capture most of the run-off, and due to them, by 2005 the river's flow had fallen below the agreed level. In years of low rainfall, the Israelis, Palestinians, Jordanians and Syrians all find themselves critically short of water, a deficit that is projected to approach about 600 million cubic meters annually even with average rainfall.

One distant hope to relieve the water shortages is the proposed Red Sea-Dead Sea Canal. Its advocates believe it would prevent the Dead Sea from drying up, generate electricity, and provide, via desalination plants, perhaps 600 million cubic meters of fresh water annually. The engineering is possible though politics and finances may prove prohibitive.

Diverting the Euphrates

To the north and east, dams on another river of Biblical fame also threaten violence. The Euphrates springs forth in the high mountains of Turkey, whose rains contribute 80% of its volume but whose rough terrain meant little was used. It flows into Syria and then across Iraq to join the Tigris at the Shatt al-Arab just before emptying into the Persian (Arabian) Gulf. Far larger than the Jordan's, the flow of the Euphrates averages 31 billion cubic meters per year. However, ambitious development plans in the three countries exceed the river's capacity by about 50%. As long ago as 1975 Iraq actually threatened war with Syria over the scanty flow below the Syria's Tabaqa Dam.

Upstream diversion of the water to fill dams and supply irrigation essentially caused the crisis, when Turkish engineers reduced the river's flow to fill the lakes behind the Keban and Ataturk dams (see Turkey, economy). The Tabaqa Dam and agricultural development project in Syria also diverted the river's flow. Alternative resources may exist for Iraq, since there is excess flow in the Tigris to the east, but development projects to use it require time and funding.

Even worse, the Euphrates and the Tigris carry a naturally high level of dissolved salts that accumulate in irrigated soils and reduce fertility. Intensive irrigation also usually raises the water level in the soil, dissolving even more salts, agricultural chemicals and fertilizers. Unless drainage ditches are constructed to carry away salty and polluted waters, the land eventually becomes useless. Thus Iraq faces not only water shortages, but the danger of water quality in its major rivers falling to a level unfit for humans, and harmful for agriculture. Though in fact designed for other purposes, Iraq's massive channel, the "Third River," may carry salty and useless water directly to the Gulf.

The nations of the Euphrates basin have not yet fought over water, but Syria and Turkey joined the anti-Iraq Coalition in the 1990–1991 Gulf War. However, in the absence of settled water rights, the potential for violence exists, and diplomatic relations remain poor. Fighting did rage across the lower reaches of the Tigris and Euphrates and the Shatt al-Arab during the Iran-Iraq War of 1980–1988. That dispute had virtually nothing to do with irrigation. Iranian demands for control of the river to mid-stream, as opposed to traditional Iraqi domain to the Iranian shore, led to the crisis that produced the war. Control and navigation rights in the Shatt al-Arab remain disputed.

The Peace Pipeline

In the 1980s the Turkish government revived older ideas and proposed two "Peace Pipelines" to carry water the unused flow of the Seyhan and Ceyhan rivers in southern Turkey to thirsty cities and industrial areas of Arab lands, some of them impacted by the loss of water from the Euphrates. While the proposal is intriguing, the proposed western pipeline to Jordan and Saudi Arabia is hopelessly uneconomic, due to the high elevations it must cross. The longer eastern pipeline would cross Syria and Iraq, ultimately supplying Kuwait, eastern Saudi Arabia, and several Gulf states. To date, the insurmountable obstacles of cost, national pride, and security have triumphed over good intentions. Oil pipelines across the Middle East have frequently been cut by government directive or politically-related sabotage. Would the water pipelines prove any more immune to interruption?

The Nile

Fortunately, the potential for conflict over the Nile River seems very low. The world's longest river drains mountainous central Africa and the Ethiopian highlands of about 84 billion cubic meters each year, making Egypt "The Gift of the Nile." For that country and northern Sudan, no other renewable water supply exists. Survival simply depends on the Nile.

In ancient times, Egyptian farmers practiced "basin agriculture." Crops flourished in fields saturated with moisture from the annual summer flood and nourished with silt that the *Blue Nile* had carried out of Ethiopia. Egyptian desire to capture more of the flow was reflected in the construction of barrages and small dams from the 19th century onwards. Negotiations to establish water rights followed; the first Nile Waters Agreement was signed with Sudan in 1929. Renegotiated in the 1950s before construction of the Aswan High Dam (see Egypt, economy), the agreement presently provides Egypt 55 billion cubic meters yearly, three times the amount allowed Sudan.

By the 1980s, severe water shortages appeared when years of drought in Ethiopia reduced the flow of the Blue Nile. (Incidentally, East African drought patterns may be associated with the *El Niño* phenomenon of the U.S. West Coast). Behind the High Dam, Lake Nasser dwindled. Conserving water for irrigation reduced the release of water for hydro electric power and some years cut drastically the

almost 40% of national electricity produced at Aswan.

Though rains later restored the Nile's flow, at least immediately, the crisis highlighted the inevitable future shortage of water in Egypt. Accurate figures are difficult to obtain, but one study suggested that the nation possibly uses 70 billion cubic meters now. With the population growing by one million mouths annually, and the government attempting to extend cultivation, water demand will naturally increase. But Egypt's present use is only possible because Sudan fails to consume its full allotment.

Despite these dire threats, millions are not yet dying of thirst. Agriculture claims more than 80% of available water and opportunities exist for conservation. The *fellah* (farmer) typically obtains his water from unlined canals, and channels it to soak his fields. Cheap water makes sense for these poor people, whose yearly income is only a few hundred dollars. Efficient, water-saving drip irrigation systems remain beyond their purchasing power. Thus, conservation will not be painless, and will impose costs, if not on very poor people, upon an impoverished government. It may also mean abandoning some lands to the insistent demands of the desert.

Fortunately, international disputes over the Nile water are unlikely to end in violence. Decades of negotiation established rights and precedents. Egypt's determination to receive its historic and vital flow is firmly advertised and well-recognized by Sudan and traditionally by the smaller, weaker nations upstream. However, these countries seem increasingly dissatisfied with their combined allocations of only 10% of the total. In 2010, Uganda, Tanzania, Rwanda and Ethiopia agreed to seek larger shares in the proposed Cooperative Framework Agreement, which Egypt has delayed since the 1980s. Ethiopia does dream of constructing a dam along the Blue Nile, but this poses immense financial, engineering and distribution difficulties.

International Cooperation
in the Indus Basin

In South Asia, two nations born in hostility faced the challenge of sharing water from the Indus River and its tributaries. By approving a technical solution, India and Pakistan brought prosperity and greater food production to the Punjab, the fertile region divided by their borders.

Simply put, the Indus is a mighty river, fed by monsoon rains and snows in the Himalayas of India and Tibet. Carrying more water than the Nile, its annual discharge reaches 97 billion cubic meters, much of it carried across the plains by five important tributaries. During British rule

a system of irrigation canals was dug. After partition, India possessed the strategic advantage of controlling the head waters, but lacked economic benefit; its water was remote and difficult to use. Pakistan, in contrast, found itself farming with water from India, but strategically disadvantaged in the event India chose to divert or otherwise interfere with the flow.

A mission from the World Bank proposed in 1951 a rational solution: consider the issue a technical, not a political, problem. In effect, the key was to base water usage on irrigation potential, not nationality. Compensation for one district's use of another country's water could be made elsewhere. Despite two wars, the system has worked. Dams built with World Bank funds, plus a complex system of canals, have enabled the two countries to irrigate the Punjab, breadbasket of the sub-continent. Once again, however, increasing needs for water and power are currently leading to tension over India's planned Baglihar dam on the Chenab River.

Besides its rivers, the Punjab's other major source of irrigation is groundwater. Unfortunately, this is increasingly dangerous to the drinker's health. A 2007 study by water pollution authorities in India discovered that 80% of the samples contained mercury far above the permissible level, and that arsenic and pesticide contamination were significant as well.

If scientists' predictions prove accurate, climate change may eventually reduce the flow of the Indus more than most other major Asian rivers. According to the models, greater global warmth will melt Himalayan glaciers, initially increasing the river's flow as the vast ice fields melt. After the glaciers retreat, however, their runoff will decline in exactly the vital spring and summer periods when irrigation is most needed on the plains of India and Pakistan. Farm output would then fall dramatically, by enough to feed perhaps 26 million people.

Opposite Extremes

Bangladesh and northeastern India struggle with entirely different difficulties—seasonally. With as much as 50% of annual rainfall occurring in less than three weeks, for centuries, Bengalis reconciled their ways of life with the seasonal flooding of the Ganges, Brahmaputra, and other rivers, whose water and silt deposits nourished the soil and produced three crops per year (see Bangladesh). With few possessions and minimal homes, farmers lived knowing that floods could strike, and river channels might be altered by hundreds of yards overnight. Nevertheless, they could hope to escape with their lives and a few possessions to begin farming anew.

Such a fate hardly appealed to modernized city dwellers living in permanent homes. In 1989 Bangladesh embarked on the Flood Action Plan to build embankments to protect cities and to confine rivers to channels. Unfortunately, confining the rivers creates the danger that silt will raise the level of the river bottoms, eventually causing them to flow *above* ground-level. If this happens, one of the poorest countries in the world will have to construct and maintain a vast system of dikes for the rivers at an enormous cost, if indeed, it can be done, considering frequent devastating hurricanes and monsoons.

Even in this region of great annual flooding, periodic droughts strike during the dry season, and rival irrigation projects highlight the need for water-sharing agreements. A proposal to divert Himalayan river water to South India also looms as a threat to Bangladesh. It shares 50 rivers with India, but only one is covered by an international agreement regarding its flow.

Global warming, by changing mountain snowfall to rain, increases flooding and reduces off-season flow. As in the case of the Indus (but probably not the Ganges), the decline of Himalayan glaciers may eventually diminish spring and summer meltwater in the Brahmaputra basin. One model predicts this could reduce agricultural output by the equivalent of food for 34 million people.

Consequences of Dams and Large-Scale Irrigation

Humans first diverted rivers in the misty years of early history. However, the large dams that tower hundreds of feet above a valley or stretch miles across a lower river basin represent a triumph, however momentary, of the 20th century. First constructed in the United States and Soviet Union in the 1920s and 1930s, the dams proved valuable for flood control, hydroelectric power, recreational use and irrigation. After World War II, building dams became a worldwide fad, and 95% of all large dams date from this period.

For all their virtues, dams in the hot climates of the Middle East and South Asia involve a variety of drawbacks. An obvious one is evaporation, largely because the sun's rays strike directly and the desert air carries little of the humidity that would slow evaporation. The loss from Lake Nasser to the air is an estimated 10 billion cubic meters a year, one-fifth of Egypt's recognized portion of the Nile's flow. Serious proposals exist to cover the entire surface of Lake Nasser with small floating plastic bubbles to reduce the water's exposure to the air, a tremendous undertaking on a surface of thousands of square miles.

On many rivers, a much more serious problem is the buildup of silt in the reservoirs back of the large dams. Engineers only recently recognized how great this problem is in warmer climates. The Ganges-Brahmaputra and Indus each carry roughly 1,700 gallons of silt in each million gallons of water. Quietly, but much faster than predicted, rivers drop this sediment in the slow waters of the reservoirs.

At the Tarbela Dam in Pakistan, for example, some 2% of the reservoir fills with soil annually, and hundreds of tons of dirt settle above the Mangla Dam. Because of the silt, the Tarbela Dam may prove useful for only 40 years, a poor investment in view

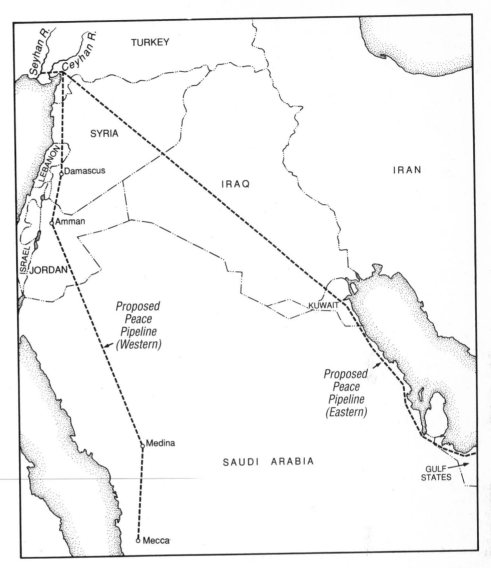

of its life expectancy of 100 years when built. In Sudan, the Roseires Dam on the Blue Nile ceased effective operation when deposits formed an island above the water intakes for the hydroelectric turbines.

Rapid silting not only spreads a dam's huge construction costs over fewer years, it also renders the location permanently useless as a dam. Unfortunately, projects conceived to reduce soil loss, such as planting trees, often proved less effective than projected.

As environmentalists and others have long pointed out, silt often plays important roles in nourishing fields and supporting the coastal ecosystem. Deprived of sediments, Egyptian and other farmers spread tons of chemical fertilizers on their soil, polluting the earth and rendering drainage water unfit for many uses. Coastlines deprived of silt may succumb to the sea, as has happened in Egypt and elsewhere.

Silting risks partly forced the scaling-back of the Narmada Valley Development Project in central and western India. Probably the largest single project in the world, its plans included 30 major dams, dozens of smaller ones and thousands of minor ones, constructed over a period of 50 years. The dams will supply irrigation water for millions of acres in the states of Gujarat, Rajasthan and Madhya Pradesh, and generate vast amounts of electricity for homes and industry. However, the new reservoirs also flood large expanses of tropical forest and forced hundreds of thousands of people from their homes. A series of court actions in 2000 finally lowered the maximum permitted height of one major dam, though it permitted construction to resume.

Alternatives

To supply thirsty homes and farms, nations in the Middle East and South Asia have turned to new sources. Infrared satellite pictures suggest that "fracture zones" stretching for hundreds of miles may hold billions of cubic meters of water in aquifers far below the level of traditional wells. Unfortunately, however, fossil water remains from moister climatic ages and is never replaced by nature. In a few decades these aquifers run dry. With government subsidies and assistance, Saudi farmers pumped this "fossil water" to irrigate farmland, but the project ultimately failed (see Saudi Arabia, economy).

In contrast, desalination transforms the free and limitless water of the seas and oceans into the sweet water necessary for human life and agriculture. Despite the higher salt content of the Red Sea and the Gulf, the oil exporting nations of the Gulf lead the world in commercial desalination. Saudi Arabia alone accounts for almost one-third of the world capacity, over one billion cubic meters annually. Kuwait and the United Arab Emirates provide another fifth. While the ancients used solar power to distill water, efficient, large-scale desalination plants today employ multistage processes for capturing steam and condensing it into water. Costs are lowest for so-called dual-purpose plants that use relatively low-temperature waste heat from power plants. In Saudi Arabia the Ministry of Agriculture, which runs desalination plants, started generating more electricity than the Ministry of Electricity and Industry.

A boat bridge across the upper Indus

Despite the availability of bright, hot sunshine, it requires far higher fuel prices—or technological breakthroughs—for solar power to become economical. The most promising method uses saline solar ponds to collect the sun's energy and use it to convert salt water into usable liquid.

Desalination is now affordable for household uses in countries with high per capita incomes—at least near the coast. It remains a hope for coastal agricultural regions, but presently the process is far too expensive for irrigating crops. Other difficulties can hardly be solved by money, however. The 1990–1991 Gulf War showed how greatly Saudi Arabia and the smaller oil-producing states depend on desalination, when a massive oil slick threatened to pollute drinking water and clog equipment. To be efficient, desalination plants must be large, but large plants mean little reserve capacity and pose tempting targets for attack and sabotage.

Experiments continue in several countries using brackish water and seawater for agriculture. The goal is to discover productive plants that need little or no fresh water and then to determine profitable techniques for growing and processing them. If successful, salt water farming could revolutionize present water use patterns. Israeli enthusiasts, for example, advocate a pipeline to carry brackish, undrinkable water from desert aquifers to farms for irrigating certain crops. Results also appear promising for growing certain oil seed crops using seawater, with the added benefit of using the plants as fodder for ani-

mals. Unfortunately the application of the discoveries will be limited and will require close monitoring: salt-water irrigation contaminates permanently any fresh ground water in an aquifer below.

The recycling of sewage and other waste-water has reached the greatest extent in Israel, where some 30% of it is reused in agriculture. The potential to recycle exists in other countries as well, but the process requires well-trained personnel and careful monitoring of pollutants. Like the use of drip irrigation, higher water prices for regular water will encourage greater use of waste-water. Unfortunately, this can be dangerous: according to data from the International Water Management Institute, 85% of cities in developing nations discharge water without appropriate treatment, risking contamination of heavy metals and other pollutants.

Many novel proposals exist to meet the looming shortage. Polar ice contains about two thirds of the world's fresh water, so giant icebergs from the Antarctic could be towed to the Middle East and melted to quench the region's thirst. More conventionally, tankers might bring drinking water from European nations with excess supplies such as France and Britain. High prices might also provide the incentive to reduce agriculture in the Nile and Indus valleys, with the water thus saved piped under the sea to cities in Arabia.

Most Americans take for granted the water that simply flows from an opened faucet. By contrast, in many parts of the Middle East and South Asia there are no

taps, and the assumption that sufficient water will be there in a decade or two increasingly looks risky. The area's limited water resources are already being developed and used to the maximum. For most countries this does not imply that water shortages now threaten living standards as does the devastating drought in northeastern Syria. But peaceful solutions require major changes and, above all, time.

Even with the best conservation methods, farming remains a thirsty occupation. Nations in the region value agriculture for its employment, the security of food supplies and realizing national aspirations. Rather than risk war over insufficient water supplies, Middle Eastern nations logically should develop other uses of their lands and work forces.

Unfortunately, logic frequently seems missing in matters of water management and agriculture. Given this region's shortages and its many failed attempts at peacemaking, trouble lies ahead. Water shortages in India have already led to fatal violence. Further west, in the words of Joyce Starr, founder of Global Water Summit Initiative, Middle East population growth is a "human explosion certain to ignite the issue of water."

BLACK GOLD: THE IMPACT OF OIL

Petroleum refining involves precision engineering and extensive equipment anywhere on earth   Courtesy: Royal Embassy of Saudi Arabia

The countries of the Middle East and South Asia enjoy few natural riches, and most of the famed mineral deposits of antiquity have been exhausted for centuries.

The great exception is petroleum. Perhaps 60% of the world's proven and probable oil deposits lie in the sedimentary basin between central Arabia and the mountains of Iran. From northern Iraq to the Strait of Hormuz, crude oil often occurs in large fields relatively near the surface. Cheap to extract, without the financial and environmental costs of drilling in deep waters or Arctic tundra, the oil is piped short distances to coastal terminals, loaded onto tankers, and shipped to refineries world-wide.

So abundant is the oil, and so efficient its production, refining and transportation, that Saudi oil probably costs under U.S. $ 0.50 per gallon to pump, refine, and transport, but it may sell for $10 per gallon in Europe and $4 in the United States. Governments and companies manage to extract enough taxes and profits from consumers to boost prices as high as other energy sources. The special physical qualities that make oil a desirable fuel also generate great wealth for those able to manipulate its price.

The Search for Oil in the Middle East

The ancients knew something about oil. Asphalt seeped to the surface in Mesopotamia. Tar paved the streets of Babylon, calked seams, and mortared bricks. Mysterious fires there and in Persia burned indefinitely, without consuming any known fuel.

Petroleum's role remained largely unchanged until the industrial revolution. By the 19th century, the new factories in Europe and the United States required great quantities of oil, for light and to lubricate moving parts. Inventors and entrepreneurs in Europe and North America dug the first wells to obtain petroleum, and after 1900 the popularity of gasoline-powered automobiles spurred demand for oil tremendously.

An integrated industry developed rapidly. The search for petroleum deposits spread to the Middle East, where prospecting began first in Iraq and Iran (then known as Persia), where the English entrepreneur William D'Arcy negotiated a concession from the Shah of Persia in 1901. After five years of disappointments, in 1908 his drillers struck the first commercial well in the Middle East, at Masjid-i Suleiman.

D'Arcy moved rapidly to exploit the find. He organized the Anglo-Persian Oil Company, which laid a pipeline to the coast and gained permission from a local chief to construct a refinery on Abadan Island at the head of the Gulf. On the eve of World War I, with the Royal Navy switching from coal to oil for fuel, Winston Churchill arranged for the British government to purchase a majority share in the company, known today as British Petroleum.

After World War I, the concessions for oil prospecting in Iraq fell to British, French and American firms who in the late 1920s formed the Iraq Petroleum Company (IPC). In the 1920s and 1930s, geologists discovered vast oil fields elsewhere in the Middle East, first in Bahrain. Then, in 1938, an American company exploring in Saudi Arabia struck commercial quantities with its seventh well. Geologists eventually recognized that quite distant oil strikes really tapped parts of one vast field, the Ghawar. Some 160 miles long, it ranks as the largest in the world, even surpassing Kuwait's Burgan field. Oil production in Qatar, the United Arab Emirates, and Oman became significant only in the 1950s and 1960s.

In contrast to plantation agriculture or modern industry, petroleum requires a relatively small but highly skilled workforce, after the initial construction of pipelines, storage facilities, loading terminals, and perhaps a refinery. Although they employed relatively few workers, the oil companies greatly affected local society. They established training programs and schools. Roads, towns, shops, medical facilities and models of new lifestyles often resulted—at least for some of the population. Another major impact was financial. Royalties, taxes, and profit-sharing flowed to the rulers, and exports supplied foreign exchange, normally scarce in developing countries.

Countries and Companies
Clash over Profits

In the Middle East, land ownership of untilled areas traditionally belonged to the government, and as a result, oil companies negotiated agreements, or concessions, from governments. These stipulated the territorial limits of company operations and specified payments to the ruler.

Companies initially bargained from strength and the rulers from weakness, because the rulers needed money and neither side knew what oil wealth existed, or if it would flow in profitable quantities. The oil industry was dominated by just a few companies—sometimes titled the "Seven Sisters"—who kept prices high and maintained large reserve capacities, so their negotiations for concessions reflected such corporate strengths.

In contrast, governments badly needed money and preferred large initial payments for prospecting rights, while accepting low royalties on output that might never occur. Thus, in 1931 Iraq agreed to royalties of only four gold shillings per ton, about twelve cents per barrel. Saudi Arabia accepted the same figure two years later. Their oil companies earned remarkable profits on their productive investments, but other investments proved complete losses despite years of exploration.

Middle East nations soon felt they deserved better, that their original concessions provided too generously for the companies and failed to reflect the changed circumstances after oil was discovered. Being sovereign, they could demand revisions in what the companies considered legally binding contracts. The first important changes came with Shah Reza's Iran in 1933. Thereafter, governments repeatedly pressed for greater revenues and for minimum annual payments. By 1950, agreements often fixed payments as 50% of gross income less production expenses. However, income was difficult to determine when oil was sold to another subsidiary of the same company.

Eventually, both sides accepted artificial "posted prices" to calculate the profits to be divided.

Iran's attempt to gain control of its oil in 1951 highlighted the limits that countries faced in their continuing struggles to gain greater benefits from oil. After Prime Minister Mohammad Mossadeq nationalized operations of the Anglo-Iranian Oil Company, the company increased output in Kuwait, and diverted its tankers to other sources. Anglo-Iranian halted payments to the government, and its lawyers prevented sales of Iranian oil in Western Europe. Eventually the two sides agreed that a consortium of companies would operate the oil fields for the National Iranian Oil Company. The lesson was clear: governments depended for their very survival on the tax revenues from oil, but the "majors" maintained sufficient excess capacity to meet their customers' needs without the exports of any one nation, and would lend oil to each other. Therefore, a single country lacked the power to force a major oil company to accept its terms.

In 1959, with world oil supplies plentiful and market prices soft, the major oil companies announced—rather than negotiated—a lower posted price for crude oil and thus reduced their payments to governments. In response, representatives of Iran, Iraq, Kuwait, Saudi Arabia and Venezuela met in Baghdad and established the Organization of Oil Exporting Countries (OPEC, 1960). From its inception, OPEC's goals concerned export prices, royalties, and the taxation of profits, but its members also desired that the companies train and hire their citizens.

Until the late 1950s, international oil companies treated Middle Eastern supplies as supplemental and set prices based on the U.S. market, thus keeping prices high in the U.S. Around 1970, however, American production peaked and soon began to decline, while U.S., European, and Japanese demand continued to grow rapidly. The increase could only be met from the Middle East. Its oil, hitherto excluded from the United States on grounds of "national security," became increasingly necessary for the world's largest economy.

Against this background, specific events gained disproportionate importance. The Suez Canal remained closed after the 1967 war, straining oil tanker capacity. A puncture in 1970 shut down the Saudi pipeline to the Mediterranean, and Libya simultaneously acted against some small oil companies for violating their concessions. Fears of world-wide oil shortages created the opportunity for OPEC to demand higher revenues.

The resulting 1971 Tehran Agreement between OPEC nations and the companies increased posted prices immediately (to less than $2 for a barrel of 42 gallons), and set them at $5 per barrel by the late 1970s. Hailed at the time as a major victory for the oil exporters, the Tehran Agreement raised revenues to the countries by 25%, enabling these nations to limit production and still pay their bills. The countries no longer needed to produce more to pay their bills—they discovered that at current conditions, they could reduce production but raise prices more. Future increases in demand would also allow them to force further price increases on the companies and consumers.

The 1973 Oil Embargo and Rising Prices

World politics provided the convenient opportunity. During the October 1973 War between Israel and the Arab nations of Egypt and Syria, hostility to the U.S. rose in the Arab world. King Faisal of Saudi Arabia won wide approval when he embargoed oil exports to the United States. To make the policy effective he also decreed a 10% cut in all exports.

Sensing their power, the Gulf oil exporters then broke the previous pattern of negotiated prices and set export prices without consulting the companies. Fears of shortages seized consumers worldwide, and prices on the spot market rose to $15 per barrel. Gas lines appeared across the U.S., service stations closed on Sundays, and President Nixon reduced the speed limit to 55 miles per hour. Recognizing the opportunity, OPEC met in December 1973 and raised the price countries would receive to $11.65 per barrel.

Great transfers of wealth followed the 1973 price increase. Prices doubled again during shortages created by the Iranian Revolution in 1979–1980, bringing inconceivable riches. Iran's revenues, for instance, rose almost seven-fold between 1973–1974 and 1977–1978. In 1981, Saudi Arabia received roughly $120 billion for its oil, over $12,000 per inhabitant. Massive purchases of foreign goods clogged ports throughout the Middle East. However, in just a few years conservation measures by consumers, cheating by OPEC members, and increased production outside OPEC brought prices down by about 50% (see box).

Price fluctuations in the 1990s

The rise of oil futures markets in the 1980s meant that OPEC members could not set world prices, but they could influence them. Given consumers' desires and non-OPEC production, OPEC members might collectively produce just enough to balance supply and demand at a target price. By the late 1980s, however, the cartel could not enforce the discipline. Kuwait and the United Arab Emirates over-

Offshore drilling requires large platforms, here arriving in the Gulf

Courtesy: Royal Embassy of Saudi Arabia

soared, gasoline prices climbed, and regular gasoline prices exceeded $2 per gallon in parts of California. So often proclaimed dead, OPEC had again revived.

High Prices since 2004: A Spike or the Future?

Oil prices rose modestly during the U.S. invasion of Iraq in 2003. This was easily predictable: the conflict halted Iraqi production and exports. Most strategists expected a rapid resumption of Iraqi exports, increasing world supplies and thus reducing prices. Instead, annual average prices climbed rapidly in 2004–05, in 2007 surpassed the 1980s peak of $85 in today's prices, and in mid-2008 refineries began to pay more than $150 per barrel.

Why?

Among many explanations, the following facts seem fundamental to any analysis:

World oil consumption rose 11%, insensitive to price: The annual price of crude oil climbed from a very low average of $12.50 in 1998 to $68 in 2007, a rise of over 400%. Economic theory suggests that consumers who face such increases would attempt to reduce consumption, but during that decade, Americans increased their consumption by almost 10%, or 1.75 million barrels per day. With the rapid spread of automobiles in China, its oil consumption rose by 84%, or nearly 3.5 million barrels per day, and other rapidly-growing Asian nations and the rest of the developing world added another 5.8 million barrels per day of consumption.

Outside OPEC, only Russia significantly increased production: Despite the high prices, U.S. crude oil output actually fell slightly, and major declines occurred in Britain (41%), Norway (18%), and several smaller producers. As a group, however, non-OPEC producers increased crude output by nearly 13%. Nearly all the increase came from territories of the former Soviet Union, and 63% came from Russia alone, as it modernized production and in 2009 overtook Saudi Arabia as the world's largest producer.

Most of OPEC pumped all it could: The 13 nations comprising OPEC lost world market share as they increased production only 7%. Nearly half the gain came from Angola, after the end of its long civil war. According to estimates of the U.S. Energy Information Administration, OPEC nations produced flat-out, with only Saudi Arabia holding any spare capacity at all (in the range of 1–2 million barrels per day). One expert, James Hamilton, disputes even this spare capacity, suggesting that the northern Ghawar field has peaked, and new projects will replace capacity, not increase it.

produced, arguing that fairness should link the size of the quota to oil export capacity, rather than to population or poverty. Consumers benefited world-wide from the lower prices, but revenues plummeted. Iraq, in financial desperation when prices plunged to $14 per barrel, invaded Kuwait in 1990 (see Iraq: history).

After seizing Kuwait, Iraq controlled the sources of roughly 20% of OPEC's exports. When U.N. sanctions on Iraq and occupied Kuwait blocked their export of oil, fears rose of oil shortages, and crude oil prices rapidly doubled. Industrial nations headed for recession, but despite Iraqi threats, OPEC approved extra output, and with help from oil in storage, a world-wide shortfall was averted.

By the mid-1990s, global use of oil had expanded, particularly in East Asia, while supplies from non-OPEC producers grew slowly during a decade of lower prices. Prices rose well above $20, and OPEC nations found that *they could cheat at their quotas and enjoy higher prices at the same*

time. However, Saudi Arabia persuaded the cartel's members to increase the total OPEC quota from 23.833 million barrels per day (m b/d) to 26.185 m b/d (without Iraq) just as East Asia suffered economic recession. When market speculators realized that some nations, particularly Venezuela, Nigeria and Qatar, exceeded even the larger quotas, prices dropped immediately and rapidly, to levels last seen in 1973. Some experts proclaimed the death of OPEC, and argued that the rational policy for Gulf producers was to earn money from volume production, even if prices reached $5 per barrel. Such prices, after all, would render oil from Alaska and the North Sea too expensive to be profitable.

After losing billions of dollars in exports and revenues, OPEC cut quotas in 1998 and 1999. Moreover, sympathetic nations outside OPEC, including Mexico, Norway, Russia, and Oman also agreed to cut exports. After several months, the cuts persuaded the markets, and every American driver witnessed the result. Oil prices

Seven years on, Iraqi output still lags: Sabotage, corruption, and inefficiency have combined to limit Iraqi production below 3m b/d.

Gasoline and jet fuel are not like "Coke": If the price of one brand of soft drink doubled, most Americans would switch to another brand. Because cars, trucks, and aircraft cannot readily switch to alternate fuels, and we would be horrified at reducing driving by, say, 25%, in the language of economists demand is insensitive to price, in the short run.

Speculative money flooded into oil futures: Seeking high returns when stock markets and housing loans offered modest profits, after 2000 hedge fund managers and others speculated in many raw materials, including crude oil. Given the tight world-wide supply, and the possibility that political unrest, terrorism, natural disaster, or simply bad luck could reduce that supply, speculators found many reasons to bid up prices, and little reason to fear a downward spiral.

What's next? Optimists think prices will moderate: Slower world economic growth might reduce consumption slightly, and other upward pressures may prove temporary, such as political difficulties in Venezuela and violence in Nigeria that created a "security premium." Iraq's proven reserves of 115 billion barrels, second only to Saudi Arabia's, will permit dramatic increases after peace and reconstruction. More exports might even be possible from Russia.

Finally, optimists quote figures from BP that show the global ratio of reserves to production stands at 40 years. This implies that during the last few decades, discoveries kept pace with increased production. The global ratio remained constant even in 2008, when reserves fell slightly, because production fell somewhat faster.

Pessimists point to "facts" as well: Demand is rising sharply in some countries, especially China and India, where hundreds of millions aspire to own a car. Based on trends earlier in the decade, the International Energy Agency (IEA) has predicted that global energy demand will soar by 60% by about 2030.

Though demand is rising, new supplies are not. During the last two decades, only a few very large-sized fields were discovered anywhere, and some, like those in very deep water off Brazil, will take years to develop. A decade ago, Kazakhstan and Central Asia promised "another Persian Gulf" of enormous supplies, but reality proved more modest. Excepting OPEC and Russia, reported world reserves equal only 12 times annual production. Global non-OPEC, non-Russian oil production

Small vessels play important roles in supply and security

Courtesy: Royal Embassy of Saudi Arabia

11

OPEC Output and Spare Capacity
(millions of barrels per day)

	OUTPUT			Spare Capacity
	1998	2006	2007	
Algeria	0.82	1.37	1.37	0.05
Angola	0.74	1.37	1.68	0
Ecuador	0.38	0.54	0.51	0
Indonesia	1.34	0.89	0.85	0
Iran	3.6	3.77	3.7	0.04
Iraq	2.15	1.99	2.08	0
Kuwait	2.09	2.54	2.46	0.17
Libya	1.39	1.68	1.7	0.02
Nigeria	2.04	2.22	2.12	0
Qatar	0.66	0.82	0.81	0.05
Saudi Arabia	8.39	9.15	8.72	1.78
United Arab Emirates	2.27	2.53	2.49	0.07
Venezuela	3.13	2.47	2.39	0.03
OPEC Total	28.97	31.34	30.9	2.2
Other Liquids	3.02	4.49	4.53	
Total OPEC	31.99	35.83	35.43	

Source: U.S. Energy Information Agency.

may have peaked in 2008, and then begin to decline. The decline is not from a lack of trying: North America and Europe accounted for 71 percent of the new drilling in the late 1990s and early 2000s, while the Middle East accounted for only 2 percent.

In the longer run, there are alternative fuels, and conservation can work magic on the ratio of reserves to consumption. However, American driving habits and China's rapid modernization could result in $4.00 per gallon or more in the years to come.

In the face of these trends, what strategies might the Middle Eastern oil exporters adopt? For the minor exporters—Egypt, Syria, Yemen, and Oman, for example—the strategy is simple: sell at the highest possible price while pumping carefully to obtain the most oil from the fields. However,

Saudi Arabia, Kuwait, Iran and the United Arab Emirates possess the potential, collectively and in Saudi Arabia's case probably individually, to set production levels that will influence world prices towards the mid-$30s per barrel, or above $120 per barrel. After the sharp decline in prices in 2008, which cost Arab economies about $2.5 trillion, modest OPEC cuts were apparently designed to raise prices to roughly $80 per barrel.

Both strategic options carry risks. Higher prices encourage the development of deepwater, Arctic and other costly oilfields that would be uneconomic at lower prices. Once those wells are drilled, their extra oil production diminishes the power of OPEC. High prices also encourage alternative types of energy. Finally, hidden in the background alternatives of strategic planners is the fear that at some point, high oil prices may lead some consuming nations to "protect world supplies" by military force.

The lower-price option also carries risks. OPEC unity could split, because other OPEC nations, enjoying the high prices for their limited production, oppose guiding prices down. Second, lower prices "for foreigners" may arouse criticism or worse among a country's citizens. For example, Saudi terrorists explicitly condemned their government for selling oil too cheaply.

The Future: The major Middle Eastern oil producers will avoid making bold strate-

Off-shore loading saves time, but requires vast tank farms

Courtesy: Royal Embassy of Saudi Arabia

WHY OIL PRICES PLUNGED ONCE BEFORE

When prices softened slightly in the early 1980s, OPEC's success still seemed to suggest that unlike other cartels (alliances of producers that limit production and raise prices), it could defy the laws of economics. Normally, a cartel's high prices lead customers to conserve and seek alternatives, resulting in reduced purchases. Typically, cartel producers then respond with secret discounts to lure customers, and to compete with producers outside the cartel. Eventually, according to theory, market forces—overproduction, cheating and outright defections—will destroy the cartel.

True to theory, in the early 1980s oil consumers reacted to high prices. They bought fuel-efficient cars, lowered winter thermostats and otherwise conserved energy. Oil use by the industrialized world fell by almost 20%. Producers outside OPEC greatly increased exploration, drilling, and output. However, the cartel did not collapse. Wealthy OPEC members initially could not spend all their revenues, and consequently cut production with few difficulties. This spared countries where cuts would be painful (and more likely ignored). This greatly slowed the decline of the cartel.

Over time, voluntary cuts proved insufficient to prop up prices. OPEC nations then agreed to cut production by an average of 40%. Again, the large producers with relatively small populations played a major "swing" role. Saudi Arabia, Kuwait and the United Arab Emirates accepted reductions in output of 50% or more, while Iran, Venezuela, Indonesia and Algeria, with much lower oil exports per person, escaped with far smaller cuts.

By 1985, however, the market for OPEC crude had tumbled to 15.4 million barrels per day, and many members cheated on quotas or provided secret discounts. Dropping its famous oil minister, Zaki Yamani, Saudi Arabia abandoned its role as a "swing producer" and determined to defend its market share. Crude flooded the world's markets, and prices tumbled briefly to below $9 a barrel in 1986. (Adjusted for inflation, this still represented a 40% increase over 1972 prices.) Greater OPEC discipline restored prices to about $18 per barrel in 1987, and for most of the next decade they fluctuated in the $15–22 range.

Consumers and alternate suppliers brought prices down once. Can they do so again?

gic moves, as President Bush discovered when he unsuccessfully appealed for higher Saudi output. Instead, they will opt for modest changes in both price and output and blame others while enjoying tremendous incomes. Evidence of softening demand, or significantly increasing supply, will continue to bring prices down. Reducing taxes on gasoline for the summer driving season, while perhaps appealing politically, will tend to push up prices further.

Sustained prices above $100 will attract the investment that is necessary to meet the world's growing demand. In the long run, that investment, plus technology and conservation, might reduce demand so much that world supplies would remain abundant for several decades. However, even if they do, the Middle Eastern suppliers will enjoy low costs of production. Their huge oilfields, high output per well, and easy access to shipping make them the most efficient sources.

HISTORICAL BACKGROUND

The Emergence of Civilization

In the earliest stage of human history people depended for food upon hunting wild animals and gathering the edible parts of plants. For warmth they clothed themselves in animal skins, and they found protection from the weather in caves or temporary shelters. Archaeologists have found evidence for this kind of life on six continents and many islands.

Climatic changes probably played an important role in the next stage of human history, known as the Neolithic or New Stone Age. As the earth warmed after the last Ice Age, rainy weather retreated northward and to the tropics. A permanent zone of high atmospheric pressure began to dominate Southern Europe and North Africa from the Atlantic to the Middle East, and Southern Asia up to monsoon-blessed India. Under the impact of successive dry, sunny days, deserts formed where previously fishermen lived, and the hunters and gatherers were forced into confined areas, particularly along river valleys, watered by rainfall trapped by mountains and highlands often hundreds of miles distant.

Beside such rivers and streams in Southwest Asia women (more likely than men) first deliberately planted seed—barley and a variety of wheat—and cultivated land, events dated by most historians to around 8,000 B.C. About the same time, people domesticated animals: culti-

vation and domestication together formed the Agricultural Revolution. Initially hardly more productive than hunting and gathering, soon farmers were capable of producing a surplus over the minimum requirements of food, clothing and shelter. Such development occurred in other areas of the world, but in later periods. Once mankind had learned how to plant grain crops and raise captive animals, a much more secure supply of food was available. It was no longer necessary for small groups of people to keep constantly on the move in search of food. They planted their fields near sources of water, their numbers increased and village life developed. The sites of the oldest villages so far discovered lie in a zone stretching from southeastern Europe across Asia Minor as far eastward as the region of the middle Tigris River.

The level of technology, combined with the tasks of obtaining food, clothing, safety, and other essentials of existence must have shaped daily activities and society during prehistory. Life was short, even for survivors of infancy and childhood. Food supplies limited the maximum size of the group, for hunters and gatherers had to move further to procure food as the group rose in size. However, high mortality for children and adults—let alone infants—decreed the importance of having many women, all either preg-

nant or about to become so. Only thus could the existence of a next generation be expected. Lacking documentary evidence, historians can only surmise that such societies regarded highly the mighty hunter and a particularly sharp stone axe. One suspects also that they stressed communal rights and obligations in contrast to individual ones, but tempered this with the recognition that adults who could not work would not survive.

Larger communities and more efficient food production allowed—and required—increased specialization of activity; farm lands and permanent buildings required greater property rights. Rulers, warriors, administrators and priests acted to protect from invaders, settle disputes, and establish moral codes. By authority, force, and religion, these new, specialized professions appropriated much of the harvest, leaving the farmers who worked the land little beyond the minimum subsistence necessary for life. Not for the last time, therefore, improvements in mankind's ability to control nature enriched the few who took advantage of the new circumstances, but left most of society little better off than before. Nevertheless, the agricultural surplus made possible a larger population, growing slowly and settling more densely. This, in turn, made possible the early steps of civilization: cities, trade, writing, metallurgy, and the opportunity to seek beauty and truth through art, philosophy, and the early sciences.

The discovery of metals, so important for the future of humanity that historians named epochs for the predominant metal, began perhaps by accident, when rocks containing copper melted around some cooking fire. Far easier to shape than stone, copper nevertheless suffered grave defects of softness and brittleness that hampered its use in tools and weapons. With the invention of bronze around 3,000 B.C., metal became more than an ornament. So important was bronze that its era lasted until approximately 1200 B.C. in Southwestern Asia.

With the new agricultural wealth concentrated in relatively few hands, trade and the production of luxuries increased. New crafts developed and old ones expanded. Artists improved their skills, notably in sculptures and reliefs, sometimes with impressive use of gold leaf. Jewelry of gold, silver and semi-precious stones like lapis lazuli and carnelian showed great concern for personal adornment among the wealthy. For the poor, seashells, colored stone, and beads of painted pottery sufficed. With even greater visual drama, towns developed, and architects experimented with new techniques for larger and more imposing buildings. Frequently the temple of the city god became the focus of town life, and its structure was often designed as much to impress the be-

CENTERS OF EARLY CIVILIZATION

ABOUT 2,500 B.C.

holder as to provide shelter for priests and rituals. Not surprisingly, temples provide some of the earliest examples of monumental architecture.

Other discoveries of the Bronze Age included improved and specialized tools, the wheel (or, more accurately, the fixed axle), and eventually the domestication of the horse. Together the last two made possible the chariot, the greatest weapon of the age. Early horses were too small to be

ridden in battle, and without stirrups proved most unstable fighting platforms, but a chariot could overwhelm infantrymen. As technology armed the defenders of the river valleys with weapons superior to those of invaders from the hills, steppes, and mountains, the opportunity arose for the three great river valley civilizations to develop. Already the greatest of their achievements must have been the discovery of writing.

15

The Spread of Civilization

The development and spread of writing systems during the Bronze Age meant that information about business transactions, deeds of kings, and knowledge about the world could be recorded and preserved, to be read in other places and later times. Around 3,000 B.C., the first true writing appeared, among the Sumerians of the Tigris-Euphrates Plain. Their wedge-shaped characters, impressed with a reed pen on wet clay tablets, produced a script now called cuneiform. Its pictographic origins predated the Sumerians, and it developed from the needs of business contracts and records in the growing cities. Cuneiform was a cumbersome and inefficient writing system, for each symbol could represent any one of several ideas or syllables, and later even sounds.

Cuneiform

Consequently, long years of training were required to become a scribe, capable of distinguishing alternate meanings. Nevertheless, cuneiform spread widely, as illustrated by one of the most dramatic recent archeological discoveries. Ebla, in northern Syria, lies hundreds of miles from Sumer. In the 1970s, archaeologists unearthed a royal library of some 16,000 clay tablets, in Sumerian and Eblian, dating from about 2,400 B.C. They provided new knowledge about the Canaanites of Abraham's time and also proof of the extent of Sumer's influence. Indeed, the writing system lingered long after Sumerian died out as a spoken language soon after 2,000 B.C., for cuneiform continued to be used for the Babylonian, Assyrian, Hittite and other languages, only dying out by the time of Christ.

Evidence suggests that writing began rather suddenly in the Nile Valley shortly after 3,000 B.C. Possibly the idea of writing, but not the system, was borrowed from Sumer. Drawings of gods, people, animals, birds and inanimate objects represented words, ideas and sounds. These so-called hieroglyphics were not a very efficient method of writing, but they were capable of recording information.

Hieroglyphics

It is not surprising that a third system of writing, the alphabet, replaced both cuneiform and hieroglyphics. Around the 12th century B.C., Canaanites living along the eastern shores of the Mediterranean assigned each symbol to represent a sound, rather than a picture, syllable, or idea. Easily applied to Semitic languages, whose words generally were characterized by three root sounds and simple vowels, the new script vastly shortened the task of learning to read and write. The alphabet thus broke the power akin to monopoly the scribes had previously enjoyed over writing. While the common man remained illiterate, merchants and officials adopted the idea of the alphabet to keep accounts and records, whatever their language.

Propelled by trade, the alphabet spread both east and west from Canaan and Phoenicia. By the 10th century B.C. it began to replace cuneiform in Babylonia, in the cursive Aramaic script whose descendants include modern Arabic and Hebrew. A century later the alphabet spread to Greece. The Greeks, in turn, used it in their far-flung trading colonies across Southern Europe, preserving in the process the name of the Phoenician city-state of Byblos, whose trade with Egypt provided Greeks with papyrus. The name remains in the English prefix *biblio* for book, and "The Book": *Bible*.

Using the Canaanite alphabet

Only after the conquest of Egypt by Alexander the Great in 332 B.C., and the rise thereafter of a great center of Hellenistic civilization at Alexandria, did the use of hieroglyphics decline. A modified Greek alphabet was devised for writing the native language, Coptic. Its use continued despite foreign rule by Greeks, Romans and Byzantines. Although after the Arab conquest, Coptic gradually fell into disuse in daily speech, it remains today in the liturgy of the Egyptian rite of Christianity, the Coptic Church.

The Rise and Fall of Empires

The sport of an Assyrian king

During the many centuries of civilization's uneven advance, life for ordinary people often proved harsh. Only in the most fortunate times did the countryside and towns enjoy peace. Instead, farmers, merchants and craftsmen alike suffered interruption of work and safety because civilization provided the incentive and means for increasingly well-organized warfare.

Sometimes there were disputes over territory between neighboring communities. This led to a new dimension in fighting when one city set out to dominate others and when one little state began to subjugate others. In modern times, mechanized industrial production has permitted populations of entire nations to enjoy lives of relative comfort and convenience. In ancient times, however, production depended on human and animal energy for power and thus luxuries and comforts could be enjoyed only by small, privileged groups—and only through taking wealth from others, both slaves within society, and increasingly by conquest. Thus, the new inventions of civilization encouraged aggressive people, at first individually, then as groups and finally as nations, to reap personal benefit from the labor of others.

In the Nile Valley, where rival cities and regions had struggled for supremacy, there arose around 2850 B.C. a leader capable of unifying the distinctly separate regions of Upper and Lower Egypt (the Nile Delta). Hardly distinct from associated myths, Menes founded the first of 30 dynasties to rule Egypt. Claiming divine descent, his successors as kings or Pharaohs exerted enormous power over society. By the 26th century B.C., the pyramid age, rulers constructed enormous stone monuments as their tombs. Amazing in size and accuracy as feats of engineering, (e.g., the Great Pyramid contains 2,300,000 blocks and varies only 9½ inches on a side) they also bear dramatic witness to the organization of society and the Pharaohs' ability to extract labor and resources from the populace. However, one of the Pharaohs' greatest weaknesses was organizational: as local governors passed office to their sons, central authority weakened and the dynasty might collapse.

Although Egypt possessed then, as now, relatively secure borders against foreign attack in the form of deserts to the south, east, and west, strong Pharaohs frequently sought conquests abroad. During the Middle Kingdom (2100–1800 B.C.) and the New Kingdom (1550–1085 B.C.), Egyptian armies defeated the Nubians up the Nile and struggled for the wealth and control of Syria against both its inhabitants and powerful kingdoms in Mesopotamia. In the 15th century, Thutmose III fought seventeen campaigns and crossed the Euphrates; hieroglyphics at the Temple of Karnak in Egypt portrayed his conquests and booty.

The growth of powerful states in Mesopotamia illustrated many features common to Egypt, including the divine origin of rulers. However, geography decreed greater difficulties for those desiring to unify the land. The broader river valleys allowed city states to develop, and peoples to retain separate ethnic identities and languages. Moreover, invaders repeatedly pierced the natural barriers of desert and mountains and established new kingdoms. Thus, for most of the 3rd millennium B.C. the dominant political organization was the city-states of Sumer. In the mid-24th century B.C., however, Sargon, ruler of Akkad to the north, conquered Sumer and proclaimed himself king of Sumer and Akkad. The next centuries, marked by rivalry between the Akkadians and Sumerians as well as invading Amorites, nevertheless witnessed another great achievement of civilization: the promulgation of codes of law.

The first recorded law-giver, Ur-Nammu, was followed by the much more famous, though significantly harsher, Code of Hammurabi.

In the struggle for territory and the wealth of civilization, empires and dynasties rose and fell. Warfare took a new turn when horses were introduced into the civilized area from the northeast about 1,600 B.C. Horse-drawn chariots could crash through a line of foot soldiers. The infantry, poorer soldiers who could not afford horses and chariots, lost status in the new military organizations.

The rise of iron-smelting in Asia Minor around 1200 B.C. apparently provided an important strength for the next dominant power of Mesopotamia, the warlike and often cruel Assyrians, with their capital at Ashur. Armed with iron weapons and heavy chariots, Assyrian troops proved invincible. They raided as far as the Black Sea and ruled to the Mediterranean, marching into captivity (and often extinction) skilled workmen and sometimes entire populations.

Enriched by conquests and the labor of subject peoples, the kings of Assyria adorned palaces and decorated impressive buildings with monuments and stone reliefs of colossal winged animals. The last powerful king of Assyria, Ashurbanipal (668–627 B.C.), personally directed an effort to collect the literature and learning of Mesopotamian civilizations. His royal library at Nineveh, excavated in the 19th century, acquired thousands of cuneiform tablets, including the Epic of Gilgamesh and the Babylonian Creation Epic. This single most important collection of cuneiform tablets provides modern historians with much of their knowledge of the culture and history of the Tigris-Euphrates Plain.

After the collapse of the Assyrian Empire, the center of power and wealth on the Tigris-Euphrates Plain shifted again to the city of Babylon. The neo-Babylonian (or Chaldean) Empire, which extended from the head of the Persian Gulf to the Mediterranean Sea, gathered wealth to give Babylon a final burst of glory before it gradually faded away.

The next great empire had its base in the mountains east of the Tigris River. The Medes were the first Iranian-speaking group to establish an empire. They dominated a large territory to the east and north of Babylonia. About the middle of the 6th century B.C. the empire of the Medes was taken over by their fellow Iranians and former subjects, the Persians. Under the leadership of Cyrus the Great and his successors, most of the civilized world except for East Asia and the defiant city-states of Greece, fell under the sway of the Persian Empire.

Like the Assyrians before them, the Persians did not hesitate to use force if the assigned taxes, or "gifts," were not sent by subject communities when due. On the other hand, many of the Persian rulers tried to gain voluntary submission of their

Ninevah: how it may have looked from ruins

subjects by showing toleration for local culture.

The vast Persian Empire was united by improved roads, a postal system for official use, uniform laws and employment of a single language for administrative purposes. The language of administration was not Persian, but Aramaic, which several centuries earlier had become dominant in business in the region between the Euphrates River and the Mediterranean Coast. The empire was divided into provinces, each with a governor (satrap) responsible to the Great King. Eventually the personal ambitions of these satraps contributed to the weakening of the empire. Another destructive force within the empire consisted of civil wars led by rival claimants to the throne. Each faction sought to gain power,

receive honor and control the wealth produced by civilization.

The extension of Persian control over the Indus Valley had significant cultural effects. Interchange of religious and philosophical ideas was one. Another was the spread of the idea of an alphabet into South Asia, apparently in the 5th century B.C. The earliest alphabet used in the Indus-Ganges civilization preserved forms of the Aramaic alphabet used in the Persian Empire. During the period of Persian domination to the west of it, the Ganges Basin was under the control of rival minor kings. The largest of the kingdoms was that of Magadha near the mouth of the Ganges River. Meanwhile, civilization was also developing in the southern part of the Indian Peninsula.

ASSYRIAN EMPIRE AT ITS GREATEST EXTENT

7TH CENTURY B.C.

Hebrews and Judaeans

In contrast to the material splendor displayed by the great empires of the river valleys, the Hebrew tribes of the plains and highlands of Canaan gave to the world an idea, monotheism. In sharp contrast to the many gods worshipped by surrounding societies, the Hebrew prophets and scriptures proclaimed that one God, Yahweh (or Jehovah), created all; His legal code stipulated ethical and moral behavior far superior to the times. Preserved by Judaism and expanded by Christianity, the unique religion of the Hebrews has influenced European civilization more than any other cultural achievement of the ancient world.

Historical research in the 20th century lends credence to the accounts given in the Jewish scriptures, which also form the Old Testament of the Bible. The first patriarch, Abraham, claimed as ancestor by both Jewish and Arab societies, roamed

Canaan with his herds, erecting in the midst of polytheism altars to Yahweh. His grandson, Jacob, also known as Israel, is generally regarded as the first Hebrew: from his sons descended the tribes of *B'nai Yisra'el*, the Children of Israel. After settling in Egypt for generations, under Moses the Hebrews escaped from captivity, to be led into Canaan by Joshua, perhaps around 1400 B.C.

Tempted by religions with visual gods— idols physically present that could be worshipped—the ancient Hebrews sometimes seem hardly distinguishable from other Canaanite tribes. They rarely ruled the entire land, and for several centuries lacked political unity even in the central highlands where their population was concentrated, running from north to south between the Mediterranean and the Jordan River. Their first king, Saul, faced invasions from the Philistines of the coastal plain and nomadic

tribes to the south and east. However, after David succeeded to the throne around 1000 B.C., the little kingdom expanded in size and military prowess, reaching its zenith in peace and prosperity under David's son Solomon (961–922 B.C.), who built the first temple dedicated to Yahweh in Jerusalem, the capital.

At Solomon's death the state fractured, with the northern tribes establishing a Kingdom of Israel in Samaria. Lacking the great religious center of Jerusalem, and prey both to Canaanite religions and invasion by foreign armies, the Kingdom of Israel lasted until destroyed by the Assyrians in 722 B.C. Under the somewhat more capable kings of the House of David, the southern Kingdom of Judah survived until finally captured by the great neo-Babylonian ruler Nebuchadnezzar in 586 B.C. His troops carried off to exile in Babylon the royal family of Judah, together with many of the upper classes and skilled workers.

After Cyrus the Great captured Babylon in 539 B.C. (and in the process ended over two thousand years of Mesopotamian empires), the liberal religious policies of the new Persian Empire allowed some worshippers of Yahweh to return to the land of their forebears, while others remained

**Israel and Judah under
King David, c. 1000 B.C.**

19

in Persia and Mesopotamia, developing a large and often prosperous center of Judaism. Despite local opposition, those who returned rebuilt the walls of Jerusalem, then the Temple itself, under tolerant Persian rule.

Far greater threats to Judaism followed the next conquerors, the Hellenistic armies of Alexander the Great in 332 B.C. Greek ideas soon came to dominate the Jewish upper classes as they discovered Greek athletics, music, and art as well as the Greek language itself. Rational religious concepts, especially about resurrection and angels, deeply impressed the wealthy, and separated them from most Jews, with their more traditional and pious values.

Direct attacks on Jewish religion and customs aroused greater resistance. When the Seleucid rulers of Syria, having captured Palestine, ordered pigs sacrificed to Zeus at the Temple, rebellion broke out. After bitter fighting, Jewish independence briefly flared anew under the Hasmonaeans, also known as the Maccabees (129–63 B.C.). Split by political rivalry, divided by religious factions and resented by non-Jewish inhabitants, the Jewish territories were easily annexed to Rome by Pompey in 63 B.C. Julius Caesar later appointed a governor named Antipater, an Idumaean from the coastal region previously conquered by the Hasmonaeans and himself possibly a descendant of the Israelites' ancient enemies, the Philistines. Converted to Judaism but opposed by the Hasmonaeans, Antipater and his sons struggled to control Judea. Finally, declared King of Judea by the Roman Senate, and aided by Roman troops, his son Herod succeeded in capturing Jerusalem (37 B.C.).

All accounts portray Herod as hated by his subjects, for many causes: a foreigner himself, a collaborator dependent on Roman rule, and a tyrant capable of killing his own sons as well as ordering the massacre of the infants of Bethlehem reported in the Gospels. Nevertheless, Herod built cities and established peace; for the non-Jews he provided festivals and Greek arts. For the Jews, he rebuilt the Temple, on a grander scale than ever before. His heirs proved less capable, and Caesar Augustus extended direct Roman rule over the area.

Increasing Jewish opposition to Rome broke into open rebellion in A.D. 66, after increasingly intolerant policies of the Emperors Caligula and Nero. Aided by rivalries for the throne in Rome, Judea became independent again, but four years later Titus defeated the Jewish armies and sacked Jerusalem after a lengthy siege. The temple, so recently rebuilt by Herod, was destroyed, and Jewish zealots holding the fortress of Masada overlooking the Dead

Solomon's Temple was made from timber brought from Tyre

Sea finally committed suicide rather than surrender. Again the Jewish population faced persecution and forced exile (called the Diaspora). After a second failed rebellion in 135 A.D. Rome made Judea a pagan colony, prohibiting Jews from living there, although believers survived in neighboring Galilee and elsewhere throughout the Roman Empire, as well as flourishing on occasion in Babylonia.

A rabbi reads from the _Torah_ in a synagogue

The Hellenistic Age, Roman Rule and Christianity

ALEXANDER

When the sudden and furious conquests of Alexander the Great shattered the dominance of Persian emperors in Asia, a new language and a new civilization began their lengthy domination of Southwest Asia. For centuries the city-states of Greece had learned from the older civilizations to the East. In the decades after 500 B.C. they fought off Persian invasions with difficulty, in heroic battles such as Marathon, Thermopylae, and Salamis. However, in 11 short years after 334 B.C., Alexander the Great, king of Macedonia though Greek in culture and education, captured the known world as far as India and established the greatest empire then known. This laid the political conditions for a new era of civilization called *Hellenistic,* meaning "Greek-like," in contrast to the previous Greek, or Hellenic.

Although Alexander's empire broke up after his death at the young age of 33, rival kingdoms succeeded him in Egypt (the Ptolemies) and Southwest Asia (the Seleucids). In both kingdoms Greeks and Macedonians who formed the urban upper class of rulers, soldiers, merchants and artisans mixed with the local population, in the process creating Hellenistic civilization. Trade flourished, from India and even China in the east to Italy and North Africa in the west. The growing wealth made possible great libraries at Alexandria and Pergamum as well as new cities and art. Science and learning advanced dramatically: among other achievements, scholars calculated the earth's circumference, founded geometry, and interpreted literature.

After 200 B.C., however, the Hellenistic world began to decline. Never solidly established east of Mesopotamia, the Seleucids retreated from the Iranian plateau and later from Mesopotamia in the face of Parthian invasions. Moreover, within the remaining territories, native populations increasingly rejected Greek beliefs, values, and language. With relative ease, then, the Roman general Pompey captured the remaining Seleucid territories (64 B.C.) and

Egypt finally fell to Octavian (30 B.C.). However, the Romans failed to conquer either Mesopotamia or Persia from the Parthians. Moreover, within those Asian territories it did conquer, Greek rather than Latin remained the language of trade and learning. Significantly, the struggle between Hellenistic and local beliefs and culture continued, most importantly in Judea.

Into this world was born Jesus of Nazareth. Educated by his mother, rather than by either Jewish scribes or Hellenistic scholars, in adulthood he preached a message of love and obedience, of humility and enjoyment of the good. As reports of his apparent miracles spread, he rapidly gained a following of Jews and others who hoped for deliverance—divinely aided deliverance—from Rome. Nevertheless, his popularity and message threatened both the Hellenized Sadducees and the carefully traditional Pharisees. Charged by the Jewish leadership with claiming to be the Son of God, he seemed to Pontius Pilate, the Roman prefect, another agitator and resistance leader. Deserted by almost all his disciples and those who desired political revolution, he was crucified as King of the Jews. Dying at about the same age as Alexander, Jesus conquered no territories, founded no cities, and overthrew no empires.

To his followers, however, Jesus conquered much more than the world. According to the New Testament, this "Only Begotten Son" of God defeated death itself. His crucifixion made possible the redemption of mankind from sin. His apparent resurrection three days later, and subsequent return to heaven, brought the assurance of a final Judgment followed by a New Earth ruled by God. Passages from the Jewish scriptures—to Christians now the Old Testament—were interpreted to show him as the fulfillment of many prophecies of the Messiah (Greek, *Christ*). Within weeks of his death an active and growing church sprang up in Jerusalem.

Christianity first spread most rapidly among Jewish communities scattered about the Roman Empire. Within a generation, however, the preaching and writings of St. Paul rendered Christianity a world religion that promised salvation to all who believed, whether Jewish or not. Both hindered and helped by occasional persecution, Christianity spread rapidly, especially among the lower classes. By the middle of the 2nd century, the major rules of the faith had been established, the Canon of Biblical books had been largely selected, and the church had been organized into a hierarchy. When persecution by the Emperor Diocletian failed to destroy the church (303–311), the church triumphed, for his successor Constantine

granted toleration and equality for Christianity while eliminating cults of the state.

In matters beyond religion, Constantine changed the face of the Roman Empire as well. In 330 A.D. he moved the capital from "heathen Rome" to Byzantium on the shores of the Bosporus. During the two centuries that followed, the eastern and western halves of the empire drifted apart, each facing invasion and struggling to maintain order and civilization in the midst of economic decay. Gradually there emerged in the east the Byzantine Empire, ruling over Greece as well as Asia Minor, geographical Syria, and Egypt. Greek in language, and Hellenistic in much of its culture, though still calling itself Rome, the Byzantine Empire mixed Christianity with the grandeur of Oriental potentates. The emperor ruled absolutely, as God's representative on earth, standing as head of the military, government, and church.

For almost a thousand years, the Byzantine Empire survived: an enormous accomplishment that contrasts with the total collapse of Roman rule in the West. During those centuries it witnessed great achievements in law, and it preserved Greek and Roman learning largely lost elsewhere. In art and architecture the stunning beauty created by Byzantine craftsmen remains at St. Marks in Venice and Hagia Sophia in Istanbul. As defenders of the faith, the Byzantine military stopped numerous invasions by infidels, and passed along to Russia and much of Eastern Europe, Orthodox Christianity and Greek-based alphabets. Nevertheless, bloodshed stains many pages of Byzantine history, and tolerance brightens few. When conflicts in theology and religion followed the same dividing lines as differences in language and culture between Greek rulers and native inhabitants of Egypt and Syria, the consequence was restlessness in those lands and weakened loyalties to the empire. When new armies appeared out of Arabia in the middle of the seventh century, Syrian, Egyptian, and North African possessions were quickly lost.

Zoroastrian, Buddhist and Hindu Cultures

When the Roman legions attempted to press eastward from Syria in the 1st century B.C., they were stopped by another military power, the Parthian Empire. This state had its origins in the 3rd century B.C. when warriors from Parthia, an area in the northeast part of the Iranian Plateau, gained local independence from Hellenistic rulers. Regarding themselves as the heirs of the first Persian Empire, the Parthians eventually expanded their control both east and west, building an empire that stretched from the Euphrates Plain to the Indus River.

Hellenistic culture declined, but was not totally eradicated, within the territory under Parthian rule. Native ideas, architecture, art and literature developed along independent lines. Although religious activity in Parthian domains is not well known, it seems that Zoroastrianism made great advances. This faith revered the teachings of Zarathustra, who lived during the 7th century B.C. In its developed form, Zoroastrianism stressed the struggle between two principal supernatural beings representing good and evil. The leading position was held by Ahura Mazda, the god of light and goodness.

About 225 A.D. the weakened leadership of the Parthians was replaced by a Persian dynasty descended from a little-known figure named Sassan. Occupying the Parthian capital of Ctesiphon on the Tigris as their own, the Sassanids presented themselves as the restorers of the purity of the first Persian Empire. Zoroastrianism took on its most highly developed form as the established religion of the government. The Sassanids increased the level of civilization in their territories by encouraging the development of cities.

The Sassanids also possessed a strong expansionist urge; this kept them in conflict with their neighbors, such as the Late Roman (Byzantine) Empire to the west, which had similar impulses. For a time in the 6th century and the first decades of the next, the Sassanid Empire was the world's leading power. In a final burst of militancy it captured Damascus and Jerusalem from Byzantium in 614, but lost them a decade and a half later. The Sassanid Empire, exhausted by the wars, succumbed to the attacks of the Muslim Arabs beginning with the fall of Ctesiphon in 637.

The golden age of Buddhism in the Indian Peninsula occurred in the state ruled by the Maurya family. At its height in the 3rd century B.C. the Mauryan Empire controlled the Ganges Basin, the Indus Valley and large regions to the south and north-west. The most illustrious ruler was Asoka (or Ashoka); during his long reign (273–232 B.C.) he turned from bloody wars of expansion to the peaceful teaching of Buddhism.

Gautama Buddha had lived several centuries earlier and it was Asoka's patronage of the Buddha's teachings which contributed greatly to the spread of Buddhism as a world religion.

Many inscribed pillars set up on Asoka's orders have been found in all parts of modern India, in Pakistan and in southern Afghanistan. These provide scholars with a picture of that early period, including Mauryan knowledge of the Hellenistic world to the west. After the death of Asoka the Great, the empire of the Maurya declined and finally ended in 185 B.C. It was replaced by many small states about which little information is available.

For nearly five centuries during which there was a notable development of trade with the outside world, attempts to build a new empire in the Indian Peninsula failed. Then in the early 4th century A.D., a territory nearly as extensive as that ruled by the Maurya was brought under the control of the Gupta dynasty. The Gupta period from the early 4th to the early 6th century is often described as the golden age of Hindu culture in the Ganges Basin, though the central and southern parts of the peninsula were to achieve their zenith of classical Hindu culture later.

The Gupta Empire reached its height from its capital of Ayodhya on the Ganges River, during the reign of Chandra Gupta II (A.D. 385 to 413). Later, particularly from about A.D. 480 to 490, Hindu civilization was badly mauled by invading Huns, who raided from bases north of the Hindu Kush Mountains. The menace of the Huns and the disturbances caused by various other peoples entering the Indian Peninsula from Central Asia did not subside for nearly a century. By then the region was again divided into a number of warring local kingdoms.

Little is known about events until the early 7th century, when a youth of only 16 years became king of a small state and attempted to build an empire. This king, Harsha, ruled well for 41 years. Not only was he a patron of art and literature, but was himself a poet and playwright. Three of his plays in Sanskrit have survived, including one called "The Pearl Necklace." With Harsha's death the last great Hindu kingdom in the Ganges-Indus region ended. Then a pattern of rival little kingdoms was a prelude to later foreign invasion.

Life-size sculpture of Buddha
Courtesy: Government of India

Muhammad and the Rise of Islam

A prayer in Tehran (late 19th century drawing)

In the rugged desert landscape of western Arabia, far from civilization's major centers, some six centuries after Christ the third great monotheistic religion arose with the preaching of Muhammad. This solemn and meditative man warned the citizens of the city of Mecca of a coming great cataclysm to end the earth, followed by a final judgment over all deeds that would grant to the righteous heaven, and to the evil, the fires of hell. From his initial messages of repentance and care of one's fellows, Muhammad's teachings expanded to fill almost all aspects of society. This religious protest first attracted a few followers, and later an entire city. Within a generation the entire Middle East lay conquered by a newly united people, and a new civilization, the Islamic, began its often brilliant rise.

Born about 572, probably after his father's death, Muhammad was orphaned as a child when his mother died. Few details of his early life are certain, but he grew up in a society undergoing dramatic social changes.

Prolonged conflict between the Sassanid Persian and Byzantine empires disrupted the traditional Mesopotamian trade route between India and the Mediterranean. One alternative route ran along the mountainous western coast of Arabia. Several Arabian tribes remained neutral in the great clash between Byzantium and Persia that stretched as far south as Yemen, and this encouraged trade. So did the religious customs that brought an annual truce to desert warfare and a pilgrimage to Mecca. Some Arab tribes, particularly Muhammad's own Quraysh, seized the opportunities, and exchanged herds for trade caravans. In the process Arab society itself changed significantly. For wealthy merchants, houses replaced tents, and the family structure strengthened as fathers viewed sons as assistants and successors. However, the increasing wealth meant greater disparities of wealth, and also a decline in loyalty to the clan and tribe. As the family strengthened, other social bonds weakened, and the poor increasingly found charity less common.

Raised by relatives and trained as a merchant, Muhammad had the good fortune to marry Khadija, a rather older widow of substantial wealth. Nevertheless, despite his financial success, he suffered inner distress over social wrongs, and meditated extensively. At the age of 40 he is alleged to have become conscious of a message from the angel Gabriel to praise the one God, Allah, as the Creator, and to care for the unfortunate.

Though living in a pagan culture, and often using the rhymed prose of common soothsayers, from his travels as a merchant, Muhammad had become familiar with the Jewish and Christian customs and beliefs. He now identified Allah as the God of their scriptures, recognized many of their prophets and considered himself the final Messenger, who recited the words sent from heaven.

Like many religious leaders, Muhammad at first appealed to relatives and friends, as well as the unfortunate. However, he aroused the hostility and anger of the leading merchants and politicians of Mecca by his vision of a dreadful judgment, by his strident demands for greater charity, and even more by his condemnation of pagan idol worship. This struck at the financial foundation of Meccan society, for pilgrimages to Mecca, with its famous black stone *Ka'aba* provided great opportunity for trade, and religion sanctioned an annual truce from raids, valuable to merchants and pilgrims alike.

Strongly conflicting with Muslim beliefs, Western scholars suggested that at one point Muhammad appeared to defuse the situation by confirming publicly that three female deities, al-Lat, al-Uzza and al-Manat, were the daughters of Allah; as such they could intercede with their Father. However, Muhammad's faithful soon recoiled at the implication of more than one god, and denounced the goddesses as mere inventions; the verses acknowledging them became the "Satanic Verses."

As pressure became economic embargo and persecution, some followers fled to Ethiopia. By 622 Muhammad himself forsook Mecca for Yathrib, soon renamed Medina, "The City" of the Prophet. Celebrated as the *Hijra*, and marking the beginning of the Muslim era, the event nevertheless supports a variety of interpretations. Did Muhammad flee from persecution, or emigrate by choice? Did he fear the Meccans because of religious opposition, or Meccan opposition to his becoming the leader of a rival community strategically situated to strangle their trade route north?

Once in Medina, Muhammad became far more than a religious leader. He had come, by agreement, as the leader of the "Ummah" or community: he was the primary secular authority. His Meccan followers abandoned the protection of the tribes of their birth by following him to Medina. Now they formed in effect a new tribe, and Muhammad became particularly responsible for their welfare, and that of the converts in Medina. Certainly, too, the visions continued, and included with the calls to repentance much practical material for the lawgiver of a new society.

The ten years Muhammad lived in Medina established the religion of "Islam" (pronounced like "this lamb"), or submission to God. Despite military defeats and political resistance from Jews and other non-believers resident in Medina, the Muslim ("One who submits") community grew and adopted the distinctive beliefs and practices that continue to the present. The individual Believer had five obligations. He must believe, confessing that "There is no God but Allah, and Muhammad is his Messenger," and bow in ritual prayer five times daily, prompted by the call from the minaret of the mosque. Annually, during the Islamic month of Ramadan, he must abstain from food, drink, and sex during the day. If possible, once during his lifetime he should undertake a pilgrimage (hajj) to Mecca. Finally, he must contribute annually a portion of his wealth as a charity or tax. Beyond these duties, the Muslim must accept the Quran ("Recitation") as the infallible word of God, interpreted by the consensus of the Islamic community as well as the traditions (or "sayings") of Muhammad carefully handed down over the generations.

Scholarly summaries of Islam, much like the paragraph above, rarely do justice to the combination of religious observances and custom in Islamic societies. The religion deliberately appeals to people of all languages and nations, and promises equality among the believers, who in forming the Ummah attempt to have religious boundaries the same as political. For centuries the Umayyad and Ab-

basid caliphates achieved this in practice, as they fused subjects of varied languages and religions into a Muslim society ruled more or less within the framework of Islamic law. Despite Muhammad's condemnation of the practices of wealthy Meccans, private property is allowed, and numerous traditions report God's favor towards merchants. The payment of interest is forbidden, paralleling original Jewish and Christian views of usury.

In social aspects, Islam reinforced the position of the husband, allowing up to four wives and divorce on (his) demand, though he was urged to limit himself to one wife if he felt incapable of treating her fairly. Nevertheless, a woman retained the right to property she brought into a marriage, a privilege enjoyed centuries before Western nations granted similar property rights to women. On balance, scholars agree that Muhammad raised the status and condition of women, in part by rigidly punishing adultery as well as condemning the practice of female infanticide.

A Muslim's worship contrasts substantially with certain aspects of Jewish and Christian traditions, yet there are many similarities: sermons, ritual prayers, and reading (or recitation from memory) of the scriptures. However, singing and other music are remarkable for their absence, as are drawings, paintings, or sculptures of living things. Friday, the day of worship, is not a day of rest, and the believers commonly gather in the mosque in the afternoon, entering without shoes after washing hands and feet. Generally in Islam there is no equivalent of a priesthood: any believer may address the congregation, who stand in rows before the pulpit, with the women meeting separately. The dead await physical resurrection and the judgment, and are mourned extensively at the funeral and 40 days thereafter.

Thanks to the media, Westerners are much more familiar with more superficial regulations of Muslim society, such as amputation for certain crimes. The Quran strictly forbids wine, and by extension alcoholic drinks of any kind. Pork, carrion, and blood are forbidden, but in great contrast to the many unclean foods of Mosaic Law, Allah is thanked for the abundance of animals created to be eaten. In dress, the veil, often the trademark of a Muslim woman, in fact reflects preexisting Persian practice rather than explicit commands in the Quran or traditions of Muhammad. Instead, recognizing the power of temptation in sexual matters, Muslims must dress modestly, an injunction interpreted in some circles as requiring a woman's upper arms and shoulders to be covered. Despite the climate, men's legs are always covered.

Perhaps the Islamic doctrine most perplexing to modern, secular societies is the concept of *Jihad*, occasionally listed as a sixth individual duty. In everyday speech the term admits many meanings such as task or burden, or even one's struggle. In the context of religion, it often, though not exclusively, implied an armed struggle for the faith, to extend the boundaries of Islam or defend them from invasion by the infidel. Scholars a generation ago frequently stressed that many kinds of work for the benefit of the Ummah could be considered Jihad. However, recent events, especially the rise of groups such as Islamic Jihad in Lebanon, leave little doubt that to a significant portion of the Muslim world, the struggle continues between Dar al-Salaam, the House of Peace (i.e., Islam) and the Dar al-Harb, the House of War (i.e., the unbelievers), fourteen hundred (Islamic) years after Muhammad's Hijra.

Then did Islam spread largely by conquest and forced conversions? Outside the Hijaz, only rarely: during the early conquests, Arab Muslims regarded with some suspicion those who wished to adopt the faith of their conquerors. In many places, it may have taken a century or two before the majority of the population accepted Islam. The converts' motives were mixed. To some, accepting the new religion removed discriminatory taxes. To others, a new community might bring different laws and personal advantages. Where missionary activity led to spiritual conviction, it often was the work of Islamic brotherhoods. Organized around a master, who initiated disciples in the ritual and beliefs of the particular brotherhood, these *Sufi* (from "one garbed in wool"; a holy man) orders reached beyond formal Islam into mysticism. They frequently incorporated ideas of existing religions, and this, like the missionary fervor of the members, advanced Islam as a spiritual force. On occasion, linked to Muslim rulers, Sufi brotherhoods also aided Islam as a conquering political force.

Islamic Expansion and Society: The Arab Caliphate

A new Mosque near Hofuf, Saudi Arabia combines traditional architecture with modern materials

For eight often precarious years after the Hijra, Muhammad struggled to maintain the Muslim community in the face of Meccan opposition. After 624, there were raids on Meccan caravans and battles as the Meccans counterattacked, as well as expulsions and massacres of the Jewish tribes of Medina and alliances struck with Bedouin tribes. Finally, in 630, Mecca capitulated, and the entire population converted. Almost all Arabia acknowledged Muhammad as politically supreme, though many tribes hardly accepted Islam. Two years later, however, at the height of his political power, Muhammad died. Although about 60 years of age, and too ill to worship in his last days, he left no messages about the future of Islamic society or its government.

As news spread that the Messenger of God lay dead, Muhammad's closest advisors met hurriedly to select a new leader of the community and thus avoid its disintegration under rival leaders. They settled on Abu Bakr, one of the earliest converts, and the next day the community publicly pledged allegiance to him. His position was imprecise, for Muhammad had been prophet, chief judge, supreme military commander, and sole legislator. Abu Bakr gained the vague title *Khalifat Rasul Allah:* "Successor to the Messenger of God," generally known in English as the Caliph. No prophet himself, but Commander of the Faithful, Abu Bakr led the Muslim community as Muhammad's secular successor and the sovereign in whose name the Friday prayers were offered.

Though only ruling for two years, Abu Bakr decided many of the crucial issues for the new Islamic state. When tribes admitting only political allegiance to Muhammad himself, and denying Islamic authority, attempted to secede, Abu Bakr sent armies under Khalid ibn al-Walid and other generals to conquer all Arabia. Quickly victorious, the Muslim armies established the central control of the Caliph, altering greatly the pre-existing Arab patterns of temporary alliances and confederations. Of additional importance, the apostate tribes soon were permitted to join the Muslim armies almost wholesale, thus turning energies long spent in violence between Arabs into a remarkable weapon directed by the Caliph.

The weapon quickly proved useful. Under Muhammad, Muslim raiders reached the fringes of the Byzantine Empire. Under Abu Bakr, out of the desert Arab columns appeared almost simultaneously, attacking Byzantine cities in Palestine and Persian troops in Iraq. The great mobility of their camel transport enabled them to strike far from the defending forces. At one crucial period Khalid ibn al-Walid's troops rapidly crossed the desert from Iraq to defeat the Byzantine army, leaving Palestine open to Muslim conquest.

Proclaimed caliph at Abu Bakr's passing, Umar (ruled 634–644) continued the policy of conquest. In 637 Arab armies defeated the Byzantine emperor at the Battle of Yarmuk, thus adding Syria to Arab conquests. The homeland of Christianity was lost to Christian rule, Jerusalem surrendering in 638. Meanwhile, at Kadisiya in Iraq, the Persian army was routed and Sassanid rule effectively destroyed. Soon afterwards, raiding forces unleashed by Umar on Egypt proved unexpectedly successful, and in 641 its last Byzantine city, Alexandria, surrendered. For the next century the Muslim expansion continued, to the east across the Iranian plateau into Central Asia, to the west across North Africa and into Spain and France.

To the European Christian imagination the Muslim conquests were a matter of religious crusades. Muhammad appeared as the anti-Christ of scripture; his conquering hordes offered captives the choice of conversion or the sword. Reality was somewhat more complicated, and explanations abound. Some causes lay within Arabia: possibly it was overpopulated, and now unified, its people sought living space outside it. Certainly religion played a great role in motivating individual soldiers, for death in battle to extend the boundaries of Islam brought God's mercy at the judgment and the promise of greater physical comforts and pleasures in heaven than on earth.

Other reasons for the dramatic rise lay outside the Muslim community. For the previous century in particular, the Byzantine and Sassanid empires had fought long and hard over Syria. Now both empires lay exhausted, separated by buffer states of Arab tribes unlikely to halt armies from Arabia. Under Byzantine rule, the Christian farmers of Syria and Egypt had long suffered heavy taxes, an alien language, and religious persecution over their theological interpretation of Christ. When Arab armies arrived, the vast majority of inhabitants did not resist: the Arabs offered not apostasy or death, but rather lower taxes and greater religious freedom. Likewise, in Iraq the native inhabitants had never become Persian; they too welcomed the Muslims. Only in Asia

Minor, with its Hellenic population, were the Arab invasions repulsed. In Iran, the collapse of the Sassanid dynasty enabled a rapid Muslim conquest, but it would become complicated in differing interpretations of Islam.

Administration of the new empire from Medina proved a difficult task. The caliph's share of the booty from the conquest provided great riches, but numerous problems arose. One was membership in the Muslim community, now a lucrative benefit, as the caliph's income from the captured territories was distributed among all Muslims, whose taxes in any case were minimal. Conversion, therefore, brought administrative difficulties: taxpayers became welfare recipients. To discourage them, converts had to be attached to Arab tribes. Despite Muhammad's message to all, regardless of tongue or nation, in some cases converts were not freed of their taxes on becoming Muslims. Later the contrast between religious appeal and fiscal expediency would fester and encourage the violent overthrow of one dynasty of caliphs.

Land ownership was another problem. Had Muslim soldiers received lands upon their conquest, their self-interest would have reduced the drive for further conquests. The issue was resolved in theory at least by keeping agricultural land as public land, the property of the caliph, with taxes on the harvest. Muslim troops were established in barracks cities on the fringes of cultivation, the better to keep them accustomed to a hard life and to separate ruling from ruled.

Where the local populations surrendered willingly, and possessed scriptures, they became *dimmis*—"protected subjects." The exact rights depended on the local surrender terms, but in general, each recognized sect received religious toleration and maintained its own laws of personal status under its chief religious leader, typically a bishop or patriarch. For example, divorce, freely available to Muslim men, remained prohibited in most circumstances in the Christian communities. (A Christian desiring an additional wife, or divorce from his existing one, could usually convert to Islam.) Laws of marriage and inheritance likewise varied by religion.

Islamic toleration, though far greater than the practices in Europe of the period, did not mean freedom or equality, but limited rights mixed with discrimination. Non-Muslim testimony against a Muslim was suspect in the courts. New churches generally could not be built, nor church bells rung often, and any Muslim who adopted Christianity (unlikely though that was) risked the death penalty for apostasy. Members of the protected sects did avoid military obligations, but paid discriminatory taxes and observed separate codes of dress and behavior.

A devout man, Umar also led his community in religious matters as well as political. Many Muslims had memorized lengthy passages of Muhammad's messages, others had been written on palm-leaves, stones, and other available materials. However, renderings could differ. Therefore Umar began the collection of an authoritative book of Muhammad's recitations: the Quran. Completed and authorized by Umar's successor as Caliph, Uthman (644–656), the original *Quran* used the *Kufic* script lacking the dots that distinguish so many Arabic letters from each other. The result, not surprisingly, was variant readings, sometimes on matters of importance between Islamic groups.

The death of Uthman at the hands of assassins revealed deep rivalries within the Muslim world, rivalries of ideology and power. His rule of a dozen years illustrated the strength of the Quraysh, Muhammad's tribe from Mecca who had nevertheless been his most aggressive adversaries. Uthman appointed many Quraysh to high office, some of them close relatives newly ac-

Pilgrims visiting the Ka'aba, sacred shrine of the Great Mosque in Mecca

quainted with Islam. Their rule created consternation among political opponents, who saw the actions undermining Muhammad's goal of a *universal Muslim community*. Their sentiments found much satisfaction in the selection of Ali as the fourth, and final, Orthodox Caliph.

Muhammad's cousin and son-in-law, Ali nevertheless entered office surrounded by suspicions that he was an accomplice to the assassination of his predecessor, Uthman. After moving his capital from Medina to Iraq, and out-maneuvered by his opponents and facing rebellion within his own supporters over his policies, Ali was murdered in 661. His major opponent, Uthman's cousin Muawiya, became Caliph in Damascus, purchasing the acquiescence of Ali's oldest son, Hasan, and established the Umayyad dynasty of caliphs.

From their capital at Damascus, the Umayyads ruled the entire Muslim world. Attacks on the Byzantine Empire were renewed; Constantinople itself came under siege in 717. In some respects Arab, rather than Muslim, in their approach to administration, the Umayyads first used the existing Coptic, Greek and Persian administrations, ranging from coinage to provincial officials. Where necessary, as in Iraq, the Umayyads ruthlessly repressed disorder and established calm, for the first time in years. Religiously, however, by opposing Ali, and especially by defeating and killing his younger son Husayn at the battle of Karbala, the Umayyads split the Muslim world into two factions. Moreover, when they sought to rule by family descent, they introduced a fatal flaw. Those who had opposed in battle Muhammad's son-in-law and shed the blood of his grandson stirred resentments that in ninety years would overwhelm their descendants.

To the strife between Ali and the Umayyads is commonly traced the origins of the major sectarian divisions in the Muslim world. In particular, as the supporters of Ali broke away to form the *Shi'a* ("Partisans" of Ali), those accepting Umayyad rule became the *Sunni*, whose name implied orthodoxy. A number of aspects set Shi'a Islam firmly apart from Sunni practice. Its followers claim that Ali's family had been marked to lead the community from the start. Therefore even the pious caliphs Abu Bakr and Umar should be cursed; the Umayyads were clearly illegitimate. More commonly, however, the Shi'a termed those God appointed over them as Imams, or leaders, who possessed special knowledge needed to guide the Muslim community. Shi'ism commonly traces a succession of Imams, beginning with Ali. To the Imams was given authoritative understanding of the

Arab tribesmen water their horses

Quran; only traditions used by them are considered genuine.

Beginning as a political and social protest movement among Arabs, and quickly spreading to the converts, Shi'ism soon included many different groups with rival interpretations and leaders. According to most Shi'a, however, the twelfth Imam disappeared in 878. While the Imam remains hidden, the law and creed would be interpreted by religious scholars as his agents. Consequently, although Shi'a Islam originally began with stress on the rulership of the family of Ali, it has evolved to allow a greater role in political affairs for the religious establishment than does Sunni Islam. In addition, it awaits the hidden Imam, the Mahdi, who will return to save humanity.

Unsympathetic Western commentators typically note two distinct beliefs of Shi'a Islam, temporary marriage and dissimulation. Despite its obvious meaning, temporary marriage need not prove brief, though it may. Instead, it established a marriage for a period contracted in advance, frequently as long as 99 years in the case of a Shi'a man who marries a Christian woman who does not convert. Dissimulation, a practice foreign to western ethics, allows, or even enjoins a Shi'a to renounce his own religion when facing persecution or difficulty.

Beyond technical differences with Sunni Islam, the Shi'a bring to religion an emotional fervency often lacking in the more rational Sunni variety. The agony and death of Husayn at the battle of Karbala are portrayed annually at the anniversary with marches and flagellation. As their own blood streams from self-inflicted wounds, the marchers feel a unity with one who suffered 1300 years ago. For this and other reasons, many Shi'a consider life on the earth a brief interlude, and death fighting for Allah brings rapidly the joys of heaven.

The Shi'a played an important, but not exclusive, role in the overthrow of the Umayyad caliphate. After an extensive propaganda campaign concentrated among converts, in 746 rebellion broke out in the name of Abu al-Abbas, and drew support from many discontented groups in the empire. First Iran, then Iraq fell to the rebels with their standards of black, and in 750 they defeated and later almost annihilated the Umayyads. The new ruling dynasty, the Abbasid, claimed descent from Muhammad's uncle and the support of Ali's family. It ushered in a religious empire for all Muslims, in sharp contrast to the Arab kingdom of the Umayyads. Symbolizing the change, Abu al-Abbas moved the capital from Damascus to Iraq; his successor al-Mansur established the new empire along Persian rather than Arab lines, and constructed for it the magnificent capital of Baghdad. Amidst the pomp and titles, the Caliph exchanged the openness of an Arab tribal *sheikh* for an Oriental despot's glory and seclusion, complete with court executioner.

Trade and agricultural prosperity brought enormous wealth to Baghdad and its caliphs, who ruled an area larger than had Alexander the Great. Products from the Indus valley reached the Atlantic coast of Morocco, all without leaving the empire, and banks developed a widespread system of checks and letters of credit. Irrigation and drainage canals in the Tigris-

Euphrates valley brought prosperity to the heart of the empire, and new foods, products and technologies spread across the vast area unified by administration, religion, and increasingly, the use of Arabic. Paper making came from China, sugar from India, and the textile centers like Damascus and Mosul enriched European languages as city names became synonymous with particular qualities of cloth (damask; muslin).

Under Harun al-Rashid, perhaps the most famous Abbasid caliph, Baghdad became the wealthiest city on earth. It hosted one of civilization's great intellectual flowerings. Scholars from a variety of ethnic backgrounds studied Greek and Hindu authors, advanced the sciences, especially optics and astronomy, adopted "Arabic" numerals from India, and invented algebra. Historians, geographers, and essayists wrote at length. In religion, Muslim scholars collected traditions attributed to Muhammad, and developed schools of law. Meanwhile, theologians disputed at length the role of logic in religion and the appropriate methods of interpreting the Quran.

From the moment they seized the caliphate, the Abbasids faced revolts and challenges to their rule, from disenchanted supporters, Shi'a splinter groups, and opportunists. In such a vast empire, control from the center often weakened along the fringes, where independent Muslim states arose. In Baghdad itself, power fell increasingly into the hands of the vizir, or chief minister, who eventually attempted to make the office hereditary. Generals intervened between rival caliphs to decide succession to the throne, and what little power remained eventually fell into the hands of the Turkish bodyguard. Although caliphs did remain, by the end of the tenth century they ceased to rule even nominally territory outside Iraq. Two hundred years after the Abbasids seized power, the reinvigorated Iranians and Turks, new to both Islam and the Middle East, came to dominate the Asian lands of Islam.

A European artist's concept of a Umayyad palace in Damascus.
European reports of Arab societies often exaggerated the exotic and the sensual.

28

The Barbarian Invasions

During the Middle Islamic Period (the 10th to 15th centuries A.D.; 4th to 9th centuries by the Muslim calendar) waves of invaders assaulted civilization in Southwest Asia. There was an enormous loss of human life in these invasions, as well as extensive damage to the economy. The Turkish and European inroads in this period were relatively temperate preludes to the far more destructive incursions of the Mongols and their allies.

Adventuring bands of Turks from Central Asia began arriving in Southwest Asia in the 10th century. Soon they started establishing themselves as a kind of military aristocracy, and by the 12th century various regions from Asia Minor to the Ganges River had overlords of Turkish origin. While introducing a new military fierceness into society, the Turkish rulers patronized writers, poets and learned men, especially Persians. They readily adopted Islam with their own modifications.

The rapid influx of Turks into Iraq in the 11th century led to the establishment of a vast empire stretching from Central Asia to the Syrian coast. This was ruled by Toghril, of the Seljuk (Saljuq) clan, who made himself Sultan in Baghdad in 1055 while reducing the Abbasid Caliph to the status of a spiritual figurehead without

power. A decade and a half later, one of Toghril's nephews, Alp Arslan, defeated the Byzantine army and made the emperor a prisoner. This victory opened Asia Minor to Turkish immigration; in 1078 these newcomers established the Seljuk Sultanate of Rum. (*Rum*, pronounced like "room" in English, was the Asian name for the Byzantine Empire, which was still called Rome).

Seljuk attacks on the Byzantine Empire and interference with European pilgrims to Jerusalem helped inspire the Pope in 1095 to proclaim a Holy War to recapture the Holy Land. The soldiers of the First Crusade had to fight their way through the Seljuk Sultanate of Rum in order to reach Jerusalem and wrest it from the garrison placed there by a Muslim government based in Egypt. These Europeans joined in the turmoil and warfare of the Eastern Mediterranean, inflicting and receiving great loss of life. On capturing Jerusalem in 1099, the Crusaders set about an indiscriminate massacre of Muslims and Jews, but in general they were neither more nor less cruel than their foes.

The Latin Kingdom of Jerusalem was established to govern the Holy Land. It lost Jerusalem to the Muslims under the leadership of Salah ad-Din (Saladin) in

1187, but regained it again after his death. The Crusader kingdom finally lost the Holy City in 1244, but held coastal enclaves until near the end of the century. At times, the Crusaders had Muslim allies against other Muslim armies, so confused were the times and intense the political rivalries.

Seljuk power was not permanent, and rival Turkish leaders displaced them. In Iran, a line of rulers known as the Shahs of Khwarezm (Khwarizm) became prominent in the 12th century, but their power was too fragile to protect the region against new invaders.

Turks also established kingdoms in Buddhist and Hindu lands. Although there had been earlier Muslim raids into the Indus Valley, the main Muslim conquerors in the northern Indian Peninsula were Turks. The rival Hindu *Rajputs* (princes) were unable to provide a unified defense against the Turkish warriors.

In the second half of the 12th century, Turkish warriors led by the Sultan of Ghur wrought great destruction on Indian civilization. Their mounted archers swept down the Ganges Valley. Hindu temples were made into mosques and attempts were made to force people to convert to Islam. Buddhism in its stronghold in Bihar had its monks massacred, its books burned and its temples destroyed. Buddhism was virtually extinguished and Hindu rule was ended in northern India. From that time onward, Muslim ruler and Hindu subject were always aware of belonging to different orders.

Muslim rule in India, established following the conquests by the armies from Ghur, took the form of the Sultanate of Delhi. In 1206 a Turkish general (and legally a slave) seized the opportunity created by the murder of the Sultan of Ghur and proclaimed himself Sultan of Delhi. Although hampered by frequent struggles over the succession, the Sultanate expanded, and reached its greatest extent in the early 14th century, when it ruled nearly all of the Indian Peninsula. In some ways, the Sultanate flourished, for despite severe taxation of the largely Hindu peasantry, great prosperity developed in trade and the production of textiles in Bengal, Lahore, and Kashmir. Nevertheless, decay set in rapidly, and during the later 14th century the Sultanate of Delhi ruled only Northern India.

Southwest Asia began to feel the full force of the Mongol Empire in 1219 when an army of some 100,000 led by Chingis Khan (Genghis Khan), invaded Iran. Seeking vengeance against the Shahs of Khwarezm for their early cruelty against Mongol subjects, the invading Mongols looted, destroyed and massacred as they advanced. Tens of thousands of people were slaughtered, while only the craftsmen were spared for use as slaves in Mongolia.

Part of Chingis Khan's hordes turned south to ravage the Indus Valley and Punjab. Delhi became a refuge for Muslims escaping from Mongol terror. Suddenly, for no apparent reason, the Mongol hordes turned back for the long journey home, laden with the wealth of the devastated lands through which they had passed.

Again in 1227 the Mongols and their allied hordes returned to plunder. For ten years they could not be withstood by any force in Iran or in the Tigris-Euphrates Valley. Of all the great Muslim centers of civilization, only Cairo escaped entirely unscathed and the Mamluk rulers of Egypt gained much prestige for defeating a Mongol force in Palestine. By the middle of the 13th century, much of Southwest Asia was either ruled by Mongols or paying tribute to them. However, the next generation of Mongol rulers adopted Islam. Soon the empire began to break up into small states and the way was open for another empire builder.

Claiming to be a descendant of Chingis Khan, Timur Lang (Tamerlane) looms prominently in the Mongol tradition. He rose to power in the second half of the 14th century, using a dubious devotion to Islam for his political purposes. On the one hand, he may be pictured as a fierce warrior on horseback, wielding a bloody sword as he leads his hordes of Mongols and Turks over civilized areas which have no power to resist. On the other hand, he may also quite accurately be visualized seated in a splendid palace, surrounded by poets and admiring rare works of art, in his capital at Samarkand.

Before his death in 1405, Timur conquered the Tigris-Euphrates Plain and all of Iran. He raided the leading cities of his time, including Damascus, Moscow and Delhi. Upon the last-mentioned, he poured such destruction that a century was required for it to recover. In the very last years of his life, he defeated the rising Ottoman Empire in battle, took its Sultan prisoner and seized control of Asia Minor. Using the wealth of his vast domains, Timur made Samarkand a center of civilization.

Timur's successors ruled a smaller territory until near the end of the 15th century. They presided over a mixed Turkish-Mongol-Iranian culture which created many masterpieces of art and literature. With the end of the invasions of Central Asia hordes, a new order could take shape.

Gustave Doré's drawing of the Crusaders storming the walls of Antioch in 1098 on their way to liberate Jerusalem from the Muslims

30

The Safavid, Ottoman and Mogul Empires

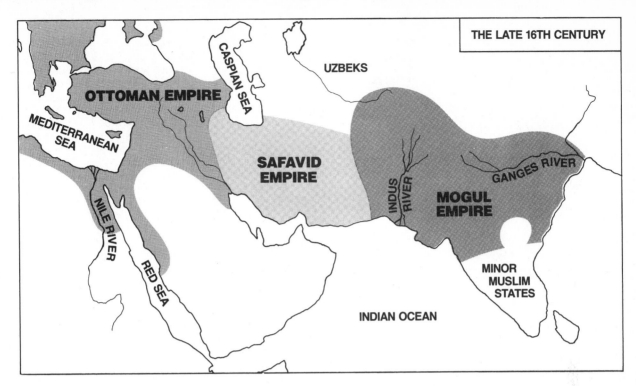

THE LATE 16TH CENTURY

UZBEKS

CASPIAN SEA

OTTOMAN EMPIRE

MEDITERRANEAN SEA

SAFAVID EMPIRE

INDUS RIVER

GANGES RIVER

MOGUL EMPIRE

NILE RIVER

RED SEA

MINOR MUSLIM STATES

INDIAN OCEAN

In many ways, Islamic civilization reached its height in the 16th century. Vigorous and ambitious, its religion and rulers dominated southern and western Asia, southeastern Europe, and all North Africa. It also swept south across the Sahara and through the savanna as far as the fringes of the rainforest. The caliphate, by now only an empty title in Cairo, failed to unite the Muslim world, and numerous independent Muslim states existed along the fringes. Nevertheless, the heart of the Muslim world divided into three major Islamic empires, each centers of an important culture.

In the middle, centered on the Iranian Plateau, the Safavid Empire split the Muslim world, for its strongly Shi'a Islam contrasted with the Sunni views both in the Mogul Empire in India and the Safavid's bitter rival to the west, the Ottoman Empire.

The provinces of Iran had witnessed numerous struggles for power after the rapid collapse of Timur's empire, especially among the Turkmen tribes of the north and west. In 1503, Ismail Safavi, a youth merely sixteen years old but hereditary leader of a Shi'a religious order, proclaimed himself Shah and Shi'ism the sole religion. Offering all the choice between conversion to Shi'ism or death, Ismail rapidly united the Iranian peasantry, urban classes and Turkish warriors into a new society and state. In time, Iranian civilians replaced warriors in the administration and central authority replaced

mystical adoration of Shah Ismail as the basis of government.

From its very beginning, the Safavid state struggled with the Ottoman Empire to the West, for it appealed to Turkish tribesmen with Shi'a leanings. Nevertheless, in battle the swords, arrows, and light firearms of Shah Ismail's warriors proved no match against Ottoman muskets and artillery. After losing much of Asia Minor, and then Iraq, the Safavids in the 17th century accepted a border between Iran and Iraq that largely remains today.

In retrospect, Shah Ismail attacked the Ottoman Empire during the zenith of its 600-year-long history. It began inconspicuously around 1299, when a Turkish warrior named Osman (Arabic *Uthman;* to Europeans, *Ottoman*) proclaimed himself sultan in northwestern Asia Minor. Welcoming all who would fight Byzantium, he allied his dynasty with *Sufi* brotherhoods and merchant guilds, and adopted Byzantine administrative techniques. Steadily the Ottoman forces advanced against Christian Byzantium. By the middle of the 14th century, permanent forces had replaced mere raiding groups across the Bosporus, isolating Constantinople. The capital itself lingered for nearly a century, spared by Timur's crushing defeat of the Ottomans in Anatolia (Asia Minor). Finally, in 1453, Sultan Mehmet II massed his armies against the Byzantine capital and captured it, ending a millennium this "Rome" had ruled Eastern Christendom. Under its Turk-

ish name, Istanbul, the city flourished as the Ottoman capital. Sultans and leading officials adorned the city with palaces and mosques, changing the skyline. Meanwhile, the conquests continued; a century later, the Balkans conquered, Ottoman troops unsuccessfully attacked Vienna.

The Ottoman Empire drew its strengths from many sources. To the uncommon valor and wisdom of the first ten sultans must be added the willingness to adopt new skills and technology. The *devshirme*, in effect a tax on Christians paid in young boys who were enslaved and educated into Islam, provided both soldiers for a standing army and administrators single-minded in devotion to the Sultan and lacking family loyalty. Financially, conquests in Europe produced great loot and tribute; in turn they enabled further aggression against Christian states. Only after 200 years did the sultans attempt significant conquest of Muslim territories. Then, under Selim I (1512–1520) dramatic conquests brought under Ottoman rule much of Anatolia and Iraq, as well as Syria, Palestine and Egypt. Under Suleyman I ("Suleiman the Magnificent"), known to his subjects as "The Lawgiver," the empire reached the height of its power and grandeur.

In contrast, by the 17th century the Ottoman Empire illustrated many signs of decay. At first Austria, then Poland and Russia pushed back the Sultan's armies in the Balkans, recapturing Hungary and parts of Yugoslavia. In the Mediterranean,

"The Golden Horn"—Constantinople in the days of yore

the Ottoman navy had suffered decisive defeat. Within the empire, anarchy spread as local administrators attempted to maintain their positions, and the sale of offices became a regular practice. The *devshirme* collapsed, and troops garrisoned in many cities rebelled. Although the capable Korprulu family *vizirs* restored administration, the Ottomans increasingly lagged behind Europe in scientific pursuits and modern learning, with unsurprising consequences for military technology. As the center of world trade shifted to the Atlantic following the discovery of the New World and sailing routes to India, the Ottoman Empire increasingly stagnated economically as well. If diplomacy and European rivalries slowed the loss of territory, the descent nevertheless seemed certain to most observers.

A Muslim Empire in India

The Mogul Empire did not rise immediately out of the ruins of the Sultanate of Delhi which had ended with a period of peace, prosperity and construction of public works, such as new irrigation canals and dams. The last important ruler let authority slip into the hands of local officials. This meant that there was no unified resistance to the hordes led by Timur Lang into the Indus-Ganges basin in 1398. Some 90,000 horsemen killed and looted without restraint, and it is said that when Timur's army returned to Samarkand, there was not a man who did not take at least twenty Indians home as slaves.

So complete was Timur's destruction of the Sultanate of Delhi that another great state did not arise in the area until the Mogul Empire was founded in about 1525. In the interim, a number of kingdoms with Muslim rulers flourished. These sultans, mainly of Turkish origin, were in general more tolerant of the culture of their Hindu subjects than the sultans of Delhi had been. Learning and the arts developed a distinctive style in this period of Islamic history in the Indian Peninsula.

The only Hindu state during the period was Vijayanagar, a name meaning "City of Victory," located on the southern tip of the Peninsula. For some two centuries after its establishment just before the middle of the 14th century, Vijayanagar defended itself against Muslim encroachment from the north and carried on Hindu cultural and artistic traditions. The combined forces of three Muslim states in the central plateau of the Peninsula finally defeated Vijayanagar in 1565 after its aged ruler was unexpectedly captured in battle and beheaded. The city of Vijayanagar was sacked by Muslim forces while many Hindus and their temples were destroyed. The fall of this state marked the end of Hindu political power.

Just after 1500, a new Islamic state was founded in Afghanistan by Babur, an adventurer from Turkistan far to the north. Barely twenty years old, and a man of taste and letters as well as the power to unite his soldiers, he claimed descent

from Timur and thus the right to rule as king. Mongol by proclamation, but Turkish in race, his dynasty nevertheless became known as the Mogul or Mughal. Invited to the plains between the Indus and the Ganges by disaffected local chiefs willing to replace their own king with another, beginning in 1524 Babur invaded northern India. His army, small in size but compact and united, possessed two great advantages: unequalled cavalry, and superior cannon from Turkey. In 1526, in a single great battle outside Delhi, he destroyed the enemy military, comprised mostly of Turkish and Afghan foreigners like himself. No national movement resisted his advance, and he found himself master of a personal domain across the plains of northern India as far east as the borders of Bengal.

Plunged into disorder on the early death of Babur, the Mogul Empire finally took shape under his grandson, Akbar. Only thirteen when he came to the throne, Akbar proved a superb general, moving armies rapidly and conquering all but the southern quarter of India. Much more than a soldier, however, Akbar established stable government that would last a century. He reached beyond mere military power to become the accepted ruler of most of India, most importantly by incorporating the Rajput chiefs, though Hindu, as governors and military commanders. Indeed, he even married a Rajput princess. As a result, the Hindu community largely accepted Akbar's empire as their own. Open-minded in religious matters, he welcomed Zoroastrians and Jesuits to his court as well as Hindus and Muslims; there was also an attempt to develop an eclectic cult centered on himself.

His successors lacked both his power and his wisdom; the empire inevitably declined. The decay came gradually, and the Moguls sponsored learning through libraries and schools, and in art perfected a distinctive fusion of Persian and Hindu styles in the Taj Mahal. However, the sixth Mogul ruler, Aurangzab (1658–1707) proved a zealous Muslim whose limited toleration of non-Muslims increased Hindu dissatisfaction and contrasted sharply with the policies of Akbar. A man of battle for much of his long reign, Aurangzab attempted to unite all India, fighting Muslim states as well as Hindu ones in the south. By the time of his death, the merchant vanguard of the next wave of foreign invaders of India had appeared, not in the traditional invasion route in the northwest, but in important ports along the coasts. After decades of disorder, British rule would replace Mogul, though the dynasty nominally ruled in Delhi until abolished by the British in 1857.

European Expansion into the Indian Ocean

Until the end of the 15th century, the direct routes from Europe to the East and its lucrative trade were blocked by the Ottoman Empire and Egypt. Europeans finally overcame the obstacle by outflanking the Muslims entirely, sailing boldly around the southern tip of Africa. When the Portuguese navigator Vasco da Gama reached the Indian Ocean by this route, his tiny fleet opened up a new era. First, only patterns of trade were altered, but in later centuries the total political organization of Southwest Asia was affected. Aggressive Europeans, possessing increasingly superior weapons and better-trained soldiers, gradually made themselves masters of the vast region.

When the first Portuguese reached the Indian Ocean in 1498, they sought only to monopolize sea trade, not to rule a land empire. By 1509 they had put an end to Arab sea power. Portugal then began building a maritime empire. Alfonso Albuquerque, who had become governor of the Portuguese settlements in India in 1509, carried forward the program of building forts at strategic locations on the coasts of India, Persia, Arabia and Africa. His fleet also continued to prevent native ships from carrying items so profitable in European markets. His nation thus gained almost a monopoly on trade in these goods, and required their transport in Portuguese ships, in keeping with the economic theory of mercantilism. Albuquerque on occasion treated with extreme cruelty rebellious subjects or Asian merchants attempting to compete with the Portuguese monopoly.

For over a century the Portuguese remained the chief traders across the Indian Ocean. By concentrating their activities on the sea and a few ports in regions without strong governments, they did not affect significantly the history of the nations of Asia, though colonies in East Africa eventually spread inland. By the end of the 16th century, however, other Europeans, eager for a share of the trade, began forcing their way into the Indian Ocean. Later, in 1650, the Portuguese position further declined after evacuation of the Arabian port of Masqat (Muscat) with accompanying loss of control of the Persian Gulf.

The 17th century belonged predominantly to Dutch merchants and sea power. They left less of a mark on Southwest Asia than had the Portuguese traders, for the Dutch preoccupation was with the spice lands farther east. The 18th century was characterized by rivalry between French and British interests seeking control of India and the approaches to it. In the end, Britain dislodged France from all but a few small enclaves, similar to those retained by Portugal.

The governments of the Netherlands, France and Britain played only secondary roles in this commercial expansion. Companies chartered by the respective kings were the leading agents. The Dutch East India Company, chartered in 1602, achieved remarkable success. With fortified trading depots at two places in Sri Lanka (Ceylon) and a number on the coasts of southern India and Southeast Asia, the company flourished during the 17th century. With aid from the strong Dutch fleet, it captured the spice trade from Portugal, despite British and French competition. When the demand for Asian spices fell, it encouraged the production of coffee, tea, and cocoa. Over two hundred years, its annual dividends reportedly averaged 18%.

The British East India Company, chartered in 1600, became even more important, both as one of the first permanent joint-stock companies and in the English company allowed in the region, it received authority to administer government where it operated. Concentrating on India, while the Dutch withdrew to the Spice Islands (Indonesia), the British East India Company established itself first at Surat on the west coast of India, with the Mogul permission. Surat rapidly developed into the most prosperous trading center in the country. Later posts followed at Bombay, Madras, and Calcutta, each to become a center of British influence. The East India Company traded especially in indigo, saltpeter, textiles and spices, often purchasing goods of greater value from India than it could sell there, and supplying silver to make up the difference.

During the 18th century the French Company of the East Indies (founded 1664) slowly emerged as the chief European rival to the British East India Company in both commerce and political influence. When the two nations fought in Europe, competition between the two companies became military in India. The British East India Company won the struggle and limited French influence to several small ports. They only rejoined India after the subcontinent's independence in 1947.

The Creation of the British Raj

George III (1738–1820)

A consistent theme in the history of the Middle East and South Asia from the late 18th century until 1947 was the expansion and strengthening of British colonial rule, often described by the Hindi and Urdu word "Raj", meaning "sway" or "rule." Beginning in Bengal, in eastern India around 1750, its encroachment elsewhere often followed the desire to protect existing possessions and trade routes.

By the mid-18th century, India lay ripe for foreign intervention. In the north, the Mogul Empire had reached a state of advanced decay, both in quality of rule and defeats by Indian and foreign enemies. Particularly threatening were the Marathas, a Hindu people adept at warfare and distinguished by their own language. They lived along the western coast and in central India, but spread across the subcontinent. In a series of wars with the Mogul Empire they exhausted its resources, but in the process the Maratha kingdom itself broke up into a loose confederation of states. While they dominated central India, they failed to establish firm central government. Henceforth the Marathas became raiders known for their rapacity and ruthlessness, plundering widely and feared by Hindus as much as by Muslims.

Then, in 1739, the Persian ruler Nadir Shah captured Delhi, plundering the treasury and Peacock Throne, and massacring the city's inhabitants. In a little more than a decade, it was the Afghan army's turn. Finally, in 1761, the Maratha army attempted to stop a renewed Afghan invasion in a battle near Delhi. The decisive defeat of the Marathas and the deaths of many of their leaders appeared to place India within the Afghan king's grasp. At this crucial moment, his troops mutinied. Thus India broke up into many smaller states, divided and lacking in direction just when Europeans sought control.

Learning from its French rival, by the 1740s, the British East India Company began to strike alliances with Indian rulers. Its weapons included interfering with the succession of Indian princes and bribery. Granting military aid to favorites often proved very effective, for European weapons and techniques increasingly outpaced local ones. With the Company's victory at Plessey in 1757, it effectively conquered Bengal, and British territorial rule began in India.

Circumstances encouraged the British domain to expand. Native attacks on Indian allies led to the retaliation and conquest. War with France in Europe led to conquest in India. Reports of great wealth in the hands of native rulers encouraged Company officials to conquer. That they succeeded so easily also was the result of the caliber of a number of Company officials who possessed the vision of conquest along with exceptional talents and freedom to operate. However, their harsh treatment of the Indian populations led to interference by Parliament in London, culminating in the India Act of 1784. This placed British rule in India under a governor-general, appointed not by the Company, but by the British government. Ironically, it was Lord Cornwallis, loser of Britain's American colonies at the Battle of Yorktown, who preserved those in India as the new governor-general.

Imperial Rule: The Raj at Its Height—and Fall

Warfare against Napoleon, in Egypt and in Europe, combined with circumstances in India to encourage the last great expansion of British rule. The British conquests were swift. In hardly more than twenty years after 1795, large territories fell: Mysore and Hyderabad in the south, the Marathas in the center, and finally the remaining Rajput states in the west. British India more than doubled in size, and unity of the peninsula within its natural boundaries became an appealing goal. Unity would end foreign intrigue and permit British commercial expansion at minimal defense costs. Moreover, ending the virtual state of anarchy in parts of India would bring peace to the inhabitants. The East India Company had traded with Indians for a century and a half before warring with them; for almost another century and a half the British would rule India.

The British Raj brought many advantages, including peace after the ravages of lengthy wars. Physically the country changed with the construction of harbors, railroads, and irrigation projects. Colleges and universities educated an Indian elite in science and medicine, and the administration became more regular and less arbitrary. *Suttee,* the practice of burning widows on the funeral pyres of their husbands, was banned. In general, though, the British granted religious toleration in areas they ruled directly, and in the many princely states allowed traditional dynasties to continue, whether Muslim or Hindu.

On the other hand, much was not well. Indian handicrafts suffered from cheap cloth manufactured in England. Each improvement in transportation rendered the competition worse, while British policies retarded the development of Indian industry. High taxes rendered the peasants impoverished tenants, and few schools served the masses. Moreover, in Indian eyes British rule involved westernization to an unsettling degree, and in 1857 the introduction of rifle cartridges greased with animal fat offended Muslim troops (over lard) as well as Hindu (over cows' grease). The Indian Mutiny of 1857–1858, at times savage and repressed sternly, brought the attention of London and reforms. The East India Company, long stripped of its trade monopoly, was dissolved. The British Raj now meant authority lay with Parliament and monarch in England.

Possession of India encouraged further British imperial expansion, for both strategic and commercial purposes. After the defeat of Napoleon in 1815, Britain's great European rival became Tsarist Russia, whose expansion towards both India and the Middle East seemed threatening. Recognizing that the traditional invaders' route to India came from the northwest, British officials extended their rule in that direction, adding the Punjab and Kashmir, then later Baluchistan (bordering Iran), and finally the North-west Frontier Province (1901). By then, only a thin, very mountainous portion of Afghanistan separated Russia from India, but in three different wars the Afghans proved far easier to influence than to conquer. Afghanistan became, in effect, a buffer state for India, as did Bhutan, Sikkim and (much earlier) Nepal (1816). Another direction of British expansion from India lay to the east, and Burma became a province of India in 1886.

Commercial conquests took place in the west. A naval force from India in 1820 forced Bahrain and rulers in Trucial Oman (now the United Arab Emirates) to recognize British authority. In the latter case, the British strongly desired to end trade in slaves and raids on shipping. At the other end of the Arabian Peninsula, British forces seized the port of Aden in 1839. Administered by the Government of India, it became an important coaling station for British ships.

Developments in Egypt inspired far greater British attention to the Middle East. The Nile Valley produced fine cotton needed by the mills of Britain, and in Egypt cotton provided government revenues. The ambition and determination of Muhammad Ali (1811–1847) so threatened the Ottoman Empire that it required careful European diplomacy, and on occasion Great Power military action to maintain the Ottoman Sultans. Under Muhammad

Victoria (1819–1901)
First Empress of India

Ali's successors, Egypt also provided an opportunity for European loans, to the ruler as well as to ordinary farmers. Finally, as overlord of the Sudan, Egypt inevitably played an active role in attempts to eliminate the slave trade from Africa.

Each of these reasons for British involvement, however, seems inconsequential beside the construction of the Suez Canal on French initiative. Already British passengers to India had reduced the long journey around Africa by using overland transportation across Egypt to the Red Sea. The canal, by enabling vessels and heavy freight to use the route, quickly became "the lifeline to India." British strategic policy in the region focused on the canal, and the Egyptian shares in the Suez Canal Company were purchased. When Egypt nevertheless went bankrupt and both anti-European riots and a nationalist uprising broke out, British troops landed in 1882 and restored order, defeating nationalist troops. Lightly disguised by diplomatic formalities and the almost total withdrawal of British troops, Egypt became a sphere of British influence though nominally part of the Ottoman Empire.

Its conquests during World War I brought the British Raj to its greatest extent in the Middle East and South Asia. When the Ottoman Empire entered the war as a German ally, Britain quickly annexed Egypt and Cyprus. Shortly thereafter, troops from India landed in southern Iraq, and despite setbacks began the slow conquest of that land. After repulsing Ottoman Turkish attacks on the Suez Canal, British, Australian, and Indian troops moved forward from Egypt into Palestine, capturing Jerusalem in 1917.

When Ottoman Turkey appealed for peace in October 1918, these forces and their Arab allies had captured all of Syria as well. From the Nile to the Ganges, and between the Mediterranean and China, no European power rivaled British influence. British goals dominated the postwar assignment of mandates of Syria and Lebanon to France and Palestine and Iraq to Britain.

Nevertheless, as the Raj reached its greatest extent, the forces of its future downfall became evident. In Egypt the 1919 Nationalist Revolution led to the creation of an autonomous kingdom three years later. Arab nationalism, the ideology of only a handful of inhabitants of the Ottoman provinces in 1912, spread rapidly with the imposition of European mandates by force of arms in Syria and Iraq, as well as Zionist immigration into Palestine. In Iran, popular opposition blocked an attempt to establish a veiled British protectorate, and Afghanistan undertook its War of Independence. In India, nationalism had showed itself a potent force, and its repression at Amritsar produced one thousand dead and wounded. Under the leadership of Mohandas Gandhi, the struggle for self-determination was becoming effective.

Thus from west to east the British Raj tottered seriously in 1919–1920. Twenty-five years later the Second World War left Britain, though armed with weapons of greater sophistication than ever before, too enfeebled to maintain the empire. In 1947 the Raj formally ended for India, though it continued for another generation on the fringes of Arabia, where ironically formal British intervention always had been smaller.

George VI (1895–1952)
Last Emperor of India

The Kingdom of Bahrain

Downtown Manama, capital city

Area: 277 square miles (717 sq. km.).

Population: 811,000 (IMF), 30% expatriate.

Capital City: Manama (pop. 148,000 city, 2008; metro 340,000, est.).

Climate: Extremely hot and humid except for a short, moderate winter. There is very little rainfall.

Neighboring Countries: Saudi Arabia (West); Qatar (Southeast).

Time Zone: GMT +3.

Official Language: Arabic.

Other Principal Tongues: English, Farsi (Persian), Urdu.

Ethnic Background: About 75% Bahraini and other Arab, with Indians, Iranians, and Pakistanis forming the largest groups of foreign workers.

Principal Religion: Islam, 65% *Shi'a* and 35% *Sunni*.

Chief Commercial Products: Petroleum products, aluminum, ship repairs, liquid natural gas, financial services and transportation services.

Major Trading Partners: Saudi Arabia, India, U.S., Japan, and Singapore.

Currency: Bahraini Dinar (1 BD = 1,000 fils).

Former Colonial Status: British Protectorate (1861–1971).

Independence Date: August 15, 1971.

Chief of State: Hamad bin 'Isa Al-Khalifa, King.

Head of Government: Sheikh Khalifa bin Salman Al-Khalifa, Prime Minister.

National Flag: A serration divides a white band at the pole from the remaining field of solid red. After Bahrain became a kingdom in 2002, its flag gained a gold crown.

Gross Domestic Product (GDP): $21.5 billion; $29.7 billion (purchasing power parity), 2009.

GDP per capita: $26,000, 2008.

The land of two seas, as its name implies in Arabic, Bahrain consists of a group of islands located off the coast of Arabia between the Gulf of Bahrain and the Persian (Arab) Gulf. The main island, some 30 miles long and 10 miles wide, is largely desert, but springs fed by sources originating on the mainland water some gardens and groves near the northern coast. By decision of the International Court of Justice, the island of Hawar near the Qatar coast also forms part of the country.

History: Bahrain's long history stretches back as far as Dilmun, a prosperous trading center that flourished some 4,000 years ago. Well placed to trade between Iraq and India, Bahrain played a role in Arab commerce during the Middle Ages, and the inhabitants became Muslims. The Portuguese conquest of the 1500s led in turn to Persian rule, but in 1783 the Arabian Al-Khalifa family, which had earlier established itself at Zubara on the Qatar coast, conquered Bahrain, seeking to gain control of its valuable pearl fishing industry. In a series of treaties beginning in 1820, rulers of this family allied themselves more closely with Britain, on occasion seeking aid against local threats. In 1861 it became a protectorate of Britain, and by 1913 that imperial power had gained control of Bahrain's defense, foreign relations and natural resources. In return, Britain promised protection to the rulers.

During World War II, Bahrain provided Britain's main naval and military bases in the Gulf, and the headquarters of the British Political Resident in the Persian Gulf was moved there in 1946. From 1926 until 1957, Sir Charles Belgrave, as personal advisor to the ruler, directed the modernization of the state's administration and economy. During that period Bahrain led economic development in the Gulf region, but nationalist and leftist sentiments created unrest. The most serious demonstrations occurred in 1956 and were suppressed with the aid of British troops. Bahrain became independent in 1971 when Britain withdrew its forces from all the Gulf states, and Bahrain decided not to join the United Arab Emirates. A constitution was issued in 1973.

In 1981 security forces discovered a plot by the *Islamic Front for the Liberation of Bahrain* to overthrow the government. The *Front* reflected both desire of the Islamic Republic of Iran to export its revolution and a renewal of Iran's longstanding interest in influencing Bahrain, despite the deposed Shah's abandonment of Iran's claims to the island after an internationally monitored plebiscite. Because a majority of the indigenous population is Shi'a, the

Bahrain

police and intelligence services—often employing foreigners—remained on the alert for subversive activity. Unrest continued to fester, and in the late 1980s police foiled a plot directed at oil installations. By the 1990s, Iranian sympathy with opposition movements was largely limited to refuge, funds and propaganda.

A dispute with Qatar long simmered over Hawar Island and several adjacent reefs and sandbanks valued for fishing rights as well as potential oil riches. Bahrain also claimed Zubara, on the Qatari peninsula, because it had been the ancestral home of the ruling Khalifa family. After Qatari troops arrested workmen building a Bahraini coast guard station on a disputed reef, conflict appeared possible, although the few thousand troops on either side were incapable of launching a concerted attack on the other.

Saudi mediation defused the crisis, at the cost to Bahrain of demolishing the construction. In 1995, Qatar successfully appealed to the International Court of Justice to rule on the rival claims. Its ruling in 2001 granted Bahrain Hawar Island, but rejected the claim to Zubara. Both countries agreed to accept the decision.

When Iraq seized Kuwait in 1990, Bahrain's government joined with other Gulf Cooperation Council member states (see Regional Organizations) in condemning the invasion and supporting the multinational force. During the Gulf War that followed, Bahrain provided airbases and ports for U.S. and British forces. Though no military action occurred on the island, the massive oil spill released by Iraq during the fighting directly threatened water intakes for drinking water and industrial use, and risked long-term devastation of the local fishing industry.

Resentment over the lack of personal rights and political freedoms led prominent Sunni and Shi'a Bahrainis to petition in 1994 for the reinstatement of the 1973 constitution (see politics). The government responded firmly, arresting a Shi'a cleric for distributing pro-democracy leaflets and later deporting him and other clerics who preached democracy. Several hundred were arrested, including women. Demonstrations alternated with repression, and in 1996, a wave of protests left 30 dead, including police.

Ominously, the discontent became strongest among the Shi'a majority, whose resentment was fueled by their perceptions of poverty, unemployment, lower-class standing and discrimination. Behind the Shi'a demands, Prime Minister Khalifa bin Salman particularly discerned "outside meddling" (code for Iran). Despite a minor cabinet reshuffle, riots and sabotage continued, along with hundreds of arrests. The regime chose not to concede reforms,

His Majesty Hamad bin Isa Al-Khalifa

though they might have divided moderate democrats from radical Islamists.

When Sheikh Hamad ascended to power in 1999 on the death of his father, Sheikh 'Isa, hopes rose that calm might be restored. The new ruler released Sheikh Abdul Amir al-Jamri, a major opposition figure, and acted to increase employment. The following year he appointed several women and a Jewish businessman to the *Majlis al-Shura* (Consultative Council). Under the slogan "Building a New Bahrain," he proposed a referendum on a "National Charter," a proposal to establish democracy and constitutional monarchy.

Sheikh Hamad's proposals initially aroused suspicions. The exiled *Bahrain Freedom Movement* considered the proposed parliament weak and opposed any referendum as long as hundreds of men and some women remained imprisoned or exiled for political offenses. It therefore called for an opposition boycott. However, Sheikh Hamad dramatically responded to the criticism by promising real power for parliament. *Even before the referendum,* he pardoned about 1,000 political prisoners, including some convicted of arson and other crimes of violence.

In an atmosphere of euphoria, most Bahraini men and women actually voted

Bahrain

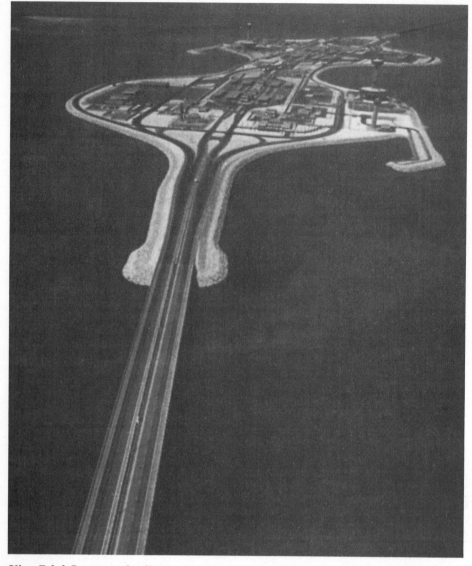

King Fahd Causeway leading to Immigration Island between Saudi Arabia and Bahrain.

Like most Arab governments, Bahrain publicly opposed the U.S. and British invasion of Iraq in 2003, and the population demonstrated against it, often vigorously. However, the government perhaps did not mind Saddam Hussein's fall from power, and Bahrain continues to serve as the headquarters for the U.S. Fifth Fleet.

Bahrain became the first Gulf state to negotiate a Free Trade Agreement with the U.S., in 2004. Such agreements provide tariff-free access for products of one country in the other, and thus, the agreement should cut the price of U.S. air conditioners in Bahrain and Bahraini aluminum in the U.S.

Politics: The 1973 constitution provided for a National Assembly composed of an appointed cabinet and 30 elected members. The first assembly was dissolved in 1975 on charges that it interfered with the functions of government. For the next quarter century, the Emir and his family held the reins of power and ruled somewhat benevolently, except for the imprisonment and alleged torture of political opponents during political unrest and rioting.

Reflecting the greater spirit of democracy after the liberation of Kuwait, in 1993 Sheikh 'Isa bin Salman appointed 30 "elite and loyal men" to form a new council, the *Majlis al-Shura*. These wealthy merchants and patriarchs of notable families possessed no real powers, but provided the Emir with advice. Soon after he came to power, Sheikh Hamad enlarged the *Majlis* and broadened its membership. By appointing a woman, he changed its character from an exclusive men's club.

The National Charter approved in 2001 replaced the *Majlis al-Shura* with an elected lower house and an appointed upper house. The lower house has the power to dismiss ministers and approve laws, though not to form cabinets from its members. The citizenry is clearly not sovereign, but Bahrain already ranks as the most democratic state of the Gulf.

In another startling move for the region, in 2004 the King dismissed a government minister, after police had repressed a demonstration against U.S. policy in Iraq.

Culture: The country's first written constitution, made public in 1973, proclaims Bahrain to be an Islamic state. A majority of Bahrainis are *Shi'a* Muslims (see Iran: Culture for details). The remaining 30% of Bahrainis, including the ruling family, are *Sunni*. Bahrain's culture is not generally distinct from that found in other Arab states bordering on the Gulf.

Bahrain has a relatively high literacy rate with universal education for all children. In addition to teacher-training colleges and various institutes, the Gulf University was

on the National Charter in 2001, and they granted it overwhelming (98%) support. Soon afterwards, despite his reputation as an opponent of democracy, Prime Minister Sheikh Khalifa suspended the notorious State Security Laws that had permitted detention without trial. The pace of reforms continued with municipal elections in 2002, when women voted and (unsuccessfully) ran for office.

Another change that same year promoted Sheikh Hamad from hereditary prince to king. The change brought neither wealth nor additional domestic power to the ruling family, but it distinguished the Kingdom of Bahrain from the emirates around the Gulf, not all of them independent.

One prominent Shi'a group boycotted the 2002 parliamentary elections because the elected lower house of parliament could be offset by the appointed upper house. Nevertheless, the elections took place successfully, and subsequently King Hamad appointed a former exile, Majid al-Alawi, as minister of labor and social affairs, and another Shi'a to the justice ministry. By 2006, Shi'a opinion shifted in favor of voting, and despite a formal ban on political parties, Sheikh Ali Salman's *al-Wifaq National Islamic Society* emerged as the largest single group, while secular candidates generally lost.

Recent small-scale riots in several areas indicate dissatisfaction with the loss of open coastline to development, much of it on reclaimed land. Allegedly, only 3% of the desert island's coastline is open to the public. The discontent is heightened by poverty, and by photographs from Google Earth showing the large enclosed estates of the elite, while the lower classes are crowded into smaller spaces.

established in Bahrain, sponsored by the smaller states of the Gulf. With facilities larger than its enrollment, it became a refuge for faculty and students from Kuwait who fled the Iraqi occupation.

The civilization of Dilmun left behind on the main island the heaviest concentration of prehistoric burial grounds on earth, some 80,000 that once covered 5% of the island. Only 6,000 mounds remain, but officials tourists will be attracted to them, as well as the National Museum, opened in 1989, the gold souq (market), portrayals of Arab nomadic lifestyle, and water sports along the coast.

Economy: Petroleum played a major role in the development of modern Bahrain, like that of every other Gulf state. Its deposits of oil, developed earlier than those of its neighbors, enabled it to begin exports in 1934. However, the country's reserves of oil remain small, and now mostly meet domestic needs; at present production levels they will be exhausted soon after 2010. In 1996 Saudi Arabia allocated its revenues from a shared off-shore field. Oil thus remains vitally important directly, as well for revenues from the important oil refinery.

Recognizing its limited petroleum reserves, Bahrain has attempted to diversify its economy away from dependence on crude oil. The oldest of its major industries, Bahrain's large oil refinery processes Saudi Arabian crude as well as local production for export. Outside petrochemicals, government policies encourage companies to invest, including low-interest loans, duty-free imports of raw materials and machinery, and personal and corporate tax waivers.

The results are an economy much less dependent on oil than most Arab states of the Gulf. Government plans call for the expansion of small and medium-sized industries, in part to absorb a workforce growing rapidly as young Bahrainis born in the prosperity of the 1980s seek jobs. Fishing employs only small numbers, and agriculture faces an uncertain future because water from the aquifer used for irrigation is turning brackish.

Abundant natural gas deposits provide energy for the region's largest aluminum smelter, Aluminium Bahrain, which opened in 1972. Later expansion projects increased capacity to 500,000 tons in 1997, the largest plant outside Russia. The prominent U.S. producer, Alcoa, negotiated a major stake in the company in 2003. The smelter processes imported bauxite, and exports mostly to East Asia and the Middle East.

After years of modest operations, the Arab Shipbuilding and Repair dry-dock began to flourish after the end of the Iran-Iraq war in 1988. Formerly, shipping companies and their insurers had sought to remove damaged tankers as quickly as possible from the zone of conflict.

Improving economic conditions in the Gulf help Bahrain's substantial offshore banking operations (those dealing with the accounts of people living elsewhere), which suffered during Iraq's wars. Financial services also play a role in the local and regional economy, with the opening of a stock exchange in 1989 that initially listed 30 companies, mostly in banking and insurance.

The construction of a 17-mile (27 km.) causeway connecting Bahrain with Saudi Arabia offers other opportunities for development. Over one million people used the causeway in the first year after its opening in late 1986, most of them weekend tourists from Saudi Arabia, coming as families and interested in shopping and amusement parks. These visitors doubled hotel occupancy rates, and the young men among them frequented the island's nightclubs and bars. However, many of the service jobs thus created in retail, tourism, and entertainment seem undignified to conservative Bahraini citizens.

Prospects of encouraging tourism from Japan, Europe, and North America improved with the expansion of the airport and with every regional cease-fire in recent decades (Iran-Iraq War, 1988; Iraqi-Kuwait War, 1991). However, prospects diminish with regional turmoil and religious-based terrorism. Although Bahrain permits the importation of liquor and taxes it highly, tourists could easily strengthen the influence of Western lifestyles and entertainment, and upset conservative Muslims. From a practical standpoint, too, non-Arab tourism requires simple and rapid immigration procedures and inexpensive air fares, both now lacking. Most of all, of course, tourism requires political stability in the region—something far beyond the control of Bahrain.

With prospects of limited oil and water supplies, and a young population rapidly joining the labor force, unemployment is expected to rise significantly during coming years among Bahrain's youth. Although about 60% of the existing workforce is foreign, many of the jobs they perform will hardly attract the country's ambitious and generally well-educated youth.

The Future: Bahrain ranks as the freest Middle Eastern economy. Nevertheless, it faces significant long-term economic and social challenges, particularly the simmering resentments of a Shi'a underclass that considers the government unfair and that thanks to Google Earth can view the walled estates of the island's wealthy and powerful.

Prosperity will depend on a greater cultural willingness to accept jobs previously left for foreigners. Besides diversification away from petroleum, traditional services like banking and transportation require greater competitiveness. The present economic downturn has created pressures on many banking firms to cut costs by reducing the number of employees.

Bahrain at night

Courtesy: Royal Embassy of Saudi Arabia

The Arab Republic of Egypt

Area: 386,873 square miles (1,002,000 sq. km.), of which only about 3.5% is arable—in the Nile Valley, the Delta and a few oases.

Population: 78 million.

Capital City: Cairo (7,450,000; 10,800,000 metro).

Climate: Hot summers, humid along the coast but dry in the south. Winters are cool with some rain along the northern coast, but drier and comfortable inland. Occasional strong winds intensify the winter chill and the summer heat.

Neighboring Countries: Libya (West); Sudan (South); Saudi Arabia (East, across the Red Sea); Israel (Northeast).

Time Zone: GMT + 2 (+3 in summer). At noon in New York it is 7:00 P.M. in Cairo.

Official Language: Arabic.

Other Principal Tongues: English and French, in school and business.

Ethnic Background: Their physical appearances vary, but nearly all consider themselves Arab and Egyptian, except a few Berbers from the western oases.

Principal Religion: *Sunni* Islam (over 90%) and Coptic Christianity.

Major Trading Partners: U.S., Italy, Germany, Japan, South Korea, Greece.

Chief Commercial Products: Tourism, Suez Canal usage, petroleum and refined products, military equipment, cotton yarn and textiles, light manufactures.

Main Agricultural Products: Cotton, sugar, rice and other grains, tomatoes, watermelons, onions, vegetables, dates, animals and flowers.

Currency: Egyptian £ (popularly the ghinnayh) = 100 piasters.

Former Colonial Status: British control, though still part of the Ottoman Empire (1882–1914), then a "protectorate" of Britain (1914–1922). Britain exercised political influence until the 1952 military *coup*.

National Day: July 23.

Chief of State: Mohammad Hosni Mubarak, President.

Head of Government: Ahmad Nazif, Prime Minister.

National Flag: Three horizontal stripes of (top to bottom) red, white and black. The eagle of Saladin in gold is centered on the white stripe.

Gross Domestic Product: $208 billion (at current prices); $500 billion (Purchasing Power Parity)

GDP per capita: $2,664; $6,390 PPP

Strategically located at the junction between Africa and Asia, Egypt holds the rank of the most populous Arab state and the center of Arab culture and entertainment. Most of its territory lies in Africa, forming the northeast corner of the great Sahara Desert. The stark desolation of gravel, sand and rock is interrupted by the Nile River, which flows from south to north for 750 miles in a valley cut through the desert. Yet for most of its length the valley floor varies in width from a mere few hundred yards to a maximum of 14 miles. Within the valley, agriculture is possible.

About 100 miles before reaching the Mediterranean Sea, the Nile divides into branches that spread out over a broad alluvial plain reaching a width of 150 miles along the sea coast. Because this triangle of fertility resembles the form of the (capital) letter *delta* in the Greek alphabet, since ancient times it has been called the Delta. The metropolis of Cairo lies at the southern tip of this Delta. At the northwest is the port city of Alexandria, named after Alexander the Great, who founded it following his conquest of the country in 332 B.C. About a quarter of the people of Egypt live in these two cities. They work as shopkeepers, government employees, in manufacturing, or at the many other jobs associated with urban areas.

Most of the remaining three-quarters of the population live in some 4,000 villages and towns scattered in the Delta and up the length of the Nile Valley. Most of them are directly or indirectly connected with agricultural production. A few people live in a half dozen remote oases in the desert west of the Nile Valley, while an insignificant and dwindling number of nomads wander with flocks of goats and camels in the desert regions that comprise about 96% of the country. There are no grasslands or forests. The highest point in Egypt, Jabal Katrina (Mt. Catherine) reaches 8,652 feet in the Sinai Peninsula, but overlooks barren rock and sands. There is total contrast between the barrenness of the desert (called "the Red Land" by the ancient inhabitants) and the tropical growth of the valley floor and Delta ("the Black Land" of the ancients).

The English name *Egypt* is derived from the ancient Greek name Aiguptos, an approximation of Hikuptah, one of the names of the ancient capital of Memphis, whose ruins are near modern Cairo. The Arabic name of the country, *Misr*, introduced with the Arabic conquest of the 7th century, originated in an ancient name used in Semitic languages. In the hieroglyphics of antiquity, the country was sometimes called "the Two Lands," referring to Lower Egypt (the Delta) and Upper Egypt (the narrow valley south of Cairo, known as *Sa'id* in Arabic).

History: The shadows of an extremely long early history lie across the modern land of Egypt—of the mighty pharaohs claiming to be gods, of Hellenistic civilization that flourished at Alexandria and especially of the brilliant Islamic civilization centered on Cairo. Yet the modern state of Egypt cannot be traced back beyond the early 19th century. Then it began to take shape under the dynamic rule of Muhammad (Mehmet) Ali, an ambitious Ottoman soldier who was neither Egyptian by birth nor a proponent of (not-yet-existent) Egyptian nationalism.

Pre-Christian civilization in the Nile Valley made enormous contributions to the development of human skills and knowledge. In fact, that civilization is considered the heritage of all humanity. Later ages also influenced the world. Roman

Egypt was one of the first fertile grounds for the spread of Christianity, and its thinkers and leaders played important roles in the history of the Christian Church. The Christians of Egypt adopted a modified version of the Greek alphabet to write their language, Coptic, the latest form of the old Egyptian language earlier recorded in hieroglyphics. The Coptic Church still plays an important role in contemporary Egyptian society.

In the early 7th century, Muslim armies from Arabia spread their rule to Egypt, little opposed by the Coptic subjects of the Byzantine Empire (639–642). During the following centuries, both the Arabic language of the new rulers and their Islamic faith were adopted by most Egyptians. When the Abbasid caliphate in Baghdad lost control of distant provinces, Egypt fell under the rule of local governors, and then Turkish dynasties, including the Tulunids, whose mosque remains impressive today.

Further elegant buildings, and achievements in the arts and learning followed under the Fatimid Caliphs (969–1171), including the founding of the University of al-Azhar, one of the oldest in the world. Claiming descent from Fatima, the Prophet

Muhammad's daughter, these caliphs espoused Shi'a Islam but maintained contact with the rest of the Muslim world. Sometimes they ruled much of it, but weak rulers and dependence on foreign slave-warriors eased Egypt's capture by Salah al-Din al-Ayyubi, known to the European Crusaders as Saladin. His Sunni descendants in turn lost authority to the Mamluks (pronounced Mam-*luke*), warrior slaves often of Turkish or Circassian origins, by the middle of the 13th century.

The most important Mamluk sultan, Baybars, checked the expansion of the destructive Mongol armies in Syria (Ayn Jalut, 1260), and defeated the remaining Crusaders as well. But despite their glories on the battlefield, and their lavish spending on works of art, the Mamluks brought few advantages to the native Egyptians. Generally foreign born, the Mamluks oppressed the Egyptians harshly, and by their intrigues and rivalries brought disorder rather than peace. After the Ottoman Sultan Selim I defeated the Mamluks and conquered Egypt in 1517, the country witnessed frequent struggles between the government in Istanbul and the remaining Mamluks, who dominated Egyptian society.

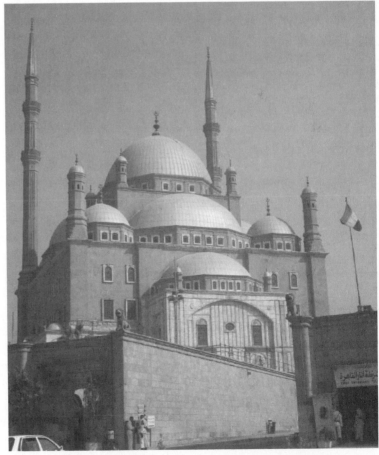

Built within Salah al-Din's Citadel, the Mosque of Muhammad Ali dominates Cairo's southern skyline.

Egypt

Napoleon's conquest and the French occupation (1798–1801) proved a vital turning point in the creation of modern Egypt. European ideas spread. More important, Muhammad Ali, an Albanian officer in the Ottoman army sent to evict the French, skillfully played off his rivals and seized power for himself while paying lip service to Ottoman rule. In 1806 the Ottoman Sultan recognized him as Pasha of Egypt.

Challenged by a barren treasury and the remaining Mamluks, he set about building a modern state. After drastically reorganizing the land taxes and taking control of foreign trade, he slaughtered the chief Mamluks in 1811. Military expeditions followed abroad, in Sudan, Arabia, and Greece. The resulting need for soldiers required imposing conscription on Egyptians for the first time. European intervention cut short Muhammad Ali's rule outside Egypt in 1841.

Modernization also attracted Muhammad Ali's attention during the four decades he and his son Ibrahim dominated Egypt. He developed a cabinet system of government, established schools, founded a government press, and attempted to industrialize Egypt with imported equipment, all without borrowing funds abroad. His attempt to monopolize trade failed, but he encouraged agricultural improvements and transferred vast domains to the state from delinquent taxpayers. Though unsuccessful in creating an empire, he separated Egypt clearly as a self-governing region from the rest of the Ottoman Empire. Some historians consider him "The Founder of Modern Egypt."

His successors provided no rival for the title. His son Sa'id, however, in 1856 signed a concession giving a Frenchman, Ferdinand de Lesseps, the right to build a sea-level canal from the Mediterranean to the Gulf of Suez, a branch of the Red Sea. By this act, Sa'id Pasha greatly altered Egypt's global strategic status, for the Suez Canal became Britain's "lifeline to India," because it reduced the length of the sea voyage from Britain to the Indian Ocean enormously, compared to the trip around Africa.

The Canal was completed in 1869, after Sa'id's nephew, Ismail, succeeded him. The new ruler elevated himself above the pashas in other Ottoman provinces by adopting the title khedive, though Egypt still remained in the Empire. Indeed, he offered the sultan tribute.

Khedive Ismail borrowed large sums from European bankers for a few good reasons, and many poor ones: mostly to finance his high living and elaborate, often unsound, schemes to develop Egypt in European fashion. Very quickly he bankrupted the state. In 1875 he was forced to sell Egypt's share in the Suez Ca-

nal to the British government. His profligate spending resulted in European supervision of Egyptian finances, and he was finally forced to abdicate.

The British Occupation

After rioters in Alexandria killed several Europeans and others associated with the strict financial administration to supervise Egypt's debt, in 1882 Britain landed troops in Alexandria. The wealthy, landowning elite, many of them Turkish-speaking, failed to unite and oppose the British. However, most Egyptians rallied to support a nationalist colonel, Ahmad Urabi (Arabi).

The two sides met at the battle of Tall al-Kabir, where British troops demonstrated an overwhelming supremacy, killing some

10,000 Egyptians while losing fewer than 80 men. Urabi soon surrendered, and the khedive became a British puppet. The British Consul General, Lord Cromer, became a virtual dictator for over 20 years (1883–1907), although Egypt formally remained part of the Ottoman Empire.

After the Ottoman government entered World War I against the Allies in 1914, Britain proclaimed Egypt a protectorate and replaced the pro-Ottoman khedive with an uncle, who received a grander title, sultan. Defended by troops from the British Empire, Egypt became an important base for the Allied conquest of Palestine and Syria.

Although wartime ideas had strengthened nationalist sentiments, after the war Britain showed every sign of planning to

Napoleon's soldiers pass an ancient temple at Thebes

42

Egypt

dominate Egypt. Sa'd Zaghlul, a nationalist activist, had long struggled against foreign rule. He and his colleagues sought to form a delegation ("wafd" in Arabic) to attend the Paris peace conference in 1919, but they were dismissed by British officials, arrested, and deported to Malta.

Within days, an insurrection spread to all parts of Egypt. Unsuccessful at repression, Britain offered a very restricted "independence," including British bases. When Zaghlul and his *Wafd Party* ensured that no Egyptian would sign such a treaty, Britain simply declared Egypt independent, with conditions. Sultan Fu'ad, became king, but proved inept in politics. (Having grown up in Italy, he was scarcely able to speak Arabic). A largely ineffective parliament was established.

The years between 1923 and the military revolution of 1953 saw few positive developments, though some progress in individual freedom. Politically the country was rent by continuing rivalry among the weak monarch, the waning influence of British officials, the increasingly corrupt and self-interested *Wafd Party*, and smaller nationalistic groups. Politicians tried to manipulate the poor for their own ends, but did little to improve their lot. King Farouk, whose reign began in 1937, became a symbol of a system which failed to meet the aspirations of ordinary Egyptians. Opposition to the monarchy mounted after the Egyptian army's loss to Israel in 1949, and the fundamentalist *Muslim Brotherhood* became increasingly active and engaged in assassinations.

Military Rule and Republic

After months of sometimes violent popular protests, on July 23, 1952, a reformist group in the Army seized control of the country and exiled King Farouk. The self-styled Free Officers sought not merely to change the ruler; they wished to revolutionize the country. Modernists at heart, they believed that an independent, honest and sincere government could reduce poverty, increase education, strengthen the armed forces and bring dignity to the average Egyptian. In keeping with these aims, they set up the *Revolutionary Command Council* (*RCC*) to handle affairs of state.

A respected older general, Muhammad Naguib, was named president, but the real leader in the *RCC* was a younger man, Colonel Gamal Abdul Nasser (or Jamal Abd al-Nasir), a tall, imposing orator with an interest in ideas. In 1954, he became president in name as well as fact.

Nasser made an enormous impact upon Egyptians, other Arabs, and people throughout the colonies and newly independent nations of the developing world. Egyptians loved him, except the wealthy

and ethnic minorities. When army officers plotted to overthrow monarchies in Iraq, Yemen and Libya, they modeled revolutionary councils after the one in Cairo. On the world stage, Nasser became a prominent spokesman at conferences of Third World nations, notably in 1955 at Bandung in Indonesia when he, Prime Minister Nehru of India, and Prime Minister Zhou Enlai of China established the Non-aligned Movement of countries neutral in the struggle between the Soviet Union and the West.

The idealistic young officers of the *RCC* seized aimed to bring progress and greater opportunity for the poor and middle classes through education, public health, and other welfare programs. Lacking experience and finding few advisors, they gradually formulated principles for building a new society, defined as "Arab Socialism." They also desired land reform, to redistribute to the *fellahin* (farmers) the large estates of the rich. As moderate socialists, but not communists, they favored government control of international trade, industry, and banks. In foreign affairs, Nasser proclaimed the ideas of Pan-Arab nationalism popular in Syria and elsewhere. Arab weakness, the philosophy explained, resulted from imperialism and dynasties

that divided what should have been one Arab nation.

In the 1950s, Egypt dominated the Arab world. Its population far exceeded those of other Arab states; it boasted the largest (if not the toughest) military, and its achievements in the arts and culture ranged from universities to movies. Inevitably, once the *Revolutionary Command Council* espoused a Pan-Arab policy, it began to champion the interests of the Palestine Arabs and to oppose Israel.

Access to weapons proved the crucial issue. In 1953 the Western allies, who dominated arms supplies to the region, agreed to limit combined Arab armaments to the level possessed by Israel. That decision preserved indefinitely the Israeli military superiority over any likely Arab alliance. In a decisive stroke to escape from Western limitations, in 1955 Egypt purchased arms from communist Czechoslovakia. The move dramatically increased Soviet influence in the Middle East.

The arms purchases sharply illustrated the contrast between the dominant Western goal in the region—defense against Soviet expansion—and Arab goals of victory over Israel or Arab rivals. When the United States reacted to the arms sale by withholding aid for a proposed high dam

Egypt

The heart of Cairo, including Maydan al-Tahrir (Liberation Square), in the 1970s.

at Aswan in southern Egypt, Nasser obtained Soviet assistance for the dam as well.

To pay for the arms, and to finance long-overdue development projects, in 1956 Egypt seized the Suez Canal Company, while promising to pay French and British shareholders the current value of their shares. Amid great international furor, Israel, Britain and France secretly plotted an invasion. Israel hoped to defeat Egypt before the new Soviet arms rendered it strong, and then to force it to sign a peace treaty. The other two nations hoped to oust Nasser in favor of a more pliable ruler.

In late 1956, Israeli forces quickly defeated the Egyptian army and occupied the Sinai Peninsula. Britain and France then used the fighting as a pretext for a joint expeditionary force to take control of the Canal Zone. This reversion to power politics entailed heavy losses of civilian property and lives, and public opinion almost everywhere condemned it. At the UN, a Canadian motion demanding a withdrawal won support from the U.S., the U.S.S.R., and nearly all member countries.

Nasser emerged from this episode as a hero to Africans and Asians who had been, or still were, under European rule. In 1958, at Syria's request, Egypt merged with it to form the United Arab Republic. Nasser became president, and his influence soared. However, the very different social and economic circumstances of the two countries made real unity difficult, and Syria withdrew from the United Arab Republic in 1961. Egyptian president continued his policy of socialism at home,

neutrality between the superpowers and support for the Palestinian cause against Israel.

The Six-Day War, June 5–10, 1967

In the spring of 1967, despite his army's continuing struggle in Yemen, Nasser allied publicly with Syria and eventually Jordan against Israel. When radicals criticized Egypt for talking tough but sheltering behind borders pacified by the UN observers, he ordered out the observers, who had separated Egyptian and Israeli forces. Nasser then announced a blockade of the Straits of Tiran, and hence the Gulf of Aqaba, to Israeli commerce. With the Suez Canal already denied to Israeli cargoes, closing the straits threatened to deprive Israel of all direct trade with East Africa, Southern Asia and the Far East. Israel publicly considered the action a cause for war, and formed a war cabinet, while Nasser moved troops into the Sinai and delivered bellicose speeches. But Egypt otherwise failed to prepare for battle, through military incompetence or perhaps miscalculating Israeli strength, or presuming the United States would restrain Israel from invasion.

Sudden Israeli attacks on Egyptian and Syrian air bases marked the beginning of the Six-Day War. In a few hours, the Arab air forces effectively ceased to exist. Control of the skies ensured victory on land, as Israeli tanks and infantry swept across the Sinai, reaching the Suez Canal, then turning back to trap retreating Egyptian units in the Sinai passes.

Nasser's miscalculation cost his army devastating losses in men and equipment.

He accepted responsibility for the defeat, and dramatically resigned, but emotional demonstrations in Cairo led him to return to power almost immediately. Other consequences of the defeat proved longer-lasting. Egypt lost the Sinai's recently-discovered oil fields. The Suez Canal remained closed, because it could not be reopened without unacceptable political and (probably) territorial concessions. The Israeli occupation impoverished the economy and soon led to a war of attrition, a period of intense shelling and air raids along the Canal.

From Attrition to Peace

When he died unexpectedly in 1970, President Gamal Abdul Nasser left a legacy of numerous economic and social reforms. Egyptian grief was immeasurable. However, in spite of the great public impression he made, his international goals involving Israel had been frustrated. Indeed, Israel enjoyed far greater military superiority than ever before. Egypt had lacked the economic and military strength to achieve his aims against a small but determined and technologically sophisticated nation determined to fight for its survival.

To replace Nasser, Egypt's leaders turned to former Vice President Anwar Sadat, one of the few original Free Officers who remained in public life. His presidency (1970–1981) marked a distinct change of economic philosophy from the state ownership of the previous decade. Hoping to lure American and other foreign investment to the country because Soviet aid and socialism had led to stagnation, Sadat's

Egypt

government lifted many, but by no means all, restrictions imposed when Arab socialism held sway. Much touted as liberalization, the reforms largely failed in their purposes. The reforms also contributed to influence peddling and profiteering by politicians, military officers and their relatives. The perennial problems of unemployment, lagging industrialization and overpopulation worsened, and the resulting dissatisfaction found both political and religious expression. Actually, Egypt was not particularly attractive to foreign investors anyway.

Initially, Sadat adhered to Nasser's foreign policy, including support for Palestinian interests and the unconditional withdrawal of Israel from the Sinai and other lands captured in 1967. The War of Attrition continued along the Suez Canal. Despite frequent warlike rhetoric, however, in 1973 Egypt dismissed the many Soviet military advisors and other personnel.

Suddenly, in October, the Syrian and Egyptian armies attacked Israeli forces occupying their territory. Egyptian troops successfully crossed the Canal and advanced into the Sinai. There, protected from Israeli bombing by anti-aircraft missiles, they fought monumental tank battles with the Israelis.

Within days, however, the tide of battle shifted. A U.S. airlift massively resupplied the Israel Defense Forces with sophisticated weapons. In a daring operation, some Israeli units crossed the Canal—into Africa, threatening Cairo and encircling large Egyptian armies. Given the risks of warfare, and its enormous human and material costs, Sadat and his advisors concluded that further confrontation with Israel was not only harmful to Egypt but also futile. Egypt accepted a truce.

Soon after the war, Sadat's policies changed dramatically. He restored diplomatic relations with the United States. Shuttle negotiations by Henry Kissinger, the U.S. Secretary of State, produced an Israeli withdrawal that returned both the Suez Canal and Sinai oil wells to Egypt.

President Hosni Mubarak

Domestically, Sadat promised economic freedom and political liberty, and he invoked Egyptian, rather than Pan-Arab, nationalism. Nevertheless, while oil exports and Suez Canal tolls provided foreign exchange, and trade increased, prosperity hardly trickled down to the masses. Likewise, peace remained only a hope.

Facing a new crisis over Lebanon in 1977, Sadat took the drastic step of offering peace with Israel. In a dramatic gesture he flew to Jerusalem and addressed the Knesset, offering to accept the legitimacy of Israel in exchange for its withdrawal from territory seized in 1967 from Egypt, Jordan and Syria. When diplomacy seemed to falter in 1978, President Jimmy Carter invited both Anwar Sadat and Israeli Prime Minister Menachem Begin to Camp David, the U.S. presidential retreat in Maryland. There, isolated from the press and their domestic political pressures, the two leaders reached terms of a peace settlement.

The Camp David Accords, signed in 1979, fell far short of Sadat's initial goals. Israel retained full control of territory captured from Jordan and Syria, and the Palestinians received only the promise of a distant and vague autonomy. Egypt, however, regained all the Sinai, including Israeli settlements. Diplomatic relations were established in 1980, and Israeli troops withdrew by 1982. In 1989, after an international tribunal verified Egyptian claims, the Egyptian flag finally returned to the beach resort of Taba, near Eilat.

The Camp David agreements aroused widespread Arab condemnation. Without settling the basic problems resulting from Israel's creation, the agreements removed Egypt from any future alliance against Israel, and thus left the Jewish state dominant militarily. Arab nations broke diplomatic relations with Egypt, and financial aid from oil exporters dwindled. Many Egyptians also viewed the accords with misgivings, and disliked having diplomatic relations with Israel, especially during periods of bloodshed between Israelis and Palestin-

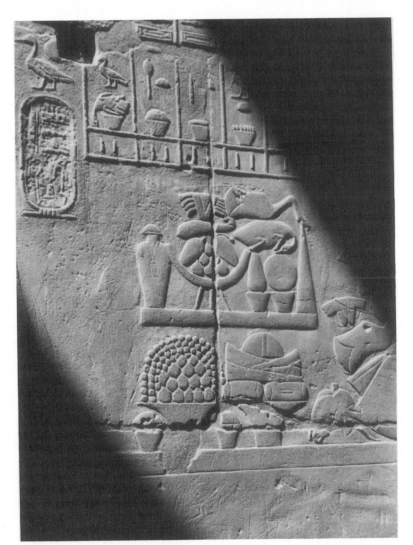

Hieroglyphs, Temple of Karnak, Upper Egypt   Photo by David Johns

45

Egypt

ians. Nevertheless, given Egypt's poverty and military weakness, the accords seemed necessary.

When Anwar Sadat was assassinated by religious zealots in 1981, there was little spontaneous outpouring of grief such as marked Gamal Abdul Nasser's death. Vice President Muhammad Husni Mubarak was sworn in as the new head of state. Yet another military officer, he generally pursued the liberalizing economic policies of his predecessor. Major attention was directed toward organizing the economy productively and reconciling the highly divergent opinions in the country. Every effort was made to present an image of stability and moderation. Mubarak also released from prison many (though not all) political opponents and Islamic fundamentalists.

Persistent Islamic Opposition

Throughout his presidency, the real opposition to President Mubarak remained the same broad movement whose militants had assassinated Anwar Sadat. The revival of Islamic values stretched from peaceful calls of professional groups to adopt Islamic law, the *Shari'a* (see Historical Background), through the *Muslim Brotherhood*, to extremist and violent groups such as *al-Gama'a al-Islamiyya* (the Islamic Group).

Until 1987, the government effectively banned the Islamist opposition from contesting elections. Partly as a result of this suppression of opinion, opposition activities took the form of demonstrations and protests, as well as arson and murder. Feeding on popular dissatisfaction with inflation, food shortages, unemployment and Israeli actions in Palestinian territories, the militants came to pose a shadowy yet significant threat to the regime. In 1992 alone, some 70 people perished in Islamist violence, among them the prominent columnist Faraj Fuda, shot despite police protection. Coptic Christians in Upper Egypt, government officials, and the police themselves suffered fatal assaults. By early 1995 terrorist attacks on buses, boats and trains had left several tourists dead, and nearly three dozen injured; more than 600 Egyptians died. As travelers avoided Egypt or stayed fewer days, the tourist industry's earnings slumped badly.

Some critics feared that the harsh government response to militant Islamic groups might heighten their appeal. Repressive measures by the police and military included widespread arrests, and rough treatment of suspects, allegedly even torture. The government also attempted to take control of all mosques in the country, a task as impossible as it was undemocratic.

To some critics, these desperate measures reflected the government's inability

Camel market in Cairo

to strike at the poverty, corruption and social distress that fostered religious extremism. However, the revival of Islamic sentiment reached far beyond the unemployed. Candidates supported by the *Muslim Brotherhood* captured the leadership of the Bar Association, while Islamic charities won recognition for responding effectively to a Cairo earthquake that killed hundreds and left tens of thousands homeless.

In response, the government struck repeatedly at the nonviolent *Muslim Brotherhood*. Though technically banned, the *Brotherhood* had been tolerated for years, while it constructed a network of charities and businesses. Eventually the government attempted to crush all Islamist opposition, with little distinction between nonviolent critics and those who attempted to assassinate Mubarak himself. Police detained hundreds of activists. Scores of leaders were sentenced to hard labor for belonging to a banned organization.

Al-Gama'a al-Islamiyya and its offshoots undoubtedly invited repression. Its extremists murdered tourists and conducted a massive attack in 1997 at the Temple of Queen Hatshepsut near Luxor that killed 62. The government interpreted these actions as the logical conclusion of moderate Islamic criticism, but human rights advocates suggested that the repression of moderates strengthened the militants. By 1998, the militant organizations apparently lay shattered. *Al-Gama'a al-Islamiyya* called for a ceasefire, and violence declined even in Upper Egypt. The next year hundreds of imprisoned Islamists were released, and leaders publicly urged a nonviolent struggle for their aims.

In 2005, two attacks on tourists in Cairo aroused fears of renewed violence as did hotel bombings in the Sinai. These proba-

bly represented individual anti-Israeli, anti-Western, and even anti-government actions rather than a systematic Islamic campaign against tourism. The new attacks seem the work of small, free-lance groups (in one case, a brother, his sister, and his girlfriend), and lack sophistication. However, they kill Egyptians and tourists alike—and their very disorganization represents a tremendous challenge to the security forces.

The attitudes of some Islamists may contribute to worsening Muslim-Christian relations, as do any forceful Christian assertions, such as a church drama about a sinful Copt turned Muslim or attempts by Muslim converts to record themselves as Christian on their identity cards. In these circumstances, permits for church construction or alterations become impossible to obtain, and Copts increasingly feel discrimination in employment. In 2009, the government's brutal attempt to slaughter all of Egypt's pigs (kept only by Christians) on the pretext of protection against the swine flu epidemic also raised protests and resentments, by animal rights advocates as well as Copts working as refuse collectors.

Regaining International Prestige

In the late 1980s Egypt emerged from the isolation that had followed its signing the Camp David Agreements. Symbolically, it returned to the Arab League in 1989, and a high-ranking Egyptian official was elected its Secretary-General in 1991. The greater prominence initially resulted from Egypt's support for Iraq during its war against Iran, as well as President Mubarak's backing for Yasir Arafat and the *Palestine Liberation Organization*. Ironically, Egypt's status outside the Arab world was enhanced after Iraq's invasion of Kuwait, when Egypt joined the anti-Iraqi coalition and dispatched 35,000 troops to defend Saudi Arabia, the third largest foreign force there. President Mubarak came to play a crucial role for the Western-led alliance as an Arab leader who supported the integrity of Kuwait. This weakened Iraqi attempts to portray events as a struggle between nationalist and Muslim Arabs on the one side, and foreigners and their puppet monarchs on the other.

Relations with Israel are diplomatically correct, but frosty, over concern about Palestinian issues and also nuclear weapons. Israel, armed with perhaps 100 nuclear weapons, has refused to sign either the original nuclear Non-Proliferation Treaty or its extension. Egyptian diplomats argue that nuclear weapons in the hands of one country of the region lead to their spread, and thus Israel should sign the treaty or propose a plan to do so later.

Domestic Economic and Political Stagnation

Under cover of war, the government adopted radical measures. It removed controls over the currency and interest rates, raised some prices to world levels, and imposed an unpopular sales tax. These measures, bitterly opposed—but probably necessary—had often been postponed, out of fears of protests by the poor, who depended on subsidized food, fuel, and medicine.

By the change of the millennium, however, the regime seemed to have lost its sense of purpose. Its privatization program faltered, leaving suspicions that favoritism had lined the pockets of some investors in profitable companies, while the many money-losing government firms continued to require subsidies. The exchange rate was controlled, then devalued, leading many investors to flee from Egypt. The stock market and economic growth slumped, even before the disastrous impact of the September 11 attacks on Western tourism. Unemployment climbed, and probably exceeded 20%. For a variety of reasons, the economy had failed to grow and produce the necessary jobs for the 800,000 new workers annually.

As Egyptians marked the fiftieth anniversary of their Revolution in 2002, they noted parallels between contemporary crises and those of the 1940s: corruption, scandals, official repression against Islamic and secular critics, and denunciations of symbolic targets like homosexuals. Uninterrupted rule by the *National Democratic Party* left a legacy of lengthy terms of office and official inertia. In response, popular opinion increasingly turned anti-government and anti-Western. Demonstrations against Israeli policies, and even stronger ones following the in-

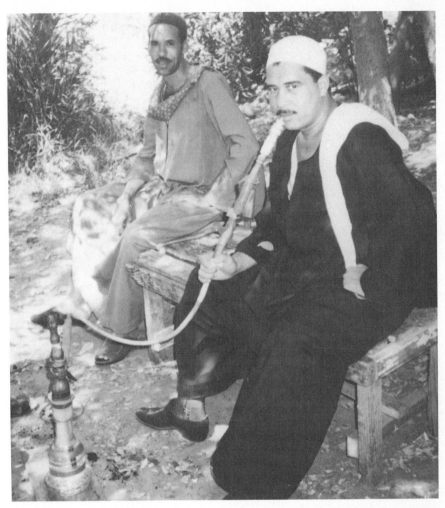

Smoking a *hookah*—which has a long flexible tube whereby the smoke is cooled by passing through water.   Courtesy: Susan L. Thompson

vasion of Iraq in 2003, took both commentators and officials by surprise.

Preparing for both presidential and parliamentary elections in 2005, Mubarak reshuffled the cabinet, bringing in a new prime minister and several younger, reform-minded ministers with business experience. Others were known as associates of Gamal Mubarak, the president's son, who is suspected of high political ambitions.

As the election approached, opposition groups formed, were prohibited, and reformed. Islamist students demonstrated for an end to the emergency regulations imposed after the death of Anwar al-Sadat in 1981. The state responded with both repression and reform. Hundreds of *Muslim Brotherhood* activists were arrested, but the government also instituted direct presidential elections. For the first time, ordinary Egyptians faced a ballot with more than one presidential candidate. However, with many voters skeptical, changing the process failed to affect the result. Husni

Mubarak won 88% of the vote from the small percentage of the population who actually voted (about 25%).

Reforms, world attention, and careful judges had more effect on parliamentary elections. Held over several weeks, they showed increasing victories for the *Muslim Brotherhood*, though its members still ran as independents. As the size of their victory increased, so did reports of intimidation, fraud, and violence. Again, the *National Democratic Party* won an overwhelming majority—over 70% of the vote. But the real election news was the *Muslim Brotherhood's* 88 seats, and the pitiful showing of secular opposition parties.

By 2008 local elections, the police and courts had locked up hundreds of opposition activists, and allowed only 20 *Muslim Brotherhood* candidates for some 50,000 local council positions. Perhaps the repression resulted from declining U.S. pressure for democracy. However, the threat of growing strikes and unrest by textile factory workers may be leading the

Egypt

**Mohammed ElBaradei,
former Director General, IAEA**

government to fear showing any signs of weakness.

Politics: The constitution of 1971, introduced by Anwar Sadat and amended several times under his successor, declares that Egypt is a "democratic, socialist" state. It provides for a strong president, who dominates the Advisory Council and People's Assembly. Until 2005, the president was not elected by contested ballot, but was first the single nominee of the People's Assembly and finally approved for a six-year term by popular referendum.

Political realities also taint elections to the People's Assembly, despite the democratic claims of Egypt's constitution. Once known as the *Arab Socialist Union* but now titled the *National Democratic Party*, the president's party always wins overwhelming victories. Official pressures, ranging from publicity and use of influence through police intervention and sometimes outright rigging, ensure a majority so large the legislature rarely serves as more than a rubber stamp.

The electoral system also helped to produce the victories. It reserved 400 of the 448 elected seats in the People's Assembly for party members. Thus in the multi-member districts, an independent candidate might receive more votes than a party, but still lose the seat to the party candidate. Furthermore, the large, multi-member constituencies have a vote threshold of 8%—and votes for parties receiving less than 8% of the district's votes are applied to the winner's total. Not surprisingly, many sophisticated city dwellers ignore the electioneering and rarely vote. In some rural districts, however, elections might be taken seriously and even violently.

Despite the obstacles, opposition parties exist, some stamped as legal by a parliamentary committee dominated by the *NDP*, others technically illegal. The small

New Wafd Party traces its origins to Zaghlul and the 1919 *Wafd*. The *Muslim Brotherhood*, technically illegal and much more than a party, runs candidates under cover, sometimes from the socialist *Labor Party*. The 2005 elections confirmed it as the only significant opposition group. Besides the small centrist *Liberal Party*, several left-wing parties reflect varying viewpoints. The major opposition groups ally to demand an end to the state of emergency, a halt to torture, and a new constitution. However, they often seem more suited to permanent opposition than to governing.

The fate of only the third new party legalized in 25 years, *Hizb al-Ghad* (*Party of Tomorrow*), symbolizes the plight of the opposition. Ayman Nour, its founder, was jailed over alleged false signatures on the party's application, although the signatures were not necessary and Nour himself had not gathered them. While in jail awaiting trial, his leadership of the party was challenged (perhaps by government agents), and the party newspaper was refused permission to publish. Released from jail in 2005, Nour ran for president, but failed to attract many votes. He was later jailed again, and only released in 2009.

Intimidation and obstacles—even the padlocking of voting locations in opposition strongholds—marked the 2007 elections for the upper house of parliament. Thanks to one reform proposed by Mubarak, the upper house will gain more significance. However, another Mubarak reform removed the supervisory judges from elections, thus eliminating one of the strongest voices for freedom and fairness.

The 2011 Presidential Elections Approach

Throughout the current parliamentary term, the government maintained pressure on the *Muslim Brotherhood*, possibly contributing to the decision of the Supreme Guide to resign in late 2009. The subsequent campaign for leadership of the organization resulted in defeat for the moderates, who generally favor engagement with society and contesting elections. By contrast, the new Supreme Guide, Mohammed Badi, seems likely to emphasize religious and social work, and reduce political involvement. Nevertheless, the government arrested several of the group's senior leaders.

Over a year before the 2011 presidential election, Muhammad ElBaradei returned to Egypt. A legal scholar and international diplomat, ElBaradei had served as Director-General of the International Atomic Energy Agency (IAEA) of the United Nations until 2009. Returning to Egypt, he indicated a willingness to campaign for the presidency, given changes to allow him to run as an independent. Though the government press has depicted him as out of touch with Egyptian conditions after living abroad for decades, representatives of several political parties and other groups joined him in forming the *National Association for Change*, a "non-party-political movement." Younger citizens often relished the prospect of a civilian candidate free of corruption, and ElBaradei's supporters turned to Facebook

Given Husni Mubarak's age and ill health, many commentators expect his son, Gamal, to contest the 2011 election. It so, it may be the closest to a genuine democratic contest in Egyptian history.

Culture: Perhaps no other country in the world is so overshadowed in the popular mind by the monuments, buildings, ruins and tombs of an ancient civilization as is Egypt. Archaeological remains from five millennia of civilization abound everywhere in the Nile Valley and the Delta.

Symmetrical and graceful beneath dramatic cliffs, the Temple of Hatshepsut

Egypt

There are royal tombs from as early as 3,000 B.C., the giant pyramids from the 26th century B.C., the magnificent tombs of kings and queens of the 15th and 14th centuries B.C. (including that of Tutankhamun), sculpture and painting from every period and innumerable elaborate inscriptions on stone in a continuous succession attesting to the cultural development of the country at a very early time.

Only a few miles separate the incredible traffic jams and skyscrapers of modern Cairo from the great pyramids at Giza on the edge of the desert. Yet the modern culture of the country has little to do with ancient civilization. New religions, crops, and ways of living largely obliterated the customs of ancient times. Even the agricultural cycle for the Egyptian farmer—known as the *fellah*—has weakened, for the Aswan High Dam prevents the Nile from flooding his lands and depositing nourishing silt for the next year's crops.

In the 7th century Islam began to mold life in the land, and the dozens of impressive mosques, some many centuries old, attest to the significance of this faith. Yet the neon lights in the cities and cotton mills in the country towns, coupled with jet aircraft and satellite TV dishes all bear witness to recent influences of the modern, industrialized world. These new influences do not merely affect the physical appearance of Egypt; they also modify ideas and social patterns. It is an ancient land in the midst of continuing social change that is felt unevenly.

Islamic values run deep in Egypt, particularly among the impoverished masses, but increasingly among students and even professionals. In contrast, some members of the upper classes, whether Muslim or Coptic Christian, attempt to follow Western styles, though most remain somewhat faithful to religious customs. The broader culture finds certain kinds of behavior and appearances offensive, while the West ignores them. Thus in 1997 the police arrested a number of students and other heavy metal fans on charges of Satanism. Possession of CDs or T-shirts with the wrong symbols—let alone long hair on men—provoked trouble. Another example: in 1999 an unmarried couple caught kissing passionately in public was sentenced to one year in jail!

Probably the most delicate difficulty that tradition presents Egypt's government and society is female circumcision. The term actually applies to several different procedures, often involving removal of the clitoris, and the practice has been defended as an Islamic solution to avoid female immorality. In fact, the custom seems largely African, rather than Islamic, and Coptic Christians continue it. Given its intimate nature, little is known about its effects on women (for example, does it render a woman uninterested in sex or increase the search for satisfaction?). On the other hand, it kills girls every year and leaves women maimed. Nevertheless, most Egyptian mothers apparently desire to have their daughters circumcised, despite a (poorly enforced) government ban on it in 1996.

Conservative social values create difficulties and obstacles for women in other ways as well. Physical abuse becomes more acceptable when, as survey data indicate, over 80% of young and middle-aged women consider wife-beating justified under certain circumstances. Despite the efforts of non-governmental organizations and the efforts of the Suzanne Mubarak, the first lady, legal equality remains distant. In contrast to fairly rapid divorce procedures when requested by a man, a woman seeking to end a marriage must either spend years in the courts, or accept a no-fault divorce that leaves her without any financial assets from the marriage.

While society frowns strongly on premarital sexual activity, economic change and education increasingly bring single men and women together. Young couples unable or unwilling to have a formal wedding sometimes turn to "urfi" marriages, traditional but unregistered marriages often kept secret even from family. If the arrangement should break down—for example, if the woman becomes pregnant but the man does not wish to be bound by his commitments—the consequences fall most heavily on the woman.

Literary Culture and Education

Though relatively poor, Egypt in many respects remains the cultural center of the Arab World, known for its novelists, short story writers, dramatists and poets. Indeed, in 1988 Naguib Mahfouz, known best in the English-speaking world for *Midhaq Alley* and *The Beginning and the End*, won the Nobel Prize for Literature. The first Arab writer to receive the honor, Mahfouz borrowed liberally from the traditions of European literature in his realistic novels of life in Cairo, because Arabic lacked a literary tradition in fiction. However, international recognition revived criticism of his work as blasphemous for portraying irreligious individuals who questioned Islam and his brave condemnation of Ayatollah Khomeini's death sentence on Salman Rushdie. Though in his 80s, Mahfouz barely survived an assassination attempt, but after recovering resumed walking the streets and alleys of his beloved Cairo until his death in 2006.

Though they lack the broad vision Mahfouz portrayed, a generation of sometimes angry young authors recently won widespread acclaim and even sales. The best known in translation is Alaa Al Aswany's *The Yacoubian Building* (2002), which reveals a society where the political corruption, sexual repression, and religious extremism flourish.

Founded in 988, the mosque school of al-Azhar in Cairo is one of the oldest universities in the world. Traditionally its professors sat at the base of one of the mosque's pillars, lecturing to students who came from many lands. There were no official examinations, but when the faculty considered a student proficient in a subject, they issued him a license to teach. Modern changes include formal diplomas, branches in medicine and other non-theological disciplines, and a women's program. The Grand Imam of al-Azhar remains an important spokesman for Sunni Islam, and offers guidance to believers on many theological issues.

In recent years Egypt lost its lead among Arab states in education, largely because of financial limitations. As in most professions, teachers in Egypt receive pitifully small salaries, so many of the best qualified have been lured to more prosperous countries to work at much higher remuneration. The quality of education at the University of Cairo and the half dozen other universities in Egypt is generally good, though in common with other Less

Statue of Umm Kahlthoum, Egypt's great 20th century singer

Egypt

Developed Countries, Egypt turns out too many liberal arts graduates, who fill (often needless) government positions or seek work abroad. In contrast, the country needs scientists, and especially skilled manual workers and technicians.

For decades education for all remained a dream rather than reality. However, the government built thousands of new schools in the 1990s, for the 90% of young boys and 80% of girls who enroll. Adult literacy climbed from 40% in the 1970s to 60% by the end of the century. However, with their salaries as low at $35 per month, teachers have encouraged the practice of guiding the best learning in private tutoring sessions, and classroom study often decays into rote memorization. Not surprisingly, many children drop out: the law requiring nine years of school cannot be enforced. After just three or four years inside a classroom, many children begin working, even in agriculture and building construction, because of family poverty.

Two new cultural events promise to enrich the country during the coming years. In Alexandria, home in ancient times of a famous library, funding from UNESCO, the government, and other sources provided a $200 million library and conference center. The international competition to design the library drew over 500 entries, and the winning entry symbolizes Egypt's ancient heritage. The disc-shaped building slants with one side in the earth, the other elevated, recalling the ancient Egyptian sun-god.

The second cultural landmark, in Cairo, recalls the Islamic heritage in its dome, geometric windows, and marble colonnades. The New Opera House on the island of Gezira replaces the 19th century landmark gutted by fire in 1971. Built with Japanese assistance as an educational and cultural center, it offers the potential of becoming much more than a mere stage for musical and other art forms in Western languages.

Health services vary greatly according to family income and education. Although the universities train doctors to the best world standards, poverty prevents adequate medical services for many. Sanitation is often deplorable. In Cairo, some two million people live in areas without sewers. Preliminary construction of a new sewer system for the city began in early 1985. Years will be required to complete this project which is an urgent matter of public health.

Popular Culture and Sport

On the popular level, Cairo's constant flow of new films and television dramas makes it the Hollywood of the region. Plots frequently dramatize the sufferings of life, particularly marriage and family problems set against a background of conflict between traditions and modern individuality, as well as the persistent issue of class-consciousness. Difficulties sometimes arise with Islamic conservatives. In one example, a film about Joseph (*Al-Mohager*, "The Emigrant") was banned for showing a prophet on the screen.

Egypt's pre-eminence in Arabic film, television drama and music made the distinctive Cairene accent familiar, and sometimes mocked, throughout the Arabic-speaking world. Other Arab countries attempted to develop their own television programming, but the arrival of music videos and satellite TV reinforced Egyptian dominance, as did the construction of Media Palace City (1995), an attempt to create a "Hollywood of the East" production center.

Egyptian musicians also dominate popular music and videos from Oman to North Africa. The "golden voice" of Umm Kalthoum captivated hearts across the Arab world during a career of six decades, and her recordings continue to sell well. By the 21st century, the country's music scene had developed a wide diversity of styles, from traditional songs and instruments to Arabic Pop, typically a fusion of traditional Arab styles and instruments with Western influences. Like popular music everywhere, romantic themes dominate, but despite the suggestive clothing of female pop stars, explicit references to sexuality are rare and would be censored, as would references to alcohol and politics.

Many Egyptians are passionate about soccer. Indeed, after Egypt lost a World Cup qualifying match to Algeria in 2009, fans stirred by media coverage rioted in Cairo and attacked the Algerian embassy. While rarely successful in World Cup competitions, the Egyptian national team, nicknamed The Pharaohs, won the African Nations Cup in 2010 for an unprecedented third year in succession. Within the country, two teams traditionally vie for championship of the football league, Zamalak and Al-Ahly, the latter with over 40 million fans.

Economy: Although systematic efforts to modernize began two hundred years ago, personal incomes remain low. A rapidly growing population, misfortune in war, misguided government economic policies and a tradition of government regulation all reduced opportunities in the past 50 years. In addition, natural resources are few. There is no timber, no coal, and outside the Nile Valley, almost no water. Mineral deposits provide little wealth for a population so large, and are limited to modest oil deposits, natural gas, salt and manganese.

Visual evidence of the mixture of poverty and progress strikes even the casual tourist, in the form of barefoot children, simple farming methods, and the ever-present unemployed. Also obvious, the gap between the poor and the rich is enormous, the latter receiving incomes some 5000% of the former. The press of millions of poor makes Cairo one of the world's most crowded and noisy cities. Indeed, a survey reported that 60% of Cairenes had used sedatives at least once against the noise and stress.

Unrelated to Cairo's noise, the population growth rate fell from more than 3% in 1985 to 2% ten years later, a welcome decline that still requires feeding one mil-

Sheep market in Cairo

lion additional mouths food every year. Almost all live in the 4% of the country's territory comprising the Nile Valley and Delta. Egypt's population is roughly seven times that of New Jersey, but lives in only twice as much territory. Moreover,

because one-third of the population is rural, average farms measure only a few acres. This overwhelms the ability of the fertile soil and warm climate to provide either sufficient food or a good standard of living.

Traditionally, agriculture formed the basis of the Egyptian economy. Famous for its desirable long-staple cotton, Egypt also produced and sometimes exported grains such as wheat and rice, as well as sugar, oranges, dates and tropical mangoes.

Before the 1952 Revolution, much farmland belonged to absentee landowners whose domains included entire villages. Under Gamal Abdul Nasser, the government attempted significant land reform, in part to break the political power of conservative landlords through limiting ownership to a maximum 50 acres in traditional farming areas. Irrigation schemes brought large tracts of desert under cultivation, and the Aswan High Dam (see page 51) provided more areas with successive crops per year. Public health and education improved in the villages.

Unfortunately, government regulations offset much of the progress. Investment in agriculture came low on the list of government priorities, while the new landowners lacked credit ratings to borrow. They often lacked formal education and technical training as well, both required to benefit from scientific advances in agriculture.

Recent reforms show the potential for substantial improvements in farm production and income. When wheat was deregulated, its price rose, and output increased by 100%. Besides rewarding farmers, this reduced somewhat the 6 million tons of wheat and flour imported yearly. Likewise, when the government permitted the private export of oranges, quantities rose by one-third, at the cost of higher prices at home. New policies towards reclaiming

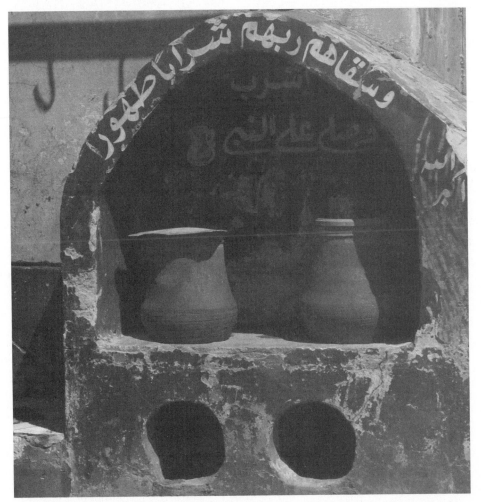

Caring for the needy: water pitchers placed for thirsty passersby in Upper Egypt

Egypt

The interior of the Bibliotheca Alexandrina

the desert stress the importance of research-intensive, low technology solutions, including the use of genetics to obtain salt-tolerant plants.

Effects of the Aswan High Dam

Above all else, Egypt under Nasser trusted the Aswan High Dam to solve poverty and raise farm output. The dam promised to store the summer floods in Lake Nasser, the largest man-made reservoir in the world and then provide year-round irrigation for many areas and water for thousands of acres of desert. A great technical achievement as well as a foreign-policy success, the dam at its completion in 1971 met these goals, and its massive turbines once generated half of Egypt's electricity.

For all its benefits, however, the High Dam also brought problems. After dropping their silt in Lake Nasser, the Nile wa-

ters flow swiftly, and now scour its banks. Some Delta lands began to subside, deprived of the fertile soil previously deposited during the annual flood. Several species of fish—especially sardines—disappeared from the coastal Mediterranean waters now denied the Nile's nutrients, though a report in 2009 raised the possibility that sewage and fertilizer run-offs apparently enriched the sea somewhat. Across Egypt, the underground water table rose, threatening historical sites, and year-round irrigation spread bilharzia and other parasitic diseases, as well as obnoxious water hyacinths.

Two predicted difficulties, rising soil salinity and the loss of silt that enriched the soil, require expensive drainage systems and chemical fertilizers. Thus the benefits of the High Dam—including protection for Egypt from years of drought in East Africa—carry several costly side effects. Furthermore, the experts are deeply divided about how much water the dam will collect. Some claim that even without major diversions upstream, early in the 21st century water shortages will appear, in part because of seepage and evaporation from Lake Nasser. Any major diversion upstream in Ethiopia or Sudan would magnify the shortfall. Complicating matters, two massive, multi-billion dollar schemes are beginning to bring irrigation to two million additional acres, one in the Sinai, the other the Toshka/New Valley project to create artificial oases west of Lake Nasser. Skeptics doubt the Nile's flow will prove sufficient for both.

World environmental issues pose other, less certain, risks to Egyptian agriculture. The low-lying Delta and coastal cities face inundation from the sea if the more alarming predictions of Global Warming prove true. Air pollution around Cairo poses a threat to plants and animals as well as humans. However, solutions to environmental problems sometimes benefit society. Alexandria's sewage, now flowing out to sea with harmful results, may be treated on land less expensively than in a new treatment plant for sea disposal. As a bonus, the nutrient-rich waste water will irrigate desert areas.

Industry: Industrial production began modestly in Egypt, partly because foreign and local entrepreneurs first sought riches from profitable government contracts. After World War I some factories began to process food and cotton textiles, logical industries given the lack of coal and iron ore. The officers that led the 1952 Revolution desired to industrialize the country, motivated by socialist ideas that encouraged national self-sufficiency and equated modernity with heavy industry. However, socialists also loathed foreign investment

The Pyramids attract all nationalities

Courtesy: Juliet Bunch

Egyptian Charm

and discouraged capitalists. As a result, the state nationalized a number of industrial companies, eventually controlling 85% of manufacturing assets. Those that remained suffered paralyzing regulations and red tape that hampered almost all trade and commerce.

Attempts to produce a complete range of manufactured goods within the country, from appliances to cars, provided expensive products of poor quality that required high tariff protection to compete against imports. (In contrast, the rapidly growing countries of East Asia follow the opposite policies, encouraging exports and foreign trade.)

Even well-intended regulations often harmed private companies. For example, to encourage investment in factories and equipment, laws decreed low interest rates on loans to industry. Perversely, this made such loans so unattractive to banks that they avoided making them.

Egypt's leadership in the Arab world also slowed economic growth. Opposing Israel militarily meant five wars (including the War of Attrition) in 25 years between 1948 and 1973. Besides the human costs of a large military force and several generations of weapons largely destroyed on the battlefield, the damage included Israeli attacks on economic targets and the devastation of cities along the Suez Canal. In addition to untold sums owed the Soviet Union for arms, the country purchased military hardware on credit from the United States, ironically during a period of peace with Israel. Paying the high-

interest loans became a crushing burden on the Egyptian economy before the U.S. cancelled the debt of $7 billion.

In contrast to past military expenses and losses, Egypt today has become a substantial and presumably profitable producer of weapons. By 1988 military exports ranked (with cotton) in fifth place among exports, earning some $500 million. Although still dependent on imports for aircraft, electronics, and other sophisticated items, reports indicated Egypt had become self-sufficient in light anti-aircraft guns, armored trucks, rockets, bombs, and towed artillery.

Four Uncommon Assets

For its present growth and future prosperity, Egypt depends on four uncommon assets: a work force employed in wealthier Arab countries, oil, tourism and the Suez Canal. Each of these benefits provides foreign exchange, vitally important for a country whose foreign debt reached $50 billion by 1991. Oil and the canal also provide alternatives to taxing the citizens.

In years of high oil prices, the export of petroleum products provided the largest foreign exchange earnings, and so enabled Egypt to import food, equipment, and

consumer goods. Although not a member of the Organization of Petroleum Exporting Countries (OPEC), it once exported larger quantities than some OPEC members. However, Egypt's oil reserves appear to be limited, despite explorations for new deposits, and domestic demand for oil is growing. Exports have fallen to around 200,000 barrels of oil and gas equivalent per day.

Fortunately, discoveries of natural gas deposits around Suez, in the Nile basin, and in the Western Desert have created a surplus of that clean fuel. The government has encouraged customers to switch to it from oil, and the first natural gas export pipeline reached Jordan in 2003.

For two thousand years travelers have marveled at the Pyramids. A century ago, the wealth and beauty of Tutankhamun's tomb rendered a minor Pharaoh a household word. For the present era of mass tourism, Egypt possesses some of the world's most spectacular archaeological treasures and monuments. Other attractions exist as well, often inexpensive and rarely spoiled by rain. They range from sandy beaches along the Mediterranean to relatively unspoiled fishing and diving in the Red Sea. They include Mt. Sinai, where

Taxi stop in Cairo

Egypt

Jews and Christians traditionally believe God gave Moses the Ten Commandments. Arabs from oil states often seek culture and entertainment in Cairo, while visitors from West and East seek bargains in the city's *souks* (or suqs, pronounced like "duke") or enjoy luxury cruises on the Nile. Despite attacks by Muslim militants, the industry earns $3 billion during prosperous years, and its employees support some one million people.

One unique Egyptian economic benefit comes from the country's location connecting Asia and Africa. Cut through the Isthmus over 10 years, at a cost of perhaps 100,000 lives, the Suez Canal reduces greatly the distance ships must travel between Europe and the Indian Ocean. Tolls from the 18,000 ships that annually make the 15-hour journey through the 100-mile long canal exceed $500,000 per trip for the largest vessels able to use the waterway. These tolls provide a very important source of foreign exchange, exceeding $4 billion annually. Further earnings come from the "Sumed," the parallel oil pipeline from Suez to the Mediterranean.

At present, the very largest tankers (Ultra Large Crude Carriers, over 300,000 dead weight tons) are unable to use the waterway. Somewhat smaller vessels would strike bottom when loaded, given its depth of only 58 feet. As a result, some loaded tankers sail around Africa to markets in Europe and the U.S., but then return, empty, to the Persian Gulf through the canal. Thanks to this practice, more vessels use the canal going southbound than northbound. Dredging to widen, deepen, and straighten the canal continues, with the goal of eventually permitting passage by any vessel.

Like the Straits of Hormuz and Malacca, or the Bosporus, the Suez Canal is one of the world's critical waterways, important economically and strategically. It was attacked during both world wars, and blocked by sunken vessels during the Suez War of 1956. Between 1967 and 1973, it was closed, and set apart the Israel and Egyptian armies. Many Egyptian nationalists care passionately about the canal's nationalization in 1956, and successful operation since 1975.

No longer the most important source of foreign currency, remittances sent home by more than two million Egyptians working outside the country still play a very important role. Before the Gulf War, nearly four million Egyptians—almost all male, mostly young, and often educated—worked abroad, primarily in the Gulf. Many were unskilled laborers, but others were teachers, doctors, and other professionals. They sought foreign jobs, some of them dangerous, difficult or dirty, because remaining at home meant unemployment or low wages. They often planned to return in a few years, with funds saved for marriage and the purchase of a little land, a house, or perhaps a business. With pay abroad often 10 times the Egyptian rate, four years hard work could equal the gain of 20 years at home. In the outstanding year of 1989/90, repatriated earnings reached $8 billion.

The Iraqi-Kuwait War and the 1990 recession in the oil states threw hundreds of thousands of their Egyptian workers out of work. As foreigners, they lacked unemployment benefits, and some could neither find work nor afford the return airfare. A decade later, the number of workers and their earnings had fallen by half.

Reforms and Continuing Challenges

Though often seeming piecemeal and halfhearted, the economic reforms of the 1990s created an environment for sustained economic growth. Difficulties like the budget deficit, inflation, and the balance of payments deficit that had plagued the country for decades dwindled to insignificance when the government, hesitantly and slowly cut subsidies and controlled its spending.

The subsidies had distorted prices badly—kerosene, for example, had cost only $.20 per gallon, and legends exist of farmers feeding bread to their animals, since it was cheaper than grains. Removing the subsidies encouraged more efficient use of resources, but Egypt's poor and middle classes found holes in their economic safety-nets. Afraid of popular backlash—in 1977 rioters had chanted at President Sadat, "Hero of the Crossing (of the Suez Canal), Where is our Breakfast?"—the cuts were scheduled gradu-

ally, and subtly. Rather than raise the price of bread, for example, the government cut the size of the pita-style loaf.

Cutting the government's large payroll and privatizing the companies it owned proved a more difficult task. In 1990, nearly one-third of all employed Egyptians worked for the government and its companies, far more than needed. A major purpose of the privatization drive was to provide jobs for the roughly 800,000 new job-seekers annually, but many legal, political and practical complications slowed the sale of government firms to private owners. Fortunately, new private companies flourished as the government removed regulations, and by 1999 only about 20% of output came from government firms, and the government's share of the workforce had fallen to 25%. Some factories proved particularly difficult to privatize, particularly in textiles, where workers understood that lifetime employment offset low wages. Strikes spread across the Delta's textile industry in 2006–07 over rising prices, lagging wages, and broken promises by management, idling some of the largest factories in the world. Given higher inflation world-wide, living conditions have often declined for industrial workers.

The Future: Although President Mubarak's lengthy recuperation from an operation in Germany received media coverage, his health and fitness remain matters closed to public discussion. His fifth six-year term expires in 2011, but he has not appointed a vice president as a prospective successor. Speculation suggests his son, Gamal, may be in line for the nomination. Many secular or moderate Muslims in the opposition have supported the former IAEA director general, Mohammed ElBaradei, in an election that could prove a crucial turning point.

Workers in the government-owned textile factories struck repeatedly in recent years, and data indicate that the lower classes may be suffering declining standards of living. Expect the usual attempts to manipulate voters and voting to achieve favorable election results for both the parliament in late 2010 and the presidency in 2011.

The Islamic Republic of Iran

Supporters of former President Muhammad Khatami celebrate his victory in 1997. The flowers faded.

AP/Wide World Photo

Area: 636,313 square miles (1,648,043 sq. km.).

Population: 75.4 million.

Capital City: Tehran (pop. 7.4 million, with suburbs, over 10 million).

Climate: Arid, except for regions of moderate to heavy rainfall in the northwest. Temperature changes are extreme, from cold winters of the central plateau and northern mountains to the intense heat of the humid southern coast

Neighboring Countries: Armenia, Azerbaijan, Turkmenistan (North); Afghanistan (East); Pakistan (Southeast); Iraq (West); Turkey (Northwest)

Time Zone: GMT +3 hours, 30 minutes

Official Language: *Farsi*, or Persian.

Other Principal Tongues: Kurdish, Baluchi, Luri, Armenian, Turkish, Shushtari, Azeri and Arabic.

Ethnic Background: People are identified mainly according to language (about 80% Persian or Iranian), but also according to tribal group or religion.

Principal Religion: Shi'a Islam (89%), Sunni Islam (10%), Baha'i (1%).

Chief Industrial Products: Petroleum and petroleum products, carpets, iron and steel, light manufactured goods, vehicle assembly.

Agricultural Produce and Livestock: Wheat, barley, pistachios, rice, sugar beets, sugar cane, potatoes, sheep, goats, cattle and chickens.

Major Trading Partners: Japan, Germany, Italy, France and the United Arab Emirates.

Currency: Rial (10 rials = 1 toman)

Former Colonial Status: Under influence of Russia and Britain (1907–1923); occupied by Soviet and British troops (1941–1945).

National Day: February 1.

Chief Executive: Mahmoud Ahmadinejad, President

"Head of the Revolution" and "Supreme Leader": Ayatollah Seyyid Ali Khamenei.

National Flag: Three equal horizontal stripes of (top to bottom) green, white and red. The edges of the green and red stripes carry 22 repetitions of the words *Allah-o-Akbar*, "God is Great." A red emblem symbolizing the Islamic Republic is centered in the white stripe.

Gross Domestic Product: $359 billion (at current prices, 2007); $861 billion (PPP).

GDP per capita: $11,400 (PPP).

The heart of Iran is neither picturesque nor fertile. Occupying more than half the country, the center is a bleak, windswept combination of desert and salt-flats—scorching hot in summer days and freezing cold during winter nights. However, the outlying mountains and watered plains support large populations, making Iran one of the three most populous Middle Eastern countries.

The least typical region is the coast of the Caspian Sea, which lies below sea level. Created by abundant rainfall and warm weather, this garden of Iran is the most densely populated area of the country. Several million people also live in the extreme northwest province of Azerbaijan, a land of mountain forests, cultivated valleys and good rainfall. Tabriz, once Iran's second largest city, is the center of this province. Other important populations of farmers and herders live in the mountainous regions along the border with Iraq on the west, and east of the Caspian Sea near Turkmenistan.

The rest of the country is largely uninhabited except for nomads who make great seasonal wanderings from north to south. The elevation of the central plateau

55

Iran

(3,000 to 6,000 feet) produces great extremes of temperature; 110° or 115° (F) during the day in the summer contrasts with sub-freezing temperatures of the winter nights. The southern coast and neighboring areas are the hottest regions of Iran; frost is unknown there. Light rainfall provides sparse pasture for livestock.

Tehran has grown in two centuries from a village to a huge city and the seat of a highly centralized government. Railroads, roads and trade center on it; industry is concentrated there. The other major cities are Tabriz and Isfahan, both of them commercial and handicraft centers with long histories.

Geologically, the country sits uneasily atop seismic zones where the Arabian and Eurasian tectonic plates meet. As the plates press against each other, they generate more earthquakes than in any other country, with small quakes striking daily. Except for Isfahan, all major Iranian cities lie in zones of high or very high seismic activity. Deprived of timber, Iranians construct homes out of concrete block or bricks, and when powerful earthquakes strike, the loss of life is often catastrophic. For example, the relatively small city of Bam in eastern Iran lost 30,000 dead in December 2003.

History: Civilization stretches back thousands of years in Iran, whose name means "Land of the Aryans," and its Indo-European peoples formed several of the notable kingdoms of ancient history (see Historical Background). Later invaders added Arab Islam and Turkish warriors to Iranian society.

So ancient is the history of Iran—or Persia, as it was traditionally known—that the modern period began hundreds of years ago, with the Safavid dynasty in the 16th century and the widespread adoption of Shi'a Islam (see Historical Background). The Safavid Empire reached its greatest power and extent under Shah Abbas (1587–1629), after whose death it declined. By the early 18th century, Persia was threatened by Turkey on the west, Russia on the north and the Afghans on the east.

After an Afghan invasion ended the Safavid dynasty, Nadir Shah (1736–1747) restored much of the country's unity and conquered additional territory. Famous for his military exploits and adventures, he returned from invading India with incredible wealth and the famous Peacock Throne, but he failed to found a dynasty. The peaceful reign of Karim Khan Zand (1750–1779) was followed by the estab-

lishment of the Qajar dynasty. Though often beset with tribal revolts and bloodshed over the succession, the sometimes—brutal Qajars maintained power until 1925. Shah Agha Mohammed Khan made Tehran his capital in 1788.

Under Qajar rule, Persia fought unsuccessful wars with Russia, the Ottoman Turks and the Afghans, and lost territory to each. Under sometimes capricious rulers, domestic politics often stagnated at best, and the country failed to advance with the times.

Rivalry between the Russian Empire and the British Empire often focused on Persia. Russia sought to expand to the warm water ports of the Persian Gulf, while Britain was concerned primarily for the security of India. Russia enjoyed more influence in Persia, though the British worked to gain favor through agents in Tehran. Finally, in 1907 Russia and Britain arrived at an agreement—without any consideration of Persian desires in the matter—providing Russia a "sphere of influence" in the north, and Britain one in the south. A strip of less important territory in the middle was left as a neutral zone.

Dissatisfaction with foreign influence and the ineffectiveness of the monarchy in resisting it grew stronger in the late 19th century, symbolized by disapproval of granting British companies a tobacco monopoly in 1890. This produced protests and a ban from the clergy on using tobacco.

Partly influenced by Western ideas of political freedom, in 1906 groups of merchants, religious leaders and reformers compelled the shah to grant a constitution and allow a parliament, known as the Majlis. Known as the Constitutional Revolution (1905–1911), these changes began an era of numerous struggles between the monarchy and the Majlis over control of the government.

During a decade and a half of struggle, marked by several closures and reopenings, the Majlis and its reformers had no more success in strengthening the country and reducing foreign influence than had the monarchy. Central authority collapsed almost entirely during World War I, as Ottoman, Russian, and British

Iran

A map of Persia from a 1560 atlas

oil exports. When Anglo-Iranian refused higher payments, in an atmosphere of emotional nationalism the Majlis in 1951 nationalized the entire petroleum industry. The elderly politician who had championed the bill, Mohammed Mossadeq, became prime minister. His government found itself unable to produce and market oil in the face of an international boycott organized by Britain, and during the next two years the country became poorer and suffered serious political disturbances. However, Mossadeq firmly refused any compromise, and demanded full national economic independence, meaning Iranian control of its oil.

The shah dismissed Mossadeq in mid-1953, but the prime minister refused to leave office. Lacking authority and fearing mobs and riots in Tehran, the shah and

President Mahmoud Ahmadinejad

forces and puppets occupied parts of the country. This set the stage for the rise of a dictator. In 1921 Reza Khan, deputy commander of the Cossack Brigade, joined a *coup d'etat*. After creating a national army to replace various foreign-influenced units, in 1923 Reza compelled the shah to appoint him prime minister. The shah then left for exile, and in 1925 Reza Khan had the Majlis depose the Qajar dynasty. Later that same year he proclaimed himself Reza Shah Pahlavi, taking the ancient name Pahlavi from Persian history because he, a commoner, needed a dynastic name.

A man of action rather than theories, Reza Shah improved and enlarged the army—then he used it, sometimes harshly, to establish obedience and order in every part of the country. He worked to gain full independence, to make himself the nation's master, and to make it as much like modern Europe as possible. He commanded the construction of roads, and a railroad from the Caspian Sea to the Persian Gulf. He introduced new secular laws and moved away from Islamic religious law. He encouraged modern technical education, forced people to dress more like Europeans, and started factories. By 1942, they employed half a million workers. Reza Shah even changed the name of the country from Persia to Iran to impress the world that things had changed. Moderate but steady income from oil exports produced by the Anglo-Iranian Oil Company financed the new projects.

After the German invasion of the Soviet Union in 1941, Soviet and British troops occupied Iran to prevent Reza Shah from allying with Nazi Germany, and to secure the country's oil and transportation routes for Allied use. Reza abdicated and went into exile, where he died.

When the Allied troops began to withdraw from Iran after the end of the war, the new shah, young Mohammed Reza faced wide opposition. Factions of many sorts, previously repressed by his determined father, vied to control the government. Great landowners, who paid nearly no taxes, attempted to dominate politics. Nomadic chieftains sought to free themselves and their tribes from Reza Shah's central authority. Shi'a religious leaders denounced secular government, and elderly politicians schemed for office. In the streets, the Communist-leaning *Tudeh Party* held sway, and foreign powers courted ethnic minorities.

In these circumstances, the Soviet Union attempted to form an autonomous Communist regime in Azerbaijan, the Turkish-speaking northwestern province. However, the United States and Britain stood by the shah, and Soviet troops withdrew in 1946. The Iranian army dealt severely with the separatist leaders.

In response to the dire economic conditions, a seven-year plan won approval from the Majlis in 1949. Because the plan's projected expenses exceeded local taxes, Iranian politicians sought what they considered a fairer share of income from

his queen fled the country. Iran tottered, near financial collapse and anarchy as Mossadeq attempted to seize more power. However, urged and financed by the U.S. CIA, forces loyal to the monarchy took to the streets, and the army arrested Mossadeq and restored order. The shah returned, and the United States provided an emergency grant to begin the country's recovery. Large-scale military and technical assistance was promised, and in 1954 a compromise agreement on the oil industry permitted exports to flow and provided fees and royalties. Thus, linked to America, the shah began to dominate the political scene in alliance with the army.

Because he faced continued opposition from such groups as wealthy landholders, extreme religious elements, politically active students and politicians of various ideologies, the shah developed several methods of maintaining his authoritarian rule. The National Security and Intelligence Organization (SAVAK) was created in 1957 to control political activity and the

Iran

press. Through arbitrary arrests and torturing of prisoners, SAVAK came to possess great power, though it made many enemies for the shah's government. While effective for a decade at suppressing Islamic fundamentalists, SAVAK also divided the modernized middle class and left it suspicious of the shah.

To win the support of peasants and moderate reformers, and decrease the appeal of leftist revolutionaries, Shah Muhammed Reza proclaimed a "White Revolution" in 1963. Two aspects of it, land distribution and greater rights for women, aroused the fierce opposition of many Shi'a clergy. They considered that the changes in the role of women threatened family morality, and the distribution of land to the peasants from vast religious foundations endangered the substantial revenues they received as administrators. While a national referendum overwhelmingly approved the reforms, they turned religious leaders such as Grand Ayatollah (Shi'a clergy's highest rank) Ruhollah Khomeini into irreconcilable enemies.

To support his government, the shah rewarded the upper ranks in the civil service and army with good incomes. Thus, he gained support from a small elite, but the almost ubiquitous bribery and other forms of dishonesty among officials contributed to the hostility of others. Increasingly, the shah proposed grand projects, and emphasized his imperial title, notably in 1971 when he spent millions of dollars celebrating the 2,500th anniversary of the founding of the ancient Persian Empire. To prevent opposition in the Majlis and yet maintain a form of representative government, the shah sponsored a royal political party, while other parties were outlawed.

Though failing, perhaps unavoidably, to meet the needs and desires of most citizens, the government attempted to assert Iran's role as a regional power with large and well-equipped military forces. This power influenced neighbors. After decades of tension, in 1975 Iran and Iraq agreed to move their border from the Iranian shore of the Shatt al-Arab to mid-channel. Because the river connects the oil center of Abadan with the Gulf, Iran gained long-sought benefits. In return, Iran halted supplies to Iraq's rebellious Kurds.

Vast increases in oil revenues during the 1970s enabled the government to rush development at home while purchasing the latest U.S. weapons such as the F-15 fighter. The guns-and-butter approach created wealth for many Iranians, but the lower classes gained little prosperity, suffered high inflation, and resented the corruption and westernized lifestyles of the rich. In between, the middle class found few legal political opportunities. With the

parliamentary opposition stifled, illegal left-wing parties and Islamic groups widened the appeal of extremists.

Riots in the religious city of Qom and in Tabriz in early 1978 showed deep popular dissatisfaction. In response, the army fired on the mobs, killing many. These deaths triggered further riots, and despite official bans, demonstrations spread to Tehran and elsewhere. Massacres by loyal troops ended all pretense of popular support for the shah, and the bloodshed united the rival opposition groups in the single goal of ousting the monarch. Despite his age (76) and long years of exile (14), Ayatollah Khomeini assumed leadership of the movement.

After months of strikes and confusion, with oil production and exports halted and the economy in chaos, Shah Muhammad Reza left the country in early 1979. As a concession, he placed the government under a long-time critic. However,

the concessions came too late. Khomeini quickly flew home to a triumphant welcome in Tehran, and appointed Mehdi Bazargan prime minister. Despite the lavish attention the shah had paid it, the army abandoned its struggle against the revolutionaries. Voters overwhelmingly approved the creation of the Islamic Republic of Iran; it became official on April 1, 1980.

The Islamic Republic immediately faced major problems. Restive ethnic minorities, many of them Sunni rather than Shi'a, threatened rebellion. The economy required emergency measures, but was largely ignored. Rival groups and individuals who had united against the monarchy now struggled violently for power. To maintain power, self-appointed "revolutionary courts" began imposing long prison terms or death sentences on former officials, accused wrongdoers or "sinners." By mid-1979 some 200 executions

Ayatollah Ruhollah Khomeini

58

Iran's Imperial Family in exile, Panama (1980).

had been carried out—often within hours of arrest. Opposing groups began political assassinations, and Khomeini had ordered the establishment of a special militia for his *Islamic Revolutionary Council*.

When militants seized the U.S. embassy in Tehran in 1979 and took 63 hostages, they won wide approval in the streets. Many political leaders approved the illegal action, but the Bazargan cabinet resigned almost immediately because it had no effective authority. Khomeini then directed the *Islamic Revolutionary Council* to take control. International pressures on Iran to release the hostages proved useless, and an American attempt to rescue the hostages in 1980 ended unsuccessfully in the Iranian desert. After the deposed Shah died in Egypt, the hostages finally were released in 1981, a gift for Ronald Reagan's inauguration.

Against this chaotic background, a plebiscite overwhelmingly approved a new constitution. Besides the typical democratic institutions of the elected Majlis (parliament) and president, the Islamic Constitution established two novel centers of power. First, the Supreme Leader (or faqih) is the chief theologian, appointed by the 86-member Assembly of Experts. He interprets religious law and acts on behalf of the Hidden Imam who disappeared in 878. The second unique source of authority is the Council of Guardians, an appointed committee of 12

clergymen charged with ensuring that proposed laws conform to Islam. Given these two innovations, supreme authority lies in Islamic law as interpreted by religious scholars, rather than in the nation's (un)sovereign people. For the first decade of revolutionary Iran, Ayatollah Khomeini held the position of Supreme Leader.

The relatively moderate Bani Sadr won the 1980 presidential election, but by 1981, facing impeachment, he fled the country. The clergy's *Islamic Republican Party (IRP)* then completely dominated government, but faced an uprising by the secular and socialist *Mujahedin-e Khalq*. The regime suppressed the uprising with great brutality and torture, executing tens of thousands of alleged *Mujahedin*, who for their part turned to bombings and assassinations, and decimated the *IRP* leadership in a single blast.

The War with Iraq, 1980–1988

Sensing that Iran had weakened from a deteriorating economy, political tensions and international isolation, Iraq launched a full-scale invasion of southwestern Iran in 1980. Capitalizing on the Iranian military's disorganization and shortages of supplies for its U.S.-made weaponry, the Iraqi forces captured border cities and drove miles into Iran. Within months, however, Iranian troops and Revolutionary Guards counterattacked, largely regaining the border by 1982. Expediently,

the government purchased military equipment and supplies from Israel, though publicly condemning it, and sold oil to the "Great Satan," the United States.

In the mid-1980s, major Iranian offensives failed to cross the marshy terrain into Iraq, despite enormous loss of life. To compensate for Iraq's superior weapons, Iran began human wave attacks with poorly-trained teenagers. Nevertheless, Iraqi tanks, aircraft, helicopter gunships and even poison gas effectively stalled the human wave and conventional attacks.

Despite the casualties and growing war-weariness, Khomeini rejected any peace that kept the Iraqi president, Saddam Hussein, in office. Desperate, the government secretly worked to release American hostages seized by pro-Iranian groups in Lebanon in exchange for arms and intelligence. Thus equipped, in 1986 troops and the Revolutionary Guards crossed the Shatt al-Arab waterway below Basra and occupied the Faw peninsula, Iran's most successful offensive during eight years of war.

Although Iraq seemed on the verge of collapse, Iranian dominance rapidly faded. Rivalries between the Revolutionary Guards and the military ended their effective cooperation, and after the Iran-Contra scandal broke, the U.S. halted supplies of anti-tank weapons, spare parts for aircraft, and other vital equipment. Iran never again mounted a successful offensive.

Iraq responded to its loss of Faw by widening the conflict. It bombed oil export centers at Khark Island and tankers hauling Iranian crude oil. When the Iranian forces responded by attacking tankers carrying crude from Iraq's Arab financial backers, the United States and other Western nations became involved and destroyed most of the Iranian navy during the so-called "Tanker War."

In late 1987, defeats followed disasters. Tehran and other major cities came under missile attacks and bombing raids. Iraqi troops quickly recaptured the Faw peninsula and advanced elsewhere. The Iranian *Mujahedin-e Khalq*, aided by Iraqi forces, attempted to "liberate" Iranian territory. Meanwhile, the obvious Iranian role in the hijacking of a Kuwaiti airliner isolated Tehran in world affairs, so that when a U.S. cruiser mistakenly shot down an Iranian airliner, Iran failed to gain a UN condemnation.

At last the leadership in Tehran recognized that continuing the war threatened the Islamic Revolution itself. Iran then quickly accepted a ceasefire (August 1988). However, the ceasefire did not ensure peace. Disputes remained over the Shatt al-Arab, and the repatriation of POWs was soon halted. Some unfortunates lingered in captivity for about 20 years.

Iran

Domestic Issues under Khomeini

The war with Iraq overshadowed almost eight years of the Islamic Revolution's first decade. After the guns fell silent the next year, debates raged within Iran over the future of the Islamic Revolution. In defeat, its leaders lashed out at possible rivals. Thousands of opposition supporters were probably executed, the savage response by a divided government to opposition viewpoints and the *Mujahedin-e Khalq's* invasion. Facing violent insurrection against the Islamic Revolution, the *Islamic Republican Party* had appealed to religion, ruled by repression, and tortured rivals. Because the *IRP* opposed any alternative loyalties, the pro-Moscow *Tudeh Party* joined the *Mujahedin* as victims. Nevertheless, the often-distorted formalities of a democratic system continued.

Single-party elections to the Majlis brought fewer clergy and other significant changes to its membership. However, the very conservative Council of Guardians repeatedly blocked significant changes, deeming them contrary to Islamic principles. The Council of Guardians also gained a major role in elections through its power to disqualify candidates.

Bitter struggles also deepened within the political elite. "Hardliners," those determined to spread the Islamic Revolution, supported the overthrow of unsympathetic Arab regimes. They also waged a vitriolic struggle against Israel and the United States. By contrast, "pragmatists" wished to use worldwide horror at Iraq's use of chemical weapons to gain closer ties with Western Europe and even the United States, and thus hasten reconstruction.

The scope for rebuilding was vast. A quarter million had died, and tens of thousands were maimed for life. Important cities and industries lay devastated, including one of the largest oil refineries in the world. Contemporary estimates placed the probable cost of reconstruction at $200 billion.

The publication abroad of the novel *The Satanic Verses* strengthened the hardliners. For a variety of reasons, all Muslims found the book offensive. Its author, Salman Rushdie, lightheartedly portrayed the Prophet Muhammad's reference to three idol goddesses as the daughters of Allah (see Historical Background) as a deliberate attempt to compromise, not a mistaken vision. In addition, Muhammad appears unable to recognize changes his secretary makes to the wording of the angelic message—but to believing Muslims, the *Qur'an* is the Word of God, dictated word-by-word to Muhammad and memorized by his followers.

When Ayatollah Khomeini sentenced Rushdie to death—a response likely considered appropriate by many religions before the modern era—he strengthened Iran's hardliners at home. However, the death sentence isolated Iran internationally: any Western sympathy with the anguish of devout Muslims rapidly disappeared in the face of death threats against an author.

In 1989, Ayatollah Ruhollah Khomeini died, just weeks after he disowned his heir-apparent. Nevertheless, the succession flowed smoothly. The Assembly of Experts appointed President Ali Khamenei as Supreme Leader. For good measure, given his modest clerical rank, he gained the rank of ayatollah as well. This appointment preserved the unity of mosque and state, at the cost of appointing a low-ranking clergyman who had succeeded in politics to the highest theological position.

Weeks later, with significant rivals blocked from nomination, the speaker of parliament, Ali Akbar Hashemi Rafsanjani, handily won the presidency. The voters also approved constitutional reforms that gave the president control over the cabinet and military.

A shrewd politician, Rafsanjani drew power into his own hands. His priority was reconstruction, and thus an end to Iran's isolation. He negotiated the purchase of Soviet factories and electric generating stations in return for natural gas. He encouraged the release of American hostages in Lebanon, and announced that Iran would not export its revolution. He removed several powerful hardliners from the cabinet. However, the regime balanced friendly gestures towards the United States with fiery denunciations of the "Great Satan," and crackdowns on the opposition.

Despite its dramatic impact on politics and the position of women, during the 1990s the Revolution remained incomplete. There were successes, especially the roads and electricity that reached many more villages, and higher rural standards of living. However, income inequality had widened. The poorest 40% of the population shared only 2.9% of national income, and the top 1% received 22% of it. Socially and politically, the country stagnated. Despite scheduled elections, the regime limited freedom. It punished journalists and artists whose independent views became too strident. For example, Professor Abdol Karim Soroush was forced into exile for suggesting that the clergy's involvement in politics might harm religion.

Soroush was fortunate. Thousands faced charges of drug offences, many trumped-up or resulting from confessions extracted by torture. Executions continued, often secretly, to complicate information-gathering by human rights groups. A Baha'i who converted to Islam but then reverted to his former faith was sentenced to death. Five authors and politicians were murdered in Tehran within a few weeks. "The work of foreign powers," claimed Supreme Leader Ayatollah Khamenei, but the evidence implicated agents from the Intelligence Ministry.

Khatami and the False Dawn of Reform

Against this background, in 1997 Mohammad Khatami, the relatively tolerant Minister of Islamic Guidance in the 1980s, upset the analysts' calculations and challenged the leading conservative for the presidency.

Even outwardly, Khatami symbolized the changes in society, for he wore both fine European-style clothes and the black turban that designates descent from the Prophet Muhammad. No secularist, his book *Fear of the Wave* proclaimed Islam superior to the West. However, from a study of philosophy, Khatami gained an appreciation of the role of freedom, the benefits of justice, and the importance of civic responsibility. Campaigning on these themes, he attracted wide support: the middle classes, the young who resented personal restrictions, women, and advocates of greater economic freedom. Leftists who desired state control over the economy supported him also, mostly to defeat the conservatives.

The election results were astonishing, particularly in the countryside, where some rural clergy had openly forbidden their followers to vote for Khatami. He won there decisively as well.

Though the conservatives lost the presidency by a landslide, they did not fall from power. The Supreme Leader and other conservatives allied with fundamentalists (those who favored Islamic law) to block change. Conservatives vetoed reformist nominees to the Assembly of Experts, and several student demonstrators were sentenced to death, without any evidence of a trial. On the streets, fundamentalist toughs attacked political rallies by moderates.

The most decisive battleground took place in the press. Brash reformist newspapers sprang up and attacked individual officials and narrow-minded policies. For example, *Neshat* questioned the role and authority of the Supreme Leader, Ayatollah Khamenei. Another paper mocked a conservative reappointed to direct the national TV network by publishing a cartoon showing a TV set as a toilet.

The police and conservative judges, beyond President Khatami's control, reacted to the explosion of criticism by arresting editors and closing papers. The leading reformer, Abdollah Nouri, was fined, sentenced to 74 lashes with a braided leather whip, imprisoned for five years, and barred from writing or publishing. Such judgments shocked reformers, but apparently most people cared little.

In 1999, police responded violently to student protests, raiding a dormitory at Tehran University, killing one student and injured many. This provoked student demonstrations in Tehran and Tabriz; when suppressed by police and fundamentalist gangs, the students turned to riots. Though the students had strongly supported Khatami's reform policies, he could not condone violence, and condemned the rioters.

Political activity exploded during the Majlis elections of 2000. For the first time, identifiable political parties appeared, rather than factions of the clergy. The most prominent of the reformist alliance was *Mosharekate* (the *Islamic Iran Participation Front*) headed by Reza Khatami, the president's brother. Election day provided reformers a two-thirds majority in the Majlis.

However, the reformist victory again aroused conservative militiamen, judges, and other government employees outside the president's authority. With the backing of the Supreme Leader, the police closed every reform newspaper and arrested many journalists. The courts convicted reformers of crimes against Islam that the Majlis could not overturn.

Although his reform program had already failed in many areas, in 2001 Muhammad Khatami won re-election, and once again, his victory strengthened the conservatives' determination to enforce strict Islamic rule. Secret trials convicted journalists, old-time nationalists, and even members of parliament for opposing the Islamic Republic. Hardliners attacked peaceful reformist rallies and infiltrated student organizations. Judges sentenced young men to public whippings for drinking alcohol or making social advances at women, heedless of the danger of alienating public opinion.

The reform era effectively ended with the 2004 Majlis elections. The Council of Guardians blocked most reformist candidates, and thus guaranteed conservative victories for nearly half the seats before a single ballot was cast. Along with some other reformist parties, *Mosharekate* chose to boycott the election. The reformers' defeat left President Mohammad Khatami an isolated lame duck.

Ahmadinejad's 2005 Victory

The unexpected victor of the 2005 presidential contest was Tehran's relatively inexperienced mayor, Mahmoud Ahmadinejad, a former member of the Revolutionary Guards. A populist, he won the election by appealing to the poor, the unemployed and others struggling with the weak economy—individuals particularly upset by corruption and possible cuts in subsidies. His other themes, including defiance of Western demands over Iran's nuclear program and opposition to Western culture, also won votes. The appeal of social liberalization proved to be limited to a relatively small, well-off, university-educated class.

In office, Ahmadinejad proved wildly popular with the rural poor, but dangerously incompetent in matters of state. He nominated an oil minister rejected by even the conservative Majlis, twice. He proposed admitting women to soccer games, and earned a decisive rejection from religious conservatives, worried about allowing women to view male legs and hear the spectators' profanities.

On the streets, yet another crackdown on morality (or, rather, women showing hair and ankles) pleased fundamentalists but angered many university students. Given the president's view of reality, he may fear a cultural "soft revolution" that would weaken the purity of the Islamic Republic. This is strengthened by the suspicions about American policy, including the $75 million voted by Congress to strengthen democracy in Iran. Several Iranian-American scholars visiting Iran were arrested, and released only months later. Paranoia became both politics and policy; Baha'is and others were targeted. The case of Roxana Saberi aroused world attention in 2009, most of it unfavorable. In what might have been a warning to the media, the U.S.-born free-lance journalist was tried and convicted of spying, but was released. By contrast, Delara Delabi was hanged despite a stay of execution for a murder committed, possibly by her boyfriend, when she was only 17.

Ahmadinejad's populist economics policies proved particularly bizarre. Though benefiting from high international oil prices—oil revenues reached $50 billion in 2006–07—his administration spent even more lavishly, and paid the bill partly by raiding the Oil Stabilization Fund, set aside by law for years of low prices. In addition, the central bank allowed the money supply to grow at 40% per year, stoking inflation.

Severe consequences appeared: by 2007 housing prices doubled, and there were shortages of some foods, particularly meat. Inflation reportedly climbed to 30%, but government figures showed less. Gasoline rationing was imposed, despite violent protests. During the cold winter of 2008, natural gas and electricity ran short, apparently due in part to unpaid bills for gas imports. The government's responses included contradictory policies like decreeing interest rates below the rate of inflation, and selling shares of government corporations to the poor for a fraction of their value. Politics apparently replaced the laws of economics, at the cost of enormous subsidies.

By 2010, with oil prices at half their 2008 peak, Ahmandinejad struggled with the Majlis to reduce $40 billion of the $100 billion cost of annual energy and food subsidies, with the president arguing, bizarrely, that doing so would cut inflation. Recognizing that such cuts would *raise* inflation and probably ignite social unrest, Parliament hesitated. However, the monthly ration of very cheap gasoline (under US $0.40/gallon) was cut from 20 gallons to 15 per vehicle, saving money on imported gasoline.

Foreign Relations: Risking Peace and Prosperity

In foreign affairs Ahmadinejad's populism proved dangerous, not merely bizarre. Republican Iran had historically opposed the West. It had condemned

Presidents Rafsanjani and Gorbachev in Moscow, June 1989   AP/Wide World Photo

Iran

peace moves between Israel and the Palestinians and sympathized with suicide attacks on Israeli civilians. Iran trained fundamentalists in terrorism, and aided Lebanon's *Hizbullah*. Consequently, Iran has remained isolated.

Ironically, the U.S. and Iran sometimes shared common interests. Both countries faced a common enemy to Iran's east—the Taliban regime in Afghanistan—as well as one to the west, Saddam Hussein's Iraq. Iran openly permitted U.S. relief supplies for Afghan refugees to cross its territory. Secretly, both countries aided the Northern Alliance.

After September 11, 2001, even the hardline Supreme Leader condemned terrorism. The U.S. invasion of Iraq in 2003 benefited Iran so greatly that some analysts suspect that Tehran planted evidence to spur the U.S. actions. The invasion ousted a hated dictator who had attacked Iran, ended the persecution of Iraq's Shi'a, and brought them to power. However, Iranian policymakers felt threatened by the presence of U.S. ground forces to the east and the west and an American fleet concentrated off the coasts. Tehran therefore acted very cautiously, and discouraged Iraqi Shi'a militias from fighting along the border. Surprisingly, relations between the U.S. occupation authorities and Iran proved workable. Many Iranians undertook pilgrimages to shrines in Iraq.

Matters turned far worse with the election of Ahmadinejad. He increased the pressure and the tension, out of conviction as well as to secure popularity among the Iranian masses. He wrote U.S. President Bush a long letter that was dismissed in Washington as nothing new, but made good propaganda on Muslim streets. The Revolutionary Guards and other organizations armed Lebanon's *Hizbullah* with the missiles that it showered on northern Israel during their 2006 war. Although Ahmadinejad was once a teacher, he repeatedly denied that the Holocaust ever took place, thus proving to the world a disregard for reality. He also promised that Israel would soon disappear (though perhaps he meant Israel as a political state rather than the annihilation of its Jewish citizens).

Ambitions for Nuclear Weapons?

Evidence of Iranian duplicity at the nuclear facilities in Arak and Natanz surfaced in 2003, thanks evidence supplied by an Iranian opposition group. The International Atomic Energy Agency (IAEA) then inspected the facilities. It discovered that in the early 1990s, Iran had launched a secret project to enrich uranium, using Pakistani guidance and equipment from North Korea, China, and elsewhere. The project repeatedly passes uranium hexa-

The tomb of Darius I, who reigned 521–486 B.C. The ancient kings of Persia had their tombs carved into cliffs so high that they could only be reached by ropes and, thus, could not be burst into to plunder.

flouride gas through centrifuges to concentrate the radioactive U-238.

The Nuclear Non-Proliferation Treaty permits enrichment for peaceful purposes such as low-enriched nuclear fuel (3.5% enriched) and research purposes (20% enriched) but not high-enriched fuel nuclear weapons (90%). Iranians of all political groups passionately defend their country's right to enrich uranium for fuel. However, nations are obligated to notify the IAEA of enrichment activities, and Iran failed to do this. Moreover, the program hardly seemed peaceful. Its facilities were secret, carefully dispersed, sometimes duplicated, and occasionally built deep underground, obviously to discourage attacks on them. The production of weapons-grade fuel would certainly be-

come a possibility, and Western intelligence analysts speculated that left undisturbed, Iran could soon complete an atomic bomb.

Fearing that enemies might use military force to prevent the development of nuclear weapons (Washington publicly sold Israel bombs designed to destroy hardened underground facilities), before leaving office, President Khatami attempted compromise and diplomacy. Iran agreed to halt enrichment during negotiations with leading European powers, but talks repeatedly floundered.

Soon after taking office in 2005, President Ahmadinejad ordered the resumption of enrichment, claiming that Iran gained nothing from negotiations. After the IAEA reported the violation to the UN, the Security Council demanded that Iran cease enrichment, but soon afterwards Tehran announced that its cascading centrifuges had achieved success. By 2007, the IAEA suspected that Iran would soon operate 3,000 centrifuges simultaneously, and planned for perhaps tens of thousands more. Although a U.S. National Intelligence Estimate concluded in 2003 that Iran had abandoned nuclear weapons production, Israelis, Western governments, and some Arab states continued to distrust Iran's intentions.

Despite the evidence of world-wide concern, Ahmadinejad refused to enter serious negotiations, and the UN Security Council twice imposed sanctions, overcoming Russian and Chinese reluctance. Concerns grew further in late 2009, when reports speculated about advanced work that could permit a warhead small enough to fit inside the existing Sahab-3 missile, and Iran declared—tardily—that it had begun work on an additional enrichment plant at Fordo, near Qom. Nevertheless, the negotiations that followed produced an apparent breakthrough, because Iran would ship most of its stockpile of 3.5% enriched uraniam to Russia and France, where it would be refined into 20% uranium and formed into fuelrods for research and medical purposes.

Within months, Iran publicly rejected the agreement, in part because of intense objections within Iran. Presumably fearing that Ahmadinejad might use the agreement to claim stature as a statesman and peacemaker, his rivals condemned it as trading "Iran's absolute right to enrich" for "Iran's absolute right to ship out uranium." In effect, Iran's domestic politics were too weak to reach an international agreement that would serve its genuine interests.

The absence of a settlement leaves Iran threatened by possible additional UN sanctions, and world powers unlikely to achieve their objectives peacefully. In reality, the U.S. and other powers hold few options. Given China's investments in Iranian oil, it is unlikely to support an embargo on Iranian oil exports and gasoline imports (which thanks to sanctions on refinery equipment provide 30% of consumption). Lesser sanctions, even if targeted at the Revolutionary Guards business interests, will likely prove uncomfortable rather than unbearable in Iran. A military strike could certainly delay a weapon, but not prevent its eventual development. Perhaps this explains the recent disappearance of some Iranian physicists, for example on a pilgrimage to Saudi Arabia.

A Stolen Election in 2009

The 2009 presidential election campaign witnessed novel political practices, including surprising media freedoms and real 1-on-1 TV debates. Mir Hossein Mousavi, an early revolutionary who served as prime minister in the 1980s, emerged as the strongest rival to Ahmadinejad's reelection. Mousavi greatly expanded political discourse. He broke tradition by appearing publicly with his wife, Zahra Rahnavard, an accomplished academic, and even demonstrated affection in public by holding her

Nada Sultan, shot dead while joining protests against the 2009 elections

hand. This appealed to women of all ages, and youth were courted by a combination of Iranian and Islamic themes, including revolutionary-era songs, mixed with Obama-style internet-based campaigning. Mousavi's campaign platform demanded social reform and changes in the economy.

A high turnout election day suggested that Mousavi had either won or forced a run-off. However, despite the complication of hand-counting over 40 million paper ballots, Ahmadinejad was declared the winner even before the polls closed. The true results of the elections will never be known. Given his strength in the countryside and among the poor, Ahmadinejad might have won a fair election. However, the evidence is strong that a group composed of the president's circle, the Revolutionary Guard leadership, and the interior ministry feared a "velvet revolution," one that without violence would reform or even overthrow the Islamic Republic. To defend it, they apparently stuffed the ballot boxes. Clearly, some ballot boxes had more votes than their precincts had registered voters, and Admadinejad's vote totals were statistically improbable in a number of locations.

Claims of fraud brought large demonstrations in the streets, often including women, and using the color green (the Prophet Muhammad's color). In reprisal, the Basij militia attacked dormitories at Tehran University and protestors on the streets, killing Nada Sultan among others. Gradually, after the Supreme Leader declared the results were divinely inspired, the Revolutionary Guards and other right-wing Islamic elements of the government re-asserted control, arresting hundreds or even thousands and blocked texting services to disrupt planned demonstrations. Show trials followed, as did reports of torture, rape, and even the deaths of some prisoners. When later public holidays and the death of Grand Ayatollah Hoseyn Ali Montazeri were marked by new demonstrations, some officials made explicit death threats against Mousavi. His nephew was murdered.

Feeroozah bazaar in downtown Tabriz, especially noted for the sale of handwoven rugs.

Courtesy: Faranak A. Benz

Iran

One aspect of the crisis often overlooked outside Iran is Ahmadinejad's weakness within the political system. While conservatives clearly dominate the Majlis and other parts of the government, many of them disrespect the populist president, and the Supreme Leader may block Ahmadinejad's policies. Thus, Ayatollah Khamenei publicly forced the resignation of the senior vice president. However, by publicly and strongly supporting the legitimacy of the election, Ayatollah Kahmenei himself has also lost legitimacy, by appearing partisan.

The protests were not completely about power: Mousavi's supporters knew the constitutional limitations on Iran's presidency. Rather, the demonstrations and the nightly calls of "Allah Akbar" protested against evident fraud, about disrespect for the individual, about desires for women's equality, and about manipulation flaunted before the nation. Although the government managed to enforce its claims of victory, the cost of the disputed election could be great. The system itself is at stake, discredited by the fraud, and by Khamenei's quick backing for the winner.

Culture: More than half the population lives in the 25 largest cities. An increasing number of urban men work in industry and government, a contrast to the past when most were merchants, craftsmen or casual laborers. Despite the restrictions placed on them, many women also find employment, and there is even a taxi service in Tehran by women for women. Life in the towns and cities is generally crowded, and wages for the less skilled cover little more than life's necessities.

Most of the rural population lives in small communities, whether peasants who farm in the Elburz and Zagros Mountains, or nomads who live in goat-hair tents that are carried from place to place as they wander in search of pasture for their flocks. These people are as hardy as their life is hard, and generally as hospitable as their environment is inhospitable.

Except for the Kurds of the Zagros Mountains, nearly all Iranians follow the *Shi'a* sect of Islam, which Ismail Shah imposed in the 16th century. Historical and theological differences divide *Shi'a* Muslims from the orthodox, or *Sunni*, Muslims who form the great majority in the Islamic world. Relations between Iran and Afghanistan, for instance, are tempered by the fact that most Afghans are *Sunni* Muslims.

Although *Shi'a* Muslims make pilgrimages to Mecca as do other Muslims (see Saudi Arabia: Culture), they also have important shrines in Iran, particularly at Meshed, where their eighth Imam, Ali Reza, was buried. Many also journey to Najaf and Karbala in Iraq, holy cities sa-

cred by virtue of the association with Ali, the first *Shi'a* Imam (and the Sunni's fourth Caliph), and his two sons. The division of Islam between *Shi'a* and *Sunni* goes back to a dispute over whether Ali and his sons, or the Umayyad clan (see Historical Background) were the rightful successors to Muhammad as rulers of the Muslim community.

A religious hierarchy dominates *Shi'a* Islam. Simple teachers and the preachers at Friday prayers in rural villages form the bottom rank. Above them are judges of religious law, then mujtahids who interpret the law, ayatollahs, and grand ayatollahs. At the top, the Shi'a Imam has remained hidden for a thousand years, although Ayatollah Khomeini's followers applied the term to him.

Iran is a country famous for its architectural monuments, some in ruin, like those of the Achaemenid Empire, but some still standing, such as the mosques of Isfahan. Museums have also been established to display the antiquities which represent every period of the country's history.

During the 1970s, the monarchy funded a rapid expansion of colleges and universities. However, the quality of education declined, as new institutions struggled to develop traditions, and students valued degrees for job placement rather than learning. Iranian education also suffered widely from a unique defect. Students who demanded high grades threatened professors by hinting at connections with *SAVAK*, the shah's dreaded secret police.

After Khomeini came to power, although *SAVAK* was demolished, the decline in education gathered speed. The Revolution shut some schools, closed the universities, and banned women from many teaching positions (and from much of public life in general). Few students could study abroad, and the lower curriculum reduced to reading, writing, arithmetic and religion. Many teachers with good training fled the country; some who stayed were executed. In 1982 the medical schools in Tehran and Shiraz were reopened because of practical needs, and the universities followed. The education crisis is now acute, as the large generation born after the revolution seeks university education.

During the Pahlavi era, many middle- and upper-class Iranians adopted external aspects of Western culture, from stylish clothing to skiing, parties and rock music. Religious conservatives and the traditional poor opposed and resented these changes; with the Islamic Revolution, such Western customs ended, at least in public. Most obviously, new laws forced women to wear *hejab* attire, notably the *chador,* or headscarf, but a much larger realm of Western culture was suppressed,

including magazines and music. Khomeini approved instrumental music only just before his death, so symphonic music may now be enjoyed, but many clergy consider rock music or female vocals sinfully enticing. Other regulations prohibit unmarried men and women from walking or dining together in public. While two girls may hitch rides from passing automobiles, unmarried couples ought not ride alone in a car, especially after dark.

Living their entire lives after the revolution, many young people now dislike these strict social controls. Risking heavy penalties if caught by revolutionary committees, some students and other young adults enjoy parties and dancing with members of the opposite sex. Pale lipstick worn by coeds in university classes, colored headscarves, and brightly colored track shoes likewise suggest widening desires for a relaxation of social regulation. There are risks: in one month an estimated 1,000 women were arrested for offenses like failing to cover their ankles or wearing too much makeup.

Advancing technology presents fundamentalists with additional targets. Parliament debated banning video-recorders, until it became obvious that leading politicians and clergy found them useful. When a western company began broadcasting TV programs to Iran by satellite, in 1995 the government banned satellite dishes, thus placing would-be TV addicts at the mercy of inspectors from the local revolutionary committees. In recent years, Iran has tried to jam satellite broadcasts, and under President Ahmadinejad the government cracked down on illegal dishes.

Drug Addiction
Probably the most severe and growing social difficulty is the swelling population of drug addicts. The numbers are frightening, and on a percentage basis place Iran as the highest in the world. Approximately 20% of all adults and teenagers probably use hashish or narcotics in one form or another, more than one million of them using opium and heroin. Given its culture and lengthy borders, Iran had a drug problem before the Revolution. In the 1980s the problems worsened, with heroin largely replacing opium, and the number of addicts growing rapidly.

As addicts lost the label "miserable persons" and became "enemy infiltrators in society," officials predictably blamed the problem on the American Central Intelligence Agency and the Mafia. Possession of more than 30 grams of heroin became a capital offense; hundreds were executed. All addicts were required to register, and many were dispatched to labor camps in distant desert regions to break the habit. Drug-related convictions accounted for

70% of Iranian prisoners. These harsh measures failed, and with an additional 600,000 users each year, *three-fourths of them women*, a variety of social agencies provide counseling, assistance, and methadone.

Such large-scale use of narcotics points to more than cheap supplies from Afghanistan. Like the riots that followed World Cup soccer games, narcotics usage indicates a society whose young are unemployed and bored. Lacking jobs and entertainment, many have lost faith in the future, a truly astounding phenomenon for a religious republic.

Youthful Rebellion & Temporary Marriage

Traditionally, Iranian families arranged marriages for their teenaged daughters and provided a dowry of furniture for the new household. In the 1980s, reflecting revived Islamic cultural values and the regime's desire for more children, the birth rate approached world record levels and population grew at 4% annually. However, planners convinced Ayatollah Khomeini of the enormous economic and social pressures such growth would create. He approved family planning shortly before his death, and in 1989 Ayatollah Khamenei declared that birth control was not against Islam. By the mid-1990s all forms of contraception (but not abortion) were available—and free. Family benefits now end with the third child. As a result, the rate of population growth fell to less than 2%.

Today society faces the challenge of educating, employing, marrying, and otherwise incorporating the children of the 1980s into adult society. Young and restless, these adults tend to present challenges to the hardline populism of President Ahmadinejad. In response, one suggestion is "make love, not dissent," that young Iranians contract temporary marriage, longestablished as a Shi'a practice. However, virginity is prized in brides of permanent marriages, so families will probably oppose a daughter's temporary marriage.

Economy: With a large population and fertile lands, thanks to its abundant and varied mineral deposits Iran possesses great industrial potential. It also benefits from large oil resources, and natural gas deposits so vast they rank second only to Russia's. The earliest crude oil producer in the region, in recent years it ranks as the second largest oil exporter in the Middle East, after Saudi Arabia.

Not surprisingly, economic policy in the country revolves around two issues: first, the policy over petroleum, the greatest producer of foreign exchange, and second, agriculture.

Agriculture always played an impressive role in Iranian history. The farms vary greatly, from the well-watered lands near the Caspian Sea to plots in the mountains and plateau that depend for irrigation on systems of underground channels.

Generally, life for farmers meant working another's land. Until Shah Muhammad Reza's land reform program in 1963, some 10,000 of the country's villages had belonged to landlords each owning five or more villages. Indeed, a few families and religious endowments dominated the lives of farmers across the country. While unsuccessful in satisfying the hopes of the peasants, the shah's land reform broke the power of the large farming families. It improved the supply of credit, seeds and agricultural techniques. Dams permitted the irrigation of additional lands, and new roads reduced transportation costs. These changes encouraged large-scale commercial agriculture, especially near rivers in the west.

All land reform proposals in Iran face a difficult choice, between equality and economic growth. Because only some 10% of Iran can be farmed, redistributing the land to all existing peasants would create miniscule, inefficient farms. But without redistribution, the great differences in wealth cause political stress, and industry and the services are not growing enough to absorb the thousands who leave farms every year.

Although demands for land reform had played a major role in the Islamic Revolution, initial attempts to seize the larger landholdings were blocked by the Council of Guardians, whose conservative clergy believed that the Qur'an upheld private property rights. Only 3% of the nation's farmland was distributed during the republic's first decade. However, feeling threatened by calls to seize their lands, the owners of large farms cautiously stopped investing in irrigation and equipment, or even repairing the vital irrigation channels.

Predictably, farm output fell. At the same time, the population rose by 3%–4% per year, one of the highest rates in the world. Until 1970, Iran had exported surplus food, but during the last years of the war, Iran spent over one-third of its oil earnings to *import* food. Millions of refugees from Afghanistan and Iraq added to the shortages.

Fishing is a substantial industry, especially in the Persian Gulf and Arabian Sea. However, it is sturgeon from the Caspian Sea whose eggs, caviar, carry the epithet "black gold." Unfortunately, pollution in the closed sea, combined with legal and illegal over-fishing, threatens the long-term future of this delicacy. Despite the annual release of over 20 million young fish, Caspian sturgeon may become extinct by about 2020.

The country's non-petroleum mineral resources include lead, chrome and turquoise, which are exported, while coal and iron are mined for domestic use, along with some sulfur and salt.

Although handicrafts are losing importance, Isfahan, Tabriz and other cities remain famous for their metalwork, carpets, ceramics and textiles. The best carpets come from the Safavid period, but those of recent manufacture deserve fame—and after oil are often the most important export.

Under the Shah's rule, Iran followed a policy of rapid economic expansion and industrialization. It exported vast quantities of oil to pay for large development projects as well as consumer goods and sophisticated weapons. Using its oil revenues on a massive scale, Iran contracted with foreign companies to build and operate entire factories. A number of different cars and trucks were assembled in the country, and dozens of other industries were founded. By 1978, the number of industrial employees reached two million. Iran's first modern steel mill was constructed in Isfahan, with technical assistance and a large loan from the Soviet Union. By the mid-1990s the country actually exported significant quantities of iron and steel.

The policy achieved one of the world's highest rates of economic growth, and the middle class prospered. Other results included inflation and resentment by the unskilled urban poor and landless peasants, who migrated to the cities in search of work.

The Economy after 1979

Despite many hopes, the Islamic Revolution provided little economic progress, though it greatly changed business conditions. It quickly nationalized the oil industry completely, thirty years after Mossadeq's failed attempt. It also took over many large manufacturing firms, and the entire banking and insurance industries, partly because many owners had fled.

However, because of their divisions over the role of private property, especially in agriculture, the ruling clergy failed to establish the economic rules of the game. Leftist clergy advocated socialism, and blamed inflation and shortages on hoarding by private businessmen. Conservatives claimed that Islam protected private ownership. The government simply intervened to suit the needs of the moment. Investors, fearing eventual confiscation, avoided long-term projects and favored trade. For those with access to foreign exchange, it became far more profitable to import than to manufacture in Iran. The result was devastating: manufacturing output fell to only 40% of capacity.

Beset by economic crises and wartime shortages, from its early days the regime

Iran

responded with price controls and subsidies. Though perhaps momentarily successful, they illustrated the absence of coherent policy, and moreover, they failed to halt inflation, which ranged from 20%–60% per year. This reduced the real value of government salaries and pensions nearly every year. Even officially, per capita income fell in half during the 1980s.

The controls and subsidies also distorted the economy. The rial became vastly overvalued, exceeding the free market rate by 2,000%. Gasoline eventually sold for the equivalent of *seven U.S. cents per gallon*, too cheap to refine even if the crude oil was free. Price controls and subsidies covered many staple items. Eventually they became unbearable even for an oil exporting nation, but reducing them in

the 1990s ignited higher inflation and aroused social discontent. Black market activities continued to thrive, because supplies of subsidized food and other essentials often ran short.

Oil policy changed significantly in the Islamic Republic. Initially, the revolutionaries favored only small quantities of exports, thinking that imports implied dependence on Western nations and Japan, and encouraged imitation of their lifestyles. Furthermore, the rush to development had created some very rich merchants and industrialists, but left most peasants and unskilled workers in poverty.

One particular difficulty facing the oil industry is U.S. sanctions. Not only do sanctions block foreign subsidiaries of U.S. oil companies from assisting Iran's

industry or providing American technology, they also threaten penalties for any foreign company that spends significant funds to develop Iran's petroleum resources. In step with Iran's nuclear enrichment, the U.S. has increased its sanctions activities, and by 2007 several major projects languished, with foreign companies negotiating for future options but avoiding investments now.

No major foreign investment has taken place since 2002, and the development of liquefied natural gas exports depends entirely on it. Moreover, the present oil production level of 4 million barrels per day will probably soon fall by 40% without further major investments, sanctions are an important issue. One major unknown is the role of China, whose need for im-

Demonstrators of all ages proclaim that victory belonged to Mousavi, Tehran, June 2009

ported oil is growing faster than any other country, and whose government does not seem to base its foreign policy on human rights issues or worry overly-much about nuclear weapons development elsewhere.

After 2003, world oil prices set new records almost annually, and the country's petroleum industry operated at full capacity. The resulting earnings greatly benefited the budget, and the national economy grew at rates of 5% or more annually, twice the rate of population growth and fast enough to begin to provide jobs for the millions of unemployed. Moreover, the Majlis finally enacted economic reforms. It slashed some business taxes and simplified the foreign investment law. Iran also announced a unified foreign exchange rate. As confidence in the economy expanded, wealthy Iranians living overseas invested again in their homeland, even though many fundamental issues remained unsolved. The stock market rose rapidly.

After the election of Mahmoud Ahmadinejad, smart money feared foreign controls or other difficulties ahead and it flowed out of the country. Economic policies took several bizarre turns, including

interest rates below the inflation rate. Prosperity languished, just as populism gave millions of people hope for a better life.

High oil revenues may even change the level of urban air pollution. For decades, the standard Iranian car was the Peykan, a British-engineered, 1950s-era sub-compact that lacked pollution controls. However, its production finally ended in 2005, and that year the country's two major auto firms, Iran Khodro and Saipa, produced nearly one million vehicles between them, of recent French, Japanese, and Korean designs. However, polluting Peykans will remain on the roads for years to come.

The Future: Few Westerners desire another Islamic nuclear power, particularly if Ali Khamenei and Mahmoud Ahmadinejad hold the triggers. President Ahmadinejad, after all, has called for the destruction of the state of Israel. Iran's nuclear adventurism represents a serious threat to world peace, even if it amounts to no more than creating the capacity to produce weapons rather than the weapons themselves.

To date, the crisis is essentially political. Military strikes would only unite Iranians

and without an indefinite occupation merely postpone the date of its nuclear weapons. However, Ahmadinejad trashes most attempts at compromises. European mediation has not succeeded, nor have recommendations of the IAEA. If economic sanctions are not successful, a beleaguered Israeli prime minister may order military strikes.

Domestically, Ahmadinejad faces a nation whose educated classes distrust him personally and (outside some seminaries) deny the legitimacy of his re-election. Structurally, the economy is a terrible mess, with annual per capita subsidies for food and fuel equivalent to three months' wages. Inflation is rising from rapid monetary growth and Ahmadinejad's populist approach—to spend more but fix little—will run short of cash if oil prices stabilize. Many members of the conservative majority in the Majlis (parliament) disrespect the populist president.

Ahmadinejad badly needs a foreign bogyman to blame for the domestic unrest, but President Obama's patient cleverness denied him the obvious target. Look for instability at home that may encourage adventurism abroad.

Scene of central Tabriz, the second largest city in Iran.   Courtesy: Faranak A. Benz

The Republic of Iraq

In April 1995, Iraqis protested the proposed UN Oil for Food Program. The next year, they celebrated it.   AP/Wide World Photo

Area: 169,235 square miles (438,317 sq. km.).

Population: 30.3 million, (UN, 2007; reliable estimates difficult).

Capital City: Baghdad (pop. 5.5 million, est. 2009).

Climate: Extremely hot in summer, moderately cool in winter; rain is limited, falling in winter. The northern mountains are colder, with snow in winter.

Neighboring Countries: Iran (East); Kuwait (Southeast); Saudi Arabia (South); Jordan (West); Syria (Northwest); Turkey (North).

Time Zone: GMT +3.

Official Language: Arabic (and in northern districts, Kurdish).

Other Principal Tongues: Farsi (Persian) and English (as language of education).

Ethnic Background: Mixed; mostly Arab (80%) or Kurdish (nearly 20%), plus some Chaldeans and Persians.

Principal Religions: Shi'a Islam (55–65%), Sunni Islam (30–35%), Christianity (under 3%; mostly Chaldeans and Assyrians), some Yazidis, and a very few Mandeans.

Chief Commercial Products: Petroleum, natural gas, petrochemicals, textiles and cement.

Main Agricultural Produce and Livestock: Wheat, barley, rice, tomatoes, watermelons, grapes, dates, rice, cotton, sheep, goats, cattle and chickens.

Major Trading Partners: (pre-war) Japan, Germany, Italy, Great Britain, France, U.S., Brazil, Turkey and India.

Currency: The New Iraqi Dinar (2004).

Former Colonial Status: British occupation and Mandate (1918–1932)

Independence Date: October 3, 1932; U.S. returned sovereignty, June 28, 2004.

National Day: Republic Day, July 14 will probably remain a holiday.

Chief of State: Jalal Talabani, President (term ending, 2010).

Head of Government: Nouri al-Maliki, Prime Minister (interim, 2010).

National Flag: Three equal horizontal stripes of (top to bottom) red, white and black, with "Allah Akbar" (God is great) on the white stripe in Kufic script. Parliament removed three stars in 2008 as allegedly Ba'thist.

GDP: $86 billion (current prices); $120 billion (PPP, 2007)

GDP per capita: Roughly $2,600–$3,800 (PPP) per year.

Iraq (pronounced *Ee-rock*, not *I rack*) is about two-thirds the size of Texas. Modern Iraq stretches across the birthplace of human civilization. Ancient Mesopotamia, the land "between the rivers," flourished because the Tigris and the Euphrates provided water. Without the rivers, nearly the entire country would be desert. About 18% of the land is under cultivation.

The two rivers flow southeast across an alluvial plain, between the rocky desert of the southwest and the Zagros Mountains along the northern and eastern borders. Except on the slopes of the mountains there is little annual rainfall, ranging from 6 inches in the south to 15 inches in the northern plains. Most of the water in the rivers comes from rain or melting snow in the mountains of northern Iraq and southern Turkey.

The people differ as much as the land. A handful of Arab nomads *(badu)* still roam the deserts. In the southern marshes upstream from Basra a few *Ma'dan* remain. These Arabic-speaking people inhabit reed huts, raise water buffalo and travel by boat. In most of central Iraq farmers live along the rivers, their tributaries and canals, while Kurdish mountain villages dot the heights and valleys in the north.

In recent decades people from all parts of the nation have migrated to Baghdad in search of work in that rapidly expanding city. They represent all the linguistic, religious and social variety of the country. It is this nationwide diversity which makes political agreement so difficult in Iraq.

History: The creation of a single, united government over the region is a modern innovation. In this land of the two rivers, some of the first cities—and city-states—evolved, and writing was first invented. Here the caliphs of Islam heard the *Arabian Nights* (see Historical Background). After serving as the capital of a vast Islamic empire, Iraq suffered invasions, the worst of all by the Mongols. In 1258, they devastated Baghdad, and most of its population was killed or forced into exile. Untended irrigation canals silted up; equally seriously, drainage canals that remove salt deposits from the fields disappeared. Today, over two-thirds of the irrigable land lies idle, sparkling in the sunshine but barren because of the high salt content of the soil.

For four centuries the Ottoman Empire ruled the region (1554–1918), and after decades of intermittent warfare, it established the border with Iran. It administered Iraq as the three provinces of Mosul (or Musil), Baghdad, and Basra. Beyond controlling the main towns, the governors attempted to maintain order among the often unruly and usually autonomous tribes. As European nations seized control of trade in the Indian Ocean and the Far East, commerce through Iraq stagnated, and little development took place. Located on the fringe of the empire, the provinces generally received few improvements. Modern schools, hospitals, and newspapers only began to appear around the turn of the 20th century, and steamboats then began regular service on the Tigris.

When the Ottoman Empire entered World War I as a German ally, British Indian troops landed in Basra and slowly moved inland. They found the population generally unsympathetic or even hostile. Politically conscious Arabs, Kurds, Turkmen and others commonly supported the Ottoman Empire or desired greater autonomy within it. Iraq as a nation—or even as a notion—did not exist. However, a small number of army officers promoted the newly-conceived idea of an

King Faisal I (1885–1933)

independent Arab nation encompassing the Ottoman-ruled areas of Mesopotamia, Syria, and Palestine.

By the end of the war in 1918, British troops occupied most of the country, and

shortly afterwards added the province of Mosul, valuing it and the region around Kirkuk because of their oil deposits. The future was uncertain: in the secret Sykes-Picot Agreement and other negotiations, France had pledged to support British rule over Iraq. However, Britain also had promised to recognize the independence of Arab lands, except the Syrian coast and Basra.

After most inhabitants rapidly recognized that Britain meant to rule the territories under the guise of a mandate from the League of Nations, a nationalist, anti-British uprising spread rapidly. To quell the rebellion, Britain sought a political solution as well as military victory, and it successfully supported Prince (Amir) Faisal, son of Sharif Husayn and commander of the Arab forces who had fought in Syria, to become king.

The new nation adopted the Arabic name for the southern part of the country, al-'Iraq, for the entire nation. The state's inhabitants, however, were not solely Arab. Kurdish tribesmen dominated the northern mountains, where Britain desired influence because of oil deposits.

69

Iraq

As a Hashemite, King Faisal traced his descent from the Prophet Muhammad through Hasan, son of Ali, the fourth Caliph (and first *Shi'a* Imam). He therefore brought a semblance of unity to the Arab population with its *Shi'a* majority but *Sunni* ruling class. Having learned from the loss of his throne in Syria in battle with the French, Faisal worked to gain independence by compromise with Britain. In 1932, Iraq received its formal independence and became a member of the League of Nations.

The Kurdish Problem

Even before it received formal independence, Iraq faced rebellion from the Kurds. Hardy and brave, but isolated from commerce and education, Kurdish tribes for centuries had maintained dialects of their Indo-European language. Lacking sea access or rail transport, and little influenced by democracy and nationalism, Kurds populated the eastern lands of the Ottoman Empire as well as western Iran. The Kurds had the misfortune to inhabit the region where three great civilizations (Arab, Persian, and Turkish) came together. Their own identity and achievements mattered less. Ruled lightly from distant capitals through tribal leaders who often challenged each other, the Kurds received little attention. They were simply Muslim tribesmen in Muslim Empires. After they adopted *Sunni* Islam, their very names often became Islamic or Arab.

Because of Britain's desire to control the oil-possessing regions of Kirkuk and Mosul, after World War I these areas were joined to Iraq despite their Kurdish majority. Although Turkey and Iran each contained more Kurds than did Iraq, its Kurds formed a large and distinct community that dominated the hills and mountains, with the Arabs centered on the plains.

In every country where they formed a significant group, the Kurds revolted, starting with the British in Iraq in 1923. A major Kurdish uprising lasted from 1930 to 1933, coinciding with Iraq's independence. Its leaders were later confined to non-Kurdish parts of the country, or fled to the Soviet Union. During World War II, a second rebellion was briefly successful. After the war, its leader, Mustafa Barzani, continued the struggle for Kurdish independence by creating, with Soviet sympathy, a republic around the city of Mahabad in Iranian Kurdistan. After years of exile in the Soviet Union, Barzani led later revolts against Iraqi regimes and died in exile supported by the U.S.

Foreign governments often sympathized with Iraq's efforts to transform its Kurdish population into orderly civilians. However, granting Kurdish demands would have threatened oil revenues, and growing nationalism blocked any government in Baghdad from ceding its territory. On the other hand, Iraq generally lacked the military force to control a fierce and individualistic people living in rugged mountains with few roads. Periods of calm and order, therefore, proved the exception.

An Independent State

After the formalities of 1932, many Iraqis recognized that they were not really independent. British military bases remained, British and French companies controlled the Iraq Petroleum Company, and British advisors played very influential roles in government. Restrictions on free elections always seemed to favor those Iraqi politicians closely tied to Britain. On the other hand there was the beginning of a modern school system. Iraqis also gained experience in the affairs of state, in politics, administration, and in modern military practices. A modern economy began to develop beside the traditional crafts and agriculture, aided significantly by exports of oil after 1934.

Military coup d'etat followed attempted coup between 1936 and 1941. The final attempt to seize power was led by Rashid Ali Gailani, a bitter opponent of Britain and Nazi sympathizer during World War II. With the help of the Arab Legion from Transjordan, Britain quelled the revolt and reinstated friendly officials. The new government declared war on the Axis in 1943 and thereby became a charter member of the United Nations.

Nationalism developed even more during the post-war years with the spread of education. During the 1940s and 1950s, a veteran Arab nationalist, Nuri Said, generally controlled parliamentary affairs on behalf of the throne—and in the opinion of many Iraqis, on behalf of the British. The rising popularity of Egypt's President Gamal Abdul Nasser and Arab nationalism isolated Nuri, as did the monarchy's policy of investing oil revenues in long-term projects that favored wealthy landowners.

On July 14, 1958, a day regarded by many Iraqis as their real day of independence, a lightning but bloody revolution by Iraqi army units overthrew the cabinet, the monarchy, and foreign influence. King Faisal II and dozens of hated officials, among them Nuri Said, were killed by troops and mobs. The new Republic of Iraq turned sharply neutralist in international affairs and renounced treaties with Britain.

Iraq

**King Faisal II (1935–58)
The six-year-old monarch, 1941**

The leader of the revolt, General Abd al-Karim Qasim, soon emerged as dictator and proclaimed Iraq democratic and united with the Arab world. A political amnesty allowed exiles to return, including the Kurdish leader Mustafa Barzani. Land reform began. However, Qasim soon clashed with his fellow revolutionaries, especially those who desired rapid unity with Syria and Egypt under Gamal Abdul Nasser. Thus, instead of uniting Iraq with other Arab states, the revolution created new rivalries between it and Egypt.

Faced with assassination attempts and an army mutiny, Qasim turned for help to the Soviet Union and the *Communist Party of Iraq.* However, Qasim grew isolated, though remaining popular among some of the poor for his spending on housing. He also decreed the equality of women before the law, thus initiating great improvements in women's status.

In 1963 nationalist military officers seized power. To prove their victory, they executed Qasim and displayed his body on television. Nevertheless, his legacy to republican Iraq remained: military rule, government control of the economy, Kurdish rebellion, and claims to Kuwait.

Iraq under the Ba'th

In 1968, one year following the dramatic Israeli military victory that discredited many Arab armies and governments, a nearly bloodless military coup brought the *Ba'th* (pronounced "Ba-ath") *Party* to power. Its members gained total control over the *Revolutionary Command Council (RCC),* the chief governing institution. Generally composed of officers, the *RCC* included a significant young civilian, Saddam Hussein. A former plotter against Qasim, he directed internal security for the party and now the regime.

Socialist and Arab nationalist rather than communist in its philosophy, the *Ba'thist* government strongly opposed the United States because of its support of Israel. It also regarded pro-American Iran as a prospective enemy, because Iran claimed the eastern half of the Shatt al-Arab waterway near Basra.

The new government dealt harshly with individuals and groups remotely capable of rivaling the regime, often discrediting them as alleged agents of foreign countries. Accusations of espionage flowed freely. Among those executed publicly were Jewish leaders, Islamic fundamentalists and even communists. Fierce disputes between the *Ba'thists* ruling Syria and those in Iraq increased the natural rivalry of the two countries. Nevertheless, in 1973 Iraqi tank units joined Syrian troops fighting Israel on the Golan Heights.

In 1979 Saddam Hussein, for years the real center of power, became simultaneously President, Chairman of the Revolutionary Command Council, and Secretary-General of the *Ba'th Party.* Saddam considered his clan from Tikrit the only trustworthy group. Some clansmen held high office; others played key roles in the country's several secret police and intelligence services. Rivals within the party were purged (and often murdered), while the public suffered kidnappings and assassinations.

Despite the dictatorship, oil revenues meant economic progress. After decades of production-disrupting disputes with foreign oil companies, Iraq gained total control of its oil production in 1973. Later that year, OPEC raised the price of crude oil four-fold (see Black Gold: The Impact of Oil). Petroleum revenues financed both economic prosperity and military equipment. Living standards rose, education expanded, and new industries and housing multiplied. Young Iraqis flocked to cities for jobs in industry and government offices.

In 1975, a compromise with the Shah of Iran moved the southeastern boundary to the center of the Shatt al-Arab, the normal international custom, instead of the traditional eastern shore. In return, Iran ceased supplying the Iraqi Kurds, who once again had risen in revolt under Mustafa Barzani. The rebellion rapidly collapsed amid deportations and executions.

A second difficulty with the mosaic of Iraqi's ethnic groups arose with the *Shi'a* population, concentrated in the south. Though Arab, and in fact the majority population, they identified strongly with many religious values of Iran (see Iran:

The Mustansiriyah University during the socially more liberal 1970s

71

Iraq

Culture). The Iraqi *Shi'a* had never played a political role appropriate to their numbers, even before independence. Thereafter, *Sunni* officers dominated the army, the focus of political power during both monarchy and republic.

Of all the nationalist groups, the secular and strongly pan-Arab *Ba'th Party* evoked particularly little following among the *Shi'a*. *Ba'th* governments, largely military and *Sunni*, traditionally spurned issues cherished by the *Shi'a*, and the absence of democratic government left the largest community in the country marginalized and often repressed.

Rivalry with Iran brought particular tension for the *Shi'a*. To oppose the modernizing Shah, the *Ba'thists* accorded refuge to his dedicated enemy, Ayatollah Khomeini. However, such support was only tactical, as the Iraqi regime allowed less religious influence on politics than did Iran, and dissatisfaction arose among Iraq's *Shi'a* as well as Iran's. In 1977, demonstrations and riots broke out in the holy cities of Najaf and Karbala. When civil disturbances in Iran threatened an Islamic revolution against the shah, Saddam Hussein expelled Ayatollah Khomeini.

After their Islamic Revolution, Iranian religious leaders, now under the charismatic Khomeini, called on the Muslims of Iraq to revolt. Disturbances in Baghdad and elsewhere resulted in stern repression. Ayatollah Muhammad Bakr Sadr, a prominent *Shi'a* leader, was executed in

Baghdad for subversion. Amid such turmoil, controlled elections to the powerless National Assembly meant little.

War with Iran

Angered by Iran's calls for an Islamic revolution, and perhaps anxious to gain territory, Saddam Hussein sensed an opportunity to force concessions from a divided and internationally isolated Iran. He therefore invaded Iran in 1980. Iraqi troops captured Khorramshahr and pushed into oil-rich regions beyond.

Despite early victories, the president miscalculated. By advancing broadly, Iraqi forces failed to deliver a fatal blow. Moreover, the war united Iranians against an ancient and often despised foe. By 1981, Iraq had lost the initiative and faced the onslaught of religiously-inspired and often fanatical Iranians determined to obliterate the *Ba'th* regime in Baghdad. Iranian naval and air attacks destroyed tanker facilities on the Gulf near Faw, and Kurdish groups rebelled in the north, supported by Iran.

To defend the country, almost all able-bodied men were drafted. Aid from other Arab governments sustained Iraq's survival. Jordan, Saudi Arabia, Kuwait and the smaller Arab Gulf states feared that a victorious Iran would export its Islamic Revolution. Consequently, although formally neutral, they favored Baghdad morally and materially. Arab oil states "lent" an estimated $35 billion, and Egypt alone sup-

Saddam Hussein al-Takriti

plied over one million workers, roughly equivalent to 20% of Iraqi manpower. Alone among Arab nations, *Ba'thist* Syria supported Iran. It halted the flow of Iraqi crude oil through Syrian ports, almost completely ending Iraqi exports of crude.

In 1984 and 1985 Iran launched massive attacks against Iraq's second largest city, Basra. Fighting on their own soil, Iraqi soldiers discovered the will to resist, aided by chemical weapons illegal under international law. The destruction of life and property in Basra, a largely *Shi'a* city, signified the failure of the Iranian Revolution to inspire Iraq's *Shi'a*.

Stalemated on the ground, the war took other forms. Iraq bombed Iran's oil export terminals, and a "Tanker War" followed when Iran retaliated against vessels carrying oil from Kuwait and Saudi Arabia. Eventually the U.S. and other nations sent naval units to escort shipping and clear the Gulf of mines. A "War of the Cities" in 1987 involved missile and bomb attacks on Tehran, Baghdad. Although limited, the attacks caused civilian casualties and created fear.

Iraqi forces finally gained the initiative in 1988. They recaptured the Faw Peninsula, damaged Iran's oil export installations, and attacked across the border. Isolated and lacking heavy weapons for defense, Iranian resistance collapsed and Tehran finally sued for peace (see Iran: History).

On the verge of military victory, Iraq engineered a crime against humanity. During the war, some Kurds had allied with Iran and "liberated" Kurdish territory. In response, the Iraqi military brutally evicted thousands of mountain villagers, demolished their homes, and moved those who survived to the hot

City Street in Karbala

Photo by William Parker

deserts. Others were buried alive. In all, perhaps 180,000 died, mostly unnoticed by the world press. However, a poison gas attack on the town of Halabja gained TV coverage of the massacred civilians. More than 50,000 Kurds, mostly women and children, then sought refuge in Turkey.

After the ceasefire, wildly celebrated in Baghdad, President Saddam Hussein promised a free press and multi-party democracy. However, demobilization proceeded very slowly, and military industrialization remained a priority. Popular generals and other officers were arrested or disappeared. Iraq defiantly executed a foreign reporter, and secrecy cloaked normal public information, such as the budget, trade, and social characteristics. Torture extended to executing children, to persuade their parents to confess.

Believing the Ba'thist slogan "One Arab nation with an eternal mission," Saddam Hussein had long seen himself the liberator of Arabs everywhere from their princes, kings and presidents. Hence he had ordered massive programs to develop chemical and biological weapons, and the "supergun," a cannon with a 1,000-mile range. He believed the U.S. was still traumatized by Vietnam and thus unlikely to fight (it continued to sell his government subsidized rice and wheat despite the chemical attack on Halabja). He also recognized that if Arab unity involved conquest, the collapse of the Soviet empire meant it must come quickly. Luckily, the closest target ranked among the richest.

War over Kuwait

In 1990, Iraq provoked a diplomatic crisis with Kuwait. It demanded border concessions near its naval base, billions of dollars to pay for Iraqi oil allegedly pumped by Kuwaiti wells, and billions more to compensate Iraq for low world oil prices resulting from Kuwait's production beyond its quota. Suddenly, Iraq broke off negotiations. Hours later its troops swiftly conquered all Kuwait.

Iraqi rule proved brutal. Officials and troops systematically looted museums, libraries, warehouses, hospitals and offices, to benefit Iraqi hospitals, universities and government offices. The Central Bank yielded foreign exchange and gold worth billions. Soon Baghdad's civilians could purchase, cheaply, consumer goods long denied them. Sharing in the booty made accomplices of thousands of otherwise honorable civilians.

Responding to the unprovoked aggression, the UN Security Council imposed an economic boycott that halted Iraqi and Kuwaiti oil exports and blocked the use of Iraqi bank accounts and financial assets. The Gulf Cooperation Council decided that UN actions were not foreign interven-

One of thousands of leaflets dropped on Iraqi troops during the Kuwait War

Iraq

tion, enabling Saudi Arabia, protector of Islam's greatest Holy Places, to accept U.S. troops for a defensive international force. Egypt and Syria later pledged troops, and smaller Gulf states provided bases and token units. Careful diplomacy by U.S. President George H. W. Bush built international support, and the UN Security Council imposed a withdrawal deadline of January 15, 1991, chosen to facilitate a cool-weather invasion.

With little real understanding about the Western world, Saddam Hussein apparently believed that Muslim protests and American anti-war emotions would deter any sustained U.S. attacks. He therefore refused to back down. One day after the deadline, Coalition aircraft and missiles began massive attacks on military and economic targets. Precision weapons reached their targets with relatively few civilian casualties.

For 38 days and nights the aerial campaign pounded weapons depots, communication links, bridges and highways, water and sewage treatment plants, refineries and factories, and the national electric power grid. Military units, especially the better-equipped Republican Guard divisions, suffered intensive bombing by B-52s. To avoid arousing Muslim and anti-war sentiments, the Coalition kept secret the casualty estimates. The deaths of many civilians in one bomb shelter nearly upset the public relations policy, but Baghdad's appeal for a Holy War failed.

To widen the war into a broad Arab-Israeli dispute and thus split the Coalition, Iraq fired Scud missiles at Tel Aviv and other Israeli targets (see Israel: History). Other Scuds landed in Saudi Arabia and the Gulf. None of the warheads carried chemical warheads, but Iraq stunned the world by pumping crude oil into the Gulf to create one of history's largest oil slicks. It destroyed wildlife and threatened the water desalination plants in Saudi Arabia and Bahrain.

Striking swiftly, Coalition ground forces punctured the dreaded Iraqi defenses with surprisingly few casualties. Tanks and airborne units, mostly American but also British and French, swept around Iraqi defenses from the west, cutting off an Iraqi retreat, while others struck at Republican Guard divisions north of the Iraqi-Kuwait border (see map). Simultaneously, Egyptian, Saudi and other Arab troops joined U.S. Marines to push northwards to Kuwait City.

After four days of fighting, President Bush announced a cease-fire; the ground fighting had lasted just 100 hours. Against some 200 Coalition deaths, Iraq lost an estimated 10,000–30,000 dead, most of its air force, and some 3,700 tanks. The physical destruction cost scores of billions of dollars.

The cease-fire did not bring peace. In Basra and other southern cities, despondent troops and Shi'a militants attempted to seize power from officials and the *Ba'th Party*. The revolt became a bitter civil war in southern Iraq; Kurdish *pesh merga* guerrillas soon revolted in the north. Iraq appeared to be disintegrating along ethnic and religious divisions.

To face the crisis, Saddam Hussein charged Ali Hasan al-Majid, who had earlier "pacified" the Kurds, with restoring control. After the U.S. refused to intervene, Iraqi troops moved methodically from city to city in the South, pounding rebel areas relentlessly. Mosques were not spared, nor the families of those resisting. The rebels lacked an over-all command, and despite fighting desperately, the Islamic revolutionaries lost Basra, the Shi'a holy cities of Najaf and Karbala, and many smaller towns. Perhaps 30,000 died in the fighting. Thousands of others were executed. Refugees flooded into U.S.-occupied territory and Iran.

After subjecting the South, the Iraqi military moved north, and their overwhelming superiority in armor and helicopter

The Highway of Death—The scorched remains of both civilian and military vehicles litter the main highway leading from Kuwait City to Basra and Baghdad. The vehicles were destroyed in allied bombing raids against the retreating Iraqi army.

gunships defeated the Kurdish fighters who had captured Kirkuk. The resulting flood of Kurdish refugees into Turkey presented Coalition leaders with a dilemma. To do nothing would arouse a sense of moral injustice: two million Kurds seemed worth defending as much as 600,000 Kuwaitis. More practically, two million refugees staying indefinitely in remote regions could create political and economic difficulties. However, any military assistance for the Kurds violated Iraqi sovereignty. This was only a technicality, but an independent Kurdish state might destabilize both Turkey and Iran. Consequently, with UN cooperation, Coalition forces forced Iraqi troops to withdraw, and then erected refugee camps inside Iraq. A Kurdish alliance took control of northern Iraq, about 10% of the country.

Post-War Difficulties in Arab Iraq

In central Iraq, Saddam Hussein and the *Ba'th* party retained power, despite military conspiracies and popular dissatisfaction. To ensure the destruction of Saddam's biological, chemical and nuclear weapons program, the UN established economic sanctions. These rapidly took bitter effect. Although they permitted imports of humanitarian goods like food and medicine, they banned the oil exports necessary to pay for them. Moreover, food for civilians was not the government's priority. So effective were the sanctions that the dearth of spare parts and raw materials reduced industrial production to one-tenth of capacity. Dire shortages of insecticides, herbicides and seeds depressed farm output, and prices rose rapidly.

To shift the blame for inflation, the regime arrested dozens of merchants and executed them for profiteering. Public works projects, from palaces to the "Third River" (designed to drain salty run-off and other pollutants), helped lower unemployment, but popular frustrations rose as family savings disappeared and heirlooms were pawned. Monthly salaries that had once provided middle-class living standards fell to $40 in 1991; by 1999 a public school teacher's monthly salary was the equivalent of only $2.

Any open expression of discontent, however, risked severe punishment. Few places on earth exhibited official brutality at the Iraqi level. Penalties initially included amputating the limbs of profiteers or farmers who hoarded their harvest, and removing an ear or tattooing the forehead of military deserters.

Slowly, UN inspectors discovered evidence of a vast prewar operation involving over a dozen factories that might produce, eventually, an atomic bomb. By 1993, Iraqi cooperation replaced confrontation, and the UN established a vast monitoring system involving planes, helicopters, ground inspectors, tagged equipment, sensors and video cameras.

In 1995, biological experts from UNSCOM, the special commission of inspectors, discovered that prewar Iraq had imported vast quantities of growth media for toxic bacteria, far more than necessary to culture and identify hospital germs. Evidence mounted that despite Iraqi denials, a large germ warfare program had existed, aiming to produce anthrax, botulinum toxin and aflatoxin.

Very possibly, the inspectors' discovery of the project caused the man ultimately responsible for it, Saddam Hussein's son-in-law, Hussein Kamal, to flee to Jordan with his wife, children, and documents. Upstaging any evidence he might give, Baghdad released further evidence of the construction of biological missile warheads and spray containers for pilotless aircraft. However, Iraqi officials claimed that these had been destroyed (contrary to agreements) soon after the Gulf War. For his part, Hussein Kamal returned to Baghdad, where he and his young sons were shot days later.

Despite the inspectors' suspicions of hidden weapons, the Iraqi people's desperation won public sympathy in many countries. Rather than lift the sanctions, the UN Security Council approved a strict "Oil for Food" program. It allowed $2 billion (later, $5.2 billion) in oil exports every six months, to pay for food, medicine, and vital equipment, plus contributions for war victims, weapons inspectors and the Kurds.

Oil for Food funds did not eliminate poverty; but they stabilized diet and improved public health. Gradually the death rate of some 6,000 children per month fell. These "silent" deaths, largely unreported by the world's media, occurred largely because of impure water supplies, open sewage, past malnutrition and poorly functioning medical facilities. However, the government manipulated the system, extracting bribes from some, and favoring sympathetic countries and companies.

Amid the popular suffering, the country's fortunate few lived well. A new luxury resort opened at an artificial lake near Baghdad in 1999, with nearly every brick carrying Saddam's initials in the manner of Nebuchadnezzar, the ruler of ancient Babylon. New presidential palaces arose across the country, and statues or portraits of the president littered almost every significant intersection.

Kurdish Autonomy in the North

Protected by a U.S. no-fly zone over Northern Iraq, in 1991 the three million Kurds found themselves free from Iraq—but short of fuel, food and the supplies needed to reconstruct hundreds of entire villages destroyed by the Iraqi army. Kurdish leaders formed their own administration, eventually known as the Kurdistan Regional Government.

Divided by geography, dialect, tribal affiliation, and personal ambitions, the Kurds were divided into two major groups. Masoud Barzani's *Kurdistan Democratic Party (KDP)*, strongest in northern and

School yard in Karbala

Photo by William Parker

Iraq

western Kurdistan, reflected the spirit of his late father, Mustafa, the legendary hero of the independence struggle. The *KDP* cooperated with the Islamic Republic of Iran. Jalal Talabani's *Patriotic Union of Kurdistan (PUK)* drew its strength in southeastern Kurdistan.

Uniting these two parties proved impossible, despite their promises to share public office between themselves. Disputes over taxes, property ownership and other matters set one party against another. In 1994, the *PUK* evicted Barzani's followers from Arbil (Erbil), the Kurdish capital. Strife continued, despite truces, and in 1996 the *KDP* invited Iraqi troops to capture Arbil from the *PUK*, in the process discovering sensitive CIA operations. However, aid from Iran enabled the *PUK* to regain some lost territory, and U.S. and Turkish pressure eventually led to a formal cease-fire. Only the rough rule of Barzani and Talabani limited the zone's descent into anarchy.

Legally part of Iraq, the Kurdish zone traded with the rest of the country and suffered UN sanctions aimed at Saddam's regime. Factories closed for lack of supplies and customers, and trade languished. The major source of taxes and trade was the (sanctions-busting) re-export of Iraqi oil and diesel fuel. Kurdistan also endured sabotage and terrorist attacks by Iraqi agents, and the zone survived largely on sanctions-busting and aid handouts.

The guerrilla war for independence launched by the *Kurdistan Workers Party (PKK)* against Turkey (see History) complicated matters greatly. The *PKK* sought refuge in Iraqi Kurdistan, and gained some freedom of action by threats to attack trade. In return, Ankara launched major invasions that inevitably destroyed homes and villages but rarely destroyed small *PKK* units in mountainous terrain.

In 1998 the two rival parties divided the territory, and formed two administrations. The *KDP* dominated the capital, Arbil, and the vital road between Iraq and Turkey through Dohuk, with its trucks carrying cheap sanctions-busting oil to Turkey. The *PUK* capital was Sulaymaniyah, a large and vibrant city despite its location outside the U.S.-imposed no-fly zone.

Despite a legacy of poverty and anarchy, by 2003 new roads crossed the land, satellite TV broadcasts communicated in local dialects, and apartments housed refugees previously living in tents. New universities were established at Dohuk and Sulaymaniyah in addition to Salahaddin University in Arbil. The UN's Oil for Food program deserved much credit for the stability and progress. It distributed Kurdistan's share of oil revenues, and did so quite effectively.

When the U.S. sought Kurdish assistance against Iraq in 2003, Kurdish leaders feared punishment or genocide if the proposed invasion of Arab Iraq failed. They clearly desired to add the city and oil fields of Kirkuk to the Kurdish zone, but they also recognized that Turkey considered Kurdish control over Kirkuk as a reason to invade. Might they lose autonomy if they were outmaneuvered in the peace settlement?

War over Saddam's Alleged Weapons

For many reasons, it was no surprise that President George W. Bush quickly abandoned the traditional U.S. policy of "containing" Saddam Hussein. The goal became "regime change." Unable to arrange a successful military coup d'etat, or unite Iraqi opposition groups to overthrow Saddam Hussein in a civil war, the U.S. determined to invade Iraq.

Especially after September 11, 2001, the U.S. focused world attention on Iraq's alleged weapons of mass destruction, worrying that these might somehow reach Islamic extremists. At the UN, President Bush claimed that such weapons threatened civilization itself. However, the "evidence" of Iraq's alleged weaponry proved flimsy or false, allegations to win public opinion rather than foundations of a policy. Furthermore, no evidence emerged of an alliance between the Iraqi regime and extremist groups like *al-Qaeda*. Historians are likely to judge the weapons issue as merely a negotiating argument and patri-

otic rallying cry, rather than genuine misjudgment. In any case, the U.S. raised the issue of weapons inspections at the Security Council, which unanimously voted for the inspectors to return to Iraq.

Facing united world opinion, Saddam Hussein yielded. Very quickly the new inspectors confirmed that Iraq was nowhere near producing atomic weapons, but they discovered some minor violations, such as missiles whose range extended a few miles beyond the limits. When no evidence appeared of biological and chemical weapons, the Bush administration strongly criticized the UN.

Diplomatic efforts to destroy Iraq's alleged weaponry ended when the U.S. and Great Britain failed to overcome threats of French and Russian vetoes, or even to gain a "moral majority" for a resolution authorizing war.

Some American "experts" (most of them civilian ideologues) argued that a small invasion force with massive air support would suffice, because Iraqis would dance for joy at their liberation. However, the regional commander, Army General Tommy Franks, desired much larger, more heavily equipped units. Because Jordan, Saudi Arabia, and eventually Turkey refused to allow use of their territories for the invasion, American and British units assembled in Kuwait and invaded from the south. Only U.S. Special Forces and the Kurdish *pesh merga* operated in the north.

The war began in March 2003, air attacks. There was never any doubt that the

The canals of old Basra

76

Masters
goes on today
Tiger eyes third title; protests
planned ▶ Preview, 1, 10-11C
By Timothy A. Clary, Agence France-Presse

USA TODAY

NO. 1 IN THE USA

Thursday, April 10, 2003

Battles still rage in the north
Kurdish fighters, above, join U.S. troops in the field, 5A

Baghdad falls

Why capital fell
so quickly, 2A

Jubilant crowds swarm U.S. troops as 3-week war topples regime; 'Game is over,' Iraqi diplomat says

History in Iraqi capital: A U.S. soldier watches and Iraqis cheer Wednesday as a 20-foot high statue of Iraqi President Saddam Hussein is pulled down in a central Baghdad square. A U.S. armored vehicle pulled it down.

Newsline

■ News ■ Money ■ Sports ■ Life

North Korea terminates non-nuclear treaty ties
Today, North Korea becomes first country to pull out of 33-year-old Nuclear Non-Proliferation Treaty, an ominous move. 10A.

Mystery illness is testing Canada's medical system
Even so, Canada is at forefront of trying to contain deadly SARS as the U.S. Department of Defense leads search for a treatment. 1D.

■ **Money: DirecTV deal**
Pending approval, News Corp. will obtain coveted foothold in USA's satellite TV market. 1, 3B.

■ **Sports: Auto racing extra**
Catching up with Matt Kenseth and NASCAR's other top drivers in full page of racing news. 12C.

■ **Life: Foot help is here**
Get soothing, expert advice today: 1-800-422-8728. 10D.

By John O. Buckley

Crossword 11D	Marketplace 11D
Editorial 14-15A	State-by-state 11A
Lotteries 15C	Stocks 4-5, 8-12B

©COPYRIGHT 2003 USA TODAY,
a division of Gannett Co. Inc.

'There is no government left,' U.S. general says

World marvels at
celebration that
war's architects
had predicted:
Iraqis dancing
in the streets,
embracing allied
soldiers, reveling in
newfound freedom

By Gregg Zoroya and David J. Lynch
USA TODAY

BAGHDAD — Saddam Hussein's government lost control of Iraq's capital Wednesday as U.S. forces extended their reach deep into the city. Jubilant crowds tore down a 20-foot statue of the Iraqi leader and dragged its head through the streets in a scene reminiscent of the fall of the Berlin Wall in 1989.

U.S. officials declined to declare victory and warned that days of fierce fighting may lie ahead. But in three weeks, the war to remove Saddam from power appeared to have reached the "tipping point" that the campaign's architects had hoped for — the moment when the Iraqi people would realize his brutal, 24-year dictatorship had ended.

"We have been in all the government buildings, and there is no government left to speak of," said Maj. Gen. Buford Blount, commander of the Army's 3rd Infantry Division. "I think we have defeated Saddam militarily." In New Orleans, Vice President Cheney said, "We are seeing the collapse of the central regime authority."

Wednesday produced the scenes of joyous Iraqis

Cover story

that Cheney and other Bush administration officials had predicted months ago. Iraqi citizens ransacked and looted government buildings. In a highly symbolic act unthinkable during Saddam's reign, a statue of the Iraqi leader in al-Firdos Square, which is at the center of Baghdad, was toppled with the help of a chain and a U.S. Marine tank recovery vehicle.

As the statue — which had been surrounded by 37 ornate white columns, each bearing Saddam's initials, to mark his 1937 birth date — fell, some Iraqis threw shoes and slippers at it, a terrible insult in the Arab world. "This was the turning point," Marine Lt. Col. David Pere said.

Marines had briefly covered its face with a U.S. flag — then replaced it with the red-black-and-white Iraqi flag — before it was toppled. "We are playing down this whole concept of American flags," Marine Lt. Gen. James Conway said. "I'll allow American flags inside the camps but not on the roads because this isn't about advancing America into the heart of Iraq. This is about liberating the Iraqi people and getting their flag back where it needs to be."

State-run radio continued to broadcast patriotic

Please see COVER STORY next page ▶

What's the status of regime's inner circle
From Saddam and his sons to Tariq Aziz, 4A

By Julian Reed, Reuters

Bush certain to reap benefits of liberation
Victory to strengthen hand in Congress, 5A

In Arab world, relief and disappointment
Cheers for "new era"; shock over speed, 10A

Allies' checklist for victory shows much work remains

Military, political
goals not yet met

By Mark Memmott
and Bill Sternberg
USA TODAY

Even as many Iraqis celebrated Wednesday in Baghdad, tough questions remained unanswered, including a basic one: how to know when the war is over.

Secretary Donald Rumsfeld said.

Last week, White House spokesman Ari Fleischer said, "Victory is when the president announces it." Wednesday, the commander of Marine Corps forces in Iraq said he didn't know whether there would ever be a traditional surrender by the Iraqi government. "I don't think we know who's calling the shots, if anyone is," Lt. Gen. James Conway said.

Even amid talk of victory, many of the coalition's objectives have

been seen since a U.S. bomb attack Monday aimed at a building they were thought to be in, but there was no firm evidence that they were killed or injured. Rumsfeld described Saddam as "not active." It was not clear Wednesday when U.S. forces could safely reach the neighborhood in Baghdad where the bombs hit.

▶ **Securing the north.** Key cities in northern Iraq, including Saddam's ancestral hometown of Tikrit, were not yet under coalition

weapons of mass destruction. The war was premised on disarming Iraq of banned weapons. Several suspicious sites have been investigated, but there was no conclusive proof Wednesday that Iraq possessed chemical, biological or nuclear weapons.

▶ **Restoring law and order and civil authority.** As coalition forces raced to Baghdad, a tide of thievery, violence and recrimination swept in behind them. Now, U.S. and British forces are trying to

fields. Only Saudi Arabia has more known oil reserves than Iraq, and 40% of Iraq's reserves are in the northern half of the country. Many are believed to have been wired for destruction, as was the case with southern fields.

▶ **Locating U.S. prisoners of war.** There are seven American POWs from this war, and 10 other U.S. troops are missing in action. One American pilot from the 1991 Gulf War, Lt. Cmdr. Michael Scott Speicher, is still listed as missing.

Iraq

only superpower could defeat the ill-paid, badly-equipped, and poorly led Iraqi forces. Unlike the 1991 conflict, no sustained bombing preceded the ground invasion, but intense raids destroyed defensive units. While some units stood and fought—often being destroyed by cluster bombs and other hi-tech weapons—many soldiers simply vanished into the population.

Because the U.S. and British planners wished to avoid casualties, the invasion tended to bypass southern cities, which were sometimes defended with determination by militiamen and irregulars. Baghdad, however, fell quickly just three weeks into the campaign, and Tikrit's surrender soon afterwards marked the end of Saddam's rule. In the north, supported by U.S. bombing, Kurdish fighters seized control of Kirkuk, long desired for its historical connections and oil wealth. At the behest of Turkey, the *pesh merga* were soon replaced by American forces, but Kurdish families began to return to homes they had fled a decade earlier, sometimes evicting their Arab residents.

From Liberation to Occupation

There were few scenes of jubilant Iraqis rejoicing at the largely American victory. Iraq's Shi'a apparently remembered the high price they had paid in 1991. The tumbling of one of Saddam's statues in Baghdad reminded foreigners of the fall of the Berlin Wall, but it proved to be a photo op by the U.S. military just outside the media's hotel, before only a few hundred onlookers. The occupation rapidly cost many more American lives from terrorism and guerrilla tactics than had the entire invasion. What went wrong?

First, popular opinion soon linked the U.S. "liberation" with the looting and destruction of stores, homes, hospitals, oil facilities, electrical generating plants, transmission lines, universities, the national museum, the national library, and much else. Priceless objects were stolen, as well as items of practical value. Some hospital equipment was even seized from the patients using it. Things too large to move were smashed or burned.

The looting, often conducted by gangs, usually occurred after U.S. and British forces had seized a locality. Iraqi security forces would have executed such criminals on the spot. As the occupying power, the Coalition forces were responsible for maintaining public order, yet they did so very selectively. American troops garrisoned the petroleum ministry but ignored pleas for protection from staff of the national museum nearby.

The looting and general lawlessness were entirely predictable. Despite the sanctity of property in Islam, Iraqis had looted Kuwait in 1990. They looted again during the Shi'a rebellion of 1991. Their brutal mob violence extends back at least to the 1958 murder of the king. The U.S. command should have instituted a curfew and required all troops and police report to barracks, partly to keep armed young men off the streets. It did not issue such orders partly because of ideology (Iraqi troops and police were often Ba'thist), partly to show the world a peaceful population that delighted at its liberation, and partly because there were too few American troops to maintain a curfew.

Although dismissed in Washington as merely the "untidiness" inevitable at the end of a dictatorship, the looting and lawlessness caused great and serious harm. Professors, hospital workers, private businessmen, and other professionals sympathetic to western-style democracy witnessed the destruction of their lifework, and sometimes their private property as well. Freed from Saddam's thugs and secret police, they now lived in fear of random arson and violence. Afraid of personal attacks, women moved about much less freely, at work or at study.

There were improvements, notably the religious freedom enjoyed by Shi'a believers to perform ceremonies connected with mourning the death of Husayn ibn 'Ali, grandson of Muhammad. Just days after their liberation, hundreds of thousands walked to Najaf in processions long banned by secular-minded Ba'thists, who feared the political potential of such gatherings and regarded the displays of emotion and self-flagellation as backward.

Bloodshed in Occupied Iraq

To the world outside, the chief feature of the occupation era was the violence and callous disregard for human life. The insurgency began with selective murders and attacks on American troops, probably by former intelligence agents and demobilized troops. However, peace did not follow the destruction of many Ba'thist cells, the deaths in battle of Saddam's sons Uday and Qusay, and the capture of Saddam himself. Instead, Islamic extremists and unidentified but sinister groups joined the Ba'thists at arms—the country became a cauldron of anti-American violence that attracted Sunni Islamists, occasionally some Shi'a radicals, and Muslim extremists from other countries.

In 2005, the Iraqi government estimated the number of insurgents at 40,000 hardcore fighters and perhaps 150,000 supporters and part-timers. A Jordanian linked to *al-Qaeda*, Abu-Musaib al-Zarkawi, became the symbol of the Islamic resistance. He and his group were specifically blamed for bombings of Shi'a gatherings and the murder of prisoners through beheading or slitting throats.

Unsuccessful against the superior firepower and tactics of U.S. troops, the rebels turned to terrorism against soft targets. One suicide bombing destroyed the UN mission, costing dozens of lives; another, the Red Cross offices. Many Western civilians left the country, or retreated to the fortified "Green Zone," Saddam's former palace area turned into the U.S. headquarters. Iraqis employed by the occupation were less fortunate: thousands died, many of them policemen and soldiers. Even in the relatively safe Kurdish zone, the major political parties suffered direct attacks.

Anti-American attitudes and attacks were, until 2007, fiercest in the "Sunni triangle," the region north and west of Baghdad. The resistance there reflected its Ba'thist past, and the privileges the region had enjoyed under its native son, Saddam Hussein. The cities of Falluja and Ramadi particularly became centers of the insurgency and illustrate the great suffering of the region. Early in the occupation of Falluja, as on occasion elsewhere, U.S. troops mistook (allegedly innocent) rifle fire in celebration of a wedding as an attack. The return fire killed civilians; demonstrations later followed. Gunmen hidden among the protesters fired at troops, who in turn shot several demonstrators.

Following the murder and dismemberment of four U.S. civilian security guards, U.S. Marines besieged the city and attempted to subdue it. After significant casualties on both sides, and widely televised pictures of civilian suffering, a political solution was found: the creation of a "Falluja Protection Force," headed by a former Republican Guard general. The novel arrangement brought temporary peace, but Falluja fell under the control of militant clerics and became a center of the resistance. The Marines renewed the invasion in 2004. Working with mainly-Shi'a units of the new National Guard, they then conquered the city, but hundreds died and nearly every building was damaged.

Large-scale Shi'a resistance came in 2004 from the *Mahdi Army* of Muqtada al-Sadr. The charismatic son of an ayatollah murdered by Saddam's regime, Muqtada appealed to the poorest sectors of society, and his fiery populism combined anti-American nationalism with Islam and socialism. After he was charged with the murder of a Shi'a cleric and his newspaper was shut for vitriolic denunciations of the occupation, the *Mahdi Army* seized parts of Baghdad and the shrine cities of southern Iraq. However, Muqtada's followers wore out their welcome. Pressured by the Shi'a leadership, especially Grand Ayatollah Ali Sistani, Muqtada accepted a political solution and his fighters were replaced by police.

Photographs of tortured and disgraced prisoners held by American troops for interrogation at Baghdad's infamous Abu Ghuraib prison deeply offended Iraqi sensibilities. Such non-lethal but nonetheless degrading and inhuman torture—or worse—was common in Abu Ghuraib during Saddam's era. But the U.S. had justified the war partly to bring human rights. To many an Arab mind, any moral superiority vanished.

Greater Roles for Iraqis

Clearly acting with insufficient forethought, the U.S. Defense Department established the Coalition Provisional Authority (CPA) to govern for several years while creating democracy and a new constitution. The CPA laid ambitious plans for reconstruction, and planned a rigidly free-market economy with some of the world's lowest taxes. It quickly spent billions of U.S. tax dollars and Iraqi oil revenues on contracts to well-connected U.S. companies, some without bids. As anti-American violence grew, the CPA administrators and military leaders concentrated in the tightly guarded "Green Zone" of western Baghdad.

The CPA reacted slowly to shortages of public services, particularly water, sewage, electricity, and fuel. Power plants, water treatment facilities and similar installations had not been targets of U.S. bombing, but looting harmed a fragile infrastructure that had suffered 13 years of sanctions. Pumping water and sewers required electricity; this in turn required generating plants that used fuel oil or natural gas. By the summer of 2004, electrical blackouts halted air conditioning and widely depressed morale. Individual acts of good will and reconstruction by U.S. troops and civilians often seemed to matter little.

Nevertheless, the CPA improved life in significant ways. It cut import tariffs from 400% to essentially nothing, thus enabling merchants to fill the markets, stores, and auto dealerships with new merchandise. It granted press freedoms, and hundreds of new papers appeared, advocated conflicting viewpoints. It repaired and reopened schools, and revised school textbooks. It paid veterans, and continued Saddam's massive food distribution policies that meant survival for over half the population. It issued a new currency, and raised wages.

Nevertheless, it was not Iraqi. Within months, American influence began to diminish. Popular demands for greater Iraqi decision-making were not satisfied by the appointment of exiles to administrative positions.

After violence rose sharply, the U.S. proposed an interim government, a new

Iraqi army was created and the police force expanded, both with American advisors. In Saddam's former Green Zone palace, the largest American embassy anywhere replaced the CPA. It supervised—and subsidized—the country. On June 28, 2004, sovereignty was publicly transferred to the interim government.

The new Governing Council selected Iyad Allawi, a Shi'a neurologist and businessman, as Prime Minister. While the new leaders thanked the U.S. for liberating Iraq, they also demanded genuine sovereignty, including the right to demand the withdrawal of occupation forces.

Constitution and Government (2005–06)

Yielding to Shi'a demands for elections, the CPA's transitional laws stipulated elections for a National Assembly that would select a government, draft a new constitution, and hold further national elections, all within a year. Besides this challenging schedule, the CPA prescribed one of the purest forms of democracy: national proportional representation, combined with the requirement that a 2/3 "supermajority" approve the cabinet, thus precluding a Shi'a-only regime.

This ideologically pure democracy encouraged politics to focus on religious or ethnic groups. The national electoral district—26 million inhabitants (more than Texas)—prohibited local notables from running independently, and reduced discussion of local issues. Political parties recognized the importance of a national presence, and as a result, they merged into "lists." In the Shi'a community, with Sistani's approval, the larger religious-based parties, *al-Da'wa* and the *Supreme Council of the Islamic Revolution in Iraq (SCIRI)* formed the *United Iraqi Alliance (UIA)* with several smaller groups. Its rival for Shi'a support was the secular *Iraqi List* of Iyad Allawi, the interim prime minister. The major Kurdish parties, the *KDP* and *PUK*, set aside their own rivalries to establish the *Kurdistan Alliance*. However, the largely Sunni insurgency denounced elections, and few Sunni politicians dared to run.

As expected, Iraqis voted their religious and ethnic identities. The *United Iraqi Alliance* won 140 of the 275 seats. To gain the required "supermajority" it formed a coalition with the 77 deputies of the *Kurdistan Alliance*. By contrast, voters decisively rejected Allawi, who gained only 14% of the vote.

However, a system cleverly designed to reward communities that voted backfired in the Sunni provinces. Only small minorities of those eligible cast their ballots, and Sunni Arab candidates, representing a quarter of the population, won only 6% of the seats. Thus the National Assembly

clearly failed to include reasonable representation of all Iraqis, a particular challenge when framing the constitution.

Immediately after the elections, the level of violence fell. The voters—58% of those registered—had spoken, and they directly rejected the insurgency. However, the coalition of just two parties took two months to select Jalal Talabani of the *PUK* as president, and three months to form a cabinet under Ibrahim al-Jaafari of *al-Da'wa (UIA)*. Much of that time was consumed by negotiations over the Sunni representatives. Meanwhile, violence returned to higher levels.

Ironically, the U.S. had sponsored the Iraq's most freely contested election in decades—to the benefit of Iranian influence. President Talabani's *PUK* had often sought military supplies from Iran, and used them to recover lost territory from the *KDP* in the 1990s. Prime Minister al-Jaafari had sought exile in Iran and Britain. His party, *al-Da'wa*, had long contacts with Iran. The deputy Prime Minister, Ahmed Chalabi, had been identified as an Iranian spy just a year earlier. Behind the scenes, other Iranian links included Grand Ayatollah Ali Sistani, who was born in Iran, speaks Arabic with an accent, and heads charitable foundations across the border.

The Jaafari cabinet ruled ineffectively during perilous times. It confronted the insurrection by incorporating Shi'a fighters from the *Badr* and *Mahdi* militias into the police. While willing to fight, these militiamen in police uniform reportedly abducted, tortured, and massacred Sunnis. Al-Jaafari's cabinet also earned a reputation for corruption, oil exports fell, and reconstruction stagnated.

Nevertheless, the cabinet succeeded in two important tasks. It drafted a constitution, and held parliamentary elections that were truly national, for they included wide Sunni participation.

The constitutional debate focused on three issues: the role of Islam, the degree of regional autonomy, and control of oil revenues. Article 2 of the draft constitution recognized Islam as the religion of the state, and "a fundamental source of legislation." It also prohibited any law that contradicted Islam's "undisputed" decisions.

Given the devout population, a formal Islamic role was inevitable, as was a retreat from gender equality imposed by secular Ba'thists. However, some clauses of the constitution left wide room for later disputes. For example, Article 2 prohibited laws contrary to democracy or human rights, and Article 14 granted all Iraqis equality. Elsewhere, women were guaranteed 25% of the parliamentary seats.

Demands for regional autonomy proved an even more vexing issue. Sunnis desired

Iraq

a unitary state, ruled from Baghdad, but Kurds insisted on their self-government in Iraq—or independence. Some Shi'a leaders also desired autonomous Shi'a regions in the south. Unable to compromise, the National Assembly approved a federal system, but left some details for later decisions.

For good measure, at least to the Kurdish interpretation, the constitution allocated oil revenues from existing fields to the central government, but those from new fields to the regions. Since the major oil deposits lie in Kurdish and Shi'a areas, Sunnis naturally opposed a clause that suggested their future impoverishment.

After a bitter six-week campaign, Iraq's voters ratified the constitution with 78% approval. However, two Sunni provinces (Anbar and Salahuddin) overwhelmingly opposed it. Voters in Nineveh also rejected it, but by only a 55% majority.

Over two hundred parties contested the 2005 elections for a permanent parliament, the Majlis. Sunni groups joined the contest, implicitly recognizing that the opportunity to participate in government outweighed the risk of insurgent opposition. This time, the Shi'a *United Iraqi Alliance* included Muqtada's *Sadr Organization,* but it lacked Ayatollah Sistani's open support.

Once again, the elections proved that voters cherished ethnic and sectarian identity above ideology and political platforms. As expected, the *UIA* (128 seats) fell short of a simple majority, and with the *Kurdistan Alliance* still lacked the 2/3 supermajority required to approve a cabinet. Sunni groups gained significant representation, with the *Iraqi Accord Front* receiving 44 seats. The major losers were secular Shi'a groups. Chalabi's alliance even failed to enter parliament.

It took five months of bargaining, rising violence, and American pressure before a "supermajority" emerged, due mostly to rivalries within the *UIA.* Eventually, the *UIA* proposed Nouri al-Maliki, deputy leader of *al-Da'wa,* as prime minister. Al-Maliki gained both Kurdish and Sunni approval and formed his cabinet in April 2006.

From any perspective, Prime Minister al-Maliki faced immense challenges. The explosions that destroyed the golden dome of the Askari shrine in Samarra had unleashed a savage reprisal by Shi'a militiamen, with hundreds of dead in Baghdad alone. Though not formally at civil war, the country suffered deadly sectarian cleansing. Thanks partly to the rapid hiring of Shi'a militiamen as government employees, some soldiers, police, and guards engaged in organized kidnapping, torture, and murder—even in Basra, where few insurgent attacks had occurred.

The UN estimated that 34,000 civilians were killed in 2006, and the International Red Cross learned that mothers deeply hoped for someone to collect the bodies from the streets before their children went to school. *Nearly 20% of the population became refugees.* Two million wealthy enough to do so moved abroad, and as many more fled to safer neighborhoods. Their homes were usually looted and then occupied by families from the locally dominant sectarian group. As the professional and business classes began to disappear, hospitals and clinics lost staff. Only the bravest university professors continued to teach; over 200 were assassinated. The Western nations most responsible for the conflict—the U.S. and Britain—accepted only a few Iraqi refugees, while Syria and Jordan hosted roughly one million each.

Non-Muslim minorities continued to face particular violence. Christian leaders were assassinated, and the laity threatened with death if they did not flee the country. Yazidis (inaccurately) face charges of worshipping Satan. The Mandaeans, followers of one of the oldest religious groups in the world, fear extinction, because Islamic extremists in Iraq are trying to wipe them out through forced conversions, rape and murder.

In 2006, Saddam Hussein was convicted by an Iraqi court for the killing of 148 Shi'a from the town of Dujail following an assassination attempt. A trial over the Kurdish massacres was also sought, but he and a few aides were rushed to execution.

Despite other successes, such as the death of Abu Musaib al-Zarqawi, who had led of one of the most fanatical insurgent groups, *al-Qaeda in Iraq,* violence against civilians increased in 2006–07. Suicide bombings, sectarian reprisal killings, improvised chlorine gas bombs and ambushes of police units proved deadly. Attacks on U.S. troops featured increasingly

Pre-war Baghdad: A high-fashion model shows off a gown

sophisticated weapons, particularly roadside bombings by "explosively formed projectiles" (EFPs), complex devices that even pierce armored vehicles.

The "Surge" Succeeds

After the Iraq Study Group warned of a slide toward chaos and government collapse, President Bush rejected calls for an American withdrawal. Instead, he ordered an increase in the U.S. military forces in Iraq to provide more troops in zones of conflict. This "surge" was expected to reduce the violence while politicians in Baghdad reached the compromises necessary to attract Sunnis and radical Shi'a groups.

The surge gradually reached in its military goals. Initially, with more American troops on patrol, their casualties climbed to some of the highest levels of the war. Some of those casualties, inflicted by EFPs supplied by Iranian groups, came from Shi'a militiamen unwilling to accept the limitations of law and order on their ethnic attacks on Sunnis. Nevertheless, violence declined in Baghdad, temporarily increased in Diyala and other provinces as insurgents found easier targets, then declined there as well. In Anbar province and elsewhere, tribal leaders who had tired of the harsh fanaticism of many insurgents formed tactical alliances with the U.S. military in return for arms and money. Mosul became the last insurgent stronghold.

With the decline in violence, many refugees began to return to Baghdad and elsewhere, in some cases only to find their homes occupied by others. Many returnees were women; like those who had remained, they found conditions worsening for women and girls. Their discouragement over the availability of jobs or fear of violence was expected. However, over three-quarters of those surveyed reported that their daughters were not allowed to attend school, a shocking outlook for the future.

Slow political progress accompanied the security surge. Parliament only tardily addressed legislation crucial to attracting Sunni support, such as reversing aspects of de-Ba'thification, the distribution of oil revenues among the regions, and possible regional units of a federal nation. Muqtada al-Sadr withdrew his party first from the cabinet, then from the *United Iraqi Alliance.* However, he proclaimed a ceasefire by his militia, the *Jaish al-Mahdi,* and asserted control over at least some of its rogue elements.

In 2008, Prime Minister al-Maliki suddenly ordered the army and police to crack down on militia activity in Basra some months after the British withdrawal. In practical terms, this meant assaulting the armed supporters of his Shi'a rival, al-Sadr, just months before provincial elections, and the *Jaish al-Mahdi* successfully fought back. Hundreds of troops and police deserted; even air support proved insufficient for a clear military victory. The fighting spread to Baghdad, but thanks in part to Iranian advice, al-Sadr agreed to a cease-fire. Thereafter, police and military patrols and roadblocks gradually asserted law and order. Al-Sadr's followers were not defeated, but stood down.

By 2009, both Basra and Baghdad had become much calmer, with some barriers down and social life resuming, and on June 30, U.S. troops formally withdrew from Iraqi cities. Hailed by the Iraqi government as a huge victory and celebrated as "National Sovereignty Day," the withdrawal was possible only because of the increased professionalism of Iraqi forces and the war-weariness of the nation. While suicide bombers later managed to devastate government ministries in Baghdad and kill scores elsewhere, the trend of violence was clearly downward, and the attacks did not ignite sectarian reprisals.

The politicians of democratic Iraq move slowly. Negotiations over the legal changes for the 2010 parliamentary elections involved repeated delays, and the elections themselves were postponed for two months without a solution to a major contentious issue, the status of Kirkuk.

The election confirmed political fractures within sectarian groups as well as between them. The Shi'a religious parties that had united in 2005 as the *Iraqi National Alliance* fractured when Prime Minister Maliki formed the *State of Law* coalition, clearly hoping to benefit from the improved security. Despite being officially secular, it appealed mostly to Shi'a groups traditionally loyal to the *Da'wa Party*. The other significant Shi'a parties, including the *Iraqi Islamic*

Supreme Council and the *Sadrists*, formed the *National Iraqi Alliance*, and split the votes of conservative, religiously-oriented Shi'a. By contrast, former interim Prime Minister Iyad Allawi's *Al-Iraqiyya (Iraqi National Movement)* appealed to Sunnis as well as some Shi'a.

To some surprise, *Al-Iraqiyya* carried every Sunni Arab province and won 91 seats in the 325-member assembly, two more than Maliki's *State of Law* alliance. Despite Maliki's charges of voting irregularities and an appeal for a recount in Baghdad, the two-member plurality held. Months after the election, at press time, it appeared possible that Iyad Allawi might form the next cabinet, Maliki's attempts to attract the *Iraqi National Alliance* (70 seats) into a coalition having met resistance from the *Sadrists*.

Former Interim Prime Minister Iyad Allawi

Culture: As Muslim Arabs, Iraqis share major cultural features with other peoples of the Middle East, ranging from the father's authority to food and religious holidays. The family remains the basic social unit, with parents, children, and grandchildren often forming a single household. Though their education may postpone it, girls usually marry young, by arrangement between her family and the groom's, and soon bear the first of many children. Large families have been encouraged by both traditional values and government policies. Consequently, the population has grown rapidly, and about half the population is less than 15 years of age.

Before the 1958 Revolution, most Iraqis lived in rural areas, typically in small, mud-brick houses except in the north, where the climate required stone. Agriculture occupied perhaps three-quarters of the population. Their living conditions were simple or even harsh, with diets restricted to bread, rice, lentils, beans,

onions, occasional mutton and dates. As oil revenues provided prosperity in the cities, they attracted a great migration, until by 1990 some two-thirds of the nation lived in urban areas, usually in neighborhoods of people from the same rural district. Agriculture, often neglected though still important, proved unable to feed the nation during the UN embargo.

After two decades of war, sanctions, and occupation, these are not ordinary times. Poverty and inadequate food rations discouraged parents from having many children. Though the family remains the basic social unit, marriage has become far more difficult, and reportedly there are now at least one million single women aged over thirty-five. Few men can afford the traditional dowry or furnish a home, while many educated women seeking a successful career preferred to remain single, at least during the last years of Saddam's rule.

Sixty years ago, large Bedouin tribes like the Shammar roamed the deserts. However, the number of nomads has dwindled to insignificance due to motor transport, resettlement programs, education, and easier sedentary life.

Modernization most visibly affected the large cities of Iraq, as the government constructed roads, shopping centers, and large buildings. The modern homes and apartment houses in the better suburbs contrast with the narrow streets of older sections. Poor migrants, on the other hand, find temporary shelter on the outskirts, often of reed matting and mud.

Formal culture in Iraq, like most other Arab countries, stresses achievements in poetry and learning, while sculpture, painting, music and drama received less interest. The great recent exception proved the rule, as the population defaced or destroyed the many statues and pictures of Saddam Hussein.

Prime Minister Nouri al-Maliki and President Bush

Courtesy of the White House

Iraq

Few of the older generation of Iraqis formally entered school, but in recent decades the government vastly extended the educational system. Primary education is compulsory, and schools now dot villages and cities alike; their renovations are one achievement of the U.S.-led occupation. A modern curriculum with post-war textbooks replaces the Quranic emphasis of the kuttabs, or mosque schools.

Beyond secondary education, universities in the major cities offer instruction in most disciplines. Although the role of women remains less public, until 2003 all schools and universities were coeducational, though this may change in the democratic post-Saddam era. Another threat to higher education comes from the killing of nearly 200 professors and other academics during the first three years of the occupation.

During the *Ba'thist* era, readership of the press remained low, a function of its predictable propaganda. However, one positive result of the U.S. occupation is a vibrant press. Over 100 papers have appeared, with titles like *New Era, Dawn of Baghdad,* and *The New Iraq,* reflecting popular desires for a better future. Daily concerns like insufficient clean water and electricity receive extensive coverage. Some private TV and radio stations compete with the government's broadcasting services and those of the two Kurdish parties.

By the 1980s, many urban men and some women selected Western styles of clothing, though the traditional gowns for men and the voluminous black *abayas* for women remained widely used, and dominated rural areas. Rural Kurds wore distinctive clothing, the men in baggy pants and women in long gowns over pants.

After 2003, Arab women generally returned to traditional dress and head-scarves, to avoid harassment, certainly, but also for their own safety after at least three students in Basra were killed for their failure to do so. During the height of the insurgency, men also faced strict demands for modesty: in 2006, the coach of the national tennis team and two players were taken from their car and shot—apparently for wearing shorts.

The Marsh Arabs

For centuries, the Marsh Arabs, known also as the Ma'dan, formed a sharp contrast to the traditional image of Arabs as herders of sheep and goats in a desert landscape. Inaccessible except by canoe, the Marsh Arabs inhabited a world of water, surrounded by vegetation and living in reed houses with high, arched ceilings. Some homes were even built on artificial islands constructed of reeds. All this was made possible by the flat terrain between the lower Tigris and Euphrates rivers, where the annual flow and flooding of the rivers created an area of permanent and seasonal marshes, lakes, and waterways that stretched across 10,000 square miles. Invaluable for fish and migrating birds, the marshes also provided an environment for rare species of otter, lizards, wild boar and other animals.

Shi'a by religion, the Marsh Arabs' lived by fishing, herding water buffalo, and weaving reed mats. They preserved several unique customs and except for limited trade, they mixed little with outsiders, rarely marrying them. During the war with Iran and later over Kuwait, military deserters sought sanctuary amidst the isolation of the marshes.

In response, the Iraqi government determined to control the region. Because irrigation and dams upstream diminished the flow of the rivers and ended the seasonal floods, some areas became accessible by roads. Later, the "Third River" drainage project diverted water to regions below the marshes. By the mid-1990s, the marshes effectively ceased to exist, and most of the Marsh Arab population had fled to refugee camps in Iran. After the fall of Saddam, efforts are being made, with international support, to restore this unique environment. However, regional drought and dams upstream in Iran, Turkey, and Syria as well as Iraq divert too much water to maintain the full scale of the marshes.

Economy: Agriculture and livestock-raising dominated the economy before the construction of a modern oil industry in the 1930s. Iraq once grew 70% of the world's dates, mostly along the rivers and marshes of the south, and wool was a significant export. Today, wheat and barley are the main winter crops of the rain-fed north, while rice and cotton grow in irrigated areas in the south. Sheep, goats, cattle and water buffalo are raised for meat, milk and hides.

Agriculture improved markedly between 1958 and the 1980s as a result of irrigation schemes and the introduction of scientific methods. After 1990, failing irrigation pumps and sanctions on pesticides, equipment, and fertilizers combined to reduce output by at least 30%. Because pesticides could not be imported, the date groves became infested with insects, and harvests fell to a small fraction of the 1980s.

The English adjective "muslin" reflects the traditional textiles of Mosul. Present industrial production includes cement, leather, shoes, cotton textiles, beer, and household articles such as matches. Small shop or home manufacturing is still important, especially for homespun woolens, rugs and reed mats.

Economic sanctions imposed after Iraq invaded Kuwait distorted Iraq's development in almost every regard. UN sanctions after 1991 essentially halted all business investment, but the era of American rule through the CPA witnessed a remarkable reduction in personal and corporate taxes. It also abolished all tariffs and permitted 100% foreign ownership of firms (aside from oil production). Iraqi-owned companies felt unprotected, but this offered foreigners a "capitalist's dream" of purchasing Iraqi land and firms exceptionally cheaply. Should these free-enterprise policies remain when peace and order eventually return, Iraq's business climate will contrast sharply with the rest of the entire region.

Insurgency, crime and corruption greatly slowed recovery from the economic collapse of 2003. Unemployment neared 50% at mid-decade, and the country desperately needs economic growth. Unemployed men become available for desperate actions, including terrorism.

Petroleum: Since the 1930s, oil exports have provided the major source of government revenue and as much as 95% of foreign exchange earnings. Iraq's proven reserves are vast; over 100 billion barrels, second-largest in the world and about 10% of the global total. Nevertheless, petroleum output has rarely reached a level appropriate to the deposits. Besides wars, friction between the Iraq Petroleum Company and the government often limited exploration and production. Geography was also a major impediment.

Reaching overseas markets from an almost land-locked country proved difficult from the start. The initial oil deposits in the northeast lay almost as far from Iraq's few miles of southern shoreline as from the Mediterranean. Therefore, a pipeline was constructed to Palestine before World War II, but it proved useless when Israel won independence in 1948. Another line to ports in Syria and Lebanon depended on their goodwill and security, and Syria interrupted exports for decades. After the discovery of oil in the south, newer technology permitted offshore loading terminals for the export of southern crude. However, that route depended on freedom to navigate the Gulf and the Strait of Hormuz, and the facilities also lay uncomfortably close to Iran and Kuwait.

Seeking other export routes, in 1977 a new pipeline was completed to the Turkish port of Ceyhan, a new direct access to the Mediterranean that did not cross Syria. Iraq also arranged construction of a pipeline across Saudi Arabia to the Red Sea, capable of raising the export capacity above the country's OPEC quota. However, both the Turkish and Saudi lines were closed after the invasion of Kuwait, and sanctions greatly hampered investment in the industry for over a decade.

While the real role of Iraq's oil in leading the U.S. to invade may never be known, some Washington think-tanks publicly advocated breaking up the government oil monopoly into smaller units that would compete with each other and hopefully destroy OPEC. The occupation authorities did move towards allowing private companies into the industry, but public opinion strongly opposed doing so when Iraqis themselves were too burdened by war to compete. However, in 2009 the government announced an auction for production contracts at about half the country's oilfields. When Exxon of the U.S. turned down the first contract, to develop and service the giant Rumaila field in the south, as unprofitable, Britain's BP

and China's CNPC accepted the opportunity. Using foreign expertise, the country hopes to expand production to possibly 12 million barrels per day, far above the 2009 level of about 2.4 million barrels per day.

The Future: *Al-Qaeda in Iraq* is reeling, casualties are down, and al-Sadr's militia is losing the ability to act at will. After months of discussion, a workable majority may emerge from the parliamentary elections. Things are looking up enough for Iraqis to report improved security—and to anticipate the official removal of U.S. combat troops in August 2010.

Challenges remain: a National Assembly unable to enact timely reforms; political fissures; the possibility that militias

loyal to political parties might return to the streets, policemen who participated in sectarian killings, inadequate government services, and widespread corruption.

The ground for hope is that Iraq's many factions—and their foreign backers—recognize the necessity of peaceful compromise. Most Iraqis wish to set violence behind them. Can they, their society, and their politicians find sufficient strength to form a stable government and defeat the insurgents who seem poised to continue car bombings and other attacks on civilians? The U.S. military claims that 80% of the leadership of *al-Qaeda in Iraq* has been removed by death, capture, defection, or flight. Even slow-negotiating politicians will appreciate that.

No cross zone in Karbala

Photo by William Parker

The State of Israel מדינת ישראל

Theodor Herzl

Introduction: Whether for its heroism during the War of Independence (1948–49) or later conflicts, its farming that "made the desert bloom," its democracy, the achievements of its citizens in music, science, or its military prowess, no other nation of the region captured the imagination of the Western world like Israel. Its immigrants from around the globe provide a more diverse culture than any other nation, and it remains a special focus even of Jews who live elsewhere by choice.

———— • ————

Area: 8,017 sq. mi. (20,700 sq. km.) within the Armistice Demarcation lines effective 1949–1967. In addition, since 1967, the West Bank (of the Jordan River), the Gaza Strip and part of Syria have been under Israeli military occupation and subject to Israeli civilian settlement.

Population: 6.7 million (UN, 2005), including over 5 million Jews and 1 million Arabs.

Capital City: Jerusalem (pop. about 750,000), more than two-thirds Jewish. Few nations recognize Israeli sovereignty over East Jerusalem (captured in 1967) so most maintain their embassies in the Tel Aviv metropolitan area (pop. 3.2 million, 2008).

Climate: Summers are hot and dry, winters mild with moderate rainfall, except in the arid south part of the country.

Neighboring Countries: Egypt (Southwest); Jordan (East); Syria (Northeast); Lebanon (North).

Time Zone: GMT +2 (+3 in summer).

Official Languages: (Modern) Hebrew and Arabic.

Other Principal Tongues: English, Yiddish, Ladino, Polish, Russian, Persian, German, French, Hungarian, Bulgarian and Romanian.

Ethnic Background: European, North African and Asian.

Principal Religion: Judaism (83%), Islam and Christianity.

Chief Commercial Products: Computer software and high-tech applications, armaments, aircraft and aircraft servicing, military electronics equipment, chemicals, cut and polished diamonds, agricultural products.

Main Agricultural Produce and Livestock: Oranges and other fruit, vegetables, wheat, potatoes, poultry, sheep and cattle.

Major Trading Partners: U.S., Japan, Germany, U.K. Switzerland, France, Italy, Hong Kong and Belgium.

Currency: New Israeli Shekel (= 100 agorot).

Former Colonial Status: Britain conquered the territory now controlled by the State of Israel from the Ottoman Empire during 1916–1918 and held it until 1948.

Israel

Independence Date: May 14, 1948. Like all holidays, Independence Day is celebrated according to the Jewish calendar, and it varies from late April to May.
Chief of State: Shimon Peres (2007)
Head of Government: Binyamin Netanyahu, Prime Minister (2009).
National Flag: White field with a broad blue horizontal stripes near both the top and bottom; centered between the stripes is a large blue "Shield of David," that is a cut-out six-pointed star.
Gross Domestic Product: $216 billion (current prices) 2009)
GDP per capita: $28,300 (PPP), 2009.

Lying on the coast of the Mediterranean Sea with the Arabian Desert at its back door, Israel has considerable variety in climate and geography. The northern part enjoys good rainfall, sometimes as much as 40 inches in a winter, but the southern part is arid desert of gravel and rock. Summers can be unpleasantly warm throughout the land, but winters are not severe, though chilly at higher elevations.

The Mediterranean seaboard is bordered by a coastal plain averaging about ten miles in width and broken only by a ridge extending northwest from the West Bank to a promontory just south of Haifa. Much of this plain is under cultivation, as it has been for many centuries. A central ridge runs south from the border with Lebanon through Israel and the West Bank, and then fans out in Israel's southern desert. The rainfall caught on the western slopes of these central hills allows a variety of fruit trees to flourish, as well as small fields of grain and vegetables. The Hula Plain north of the Sea of Galilee has been partly reclaimed from marshes. A fertile plain lying to the southeast of Haifa has been a source of grains and other foods since ancient times.

Flowing from sources on the slopes of Mt. Hermon and the Golan Heights, the Jordan River provides the major source of fresh water in the region. South of the Sea of Galilee the Jordan Valley lies entirely below sea level, and at the Dead Sea it reaches the lowest point on earth (about 1300 ft. below sea level, and falling). South of the Dead Sea, the deep valley rises gently to the Gulf of Aqaba and Israel's southern port, Eilat.

History: Proclaimed independent on May 14, 1948, Israel represents the triumph of modern Zionist dreams for a Jewish state. Its origins reach back, however, for centuries. After the Romans crushed Jewish revolts in Palestine during the first and second centuries A.D., Jews overwhelmingly lived scattered outside their Promised Land, forbidden for centuries to reside in Jerusalem by pagan Rome and

then Christian Byzantium. The small Jewish minority in Palestine welcomed Arab rule (635–638), and Jews began to return to Jerusalem after the Muslim conquest. The restoration of Christian rule, in the form of the Crusades, meant the massacre of almost all Muslims and Jews in Jerusalem (1099).

The restoration of Muslim rule after the defeat of the Crusaders improved Jewish fortunes in Palestine, and a trickle of immigration began, in part by refugees from

ZIONISM: For centuries Zionism reflected the yearning of Jews to return to Zion, meaning the citadel at Jerusalem, and even the entire Holy Land. After increasing nationalism in Europe, Theodor Herzl and others transformed cultural and religious Zionism into a political ideology. It holds that Jews everywhere form *one people*, whose protection requires a Jewish state.

Israel

persecutions and expulsions in Western Europe. Despite ravages of the Black Plague, famines, and rival rulers, the Jewish communities survived. They strengthened after 1492 with a rapid influx of Spanish Jews expelled from their homeland. Ottoman rule (1517) decayed relatively quickly in Palestine, however, and amidst insecurities and disorders the Jews suffered alongside Christians and Muslims. By 1800 the Jewish presence in Palestine had dwindled to the lowest level for centuries, and nations like the United States and France had removed all legal disabilities of Jews. Events took the unexpected turn, however: a century later, Zionism had infused the Jewish world with the idea not merely of Jewish settlements in the Promised Land, but of a *Jewish state* there.

The Birth of Political Zionism

The origins of Zionism lay far from the traditional and pious Jewish settlements in Palestine. Persecutions (pogroms) in Eastern Europe, especially in Czarist Russia and Poland, led Leo Pinsker to demand a home for oppressed Jews in 1882; a colonization society sprang up. By 1900 thousands of Jews fleeing the anti-Semitism of Eastern Europe entered the Holy Land to pioneer new settlements with the goal of developing a self-supporting economy based on agriculture. The number of Jews in Palestine thus increased to an estimated 45,000.

Against the backdrop of this often religious migration, the concept of political Zionism arose, the belief that the Jews scattered across the world constituted a single nation, that their right to liberty and independence—perhaps even their survival—included a return to the Promised Land and the establishment there of the State of Israel. Its best known early advocate was Theodor Herzl, who published *The Jewish State* in 1896 and organized the movement with the first Zionist World Congress of 1897 in Basel, Switzerland. Under the influence of European anti-Jewish persecution and discrimination, he envisioned "the establishment for the Jewish people of a home in Palestine."

Only accepted by a handful at first, this application of 19th century European territorial nationalism to Jewish existence began to grow steadily. Eventually the main ideas of political Zionism included (1) the concept of "a Jewish People," not merely various communities following the religion of Judaism; (2) the inevitable recurrence of anti-Jewish persecution; (3) the impossibility of Jews living full and complete lives outside a distinctive and territorial state; (4) the historic right of "the Jewish People" to *Eretz Yisrael,* the Land of Israel (see Historical Background) and

Entrance to the Dome of the Rock, a sanctuary erected in the 7th century by Muslims on the site of the Temple of Solomon and the Second Temple, then in ruins. This is one of the most sacred of all Islamic shrines.   Photo by Linda Cook

(5) the duty of all Jews everywhere to support the national cause. These ideas formed the basic ideology in building the State of Israel and in its history to the present.

Before World War I, the desire Land of Israel was part of the Ottoman Empire. Most Ottoman authorities did not favor the Zionist immigration and land procurement because of local Arab opposition, but they were only partly able to resist external European support for Jewish immigration, as well as internal subterfuges and bribes that provided land to Jewish settlers, if expensively.

The vigor and ideals of a new generation of Zionist immigrants, known as the Second Aliyah, influenced deeply the founding of modern social institutions by 1914: they established newspapers, trade unions, and political parties. Hebrew became the language for Jewish schools, the first secondary school started, and land was purchased for a university. Moreover, the character of Zionist settlement had been formed. The native Jewish settlements were primarily urban, and other Jewish immigrants lacked a clear philosophy of purpose, some producing wines

1947 UN Recommendation

86

for export using French experts, Arab labor, and Baron Edmond de Rothschild's subsidies. In contrast, socialists within the Zionist organization sought to build a society of collectives where Jews worked together at even the most menial tasks and refused to employ (cheap) Arab labor. By the beginning of World War I, about 100,000 Jews lived in Palestine, compared to roughly 550,000 Muslims and 70,000 Christians.

World War I proved a major turning point for Zionist hopes. Having agreed secretly with France to internationalize Palestine, Britain also implied to Sharif Husayn, leader of the Arab Revolt then in progress, that Palestine would form part of an independent Arab state. However, the persuasive influence of a prominent scientist, Dr. Chaim Weizmann, led on November 2, 1917, to the Balfour Declaration. It promised British favor for the establishment of a "national home for the Jewish people" in Palestine, although it expressed support for the civil and religious rights of the non-Jewish populations. Most Palestinians opposed the declaration, and testified their opposition to the American King-Crane Commission during the peace talks. Nevertheless, incorporated into the 1920 San Remo Agreement that divided the Middle East between France and Britain, the Balfour Declaration also formed part of Britain's Mandate for Palestine in 1923. Unlike other Arab mandates it did not prescribe a constitution and eventual independence.

Jewish Achievements during the Mandate

With the end of war and a sympathetic nation in control, Jewish immigration rapidly expanded, with predictable Arab reactions. In 1920 serious rioting broke out, as it did frequently during the Mandate. Jewish immigration rose sharply after Hitler gained power in Germany. By 1939, despite Arab riots and consequent British reductions in permitted immigration, nearly one-third of the population was Jewish. The relative prosperity of Palestine also attracted Arab immigrants, though those numbers are poorly documented. In any case, Zionist leaders could plan for the day when Jews formed a majority of the total population. Until then, Jewish organizations bought land, settled it, and established industry.

Jewish land purchases provided a major source of Arab resentment. Fertile, watered farmland rarely lay vacant, and it frequently cost far more than similar land in the United States. Although many acres remained idle, their cultivation was handicapped by qualities the twentieth century would change: the low level of agricultural technology and education,

the absence of engine-powered pumps, incursions by Bedouins, expensive animal transportation, and blocked foreign markets.

Against this background, the Jewish National Fund purchased farmland from Arab landlords. The land had rarely been owned by those who farmed it, however. Significant purchases came from absentee landlords residing in Syria and Lebanon.

With the change of ownership, any Arab tenant farmers became dispossessed, for whether a communally-run *kibbutz* or a *moshav* with private ownership, a Jewish settlement stressed the dignity of Jewish labor. Moreover, once purchased, the land became the inalienable property of the Jewish community. Superior in education, technical knowledge, machinery and incentives to the Arab tenant farmers they replaced, the Jewish settlers often succeeded in bringing the desert to bloom. Indeed their example influenced the remaining Arab farmers, whose production increased substantially. Jaffa's oranges won fame as Jewish exports, but Arabs had cultivated them for centuries and still accounted for about half of all orange exports in the 1930s.

The social development of the Jewish community continued apace before World War II. The Hebrew University was founded in 1918, and universal elementary education was achieved in the 1930s. The Jewish Agency was established in 1929 to assist in fostering the immediate goals of immigration and the acquisition of land, as well as the promotion of religion and the use of Hebrew. The Jewish Self-Defense Force, the *Haganah*, developed in secret, coming to possess a strong organization and significant weapons.

Nevertheless, the Jewish community was not united. One minority, firmly orthodox, feared that the nationalism of Zionism destroyed the religious basis of Judaism. At another extreme, the Revisionists led by Vladimir Jabotinsky demanded the immediate fulfillment of the Jewish national home, on *both sides* of the Jordan River, thus including the East Bank or Transjordan.

Arab Palestinians failed to achieve similar progress under the Mandate. By 1936 their frustration reached the point of a general strike, violence, and rebellion. Again the British government investigated, and again promised, this time in the 1939 White Paper, to limit Zionist immigration and implied future self-government for Palestine. World War II and the death camps of Hitler's Germany, however, placed Zionism deep in the imagination of most Western peoples. Moreover, particularly to American fundamentalists, a restored Israel seemed to fulfill Biblical prophecies.

The War for Independence, 1948–1949

In this climate, skillful Zionist leaders in America, cooperating with David Ben-Gurion, managed simultaneously to uphold U.S. limitations on Jewish immigration, and to encourage President Truman to urge it publicly for Palestine. No longer a great power, and no longer valuing the Suez Canal as a route to India, Britain found the difficulties of ruling Palestine too great and turned the problem over to the new United Nations. The Zionists won a major legal and psychological victory in late 1947 when the General Assembly voted by a narrow margin to recommend the political partition of Palestine. It assigned about 60% of the territory to a "Jewish State" although the Jewish settlers comprised only a bare one-third of the population. The Security Council did not endorse this recommendation nor did it provide any enforcement. As Britain had announced its plan to withdraw from Palestine by May 15, 1948, the issue was left open to resolution by force.

Within Palestine, force pitted the Arab majority against the Jewish minority. The latter were organized militarily into three groups. Representing the mainstream Zionist movement, the *Haganah* counted some 60,000 fighters, armed even with a few tanks and backed by a supply system that smuggled arms from Europe. In contrast, the Revisionists of the 1920s influenced the two right-wing and smaller groups, the *Irgun* of Menachem Begin, and the *Stern Gang*. Sabotage of British military and transport installations already showed their capabilities. The *Irgun* and *Stern Gang* in particular adopted methods which today are considered terrorist. In one of the most daring examples, in reprisal for British arrests of Jewish leaders, the Irgun blew up the British headquarters at the King David Hotel, killing 91.

The Palestinians, by contrast, organized no comparable military force, but counted on help from the surrounding states. As the British forces withdrew, Syrian volunteers and army officers entered Galilee (January 1948), and an Arab Liberation Army formed, financed and supplied in part by Egypt and Iraq. By April 1948 full-scale war broke out on many fronts, as both sides fought for as much land as they could obtain, regardless of the UN partition plan. Jewish forces quickly gained the Galilee region and Haifa, according to the partition part of the Jewish state. In addition, they captured Jaffa and Akka (Acre), allocated to the Arab state.

The fighting involved entire communities, and descended quickly to brutality. The *Irgun* attacked the Arab village of Deir Yasin, near the vital road to Jerusalem, and massacred some 250 people, many of them women and children. In response, Arabs at-

Israel

Prime Minister David Ben-Gurion signs the independence declaration, May 14, 1948
AP/Wide World Photo

tacked a convoy headed for the Hebrew University and Hadassah Hospital outside Jerusalem; 77 professors, students, and medical personnel perished. Thereafter, hundreds of thousands of Arabs fled from exposed villages and cities captured by the Zionists, in fear, to escape the fighting, or pressured by Jews. The Jews had nowhere to flee and fought rather better.

As the Mandate drew to a close, on May 14, 1948, in Tel Aviv David Ben-Gurion proclaimed the establishment of the State of Israel, and won immediate recognition from the United States. The next day, backed by resolutions of the Arab League, armies of Egypt, Iraq, Transjordan, Syria and Lebanon entered the war. The first war between Israel and the Arab states began, with the Israelis fighting for their independence and very existence as a separate state. The Israeli army outnumbered the Arab forces in Palestine and soon gained the offensive, striking at enemy targets in turn. Poorly coordinated on separate fronts, their equipment often obsolete or defective, the Arab armies also failed to evade a United Nations arms embargo successfully. Like the four major wars that followed, this ended in Israeli victories almost everywhere, though one Jew of every 100 in Israel died.

Building the State of Israel
The boundaries of the various armistices of 1949 found Israel much enlarged

from the partition plan, with about 70% of the mandate's territory. The highlands of the West Bank remained largely Arab and controlled by the Arab Legion of Transjordan, except for a Jewish sector including part of Jerusalem. The only remaining portion of Palestine not under Israeli rule was the Gaza Strip in the southwest, inhabited mostly by wretched refugees and administered by Egypt. Equally important for the future, 700,000 Arab refugees fled what was to become the State of Israel.

For Israelis, independence meant a national government. Chaim Weizmann was elected to the largely honorary position of president in 1948, while the next year elections were held to the *Knesset*, the national parliament, whose majority leader is the Prime Minister. Israel's electoral system is one of the fairest in the world at translating preferences for political parties into seats in the legislature. With only one electoral district (the entire country), and proportional representation, each party's number of seats in the 120-member Knesset reflects very closely its percentage of the national vote.

Many parties seized the electoral system's opportunities in 1949, and have ever since. David Ben-Gurion headed the largest, *Mapai*, (the core today of the *Israeli Labor Party*), but it never won a majority in the Knesset although it dominated every cabinet until 1977. Consequently, Israeli governments have always been coalitions, in the

early years largely between *Mapai* and the *National Religious Party*. The need to form a parliamentary majority often gives small parties disproportionate weight in forming a coalition.

The first government faced an immediate economic crisis. War had disrupted trade and production, and an Arab trade embargo blocked logical industrial development by cutting the oil pipeline to Haifa from Iraq and destroying dreams of Jewish capital and knowledge uniting with Arab labor. To help in the crisis, aid flowed in from private sources, especially the United Jewish Appeal in the United States, as well as from the American government. Well into the 1960s a major source of funds came from West Germany in the form of reparations for the Holocaust. Nevertheless, in a poor parcel of Asia, Israelis enjoyed living like Europeans, and the balance of payments often reflected a sharp deficit.

Besides the burden of defense, the government budget faced enormous costs of absorbing Jewish immigration. One of the first enactments of Israel, the Law of the Return, granted citizenship to all Jews who landed in Israel. In the first four years of independence, some 700,000 responded, many of them relatively poor and less-educated from Arab countries such as Morocco, Yemen, and Iraq. In contrast to the Eastern European *Ashkenazi* Jews who had dominated the Zionist movement and Israeli society, the new immigrants were overwhelmingly *Sephardic* Jews, with differences significant for Israeli politics and society (see Culture). Another important project was the Israel National Water Carrier, a system of canals and pipelines bringing water from the Jordan River to the coastal plain and then the Negev desert for irrigation.

The Arab Minority
For the Arabs who remained, Israeli rule brought the second-class citizenship of a discontented and distrusted minority. The symbols of state reminded them that they had lost: the Star of David on an alien flag and an official language they could not speak. Israeli development often removed all traces of previous Arab habitation, even buildings and cemeteries, so Arabs witnessed the destruction of the memories of their past. The annual commemoration of Land Day (March 31) protests the confiscation of Arab land.

Less educated and relatively impoverished, with a high birthrate, Arab towns often failed to develop municipal services in a country where welfare came from charitable organizations more than from the state. Except for members of the Druze community (see Lebanon: Culture), Arabs are relieved of military service and thus of veterans benefits. Nevertheless, their economic progress generally exceeded that of most of the Arab world. Israeli Arabs also enjoyed the right to vote in genuine multi-party elections, in contrast to most Arabs' lives under dictatorships and authoritarian rulers.

After living on the margins of national life for decades, in the late 1990s many Israeli Arabs became more assertive, electing Arab members of the Knesset rather than voting for *Labor*. They joined the protests that initiated the "*al-Aqsa Intifada*" in 2000, and suffered pillage and vandalism by Jewish mobs. The police shot Arab demonstrators, but put their weapons away when facing Jewish mobs. Further Arab-Jewish riots rocked Acre in 2008

The harshest current Jewish criticisms of the Arab minority currently comes from the political party *Yisrael Beiteinu—Israel our Homeland*. Ironically, it is the party of recent immigrants from the former Soviet Union, the least locally-born group in society.

The Suez Wars, 1956 & 1967

Although armistice agreements formally took effect with neighboring states in 1949, armed Palestinians crossed into Israel and inflicted damage or injury, sometimes killing civilians despite the efforts of the UN Truce Supervision Organization. To satisfy Jewish public opinion that something was being done, in 1953 Israel adopted a policy of "retaliatory" military raids. These destroyed property and civilian lives on the Arab sides of the demarcation line. Roughly ten times as many Arab civilians died as Israeli civilians through violations of the armistice lines.

After rising tensions on the border with Egypt for more than a year, in October 1956 Israel launched a massive surprise attack on Egypt. Within ten days Israeli forces occupied almost all the Sinai Peninsula, including Sharm al-Sheikh, which controlled the Straits of Tiran at the entrance to the Gulf of Aqaba and thereby Israel's maritime route to East Asia. France and Britain had secretly joined plans for the aggression (see Egypt); they then invaded the Suez Canal Zone. However, with the agreement of the United States and the Soviet Union, the UN halted the fighting and supervised the withdrawal of foreign troops. A UN Emergency Force took up positions on the Egyptian side of the frontier to prevent incidents, and the Straits of Tiran remained open for Israeli shipping.

For most of a decade, Israel progressed economically and socially. However, in 1964 the Arab states voted to strengthen their armed forces and divert their major tributaries of the Jordan River. These actions threatened Israel's major source of fresh water. Equally troublesome, Palestinian guerrilla raids increased. Against this background, in early 1967, Egypt moved troops into the Sinai, ordered out the UN Emergency Force posted along the borders, and announced the closure of the Straits of Tiran. As world diplomacy sought to relax the tensions, Israel demanded that the Straits remain open, and Jordan and Syria formed a united front with Egypt.

On June 5, 1967, Israel launched a new war in full force. In hours the air forces of Egypt and Syria were destroyed on the ground, Jordan's airports were bombed to uselessness, and the Iraqi air force was largely disabled. By the end of fighting on June 10, Israel had occupied the Sinai Peninsula, the Old City of Jerusalem, the West Bank, and a strip of Syria's Golan Plateau about 20 miles wide.

Diplomatic wrangling in the UN Security Council postponed until November 1967 its formal conditions for peace. Underneath a bland exterior, Resolution 242 masked strong divisions of interpretation. Israelis stressed the need for peace and acknowledgment of their right to sovereignty. Thus, withdrawal "from territories occupied" meant withdrawal to secure boundaries. To Arabs, however, it meant the evacuation of *all* territories occupied. A "just settlement" of the refugee problem held no common meaning, and Palestinians resented being classified merely as refugees, not as a nation.

From the victory Israel gained much, at a relatively small cost in lives and

---

SPECIAL DOCUMENT

UN Security Council Resolution 242

On November 22, 1967, the Security Council of the United Nations unanimously approved—and has subsequently reaffirmed—a resolution outlining the basis for peace between the State of Israel and the Arab countries with which it is in conflict. The United States, Israel and Egypt, in the Camp David accords of September 1978, specifically endorsed the implementation of this resolution "in all its parts." The following is the text of that resolution:

The Security Council,

Expressing its continuing concern with the grave situation in the Middle East,

Emphasizing the inadmissibility of the acquisition of territory by war and the need to work for a just and lasting peace in which every state in the area can live in security,

Emphasizing further that all member states in their acceptance of the Charter of the United Nations have undertaken a commitment to act in accordance with Article 2 of the Charter,

1. Affirms that the fulfillment of Charter principles requires the establishment of a just and lasting peace in the Middle East which should include the application of both of the following principles: (a) Withdrawal of Israel armed forces from territories occupied in the recent conflict; (b) Termination of all claims or states of belligerency and respect for and acknowledgment of the sovereignty, territorial integrity and political independence of every state in the area and their right to live in peace within secure and recognized boundaries free from threats.

2. Affirms further the necessity: (a) For guaranteeing freedom of navigation through international waterways in the area; (b) For achieving a just settlement of the refugee problem; (c) For guaranteeing the territorial inviolability and political independence of every state in the area, through measures including the establishment of demilitarized zones.

3. Requests the Secretary-General to designate a special representative to proceed to the Middle East to establish and maintain contacts with the states concerned in order to promote agreement and assist efforts to achieve a peaceful and accepted settlement.

4. Requests the Secretary-General to report to the Security Council on the progress of the efforts of the special representative as soon as possible.

Israel

wounded. President Johnson did not demand withdrawal to the 1949 Armistice lines, as happened in 1956. The new cease-fire lines stretched fewer miles but encompassed three times the territory of 1949. More importantly, the Jewish *Diaspora* again felt deeply its attachment to Israel. Thousands came to fight or replace men and women called to battle; funds flowed to aid society and government. Discouraged and worried about emigration before the war, Israeli self-confidence returned with victory.

While postponing decisions on the fate of most occupied territory, Israel moved quickly to incorporate East Jerusalem into Israel itself. Within the Old City lies the Wailing Wall, remaining from the Second Temple and the most sacred Jewish shrine. Prohibited from worshipping there during Jordanian rule, the Israelis rapidly bulldozed neighboring houses for better access. (Greatly complicating the achievement of peace, the Wailing Wall borders the Haram al-Sharif, one of the holiest Muslim shrines, containing the Dome of the Rock and al-Aqsa Mosque.) Reconstruction of the old Jewish quarter commenced, and under Mayor Teddy Kolleck, one of the most remarkable leaders in the Middle East, the city administration of Jewish Jerusalem stretched east.

In the years after 1967 Israel continued its rapid economic growth. Industry expanded and personal incomes climbed rapidly. Under the influence of prosperity, the idealistic culture of early Zionism matured increasingly into materialism. Arab labor from the West Bank and Gaza filled menial and low-paid jobs, and the territories provided new markets for Israeli products. Traditional problems continued:

military expenses devoured the national budget and foreign charity failed to cover the trade deficit, so the currency depreciated. However, Israel found its new arms supplier, the U.S., willing to turn its loans into grants, thus easing the financial burden.

Defense difficulties continued, despite the overwhelming victory. By 1969, battles along the Suez Canal escalated to become the War of Attrition. Though its aircraft wreaked havoc on Egypt, the cost to Israel in lives and funds was not insignificant. Moreover, Israel's 1967 victories strengthened Yasir Arafat's conviction that only guerrilla warfare could regain Palestine. Civilian casualties had been relatively small in 1956 and 1967. They now climbed, from Palestinian raids and Israeli punitive reprisals.

The October 1973 War and Disengagement

On October 6, 1973, while Israel observed *Yom Kippur*, the Day of Atonement, simultaneous attacks by Syria and Egypt opened the next Arab-Israeli War. Technically, the Egyptians and Syrians never reached Israel; rather, they attacked Israeli forces on their own national territories. Egyptian armies crossed the Suez Canal, pierced the Bar Lev Line, and entered the Sinai. Syrian troops also advanced, capturing Israeli positions on the Golan Heights.

Rapidly mobilizing, the Israel Defense Force (IDF) counter-attacked, and the intense tank battles destroyed perhaps 2,000 tanks and 500 aircraft. Sensing a weakness and benefiting from advanced arms and technical superiority, General Ariel Sharon led his troops across the Suez Canal into Egypt itself, encircling an entire Egyptian

army and leaving Cairo almost defenseless. The Syrians likewise retreated, but the enormous cost of the war convinced many on both sides of its futility. Three weeks after it began a ceasefire took effect.

Disengagement agreements mediated by Henry Kissinger, the American Secretary of State, followed the ceasefire. In 1974–1975 Israeli troops withdrew into the Sinai, returning the Suez Canal and oil fields used since 1967. Egypt allowed non-military cargoes for Israel through the newly-reopened Canal. Separately, Israeli troops returned portions of the Golan Heights to Syria, including the devastated town of Qunaytra.

When elections approached in 1977, the *Labor* government disintegrated under charges of mismanagement and corruption. Supported strongly by Sephardic Jews, *Likud* triumphed, and ended *Labor's* unbroken hold on government. Menachem Begin, former leader of *Irgun* and a long-time advocate of keeping all occupied territories, formed a coalition with a diverse group of parties. Rejecting socialism, the government raised taxes, devalued the currency, and reduced subsidies. The labor unions went on strike.

Peace with Egypt and Camp David

Foreign relations suddenly altered in 1977 when President Sadat of Egypt offered to visit Jerusalem in quest of genuine peace. For the first time, an Arab ruler publicly met with Israel's prime minister and talked directly to Israelis in their country. Sadat offered full peace; in exchange he asked for the principle of withdrawal from the occupied lands and the right of their Palestinians to determine their own future.

Sadat's dramatic moves posed a difficult political decision for Israel: the choice between territory and peace. After weeks of equivocation, Prime Minister Begin responded that his government could not give up "Judea and Samaria" (to others, the "West Bank") because they formed part of the "historic land of Israel." Instead he offered Palestinians "living in the Land of Israel" civil autonomy under Israeli control.

Against a background of terrorist attacks by Palestinians and an Israeli invasion of Southern Lebanon, President Carter invited the Israeli and Egyptian leaders to Camp David, the presidential retreat. Secluded from the press and political pressures, for nearly two weeks Menachem Begin and Anwar Sadat negotiated, and finally signed agreements at the White House. Israel obtained one of its major policy goals: a peace treaty with Egypt, the most powerful Arab state. In return, Israel promised to return the Sinai to Egypt.

The West ("Wailing") Wall within Jerusalem where Jews pray. Tradition is that the wall was partially built of materials from Solomon's temple. Photo by Linda Cook

Israel

After a formal peace treaty between Egypt and Israel in 1979, Israeli troops withdrew from Sinai, and Begin's promise that no other settlements would ever be removed became *Likud* policy and effectively ruled out exchanging other occupied territories for peace.

With Palestinians increasingly restive in the West Bank and Gaza, the Begin cabinet worried about the growing Palestinian military in Lebanon. Under secret plans drawn up by Defense Minister Ariel Sharon, in 1982 Israeli forces used a pretext to launch a massive invasion of Lebanon. The IDF eventually reached Beirut's suburbs and linked up with the Maronite Christian enclave (see Lebanon: History). Outside Beirut, Israeli casualties began to mount, eventually making the invasion of Lebanon Israel's most costly foreign war, measured in lives. Moreover, Israeli troops permitted Maronite militiamen to enter captured Palestinian camps, where they massacred nearly 1,000 men, women, and children. Israeli opinion grew increasingly divided. Many citizens, including some officers, demonstrated for a withdrawal from Lebanon; the *Peace Now* movement reflected such concerns.

Soviet Immigrants Change the Demographics

Jewish immigration from the Soviet Union and the Palestinian *intifada* combined to challenge Israel's occupation, politics and society in the early 1990s. Aided by changes in Soviet society, tens of thousands of Jews and their spouses emigrated from Russia to Israel. This massive population transfer touched the very basis of Zionism. Soviet immigrants boosted the productive population, and they postponed the threatened Arab majority for decades. Further immigrants were airlifted to Israel from Ethiopia in 1991. In time, the immigrants changed Israeli society, with Russian newspapers and even Orthodox churches appearing. Politically, the new immigrants generally opposed withdrawal from the occupied territories, and their politicians initially allied with *Likud*. They later supported the secular nationalist platform of *Yisrael Beiteinu*, "Israel is our home."

Consideration of a Palestinian State

The first twenty years of Israeli's occupation of the lands captured in 1967 brought few serious challenges. However, the seven years from 1987 to 1994 changed the entire focus of Israeli-Palestinian relations.

The strikes, civil disobedience, rock-throwing and other violence of the first Palestinian *intifada* began in late 1987. Coordinated in secret, it took Israeli leaders by surprise. The *intifada* marked a distinct change from the physical threats posed by

Presidents Sadat, Carter and Prime Minister Begin, September 17, 1978, at the White House
Courtesy: Jimmy Carter Library

Arab armies in past wars. Because the *intifada* stressed defiance, not attacks on Israel, it contrasted sharply with attacks by Palestinian guerrillas. Indeed, only 15 Israelis died in its first year, compared to more than 360 Palestinians.

Crushing the uprising meant using one of the world's most highly rated war machines against teenagers throwing stones and Molotov cocktails. Annual reserve duty was extended, and troops adopted lethal tactics. Nevertheless, military force did not crush the political uprising: rather, the *intifada* focused world attention on the Palestinians. The U.S. attempted a peace shuttle, and officially accused Israel of violating human rights and inflicting "many avoidable deaths." Yasir Arafat, Chairman of the PLO, successfully used world concern over the *intifada* to win UN General Assembly approval of an international peace conference which would grant Palestinians "official observer" status. The *Likud* resistance to land for peace had lost its foreign support: the United States seemed to change sides, and many American sympathizers and major Jewish groups supported Israel-PLO talks under certain conditions.

Israeli opposition to a Palestinian state includes many strands. The 1967 West Bank threatened vital highways and Tel Aviv's suburbs, while the Jordan River provides the shortest and most defendable border. Another strategic argument holds that any Palestinian state would sometime fall to extremists. Continuous occupation may be less damaging in Israeli lives and world opinion than terrorist raids and reprisals.

Other reasons to keep the territories lie in ideology. Revisionist Zionists, from Jabotinsky in the 1920s to ultra-Orthodox Jews today, stress that Israel must occupy the whole of the Biblical Promised Land.

Over Jerusalem the refusal to withdraw becomes almost universal. Arab East Jerusalem physically forms part of a city almost all Jews promise never to divide. Moreover, Judaism's most sacred shrine, the Wailing Wall, lies within the largely-Arab Old City.

Political reality presents another major hurdle. The policy of "creating facts" involved the settlement of 250,000 Jews in the West Bank by 2005, in addition to perhaps 200,000 near Jerusalem. Though less than 10% of the electorate, these settlers form a major political force with one overriding issue: "No withdrawal." Finally, there are economic reasons, among them that the surplus of water of the West Bank provides that vital resource for Israel itself.

Pressures do exist for compromise. One is the difficulty of indefinitely occupying a land and depriving its inhabitants of self-determination. Ruling the restive population requires military control, and increases military influence in public and private life. Moral questions arise also, symbolized by predictions that the greater Arab birthrate will eventually create more Arabs than Jews between the sea and the Jordan River. The occupation inevitably complicates foreign relations, and difficulties at the United Nations.

General Rabin & Negotiation from Strength

Iraq's seizure of Kuwait in 1990 seemed a grave threat to Israel's security, because Saddam Hussein claimed a war over Kuwait was actually a war for Israel. The IDF placed its airmen on alert, and the government issued gas masks. Hours after coalition forces attacked Iraq in January 1991, the first of 39 Scud missiles landed in Tel Aviv, destroying and damaging homes in a residential area. Scores of injuries and a few deaths resulted from

Israel

The "government of national unity," September 1984

the attacks. Remarkably, Israel did not retaliate: the transformation of the Gulf War into a general Arab-Israeli conflict would have benefited Iraq but not the United States or its Arab allies. Patriot missile crews arrived to defend Tel Aviv, and coalition aircraft renewed attacks on well-hidden Scud launchers in western Iraq. Israel sought hundreds of millions of dollars in aid to cover missile damage, military expenses, and economic losses such as the decline in tourism.

The Gulf War confirmed Israeli military superiority in the Middle East and left its most threatening Arab rival in shambles. Military security was completely assured. Moreover, thanks to immigration from the Soviet Union, the Arab demographic time bomb—the threat of an Arab majority in Israel and the territories—was postponed for two decades.

For the 1991 elections, *Labor* selected the more popular Yitzhak Rabin as its leader rather than Shimon Peres. Though a tough general, he favored Palestinian autonomy and peace through concessions over occupied territory. *Labor* won a decisive victory. Acting decisively on several issues, Rabin halted the construction of new communities in the Occupied Territories (though permitting security outposts to expand). This won American loan guarantees for housing construction within Israel and raised hopes at the peace talks. Rabin's negotiators even conceded a possible withdrawal in the Golan Heights in return for peace with Syria.

The *intifada* proved the most pressing and increasingly lethal problem (see Palestine: History). Finally, Rabin closed Israel to the 60,000 workers from the Occupied Territories, thus halting most contacts between Israelis and Palestinians. As calm returned, most Israelis favored a permanent ban, despite labor shortages in some industries and recognition that unemployed and destitute men probably become more militant. On the deeper level, many also recognized that the practical separation of the Territories made some later withdrawal likely.

After secret negotiations in Oslo produced a Declaration of Principles for an eventual peace agreement, Prime Minister Rabin and PLO Chairman Yasir Arafat publicly shook hands at the White House in September 1993. The Declaration stipulated a withdrawal from most of the Gaza Strip and Jericho and the creation of a Palestinian Authority to administer them. It also specified later Israeli administrative and military withdrawals from much of the West Bank.

The Oslo Accords were clearly not a peace agreement. They deliberately left many matters undecided. Very difficult issues, such as borders, Palestinian refugees, and East Jerusalem (claimed as the Palestinian capital) remained for the final agreement, to be reached after confidence-building measures provided greater trust between the two sides. Radical Jewish and Arab opponents of peace sought to destroy the peace process through violence

that often took the lives civilians and children. Each unfortunate case required revenge that in turn incited reprisals that continued the cycle of violence. However, "Oslo" had established a timetable, and after last-minute bickering, in 1994 the Israeli flag was lowered over Gaza and Jericho.

The withdrawal brought neither economic bonanza nor safety to Israel. Suicide attacks by *Hamas* and the *Islamic Jihad*, particularly against buses, killed scores of Israelis. In response, the cabinet again sealed the border with Gaza and the West Bank and halted the agreed release of prisoners. Fearing for the safety of isolated settlements, the cabinet halted further withdrawals. In turn this postponed the Palestinian elections scheduled by the peace agreement.

Despite mixed success with Palestinians, the Oslo Accords brought welcome progress towards peace with some Arab states. Morocco established diplomatic relations. More dramatically, Jordan signed a peace treaty, after settling its demands for water rights and the small occupied territory (145 square miles) along the border. Visionaries predicted broad trade and development links, as well as hydroelectric and desalination schemes at the Dead Sea. Peace with Syria proved more difficult, given the domestically hazardous issue of the Golan Heights. Syria demands the entire territory. However, Golani settlers vote *Labor*, and many Israelis fear losing important strategic advantages from a withdrawal. Repeated negotiations have accomplished nothing—but occasionally provided a distraction when a prime minister needs relief from domestic pressures.

The Assassination of Yitzhak Rabin

Despite vicious attacks by right-wing extremists, including posters depicting Prime Minister Rabin as a Nazi, in 1995 the cabinet approved a withdrawal from several West Bank cities as a prelude to Palestinian elections. Two months later, after the usually unsmiling Rabin celebrated at a peace rally in Tel Aviv, a fanatical Orthodox law student shot him in the back. The assassin murdered, he said, because Rabin had negotiated away Israel's God-given land and endangered settlers' lives.

Immediately after Rabin's death, the vast majority of Israelis supported the peace negotiations. However, once again suicide attacks, targeted assassinations and an economic closure weakened advocates of peace on both sides. Israelis buried the dead while elections approached.

Stagnation, not Peace, under Netanyahu

In the 1996 elections, voters cast two ballots, the second one offering the novelty of voting for a person, for a prime minister. Its purpose was to speed the process of forming a government, and it worked. The Knesset proved more divided than ever, but Binyamin "Bibi" Netanyahu of *Likud* defeated Shimon Peres by less than 1%.

A forceful and complex personality, Netanyahu was young, telegenic, and an opportunist. *Likud* had opposed the whole Oslo process, but in a last-minute gesture that clinched his victory, Netanyahu accepted Oslo, promising to win a more secure peace.

In reality, stagnation resulted, not peace. Trouble followed construction of a Jewish settlement, *Har Homa*, on traditionally Arab land between East Jerusalem and Bethlehem. Symbolically and literally, the project completed the Jewish encirclement of Arab East Jerusalem and cut it off from access to the West Bank. When the bulldozers moved in, Palestinian leaders halted the peace negotiations.

Within Israeli society, serious fractures appeared. Russian and Ethiopian immigrants demanded spending to meet their needs, while many Sephardim (descendants of Middle Eastern Jews) sensed the Ashkenazi (European-descended) elite looked down on them. Students went on strike for lower tuition, and government workers for higher pay. The divide between religious and secular Jews became a greater issue than peace, and the resulting emotions challenged the integrity of government. When the Supreme Court

ended the draft exemption for the Orthodox and allowed farms to operate on the Sabbath, a mass rally attacked the court. Similarly, supporters of *Shas* (the ultra-Orthodox *Torah Observing Sephardim Party*) believed their leader, Rabbi Arie (Aryeh) Deri, was convicted of corruption because of his ethnic and religious position. Secular Jews objected to the automatic draft deferments for ultra-Orthodox (*Haredim*) students in yeshivas.

Burdened by American pressures to hold to the Oslo Accords as well as by personal resentments and political instability (four finance ministers in 30 months), Netanyahu's coalition collapsed.

The 1999 election campaign rapidly became a referendum over Netanyahu, leaving "Bibi" challenged only by Ehud Barak of *Labor*. Barak waged a careful campaign, neither too leftist nor sympathetic to the

Israeli occupied territory

Israeli settlements in the occupied territories

(See also Palestine)

GOLAN HEIGHTS

WEST BANK

Jordan River

Tel Aviv

Jerusalem

Dead Sea

GAZA STRIP

0   25 Miles

Palestinians. Netanyahu desperately attempted to stir up Palestinian passions, but there were no significant terrorist attacks, and Barak won a resounding triumph.

Barak: Worthy Goals Unfulfilled

An Ashkenazi and "Israel's most decorated soldier," Barak desired a strong cabinet to represent the nation, rather than merely parties. However, his personal win carried no coattails: *Labor* lost seats. For support beyond traditional allies on the left, Barak drew in *Shas* and another religious party.

The cabinet tackled difficult and divisive issues, against the background of increasingly harsh culture wars between secularists and practicing Orthodox and ultra-Orthodox Jews. Barak moved to end the abuse of draft deferments by ultra-Orthodox men. Yossi Sarid, the minister of education, changed the history curriculum to reinterpret the War of Independence and admit Israeli mistakes. He also added a Palestinian nationalist poem. For this, the leader of *Shas* described Sarid (a cabinet ally) as a "Satan" to be wiped from the face of the earth. Through its brinkmanship over the budget, *Shas* retained large subsidies for its badly-run school system.

For many Israelis, the difficult work of government reform seemed overshadowed by scandals. President Ezer Weizmann, accused of receiving illegal payments from a French businessman, fell from office, as did Deputy Prime Minister Yitzhak Mordechai, over allegations of sexual assault. Binyamin Netanyahu was blamed for corruption and misuse of gifts he received as prime minister, though the charges were dropped. A few years later, President Katzav was charged with rape. Further from politics, financial irregularities in some *yeshivas* vied for publicity with the national soccer team. Its players lost a match after a pre-game visit to a brothel.

In foreign affairs, Barak sought solutions to all remaining conflicts. He negotiated with Syria, and bluntly accepted an eventual Palestinian state. Overcoming right-wing criticism, he opened a 27-mile route connecting the Gaza Strip with the West Bank. Ten unauthorized Jewish settlements on the West Bank were closed (though dozens remained).

Although Barak often proved a tough defender of Israel's interests, his reputation came to rest on the withdrawal from South Lebanon. Unable to negotiate a departure from territory occupied for two decades, the IDF withdrew under pressure in 2000. The collapse of its local ally, the *South Lebanon Army*, brought forth comparisons with Vietnam, even in Hebrew papers.

Israel

For your shopping convenience
THE JERUSALEM POST BOOK DEPT.
is open Sun. - Thur.,
9:00 a.m. - 3:00 p.m.
Fridays 9:00 a.m.-1:00 p.m.
10 Harav Kook St.
Downtown Jerusalem.
Tel. 02-241282

THE JERUSALEM POST

SECOND EDITION

VOLUME LXIII, NUMBER 19113   SUNDAY, NOVEMBER 5, 1995 ● HESHVAN 12, 5756 ● II JAMAD 12, 1416   NIS 4.20 (EILAT NIS 3.60)

RABIN ASSASSINATED

Peres pays tribute to longtime rival, partner

DAVID MAKOVSKY, BATSHEVA TSUR and agencies

AN empty chair draped in black marked Prime Minister Yitzhak Rabin's place at the cabinet table as the nation's leaders met in emergency session and declared a transition government hours after he was assassinated at a peace rally.

Ministers wept while acting Prime Minister Shimon Peres paid tribute to his long-time political rival and partner in

forging peace with the Palestinians.

"He was a rare leader in Jewish history...in the last three years as Israeli prime minister he effected a revolution in the positive sense in the Middle East," Peres said in televised remarks.

"I asked myself if this happened to me, what would I want to happen later," Peres

(Continued on Page 12)

A black day for the whole Jewish nation

EDITORIAL

THE shock is universal. No Israeli, no Jew, no decent human being anywhere can help being shaken to the core, shattered to the depth of his and her soul by the news of the assassination of Prime Minister

Pronounced dead at 11:15 p.m. after being shot

RAINE MARCUS, SARAH HONIG and ALON PINKAS

PRIME Minister Yitzhak Rabin was assassinated last night by a 27-year-old Herzliya law student, who fired three bullets from a pistol at him at point-blank range. Rabin was felled as he was entering his official car at 9:50 p.m. at the conclusion of a massive peace rally in Tel Aviv's Kikar Malchei Yisrael attended by some 100,000 people.

Rabin was pronounced dead at 11:15 p.m. by doctors at Ichilov Hospital, where he had been brought with wounds to his back, abdomen, and chest. He died on the operating table from massive hemorrhaging and heart failure, without regaining consciousness.

The prime minister was not wearing a bullet-proof vest,

that he "did not regret his deed," which he said was "planned for some time."

A police source said that Amir had twice before attempted to assassinate Rabin, but no more details were available. In the two previous attempts, said the source, Amir tried to get close to the prime minister and was armed both times.

Amir was apprehended immediately after the shooting by police and pressed up against a cement wall, as dozens of policemen surrounded him.

Eyewitnesses reported seeing Rabin collapse. His bodyguards pushed him into the car and whisked him off to Ichilov Hospital, some 500 meters away. One of Rabin's bodyguards was also wounded by bullets.

Health Minister Ephraim Sneh told reporters at midnight that Rabin sustained bullet wounds in

---

Failure at Camp David

Conscious of the rapidly approaching deadline to complete the Oslo Accords (September, 2000) and seeking an agreement before the end of his term, President Clinton summoned both Prime Minister Barak and Chairman Arafat to Camp David in summer 2000. Removed from the media spotlight, he attempted to resolve the outstanding issues: borders, settlements, refugees, and East Jerusalem. Conceding what no Israeli leader had yielded previously, Barak offered Arafat a Palestinian state with a capital in the Jerusalem suburbs, some local control in Arab districts of the city, and possibly international sovereignty over the Muslim Holy Places (the Haram al-Sharif). A small number of refugees would be reunited with families in Israel.

This offer defied the almost universal Israeli desire for a united Jerusalem. It outraged the settlers, *Likud,* and most religious parties. Vague talk of treason and assassination prompted increased security for the prime minister. But Yasir Arafat rejected the proposal because it failed to meet one minimum Palestinian demand: Arab sovereignty for Arab Jerusalem. (This outright rejection was a grave practical mistake. Immense suffering and thousands of dead since then have failed to produce so favorable an offer.) On his return, Barak resigned, forcing an election only for the office of prime minister.

Likud's nominee was the portly party leader, General Ariel Sharon. Sharon's aggressive career had contributed to the deaths of many Arab civilians, and his widely publicized visit to the Haram al-Sharif in September 2000, asserting that the Temple Mount was not negotiable, had set ablaze passions already very hot. A new *intifada* broke out, this one much more violent. Without a proposed peace agreement, the election failed to offer voters a referendum on peace. Instead, it focused on personalities and approaches

Ariel Sharon Dominates Politics

After his 2001 landslide victory (62%), Sharon formed a government of national unity, including *Labor* leaders in sensitive positions (Shimon Peres, foreign ministry; Binyamin Ben-Eliezer, defense).

The new *intifada* brought the Oslo peace process to collapse, and violence escalated on both sides. In response to terror attacks, Israeli troops surrounded Palestinian-controlled areas, blocked travel and trade, and squeezed them economically. Targeted assassinations killed dozens of alleged terrorist leaders, and often innocent bystanders. Palestinian security forces became frequent targets. Yasir Arafat was limited to the city of Ramallah, then, after renewed Israeli occupation of much of the West Bank, to two rooms in his headquarters (see Palestine), until Israeli troops withdrew under U.S. pressure.

American, Egyptian, European and other mediators vainly tried to calm the crisis, but found themselves blocked by the interplay of Palestinian attacks and Israeli intransigence. Sharon's cabinet refused to talk peace during violence, and demanded seven days of calm before opening talks or implementing peace proposals. But Sharon excluded from "violence" Israeli assassinations of Palestinian leaders. Historians may well conclude that Prime Minister Sharon bore significant responsibility for the hostilities; at least since 1982, he had carried a personal grudge against Yasir Arafat. Sharon gave Israeli troops great freedom to attack Palestinian suspects, and eyewitnesses claimed the killing of men and boys sleeping or otherwise unarmed. Nevertheless, Sharon frequently faced harsh right-wing critics whose solutions often included ethnic cleansing.

Objectively, Sharon had promised peace, but blood flowed in Jewish streets. The economy had nosedived into recession, and 20% of the population lived in poverty. A poll found that most Israelis felt they had never had it so bad. Serious cuts in government services were likely. Media accounts of financial sleaze reached all the way up to Sharon himself, for past violations of campaign finance laws.

Nevertheless, Sharon and the *Likud* easily won the 2003 elections, while the left-wing of Israeli politics—*Meretz,* and *Labor*

Former Prime Minister Ehud Olmert

itself—fell badly, as did *Shas*. *Likud* almost doubled its seats in the Knesset. Clearly, Israelis had reacted to the suicide bombings by blaming *Hamas* and other Palestinians, not the grandfatherly general who was doing as well as anyone could expect. Many Israelis deserted the parties inclined to compromise for peace.

The Roadmap, Gaza, and Kadima

Peace gained further importance because of a "roadmap" developed by the U.S., the UN, the European Union, and Russia. Backing a two-state solution, the roadmap proposed a provisional Palestinian entity by 2003 and a complete agreement by 2005. The roadmap reflected Israeli and American rejection of Yasir Arafat as a trustworthy Palestinian leader, but it clearly accepted a Palestinian state. This dismayed many settlers, other right-wing Israelis, and their American fundamentalist supporters, whose typical solution is an ethnic cleansing of Judea and Samaria by removing all Palestinians to Jordan. Despite their warnings, President Bush backed the roadmap. Prime Minister Sharon initially refused to accept the plan, but eventually his cabinet bowed to foreign pressure and did so—by a narrow majority, with 14 reservations.

The roadmap's first steps included, on the Israeli side, withdrawal from the recently occupied towns and cities, a halt to settlement activity, and the dismantling of illegal (by Israeli definition) and some legal settlements to permit contiguous Palestinian areas. For their part, the Palestinians needed to achieve political reform (including elections) and end the violence.

Ariel Sharon had always backed Jewish settlements. For decades his vision of a Palestinian state had been Arabs densely packed into several small clusters with municipal self-government but not much else,

divided from each other by corridors of Israeli roads and military posts. Sharon's approval of the roadmap was likely a momentary acquiescence to be followed by later obstruction. Certainly, he remained committed to building homes in West Bank settlements, despite U.S. objections.

Nevertheless, Sharon's ideology split from the hardliners because he recognized that the Arab population of Gaza was too dense and crowded for Jewish settlements to succeed, while the price for holding Gaza was continuing casualties. Moreover, *Sharon realized the impossibility of Israel's long-term control of Palestinian cities.* As he told the UN General Assembly in 2005, "The Palestinians will always be our neighbors. We respect them and don't aspire to rule over them. They also deserve freedom and a sovereign national entity in their own country."

His solution was to withdraw from the entire Gaza Strip, unilaterally, and for good measure, also from four unofficial West Bank settlements. The roadmap was incidental: other settlements would remain. Most Israelis backed the withdrawal, but, the settlement movement bitterly attacked it, and their vigorous campaign led *Likud* to reject it. The prime minister won cabinet approval for a modified plan, but his coalition frayed.

The Gaza plan represented a one-sided solution to the Israeli-Palestinian conflict. Its logical outcome was not a negotiated permanent peace, but an Israel beyond Palestinian violence, leaving the Palestinians to live in poverty and, if they were inclined, anarchy. The same philosophy motivated construction of a 300-mile long barrier to separate the Arab West Bank

from Israel—comfortably encircling major Jewish enclaves at Palestinian expense. It cuts off considerable Arab land (one estimate exceeds 40% of the West Bank) and some homes. UN reports condemned it and the International Court of Justice, in an advisory opinion, claimed it illegal. In 2005, the Israeli Supreme Court ordered a review of some small sections.

To deter any boasts that Israel had been forced out of Gaza, as had been claimed for South Lebanon, IDF raids destroyed the infrastructure and workshops of *Hamas* and the *Islamic Jihad*. An invasion of the Jabaliya camp in northern Gaza killed more than 100 Palestinians. Success for a unilateral withdrawal also meant the targeted assassination of extremist leaders, most prominently Sheikh Ahmad Yassin, the so-called "spiritual leader" of *Hamas* and its unifying figure.

Strengthened by these military successes, and by polls showing a majority of popular support, Sharon rejected demands for a national referendum. When *Likud* cabinet ministers failed to approve the withdrawal, he dismissed them. With his right-wing coalition in tatters, he invited *Labor* to join a national unity government.

On schedule in 2005, Israeli troops smoothly removed the 8,500 settlers who clung to the 21 small colonies of Gaza. Building on success, Sharon overturned the political landscape by abandoning *Likud* and forming a new, centrist party, *Kadima* ("Forward"). A veritable tidal wave of leading politicians, including Shimon Peres, abandoned their parties and joined *Kadima*, destroying decades-old political and social boundaries. Competitors fumed that *Kadima* lacked ideology and

Bitterness and frustration: Palestinian youths defy the Israeli army

Israel

apparent insignificance, with about 10% of the vote, similar to the Russian émigrés' hardline *Israel Beiteinu* and *Shas.* Within weeks, Ehud Olmert negotiated a coalition with *Labor, Shas,* and the *Pensioners' Party.* However, Olmert's honeymoon with the public appeared on the wane. Press commentaries savaged several appointments, and noted the lack of military experience in a cabinet determined to draw the nation's boundaries. One opinion poll suggested half the population had misgivings about the new prime minister.

The War with Hizbullah, 2006

Hizbullah guerillas crossed the Lebanese-Israeli border in July 2006, attacked an isolated patrol, and captured two Israeli soldiers. The raid apparently sought hostages for bargaining and to embarrass Israel's newly-formed cabinet. The Olmert cabinet, determined to rescue the captives, escalated its response to the raid into a war to destroy *Hizbullah.* The IDF attacked *Hizbullah's* military positions, and bombed widely: the party's political offices, its television station in Beirut, and even the home of its leader. If the outside world considered this harsh, it was expected. However, Israel also targeted non-*Hizbullah*-Lebanon: Beirut's airport, vital road bridges, gasoline service stations, factories, and road traffic far from battlefields.

Hizbullah responded by launching missiles—several thousand—far deeper into Israel than ever before. They reached Haifa and most of northern Israel; some Israelis temporarily moved to safer regions. It also fought the poorly-executed Israeli ground assault well enough to boast, eventually, of divine victory in a conflict whose human cost was heavy for Israel (40 civilians, 112 military personnel). The fighting finally ended when the Security Council established a ceasefire (see Lebanon: history).

The Israeli public quickly concluded that the war had been bungled by an incompetent cabinet and military. Commissions investigated the failures, and resignations followed, including those of the chief of staff, and of *Labor's* Amir Peretz, who, though inexperienced at military command in a nation of veterans, had been appointed minister of defense. Once again, Binyamin Netanyahu emerged as Israel's most popular politician, and *Labor* selected Ehud Barak as its new leader.

Combined with missile attacks on southern Israeli towns from Gaza, the war led many Israelis to question the very possibility of a two-state solution. After all, *Hamas* and *Islamic Jihad* on the southern border and *Hizbullah* along the north rejected Israel's very right to exist. Will any Israeli borders ever achieve moral significance to them?

was dominated by one man. Regardless, with elections approaching, it took a great lead in the polls.

Months before the 2006 elections, a massive stroke struck the 77-year-old prime minister. The shocked nation compared Sharon's fate with the assassination of Yitzhak Rabin a decade earlier. Once again, a traditionally hawkish leader was struck down on the verge of dramatic actions for peace. Some radical settlers quietly gave God the credit for both incidents.

As deputy prime minister, Ehud Olmert assumed control of both the government and the party. Pledging to draw the final borders by 2010, he maintained *Kadima's* unity and rallied the nation around Sharon's legacy. The other parties fared less well. Though he won the *Likud* leadership, Netanyahu failed with the electorate, who remembered his vacillation over Gaza, because he had clung to his cabinet post until just before the withdrawal. Centrist and secular, *Shinui* even lost its founder to *Kadima.* Only *Labor,* under the Moroccan-born Amir Peretz, managed to present a thoughtful campaign, concentrating on domestic issues.

Kadima won 29 seats, and became the Knesset's largest party. *Likud* tumbled to

Despite the war and the resulting political crises, life in Israel continued its patterns. Until the world recession of 2008, the stock market held its value remarkably well, and the economy continued to grow. The United States committed another $30 billion in military assistance over ten years.

Cultural conflicts also continued. Rabbi Ovadia Yossef, spiritual leader of *Shas*, said God helped soldiers when they "believe and pray" and they did not get killed. In fact, many observant soldiers had been killed in 2006, and linking of military deaths to secularism stoked another round in the culture wars. At the behest of religious conservatives, the national bus company, Egged, designated "modesty buses" that separated the men (in the front) from women (to the rear, of course).

Olmert Stumbles, Launches Gaza War

A man with an appreciation of luxuries, Ehud Olmert over the years received funds from questionable sources. By 2008 he had been investigated several times before charges were dropped. However, the court testimony of an American businessman, Morris Talansky, that he had passed envelopes stuffed with cash for the prime minister's political campaigns threatened the ruling coalition. Polls indicated that nearly 70% of Israelis desired Olmert to step down. Minister of Defense Ehud Barak threatened to pull *Labor* from the cabinet. The foreign minister, Tzipi Livni, *Kadima's* deputy leader, called for a party primary to select its leader. Olmert agreed to go, but remained in office pending Knesset elections in early 2009. National

security issues dominated his last months in office.

After *Hamas* gunmen gained control of Gaza in 2007, the territory provided a base for missile and other attacks on Israel, but lacked a government willing to negotiate with Israel, or that Israel could recognize. The simple, home-made Qassam missiles fired by *Hamas* and *Islamic Jihad* at the closest town, Sderot, and the city of Ashkelon did not constitute a strategic threat, but they inflicted casualties. They also posed the eventual risk of longer-range missiles with larger warheads. Ariel Sharon's entire policy of disengagement/unilateral withdrawal collapsed.

In response, the Olmert cabinet declared the Gaza Strip a "hostile entity," and to pressure *Hamas* to halt the attacks, it restricted deliveries of fuel, electricity, and almost all supplies, eventually including food. This effectively crushed the territory's economic life. Virtually the entire population came to subsist on international assistance (see Palestine: history). A truce negotiated in mid-2008 reduced the rocket fire significantly, but the border blockade remained. The truce broke down in response to an Israeli attack on an alleged tunnel from Gaza into Israel, and was not renewed.

Striking by surprise in December 2008, the Israeli air force opened the Gaza War when it attacked Gaza, demolishing *Hamas* militia bases, rocket launching sites, police facilities, and government offices. Civilian locations were also targeted—homes, mosques, hospitals, schools and others, on grounds they were used by *Hamas* fighters or stored weapons. After a week of aerial bombardment, the Israeli army invaded

Former Prime Minister Sharon

the Strip, eventually entering parts of the city of Gaza itself.

After three weeks of fighting, Prime Minister Olmert declared a unilateral ceasefire and promised a withdrawal from the Strip if rocket attacks ended. With the Gaza Strip bisected and most Palestinian population centers surrounded, the major objectives had evidently been achieved. Soon after, *Hamas* also ended its major hostilities, though in the months following some rockets were fired at Israeli towns.

The Gaza War was planned months before the pretext for launching it, and its major goal was to deter possible future attacks by any enemy, by demonstrating the power and effectiveness of the military's response. Despite *Hamas* claims, this was largely achieved, as evidenced by the vastly different casualties suffered by each side. Although precision weapons were often used by the Israeli forces, the fighting claimed the lives of hundreds of *Hamas* combatants as well as hundreds of civilians. By contrast, just three Israeli civilians and 10 soldiers were killed. Critics claimed that Israel had committed war crimes, including the disproportionate use of force, and the U.N. Human Rights Council demanded a credible investigation of charges of war crimes. However, disproportionate force is fundamental to an effective deterrence.

Netanyahu's Isolation and the Flotilla Attack

More than most wars, the Gaza invasion was scheduled by politics. To maintain good relations with the United States, it needed to end before the inauguration of President Obama. With Knesset elections scheduled for early 2009, it also needed to impress public opinion with the abilities of the cabinet, two of whose

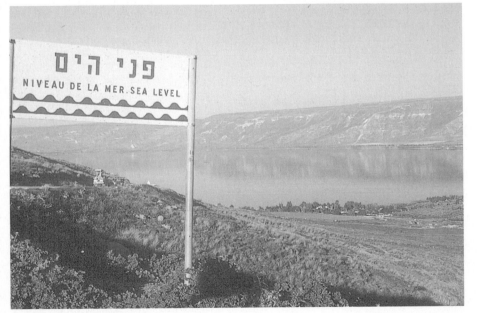

View of the Sea of Galilee

Photo by Eugenia Elseth

THE JERUSALEM POST

VOLUME LXIII, NUMBER 19216 • MONDAY, MARCH 4, 1996 • ADAR 13, 5756 • SHAWAL 14, 1416 • NIS 4.20 (EILAT NIS 3.60)

Hamas suicide bomber kills 18 in Jerusalem

Peres: We are at war with Hamas

BILL HUTMAN

PRIME Minister Shimon Peres declared that Israel is at war with Hamas, following yesterday's deadly suicide bus attack in Jerusalem.

A Hamas suicide bomber blew up a No. 18 Egged bus on Jaffa Road in Jerusalem yesterday morning, killing 18 and seriously wounding seven, exactly a week after another suicide bomber took 25 lives on the same line.

An angry Peres listed new security measures to be enacted, and declared his commitment to "separation" between Israeli and Palestinian peoples. (See story below).

The bomb was similar to the ones used in last week's attacks in Jerusalem and Ashkelon, a senior police source said.

"The evidence points to the same hand being involved in all the attacks," the source said. In all the attacks, 15 kg.-20 kg. of TNT were used and metal scraps, in

Security and medical personnel run for help immediately following yesterday's deadly bus bombing.   (Brian Hendler)

Bodies were flung into the air, and glass flew everywhere," he said.

"The rescue work was finished within minutes," Amit said. "It's sad to have to say that we have become experts in dealing with this type of event."

Light rain began to fall after the injured had already been evacuated, and did not appear to affect the police work.

Several police officers commented that the location of the attack, even if coincidental, near the police station and City Hall, made it that much more enraging.

Prime Minister Shimon Peres came to the scene about two hours after the attack to see the devastation first-hand. There were a few anti-government calls from the crowd during the short briefing Peres received from Amit and Inspector-General Assaf Hefetz.

Amit and Hefetz later met with Peres at the Prime Minister's Office, where they discussed the government's planned security moves, including beefing up police and army presence in the capital.

There were brief pushing and shoving matches between police and the crowd of several hundreds onlookers, including many who openly expressed their outrage by chanting "Death to Arabs," and "Peres go home."

Amit said police were bracing for demonstrations and possible attempts by Jewish extremists to carry out revenge attacks on Arabs. Dozens of protesters chanting "Death to Arabs" rushed toward the Old City in the afternoon, but were halted by police.

Mayor Ehud Olmert called for restraint from the crowd. "I understand that people are angry, but this type of behavior is not helpful at this time. It only makes the work of the security forces

---

members, Tzipi Livni (foreign minister, *Kadima*) and Ehud Barak (defense minister, *Labor*) were their party candidates for prime minister. However, the war failed to bring this political victory. Instead, although *Kadima* finished ahead of *Likud* by one seat, the greatest political beneficiaries of fighting were the more extreme right-wing parties whose nationalism opposes any Palestinian state (see table).

With effort, Binyamin Netanyahu of *Likud* formed a coalition with *Yisrael Beiteinu*, *Shas*, smaller right-wing partners,

and *Labor*. The most contentious appointment is probably Avigdor Lieberman of *Yisrael Beiteinu* as foreign minister. He rejected U.S. calls for a halt to the growth of settlements and his hard line on negotiations with the Palestinians implied difficulties with the Obama administration and the E.U. Meanwhile, within the country his party's electoral slogan, "No loyalty, no citizenship," heightened tensions over the Arab minority.

Prime Minister Netanyahu himself deftly attempted to deflect U.S. demands

for a two-state solution by announcing his support for a demilitarized Palestinian state. However, words were not enough: embarrassed by the announcement of new settlement housing during the visit of Vice President Biden, the U.S. demanded a real halt to settlements, including in East Jerusalem. While Netanyahu did halt new home construction, he also announced that the freeze was temporary, and did not apply to municipal buildings and the 3,000 homes already under construction. This avoided the need for the cabinet to take hard choices.

A new twist to the Palestinian crisis occurred in 2010 when Israeli commandos seized the *Mavi Marmara*, a Turkish ferry used by pro-Palestinian human rights activists to challenge the blockade of Gaza by attempting to deliver supplies of cement, paper and water purification tablets. The commandoes boarded the vessel in international waters, in the process killing nine Turkish citizens.

World opinion overwhelmingly condemned the operation, which brought far more attention to the plight of Gaza than any Palestinian public relations campaign had ever done. Enraged by "state terrorism" against its vessel and the killing of its civilians, the Turkish government halted

---

The Knesset Political Spectrum, 2009

4	*Hadash*	far left, mixed Arab, Jewish
3	*Meretz*	left-of-center
13	*Labor*	center-left
28	*Kadima*	center
27	*Likud*	center-right
11	*Shas*	populist; religious—Sephardic
15	*Yisrael Beiteinu*	far right nationalist
4	*National Union*	far right nationalist
5	*United Torah Judaism*	religious—ultra-Orthodox
3	*Jewish Home*	religious Zionism
4	*United Arab List*	Arab nationalist
4	*Balad*	Arab nationalist

President Shimon Peres

Prime Minister Binyamin Netanyahu

military cooperation with Israel. Very likely, the raid will cost Israel its one allied Muslim state and weaken other relations. Embarrassed by attention to its own blockade of Gaza, Egypt permitted individuals to cross the border. President Obama called the plight of Gaza unsustainable.

The embargo was imposed, with broad initial support in the West, to block weapons from reaching terrorists. It served to pressure the *Hamas* administration in Gaza, and was maintained partly to secure Gilad Shalit's release after the soldier's capture in 2006. However, widespread smuggling through the tunnels provided Gaza's militants with some weapons, and its rich with cars and consumer goods. The suffering population could hardly remove their *Hamas* rulers, and Shalit's release very likely hinges on an exchange for Palestinians held by Israel.

In the face of demands for an international inquiry, Israel appointed its own commission, but limited its scope. It relaxed the embargo on items such as food, clothing, and toys, and also announced that supplies for UN agencies would be permitted.

Israel found itself isolated by the 2010 conference of the nearly 200 nations who have signed the Nuclear Non-Proliferation Treaty (NPT), because it likely maintains a nuclear arsenal and has not signed the NPT. By calling for a 2012 conference on nuclear activities in the Middle East, the conference also focused future attention on the issues. As an added insult, the conference report did not mention Iran's nuclear enrichment program, widely-suspected of preparing materials for nuclear weapons.

Prime Minister Netanyahu's greatest security concern has been Iran's uranium enrichment program, given its potential for nuclear weapons. A successful military strike could delay or even remove the threat, and also strengthen regional respect for Israel's military prowess. However, it would also isolate Israel further.

Culture: As the Zionist settlers of the pre-independence period were mainly Europeans, their culture has tended to dominate, with attempts to Europeanize the later waves of immigrants from Persian, Afghani, Kurdish, Yemeni, Iraqi or North African backgrounds. These Sephardic Jews now outnumber European Jews, and they increasingly assert their own cultural values.

Israel in fact enjoys cultural diversity as great as that found anywhere, because its people have come from the symbolic four corners of the world. Approximately half of all Israelis were born in some other land, and they brought a variety of cultures with them. Though Jews, they neither act alike, nor think alike, nor look alike, though most now wear European style clothes.

The non-Jewish minorities are almost entirely Arabic-speaking and comprise about 750,000 Muslims, 150,000 Christians and 60,000 Druze (see Lebanon: Culture). In general these minorities suffer lower standards of living, and receive less education. One recent study found 48% of Israeli Arab families living below the poverty level, and the high school drop out rate 50%. However, there was not much benefit to remaining in school: in one sample, educated Arabs suffered 33% unemployment.

The complex educational system includes both state and private schools, but even the private schools are partly subsidized and controlled by the government. Within the state schools there are three systems: secular, religious, and Arabic-speaking. Secondary schools receive no direct public financing, but the government helps pay the fees for qualified students on the basis of need.

Of the several institutions of higher learning, the oldest and most prestigious is the Hebrew University of Jerusalem. Many faculty members have been educated in Europe or North America, and there is significant interchange with universities on those continents. In terms of its research accomplishments, publications, and student quality, the university outranks all others in the Middle East. However, between 2001 and 2005, the Israeli government cut its funds to higher education by about 15%, leading to student strikes supported by academic administrators who feared that further cuts could cause the system to collapse. Strikes by professors and others marred the 2007–08 academic year.

At independence, Orthodox Judaism became the established religion of the state. Today a minority of Israeli Jews adhere to this branch of Judaism. Many Jews consider themselves secular, or worship at Reform synagogues, but the fastest growing congregations are the ultra-Orthodox. Differences between members of these groups have led to intellectual disputes, sometimes labeled culture wars. At one extreme, a secular Jew might regard anyone as a Jew who considers himself or herself such, even though an atheist. In contrast, many Orthodox and ultra-Orthodox hold secular Jews responsible for the loss of Jews through assimilation in other societies. A few consider this a loss to Jewry equivalent in numbers to the Holocaust.

Lifestyle issues also divide society, and sectarian tensions have escalated dramatically in recent years, with antagonisms ranging from cultural events to advertising regarded as immoral. Fans of specific soccer teams, for example, often share common religious and political perspectives. Sabbath observance by public transportation and industry is a heated point of conflict: buses stop, and stores close in Orthodox areas. Marriage often involves conflicts as well, because only Orthodox weddings are legally binding. Many secular couples must therefore submit to Orthodox rituals they find sexist—or marry elsewhere. Each year, over 25% of all Jewish couples who marry do so outside Israel, often in Cyprus.

Disputes over religion extend to immigration law. Ultra-Orthodox groups have sought to amend the "Law of Return" to exclude converts according to Reform, Conservative and Reconstructionist Judaism. But some 90% of American Jews belong to these groups, and such a law would reflect badly on their rabbis.

Israel

In recent years, most immigrants have come from Russia, after the U.S., the other Jewish population center outside Israel. While valuable in boosting the non-Arab population, many Russian immigrants come from mixed backgrounds, and their spouses may even claim Christianity.

In the first decades of Israeli statehood, reported crimes were relatively few, a feature of citizens bonded together by the experiences of the Holocaust and winning independence. Zionism unified diverse populations, and the socialist ideology minimized differences of wealth and income among the population. Concern with morality even delayed the introduction of television to Israel.

As Israeli society matured, individualism played a greater role, and distinctions grew between economic classes. Against this background, and in common with many other developed societies, the crime rate began to rise. Reaching on occasion from high government officials to youths from the less prosperous *Sephardic* Jewish and Arab communities, the criminal acts range primarily from fraud and corruption to burglary. In addition, the occupied territories continue to witness high levels of crime, including murder, often between Israeli settlers and Arabs.

Economy: During the first two decades of its existence, Israel enjoyed one of the fastest rates of economic growth of any country, despite insignificant oil, natural gas, and coal deposits. Following a basically socialist pattern, the government established new towns for immigrants and subsidized worthy essentials like bread

and milk. Extensive medical care and other benefits came through the widespread system of labor unions. Some of the highest taxes in the world accompanied these social advantages, with rates as high as 70% on upper middle class income. Not surprisingly, budget deficits, inflation, and trade deficits accompanied the rapid growth.

By the late 1970s it became clear that economic development faced increasing difficulties despite massive U.S. aid amounting to nearly $1,000 per citizen. A 1988 Israeli study termed the economy a "relic" incapable of supporting national defense or attracting immigrants. Personal income hardly grew after allowing for inflation and population growth. With a trade deficit almost twice as large per person as the United States, a $26 billion foreign debt, historically high unemployment and short-term interest rates exceeding 20% after adjusting for inflation, in the later 1980s Israel suffered net emigration until the influx of Soviet Jews.

A number of causes contributed to the economic difficulties. Besides the heavy defense burden (10% of GNP), economists blamed the marriage between socialism and Zionism that produced a bloated bureaucracy, government regulations, and heavy taxation. To some extent, too, the high unemployment and low growth rates resulted from the successful fight against inflation. After it exceeded 400% annually, Israelis ceased using their own currency for most business activity. Government policies then successfully cut it to about 20%, aided by additional U.S. grants and the drop in world oil prices. However, the

bloated bureaucracy remained largely unchanged. The large budget deficit continued despite high taxes, and only a few failing non-profit companies were forced to close.

The government and labor unions own major portions of the economy. By 1985 the 192 state-owned firms employed 65,000 workers, and produced a significant portion of the country's total output. The largest industrial conglomerate, Koor Industries, is owned by the labor federation *Histadrut*, and another major source of manufactured goods is the collectively-owned farms (*kibbutzim*). Typically, then, about one-third of business value comes from non-profit sources. In 1995 the government began to privatize *El Al*, the nation's airline, 13 years after it faced bankruptcy. In 2007 privatization was still continuing.

International Trade

Two international developments in the mid-1990s offered greater opportunities for the Israeli economy. First, the Arab boycott of companies doing business with Israel, a form of secondary boycott illegal in many countries, shuffled towards final collapse when the Gulf States abandoned the boycott. Second, the Free Trade Agreement between the United States and Israel came into full effect in 1995, and included Israeli agricultural products excluded by the Free Trade Agreement with the European Union.

Agricultural output has expanded enormously since 1948. The introduction of new crops, chemical fertilizers and irrigation systems increased production more than 500%. Sparse grazing lands turned into farms, thanks to irrigation from the Jordan River and the most advanced dry-climate agricultural cultivation methods. Israel imports basic foodstuffs, including beef, but exports high-value and out-of-season fruits and vegetables to Europe and even the U.S.

For a small country, Israel produces a wide variety of industrial products, from simple furniture to cut diamonds to satellites. The armament and related service industries employ over 10% of the national workforce, and produce a leading category of exports. These have included guided missiles, artillery, and fighter aircraft as well as the most famous, the Uzi submachine gun. Customers range from the United States to Taiwan, South Africa, and a number of Latin American nations. Israel Aircraft Industries had hoped to become a major producer of high-technology fighters, but financing failed, and the pride of the aviation industry is now the Arrow anti-ballistic missile system developed with U.S. assistance and technology.

Panoramic view of Tel Aviv

Courtesy: Embassy of Israel

Another noteworthy product is the Phalcon battle management system that will fit inside a large military transport aircraft. Because the system was developed without U.S. assistance, unlike the Arrow it may be sold without American permission, as it was to India. However, Israel heeded U.S. pressures not to sell Phalcon to China, because of its possible use in battle against Taiwan. Despite such complications, and the bankruptcy in 2005 of Israel Military Industries, the producer of the Uzi, Israel typically ranks as the world's fifth largest arms exporter.

In the 1990s, Israel's talented and highly educated workforce proved particularly adept at high technology, particularly computer software. Hundreds of startup companies worked with U.S. firms and made the country one of the world's centers for innovation in computing.

Another prominent industry in terms of foreign exchange earnings is tourism. Jerusalem contains the holiest shrines for both Jews and Christian pilgrims. Numerous Biblical and historical sites elsewhere also attract visitors, and there are beaches and other attractions both scenic and cultural. Understandably, tourist arrivals suffer from fears of terrorist attacks, and the Gulf War discouraged tourists whose idea of pleasure did not include gas masks. Tourism fared better with the peace treaties, however, and reached 2.7 million visitors in the year 2000. By the following year, many hotel rooms were empty again, a byproduct of the renewed *intifada*.

Given its outstanding—and growing—scientific and technical talent, its pioneering research in desert agriculture, and the enterprising nature of its people, Israel retains the promise of prosperity. However, as they have ever since independence, two major difficulties stand in the way. First, government regulations now appear as some of the most bothersome outside the Less Developed Countries. Second, a ceasefire without peace diverts too many resources to military use.

The Future: Four issues will dominate headlines short-term. First, U.S. President Barack Obama opposes settlement growth and seems determined to work for a two-state solution. Balance towards the region might replace intimacy with Israel as the major U.S. outlook.

Second, Prime Minister Netanyahu's allies desire a successful military strike against Iran's nuclear program. The political turmoil following Iran's 2009 election suggests President Ahmadinejad desires a foreign enemy to unite his divided country. It is unclear how Israel should react.

Third, the major issue remains "what to do with the Palestinians?" The time bomb ticks: this decade Arabs will likely exceed 50% of the population inside the boundaries Israel now controls. It seems impossible to deny them democracy in perpetuity, despite the arguments from far-right Israelis and their sympathizers that military force will achieve Arab submission.

There are few options. Right-wing extremists advocate ethnic cleansing to achieve a Jewish-only state between the sea and the Jordan River. But population removal by force is a crime against humanity, so seems impossible. Without it, a single-state solution would deny the essence of Zionism, the creation of a Jewish state.

The favored international response, a largely-Jewish Israel living beside a Palestinian state, seemed possible in the 1990s after the Oslo Agreement. However, it has been weakened by Palestinian militancy, the ascendancy of *Hamas* and its rejection of any permanent peace with Israel, and the "facts on the ground" created by Jewish settlements in the West Bank.

Is peace even possible? Perhaps not. Israeli public opinion clings to existing settlements. A Jewish civil war would result from an attempt to close them. Contrary to the Bush-era "roadmap," politicians plan their expansion even into areas regarded by the U.S. as logically Arab land. But the question may fairly be asked: is there a legitimate Palestinian organization with a desire for a peaceful, two-state solution and with the authority to govern?

For the short-run, expect the Cyprus model: a conflict without a solution. To quote Foreign Minister Lieberman, "We will not be able to reach agreement on core and emotional subjects like Jerusalem and the right of return of Palestinian refugees." Those who think agreement possible "do not understand reality and are sowing illusions." However, nature abhors a vacuum, and unlike Cyprus, the two populations are not separate, self-governing, and protected by national armies. International realities will likely force the U.S. to attempt negotiations.

Palestinians are not the only demographic time-bomb. The growing ultra-orthodox, or Haredim, community seeks to contribute to the non-material, spiritual vibrancy of the country. But its young men are not subject to the draft, its parents oppose their daughters being schooled with Sephardic girls, and many men receive welfare as they study rather than earn a living. In effect, the Haredim seek benefits from wider Israeli society without contributing proportionally to it. The time is coming when, to quote demographer Mencahem Friedman, either the Haredim will have to change their ways or "the government will force them" to contribute more to the economy and defense.

The Knesset through Palombo Gate

The Hashemite Kingdom of Jordan

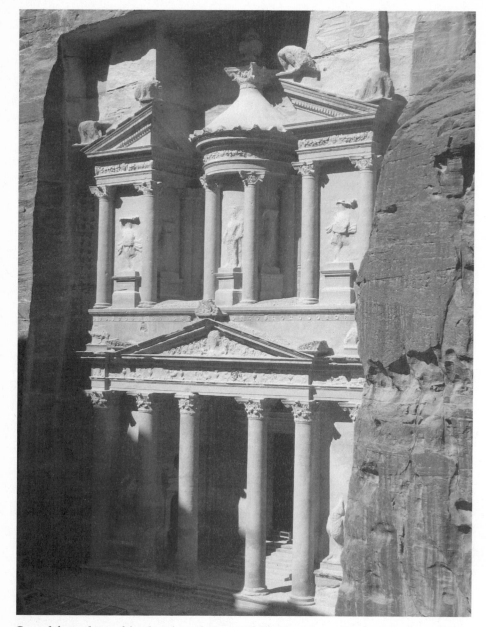

Carved from the multi-colored sandstone cliff, the Treasury at Petra symbolizes the ancient Nabataean center of trade and wealth. It creates a dramatic impression on visitors emerging from the long, narrow entrance gorge known as the Siq.   photo by the author

Area: 34,495 square miles (89,342 sq. km.).
Population: 6.1 million.
Capital City: Amman (pop. 2.6 million)
Climate: Hot and dry in the summer, but winter can be cold with moderate rain and even snow in the northwest. The Jordan Valley and Aqaba area are warmer. The eastern and southern regions are desert.
Neighboring Countries: Syria (North); Iraq (Northeast); Saudi Arabia (Southeast); Israel and Occupied Territories (West).
Time Zone: GMT +2. When it is noon Pacific Standard Time it is 10:00 P.M. in Jordan.

Official Language: Arabic.
Other Principal Language: English is widely used.
Ethnic Background: Arab except for small Circassian communities; a majority originally Palestinian.
Principal Religion: Sunni Islam (about 91%) and Christianity.
Chief Commercial Products: Phosphate, olive oil, tomatoes, wheat, barley, figs, lentils, tobacco, sheepskins, hides, cement, salt and refined petroleum products.
Major Trading Partners: Saudi Arabia, U.S., Germany, Iraq, Japan, U.K., Syria and India.

Currency: One Jordanian Dinar = 100 piasters.
Former Colonial Status: Under British control (1918–1946).
Independence Day: May 25, 1946.
Chief of State: Abdullah II (Abdullah ibn Hussein al-Hashimi), King.
Head of Government: Sami al-Rifai, Prime Minister (2009).
National Flag: Three horizontal stripes of black, white and green and a red triangle at the pole bearing a white seven-pointed star.
Gross Domestic Product: $24 billion (current prices); $35 billion (Purchasing Power Parity), 2008
GDP per capita: $5,800 (PPP), 2008.

The borders of Jordan, like those of many other countries drafted by colonial powers, often fail to reflect either natural features or differences in populations. In the years immediately following World War I, the boundaries were drawn to suit British policy, and they have been modified little since. The country takes its name from the Jordan River, which with its tributary, the Yarmuk, is the only real river in the area, and provides the only natural boundary.

The Jordan River, deprived of an estimated 95% its fresh water by diversions, is only a small stream when it empties into the salty Dead Sea, the lowest body of water on earth. Its surface lies more than 1,300 feet below sea level. Because the Jordan's scanty flow falls short of the very rapid evaporation caused by the heat and solar rays in the depression, the Dead Sea is drying up. About 50 miles long from north to south just a generation ago, as shown on the map, it has lost the southern third. However, the sea will not quickly disappear: its maximum depth reaches about 1,300 feet. The salt concentration is almost ten times that of ordinary sea water. This great density allows bathers to float easily and in fact to read the newspaper while sitting afloat, but they suffer stings at every scratch on their skin.

Immediately east of the Jordan Valley the land rises steeply to the edge of a high plateau. The strip along the edge of the plateau, wider in the north, receives moderate rainfall (about 25 inches annually). As the plateau drops in elevation to the east and south, rainfall diminishes rapidly to nothing. Only the hardiest *badu* nomads wander out into that area in search of a livelihood.

Amman, the capital of the country, lies on the plateau, spread onto the sides of several converging valleys. In 1925 only a small Circassian village built among the ruins of ancient Roman Philadelphia, Amman has grown into a large, modern, and fairly comfortable city.

102

The Royal Family of King Abdullah II

History: Although the high plateau was farmed extensively during the Roman and Byzantine eras, and Umayyad caliphs built palaces in the desert, for most of the last thousand years Bedouins dominated the country. During the 19th century, settlement increased, as did Ottoman control, and the Hijaz railroad was built through the territory from Damascus to Medina a decade before World War I. During that conflict, the troops and Bedouin allies of the Arab Revolt fought against the Ottoman forces along the railroad, and the port of Aqaba became the first important Arab conquest outside the Hijaz. Under Emir Faisal, and supported by British supplies and advisors such as T.E. Lawrence (Lawrence of Arabia), the Arab forces used their mastery of the desert to outflank the Ottoman forces, tying down large numbers of them in garrison duties.

After the war, Jordan fell under Arab rule from Damascus, and thus in 1920 part of Faisal's Kingdom of Syria. However, French forces soon marched on Damascus, ousted Faisal, and subjected Syria to the French mandate. Jordan, though the southern portion of Syria, lay in territory that by Anglo-French agreement fell under British influence. Hence France did not occupy it. Several weeks later, Faisal's brother Abdullah arrived in Amman from the Hijaz, hoping to regain all Syria for Arab rule, but only minor raids took place against the French.

Acting on the wishes of Britain and France, the League of Nations granted Britain control over the territory within the Palestine Mandate (the term "Jordan" then referred only to the river and valley). However, conditions contrasted greatly between the two banks of the Jordan River. The western territory had cities and towns, settled farmers, and Zionist immigrants.

The East Bank resembled a frontier society. There were no cities, a mere scattering of towns, and only the skeleton of modern government. Tribes of nomads and semi-nomads raided each other and the few settled farmers. For the practical reason that Abdullah already ruled the area as Faisal's replacement and as a reward for his family's alliance, Britain formed the Emirate of Transjordan for Abdullah. Claiming descent from the Prophet Muhammad's family, and thus a Hashemite, Abdullah eventually gave his family name to the state.

Aside from settled areas around the towns of al-Karak, al-Salt, Ajlun and Irbid, nomadism remained the dominant way of life. Abdullah selected Amman as his capital. An impressive city in ancient times, it was located on the Hijaz Railway, and a few Circassian refugees from Russian expansion in the Caucasus had settled nearby. During the 1920s Emir Abdullah attempted to establish law and order, protect the frontier, settle nomadic tribes, and undertake the beginnings of modern government.

The military, known as the Arab Legion, became the instrument that brought order to the countryside. Composed of Arab soldiers with British officers, during World War II it also fought for the Allies in Syria and Iraq. As the Emir's government showed more competence, the treaty with Britain was revised several times, each revision giving his officials more authority. Finally, negotiations in 1946 led to a treaty recognizing the independence of Transjordan, and Abdullah proclaimed himself king. A mutual defense treaty permitted British troops to remain in the country, and British officers technically under Abdullah's orders commanded the Arab Legion.

When the United Nations voted in late 1947 to partition Palestine between Jews and Palestinians (see Israel: History), King Abdullah saw the opportunity to realize one step in his cherished dream of ruling a kingdom of "Greater Syria," including Transjordan, Syria, Lebanon and Palestine. When Britain's mandate over Palestine expired, he sent the Arab Legion to

Administered by Jordan, 1949

0   20   40   60   80   100 Miles

Jordan

King Abdullah of Jordan (1882–1951)

fight the newly proclaimed state of Israel. Other Arab states acted likewise, but in the War of Israeli Independence (1948–49) Arab armies suffered defeat. Israeli forces occupied areas reserved by the United Nations partition plan for the Arab state. The Legion fared better than most Arab forces, capturing the Jewish section of Jerusalem's Old City, but before the final armistice, it was forced, by Israeli ultimatum, to pull back elsewhere.

Most Palestinians thought King Abdullah had intervened in Palestine as much for dynastic gain as to repulse the Israelis. As the fighting ended, he secretly met Israeli officials to assure them of his limited intentions. Later he convened a congress of Palestinian notables that proclaimed him King of all Palestine; in 1949 he annexed formally the central portion that his troops controlled. Except for Gaza, all Arab Palestine became the West Bank of the Hashemite Kingdom of Jordan, and Abdullah came to rule the holy places in Jerusalem, Bethlehem and Hebron.

However, Jordan also gained a large and restive population, including several hundred thousand refugees on both sides of the river. They widely opposed Abdullah, considering him an agent of Britain and a traitor to the Palestinian cause. Furthermore, because of their greater achievements in education, larger population, and greater sophistication, Palestinians considered Transjordan as backward. Not surprisingly, tensions arose between the Palestinians and the Transjordanians.

In 1951 a Palestinian assassinated King Abdullah as he walked in Jerusalem. His young grandson, Hussein, then became king, although guided by a regency council until he turned 18 in 1953.

At first, Hussein permitted political activity and allowed parties to organize and govern through parliament. Most politicians were extremely nationalistic and anti-Western, critical of the roles played by Britain, France and the United States in the creation of Israel. In a showdown in 1957, King Hussein, dissolved parliament, arrested the cabinet, ended the Anglo-Jordanian defense treaty and dismissed Glubb Pasha, the British commander of the Arab Legion for two decades.

These events marked the young king's assumption of personal authority. To replace British aid, he sought financial, military and technical assistance from the United States. Nevertheless, following the Iraqi Revolution in 1958 that overthrew and murdered Hussein's cousin, Faisal II, British troops returned to Jordan to uphold the monarchy.

Between War and Peace with Israel

Given Israel's military strength, Jordan recognized the importance of preserving the 1949 armistice agreement with Israel. However, most Palestinians, especially those exiled from homes in Israel, wanted Jordan to join other Arab nations in a military confrontation against it (see Palestine). Tensions between several Arab states and Israel led Egypt's Nasser to deepen the crisis in May 1967 (see Israel: History). King Hussein was drawn unwillingly into a military treaty with Egypt, and then into war with Israel in June.

In four days of fighting, the vastly superior Israel Defense Forces crushed all Jordanian units west of the Jordan River, and seized the richest portion of the kingdom. With nearly half the population lost, and economic benefits from the major tourist locations around Jerusalem ended, Jordan faced great economic, political, and social difficulties.

Nearly 400,000 Palestinians fled to Jordan, creating a new wave of refugees, adding to the large communities of displaced Palestinians from 1949 around Amman, at Zarqa and elsewhere. New camps were set up with international aid, to provide food and shelter for the flood of persons crossing the river. The burden of the refugees stretched Jordan's finances; their numbers swamped the available jobs.

Both old and new camps became fertile recruiting centers for *al-Fatah* and other guerrilla groups linked to the *Palestine Liberation Organization (PLO)*. Claiming they would succeed against Israel where the combined Arab armies failed, these groups launched attacks against Israel and Israeli-occupied areas. Israeli reprisals turned much of the Jordan valley into a zone of sporadic battles, but at Karameh in 1968 the guerrillas held their positions against an Israeli raid, consequently gaining fame and support in the Arab world (see Palestine: History).

The late King Hussein of Jordan

After first permitting the guerrillas to operate in its territory, Jordan feared both their growing power as a "second government" and Israeli reprisals for guerrilla raids. The government therefore attempted to curtail the armed groups. Finally in "Black September" 1970, King Hussein ordered his army to crush the guerrillas. Perhaps 10,000 people, most of them Palestinians, died in Amman during the fighting; much of the city was heavily damaged. A tank invasion by Syrian-based units of the Palestine Liberation Army met defeat from Jordan's small air force, while troops set free Western passengers hijacked by Palestinian radicals.

The firm suppression of the fashionable guerrillas evoked fierce hostility from Palestinians and other Arabs, but after sometimes bitter fighting the military had regained control everywhere by 1971.

In the 1980s Jordan developed a deep friendship with Saudi Arabia, ironically ruled by the very family that forced King Hussein's great-grandfather out of his kingdom in the Hijaz (see Saudi Arabia: History). Along with the smaller Arab Gulf emirates, Saudi Arabia provided funds toward Jordan's expenses as a frontline state in the conflict with Israel.

Sensing the threat to the Arab oil states from Iran and its "Islamic Revolution," King Hussein offered full support to Iraq in its war with Iran. Technically at war with Israel, threatened politically by Syria and risking subversion from Iran, Jordan entered an informal alliance with Iraq that increasingly brought the two countries together in economic and foreign policy issues.

The widespread nationalist uprising (*intifada*) that began in 1987 in the Israeli-occupied territories showed again that the inhabitants of the West Bank considered themselves Palestinians, not Jordanians. The 1974 Arab summit had proclaimed the *PLO* to be the only representative of the Palestinian people, thus denying Jordan's claim to the West Bank. However, Jordan continued to pay the salaries of some civil servants in Palestine. As the *intifada* gathered strength, however, such links aroused widespread criticism from Palestinians and other Arabs. Consequently, in 1988 King Hussein dramatically recognized the Palestinians' wish to form their own country.

King Hussein's last decade

Iraq's invasion of Kuwait in 1990 plunged the Jordanian economy into a major depression. UN sanctions halted the transit trade and Jordan's own exports to its main customer, Iraq. Some 200,000 Jordanian workers returned from the Gulf states, reducing the annual remittances sent to families, and raising the unemployment rate to nearly 30%.

Though the king condemned the invasion, he proposed Kuwaiti border concessions and subsidies to Iraq. This "Arab solution" avoided placing non-Muslim troops on Saudi territory (traditionally prohibited to non-believers), and reduced the chance of conflict between a chemically-armed Iraq and nuclear-equipped Israel. Hussein noted, too, that for 23 years UN Security Council Resolution 262 had called in vain for an Israeli withdrawal from the Occupied Territories. The Palestinian problem called for parallel treatment of Kuwait.

Though politically popular among both Palestinians and Islamists, King Hussein's perspective brought financial disaster internationally. For years, Saudi Arabia and other Gulf states had provided subsidies and cheap oil. Now an isolated Jordan found itself cut off financially.

In the aftermath of the war, King Hussein ended martial law imposed in 1967. He issued a "National Charter" that reestablished multiparty democracy and secured allegiance to the king. Prime ministers followed in rapid succession, and some 15 political parties, including the *Islamic Action Front* of the Muslim Brotherhood, contested the 1993 elections. However, the new and sometimes uneven electoral districts weakened parties, by allowing voters just one vote even if there are multiple candidates in the district. This helped independent candidates from traditionally important families to triumph. The *Islamic Action Front* gained 16 seats, and as the largest group, it led the opposition of Arab nationalists and leftists.

In the shadow of the Madrid and Oslo peace processes between Israel and the Palestinians, quiet and symbolic diplomacy tackled and resolved the major disputes with Israel. In 1994, a peace treaty formally ended 46 years of belligerence, and regained some small bits of land (totaling 145 square miles) occupied by Israel, although the *kibbutzim* cultivating them leased some property back. More importantly, the treaty also restored water rights in the Jordan and Yarmuk valleys, and the U.S. promised to waive repayment on loans of nearly $1 billion. Jordan gained a privileged role at Muslim sites in Jerusalem, though it promised to turn them over to Palestinian authorities once Israel withdrew.

Amman, a city built on seven hills. Against the slope of one is this large Roman amphitheater now restored and being used for performances as it once was almost 2,000 years ago.

Jordan

Wadi Rum drivers taking a break   Photo by Susan L. Thompson

Peace required Jordan to amend its anti-Israeli laws and permit trade with Israel. However, popular opposition made this difficult. Some professional associations banned their members from dealing with Israelis. Islamic, leftist and Pan-Arab parties demanded that the treaty be scrapped. The opposition gained strength because the first visible benefits seemed limited to short-term tourists bound for Petra. However, critics failed to anticipate the opportunity for exports of light manufactures to the U.S. under the accompanying free trade agreement, and by 2002 the U.S. had become Jordan's largest export customer.

The last months of King Hussein showed again that real power in the country lay not with parliament but with the royal family. Stricken with cancer, Hussein left his treatment at the Mayo Clinic in 1999, to fly home to Amman, where he very publicly designated his eldest son, Abdullah, as heir, in place of his brother, Hassan, the crown prince since the 1960s. Days later, after final medical efforts at the Mayo Clinic failed, King Hussein returned home to die.

Hussein had ruled Jordan for nearly 47 years, many of them tumultuous, and he cut a much larger figure on the world stage than his country's population and wealth merited. A vast assembly of world leaders gathered for the funeral—the only significant absentee seemed to be Saddam Hussein of Iraq.

The son of Hussein's British second wife, Abdullah had spent almost his entire life in the military, commanding the special forces. Educated in Britain and the U.S., he had long accepted his uncle as the next king. Nevertheless, commentators commended the initiative and energy he displayed as a ruler. Within weeks, Abdullah visited most Arab capitals, where he improved relations with political opposites like Syria and Kuwait. During trips to Western capitals, he sought economic concessions, particularly debt relief.

In Amman, Abdullah proved adept at popular symbolic gestures, appearing in the streets disguised as an ordinary individual for direct evidence of public opinion. He also appointed a new prime minister, whose cabinet included both modernizers and Islamic critics of previous regimes. However, the cabinet failed to move as quickly as the king desired, and a succession of cabinets failed to achieve substantial change.

Water Shortages

After several years of low rainfall, by 1998, Jordan faced a prolonged and devastating drought. Piped water in Amman became foul-smelling and highly contaminated with bacteria, apparently from pollution at the main reservoir. Normal winter rains nearly disappeared from the region in 1999. Wheat and other crops that depended on rainfall failed. Many herders lacked water for their flocks to drink and stubble for them to eat. Israel announced it could not supply the water agreed in its peace treaty with Jordan.

Heavier rains and even significant snowfalls during recent winters raise hopes that weather patterns were turning "wetter," but even parts of the capital city receive tap water only one day per week during the summer. In the short run, little can alleviate a water shortage shared with neighboring countries, and irrigation-based agriculture, which accounts for 75% of water use, may need to be curtailed. In King Abdullah's words, "Drinking water remains the most essential."

For the longer term, there are plans to tap the Disy acquifer deep in the southeastern desert, and proposals exist to desalinize seawater and create hydroelectric power in the valley south of the Dead Sea. However, that source of fresh water will be distant, expensive, and require an international agreement with Israel and the Palestinians. The Wahdah Dam project with Syria on the Yarmuk River may provide the expected 50 million cubic meters of water to Amman and to agriculture in the Jordan valley, but it will not satisfy the country's needs. Indeed, Syrian dams upstream threaten to divert much of the flow.

After September 11, the growing crisis between Washington and Iraq threatened Jordan with a repetition of the 1990 Kuwait crisis. The U.S. provided the largest amount of foreign aid ($300–$450 million per year) and a growing market for ex-

The 1989 elections in Jordan demonstrated vividly the deeply-held differences between Muslim fundamentalists and women influenced by Western concepts of equality and women's rights.

In her campaign for parliament, the TV personality, Toujan al-Faisal, raised a number of social issues, including child abuse, polygamy, and wife-beating. For this, she was charged in Islamic court by two Muslim radicals, one a deputy to the Mufti (legal scholar) of the military, on grounds she had "defamed Islam." As punishment, her critics demanded the court declare her legally incompetent, dissolve her marriage, remove her children, and grant immunity to anyone who shed her blood.

The Islamic court dismissed the case, possibly at the urging of the royal palace. Neither Toujan al-Faisal nor any other woman won a seat in the elections, but soon after King Hussein did appoint Layla Sharaf the first woman in the Senate.

Ms. al-Faisal later became the first woman elected to Parliament, but after she posted an article on the internet that accused the prime minister of corruption, she was imprisoned. Toujan al-Faisal was pardoned by King Abdullah in 2002.

King Abdullah II

ports, but Iraq supplied half of all oil imports for free, and accepted food as payment for the rest. At the price of treading on domestic democracy, King Abdullah steered the country through the crisis with few international difficulties.

Proclaiming a "Jordan First" policy, the king dissolved parliament and delayed its elections. In the vacuum, he issued temporary laws that tightened controls over the press and banned unapproved public meetings. The army flexed its strength in rounding up known extremists. Such measures reminded political activists that war in Iraq should not become the occasion for violent demonstrations.

Overdue elections in 2003 reestablished parliament, and expanded it, after two years of rule by royal decree. Voters of the newly designed districts overwhelmingly favored independent candidates, a goal of the electoral system. The *Islamic Action*

Front won only 20 seats, and both women and leftists failed to win a single contested seat. However, women had been guaranteed nine seats by recent reforms and the remainder could be appointed.

Coordinated attacks on three foreign-own hotels in Amman killed dozens of Jordanian wedding guests, and a few foreigners in 2005. King Abdullah rallied public opinion in the shocked nation against Abu Musaib al-Zarqawi, the Jordanian leader of al-Qaeda in Mesopotamia, who claimed responsibility for the attacks. The televised confession of an Iraqi woman whose explosives failed to detonate strengthened the king's claims, and increased popular opposition to terrorism. No doubt the public support will be appreciated. Jordanian intelligence agencies keep close track on Jordanian activists and plotters, but identifying foreign terrorists becomes a difficult challenge.

Jordanians could be forgiven for cynicism about the results of the 2007 parliamentary elections, when pro-government candidates won 104 of the 110 elected seats in the lower house. The opposition *Islamic Action Front* of the *Muslim Brotherhood* (probably linked to *Hamas* as well) lost 11 of its 17 seats, and claimed fraud, but most commentators agreed that the count was not so fraudulent as the system was rigged. Districts in cities likely to return pro-Islamist, Palestinian, or liberal critics of the government are sometimes ten times the population size of rural constituencies of faithful conservatives.

Apparently unhappy with the failure of parliament to enact desired legislation, in late 2009 the king dismissed parliament and appointed as Prime Minister Samir al-Rifai, a businessman whose father had

served as prime minister. With elections not expected for nearly a year or more, the new prime minister and king may seek to address parts of the king's reform agenda by decree, including economic reforms and a new election law that somehow manages both to satisfy public opinion and provide a parliamentary majority of the right sort of people. Surprisingly, half the population still votes, apparently valuing order and security above mechanistic democracy.

Culture: Antiquities lie strewn profusely across—and beneath—the landscape of Jordan. Perhaps as many as 500,000 identifiable archeological sites exist, and teams of workers from many lands descend annually to discover remains dated from the Paleolithic to the Ottoman periods. In years of good fortune, they unearth seals, broken pottery, and occasional pieces of jewelry. In the popular imagination, however, the foreigners must come for gold. As a result, archeological pillaging constitutes a widespread crime.

Although desert palaces of the Umayyads and the Byzantine mosaics at Madaba constitute a priceless treasure, the most impressive ruins date from the Roman era. Now the scene of a cultural festival, the columns, buildings, streets and amphitheater of Jerash rank as one of the Empire's best preserved cities outside Italy. By contrast, Semitic Nabateans carved residences and tombs in the nearly vertical limestone cliffs of a narrow gorge. The home of enterprising merchants, Petra flourished for about 200 years after 100 BC. Already in decline by the Arab conquest, it became a lost city, rediscovered only in the 19th century. Tourists today endure sand and sunshine to marvel at the intricately carved columns, the splendor of

T. E. Lawrence described Wadi Rum as "vast and echoing and God-like."
Photo by Susan L. Thompson

Jordan

sunlight on rose-colored sandstone, and carved channels that brought water from a distant spring.

Universal, compulsory education through six elementary and three preparatory ("junior high") years has almost been attained, partly due to facilities provided for children by the UN Relief and Works Agency for Palestine Refugees. The quality of instruction tends to be good, if traditional, in Arabic language and literature, as well as in mathematics, where Jordanian test scores approached U.S. levels.

The University of Jordan opened on the outskirts of Amman in 1963, and remains the most prestigious in the country. Yarmuk University was established at Irbid in 1976, while the 1980s saw the beginnings of Mu'ta University in the south. In the 1990s, numerous private colleges and universities sprouted across the landscape, often to serve students whose families had lived in the Gulf States.

The modern culture of Jordan is essentially similar to that found in Syria and parts of Lebanon, with stronger nomadic and Saudi influences in the eastern and southern deserts. Nevertheless, observers often notice differences in Jordan, including greater respect for standing in line and obeying traffic regulations.

For most inhabitants, entertainment means spending time with friends and relatives, typically in segregated circles of men and women, drinking coffee and tea. Entertainment may also mean watching television; some Bedouin tents even boast a set. One key difference from American customs is the relative absence of single men and women mingling together. Ro-

mances are rarely conducted openly, and few girls or women would consider going to the movies without a group of relatives or friends. A wide variety of sports attract some enthusiasts, but in a small country there are no professional teams. Soccer is played at the high school level and by some men's teams.

Economy: A century ago life in Jordan revolved around nomadic and semi-nomadic herding and farming, with a handful of small towns. Today, some herders do remain, and Prince Hasan bin Talal's Badia project attempts to encourage ecologically sound ways of life. Where rainfall and irrigation permit, settled farmers cultivate a variety of crops, ranging from grains and other staples to tomatoes, melons and warm-weather vegetables. Agricultural exports account for around one-fifth the total, but many foods must be imported. The climate and soil usually ensure that farmers, many of them tenants paying one-third of the crop to the landlord, achieve only a modest standard of living. After independence the government undertook a series of irrigation projects and other assistance for agriculture, particularly the East Ghor Project to use water from the Yarmuk River for farms in the Jordan Valley.

Unlike its Arab neighbors to the northeast and south, Jordan contains no significant oil deposits. The country plays a modest role as a regional trade and commercial center, partly because its drier, cooler climate contrasts favorably with the Gulf, partly because Westerners find their lifestyles less restricted. Amman also served

as a base for many companies and organizations attempting to operate in Iraq.

Besides encouraging trade and tourism, economic development projects have included exploiting the phosphate deposits that account for about 25% of the nation's exports. Ambitious plans also exist to exploit the Dead Sea for potash.

The economy has alternately suffered and prospered because of international events. Disputes with Syria often cut access to the Mediterranean. War with Israel in 1967 inflicted 400,000 new refugees, the collapse of tourism, and the loss of the most highly-developed portion of the kingdom, which accounted for 40% of GNP. Financial aid rewarded Jordan's rejection of the Camp David Agreement (1978), and the economy grew at 10% annually. While many Jordanians (330,000 in 1988) worked abroad, often as skilled professionals in oil-

Hospitality in a Jordanian family

exporting countries, some 200,000 other Arabs filled low-paying jobs in Jordan.

The collapse of world oil prices in 1986 initiated an era of economic retrenchment. Aid from Arab oil exporters fell, and job prospects weakened abroad. Interest and repayment on the foreign debt soared, and foreign exchange reserves fell. The dinar fell steeply against the dollar, losing as much as 50% of its value in one year. Thus, by early 1989 several economic difficulties hit simultaneously: lower aid, debt repayment, precarious reserves, inflation, rising imports, and a budget deficit surpassing 20% of GNP (the U.S. then: 2–3%). Clearly Jordanians had lived beyond their means, and could no longer borrow to do so.

Although the government responded with economically-reasonable measures such as higher indirect taxes, cuts in subsidies, and canceling new weapons purchases, popular resistance led to riots and political change (see History). Friendly Arab nations responded with promises of modest aid, and rescheduled debt repayments. The cabinet cut spending for investment projects, and devoted more to debt repayment. In these ways the country survived the immediate crisis, only to suffer lost subsidies and disrupted trade during the Gulf War.

Flooded with hundreds of thousands of new Palestinian refugees, this time from the Gulf, the economy recovered surprisingly rapidly after 1991. Construction boomed, as former workers in the Gulf invested their savings in homes, offices, and apartments. Foreign exchange reserves rose, the economy briefly grew rapidly (over 5% per year), and yet inflation remained modest.

For the medium-term, however, Jordan lost its major export market, Iraq, to UN sanctions. The lost transit earnings themselves reached billions of dollars. Despite fanfare and hopes, peace with Israel brought no great economic dividend. In the late 1990s the country entered a significant recession. Unfortunately, economic policy could not be used to restore output. Fiscal policy was immobilized: massive budget deficits, covered partly by foreign aid, marked good years as well as bad. Monetary policy was equally ineffective: a rapid increase in the money supply would lead the wealthy to send it abroad, before the *dinar* fell in value. As an importer of natural gas and petroleum, the country suffered again when oil prices rose in 2008, requiring 20% of GDP to pay for energy imports.

With a rapidly-growing workforce, the economy must grow by 5%–7% annually to create the number of jobs needed for those newly seeking work. However, after 1996, the population grew faster than the economy, and by 2002 total unemployment perhaps reached 25% of the labor force.

A free trade agreement signed with the U.S. provides easier access for Jordanian goods, especially textiles produced in Qualified Industrial Zones using some Israeli inputs. In recent years these exports grew rapidly, and the zones employ 35,000 workers. However, Jordanians apparently lack the skills or the desires to work in textile factories, and about 75% of the employees come from South Asia and China.

The recent discovery of substantial uranium deposits in the desert south of Amman offers the possibility of creating a nuclear industry that could generate electricity, power desalination and irrigation projects, and export nuclear fuel. However, the U.S. generally opposes the spread of nuclear enrichment facilities, and Israel may also raise objections behind the scenes to the construction of civilian nuclear power plants.

The Future: In King Adbullah's own words, he desires Jordan in the future to be "secure, stable and prosperous." The king and prime minister reflect their experience in the military, so expect the kingdom to make every effort to deter further terrorist attacks.

In the long run, royal reforms must meet the acid test of satisfying the man on the street, rather than the favored few. Expect discussion about reforms of laws regulating politics and elections, an emphasis on economic development, and more talk about the "National Agenda," a 10-year reform program. However, the Jordanian elite have no desire to be overthrown. Security issues will continue to trump democratic ones.

Jordan's desire to enrich its own uranium for nuclear fuel poses a potential difficulty with the U.S.

Arab hospitality quickly means hot tea

Photo by Michael Russell

The State of Kuwait

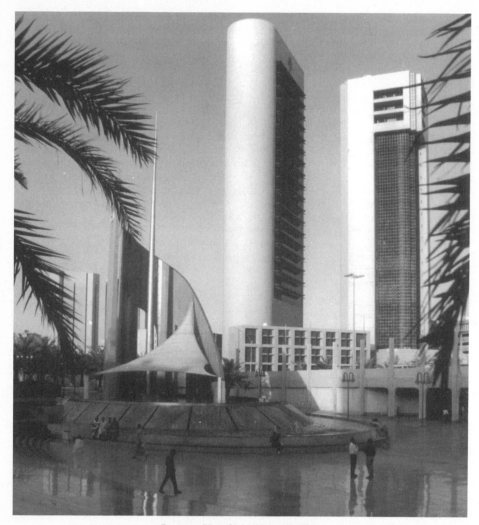

Luxury Hotels in Kuwait City

Area: 6880 sq. mi. (17,819 sq. km.; estimates differ).

Population: 3.6 million (under 40% native Kuwaiti).

Capital City: Kuwait City (1.7 million).

Climate: Very hot except for a short comfortable winter, which usually brings a few inches of rain.

Neighboring Countries: Saudi Arabia (South) and Iraq (North).

Time Zone: GMT +3.

Official Language: Arabic.

Other Principal Tongues: Persian and English.

Ethnic Background: Overwhelmingly Arab, with communities of Persians, Indians and Pakistanis.

Principal Religion: Islam.

Chief Commercial Products: Crude oil and refined products.

Major Trading Partners: Japan, U.K., U.S., Netherlands, Italy, Germany, South Korea and Singapore.

Currency: Kuwaiti Dinar (= 1000 fils).

Former Colonial Status: British Protectorate (1914–1961).

Independence Day: June 19, 1961.

Chief of State: Sheikh Sabah al-Ahmad al-Sabah, *Emir*, or Ruler.

Head of Government: Sheikh Nasser Muhammad al-Ahmad al-Sabah, Prime Minister (2009).

National Flag: Three horizontal stripes of green, white and red, with a black trapezoid at the pole.

Gross Domestic Product: $135 billion (at current prices); $144 (Purchasing Power Parity), 2008.

GDP per capita: $40,000 (PPP), 2008.

Kuwait (pronounced *Kwait*) is a tract of flat desert at the head of the Arab (Persian) Gulf. There are only a few natural oases in the country and no significant supply of fresh water for the city of Kuwait, which gave its name to the state.

Most of the population lives in the modern suburbs, a vivid change from the old town of mud houses that existed a generation ago. The wealth produced by oil attracted hundreds of thousands of immigrants, who with their descendants amount to over 60% of the population. The Arab world, especially the nations from Egypt to Syria, provided teachers, engineers, doctors, office staff, and skilled workers. Sharing language (but not dialect), culture and usually religion with native Kuwaitis, before 1990 these immigrants formed a majority of the population.

Aside from some Iranians, the other immigrants present a physical contrast. Indians, Pakistanis, and other Asians fill service jobs, and even build *dhows*, the boats that for generations established Kuwait as a trading center and base for pearl diving. The few European and American expatriates work in the oil industry and hold scattered positions in finance and commerce.

History: Although ancient ruins on Failaka island show human settlements thousands of years ago, for centuries the inhabitants were essentially nomadic. Then, in 1756, Anayza tribesmen from central Arabia, probably searching for pastures during a drought, settled and built a fort where the city of Kuwait now stands. In Arabic, Kuwait means "Little Fort," and the little collection of mud huts, benefiting from a natural harbor, grew into a trading outpost and pearl-diving center. It eventually came to possess a defensive wall.

The ruling family of Kuwait descended from the first ruler, and carries his name, al-Sabah (pronounced es-sabah). Though formally titled emir (prince), the ruler and other important members commonly use the honorary Arab title of sheikh. Arab custom and a tradition of consultation limited the sheikh's autocratic powers, and senior men in the extended family selected the most appropriate successor. Because the early emirs proved to be long-lived, there was less opportunity for interference by the swiftly-growing Ottoman Empire, which claimed the territory as part of the wilaya ("province") of Basra.

At the end of the 19th century, Emir Mubarak faced a critical decision. Fearing the increased ability of the Ottoman Empire to rule its distant territories, in 1899 he negotiated a secret treaty with Britain that placed Kuwait under its protection. Then, when the Ottoman Empire entered World War I in 1914, Britain easily declared Kuwait a protectorate. The Sabah family retained internal authority over the town, which remained an uninviting and lonely little trading center.

On the death of Sheikh Mubarak in 1915, the succession passed to each of his sons, Jabir and Salim. This established a pattern of the succession, alternating between their two families. Thus, until 2005, a "crown prince" was not the son of the current emir,

Kuwait

The late Sheikh Jabir al-Sabah

but rather a cousin who traced his paternal ancestry through a different line.

As geologists searched for oil deposits near the Gulf, British and American companies formed the Kuwait Oil Company and received a concession from the Emir. The company began drilling for oil in 1936, and soon discovered some of the richest deposits in the world. Exports began after World War II, and oil production and revenues soon made a startling impact on the dusty little town as it began the awkward change into a large, modern city.

Sheikh Abdullah al-Sabah became ruler in 1950. A benevolent monarch, he presided over the early period of economic growth. He initiated the policy of using the fabulous oil revenues for the benefit of all through a program of public works. In spite of this, much of the money was squandered.

The British protectorate ended in 1961, when Kuwait became independent. President Qasim of Iraq immediately claimed the state, threatened to invade, and blocked Kuwait's membership in the UN. However, Britain remained an ally, and its troops returned quickly, until Arab League forces replaced them. After the overthrow of Qasim in 1963, the *Ba'thist* government in Iraq recognized Kuwait's independence, reportedly in an arrangement involving money. Several treaties followed between the two states. One difficulty remained the boundary. The 1932 demarcation agreement between (British-protected) Kuwait and (British-influenced) Iraq contained neither map nor detailed descriptions, so that Kuwaiti territory began "south of the southernmost palm tree at Safwan."

After independence, Kuwait moved towards democracy. Elections in 1961 selected twenty men to serve with members of the ruling family in a Constituent Assembly that would draft a constitution. Their 1962 Constitution retained the Emir as the chief executive of government, assisted by a prime minister and cabinet. An elected National Assembly received the power to make recommendations and serve as a forum of discussion. The electorate, however, extended only to males whose family possessed citizenship in 1920. The Constitution even prohibited Kuwaiti-born males of a non-Kuwaiti father from voting. Only about 10% of the population could vote.

In its early years the National Assembly worked reasonably well. However, in the late 1960s the ruler, faced a series of difficulties—foreign military tensions, the hijacking of Kuwaiti airliners, and terrorist violence. He reacted by suspending the Assembly and imposing press restrictions. This halted inconvenient criticisms from its members, and press censorship discouraged unflattering commentary by journalists. Kuwait reverted to government by decree, in common with the other Arab Gulf states.

During the 1980s, the war between Iran and Iraq pitted two ideological opponents

of monarchy against each other: socialist republican Iraq against Islamic republican Iran. Fearing Islamic revolution more than the traditional threats of its large Arab neighbor, Kuwait loaned more than $10 billion to Iraq interest-free, and sold oil on its behalf against promise of repayment. Kuwait also allowed Iraqi military supplies to pass through its territory.

When the combatants attacked neutral vessels in the Gulf, Kuwait sought assistance. The U.S. provided naval protection. After an Iranian missile attack on the main oil terminal in 1987, Kuwait purchased military hardware and sought closer ties with other Arab Gulf states, Egypt and the United States.

Invasion, Occupation and Liberation

After the 1988 cease-fire between Iran and Iraq, popular protests swelled among Kuwaitis anxious to end censorship and restore parliament. Some politicians even questioned the royal family's role in a stock market crash. At this the government balked, and police used unexpected violence on the wealthiest demonstrators in the world. In 1990 Sheikh Jabir ordered elections for a *Shura*, a consultative council rather than the legislature. Members of the former Assembly boycotted the elections, complaining that the *Shura* "lacked teeth," and condemned the arrest of critics.

Tensions with Iraq mounted rapidly in July 1990, when President Saddam Hussein fiercely denounced Kuwait, warning that "cutting necks is better than cutting the means of living." Iraq complained, first, that Kuwait had exceeded its OPEC quota and thus (possibly) drove down oil prices, costing Iraq $1 billion annually for

111

Kuwait

Kuwaiti women weep at the graves of relatives killed by the Iraqi army during the 7-month occupation

AP/Wide World Photo

every $1.00 decline in oil prices. After the long war with Iran, Iraq could not afford the loss.

Second, Iraq demanded money: billions in aid besides writing off the wartime loans, plus compensation for $2.4 billion worth of Iraqi oil allegedly pumped from the Rumaila field that straddles the border. Finally, Iraq demanded long-term leases on the islands of Bubiyan and Warba, to protect its naval base and access to the Gulf.

Hours after Saddam's diplomats suspended negotiations, Iraqi forces attacked Kuwait. Caught by surprise, Kuwait's military offered piecemeal resistance. By nightfall, Iraqi troops had crushed all opposition. Sheikh Jabir and the crown prince barely escaped to Saudi Arabia; other members of the ruling family were arrested.

Initially Iraq claimed it had acted to support Kuwaiti revolutionaries. However, courageous Kuwaiti opposition leaders refused to join the "Provisional Free Kuwaiti Government." Deprived of any Kuwaiti authenticity, Iraq annexed Kuwait six days after the invasion (see Iraq: History).

In exile, the government reformed. The Kuwait Investment Office and other funds in London funded the government and supported hundreds of thousands of citizens who fled the fighting or were trapped abroad. The government also lent to Kuwaiti banks, preserving them from default, and promised $5 billion to the coalition forces gathering against Iraq. Further billions were pledged to countries suffering severe hardship from the invasion and economic sanctions against Iraq.

The ruling family also undertook to unite its citizens. Sheikh Jabir met with

opposition figures, and the crown prince pledged trust in the 1962 Constitution and parliament. For its part, the opposition agreed to support the dynasty.

Meanwhile, Iraqi forces plundered Kuwait: gold and foreign currency worth billions, truckloads of consumer goods, cars stolen from the streets. Hospital equipment and library books disappeared; even traffic lights were stolen, along with cadavers from the medical school. Iraqi university officials apparently divided the academic spoils before shipping them home. The vast booty depressed prices in Baghdad.

Such pillage greatly encouraged resistance by the 200,000 citizens who remained. Government employees stopped work, and at night, defiant women shouted "Allahu Akbar," from rooftops, implying that Allah, not Saddam Hussein, was great. The resistance undertook some military actions, helped subvert Iraqi rules, and aided foreigners sought as hostages by the Iraqis. Equally important, it maintained morale and social order.

In response, the Iraqi forces deported thousands of Kuwaitis; other thousands were killed. Many of those who were deported were apparently executed, in several Iraqi cities, and buried in mass graves. Hundreds of others remain missing two decades after the conflict.

During the battle to liberate Kuwait, Iraqi forces deliberately sabotaged industry and the environment. Eight million barrels of crude oil were dumped into the Gulf, creating one of the greatest oil slicks in history that coated hundreds of miles of beach and damaged marine life. A decade later, local coral reefs had still not recovered.

Iraqi units also set afire 732 of the nation's 950 oil wells. The fires burned up to 6 million barrels of oil daily, about 10% of all petroleum consumed world-wide and their smoke damaged neighboring countries with soot, acid rain, and other pollution. Led by the legendary Red Adair, teams from nine nations extinguished the fires far ahead of schedule. However, the escaping oil reduced underground pressure in the oilfields, thus permanently reducing the nation's oil potential.

Liberated by coalition forces, Kuwaitis rejoiced. However, their euphoria soon yielded to concern. Destroyed water mains and electrical generating plants took time to repair, despite stockpiled equipment and parts. Within days, leaflets condemned the government for the lack of food and utilities, apparently delayed because of bureaucratic fumbling. Critics demanded the ending of martial law, a broader-based cabinet, and restoring the Constitution. In response, Sheikh Jabir promised to restore the National Assembly.

Sheikh Nassser Muhammad al-Ahmad al-Sabah, Prime Minister

Copyright: Brian McMorrow

Domestic Politics after Liberation

Despite the demonstrations in 1991, the 1992 National Assembly elections proved honest and even festive. Given the few thousand male voters in each two-member district, the numerous candidates met the electorate at *diwaniyas* (see Culture) to chat about politics and society. Lacking political parties, voters could chose between candidates sympathetic to the ruling family or opposition candidates reflecting three broad groupings: the *Democratic Forum* (secular liberals), Islamists, and traditional politicians. By winning 35 of the 50 seats, this "Opposition," really nothing more than unstructured and shifting alliances—dominated the Assembly. Though it represented a majority on some issues, it could not form the government, and its options were, and remain, limited: the grilling of an unpopular minister, and even voting no-confidence in the individual, but not the ministry.

As a result of the system, in practice, the Assembly proved a debating society incapable of effective action. Neither it nor later assemblies addressed the challenges common to many Gulf states: severe budget deficits in years of low oil prices ($5.6 billion in 1994, some 20% of GDP), an over-large bureaucracy, and inefficient government-owned companies.

To no one's surprise, the opposition majority in successive assemblies provoked legalistic wrangling. At one point, Sheikh Jabir dismissed the Assembly when it attempted a motion of no confidence because free copies of the *Qur'an* had been distributed despite a missing verse. (Muslims believe the book is the uncreated Word of God, so such an error is more significant than, say, a printer missing a few verses of the Bible). The Assembly had passed only four laws in two years.

Displaying a flair for getting things done, in the two months from dissolution to elections the government decreed 60 new laws, including one to grant the vote to women. Constitutionally, all the decrees stood unless rejected by the new Assembly.

After liberals and Islamists gained seats, press reports predicted that the new Assembly would let women's suffrage remain. However, tradition triumphed instead, and the deputies narrowly rejected the decree. In 2005, prodding from the emir and the prime minister finally persuaded the Assembly to grant women the right to vote.

In 2006, Sheikh Jabir died. The planned succession faltered when Crown Prince Saad proved too ill to recite the oath of office. After a few days of uncertainty, both a family majority and the National Assembly elected Prime Minister Sheikh Sabah, the younger half-brother of Sheikh Jabir, as emir. He in turn chose his brother, Sheikh Nawaf, as crown prince, and his nephew, Sheikh Nasser, as prime minister. These appointments destroyed any semblance of alternation between the al-Ahmad and the al-Salem branches of the family.

Reformers in the Assembly and Kuwaitis in general welcomed the promise of a more active leadership. However, within months the long-simmering demands for electoral reform suddenly caught the public's attention. Reformers claimed that, in the absence of political parties, the system of 25 two-member electoral districts encouraged corruption, exaggerated tribal influence, and favored local notables, "service politicians," concerned with petty local issues. Both the government and loosely-linked opposition recognized the need for reform. The cabinet favored 10 districts, the opposition, just five.

Adopting the slogan "5 for Kuwait," a small group of young and educated activists launched a campaign of public protest to demand change. Focusing on just one issue, the activists communicated by text messaging and blogs, and cut strips of orange cloth for sympathizers to wear. Night-time demonstrations outside the National Assembly surprised the nation. Orange-clad protestors filled the Assembly's visitor galleries. Emboldened, the Assembly demanded, without precedent, to question the prime minister, and opposition members walked out. A constitutional crisis threatened. To defuse it, in 2006 Emir Sabah called early elections. For the first time women, could vote and run for office.

The hurried election campaign united various opposition groups—Islamists, nationalists, and liberals—to pursue redistricting. Candidates pursued women's votes, usually with separate receptions for them, a notable change. The *Orange Movement*, incorporating groups like *5 for Kuwait*, beamed satellite broadcasts and streaming video of opposition speeches.

The results disappointed women candidates. Women's issues such as the financial problems of divorcées, widows and children, the unequal treatment of women married to non-Kuwaitis, and health care, received less attention than redistricting and alleged government corruption. No women won.

The new cabinet, again under Sheikh Nasser, backed legislation for just five electoral districts, but within months conciliation failed. Disputes with the Assembly led the cabinet members to resign, and Sheikh Sabah called for new elections in 2008, the first to use only five districts. Again, women failed to win, and the most striking change was the decline of the largest previous group, the *Islamic Constitutional Movement (HADAS)* affiliated with the *Muslim Brotherhood*. Many voters apparently favored the more rigid *Salafi* Islamists instead. Within a year, the Assembly clashed with the cabinet, and rather than face questions about the economy and corruption, the prime minister resigned again.

The subsequent elections in 2009 provided a substantially difference set of vic-tors. Dr. Maasouma Al-Mubarak, the first woman to hold a cabinet position, received the most votes in the first district, and three other women—all holders of doctorates from U.S. universities—also won seats in the Assembly. Their gains came at the expenses of Islamic conservatives. The Assembly now includes such a variety of blocks—tribal representatives, Shi'a, Sunni Islamists of different perspectives, and even a few liberals—that in the absence of a party system to structure politics, fractious discord marked the first sessions.

Searching for Security: Foreign Relations

After 1990, Kuwait's search for security surpassed many traditional concerns. The post-war demarcation of the border placed several oil wells, a ship channel, and the major Iraqi naval base within Kuwait. Though approved by Saddam Hussein's rubber-stamp parliament in 1994, international disputes over the new border seem inevitable.

After its liberation, Kuwait spent more per capita on arms than any other country. Defense spending exceeded 20% of the total budget, but it will take time for troops to master the tanks, aircraft and missile boats.

Seeking allies from outside the Gulf region, Kuwait signed a defense pact with the U.S. in 1991 (renewed in 2001) that covers joint training and military exercises, as well as U.S. stockpiles of equipment. Similar arrangements provide French and British support in time of conflict.

In a rare move for an Arab country, during a 1998 crisis over UN inspection in Iraq, Kuwait agreed to let UN forces use its airbases. After U.S. and British bombers used those bases to attack Iraq in 1999, Saddam Hussein denounced Kuwait's sovereignty. However, threatened by a U.S. invasion, in 2002 he softened this stand and even returned some of the seized National Archives.

KUWAIT'S 4 WOMEN ELECTED TO THE NATIONAL ASSEMBLY

Dr. Maasouma Al-Mubarak

Dr. Rola Dashti

Dr. Salwa al-Jassar

Dr. Aseel al-Awadhi

Kuwait

A Kuwaiti oilfield worker kneels for midday prayers near a burning oil well
AP/Wide World Photo

Alone in the Arab world, Kuwait publicly backed the U.S.-led attack on Iraq in 2003. Most Kuwaitis delighted in the destruction of Saddam Hussein's regime in Baghdad, but the thousands of foreign troops passing through the emirate presented targets for international terrorists and grounds for Islamic criticism. In 2005, several fatal shoot-outs occurred as security forces attempted to capture Muslim militants, some of them foreigners. Partly in response, the government announced moves to curb militancy by removing intolerant school textbooks and closing unofficial mosques.

The U.S. defeat of Saddam Hussein's Iraq ended the constant threat of an Iraqi invasion and promised international calm if good relations can be maintained with Iran. This may reduce the need to host U.S. troops and thus ease the tensions that inevitably occur when American troops, and their families, live in a strict Muslim state.

Culture: Kuwait shares the basic culture of its neighbors. Until the affluence resulting from oil production, its population of less than 100,000 wandered with flocks, engaged in trading in the town, or worked as seamen on the sailing vessels that plied as far as India and East Africa. Its culture was indistinguishable from that of southern Iraq or eastern Saudi Arabia. Some of its inhabitants were the *bidoun*, literally, "those without," desert Arabs whose families wandered across national boundaries in the region. The *bidoun* lacked citizenship because ancestral residence could not be proven.

Oil wealth following World War II changed the face of the town and the people. The poverty-stricken *badu* virtually disappeared, as did the Kuwaiti sailors, while poor shopkeepers became wealthy businessmen. Mud huts gave way to air conditioned houses, often of palatial proportions. Kuwaitis often hold the world's top ranking in ownership of many consumer items, from cars to boats to electronics.

Non-Kuwaiti professionals and even workers have benefited from free medical service, educational facilities and other welfare programs. The educational system in Kuwait is the best financed in the world; students are not only provided with free education, including books and other equipment, but are given at least one free meal a day. Secondary school students receive living allowances.

The University of Kuwait, founded in 1966, grew to be one of the best in the region, with the pre-war student body numbering over 10,000. About half of the students came from Kuwait, a quarter from other Gulf states and the rest from various Asian and African nations. The faculty was drawn from Egypt, Syria, Iraq and other Arab countries. In recent years, a number of private colleges and universities have been established, some with American links.

For the past twenty years, women have formed a majority of the graduates at the University of Kuwait. This achievement reflects the surprising roles held by women in the country's liberal professions and business community, and provides the educated women who enable that role to continue. Kuwaiti women drive, shop, and otherwise play a much more public role than women in other Gulf countries, and in 2009 the constitutional court ruled that married women may obtain passports without the consent of their husbands.

In a society without alcohol, nightclubs, and social restrictions separating men and women, *diwaniyas* play an important role in Kuwaiti society. Held in the relaxed atmosphere of private homes, with segregation by gender, these evening gatherings bring together the relatively small number of citizens. In recent years they provided forums to discuss political and social issues, and increasingly seem to take the function of political parties, which are banned.

Economy: Fifty years ago Kuwaitis earned their living by pearling, nomadic herding, and trading with sailing vessels. By 1990, they became the first country in history whose earnings on foreign investments exceeded those of trade. The key to the transformation was petroleum. After reconstruction, it regained its position as the source of almost all (roughly 95%) exports, nearly half (45%) of the GDP, and most government revenue.

Despite its small size—about that of New Jersey—Kuwait sits atop the Burgan field, one of the largest oil fields in the world. The traditionally country ranks fifth in world oil reserves, about 10% of the total, slightly below Iran and the United Arab Emirates. Given the small population, a very modest share of global oil out-put provides one of the highest per capita incomes.

Oil revenues allow Kuwaitis to live in substantial comfort despite the climate. In a desert land, they each consume an average of 22,000 gallons of fresh water annually. While some springs have been tapped, five giant desalination plants provide most of the flow. Brackish water from springs serves for street cleaning, livestock watering, and when mixed with fresh water, for irrigation.

That any agricultural production takes place is surprising, given wealth and climate, and government aid is critical. Besides an annual stipend, farmers receive interest-free loans, seeds and other supplies at 50% of cost, and subsidies for drilling wells.

After immediate development needs were cared for, in 1966 Kuwait established the Reserve Fund for Future Generations. Its income from oil revenues was to be invested but not consumed until the 21st century. In 1990 its assets approached $60 billion, or over $100,000 per citizen. Additional government funds brought total assets to roughly $100 billion. So large were the accounts that the Kuwait Investment Office (KIO) found it difficult to invest the money abroad without arousing opposition. For example, in 1988 it purchased nearly 22% of the shares of British Petroleum, but was forced by the Thatcher government to reduce its holding to less than 10%.

A rapidly growing economy in the 1960s and 1970s offered many business opportunities, but the collapse of the uniquely Kuwaiti *Souk al-Manakh* in 1982 depressed the financial sector. This souk was an unofficial stock market in a parking garage, whose participants played for very high stakes—half the investors placed over $860,000 apiece. Unfortunately, much of this money was lent by banks against little collateral, and the souk's crash left $15 billion in unsecured debt. For years the banking industry struggled to cover its losses, and a final settlement was often postponed. Finally, in 1995 the government completed buying up the bad debts of local banks, some $24 billion involving 7,000 debtors, thus ending the crisis as well as the banking difficulties resulting from the Gulf wars.

The Iraqi occupation in 1990–1991 imposed enormous economic devastation on the small country. Wartime expenses, subsidies to Coalition allies, and the costs of reconstruction reduced the value of KIO assets by about $50 billion. Deliberate sabotage damaged the entire oil industry, including all three refineries and almost every well. Seeping and burning wells destroyed an estimated $20 billion of crude petroleum. However, reconstruction moved rapidly, and both oil exports resumed in 1991. The pace of reconstruction surprised the experts, and the next year oil production rose to its pre-invasion quota. By 1993, Kuwait's higher exports prompted other OPEC nations, who had waived the country's quota, to demand cuts as part of an effort to balance world supply and demand.

Revenue from oil sales helped fund reconstruction costs, estimated at $20 billion rather than the initial $60–$100 billion. By 1994, many major rebuilding projects had

been completed and refinery capacity had climbed to 800,000 barrels per day. However, despite its greater OPEC quota, and oil revenues exceeding $10 billion annually, the government had to borrow massively to fund subsidies, the bureaucracy, and military rearmament.

When oil prices set new lows in 1998–99, Kuwait received only about U.S. $8 per barrel of crude, and government revenues fell in half. To cover the resulting deficit, the cabinet promised comprehensive economic reforms, including higher prices for subsidized electricity and fuel. Other proposed reforms included privatizing some 60 companies owned at least partly by the state, and cutting the government bureaucracy. However, until education prepares students for private sector jobs, cutting government workers clashes with the pol-

icy of keeping unemployment low by giving jobs to university graduates.

The necessity for such unpopular measures disappeared after OPEC cut production and oil prices recovered in 1999–2000. With share prices depressed by economic and political concerns, much of the economy remained stagnant, but the state again received enough revenue to continue providing a comfortable life for its citizens.

The occupation raised anew the question of the economic future of Kuwait. It cast doubt on its ability to survive as a workplace for foreigners (82% of the workforce). If the government reduces the number of foreigners permitted to work, citizens will then have to survive with fewer employees and servants. Kuwaiti women face traditional cultural objections to their working, but they now form about one-quarter of the indigenous workforce.

The Future: The 2009 election results suggest opportunities for cooperation between the Assembly and the ruling family, if those newly elected prove more amenable to constructive government than some previous parliamentarians. Accomplishment is needed for the country to update its investment laws and address its future. However, members of the Sabah family dominate the major positions (defense, interior, foreign affairs, and more) in the cabinet announced after the May 2009 elections, so there is danger that the new Assembly will prove an expensive and ineffectual, debating club just like its predecessors.

The good life in Kuwait depends on the continued flow of oil. An estimate in the *Petroleum Intelligence Weekly* claimed that only 24 billion barrels of proven reserves remain, rather than the official 99 billion barrels. If that is correct, lean times are ahead much sooner than anticipated, and politicians of all varieties will face immense challenges.

Dressed in orange and carrying signs proclaiming "5 for Kuwait," demonstrators pressured the cabinet to resign and call early elections, 2007.

The Republic of Lebanon

The Souk al-Nasr, a colorful Beirut market, with beautiful materials, sacks of flour, exquisite handicrafts, and fresh vegetables.

AP/Wide World Photo

Area: 4,036 square miles (10,452 sq. km.).

Population: 3.9 million (2008), including about 450,000 Palestinians. Last census: 1929.

Capital City: Beirut (pop. about 1.6 million, plus suburbs).

Climate: Summers are hot and humid on the coast, cooler and drier in the mountains. Winters are mild on the coast, but colder and snowy in the high mountains. Rainfall is normally plentiful in winter, but rare in summer.

Neighboring Countries: Syria (North and East); Israel (South).

Time Zone: GMT +2. When it is noon Central Standard Time in the U.S., it is 8:00 P.M. in Lebanon.

Official Language: Arabic.

Other Principal Tongues: French, English and Armenian.

Ethnic Background: About 93% of the people are Arab, based on language. The largest cultural minority is the Armenians, who comprise about 6% of the population.

Principal Religions: Islam (more Shi'a than Sunni), Christianity (mainly Maronite and Greek Orthodox) and the Druze faith.

Chief Commercial Products: Citrus fruit, apples, olives, wheat, potatoes, tobacco, leather goods, vegetable oil, cotton textiles, cement and chemicals.

Major Trading Partners: Italy, United States, United Arab Emirates, France, Germany, Syria and Switzerland.

Currency: Lira or pound.

Former Colonial Status: French Mandate (1920–1943).

Independence Date: November 22, 1943.

Chief of State: Michel Suleiman, President (2008).

Head of Government: Saad Hariri, Prime Minister (2009).

National Flag: Three horizontal stripes, with a green cedar tree centered on the wider central white stripe between two red ones.

Gross Domestic Product: $35 billion (at current prices); $56 billion (Purchasing Power Parity), 2007.

GDP per capita: $14,500 (PPP), 2008.

Lebanon

The smallest mainland nation of southwest Asia, Lebanon historically connected the interior of the *Fertile Crescent* with lands across the Mediterranean Sea. Over the centuries, ideas, (including the alphabet), the military (the Persian fleet against Greece) and a variety of products made the journey in one direction or the other. After World War II, Lebanon became an intellectual and commercial center for the entire Arab world, but disputes among its peoples—disputes that involved how closely it should link with the West or East—plunged the nation into a civil war that nearly destroyed it.

Four geographical zones run the length of the country from north to south and resemble layers of a sandwich. First, a narrow plain hugs the coast; the largest cities are all located in this zone. Moving inland, the slopes of Mount Lebanon (a range rather than one mountain), with peaks exceeding 9,000 feet above sea level, comprise the second zone.

On the inland side of the Lebanon range lies the third zone, the *Biqa'* (or Biqaa) valley, a plain up to 15 miles wide. Its rich soil and flat fields provide most of the country's grains and vegetables. The Litani, the only significant river entirely in Lebanon, flows southward through most of the plain before turning sharply to the west to empty into the Mediterranean. The Orontes River begins in the northern part of the Biqa' Plain and flows north into Syria.

The last and easternmost division is the Anti-Lebanon Mountains; these form the border with Syria on the east. Near the southern end of this range is Jabal al-Sheikh or Mount Hermon, a snow-capped peak visible in clear weather from the tropical Jordan Valley to the south. Lebanon has no desert.

Winter and early spring constitute the rainy season. Much of the country receives at least 30 inches of precipitation annually, some areas much more. Snowfall is often heavy in the higher mountains, making the area suitable for winter sports.

In their physical appearance, culture and linguistic dialects, the inhabitants resemble those of neighboring Syria. In both cases, the vicissitudes of history have left a variety of traits.

History: Homeland of the ancient Phoenicians, its strategic location made Lebanon a battleground in ancient times. Inscriptions at the Dog River commemorate conquerors ranging from Egyptian pharaohs and Babylonian kings to Roman emperors. The territory fell to the Ottoman Empire in 1516.

Given its rugged terrain, Mount Lebanon traditionally provided a haven for persecuted minorities, who often gained autonomy under their local leaders. Three religious communities dominated the mountains. The Maronite Christians in the north eventually linked with Roman Catholicism. In the center, the secretive Druze split from orthodox Islam in the Middle Ages. Like the Maronites, the Druze were uniquely Lebanese (see Culture). In the south and east, Shi'a Muslim villagers shared religious ideas and practices with fellow Arab Shi'a in Iraq.

During the 17th Century the powerful Druze chieftain Fakhr al-Din extended his control beyond Mount Lebanon to parts of Syria and Palestine, but conflict with the Sultan in Istanbul led to his execution. After years of little change, the 19th Century witnessed greater trade and missionary activity, especially schools. A decade of Egyptian occupation brought greater rights for Christians as well as (hated) conscription. After communal violence in 1860, to protect the remaining Maronites from further massacres and mistreatment,

France landed troops, and forced the Ottoman Sultan to grant Mount Lebanon a special legal status under a Christian governor.

As European nations sought zones of influence in the Ottoman Empire, France's traditional protection of Roman Catholic Christians naturally led it to expand its contacts in Lebanon.

When Ottoman Turkey allied with Germany in World War I, its officials seized French documents that compromised many leading notables, both Christians and Muslims, and several were executed. As a further punishment, the Ottomans prohibited the transport of grain into Mount Lebanon, and thousands starved to death, particularly after an attack by locusts.

Secret wartime negotiations between Britain and France, formalized as the Sykes-Picot Agreement, assigned the coast and the Syrian interior to France. Thus, soon after British forces liberated the inhabitants from Ottoman troops in 1918, a French detachment landed in Beirut and occupied the coast and Mount Lebanon. However, they did not take control of the Arab-ruled Biqa' valley and Anti-Lebanon mountains until 1920, when a French invasion defeated the nationalist government in Damascus.

While the League of Nations prepared a mandate for the region, in 1920 the French High Commissioner divided Syrian territory into four districts. "Greater Lebanon" included the coast, Mount Leb-

117

Lebanon

The cedars of Lebanon

anon itself, and the entire Biqa' plain. Nearly twice the size of Ottoman Mount Lebanon; its population was evenly divided between Christians and Muslims. In 1926 France proclaimed this the Republic of Lebanon.

Public opinion divided sharply over the new state. Many Christians favored a separate Lebanon under French protection, thinking it would provide them political power and safety. However, most Muslim Lebanese opposed the mandate. Between 1926 and 1939, the occasional outbursts of violence against French rule proved local affairs, discouraged by concentrated French military forces in the country. The Lebanese government received internal autonomy subject to veto by the French High Commissioner, while France continued to control international relations.

After France surrendered to Nazi Germany, British and Free French troops invaded Lebanon and Syria in 1941, and the Free French commander afterwards proclaimed the two countries independent. However, in 1943 the French arrested the elected Lebanese president and his cabinet. This united Christian and Muslim politicians in favor of independence, and pressure from Great Britain and the United States forced France to free the officials and grant independence.

Traditional political leaders began maneuvering for the interests of their com-

munities even before the French withdrew, and formalized the agreement as the National Pact. Broadly revered as the unwritten constitution, this stipulated a *Maronite* president, a *Sunni* Muslim prime minister and a *Shi'a* Muslim speaker of the parliament. Citizens of the various smaller religious groups were thus barred from the highest offices (see Politics). Unfortunately, Bishara al-Khuri, the first president after independence, manipulated the political system for corrupt ends. He was forced from office.

During the presidency of his successor, Camille Chamoun (1952–1958), Arab nationalist ideas associated with Egypt's President Nasser further stirred the tensions in Lebanese society. The champion of conservative Maronites who insisted that the Lebanese were not "Arabs," Chamoun sought support from the U.S. and from monarchial Arab regimes trying to stop Nasser's radical ideology from spreading.

With foreign money, some reportedly from the CIA, Chamoun organized the election of sympathetic candidates in the 1957 elections, filling the Chamber of Deputies with his men. He then proposed to change the constitution so he could have a second six-year term. This would have allowed him to orient Lebanon to the West, strengthen Maronite supremacy and subdue the opposition.

1958 Disturbances

Dissension caused by the president's actions led to a restrained civil war in 1958. This divided both the country and the capital city into zones controlled by local political bosses and their private armies. Muslims sympathetic with Pan-Arabism and Nasser fought Maronites sympathetic to Chamoun. The national army remained neutral, and used its strength to police danger zones and minimize conflicts.

After a revolution overthrew the pro-Western king of Iraq, at Chamoun's request U.S. Marines landed at Beirut, ostensibly to support Lebanon's independence from communist threats. Chamoun's attempt to garner further American support for his power play failed, however, and he left office when his term ended.

The crisis of 1958 settled none of the basic issues facing the country. When the Chamber of Deputies met to select a new president, opinion overwhelmingly favored Fu'ad Chehab, the army commander. A neutral and less partisan figure, Chehab's presided over the country's brief golden age of progress and tolerance. However, during the rule of his successors in the late 1960s and early 1970s, dissatisfactions smoldered, factionalism persisted, the gap between the rich and poor widened, and animosities grew. Handicapped by a lack of consensus regarding national goals and the virtual monopoly on power held by a few communal leaders, governments rarely acted positively or decisively.

Necessary steps were not taken. Lebanon was unable to impose fair taxation or finance free public education. Attempts to build a strong, unified army were blocked by leaders fearful that such a force might override their individual communities. In time, solutions might have been found, but regional issues forced their way into Lebanon, and its governments could never formulate a widely-accepted policy toward Palestinian activity within Lebanon.

Neutrality

After playing only a nominal role in the 1948 war with Israel, Lebanon's small military avoided the 1956 and 1967 conflicts. Soon afterward, however, the country became the hapless victim of Israeli reprisal raids against Palestinians who launched guerrilla raids into Israel from Lebanon (see Palestine: History). Both Palestinians and Israelis resorted to tactics directed at civilian targets, including an Israeli raid on Beirut airport that destroyed many of Lebanon's civilian airliners. Concerned about the reprisals and national sovereignty, but pressured by Arab states and political opinion among the growing Muslim majority, the government proved unable to assert control over the Palestinians.

By 1975, both society and government exhibited classic signs of failure. Assassinations and small-scale violence erupted between rival groups. Journalists were kidnapped. Armed Palestinian units operated freely in parts of the country, scrutinizing—and sometimes seizing—Lebanese travelers at checkpoints along roads and streets. In the atmosphere of lawlessness and disorder, frustration mounted. Slogans of the 1960s, suitably adapted, appeared on the walls, among them, "Lebanon: Love it or Leave it."

Militia and Proxy Warfare

As tensions rose, Maronite militias trained for battle, and political rallies featured armed supporters. Most Maronite leaders hoped to regain Maronite supremacy, restore order, and rid the country of all Palestinian fighters. In early 1975 Maronite militiamen attacked a bus loaded with Palestinians. Palestinian forces retaliated, and for 19 months, war engulfed the country and especially its capital region.

Described abroad as a struggle between Christians and Muslims, the fighting was not purely sectarian. Palestinian and leftist groups joined together and though overwhelmingly Muslim, they included a few Christians. Nevertheless, many civilians were murdered or maimed solely because of their religious identity, obvious usually from names and certified by the national identity card.

Foreign involvement added further complexity. Weapons, supplies, finances and advice fueled the conflict. Besides representing a struggle for power in Lebanon, the war served as a battlefield for the Arab struggle with Israel. To accomplish their national aims, first Syrian (1976), then Israeli (1978) troops invaded parts of Lebanon. Syria initially invaded to limit the Palestinians and Lebanese leftists, and relieve the Maronite forces. Other foreign troops played a peace-making role, with the United Nations (UNIFIL, in the South) and the Arab League. Neither proved successful. By the early 1980s, however, violence became more infrequent, crossing the previously-deadly Green Line that divided Muslim and Christian Beirut became more common, and some attention focused on reconstruction.

Israel's War in Lebanon (1982)

Chaos returned, however, when Israel again invaded in mid-1982, publicly to gain "peace in Galilee" but actually attempting to implement General Ariel Sharon's secret plans to destroy Palestinian military forces and create a zone of influence in Lebanon. The massive assault occupied the southern half of the country and besieged the capital. Saturation bombing ahead of the Israeli advance kept Israeli casualties to a minimum; about 90% of the 20,000 killed were civilians. Material devastation was extensive; nearly a quarter of all the buildings in Beirut were damaged. However, Beirut did not fall. As its siege stalemated, international pressures grew on Israel, and negotiations produced the evacuation of Palestinian forces from the city.

Through war and occupation, Lebanon's political system struggled to function. With elections due for a new president, the Chamber of Deputies met, surrounded by Israeli soldiers and Maronite militiamen. Its members elected Bashir Gemayel, head of the right-wing *Phalangist Party* as president. Before he could take office, however, a massive bomb killed him at his headquarters, the work of one of his many enemies, Lebanese or foreign. Parliament then selected Bashir's brother, Amin, as president, though he lacked Bashir's political and military authority.

In response to Bashir's assassination, Israeli forces extended their control around

Beirut "Paris of the Middle East" before the ravaging civil war

Lebanon

Stylish, bustling Beirut in times before invasion and civil war

Credit: National Council of Tourism in Lebanon

Beirut. Fatefully, they allowed pro-Israeli Christian militiamen into the Sabra and Chatila Palestinian refugee camps south of the city. There the militiamen sought revenge for their past losses by murdering about 1,000 civilians while the Israeli military ignored the gunfire.

It took U.S. and European troops to restore order from the chaos. They maintained public order as Israeli units withdrew; they then helped reorganize the Lebanese army. Soon, however, the army joined the political and sectarian fighting, and the peacekeepers' role became partisan. After a suicide truck bomb killed 241 U.S. Marines in their barracks, the remaining American forces withdrew, and Lebanon returned to its usual wartime patterns. The president governed the palace, but the rest of the country fell under the control of local militias or foreign troops. Some technical departments still attempted to function.

The worst violence continued in the south, where forces within the Palestinian, Druze, and Shi'a communities fought each other and the Israelis. In central Lebanon, the *Lebanese Forces* collected taxes and imposed some order and administration on East Beirut and the surrounding countryside, while near-anarchy prevailed in West Beirut.

General Aoun Takes Control

The aging parliamentary deputies failed to select a successor to President Gemayel in 1988. Minutes before his term expired, he appointed General Michel Aoun, Commander-in-Chief of the (divided) Lebanese Army, as prime minister. This highly

Civil War Zones, 1983–1990

unusual action placed a Christian in the highest office reserved for Sunni Muslims. The incumbent prime minister and cabinet refused to resign.

A straightforward general determined to reunite Lebanon and expel all foreign troops, Aoun blockaded small ports where militias imported goods and military supplies duty-free and often exported illegal drugs (the only profitable exports during the war). Many Maronites initially supported the general, though fewer after his troops battled the *Lebanese Forces* for control of the Maronite heartland.

As a patriot, Aoun led his troops into intense battles with Syrian troops marked by indiscriminate shelling (mostly by Syrians) of civilian targets. One million fled; hundreds died, and survivors spent days and nights underground, often without electricity, fuel, or running water. Industry ground to a halt, and most factories were damaged. Unable to force a Syrian withdrawal, Aoun hoped for foreign pressure to remove them. But no nation intervened when Syrian troops attacked his headquarters in 1990, the last major action of a civil war that officially claimed over 144,000 dead, another 17,000 missing, and 184,000 wounded.

Under pressure from Saudi Arabia, in 1989 most Lebanese parliamentary deputies met in Taif, Saudi Arabia, and hammered out a new constitutional arrangement (see Politics). The deputies also accepted the Syrian occupation, at least temporarily. After their first choice as president was murdered, the deputies elected Elias Hrawi, a Maronite, to the post. He quickly recognized the Muslim prime minister and gained support from important Maronite elements, including the *Phalange Party* and the *Lebanese Forces* militia.

Joyless Peace under Hrawi

Seizing the initiative after General Aoun's defeat, President Hrawi asserted control over East Beirut and began to destroy the many walls dividing Lebanon. The Green Line defenses came down, and the Christian, Druze and Shi'a militias started to disarm. The army took over small ports previously valued by the militias for customs revenues and drug exports. Daily life improved, business activity strengthened, funds flowed into the country and schools reopened. The new cabinet included many militia leaders, in an attempt to link them to the success of the new order.

The army moved to regain control of South Lebanon in 1991. Troops entered Sidon and Tyre to public cheers, and they defeated *PLO* units that refused to yield their heavy weapons. However, possibly under Syrian influence, the army did not move against *Hizbullah* units, which continued to attack Israeli troops and the

South Lebanon Army in the Israeli Security Zone. Israel retaliated. Despite worthy attempts and the release of Western hostages, sovereignty and peace proved elusive. Car bombings occurred even on the American University campus.

The government met little success with its economic policies, but it produced raging inflation. It doubled official salaries despite an empty treasury and printed money to cover the costs. The *Lira* fell drastically against other currencies. Allegations of corruption forced the prime minister to resign.

Deep controversy arose over elections scheduled for 1992, the first in 20 years. Politicians sympathetic to Syria considered the elections a major step towards peace, but critics—including the Maronite patriarch—faulted elections held under foreign occupation. Moreover, hundreds of thousands of refugees could not return home safely to vote. Despite the objections, the elections went ahead. True to tradition, political parties did not dominate the results, but *Hizbullah's* alliance proved the unexpected "winner," gaining 12 seats of the 128. Observers credited these wins to popular support for the party's social welfare programs and its attacks on Israel. Because most Maronites had boycotted the election, many Christian seats were captured by pro-Syrian figures elected by Muslims. This left the Maronite community isolated and its leaders outside parliament. The nation remained badly divided.

President Hrawi selected Rafiq Hariri as his new prime minister. Born in Sidon, his business activities in Saudi Arabia had made him a billionaire and brought him close friendship with its king. Hariri had maintained close ties with Lebanon and had provided scholarships to thousands of Lebanese. As a man expected to give Lebanon far more than he might (corruptly) take, he won support even from traditional Maronites.

Hariri aimed to fight corruption, cut the bloated bureaucracy, and restore government schools, hospitals, electricity, water and telephones. He sought foreign aid and extended army control to the Shi'a suburbs south of Beirut. However, *Hizbullah* retained considerable freedom to strike at Israeli forces and the *South Lebanese Army* in the Israeli-occupied territory.

The prime minister faced three great difficulties: building national unity, reviving business confidence, and restoring government authority. Meanwhile Syria, Israel, Iran and other countries continued to manipulate events for their own purposes. Thousands of Syrian troops remained, to their supporters, peacekeepers, but critics condemned them as occupiers. They indirectly assisted *Hizbullah*, and they provided an excuse for Israel to occupy the south as a "security zone."

The connection with Syria extended beyond military matters. Treaties signed in 1991 linked the two countries politically and diplomatically. By prohibiting media

Bleeding Beirut: bomb blast killing 30 people, July 1986

Lebanon

The Faraya ski resort—a far cry from the desert heat found in neighboring nations.

attacks on Syria, the treaties clearly violated the traditional freedom, bordering on license, exercised by the Lebanese press.

The Syrian link alienated most Maronites, who perceived political discrimination in many ways, including selective prosecution of Christians for violent crimes. Prime Minister Hariri attempted with little success to mend fences by appointing several important Maronites to the cabinet.

Attempts to regulate the small country's 38 TV and 150 radio stations, a technical necessity but proposed in a fashion to benefit Hrawi's allies, symbolized critics' claims of the misuse of power. Further alienation resulted from parliament's decision in 1995 to extend President Hrawi's term of office for three years, thus avoiding another awkward election with Syrian troops present.

Lebanon's recovery from the devastation of nearly two decades of war proved uneven and slow. Annual economic growth rates as high as 7%, though impressive as statistics, failed to bring the expected prosperity. International aid came only in trickles, and by the mid-1990s taxes still reached only 50% of expenditures, and exports only about 10% of imports. Government salaries fell behind the comparable private sector. Teachers, whose salaries hardly exceed the minimum wage, struck for a pay raise. To address general labor discontent, in 1996 the prime minister proposed higher wages for the worst-paid, but this failed to satisfy labor and angered business.

Nevertheless, Hariri pushed ahead with reconstruction. He established Solidere, a

$1.8 billion company to rebuild the heart of Beirut. Funds poured into real estate development, and hundreds of buildings were torn down. As the bulldozers moved in, archaeologists found remarkable ruins from almost every era of history, adding another complication to reconstruction. Rebuilding central Beirut was largely complete by the late 1990s. Prosperity, however, still eluded the country.

Lahoud's Election and the South Liberated

When President Hrawi's extended term neared its end in 1998, Syria approved the nomination of army commander, General Emile Lahoud, as president. Parliament quickly amended the constitution to permit the election of a government employee and later unanimously elected the general, a Maronite. Personality differences soon led Lahoud to replace Hariri as prime minister, but the new president pledged to work within the law, fight corruption (it had obviously worsened despite Hariri's pledge to combat it), and cut the budget deficit. The most significant developments, however, came in South Lebanon.

When Hizbullah's attacks on Israel's self-proclaimed security zone and northern Israel had sharpened in 1996, Israel responded with large-scale bombardments from land, sea, and air on both military and economic targets, including a water reservoir and an electricity installation in Christian Beirut.

In many ways, Hizbullah emerged the winner. Only a few of its fighters died, and the rocketing continued. But Israeli gunners, deliberately or carelessly, shelled civilians sheltered at the UN post at Qana, killing about 100 and drawing international condemnation. Tel Aviv and Washington had initially proposed peace terms that disarmed Hizbullah "terrorists." After the slaughter at Qana, "terrorist" hardly seemed a label for one side alone. Shuttle diplomacy only restored the earlier understanding in written form: no cross-border attacks.

Continuing casualties, sometimes as many as 30 soldiers killed annually, led Ehud Barak to promise, during his successful campaign for prime minister in 1999, to withdraw from Lebanon. The difficulty, as always, was security: Lebanon and Syria refused to provide a guarantee of the safety of northern Israel, arguing that UN resolutions demanded an unconditional withdrawal. While Hizbullah attacks continued, morale declined in the South Lebanon Army (SLA) and among Israeli troops. Slowly disintegrating, the SLA withdrew from the Christian town of Jezzine in 1999.

Abruptly, Israel withdrew from the entire zone in 2000, months ahead of Barak's deadline. The collapse of the SLA forced a

rapid retreat that saved Israeli lives but meant abandoning supplies and equipment. Hizbullah had forced an Israeli retreat; the war for Lebanon seemed the only Arab victory in a century-long struggle. The retreat largely ended the violence. Hizbullah had previously attacked Israeli towns and farms across the border. After the withdrawal, Israeli Arabs could talk across the border fence to relatives not seen for over 50 years, though brash adolescents chanted anti-Israeli slogans.

One significant border dispute remained: the Shabaa farms region on the slopes of Mt. Hermon. Only a few hundred acres, they were claimed by Lebanon historically, but occupied by Syria and captured by Israel in 1967. The UN considers them part of the occupied Golan Heights. Death stalks within the Shabaa farms, and Hizbullah has ambushed Israeli soldiers in operations designed to gain counter-hostages for the dozens of Lebanese imprisoned in Israel.

Despite predictions of a bloodbath for collaborators, South Lebanon remained calm under Hizbullah control; Lebanese administrative control only gradually returned. The SLA collapsed completely. Its members who remained were tried and often sentenced to short prison terms. Others members fled to Israel with their families.

Continued Occupation and Economic Distress

Gerrymandering, manipulated regulations, and intimidation marked parliamentary elections held after the Israeli withdrawal in 2000. Nevertheless, in a political system where personalities matter more than parties, voters decisively favored candidates linked to former Prime Minister Rafiq Hariri. Despite personal animosity between the two men, President Lahoud reappointed him.

In fact, the campaign rhetoric overshadowed the actual winners. Some candidates openly raised the issue of foreign—meaning Syrian—domination. Walid Jumblatt, the Druze leader long close to Damascus, called for a new relationship between the two countries. Clearly, Lebanese across the political spectrum felt that the end of Israeli occupation removed the rationale for the Syrian occupation as well.

In response, Damascus withdrew its troops from Beirut in 2001, removing an eyesore. However, strong Syrian influence remained, exercised through the Lebanese intelligence services, political manipulation, and some 25,000 troops in the north and east. To counter any sense of declining Syrian prestige, the security forces (rather than regular police) arrested hundreds of Maronites on flimsy charges. Although most were soon released, several prominent personalities, including inter-

Lebanon

national journalists, were charged with treason for communicating with Israel. Such maneuvering further weakened any desires for reconciliation.

Still a billionaire himself, in his second term Hariri governed a country whose debt of over $30 billion roughly equaled two years' GDP. Interest ($3 billion annually) and debt repayment exceeded tax revenues, making Lebanon the most indebted country in the world. While appealing to foreign governments for assistance, Hariri took one well-noticed public action: he closed the government television station for months and laid off its personnel.

In 2001 and 2002, Lebanon built pumping stations on the Hasbani River and its tributary, the Wazzani, to bring irrigation water to a few parched (and impoverished) villages along the southern border. But because the Hasbani flows into the Jordan River, a major source of Israel's water supply, its Prime Minister threatened war over the pumping. However, project usage fall within the limits proposed by an official U.S. plan in the 1950s, and since the European Union funded the projects they are likely to succeed.

The Cedar Revolution

Before President Lahoud's six-year term expired in late 2004, Syria summoned the Lebanese cabinet to Damascus. It returned in favor of a constitutional amendment to extend the president's term by three years, and despite the anti-Syrian opposition, parliament agreed. However, the UN Security Council, led by the U.S. and France, voted for the withdrawal of all foreign (i.e., Syrian) troops, the disarming of all militias (*Hizbullah*; Palestinians in camps), and fair elections.

Syria withdrew its troops near Beirut, but kept units in the north and east. *Hizbullah* retained its arms. Lahoud remained in the president's office, but Rafiq Hariri resigned, and formed an anti-Syrian alliance with traditional Maronite politicians and the Druze leader Walid Jumblatt, thus uniting three of the country's four sectarian groups.

On Valentine's Day, 2005, a massive bomb killed the ex-prime minister and dozens of others as his motorcade passed through the hotel district. The very sophisticated assassination plunged the country into crisis. Many Maronites and Druze condemned the Syrian and Lebanese intelligence services directly. Others blamed the security forces' failure to protect an obvious target after opposition politicians had warned of death threats against them. However, most Shi'a suspected that Israel or the U.S. had engineered a murder that would damage Syria's reputation. A UN report later claimed that Syrian President al-

Asad had threatened Hariri, that top Syrian intelligence officials were implicated, and that Lebanese authorities had utterly failed to conduct a competent investigation. Everyone but the security services, it seemed, had heard of threats against Hariri.

As protests mounted in central Beirut, Hariri's sister and his son, Saad, spoke passionately for justice and freedom. Political opinion swung strongly against Syria. Perhaps 25% of the country's entire population massed in Beirut's central square on March 14, 2005 to demand justice and the complete withdrawal of Syrian troops.

To the surprise of many, Syria responded to the crisis by withdrawing all its troops and (most?) intelligence agents from Lebanon. However, many blamed Syrian intelligence and its Lebanese allies for continued bombings in Christian areas and the murders of prominent journalists and politicians critical of Syria.

As Lebanon prepared for elections, under a gerrymandered system that most Maronites opposed, the Hariri-Jumblatt-*Lebanese Forces* alliance took the label "March 14" forces. The election results showed a starkly divided country. Saad Hariri's alliance carried all of Beirut's seats, and did well in the north and east, while the rival *Hizbullah-Amal* coalition took every seat in the south. In Mount Lebanon, Jumblatt demonstrated his wide support from the Druze community.

Maronite voters, however, sharply rejected Hariri's *Lebanese Forces* allies in favor of General Aoun, the former ruler during the Civil War who had returned from exile to contest the elections. A decade earlier, Aoun's defiance of Syria had cost the lives of hundreds of soldiers and perhaps thousands of civilians. Now he formed pragmatic alliances with pro-Syrian politicians. The elections thus emphasized the sectarian nature of Lebanese society, with each sectarian group's heartland uniting behind one leader.

Despite his solid majority, Saad Hariri refused office, and his alliance nominated Fouad Siniora as prime minister. Short of the two-thirds majority required to remove President Lahoud from office, Siniora formed a unity cabinet that included pro-Syrian representatives from *Hizbullah* and Aoun's *Free Patriotic Movement*.

The fate of President Lahoud dominated Siniora's first year in office. Suspicion over his involvement in Rafiq Hariri's murder followed the arrest of his intelligence chief and the commander of the presidential guard. However, the Maronite community hesitated to remove their own president.

The Year of Lebanese Turmoil (July 2006–07)

Breaking six years of relative calm along the internationally-recognized Israeli bor-

der, in July 2006, *Hizbullah* guerillas captured two Israeli soldiers and killed several others. Besides hostages for bargaining, the guerillas likely sought to embarrass Israel's newly-formed cabinet, and divert attention from Iran's nuclear processing.

Israel's inexperienced cabinet under Ehud Olmert seized the opportunity to turn the border raid into a war, aiming to free its soldiers, crush *Hizbullah's* military force, and perhaps demonstrate Iran's inability to protect its ally. The Israel Defense Forces (IDF) launched a missile and bombing blitz of *Hizbullah's* military in the South, its offices and television station in Beirut, and even the home of Hassan Nasrallah, its leader. Non-Shi'a Lebanese often thought this appropriate retaliation for a reckless provocation, though unfortunate in the civilian casualties.

When the Israeli cabinet held Lebanon directly responsible for the soldiers, it ignored the common Lebanese distinction between *Hizbullah's* territory and sovereign Lebanon. Long powerless over *Hizbullah,* Beirut also proved powerless when Israel attacked businesses, Beirut's airport, vital road bridges, gasoline service stations, and even individual commercial trucks. A raid on Beirut's generating station created an enormous slick of heavy oil—possibly the Mediterranean's worst. An air and sea blockade halted the economy and caused several billion dollars in damages. Tens of thousands evacuated, both foreigners and Lebanese.

Hizbullah retaliated by launching missiles far deeper into Israel than ever before, reaching Haifa, then further south. The missiles, supplied by Iran through Syria, killed over 40 civilians and wounded scores more. By contrast, Lebanese civilian casualties from Israeli fire exceeded 1,000

Former President Emile Lahoud

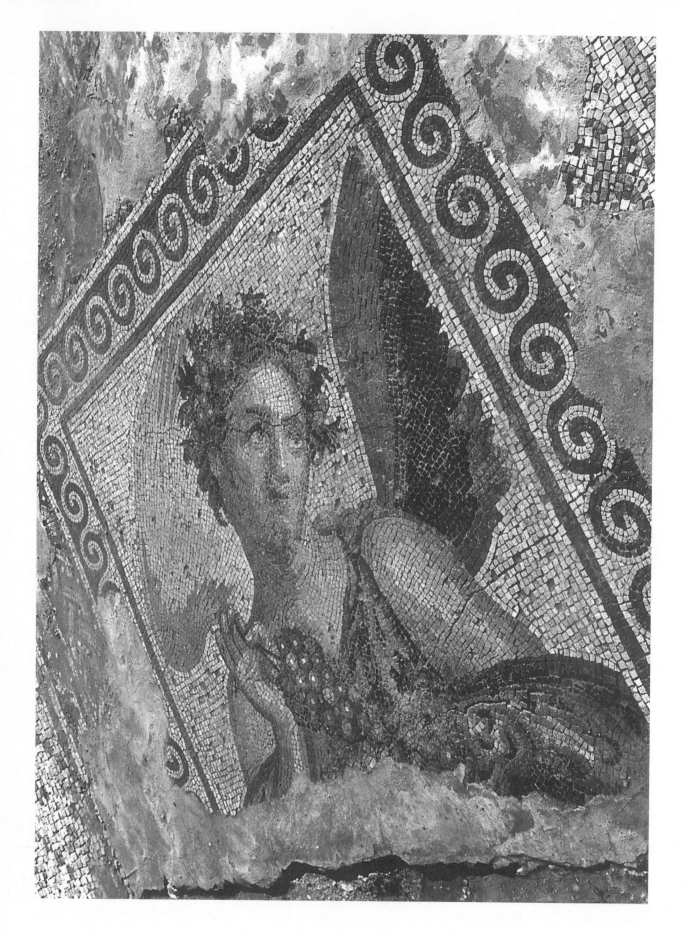

Lebanon

dead, plus thousands injured. Nearly 25% of the population fled their homes.

After weeks of air strikes, the IDF launched ground assaults into South Lebanon, apparently intending to occupy territory up to the Litani River. However, by the standards of past Israeli triumphs, the troops were unprepared, or the plans were flawed, and *Hizbullah* fighters inflicted unexpected casualties. The world clamored for a ceasefire, but in hopes that Israel would destroy *Hizbullah,* the U.S. obstructed a Security Council decision. After a month of fighting, with no Israeli victory in sight, the Security Council finally voted Resolution 1701. It called for the return of the two captured soldiers, the disarming of *Hizbullah,* government control over the Lebanese south, and a strengthened UN presence.

Having battled to perhaps a draw, *Hizbullah* rapidly won the public relations victory during the peace. Its officials poured a "river of green" on Lebanese eager to rebuild their destroyed homes, $12,000 in cash, with virtually no paperwork. *Jihad al-Bina'*, the party's construction arm, quickly cleared ruined apartment blocks. In a play on Hassan Nasrallah's name, the party posted signs proclaiming "Divine Victory," in Arabic "Nasr min Allah."

By contrast, the widespread attacks on Lebanon weakened the democratic and anti-Syrian government. With U.S. diplomatic backing, Israel had devastated a pro-Western country, but left untouched Syria and Iran, *Hizbullah's* key suppliers. This strengthened Syrian sympathizers in Lebanon, and Islamist extremists worldwide. *Hizbullah* and its allies left the national unity cabinet, leaving it short of any Shi'a minister, and then declared the government illegal. Whether to block a UN tribunal over Rafiq Hariri's assassination for Syria's benefit, or to extend its own power, *Hizbullah* demanded a unity government and sponsored months of demonstrations in central Beirut, including a protest camp outside Parliament.

The aftermath of the war proved particularly discouraging to Lebanese who had hoped, before the war, for prosperity and development after liberation from Syrian occupation. Bombings and assassinations targeted anti-Syrian figures, most prominently members of parliament and leading journalists—men with names like Gemayel (Minister of Industry), Tueni (MP and respected journalist), whose fathers and grandfathers were pillars of Lebanese society, and a brave TV anchorwoman, May Chidiac, who survived an assassination attempt that cost her an arm and a leg. The assassins were never found.

President Lahoud's term expired in 2007 with Parliament immobilized, and the country began a period of anxious uncertainty. Although nearly all political groups accepted the military commander, General Michel Suleiman as a compromise candidate, the opposition rejected the authority of the cabinet to propose legislation to let the military commander run for office. So the election was held hostage until *Hizbullah* had gained wider goals.

After months of crisis, in May 2008 the cabinet attempted a show of authority. It dismissed the military commander of Beirut airport and declared *Hizbullah's* landline telephone system illegal. *Hizbullah's* response was firm: street blockades and violence quickly spread, and its militiamen seized Sunni sections of West Beirut, demonstrating their military superiority over Sunni militias. The military maintained its unity by taking no action, though it threatened to do so if gunmen did not leave the streets.

In Washington, President Bush proclaimed, "The international community will not allow the Iranian and Syrian regimes, via their proxies, to return Lebanon to foreign domination and control." However, the U.S. had no proxies to support the cabinet, and outmaneuvered, the cabinet backed down. In response, *Hizbullah* reopened roads and the international airport. Even more important, both government and opposition accepted an invitation backed by the Arab League for talks in Qatar.

With diplomacy and arm-twisting by the Prime Minister of Qatar, Sheikh Hamad bin Jassim, the two sides agreed a major political compromise. Presidential elections would be held, almost immediately. The new cabinet would include a blocking minority from *Hizbullah* and its allies, with the remainder appointed by the new president. Re-drawn parliamentary districts would concentrate sectarian voters, strengthening their ability to elect their own, and no group would be allowed to use arms to settle disputes. Finally, the opposition promised to disband the protests that had paralyzed downtown Beirut for months.

After 19 failed attempts, the Chamber of Deputies met and quickly elected Michael Suleiman president. The next day he took office, and reappointed Prime Minister Siniora. One year later the country successfully conducted parliamentary elections.

Successful Elections, 2009

Many Western commentators interpreted the election of a new parliament in geo-strategic terms, portraying Lebanon as a contest between the pro-American, anti-Syrian March 14 bloc and the pro-Iranian/anti-Israeli/Muslim extremist *Hizbullah* bloc. Though partly truth, that explanation ignored local realities, personal rivalries, and *Hizbullah's* desire to avoid direct control. It also neglected the powerful role played by fear. For example, Sunnis felt apprehensive of Shi'a encroachment, with Syrian and Iranian backing, while Shi'a opinion feared the government's alignment with the West would leave Lebanon weakened in another war with Israel.

Although *Hizbullah* had nominated only 11 candidates of its own, to avoid overwhelming other groups, its 2008 victory in the streets of Beirut likely increased apprehension in other communities. Outside money flooded the country and thousands of overseas Lebanese returned to vote. In fact, there were no close contests for about 100 of the 128 seats. The remaining seats were mostly Christian, and fear motivated enough Christian voters to elect Christian candidates aligned with the March 14 alliance.

Post-election politics revolved around the appointment of a cabinet that would reflect all factions of the country without giving the victors too much power. Indeed, Lebanon's government is a rarity among nations: the political opposition insisted that democracy meant power-sharing. After months of bargaining, a cabinet of 30 members was divided 15 for the victors, 10 for the opposition, and five members loyal to the president. Thus Prime Minister Saad Hariri must obtain consensus to act, and with the support of the presidential group of five, the opposition can veto proposals.

Politics: Dating from the French mandate, the Lebanese constitution stipulates a Chamber of Deputies (parliament), and a president elected by it for a single term of six years. The president is the most pow-

President Michel Suleiman

Lebanon

erful authority, for he selects and may dismiss the prime minister, subject to parliamentary approval.

Representative democracy really means representation of religious groups. The *National Pact* of 1943, an unwritten amendment to the constitution, reserves the presidency to a Maronite Christian, the premiership to a Sunni Muslim, and the speaker of parliament to a Shi'a Muslim. Similar sectarian restrictions apply elsewhere, so that the army commander must be a Maronite. Christians historically dominated the Chamber of Deputies by a 5:4 ratio, but the 1989 Taif Accord equalized the membership of the 128 deputies. The accord also determined the number of seats for the country's six districts based on political compromise, not the actual number of residents.

In practice, the formal democracy becomes a feudal system based on traditionally important families, sometimes abetted by voting practices that trespass on the secrecy of the ballot. Voters support a local leader, known as a *za'im*, from an important family of their own faith. Once elected, a *za'im* develops a patron-client relationship, using the political system to obtain benefits for his district and his family, a sometimes foggy distinction. While they cling to privileges for their communities, *za'ims* recognize the benefits of cooperating with leaders from other sects, who often share their economic wealth. Alliances might even be formed across the sectarian divide against rivals of the same faith.

Thanks to this system, there are no significant national parties. Ideology and typical political issues are diminished as sons—Chamoun, Jumblatt, Karami, and many others—replace fathers in politics and often in parliament. There is never a landslide that "throws the rascals out" no matter how disillusioned the voters.

At one time the size of the Maronite community justified its dominance. But Maronites emigrated more often than Muslims, and as they became wealthier more quickly, they preferred fewer children. By the 1970s, Maronites (probably) fell to third place demographically, but they refused to relinquish the presidency and command of the army, for they remembered past Muslim domination and persecution.

Long the country's neglected community, the Shi'a community's rise to greater recognition followed the replacement of feudal *za'ims* by *Hizbullah*. Because it supported Palestinian groups that murdered Israeli civilians and maintained links with suspected hijackers and the 1983 Marine barracks bombers, *Hizbullah* is often derided in the U.S. as merely a group of terrorists.

But in today's Lebanon, the *"Party of God"* runs schools, dispensaries, and public works projects. It provides fertilizers and agricultural advice to thousands of farmers, and clean drinking water in slums. With 11 representatives in parliament, the effectiveness of its organization far exceeds any other political group in the country, possibly including the government bureaucracy. Across the Arab world it was hailed for liberating South Lebanon and defeating Israel (i.e., holding its own) in 2006. These achievements render *Hizbullah* too strong for the Lebanese government to challenge, regardless of U.S. desires to freeze the organization's financial assets as a terrorist group and the UN vote to disarm it.

In a related matter, the party's political strength led the Hariri government to support the right of the "resistance" against Israel to maintain arms, contrary to U.N. decisions. While the *Party of God* undoubtedly possesses thousands of rockets, contrary to Israeli claims it probably is not armed with SCUD missiles, if only because the older, liquid-fueled weapons are too large to hide and too cumbersome to use.

Culture: Though often Western in dress, material possessions, and television, most Lebanese naturally retain their own social values. A more traditional life and dress is found in small towns and villages, especially in those inhabited by Shi'a Muslims. The traditional culture differs very little from that of Syrians and Palestinians.

The Maronite (Arabic *Maruni*) Church is unique to Lebanon. Formed as a distinct group in Syria about the 6th century, the Maronites have preserved many ancient customs in the mountains. Arabic and Syriac are both used in the liturgy. The marriage of priests is permitted, but the Maronite Church has been in communion with the Roman Catholic Church since the First Crusade. In recent centuries, Maronites have been rivals with the Druze for control of the Chouf Mountains overlooking Beirut. In 1860, when Maronites suffered defeats at the hands of their enemies there, French soldiers intervened on behalf of the Christians. Many Maronites, including monks who own some of the best land, still believe that Western Christians have a duty to help the Maronites gain victory over their non-Christian rivals.

Long before the Israelis adopted the argument, Maronites presented themselves as isolated defenders of the "values of Western Civilization" among unruly Arabs. However, the continued bloodshed typical between rival Maronite factions indicates a perverse understanding of "western values." For example, in 1988 presidential bodyguards killed two officers of the *Lebanese Forces* over some petty dispute. Four

days later, two of the president's supporters were murdered in retaliation, following the age-old principle of the vendetta.

The Druze (Arabic *Duruz*) form a cohesive community whose origins lie partly in Shi'a Islam. Several Christian ideas and practices have also been incorporated into the sect along with unique beliefs and interpretations belonging only to the initiated. Besides their stronghold in the Chouf southeast of Beirut, they are also found in Jabal al-Druze in southern Syria.

Traditionally inhabiting the southern mountains and the *Biqa'* valley, the Shi'a often suffered exploitive landowners and received few government services. In the 1970s and 1980s, their towns and villages suffered Palestinian occupation and then Israeli invasions. Less educated, the Shi'a formed the poorest religious community, but after they migrated to Beirut's southern suburbs, they gained significant military and political clout, especially with the formation of *Hizbullah*.

Nearly all Lebanese value education very highly. Thanks to its mixture of state, private and church-supported schools and universities, the country long enjoyed the distinction of some of the finest education in the Arab world. The American University of Beirut attracted students and faculty from many lands; so did other colleges and universities, helping to maintain Beirut's status as an intellectual center. However, while the government developed a public school system after independence, its teachers or facilities often lack the qualities and advantages of the better private schools.

For many years, the highlight of Lebanese cultural activities was the summer Baalbeck Festival. World-class orchestras, pop stars, and dramatic groups performed against the imposing backdrop of some of the greatest Roman-era ruins. A wartime casualty, the festival returned to the hearts of Lebanese when Fairouz, one of the Arab world's most famous singers, returned to the stage in 1998. During the civil war, she had refused to perform anywhere in Lebanon, and though a Christian she had remained a national symbol. Thus her return to Baalbeck represented the return of normalcy.

Younger Arab men and women often prefer the sounds—and gyrations—of the rock stars of music videos, and Lebanon's Nancy Ajram and Haifa Wehbe attract a large following in the region while scandalizing Middle East conservatives. Members of Bahrain's parliament nearly unanimously sought to ban what they imagined would be a sexually provocative concert—despite Wehbe's promise to cover up. The incident provided many Lebanese, more worldly-wise, respite from the immorality of communal bloodshed.

Another cultural challenge is the recovery of antiquities looted from museums or kept privately, contrary to the law. Officials have seized thousands of works, including mosaics and sarcophagi, and recently even regained full control of Beit al-Din, the 18th-century capital and one of the most famous historical sites in the country.

Economy: In the first decades of independence, many Lebanese prospered from their country's role as a center of international banking and trade. Beirut became the natural Middle Eastern headquarters for many companies. Tourism flourished, transit fees on Iraqi and Saudi Arabian oil helped meet the government's budget, and Lebanon visibly achieved the highest Arab standard of living outside the oil states.

Two decades of civil and international war destroyed much of the formal economy. Artillery salvos gutted banks and factories, the transit trade collapsed and government revenues plummeted as militias collected customs duties for themselves in the many small ports. Once aspiring to a moderately wealthy standard of living, many Lebanese faced destitution.

The collapse of the Lebanese Lira symbolized the wider economic catastrophe. The lira initially maintained its value remarkably well. However, sometimes the government printed money to pay its bills, especially after 1986. The resulting inflation drove the exchange rate so low that one lira became worthless. Money, in fact, became cheaper than wallpaper. The human effects of inflation were often disastrous. It wiped out the lifetime savings of many people, and because wages failed to rise equally with prices, impoverished most others.

The chaos of civil war provided a little-noticed example of the unacceptable face of unregulated capitalism. An Italian company, Jelly War, shipped thousands of barrels of toxic waste to Lebanon, burying the containers in the mountains or near the sea. Complaints led the Italian government to repossess much of the material, but Greenpeace claimed that several thousand barrels remained.

The task of reconstruction was enormous. Wartime destruction and neglect proved particularly devastating to utilities, the networks of electric and telephone cables, water pipes and sewer lines. Enterprising Lebanese often coped by makeshift arrangements that conveniently avoided payment for the erratic services, but massive rebuilding was required. In the late 1990s government reconstruction funds had reached about $20 billion, and a construction boom brought new housing as well as roads and commercial buildings. The capital again enjoyed electricity a full 24 hours per day, though often through a tangle of wires. Most construction workers were not Lebanese, but Syrians and other Arabs, who formed roughly 20% of the workforce. After 2006, they were needed again, for reconstruction after Israeli attacks.

The Future: The Cedar Revolution reflected deep desires for freedom from Syrian interference, but its liberal, anti-Syrian tilt was limited by divided Christian loyalties and *Hizbullah's* ability to control the streets. General Aoun's failure to deliver the Christian vote in 2009 modestly improves the opportunities for effective government. The creation of a cabinet that includes members of all major sectarian groups without producing gridlock was no mean feat.

Thanks to wide acceptance of the 2008 Doha Agreement, the country now enjoys a president and a democratically-elected parliament. Beirut is restored after the lengthy sit-ins, and tourist resorts in mountain villages can hope for prosperous summers. The dreams of Washington or Tel Aviv that somehow the government would disarm *Hizbullah* have been shattered. But in the long run, can the Lebanese unite to make things work? Do the leaders of the political classes even want to reach across sectarian and ideological lines?

In many regards, Lebanon lives on borrowed funds and borrowed time. The achievements of its citizens are impressive, but they come with the world's deepest foreign debts per capita. Doha provided a life-restoring transfusion; the 2009 elections maintained the flow. May the revival not be wasted fighting as proxies in the regional rivalry between the U.S.-Israeli alliance and that of Syria and Iran.

ناديـن

تـاكسـي:
أنا الثانية ورجهلانة،
ولست مغرمة وحلمي
لحن من ملحم بركات

راغب
علامة
ينصح
بالابتعاد
عن
مطربة
النبريش

هيضاء:
الذين يحاربونني
حشرات
والله يسامح
أختي رولا

نوال الزغبي
تمنع كلبها من
مشاهدة روبي

عقد قران
أصالة
وطارق العريان

إيلي نحاس:
أنا الأول
واستأجرت 3 طائرات
لإحياء عيد ميلاد
ابن القذافي

ربيع الأسمر
يحكي قصته
مع سحر وابنها

Lebanese rock star Nancy Ajram

The Sultanate of Oman

Small village in the interior of Oman

Area: About 119,500 square miles (309,500 sq. km.).

Population: 2.8 million (2008), including 400,000 South Asians.

Capital City: Muscat (pop. 800,000).

Climate: Extremely hot and dry except for the short winter season which is comfortable in most areas, cool in the mountains. Winter normally brings adequate rainfall at higher elevations.

Neighboring Countries: United Arab Emirates (North); Saudi Arabia (West); Yemen (Southwest).

Time Zone: GMT +4.

Official Language: Arabic.

Other Principal Tongues: Baluchi and languages of the Mahri group.

Ethnic Background: Predominantly Arab, with significant African and Asian intermarriage. Small communities in Dhofar preserve the remnants of older linguistic and ethnic groups.

Principal Religion: Islam.

Oman

Chief Commercial Products: Petroleum, dates, dried fish, grain, pomegranates, limes, goats, cattle and camels.

Major Trading Partners: Japan, United Arab Emirates, U.K., U.S., West Germany, Netherlands.

Currency: Rial (1 rial = 1000 biaza).

Former Colonial Status: Independent but under British influence, mid-19th to mid-20th centuries.

Chief of State: Qabus bin Said, Sultan.

National Flag: At the pole there is a vertical stripe of bright red bearing the national emblem (crossed swords behind a broad dagger on a belt) at the top; the remainder of the flag consists of three horizontal stripes, white, red and green, top to bottom.

Gross Domestic Product: $59 billion (current prices); $76 (Purchasing Power Parity), 2008.

GDP per capita: $27,000 (PPP), 2008.

One of the hottest and driest countries on earth, Oman lies on the southeast corner of the arid Arabian Peninsula. Facing the Gulf of Oman to the northeast and the Arabian Sea on the south, it extends along 1,000 miles of coast. It is the oldest independent Arab state.

Stretching from Sur at the eastern tip on the country toward the northwest, the Hajar Mountains form one of the major geographical features of Oman. The highest part of the range, with peaks rising more than 9,000 feet, is *Jabal Akhdar,* the "Green Mountain." Average annual rainfall on the upper slopes is a modest 20 inches per year, far exceeding the country's typical precipitation of only 3"–4" annually. By contrast, then, the mountains are green.

Between the Hajar Mountains and the sea from just north of Masqat to the UAE border beyond Sohar lies the Batina Plain. Watered mostly by mountain rainfall that flows underground toward the coast, its inhabitants mostly depend on water raised from shallow wells. Nearly all sedentary Omanis live on the Batina Plain, in Masqat or its twin city Matrah, or on the eastern slopes of the mountains.

The remaining three-quarters of the country is mostly arid steppe, with no standing water. The scant pasturage for goats and camels is found in river valleys. One unusual climatic feature helps a few varieties of wild animals survive in otherwise uninhabitable regions. Sea breezes moving inland bring fog and dew. To survive without streams or drinking holes, animals must lick the moisture off the leaves of plants. In one such area conservationists are attempting to reintroduce the locally-extinct Arabian oryx with animals bred in captivity in the United States.

In the southwestern corner of the kingdom lies the smaller coastal plain of Dhofar, with the town of Salala. Rising behind it, the Qara Mountains receive enough moisture during the summer monsoon to support cattle and goats. In ancient times, Dhofar flourished as a supplier of frankincense, the fragrance famed in the Biblical story of the Three Wise Men. In the late 1990s, the moist climate of Salala began to attract Arab tourists who found vacationing in clouds and rain cheaper and more congenial there than in Europe.

History: Before the 19th century, the history of Oman was largely a series of tribal wars, peaceful interludes under powerful rulers, and foreign invasion from other parts of Arabia or Persia. Saif bin Sultan, who died about 1711, extended Omani control over ports of East Africa and Zanzibar, establishing an empire.

The present line of rulers, who belong to the Al Bu Said family, was established about 1744 with the expulsion of the Persian invaders from Masqat and other coastal towns. In an age when Britain ruled the seas, the reign of Said the Great (1804–1856) saw Oman as the strongest native power in the Indian Ocean. The newly established cloves plantations on Zanzibar and—until curtailed by the British—the slave trade accounted for Said's wealth, along with his active fleet of sailing craft. When he died, his empire was divided between two sons. One took Zanzibar (now a part of Tanzania), where his descendants ruled until the last was deposed in a 1964 revolt by his African subjects. The other received Oman, which then played a less important international role. Gradually, Oman came under increasing British influence, though it retained its legal independence.

Sultan Taimur, a great-grandson of Said the Great, abdicated in 1932, to retire in India. He left the throne to his young son, Said, who became the thirteenth member of the Al Bu Said to rule. Unlike his father, Said took to the job readily, though after two decades of uneventful rule, he faced two crises.

The first was a dispute over Buraimi Oasis, which Oman shares with Abu Dhabi

Oman

A young couple in traditional dress

(see United Arab Emirates). Saudi Arabian soldiers occupied this collection of villages in 1952, and a Saudi governor took up residence. Eventually, after several years of adverse publicity, Sultan Said reoccupied the villages he claimed with the aid of British-trained and British-led soldiers from Trucial Oman (now the United Arab Emirates).

The second major crisis was an armed rebellion (1957–1959). Ghalib bin Ali claimed both the religious title of Imam and an independent state in the interior, with its capital at Nazwa. Ghalib's followers received weapons and training in neighboring Saudi Arabia. Returning to Oman, they seized control of Nazwa before the Sultan had time to act.

The rebellion was suppressed with the aid of British soldiers and aircraft after a few months duration. After hiding on the summit of Jabal Akhdar until early 1959, the rebel leaders escaped to exile, where they condemned Sultan Said as an agent of British imperialism.

A palace coup deposed Sultan Said in 1970. His only son, Qabus (also spelled Qaboos) swiftly seized power and quickly began careful modernization. To symbolize his new policies, he changed the name of the Sultanate from "Muscat and Oman" to simply "Oman."

The scope for social reforms was vast. Committed to preserving the traditional lifestyle, Sultan Said had failed to spend for social purposes the new revenues from oil exports. The country's sole hospital had 12 beds, and only six miles—10 kilometers—of road had been paved. Fewer than 1,000 students attended primary

school; no high school existed. Communications likewise languished, with only 550 telephone subscribers, and infrastructure items such as ports, airfields and public utilities remained primitive. The new Sultan's government attempted to develop all these areas, as funds permitted.

Under Sultan Qabus the country also began to emerge from diplomatic isolation. It joined international organizations and allowed foreigners to enter. Oman was admitted to the League of Arab States and the United Nations in 1971. That same year, diplomatic relations were established with Saudi Arabia, the most important neighbor and a past supporter of rebel movements in Oman.

The first six years of Sultan Qabus' reign fell under the shadow of the Marxist-oriented rebellion in Dhofar, which his father had failed to restrain. Supported by the People's Democratic Republic of Yemen, the leaders of the rebellion ultimately aimed to overthrow all the conservative rulers in Arabia and thus control vast oil-producing regions. Advised by British officers and aided by Iranian units supplied by the Shah, Omani forces claimed victory in 1976. This freed the government's attention for economic development.

In the 1980s relations between Oman and South Yemen improved, and Oman came to play an important role in the Gulf Cooperation Council, though it frequently follows its own initiatives in foreign and defense policies. Its troops joined the war against Iraq over Kuwait (1991), and U.S. and British forces use its military bases.

Widening its diplomatic contacts substantially, in 1994 Oman hosted Israel's

Prime Minister Yitzhak Rabin for discussions, the first known visit by an Israeli leader to a Gulf state. Radical Palestinian groups and Iran strongly condemned the visit. However, Oman essentially seeks peaceful relations in the region. It cooperates with Iran in developing joint oil and gas fields, and has sent observers to Iranian military exercises.

Like other oil producers, Oman often suffers a substantial budget deficit because when oil prices drop, government spending for social improvement and development plans exceeds revenues. In 1995 it announced plans to cut the deficit to zero by the end of the century, partly through privatizing state-owned companies. However, declining crude oil prices automatically reduced government revenues and made a balanced budget impossible. In 1999 the deficit doubled, and the government responded with several new taxes and cuts in spending. But higher oil prices after 2000 brought much larger revenues.

Seeking to modernize the government as well as the economy, Sultan Qabus has gradually increased popular participation in political decisions. His first step in the early 1990s was to propose a Consultative Council (Majlis al-Shura) free of official appointees, and thus more open to citizen viewpoints. To select the Council, the Sultan instituted the country's first, but limited election: only selected tribal sheikhs, religious leaders, and businessmen voted.

In 1996 Sultan Qabus extended the government's structure by decreeing a "Basic Law" or constitution that included a supreme court and nudged the Council towards becoming a legislature by adding an upper house and calling it the Council of Oman. However, the sultan apparently sensed that the political elite seemed more

His Majesty the Sultan Qabus

interested in personal success than the national good. In response, he reshuffled the cabinet to involve more reformers, and he appointed women to both houses of the Council.

In the Council's 2003 elections, for the first time all adult Omani citizens held the right to vote. Another first that same year was the appointment of a woman as cabinet minister. Despite these formal changes, some analysts suggest that many Omanis felt apathetic towards an advisory group that could not address issues like defense, foreign policy, or other matters declared sensitive.

Conceivably the Sultan, born in 1940, plans to lead the country towards representative government in his lifetime. However, the Omani public seems to prefer his benevolent though autocratic rule to most alternatives.

The succession is not clear: Sultan Qabus never married and never named an heir. The Basic Law stipulates that male members of the ruling family determine the succession within days of his death. If no agreement is reached, Qabus's secret nominee will be designated. Meanwhile, the security forces maintain close watch over potential trouble-makers, arresting alleged Islamic extremists in 2004 but releasing them the next year.

A desert country whose scant rainfall falls partly in scattered summer thunderstorms, in 2007 Oman unexpectedly suffered the most severe storm ever recorded to hit the Arabian peninsula. When Cyclone Gonu, a category 3 hurricane, passed along the eastern coast, its winds, waves and rainfall killed over forty people, knocked out power in Muscat, and flooded roads, homes, and cars.

The government reacted effectively to the disaster. It evacuated people from flood areas, closed shops ahead of time, and ordered everyone indoors. Repairs to roads and electric systems began almost immediately, and both of Muscat's water desalination plants returned to operation a few days later. Despite economic losses estimated at about $1,500 per inhabitant, Sultan Qabus politely declined offers of aid from Gulf nations and the U.S.

Culture: Oman has one of the highest percentages of nomads of any country in the world. Over half its people spend most or all of the year wandering with their herds. The remainder of the population is divided between farmers and townspeople. In the principal ports of Masqat and Matrah, many Baluchis and Indians work respectively as laborers and merchants.

Most Omanis follow the teachings of the *Ibadhi* sect of Islam, whose origins lie in the *Khawarij*, a faction that disagreed with Ali, the fourth Caliph of Islam. Many traditions and rituals found in Sunni and Shi'a Islam are not followed by the *Ibadhis*, who stress the importance of proper belief, righteous conduct and the supreme authority of the Qur'an.

Through much of *Ibadhi* history, a leader called the *Imam* led the community in both religious and secular domains. He was selected in theory by all believing males, but in practice by tribal leaders. His duty was to rule the true Muslims, i.e., the *Ibadhis,* and force heretics—Sunni or Shi'a—to follow him. Outside Oman, there are only scattered *Ibadhi* communities in North Africa, India and Pakistan.

The Dependency of Dhofar is administered separately from Oman itself, and has

communities that are distinct from other Arabians. Most important among them are the *Qara* people, who give their name to the mountains in which they live. Their language is distinct from Arabic, though related to it. They dress distinctly, and follow different social habits. They are the only Arabians who depend primarily on cattle rather than on goats and camels for a livelihood. Their cattle are very small, about half the size of usual breeds.

One of the most important recent developments in Oman has been the expansion of educational facilities. In 1970 there were scarcely half a dozen schools. Today, hundreds of schools, with thousands of foreign teachers, many of them Egyptian, enroll over 300,000 students, more than half of them girls. Evening classes provide learning for adults.

Sultan Qabus University opened in 1986 with a largely Western curriculum. In common with many other Arabs, Omanis find the study of the humanities, Islamic studies, and the behavioral sciences more appealing than technical skills, engineering and the physical sciences. Around one-half of the university students enroll in the former programs, although the country needs technicians and scientists. The expansion of education now includes a university at Nazwa.

Thanks to the classical music tastes of its sultan, Oman boasts the only professional symphony orchestra of the entire Arabian Peninsula. When the Royal Oman Symphony Orchestra was founded by the Sultan's decree in 1986, there were no pianos or violins worth mentioning in the entire country. No Omanis had studied music, and the first high school was only a decade old. British instructors conducted a talent search and identified musically talented children. Now aged twenty-something, these young Omanis form the national orchestra. Its performances, though considered surprisingly good by Western critics, lie outside the country's culture and tastes, so Omanis generally ignore them.

Economy: Unlike the smaller, oil-rich nations of the Arab Gulf, Omanis acquired a strong agricultural tradition over the centuries. This provides a significant focus for economic development. Even with oil revenues, farming, herding and fishing remain vital parts of the economy; the government, however, no longer depends on taxing produce and livestock to meet its budget.

Three years after the discovery of petroleum deposits, Oman entered a new economic era in 1967, when oil exports began and revenues flowed to the ruler. After Sultan Qabus seized power, development activities increased rapidly. Agricultural

The highway at Matrah

Oman

projects improved water supplies and crop varieties for farmers. Investment in up-to-date shipping facilities at Matrah and an international airport improved transportation links with the rest of the world, while paved roads and airfields eased travel within the country. Electrical generating plants, housing projects, and radio stations increased the enjoyment of life, while modern hospitals and public health programs extended the lifespan.

Given these favorable conditions, private businesses also expanded rapidly, in the retail trade, services, and other areas. In 1989 the Stock Exchange opened, with 71 companies, mostly in services such as insurance and transportation. The pace of economic development attracted foreigners as well.

Like other Gulf states, Oman will face growing difficulties finding suitable jobs for its young. Half the population is 15 years of age or younger, but already some 4,000 youth graduate from high school annually. They often aspire to government jobs that, compared with private businesses, pay higher salaries, offer greater job security and require shorter hours. However, even by replacing its foreign employees, the government cannot absorb many of the job seekers. In the private

economy Pakistanis and Indians accept far lower wages and often fill lower-status jobs. Legislating higher wages for Omanis, or forcing out foreign workers, will merely raise the cost of doing business.

Although income from oil constitutes about 80% of government revenues, known reserves are estimated at a modest 5 billion barrels. Peak production only reached 800,000 barrels per day, and by 2006 had fallen to 630,000 barrels per day, due partly to disappointing declines in output. Recent efforts at steam injection, which heats oil in the rock, and facilitates its flow, are among the largest in the world. By combining steam and gas injection methods (known as enhanced recovery), the country hopes to raise the recoverable portion of oil deposits from 10–20% to nearly 40%. As a minor producer, Oman never joined OPEC.

Natural gas offers more promise of long-term benefit. In the mid-1990s an ambitious program to develop natural gas resources raised confirmed reserves to 25 trillion cubic feet. The government created Oman LNG, a joint venture with oil companies and private firms to build a multi-billion dollar plant to export 6.8 million tons of liquefied natural gas annually. The first shipments took place in 2000.

Oman also seeks diversification outside the energy sector. Copper is mined, refined and exported, and Japan has assisted the search for further copper and gold deposits. Though encouraged, industrial output is small, and large projects to produce aluminum, fertilizers and petrochemicals remain incomplete. Oman's few manufactured exports enter the U.S. under a free trade agreement ratified in 2006.

In 1999 the Raysut transshipment terminal was opened not far from Salala. A major deepwater port costing over $250 million, the project was designed to unload the Gulf-bound cargoes of large vessels for transport into the Gulf on smaller ships. A direct competitor to Jebal Ali in the UAE, the project will only succeed if it operates efficiently and if major shipping firms prefer to avoid the sometimes troubled waters of the Gulf.

The Future: Political stability seems set to continue, especially because the Sultan continues to rule, and rule well. Relaxed relations with united Yemen also help. However, the time bomb of rapid population growth ticks away, and while not critical yet, the problem of creating suitable jobs for the young will assume serious proportions soon.

The Qurum Natural Park in the Heart of Muscat

Courtesy: Royal Embassy of Saudi Arabia

132

The Palestine National Authority

CAN THIS FRAGMENTED HOMELAND SUCCEED?

Palestinians unite around a common flag, a common Arab culture, and a love of their ancestral homeland between the Mediterranean and the Jordan River. However, nearly two decades after the Oslo Accords promised an eventual Palestinian state, sovereignty still eludes this long-suffering people. A legal framework exists in the Palestinian Authority (PA), complete with legislature and executive. But the PA lacks a capital, governs only 17% of the West Bank, survives only on foreign assistance, and controls no borders. Its police forces—several of them—sometimes shoot each other, and the Gaza strip, controlled by *Hamas*, defies the president. Limits on media freedom come from PA censors rather than Israelis. The advances toward statehood merit the inclusion of Palestine among the formally independent states of this volume. However, the nation-state of Palestine is not an accomplished fact. Critically, popular acceptance of peace with Is-

rael, vital to the PA's very existence, is lower today than a decade ago.

After suffering many calamitous events during the twentieth century, the Palestinians now reside in four distinct categories:

1. Palestinian Authority Territory: Gaza and most Arab areas of the West Bank

Area: Gaza: about 136 square miles. West Bank: Palestinian autonomy in a few square miles of the 2,140.
Population: 3.9 million (UN, 2007), of whom 1.5 million in Gaza
Capital City: Ramallah (legislative). The desired capital: East Jerusalem.
Climate: Mild winters; summers hot (Gaza) to very hot (Jericho).

Neighboring Countries: Israel and Egypt (west of Gaza).
Time Zone: GMT +2.
Official Language: Arabic.
Other Principal Languages: Hebrew (used by Israeli settlers); English.
Ethnic Background: Arab.
Chief Commercial Products: Citrus, including oranges; olives, grapes, figs, vegetables, flowers, grain, handcrafted items and services.
Major Trading Partners: Israel; Arab states (for oil imports).
Currency: Israeli New Shekel; dollars preferred.
Colonial Status: Still subject to Israel; previously under direct Israeli occupation (1967–1994; parts reoccupied) and rule by Egypt (Gaza) and Jordan (West Bank) (1948–1967). Britain ruled the area under League of Nations Mandate after World War I.
Official Holiday: November 15, commemorating the National Council's declaration of independence of the West Bank and Gaza, 1988.
Leader: Mahmud Abbas, President of the PA and PLO chairman.
Head of Government: Salam Fayyad, Prime Minister (2007, West Bank; Ismail Haniya, claimant Prime Minister, Gaza).
National Flag: Three horizontal stripes of black, white and green and a red triangle at the pole.
Per capita income: Less than $1,000 annually, but 60% live on less than $2 per day.

2. East Jerusalem and other Israeli-controlled areas

Area: Desired by Palestinians: about 25 square miles annexed to Jerusalem in 1967; other areas near strategic locations or Jewish settlements.

3. Israeli Arabs

Population: 1.2 million, est.

4. Refugees and Emigrants Abroad

Population: Perhaps 4 million, 10% living in refugee camps. Major concentrations live in Jordan (2,250,000), Saudi Arabia and other Gulf States (450,000), Lebanon (350,000), Syria (300,000) and Egypt (100,000). These estimates are often supplied by those with political or financial interest in the numbers.

Palestinian-administered territory lies in two portions of the ancient Biblical holy

Palestine

land. The smaller but more densely populated is Gaza, a narrow strip at the southern end of the coastal plain. The larger region, whose boundaries perplex negotiators, is the West Bank, located on the ridge of hills between the Mediterranean Sea and the Jordan River. The western slopes of the hills enjoy substantial rainfall that seeps into important aquifers that extend into Israel. By contrast, the barren eastern slopes and Jordan valley receive little precipitation.

History: Civilization extends back into pre-history in the land between the Jordan and Mediterranean. Jericho, for example, is one of the oldest continuously-occupied towns in the world. Given the light rainfall, much of the population must have herded flocks of sheep and goats and lived outside the villages and towns. The Biblical narrative of Abraham, and similar accounts in the Quran, suggest a semi-nomadic life under the authority of a family patriarch.

Some 3,000 years ago two new peoples settled among the Semitic Canaanites who had inhabited the region. From the east, the *Bnei Israel* (Sons of Israel) crossed the Jordan River and seized the central hill region. Their Semitic language resembled the Canaanites', but religious, intellectual, and tribal matters set them apart. From the west, the Philistines, a sea people, landed and occupied the coastal plain. Influenced by the Greeks, the Philistines enjoyed superior iron technology and sometimes physical (Goliath?) superiority, but their power eventually weakened. Nevertheless, the Philistines contributed their name to the region's Greek and Roman occupiers. Jewish revolts against Roman rule in the century following the death of Jesus of Nazareth led the Romans to expel most Jews from the territory.

The Arab conquest of Palestine (635–638) brought major changes in religion and language. Most inhabitants initially remained Christian, as subjects under Muslim rule, but during the following centuries a majority converted to Islam. With the exception of the Crusaders' conquests, the chronological record of Palestine differed little from those of neighboring territories (see Historical Background).

Modernization impacted the region visibly during the 19th century, and the first substantial Jewish immigration took place at its end (see Israel: History). Nevertheless, the population remained largely Muslim and overwhelmingly Arab. Only about 10% of the inhabitants were Jewish when British forces defeated Ottoman armies during World War I and ended Muslim rule.

Arab nationalism grew rapidly during the early twentieth century, but Palestinian identity only came later. In 1919 most Christians and Muslims desired to form part of a united Arab state, as they indicated to the King-Crane Commission sent by U.S. President Wilson. Nevertheless, the 1923 San Remo Conference granted Britain a mandate whose terms incorporated a Jewish national home.

For both Muslim and Christian Arabs, life under the mandate witnessed multiple setbacks. Misled by Hajj Amin al-Husayni, the Mufti of Jerusalem and president of the Muslim Council, the Palestinians failed to develop pragmatic leaders. Their traditional culture encouraged the leading families to consider each other as rivals, rather than as allies against Zionism. They lacked quiet methods to influence the government in London, and the struggle with Zionism led them to perceive themselves distinct from Arabs in Transjordan, or Syria.

There were other weaknesses. Arab society lacked funds for investment, and because the mandate deliberately left health and education to the communities, rather than government, Arabs fell further behind Zionist settlers. While material living conditions did improve, dissatisfaction marked all classes. Leading families desired the prestige, authority, and financial rewards that politicians received in Beirut, Damascus, and Baghdad. The poor resented the domination of an alien gov-

The Arab headdress—the kufiyya—served as a valued identity mask.

134

Palestine

ernment, and the politically aware opposed a colonial power that promised their own birthplace as National Home for immigrant Jews.

Lacking a coherent ideology, the Arab population condemned the loss of Arab land to Jewish settlements. They realized that if immigration continued, Arab Palestinians would eventually become a minority in a Zionist state (see Israel: History). In desperation, Palestinians turned to large-scale communal violence in 1929 and a lengthy general strike in 1936, when Britain responded to Zionist pressures and dropped plans for self-government. When a British commission proposed the partition of Palestine, virtual civil war broke out, with Arabs fighting both the British and Jews. Britain attempted to calm passions with a 1939 "White Paper" that proposed limits on Jewish immigration and land purchases and eventual self-rule. Together, these suggested an Arab majority.

Social changes increased the difficulty. The Arab population grew fastest in the same urban areas as the Jewish population: along the coast at Haifa and Jaffa, and at Jerusalem. Thus any partition that granted these areas to a Jewish state would confine Arab rule to the relative backwater of towns like Nablus and Jenin along with the less fertile hill country.

Origins of the Refugee Problem

After the mandate ended with partition voted by the United Nations (1947) and

PALESTINE: Partition Plan recommended by the UN General Assembly, November 1947

growing violence (see Israel: History), Palestinians began the flight that divided them into four groups. Historians continue to dispute, often very bitterly, the reasons why some 700,000 Palestinians fled their homes during the 1948–1949 Israeli War for Independence. Interpretations sympathetic to the Palestinians stress the Jewish warnings to flee, or outright expulsion. Moreover, on occasion Arab homes were simply demolished.

Israeli apologists sometimes accuse Arab radio broadcasts of warning the inhabitants to move from the path of advancing Arab troops. However, no credible evidence exists for this claim, and clearly in some locations Israeli troops ordered the inhabitants out. At least in Haifa, the Jewish mayor urged the Arabs to remain. Often, as the fighting drew near, the sight of refugees encouraged other families to seek greater safety while they awaited the verdict of battle. After atrocities such as a massacre of Arab civilians at Deir Yasin, and the reprisal murder of Jewish medical personnel on Mt. Scopus, many families must have felt their lives were at stake.

The Palestinians who fled to refugee camps enjoyed few of civilization's amenities. Usually illiterate peasants, the refugees posed a significant welfare burden on newly-independent countries whose own populations were very poor. Consequently, policies of separation were economically expedient, and despite sharing language, history, and religion, most Arab states discouraged the integration of refugees. Often, Arab regimes did little but police the camps and proclaim the refugees' distress as evidence of the moral wrongs inflicted by Zionism.

The refugees themselves also rejected assimilation. They argued that they should return to homes in Palestine; some, indeed, could see their houses and lands across the armistice lines. Resettlement in other Arab countries might weaken their claim for justice. Of course, Israel consistently rejected any form of repatriation.

For over 60 years the refugees and their descendants have yearned for their day of return. While waiting, they lived first in tents, then crowded into houses of concrete block and galvanized roofs. Many lacked running water, and the buildings proved cold in the winter and hot in the summer. Often unemployed and nearly always poor, the refugees remained a fertile ground for political agitation. Minimal levels of food and clothing provided by the United Nations Relief and Works Agency (UNRWA) ensured that none starved. Ironically, UNRWA schools, employing Palestinian teachers, made the Palestinians among the best-educated Arabs. They also instilled an intense nationalism in their school children.

The West Bank

In 1949, after his Arab Legion proved at least partly effective against Israel, King Abdullah united the West Bank with his existing state of Transjordan and proclaimed the Hashemite Kingdom of Jordan. For the West Bank Palestinians, the union with Jordan proved difficult. Although the Palestinians outnumbered East Bank Jordanians and had achieved higher levels of education and political sophistication, East Bank Jordanians dominated government and the military.

Most of all, Palestinians distrusted Abdullah's moderation towards Israel. They interpreted his annexation of the West Bank as enriching his dynasty; their passion was Arab nationalism and the desire to destroy Israel. Abdullah enjoyed his enlarged kingdom only briefly, for he was assassinated by a militant Palestinian in 1951. King Hussein, his grandson and successor, continued the royal moderation; Palestinians retained their suspicions. Investment was concentrated in the East Bank, an astute policy in view of the increasing military superiority of Israel, though naturally unpopular on the West Bank. Progress towards democracy faced frequent reverses, and the Hashemite Kingdom greatly depended on foreign aid (see Jordan: History).

Conditions were materially worse for the Palestinians in Gaza, a strip about 25 miles long and five miles wide administered by Egypt but not annexed. The 200,000 refugees overwhelmed the existing population of 70,000, and the dense population limited agricultural development. With its own impoverished millions, Egypt lacked funds to develop Gaza, and in fact Cairo discouraged the refugees from settling in Egypt.

Israel's conquest of the West Bank and Gaza Strip in June 1967 ushered in a new era. East Jerusalem was annexed, and its inhabitants therefore gained the vote. The rest of the West Bank came under military administration. Absent a peace agreement, its inhabitants officially lived in occupied Jordan, but West Bankers grew increasingly separate from it despite financial aid and salaries from Amman.

Although Security Council Resolution 242 called for an Israeli withdrawal from territories occupied during the war, Israel increasingly intended to remain. Any proclamation of Palestinian identity met Israeli hostility. Flying the Palestinian flag became illegal, along with nationalist activities.

Moreover, Israelis "created facts." They established settlements on Arab lands, particularly around Jerusalem, at strategic points along the Jordan River, and places where Jewish settlements had existed before 1948. Within 20 years, the 60,000 set-

Palestine

tlers came to control about 50% of the West Bank's land, and 34% of that in the crowded Gaza Strip. Settlers also claimed a disproportionate share of water, using almost four times as much per person as the natives.

The Israeli occupation brought substantial economic changes. At first, commerce and industry expanded. Tens of thousands found jobs in Israel, at higher wages. Private education increased, several colleges and universities were founded, and social support organizations provided mutual aid. However, in the 1980s, the growth rate fell; given the high birth rate this meant stagnant living standards. In addition, many Palestinians resented the occupation's hardships. Israeli permits reportedly protected Israeli farmers from Palestinian competition. Exports to markets in Europe often proved impossible. Tax revenues from the territories exceeded aid to them, and the Palestinians purchased far more from Israel than they sold there.

Nevertheless, until 1988 the occupation failed to arouse significant criticism in Israel or the United States. Only then, deprived of hope that diplomacy might bring freedom, did Palestinians slowly turn to direct action. Strikes and protests became a common weapon, often engulfing the occupied territories for weeks.

Israel responded sternly, sometimes violating the Geneva Convention. Strike leaders and suspected activists were deported, and hundreds of others detained without trial. Several thousand houses belonging to the families of militants were demolished, and lengthy curfews frequently punished all inhabitants of an area. Little scope existed for legal activities opposed to the Israeli occupation, and youths hanging the Palestinian flag from electrical wires were forced at gunpoint to remove them, risking death by electrocution.

Palestinians in Exile

By contrast, Palestinians abroad felt far greater hope soon after 1967. The 1964 Arab Summit Conference established the *Palestine Liberation Organization (PLO)*. Subsequently, the Palestine National Council was formed to reflect Palestinian opinion, and the Palestine National Charter established the PLO's goals. These called for a "One State Solution"—replacing Israel with a secular and democratic state where individuals of all religions could live together. Such phrases perhaps seem innocent, but the Charter also called Palestinians to liberate their land by force and denied Jewish immigrants a place within Palestine. Even without Zionism's emphasis on a special state for Jews, Israelis would hardly accept a solution that expelled most of them from their homes.

Also in 1964, Yasir Arafat founded *al-Fatah*. Consciously modeled after successful anti-colonial guerrilla movements elsewhere, *al-Fatah* undertook a variety of small attacks on Israel from Syria and Jordan, actions that drew Israeli reprisals that in turn led to the June 1967 War.

That war exposed the futility of Arab military goals to defeat Israel, and it discredited virtually every Arab leader. Only the guerrillas "who sacrificed themselves," the *fida'iyin* remained. When they fought back bravely against an Israeli raid on Karameh in Jordan, they became heroes. Guerrilla groups multiplied; among the many were the *Popular Front for the Liberation of Palestine (PFLP)*, the *Popular Democratic Front (PDFLP)*, and *Saiqa*. The first two groups reflected leftist ideologies, complete with class struggles and the necessity of political and social revolution throughout the Arab world. Others were basically paid agents of particular Arab regimes.

Above all, Palestinians and their financial backers turned to the straightforward nationalist views of *al-Fatah*. Its founder, Yasir Arafat, became Chairman of the *PLO* in 1968 and symbolized Palestine as no other leader had. The *PLO*, in turn, became an umbrella organization for the various *fida'iyin*, running the refugee camps and conducting Palestinian publicity and diplomacy.

Inevitably the guerrillas disturbed Arab governments. Raids into Israel provoked retaliation, against both commando groups and the host country. The *fida'iyin* sought sophisticated weapons and fortified bases, and became armed units operating within an Arab state, often better paid and more glamorous than the national army. Furthermore, to avoid Israeli retaliation on economic targets, governments had to halt guerrilla raids from their territory or watch their citizens' standard of living destroyed. Syria quickly controlled its local guerrillas. Egypt permitted none. For Jordan and Lebanon the experience was bitter, but the refugees themselves suffered the greatest loses in inter-Arab fighting.

Its long border with Israel and large Palestinian population made Jordan a naturally desirable base for the *fida'iyin*. Their desire to liberate all Palestine—including freeing the West Bank from Hussein's kingdom—led to tensions. In 1970, the *Popular Front* hijacked Western jetliners to a desert landing strip in Jordan. In part to free the passengers taken hostage, the Jordanian army fought bitterly against Palestinian guerrillas in Amman. Thousands died, many of them civilians, and the surviving Palestinians called it Black September. (Later a secret terrorist group linked to *al-Fatah* adopted the name as a memorial.) King Hussein regained control of his capital, and after further fighting, expelled the *fida'iyin* from Jordan.

They transferred their activities to Lebanon, a country too weak to limit their activities or prevent Israel from striking at will. Scores of problems developed between the Palestinians and the Lebanese, ranging from unpaid traffic tickets and electric bills to guerrilla checkpoints and gun battles. Against a background of political wrangling between Lebanon's Muslims and Maronites, in 1975 a Phalangist ambush of a Palestinian motorcade marked the beginning of the Lebanese Civil War (see Lebanon: History).

In the war's first stage, the *fida'iyin* and their leftist and Muslim allies nearly defeated the Christian Maronite militias. However, Syria—long a political and military ally of the Palestinians—turned the battle against them. The major refugee camp at Tel al-Za'tar fell after a bloody struggle. In 1978, though, the Palestinians and Syrians reunited. In revenge for Palestinian attacks, Israel invaded south Lebanon in 1978. Thousands of Palestinians and Lebanese perished in 1982, when a full-scale conventional attack brought Israeli troops to the suburbs of Beirut (see Israel: History). Still more civilian deaths resulted when Israeli troops allowed Maronite militiamen to enter Palestinian refugee camps outside Beirut and massacre—unopposed—hundreds of women, children, and old men.

The long years of fighting brought few benefits to Palestinians, and the hopes kindled by Karameh waned. The *fida'iyin* killed many times more Arabs—Jordanians, Lebanese, Syrians, and others—than Israelis. Likewise, the refugees suffered more deaths from Arab weapons than from Israel. Despite their great popularity in some Arab and Third World circles, the *fida'iyin* had by their terrorist actions aroused intense dislike in Western public opinion. Fortunately for the Palestinians, world attention turned in 1988 from the exiled Palestinians to those living in the West Bank and Gaza Strip.

Resisting Occupation: The Intifada

The popular rebellion known as the *intifada* began in 1987. Against the Israel Defense Force, one of the world's most admired military organizations, civilians of the West Bank and Gaza used strikes, civil disobedience, rock-throwing, other petty violence and boycotts of Israeli goods. Rock and bottle-throwing youths damaged thousands of passing cars and buses; firebombs gutted others. However, the violence was not deliberately lethal, and the statistics for 1988 firmly established the one-sided nature of fatal violence: 366 Arab deaths and 11,000 wounded compared with 15 Israeli deaths and 420 injured. The *intifada* reflected a deliberate attempt to defy Israeli rule rather than to kill Jews.

The first *intifada* began with protests and stones

The youthful activists earned wide television coverage, but the *intifada* involved many elements of Palestinian society. Middle-aged, middle-class merchants accepted repeated general strikes designed to show the authority of the resistance movement. Traditional Israeli controls—for example, smashing shutters on closed shops or welding them shut—failed to break the strikes.

Other economic actions included the boycott of Israeli cigarettes and soft-drinks, and widespread resistance to taxes. The 140,000 Palestinians who provided the major source of cheap unskilled labor in Israel's construction and other industries obeyed strike calls and disrupted the Israeli economy.

The *intifada* inflicted heavy costs on the Palestinians. Besides the deaths—many of them avoidable—there were beatings, deportations, and tens of thousands of arrests. Attempting to break the uprising, Israel closed professional associations and charitable groups. It destroyed the homes of families whose teenagers were suspected of throwing gasoline bombs.

The *intifada* dramatically changed world opinion about Palestinians. They had been refugees first, then terrorists who hijacked airliners, murdered Olympic athletes, and massacred hostages. Such acts provoked outrage and extreme hostility in the Western world. After the *intifada*, they became a defenseless people, beaten and shot by alien soldiers. Even in America, the televised sufferings of Arabs eroded the prevailing belief in the moral rightness of the Israeli occupation. Closer to home, witnessing the intense nationalism, King Hussein of Jordan withdrew his claims to the West Bank.

These strengths enabled Yasir Arafat to take the diplomatic initiative in seeking an independent Palestine limited to the Occupied Territories. When the Palestine National Council met in Algiers in 1988, Arafat's carefully worded policy triumphed. Despite years of condemning it, the delegates voted to accept UN Security Council Resolution 242, linking it to the Palestinian right to self-determination (see Israel: History, Resolution 242). The resolution also implicitly abandoned the PLO's goal of eliminating Israel, and condemned terrorism of all kinds. The Council balanced these actions by declaring Palestine independent, using words that mirrored Israel's similar declaration in 1948. However, the acceptance of a state on the West Bank and Gaza—the "Two-State Solution," split the Council into moderate and rejectionist camps. It also failed to win recognition from European nations and the United States, who insisted that accepted territory and boundaries must precede formal recognition.

Soon afterwards, Arafat addressed a special session of the UN General Assembly, held in Geneva because the U.S. considered him a terrorist and refused him a visa. Posing as a statesman, he detailed the positions adopted by the National Council, and gave away the ultimate Palestinian bargaining chip—recognition of Israel. He hoped, in response, for negotiations to free the occupied territories and form a Palestinian state. The votes in Algiers and the speeches in Geneva gave Arafat the diplomatic initiative. Within days the U.S. held talks with the PLO. After more than two years of the *intifada*, Palestinians had restored their self-respect and unity, and gained Western sympathy. But neither the *intifada* nor Arafat's recognition of Israel had gained an inch of territory or improved the harsh military occupation. Israel's new hard-line cabinet under Yitzhak Shamir fundamentally opposed ceding any territory of Eretz Israel for peace.

Moreover, the facts on the ground worsened. In its last days, the Soviet Union reversed policy and allowed its Jews to emigrate; some one million Jewish immigrants were expected. They placed a very long fuse on the "demographic time bomb" of an Arab majority between the Jordan and Mediterranean. Settlement activities also increased in the territories, subsidized by the government despite international condemnation. Within Palestine, the *intifada* showed signs of disintegration, as its targets became alleged collaborators or Palestinians charged with moral failures like corruption, homosexuality or prostitution. The *intifada*, itself a struggle against the powerful, was creating its own victims. To some extent, the violence between Palestinians resulted from Israeli success in rounding up or eliminating leaders and activists. Some 10% of the population suffered imprisonment, injuries requiring hospital care, or material losses such as destroyed crops or confiscated possessions.

The Price of Backing Saddam

Many Palestinians enthusiastically supported Iraqi President Saddam Hussein in 1990 when he seized Kuwait, because he then demanded a peace settlement involving Israeli-held lands. Yasir Arafat publicly embraced him. This obviously marked the triumph of emotional desperation over reason. Diplomacy had produced nothing and the *intifada* little but casualties. As a result, Palestinians welcomed a strong leader who threatened Israel, defied the West and promised to unite the Arab nation. Few considered the flawed logic of demanding nationhood for one group of Arabs, while supporting the invasion and seizure of another Arab state. If Palestinians supported Arab unity and one Arab nation, then logically Israel was right: there was no need for a twenty-first Arab state.

Palestinians suffered more from the Gulf War than any nation besides Kuwait and Iraq. In Kuwait, though divided in their response to the invasion, they suffered collective reprisal. Thousands lost their jobs and life savings. Hostility, revenge, and deportations decimated the community. Palestinians in other Gulf countries found themselves under suspicion, and unable to renew visas. Losing residence and employment, they became refugees yet again.

In the West Bank and Gaza, support for the invasion cost Kuwaiti support for hospitals, schools, and the *intifada* just as Israeli curfews worsened living conditions. Gulf rulers halted aid estimated at $100 million per month to the PLO. The official

Palestine

PLO position swung to "neutrality," over Kuwait, but popular feeling in refugee camps and the Occupied Territories openly supported Saddam Hussein and cheered Scud attacks on Israel. It was yet another public relations disaster to a cause prone to self-destruction.

Despite their misfortunes, Palestinians won representation at the 1991 peace negotiations in Madrid because the Jordanian delegation attached Palestinian intellectuals outside the PLO. These negotiators won wide respect. Their spokeswoman, Hanan Ashrawi, presented their case to Westerners far more persuasively than Yasir Arafat ever had. Nevertheless, the discussions produced nothing of substance, partly because Israel intended to yield nothing, as its prime minister later confessed. Meanwhile, led by *Hamas* and other militant Islamic groups, Arab opposition grew strengthened against the talks.

After the 1992 Israeli elections, the new *Labor* government halted most new settlements outside Jerusalem. However, when the killings of Israeli soldiers and civilians continued, Prime Minister Rabin refused Palestinians entry to the Occupied Territories, even for work. Immediately unemployment soared to 50% or more in some places. The closed border carried momentous consequences. Israelis realized that they preferred life without Palestinians, and support rose for a break with the Occupied Territories.

Against this background, Israeli and *PLO* negotiators secretly met in Oslo in 1993, and agreed to create a Palestinian administration in Jericho and Gaza by April 1994. A now-famous handshake at the White House formalized the Declaration of Principles between two men who had been bitter enemies for decades, Prime Minister Rabin and Chairman Arafat.

Progress towards Palestinian Autonomy

Though the Oslo Accords won wide support in the world's press, many Palestinian groups condemned them, both on the left (the *Popular Front* and the *Democratic Front*) and the religious right (*Islamic Jihad* and *Hamas)*. They considered two disconnected parcels of land under limited self-rule far too small a reward for ending the struggle to replace Israel with a Palestinian state. Opposition also arose within the Palestinian leadership. Calls grew for democracy, and Hanan Ashrawi chose to serve on a human rights group rather than on the administrative council.

The Oslo Accords envisaged complete agreement by December 1993, followed by a phased Israeli withdrawal, zones of self-government, and elections in 1994. However, each side desired the immediate steps to reflect its vision of the final arrangements. And over the final arrangements there had been no agreement. Officially, Israel still regarded the Palestinian future as up for negotiation, and it sought to protect every Jewish settlement and access route, even those surrounded by tens of thousands of Arabs at Hebron and Gaza. In contrast, Palestinians considered their zones the embryo of an independent state, and sought the trappings of statehood: tariffs and economic regulations, currency (even if only symbolic), passports, stamps and telephone area codes. Their leaders also included Palestinians from East Jerusalem, despite Israeli objections that this involved the fate of the city. From its beginnings, the Oslo process fell behind schedule, and the slow pace of negotiations weakened support for peace.

Nevertheless, important forces on both sides sabotaged the peace process, and Palestinian history between 1993 and the present ultimately reduces to the conflicts these forces provoked. Unwavering in their rejection of the Oslo Accords, *Hamas* and *Islamic Jihad* launched terrorist raids that ranged from the isolated murder of soldiers to suicide attacks that killed dozens. His mentality shaped by his years as a guerilla, Yasir Arafat proved unwilling or unable to enforce the security that Israeli leaders saw as the basis of peace. On the other side, Israeli cabinets often pressed tactical demands about negotiations at the cost of setbacks to the strategic goal of peace. Border closures inflicted unemployment and other hardships that likely created additional recruits for the most militant groups. Targeted assassinations—the selective murder of militants by intelligence agents or missile strikes—often provided justification in Palestinian minds for further suicide raids.

Against this background, there were moments of achievement. In 1994, the first step towards Palestinian autonomy occurred when the *PLO* took control of Jericho. Middle-aged soldiers from the Palestinian Liberation Army arrived to become policemen in Gaza and Jericho; crowds of well-wishers cheered them. The rapid pace of events caught Palestinian leaders unprepared. The post office had no stamps; the police, no telephones. The near-bankrupt *PLO* used a U.S. grant of just $5 million for initial expenses, but the Palestinian flag flew over Gaza and Jericho. After later negotiations, the occupiers departed Ramallah and other towns, but two-thirds of the West Bank still remained under Israeli control, including military bases, 128 settlements, and access roads, in a territory half the size of Connecticut.

Freed from the occupation, in 1996 voters overwhelmingly elected Arafat "Ra'is," or president. His supporters likewise won a majority in the Palestine National Council. Arafat then kept a very significant promise. He summoned the Palestine National Council to Gaza, where after decades of exile, it met and voted overwhelmingly to delete the Charter's call for the destruction of Israel. The Israeli *Labor Party* hinted acceptance of an independent Palestine, and talks began on the final, most difficult issues: East Jerusalem, refugees, water, and settlers.

During the elections that followed the assassination of Yitzhak Rabin, Palestinian suicide bombers demonstrated the insecurity of the peace process, and thus helped secure victory for Binyamin Netanyahu, whose *Likud Party* had opposed the Oslo Accords, and in fact any Palestinian state. While Netanyahu met Arafat and withdrew troops from part of Hebron, he also permitted the start of a new Jewish settlement, Har Homa (Jabal Abu Ghnaim), in the vital stretch of Arab-inhabited land between Bethlehem and East Jerusalem. The Peace Process continued to disintegrate. Suicide bombings by *Hamas* in Jerusalem provoked an internal closure on Palestinian areas. This shut down travel and trade *between the individual Palestinian towns*, a blow far worse than Israel had inflicted before the Oslo Accords. Unemployment afflicted half the working

Intifada

population, and many individuals had incomes of under $2.00 per day.

The city of Hebron, the largest Arab community with nearly 100,000 inhabitants, has remained an intense source of conflict and resentment. To protect some 450 Jewish settlers and students, Israel retained 20% of the entire city, including its commercial and religious center. On the outskirts, other settlers used any available pretext to seize Arab farmlands and demolish homes built or extended without permits.

Near-success, then Diplomatic Collapse

The greatest opportunity for peace occurred in 2000. During the final days of his presidency, President Clinton invited Arafat and then-Prime Minister Barak to the Camp David presidential retreat. During intense negotiations, Barak conceded a greater Palestinian role in East Jerusalem than any Israeli leader had ever discussed in public, but would not yield actual control over the Arab parts of the city. Mindful of both political opinion at home and his place in history, Arafat rejected the concession, insisting that "the Arab leader has not been born who will give away Jerusalem."

Ariel Sharon's visit to the Haram al-Sharif, the Muslim holy places on Temple Mount with a security detachment of 1,000 plunged the two sides into violence. The leader of the opposition *Likud* party, General Sharon had earned a reputation for aggressive behavior towards Arabs (the Qibya massacre, Jordan, 1953; ignoring a cease-fire, Egypt, 1973; permitting militiamen to enter Palestinian camps, Lebanon, 1983, where they murdered hundreds). Angry Muslims considered his visit a sacrilege and protested by stone-throwing; the police shot dead some rioters. This marked the beginning of "al-Aqsa intifada," a bloody resumption of protests and violence against the occupation (see also Israel: History).

Certainly, the Palestinians frequently initiated violence, but they overwhelmingly suffered the casualties. Under *Labor's* Prime Minister Barak, troops shot to kill, and half the casualties came from gunshots to the neck and head. The televised death of Muhammad Dura, a twelve-year-old boy shot while huddling with his father, won sympathy (but little else) in Arab countries and the West. Instituting a collective punishment over all the territories, Israel re-imposed its closure system, cutting the Gaza into six enclaves, and the West Bank into 24. Economic conditions, never prosperous, again became desperate. Families shared what they had, but many survived only on UNRWA food subsidies and aid from abroad (perhaps averaging $500 per person in 2001).

**The late Yasir Arafat,
PLO chairman and PA President**

Seeing little progress, Palestinian popular opinion increasingly accepted the militants' argument that the Oslo peace process had created little else than a powerless and undemocratic Authority mismanaged by President Arafat. The Palestinian police even did Israel's dirty work: the occupied provided security for the occupier. Because Israel was unwilling to grant Palestinian demands, reasoned the militants, the *intifada* must continue until victory.

Yasir Arafat, alternating between his role as president and a manipulator seeking negotiating strength, permitted or (allegedly) encouraged violence if that might strengthen Palestinian interests. He possibly used terrorism to force concessions from Israel, striving to keep the territory and power gained by Oslo without delivering the promised security. Certainly *Likud's* new Prime Minister Sharon held him personally responsible for the terrorists' bloodshed.

Whatever the initial relationships, the militants soon escaped official control. Religious and secular groups joined the armed struggle. Besides *Hamas* and *Islamic Jihad*, they included the *al-Aqsa Brigade* of Arafat's own *Fatah* movement. This placed the Palestinian security forces in impossible circumstances. Israel and the U.S. demanded that Arafat end terrorism and arrest its perpetrators before negotiations. To make those arrests required the police, but widespread public support for these groups sometimes blocked Palestinian police who attempted to arrest alleged militants. The police also became particular targets of Israeli fire, as targets in reprisal killings.

After an explosion killed 25 elderly Jews gathered for Passover in the spring of 2002, Israeli forces systematically attacked the major West Bank cities in an effort to destroy terrorist cells. Over 200 Arabs died; tens of thousands endured hardships ranging from battle wounds to confinement indoors. Government offices, police offices and stores suffered vandalism. After a carefully planned ambush in the Janin refugee camp took the lives of Israeli soldiers, the Israel Defense Forces left destruction compared by eyewitnesses to an earthquake zone. Accounts verified by Human Rights Watch suggested war crimes occurred, such as the use of civilians as human shields, or the prevention of medical assistance to the camp for five days.

In Ramallah, the Israelis deliberately spared part of Yasir Arafat's headquarters, but confined him to two rooms, and prevented him from attending an Arab summit conference. Thus imprisoned, he regained some of the respect as a leader that his inept administration had destroyed. Released after American pressure, Arafat later promised reforms and elections, the first to the legislature in six years. However, suicide bombings led Israel to seize and hold most Arab cities and towns, and Arafat probably did not desire genuine elections; they were postponed. His popularity, overwhelming while he was besieged, fell rapidly in the face of demands from nearly everyone—Palestinians of all parties, Americans, Israelis—for improved security, an attack on corruption, and the rule of law.

Fatah Fractures; Hamas Wins

Beyond symbolism, in almost a decade the Palestinian National Authority had achieved little. Israel controlled the electricity, water supply, and telephone lines, and divided Palestinian islets from one another by roads to the growing settlements. Financially, the PA depended almost completely on foreign aid. In fact, most of its own taxes are collected by Israel on trade, thus enabling Israel to block them when desired. Arafat's employees felt underpaid, and the Palestinian public resented corruption and the creation of monopolies. The heavy-handed police often acted repressively. When twenty academics and legislators signed a severe attack on the Arafat administration and called the Oslo peace process a "conspiracy" against the nation, the security forces arrested half the signatories without charging them.

Arafat's death in 2004 offered the possibility of a new start. Long the personal symbol of the Palestinian struggle, in Israeli and American eyes he often represented the causes of his political rivals, the

Palestine

The Palestinian Red Crescent Society offices, directly targeted   (Photo by Said Abedwahed)

suicide bombers. As president, he also bore responsibility for an incompetent and failing administration. His death left a nation so fractured politically that commentators speculated about the possibility of anarchy, or that Islamic militants might seize Gaza and split it from the West Bank.

In the presidential race that followed *Fatah* united around Mahmud Abbas, a long-time aide to Arafat. Despite his moderation and opposition to the violent *intifada,* Abbas won an overwhelming majority in a light turnout. He adeptly negotiated a ceasefire with Israel that required a halt to Palestinian violence. In return, Israel agreed to withdraw from some West Bank cities, stop assassinations, and release hundreds of prisoners.

Abbas fared less well with domestic politics. His first appointed prime minister failed to win a majority for his cabinet. He also failed to combat corruption effectively, or to halt the growing anarchy when *Fatah's* own multiple security forces confronted each other and those of *Hamas* on the streets of Gaza. However, he did persuade the various armed units to halt suicide operations in 2005, thus making possible the Israeli withdrawal from Gaza.

Recalling the Arab sense of victory that followed Israel's withdrawal from Lebanon, the Sharon cabinet determined to erase any doubts about Israeli power before withdrawing from Gaza. Israel Defense Forces assassinated a number of militants, notably Sheikh Ahmad Yassin, the elderly leader of *Hamas* who died in his wheelchair. After his successor was assas-

sinated a few weeks later, *Hamas* kept its leadership secret.

Besides exterminating the militants' leadership, the Israeli military also targeted supply depots, workshops and other possible military targets. Its units inflicted such destruction on the Rafah refugee camp that the U.S. abandoned its usual veto and allowed the UN Security Council to condemn the operation.

In the end, the Israeli withdrawal initially brought a great sense of freedom to

Gaza, but within months, the predictions of anarchy began to come true. Abbas's own party, *Fatah,* splintered between the Old Guard around Abbas and supporters of younger militants like Marwan Barghouti, a hero imprisoned for life in Israel for approving attacks on civilians. Without Barghouti, *Fatah* symbolized a policy blamed by the public for corruption and the economic depression. By contrast, *Hamas* decided to contest legislative elections, and it entered the contest united and disciplined. *Hamas* won decisive victories in most locations, the highest share of the national vote, and it captured 72 of the 132 seats.

By exercising their democratic right to vote for the party of their choice even though it refused to recognize Israel, Palestinian voters plunged themselves into difficulties. *Hamas* found no allies; its prime minister, Ismail Haniya, immediately faced a cut-off of almost all government revenue—taxes collected by Israel and foreign aid from the U.S. and Europe. On the surface, these governments refused to contribute funds to a group committed to Israel's destruction. Conveniently, this same tactic might financially strangle the Palestinian Authority to death and thus also discredit *Hamas.*

Israel could hardly be expected to finance those committed to its destruction. However, the financial strangulation carried somber consequences. Following a relatively free election, the West punished the Palestinian people for voting out a decrepit and divided party. Arab democracy, it seemed, was desired—but only as long as voters selected those approved by America. Although unwilling to recognize

A wounded Palestinian being evacuated. Palestinian and Israeli accounts conflict dramatically over the identity of those killed and wounded. The lack of a uniform does not imply a civilian casualty.

Israel, Ismail Haniya was willing to pursue a truce with it.

The results of the financial blockade were as predictable as they were perverse. Without the tax revenues collected by Israel, Palestinian revenues covered perhaps one third of salaries. Utterly unable to pay them, the regime floundered. The economy continued in depression. Western nations and organizations therefore funded relief activities and even paid salary support for civil employees. In fact, *they actually spent more money on Palestinians during the blockade* than they would have without it. Arab government aid, though, could not reach Haniya's legitimately elected government.

Gaza under Hamas

Sporadic fighting broke out between Islamic militants in Gaza and the Israeli military. A brazen raid by militants over the border into Israel captured 19-year-old Corporal Gilad Shalit, and during 2006, while Israel fought Hizbullah across the northern border, it also launched attacks on militants in the Gaza Strip. While world attention focused on Shalit, the bloodshed proved highly one-sided. During the year after the withdrawal from Gaza, two Israeli civilians died from the militants' simple rockets. By contrast, according to the human rights group B'Tselem, the retaliatory air strikes and tank invasions killed about 400 Palestinians. This mirrored the wider balance of casualties, including the West Bank, with 660 Palestinians killed by Israeli security forces in 2006, nearly a quarter of them children. During the same period, only 23 Israelis died from Palestinian hostilities.

**President Mahmoud Abbas
of Palestine**

In 2007 King Abdullah of Saudi Arabia pressured *Hamas* and *Fatah* to form a cabinet of national unity, in hopes of lifting the blockade and ending the frequent clashes between their militias in Gaza. However, Ismail Haniya remained prime minister, and he continued to refuse to recognize Israel, so the blockade continued. That summer, clashes between the two parties' militiamen in Gaza reached a crisis. *Hamas* rejected President Abbas's attempts to control the security forces, and arrested or killed *Fatah's* fighters in Gaza. In response, Abbas dismissed Haniya's cabinet. Almost immediately, the financial blockade was lifted. Since *Hamas* members still formed the parliamentary majority, Abbas governs only the West Bank, and contrary to standard democratic practices. Gaza remained under *Hamas* rule.

Once *Hamas* ruled Gaza, Israeli restrictions gradually halted Gaza's economy.

The level of goods entering Gaza fell to 10% the year-previous level. Construction stopped completely, 90% of private industries shut down, farms became free-fire zones for Israeli tanks, and 80% of the population only survived thanks to food aid. The power generating plant failed to operate well after it was attacked, and Israel cut the levels of electricity and fuel permitted into the Strip. Hospitals fell short of medicines, but animal vaccines were rushed into Gaza, to avoid communicable diseases.

In desperation, *Hamas* militants broke through the border to Egypt. For two weeks hundreds of thousands of Palestinians purchased cheap Egyptian goods at border towns. When Egypt re-sealed the border, trade continued underground, through tunnels where smugglers brought consumer goods—eventually, even new cars—and undoubtedly military supplies. Ironically, since *Hamas* taxed the smugglers, its control over the economy increased—it now gained revenue from trade without Israel collecting the taxes.

By late 2008, neither side had gained its desired goals. A truce had committed Israel to permit increased trade, in response *Hamas* halting all attacks by all groups on Israel. But attacks never quite stopped, and trade never resumed its peace-time levels. After the formal expiration of the ceasefire, Israel launched an intensive bombing campaign followed by a land invasion of Gaza, seeking to destroy the rocket-launching capabilities, reduce or eliminate *Hamas* as an armed organization, and re-establish respect for its military after the inconclusive war against *Hizbullah* in 2006 (see Israel: **history**).

Hamas fought back with tactics borrowed from *Hizbullah* and Iran. Its fighters dispersed among the population to fight in civilian areas, with weapons stored in many homes and mosques. To avoid air attacks, fighters moved directly between homes, or used tunnels and underground command posts—a headquarters was reported underneath the largest hospital. Clearly, these tactics did not seek to minimize civilian casualties, and Amnesty faulted *Hamas* for endangering Palestinian civilians by firing rockets from residential neighborhoods. For their part, Israeli troops rarely entered houses by the door, fearing booby-traps, and combined the use of precision weaponry with heavy, short-range firing at points of resistance. Inevitably, hundreds of Palestinian civilians were killed, some of them sheltering beside UN compounds or in a UN school. Thousands were wounded.

Charges of war crimes quickly arose against both sides. Israel received the most condemnation (e.g., from the UN, the Red Cross, Amnesty International), for

Israeli missiles score direct hits on Gaza University, suspected of harboring Hamas military activities

Palestine

its use of civilians as shields or to enter suspected booby-traps, for using white phosphorous bombs, for obstructing access to medical care, and the "wanton and deliberate" destruction of homes, businesses, and public buildings. However, *Hamas* was blamed for its rocket attacks on civilians. Israel also claimed that *Hamas* fighters abandoned uniforms to mix with the population, violated rules on the use of the white flag, sheltered behind civilians, and generally fought in ways that endangered civilians.

The three-week war ended when first Israel and then *Hamas* independently announced cease-fires. It left enormous destruction, including neighborhoods and an industrial area flattened by bulldozers and shells. Along with other infrastructure, damaged sewer and water pipelines may take years to repair. Nevertheless, the fighting had failed to create new rules of the game. *Hamas* remained in power, the blockade continued, and the world perceived Gazans as the victims, but did little about it. Smugglers quickly resumed their trade through the tunnels, no doubt importing weapons as well as consumer goods.

Although the United Nations, the International Committee of the Red Cross, and other organizations long warned about the consequences of the blockade of Gaza, for three years Israel successfully defended it in Western public opinion as a necessity for security against home-made missiles. The gradual release of information about details of the restrictions—for example, mineral water could be imported but not fruit juice, the UN had trouble reconstructing its buildings, and prohibited repairs to the sewer treatment plants threatened health—failed to change perceptions.

When Israeli commandos stormed the *Mavi Marmara* in international waters and killed 9 peace activists, world perceptions shifted radically. The Turkish ferry was part of a flotilla organized to challenge the blockade by attempting to carry humanitarian supplies to Gaza, and Israel claimed the commandos fired in self defense against activists armed with "clubs, knives, and other weapons." Nevertheless, world perceptions changed, even the U.S. president recognized that conditions in Gaza had become unsustainable. Egypt opened the Rafah crossing.

Within days, in the face of proposals that the European Union might supervise cargoes for Gaza, the Israeli cabinet reduced the scope of the embargo. Food items, toys, and kitchen utensils reportedly will be permitted, as well as material for the U.N. Sea shipments to Gaza are still prohibited, and given Egyptian cooperation, total control over imports remains. Israeli dominance is thus still asserted, and the collective punishment of Gaza continues, though presumably less harshly.

Meanwhile, Israeli restrictions continue to make life "extremely hard" for Palestinians in the West Bank. Getting to school, work or hospital is often virtually impossible, and restrictions linked to Israeli settlements deprive many Palestinian farmers of their land. An estimated 50% of the West Bank's population lives in poverty

Political Instability Discredits the PA

When his already-extended presidential term approached its end in 2009, Mahmud Abbas suggested that he might not run again. However, with the PA divided between *Hamas*-ruled Gaza and the West Bank under *Fatah,* free and open elections seemed improbable. Moreover, if Abbas would not run, *Fatah* lacked a viable nominee besides Marwan Barghouti, still imprisoned. To avoid the crisis, in January 2010 the *PLO* met the difficulty by extending, once again, the terms of both the president and parliament. Predictably condemned by *Hamas,* the decision hardly strengthened popular support for the PA. Internationally, the entire matter left the Palestinian Authority a poor partner for the indirect "proximity negotiations" widely considered the only route leading to a two-state solution. However, the negotiations were also likely to fail on the Israeli side, with a cabinet unwilling, or a country unable, to halt settlement growth for a sustained period.

One somewhat surprising positive development is the economic recovery taking place on the West Bank, prodded by the Prime Minister, Salam Fayyad.

Culture: As Arabs, and most often Muslims, Palestinians share many cultural values of the surrounding countries. Customs regarding food, dress, and limitations on young men mixing with young women are much like those in Jordan. However, the diversity of personal experiences provides a greater variety of cultural impacts than in most Arab states. Most refugees in Gaza, for example, lack the financial sophistication of an engineer in Saudi Arabia, or the intellectual breadth of an educated woman from East Jerusalem.

Heavily influenced by Marxism and other secular ideas, the *Palestine Liberation Organization* accepted women as professionals, and many of them dressed in Western styles. With the growth of Islamist militancy, however, women in Gaza and other bastions of *Hamas* increasingly choose to wear at least a head covering, and conservatives clearly consider a woman's significance to come from her husband or family. Islamists in recent years also discouraged concerts of popular music and dancing. There is only one movie house in the entire Palestinian authority.

The most-recognized Palestinian intellectual in the Western world was undoubtedly Edward Said, the eloquent literary critic and author of *Orientalism*, a serious attack on much Western writing about the region. Far closer to contemporary passions, the feature film *Paradise Now*, a joint production of Israelis and Palestinians, portrayed the emotions of two young men recruited as suicide bombers. The movie was nominated for an Oscar in 2006 as best foreign film and it won that category at the Golden Globes.

Gaza University leveled by direct Israeli attacks.

Economic Prospects: Several recent studies attempt to predict economic conditions in the first years of an independent state. Given the high birthrate, and the possible return of some refugees, the population of the PA will climb significantly from the three million at the turn of the century. Water use for irrigation, industry, and households by such a dense population would place severe pressure on resources, and imply that current Israeli dependence on West Bank supplies must cease.

Estimates of the cost of establishing a Palestinian state exceed $14 billion, with large investment in housing, business, industry, and the infrastructure. Because independence will likely permanently reduce the number of jobs in Israel, it will require greatly enlarged economic opportunities in the West Bank and Gaza. Companies linked to Israel would need to shift to other export markets, or find alternative suppliers. Given such substantial financial burdens, an independent Palestine located between Israel and Jordan can prosper only with large subsidies from other Arab states.

The Future: The 2009 Gaza War reduced Palestinian rocket and mortar attacks on Israel, but did not quite end them. Israelis and Palestinians alike would rather increase their honored dead than accept a compromise peace. Many Jews care too deeply about Zionism, and many Arabs dwell too fervently on their past injustices, to recognize those across the security wall as genuine humans. The kindest and wisest Palestinian leaders condemn the folly of alienating world opinion by blowing up innocent civilians, but they are a minority. In contrast, militants argue that honorable death is preferable to living under an occupation that dehumanizes, assassinates, and annually seizes more land.

The "roadmap" presented to Israel and Palestinians in 2003 made sense on the surface. The Annapolis negotiations between the U.S., Israeli, and Palestinian leaders also sounded good. But the outside world provided each side sufficient resources to continue the struggle. Without a conclusive defeat, neither side will compromise. Therefore, the international community bears the burden of providing the outlines of a reasonable settlement and then ensuring its implementation.

Since Israel's independence, the creation of two national states, Jewish and Palestinian Arab, has seemed the logical solution to the dispute over the Holy Land. But Palestinian autonomy is a mockery, with a quarter-million settlers moving to lands claimed by the Palestinians since the peace process began in Oslo. Barack Obama will be the last U.S. president to press for a viable two-state solution before it is time for a radical re-think.

Given world pressure after the attack on the humanitarian flotilla, expect Israel to reduce the Gaza embargo in ways that raise living standards slightly. But the fundamental circumstances will not change. Very possibly, there is no happy ending for this generation or the next.

A Palestinian girl in Gaza

The State of Qatar

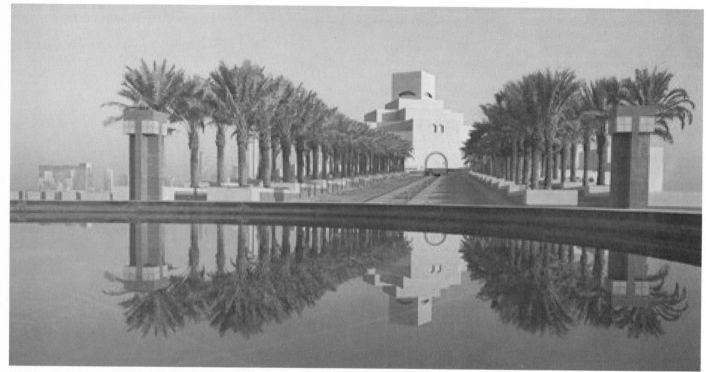

The Museum of Islamic Art, Doha, designed by I. M. Pei

Area: 4,416 sq. mi. (11,437 sq. km.).

Population: Perhaps 1.3 million. About 20% are native Qataris.

Capital City: Doha (pop. 300,000, estimated).

Climate: Extremely hot and humid except for moderate and dry winters.

Neighboring Countries: Saudi Arabia (South); Bahrain (off Northwest coast); United Arab Emirates (Southeast).

Time Zone: GMT +3.

Official Language: Arabic.

Ethnic Background: The Arab majority is less than half Qatari. The workforce is often Iranian or Pakistani.

Principal Religion: Islam.

Chief Commercial Products: Liquefied natural gas (LNG), petroleum and petrochemicals; iron and steel; urea and ammonia fertilizers; some vegetables during the winter.

Major Trading Partners: Japan, U.S., Germany, U.K., France, Thailand.

Currency: Riyal (= 100 dirhams).

Former Colonial Status: British Protectorate, 1916–1971.

Independence Date: September 3, 1971.

Chief of State: Sheikh Hamad bin Khalifa Al Thani, Emir.

Head of Government: Sheikh Hamad bin Jassem Al Thani, Prime Minister.

National Flag: An unadorned maroon field with a broad, serrated vertical band of white at the pole.

Gross Domestic Product: $128 billion (current prices and Purchasing Power Parity, 2008.

GDP per capita: $95,000 (PPP), 2008

Qatar, (pronounced *Gah*-tar, stress on the first syllable) occupies a peninsula jutting northward into the Arab Gulf from the mainland of Arabia. It is little more than 100 miles long and varies from 35 to

50 miles in width. The terrain is almost entirely a barren desert of gravel, rock and sand. Sources of fresh water are extremely scarce. Aside from a few date palms and agricultural experimental stations, the little vegetation is hardy desert scrub.

History: The Late Stone Age inhabitants looked to the sea for their livelihood. Fishermen who traded some goods with the outside world, they shared a common way of life with other societies along the coast of Arabia. Evidence for this comes from pottery discovered in Qatar that bears ornamentation patterns found as far north as Iraq. These two fundamentals—the sea for livelihood and a shared culture in the region—influenced life in Qatar for the next 5,000 years.

Given its meager water supplies, Qatar played no significant role in the region's conquests, whether by Alexander the Great's navy, Muslim Arabs nine hundred years later, or occasional Persian rulers. However, archaeological remains from the Muslim Abbasid era (9th century) suggest that the inhabitants used greater wealth, perhaps from selling pearls, to construct better homes and public buildings. When the Abbasid prosperity declined in Iraq, so did the population of Qatar. By the 13th century an Arab geographer considered it just a village.

After Portugal's brief predominance in the Gulf ended, Safavid Persia claimed the area in the 18th century, and taxed coastal communities for their pearling activities. In 1793, the villagers of Qatar provided refuge to refugees fleeing from Saudi conquests in Arabia. Two years later Saudi forces captured the important fort of Zubara. The Saudis appointed a governor in 1809, but within a decade the Saudi state collapsed (see Saudi Arabia: History).

Sporadic confusion and disorder marked the 19th century. Raids by Gulf towns on each other and on merchant shipping led Britain in 1820 to draft a treaty that committed most Gulf ports to honor a regional truce. Lacking an acknowledged ruler, Qatar could not sign the document. Fighting later broke out with its traditional rival, Bahrain, whose forces razed the largest town, Doha. Following inconclusive skirmishes in 1868, Britain negotiated a settlement with Muhammad bin Thani, a leading tribal leader, whose authority gradually spread to the entire peninsula.

In the 1870s, Ottoman Turkish troops landed, and appointed Muhammad's son, Qasim, as the local administrator. However, Qasim later fought against an Ottoman detachment, and the revival of the Saudi state led him and most of the population to embrace *Wahhabism*. By the early 20th century, four states desired to influence the territory: Bahrain, the Saudis, the Ottoman Empire and Great Britain. Despite the rivalries, Qatari pearling activities reached their zenith, with hundreds of pearling boats carrying nearly 13,000 crew and divers.

After World War I began, the Ottoman detachment withdrew, and the 1916 Anglo-Qatari treaty ended nearly centuries of legal limbo. It recognized British influence

as paramount, gave protection to the pearling fleet, and forbade the slave trade. Qatar was allowed to govern itself under the Al Thani (Al translates "family;" al-means "the"). Its formal society, politics and culture remained almost completely undeveloped, with virtually no medical facilities and only a solitary modern grade school.

The 1930s proved devastating. World demand for jewelry, and thus pearls, fell greatly during the Great Depression. Even worse, the Japanese discovered a method to raise cultured pearls. This created devastating competition and sharply falling prices. In 1935 another agreement with Britain granted the (British) Anglo-Persian Oil Company exclusive rights to search for oil. Commercial deposits were discovered in 1939, but World War II postponed development, and oil exports only began a decade later.

Oil changed Qatari society. The ruling family inevitably squandered some of the new wealth. Nevertheless, oil revenues financed roads, schools, and hospitals. A shortage of local labor led to a steady influx of workers and professionals from other Arab and Muslim nations. Soon Qataris found themselves a minority in their own state.

With British withdrawal from the Gulf on the horizon, Qatar considered federating with Bahrain and the seven sheikhdoms of Trucial Oman (see United Arab Emirates). However, old rivalries stirred distrust, and satisfactory terms could not be negotiated. Qatar then proclaimed its separate independence and in 1971 it gained membership in the League of Arab States and the United Nations.

As independence neared, the emir approved a basic law for the state. While no charter of democracy, this included a bill of rights and provided a Council of Ministers and an Advisory Council—both appointed by the ruler himself. Soon after independence, a more cautious and hard-working cousin, Sheikh Khalifa bin Hamad, seized power, blaming his predecessor for squandering financial resources. The ruling family and most Qataris approved the change.

The new emir energetically devoted some oil income for economic development, including steel and fertilizer projects. He appointed an advisory council in order to learn opinion outside the ruling family. Internationally, he donated generously to Palestinian and other Arab causes.

Given the historically insignificant value of the surrounding uninhabited coral reefs and expanses of desert, even after independence some of Qatar's boundaries had never been demarcated. In 1986 a dispute with Bahrain heated up over Hawar Island, an outcropping of reef whose possession conferred sovereignty over potential oil deposits (see Bahrain). Failing to obtain a mediated settlement in the Middle East, Qatar asked the International Court of Justice to determine its rightful owner. In 2001 the court ruled that Hawar was indeed Bahraini territory, but that the contested town of Zubara belonged to Qatar. Both sides accepted the ruling.

As a member of the Gulf Cooperation Council, Qatar joined the multinational coalition to liberate Kuwait. Its forces fought in the first ground victory of the war, defeating an Iraqi attack on the Saudi city of Khafji.

After years as the prime minister, in 1995 Sheikh Hamad overthrew the emir, his father, Sheikh Khalifa Al-Thani. Much younger than many Gulf rulers, Sheikh Hamad, assisted by his foreign minister, displayed a distinctively independent foreign policy. He approved military facilities for U.S. forces, and hosted visits by Israeli officials. Both earned condemnation from many Arabs. However, he also expressed sympathy with both Iraq and Iran.

Sheikh Hamad took initiatives in both domestic and international politics. He reduced press censorship and encouraged media discussion of serious issues such as the role of women. Along with greater freedom of speech, he instituted municipal elections. This proved a success with the voters, and six women ran for office, though they did not win.

The constitution issued by Sheikh Hamad and approved in 2003 created a partly-elected advisory parliament and provided a level of democracy surpassed by only Bahrain and Kuwait on the Arab side of the Gulf. Sheikh Hamad has also

H.H. Sheikh Hamad bin Khalifa (left) with Sheikh Jabir, Emir of Kuwait.
Courtesy: Royal Embassy of Saudi Arabia

Qatar

An exciting and highly competitive camel race across the desert

emphasized the separation of family and state finance. In 2003 he also transferred the designation of crown prince to a younger son, Tamim, a British-educated soldier.

In economic affairs, Qatar diversified away from oil and developed its North Shore natural gas deposits, part of the world's largest single field. Since most potential customers live in East Asia or on other continents, selling the gas means liquefying it. Qatar aims to become the greatest exporter of Liquefied Natural Gas (LNG) in the world and by 2030 supply 25% of all U.S. LNG imports (see Economy). While attracting billions of dollars of foreign investment, the government also extended a number of financial benefits to Qataris working in the private sector, to reduce the appeal of government jobs and reduce the cost of hiring Qataris rather than foreigners.

During the 2003 invasion of Iraq, the U.S. increasingly used the al-Udaid military base south of Doha. It became a politically safe location because Qatar's small population seemed too rich to protest about the bases, whereas many Saudis opposed the presence of U.S. troops. The U.S. military concentrated its information activities in Doha and installed the latest command facilities at al-Udaid, which became the primary U.S. base in the region.

Culture: Qatar is the only country besides Saudi Arabia with a sizeable Wahhabi community. As most Qataris (but few of its foreign workers) follow Wahhabi practices, strong historical ties link the state with Saudi Arabia.

Traditional ways of life changed drastically in Qatar as people became accustomed to the mechanical conveniences and processed food of the industrialized world. Social values are also in a state of rapid change, particularly with the expansion of free and compulsory education up to the age of 16.

Like most Arab countries, Qatar's school system provides six years of elementary school, three preparatory, and three secondary. More than 50,000 children and young people enroll in this twelve-year system. There are also technical schools, a teacher-training school and a religious institute. The University of Qatar, completed in 1985, has an enrollment of about 4,000.

In the late 1990s, the Qatar Foundation for Education, Science and Community Development, a non-profit of the ruling family, established Education City. Five prominent U.S. universities, including Cornell and Carnegie Mellon, share an impressive 2,500 acre campus that reflects Qatar's determination to become a leading educational force in the Middle East. The curricula and textbooks are the same as the home campus, and all instruction is in English. On-campus, even the traditional gender separation is relaxed, at least in some disciplines.

The goals underlying Education City are relatively straightforward. Young people, particularly women, desire a first-rate education, but especially since 2001 are reluctant to study in the U.S. In addition, the universities attract wealthier expatriates, and hopefully students from abroad.

Qatar's Al-Jazeera satellite TV station, government-financed but operated independently, broadcasts sophisticated critiques and interviews, including some of Saddam Hussein's attacks on Arab rulers. Although some governments occasionally shut down Al-Jazeera's offices, and a group of Arab governments in 2008 at-tempted to crack down on satellite channels that "offend the leaders or national and religious symbols" of Arab countries, or fail to "protect Arab identity from the harmful effects of globalization," surveys indicate that audiences over most of the Middle East enjoyed its fresh approach.

Al-Jazeera's journalistic independence brought it exclusive interviews with Osama bin Laden after the September 11 massacres. During the U.S. attacks on Afghanistan, the Taliban rulers expelled all foreign correspondents except those from Al-Jazeera. However, such journalistic initiative, combined with extensive coverage of events in Palestine from the Arab perspective, often antagonized Israel and Western governments. During the invasion of Iraq in 2003, the news service provided extensive and graphic coverage of the conflict, often from inside Iraq. By interviewing U.S. POWs and showing civilian casualties, it aroused fresh criticism in the U.S.—and won greater loyalty among Arab viewers.

In 2008 the dramatic Museum of Islamic Art opened to rave reviews of its collection of priceless objects from throughout the Islamic world. The country's cultural statement to the world, the museum is set in a building designed by I. M. Pei with influences from the Mosque of ibn Tulun in Cairo.

Economy: Though the traditional Arab lifestyle of nomadic herding existed for centuries, culturally and economically the most important industry was pearling. In the relatively shallow waters around the peninsula, mollusks grew thickly enough to permit a flourishing trade involving hundreds of boats and, at its peak, over 13,000 sailors and divers. Life aboard the

Qatar

The ultra-modern Doha Sheraton Hotel

The North Shore gas field below the waters of the Gulf is enormous. Its reserves, estimated at 900 trillion cubic feet, suffice to place the country third in global proven reserves, behind Russia and Iran. Since world demand for LNG is limited mostly to electric generating plants, Qatar seeks additional uses for natural gas. A joint Qatari-South African venture opened a gas-to-liquids refinery in 2006 to produce environmentally cleaner low-sulfur diesel. However, the process is tremendously expensive, and with a competitor's plant expected to cost $18 billion, in 2007 ExxonMobil abandoned its project.

With both gas and oil exports immensely profitable in recent years, Qatar's per capita incomes rank among the highest in the world. The government's Qatar Investment Authority has acquired perhaps $60 billion in assets now, and its revenues in the next few years may reach $30 billion annually. It recently purchased 20% ownership of the London Stock Exchange, and bids are expected for other prominent Western companies.

The Future: High energy prices and further development have postponed the expected date when oil output will run dry. Natural gas revenues are expected to climb by four times in the next several years.

Great income, cultural homogeneity, and careful planning make Qatar a very stable state. Social unrest is limited and political violence by Qataris is unknown. Those must be important reasons for the recent decision to permit labor unions, and there is growing general interest in human rights. This is not a democracy, but elections probably would not produce a wiser and more stable leadership. Expect Sheikh Hamad (the Emir) and Sheikh Hamad (the Prime Minister) to foster development in the wider sense, politically, socially, and economically.

pearling vessels was difficult, for the sailboats would be gone most of the summer. With no underwater supply of air, most divers sought banks of oysters at depths of about 50 feet, descending rapidly and returning to the surface within a minute. The most daring might descend 80 feet, but breathing and other health problems were not uncommon.

The international price of pearls climbed rapidly after the 1870s, and an economic system developed to finance pearling expeditions. However, in the 1930s the Japanese development of cultured pearls undercut the industry, with devastating effect.

After the discovery of oil in Bahrain and Saudi Arabia, it was not surprising that the Anglo-Persian Oil Company (ancestor of today's British Petroleum) found modest quantities of commercial deposits in Qatar. Thanks to its deep port, Umm Said became the center of petroleum operations and industry, with the result that although Qatar today is relatively industrialized in terms of output, industry is concentrated in a relatively small area.

The great oil price increases of the 1970s provided enormous wealth. The government bought out the subsidiaries of foreign companies producing in the country, and by 1977 all production came under its Qatar General Petroleum Company. The 1980s proved less favorable, with declining oil prices along with lower production quotas from the Organization of Petroleum Exporting Countries. Exports fell by

millions of dollars per day, and declining oil revenues plunged the government's budget into deficit. In the 1989 budget, for example, the deficit reached almost $5,000 per inhabitant—roughly five times the celebrated U.S. deficits of the time.

Recognizing that its oil deposits were fairly small, the government adopted a deliberate policy of diversification away from petroleum. By the late 1990s, exports of steel, aluminum, fertilizers and other petrochemicals based on natural gas partly offset the decline in oil revenues. Qatar is becoming the Middle East's largest producer of ammonia and urea fertilizers, with export markets in India, China and Japan.

The most important diversification was the production and export of Liquefied Natural Gas (LNG). While liquefaction is the only practical means of transporting natural gas to markets that lack pipelines to them, it requires highly expensive refineries, known as "trains," to convert the gas to a highly explosive liquid at −256° Fahrenheit and only 1/600th the original volume. Specially designed ships then carry the liquid to another "train" near the consumer, which transforms it back to gas. In 1997, Qatar shipped its first exports of LNG, and most current exports go to East Asia. However, in 2005 Qatar Petroleum and ExxonMobil agreed to build the world's largest LNG refinery at a cost of $14 billion. Its two "trains" will produce 15 million tons of LNG per year for the American market.

Qatari woman weaving intricately designed heavy rugs

147

The Kingdom of Saudi Arabia

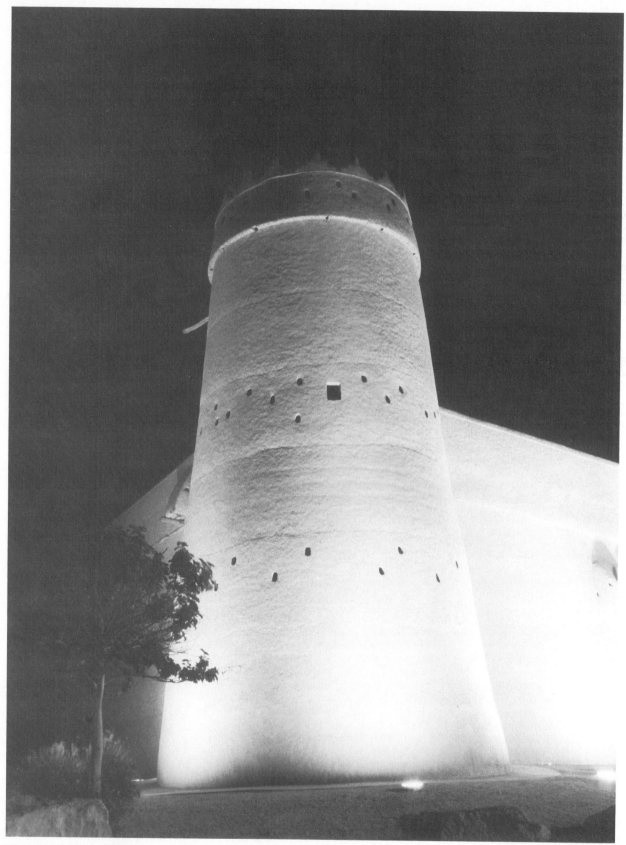

Masmak Fortress Riyadh

Courtesy: Royal Embassy of Saudi Arabia

Saudi Arabia

Area: About 864,870 square miles (2,240,000 sq. km.).

Population: 25.8 million (UN, 2007); some estimates lower.

Capital: Riyadh (pop. 5.3 million, estimated).

Climate: Very hot and dry, but humid on coasts; at higher elevations nights are cool. Rain is negligible except in the southwestern highlands.

Neighboring countries: Jordan (Northwest); Iraq (North); Kuwait (Northeast); Qatar (East); United Arab Emirates (East); Oman (Southeast); Yemen (South).

Time Zone: GMT +3. Solar time, calculated daily from sunset, is used for religious purposes.

Official Language: Arabic.

Other Principal Tongues: English, in commerce and in some schools.

Ethnic Background: Generally identified as Arab, including dark-skinned communities found in coastal towns.

Religion: Islam (officially 100%, except for foreign residents).

Chief Commercial Products: Petroleum, dates, salt, gypsum, cement, wool, grain, hides, fish, chemical fertilizers, plastics and steel.

Major Trading Partners: U.S., Japan, France, Italy, Germany, Netherlands.

Currency: Riyal (= 100 halalah).

Former Political Status: Ottoman rule in the west; British advisors in the east.

National Day: Only religious holidays are officially observed.

Chief of State: Abdullah ibn Abd al-Aziz Al Saud, King and Prime Minister.

Leading Royal Aide: Sultan ibn Abd al-Aziz Al Saud, Crown Prince and Deputy Prime Minister.

National Flag: The Islamic creed in ornate Arabic script is written in white on a green field; beneath the writing is a horizontal sword, also in white.

Gross Domestic Product: $422 billion (at current prices); $630 (Purchasing Power Parity), 2008

GDP per capita: $24,000 (PPP), 2008

Covering more than two-thirds of the Arabian Peninsula, Saudi (pronounced phonetically *Sah-oo-di*) Arabia is one of the bleakest desert countries in the world. It has no rivers, no perennial streams and no lakes. Most of its total surface is rock, gravel or sand. Less than 1% of the land has enough natural moisture for agriculture of any kind. There are no real forests; only sparse desert plants survive. Nearly one-third of the area is used seasonally as scrub brush grazing land.

From west to east, the country's terrain begins in the Hijaz, with a coastal plain along the Red Sea. A chain of mountains then rises steeply, from Jordan in the north to Yemen in the south. With peaks ranging up to 10,000 feet, the mountains in the south catch some precipitation and allow limited agriculture. Further inland, the land slopes down gradually toward the Persian (Arab) Gulf. The central region, known as *Najd* ("steppe"), receives only two or three inches of rainfall annually, while much of the southern area receives none at all in most years.

Known as the *Rub' al-Khali,* or "Empty Quarter," the south contains virtually no permanent habitation, but the largest stretch of sand in the world. It is a region of giant, seemingly endless sand dunes, often several hundred feet high and miles in length; eternally shifting, pushed by the hot desert winds. Finally, along the Gulf coast stretches the Eastern Province, Hasa,

with a hot, humid climate and an abundance of oil.

History: A land of nomadic tribes and scattered oasis settlements, Arabia was never united until Muhammad proclaimed his prophetic messages and established an Islamic government with its capital at Medina (see Historical Background). However, after Ali, the fourth caliph, moved the capital to Iraq, Arabia lost much of its political importance, though Mecca and Medina retained significant religious roles.

When the later caliphs in Damascus and Baghdad lost control of the united Muslim world, most of Arabia returned to tribal rule. Outside influence was greatest in the Hijaz, thanks to the pilgrimage and the general prestige of Islam's origins. Ottoman sovereignty was proclaimed there in the 1500s.

The origins of the Saudi kingdom lie in the 17th century, when Muhammad ibn Saud, a tribal leader in Najd, accepted the teaching of Muhammad ibn Abd al-Wahhab. After study in Damascus and Baghdad, Abd al-Wahhab had become convinced of the need to reform and purify Muslim society of pagan practices among

Saudi Arabia

Abd al-Aziz Al-Saud, King of Saudi Arabia, 1932–53

the Bedouin and philosophical and secular influences in the cities.

Strengthened by the appeal of these teachings, known to Westerners as Wahhabism, during the 18th century Saudi troops and Wahhabi believers conquered large parts of central Arabia and raided north into Syria. During the Napoleonic wars, the Wahhabis conquered the Hijaz, seizing from the Ottoman sultan the holy places of Mecca and Medina that he claimed to protect. However, the Wahhabis had overextended, Muhammad Ali, the ruler of Egypt, defeated the Saudi fighters and even destroyed their capital. Rival Arab rulers encroached on Saudi lands.

By 1902, the heir to leadership was a 22-year-old exile, Abd al-Aziz Al Saud (*Al* in Arabic means "House," or "Family;" it differs from *al-*, meaning "the"). With only a handful of followers, he undertook a daring mission to restore family fortunes, seizing Riyadh, the capital, from the rival family of Rashid.

A tall and powerful man with a natural gift for leadership, Abd al-Aziz gradually enlarged the area of his control by victories over rival tribes. In 1913 he conquered the eastern coastal district of Hasa from the Ottoman Turks, not knowing that years later the oil under its sands would make him one of the world's wealthiest men. During World War I, Abd al-Aziz promised the British that he would not join the Turks against England; for this he was rewarded with $25,000 a year.

Dominant in central Arabia by 1921, Abd al-Aziz turned against his remaining, and irritating, rival, Sharif Husayn (Hussein) of the Hijaz. Supported by Britain during his revolt against the Turks, Husayn was a difficult character, and harbored great ambitions. In pursuit of them, he adopted the imprecise title "King of the Arabs" and hinted at proclaiming himself caliph, thereby outraging Arabs of many different backgrounds.

Abd al-Aziz's followers, the militant *Ikhwan* ("Brotherhood") who relinquished

tribal loyalties for Wahhabism, were eager to cleanse the holy cities of Mecca and Medina from what they considered sacrilegious traditions. At the end of 1924 the *Ikhwan* entered Mecca and within a year took Medina also. In 1926 Abd al-Aziz was proclaimed "King of Hijaz." After repressing a revolt by the *Ikhwan*, in 1932 he formed his various domains into the Kingdom of Saudi Arabia. Satisfied with his conquests, and blocked from further expansion by Transjordan and Iraq, King Abd al-Aziz turned to consolidating the country he ruled.

Unhampered by a constitution or democracy, his autocracy nevertheless faced limits from the Wahhabi religious leaders and from the ruling family, enlarged by his many marriages to daughters of tribal leaders. Moreover, the kingdom was poor: for many years pilgrims visiting the Hijaz were its economic mainstay.

The discovery of oil in Hasa in 1938 marked the beginning of a new era in Saudi Arabia, but significant petroleum production was delayed by World War II (see Economy). By the late 1940s, oil revenues began to pour into the country, and the aging Abd al-Aziz faced the challenges of corruption common to the arrival of such wealth. His numerous sons and relatives squandered millions of dollars monthly and every transaction involved the payment of suitable bribes to officials.

Reforms under Faisal

For over fifty years, Saudi Arabia has been ruled by one of the 37 sons of Abd al-Aziz. The reign of the second to rule, Faisal, witnessed gradual but limited reforms. He greatly increased the budgets for education, medical care and transportation facilities, though his government rejected many aspects of westernization and made little effort to promote social change. It refused to allow free political expression or formal public participation in government. The traditional Saudi social system spread responsibility over a large number of relatives, and politically it provided access to the royal family for even the poorest citizen. Rather than replace these features, Faisal worked to render them more honest and efficient.

In international affairs, Faisal proved a cautious conservative willing to work quietly for his goals. He sought better relations with neighboring states, and naturally opposed any communist or other revolutionary influences in the Arab world. Only after Egypt's defeat in the 1967 Arab-Israeli War, and the end of its revolutionary propaganda, would Faisal cooperate with it.

Another pivotal Saudi issue was support for Palestinian Arabs against Israel.

Faisal considered Jerusalem to be Islam's third holiest city, and he wished to pray there under an Arab and Islamic flag, rather than a Jewish one. To that end, Saudi Arabia paid funds directly to Yasir Arafat and the Palestinian leadership, to "confrontation states," (the Arab countries partly occupied by Israel in 1967), and to the UN, to care for the refugees.

During the Arab-Israeli war of October 1973, Saudi Arabia interpreted the issues mainly in terms of religion. King Faisal proclaimed an embargo on all oil shipments to the energy-short U.S. until he was "able again to pray in Jerusalem under an Arab flag." However, at the urging of Egypt, he ended the embargo in 1974 in exchange for vague assurances concerning Israeli withdrawal from Jerusalem.

While the embargo was not fully effective—oil can transfer ownership rapidly on the high seas—the embargo was accompanied by a reported 10% cut in Saudi oil exports. Against the background of tight world oil supplies, these Saudi moves provided the conditions necessary for the Organization of Petroleum Export-

ing Countries (OPEC) to raise the price of oil about 400% (see Introduction: Black Gold). A flood of oil revenues resulted, and Faisal reaped a great increase in prestige at home and abroad.

King Faisal was shot fatally in 1975 by a nephew. There seemed to be no rational political motive, and succession went smoothly. His brothers who succeeded him as Saudi monarchs continued to make serious attempts at close political and economic cooperation with the United States, desiring American technological skills and experience, while the U.S. was greatly helped by Saudi purchases of American goods. Both countries also shared the common goal of protecting the region from communist encroachment. Saudi Arabia used its own foreign aid to make allies and reduce Soviet influence in several poorer states.

The government, royal family, and outside world were stunned in 1979 when Islamic extremists seized the Grand Mosque in Mecca and called for revolution. After crushing the rebellion and executing some participants, the Saudis responded with

reforms, in particular for the Shi'a inhabitants of the eastern province bordering on the Gulf. The mosque's takeover emphasized the importance of maintaining the royal links with the *ulama'*, or Muslim scholars, and it also served to warn that social changes should not overtake cultural and religious values.

Invasion and the Gulf War, 1990–91

The 1990 Iraqi seizure of Kuwait placed Saudi Arabia in grave peril. The Iraqi forces in Kuwait alone numbered three times the total Saudi military (though the Saudis enjoyed vastly better equipment). Baghdad threatened to attack if its oil exports across Saudi Arabia were halted, as the UN Security Council demanded. Enormously complicated oil installations—wells, pipelines, tank farms, refineries, ports—lay within range of Iraqi missiles and bombers. Moreover, if he kept Kuwait's oil wealth, Iraq's President Saddam Hussein would control reserves and output rivaling Saudi Arabia's, upsetting the balances of power in both the Arab world and OPEC.

The political threat seemed as substantial as the military. Saddam Hussein's invective against the Kuwaiti ruling family mocked all Gulf dynasties, including the Saudi. Demands that Arab oil wealth support all Arabs stirred popular resentment among poor Arabs everywhere. Such claims threatened revolution within Saudi Arabia, and isolation from the Arab world.

By contrast, the United States offered to defend Saudi Arabia and liberate Kuwait. However, such an alliance carried risks. To many Muslims, the Protector of the Holy Places must not depend on "infidel" troops. (Baghdad later charged, falsely, that American soldiers were actually based in the Holy Places of Mecca and Medina.) Some Arab nationalists opposed an attack by Israel's ally (the U.S.) against Israel's strongest enemy, Iraq. The presence of foreign troops also risked foreign politicians, journalists, and unflattering attacks on the lack of Western-style democracy. Domestically, an alliance with the U.S. meant arousing scorn about defense by "Jews and women" as well as offense at the display of Western lifestyles ranging from Christmas to women actively serving in the military.

Despite these risks, King Fahd and his government quickly requested troops from Arab, American and other nations. The kingdom pledged money to its allies and to nations victimized by the occupation of Kuwait. The government also sought approval for its stand from the World Muslim League and Arab nations.

After the United Nations deadline passed for Iraq to evacuate Kuwait (Janu-

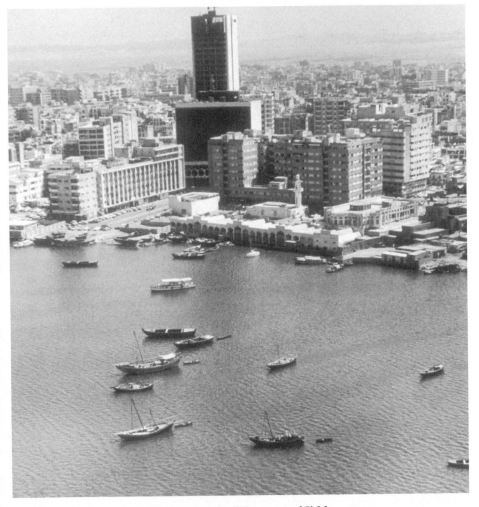

The modern Red Sea port of Jidda

Saudi Arabia

ary 15, 1991), Coalition aircraft, often from Saudi bases, launched a massive destruction of Iraq's military and infrastructure (see Iraq: History). In response, Iraqi Scud missiles were targeted at Riyadh and apparently at oil and military targets in the Eastern Province. Although Patriot missiles intercepted some Scuds, damage did occur, notably to a Muslim religious college in Riyadh and barracks housing Americans in Dhahran. An Iraqi tank column also assaulted the city of Khafji, but was repulsed by Saudi and Qatari troops. Rather than undermine the government, the attacks generally served to increase patriotism among Saudi civilians, including the minority Shi'a of the Eastern Province. Saudi ground forces played an important role in the recapture of Kuwait City, and a Saudi pilot scored the only double kill of the war.

Like many wars, this one with thousands of foreign soldiers created expectations of reform. Partly in response, in 1992 King Fahd proposed a formal, written constitution, with a *Majlis al-Shura*, or consultative council, and he appointed the council's 90 members, but gave them no executive powers. The country was not becoming a democracy: the king remained commander of the armed forces, chief administrator, and dispenser of the royal treasury.

Economic Challenges of the 1990s

During the 1990s, national attention often focused on economic issues. Petroleum output fell, as Saudi Arabia attempted to hold OPEC together by enduring proportionately larger production cuts than smaller producers. Essentially, the kingdom is a "windfall economy," where outside forces may be as important in determining the level of earnings as changes in the actual amount of work. Put differently, windfall economies break the link between work and reward: the lazy procrastinator suffers some years, but does very well in others. In 2000, just when the Saudi public recognized that major reforms were absolutely necessary, a combination of production cuts and Asian economic recovery sent the price of oil soaring. Serious but boring issues like the need for reinvestment in the oil fields, or increasing electric generating capacity, lost their urgency.

Foreign Challenges & Domestic Perils after 9-11

By 2001, relations with the United States—the country's major ally—showed signs of difficulty. Most Saudis sympathized with the Palestinians, and felt that the Bush cabinet favored Israel. This sentiment led officials to call off high-level military talks in Washington just days before the September 11 terrorist attacks.

King Abdullah of Saudi Arabia talking with Secretary of State Condoleezza Rice.
Courtesy, U.S. State Department

News that 15 of the 19 men identified as terrorists came from Saudi Arabia unleashed Western disparagement of nearly everything Saudi and placed the kingdom on the ideological defensive. In addition to repeating long-standing concerns about human rights violations like harsh justice and the treatment of women, critics made three particular allegations.

First, Saudi policy had created a society that encouraged radical fundamentalist religious groups. Extending its long-standing alliance with doctrinaire Wahhabi leaders, during the 1990s the state had funded a rapid increase in religious schools. A decade later, their graduates, ill-equipped for employment in business or technology, formed a pool of potential extremists.

Second, *al-Qaeda* and other militant Islamic groups had been funded, knowingly or not, by contributions to various charities. Critics suspected that the regime had reached an unspoken understanding with the religious militants. If they spared the kingdom from their violent attacks, militant organizations could raise funds for various causes.

Third, some U.S. critics claimed, the kingdom was not a genuine ally. It refused permission for U.S. bases in the kingdom to launch aircraft against the *Taliban* and *al-Qaeda* in Afghanistan. The government also rejected use of its territory for an attack on Iraq, even if the UN approved the invasion.

With limited success, Crown Prince Abdullah and others explained that the West's enemy was not Islam, but rather a few misguided individuals. In addition, they argued, Western nations' support for Israel weakened moderate Arab governments friendly to the U.S. Abdullah promised that his nation would meet any shortfall in world oil supplies. Saudi Arabia kept this promise during the Iraq War of 2003, using its spare capacity and stockpiled crude to replace Iraqi output.

Nevertheless, the monarchy found itself trapped between American policy and the Islamic and Arab values of its population. It proposed a comprehensive plan for Arab-Israeli peace, but Washington ignored the proposal, and some preachers at home condemned it as compromising. The two governments announced the closure of American bases, but within a month, suicide bombers struck Riyadh anyway.

Pressures for Reform and Counter-terrorism

Confronted by declining standards of living, high unemployment, allegations of corruption, and heavy-handed policies by the justice system and religious police, many Saudi civilians strongly desire change. However, public opinion is deeply divided about the desired direction of reform. Advocates of greater personal liberty inevitably clash with preachers blaming lax morality for social decline. Because each side's essential reforms reach deep into personal lives, the pathway to reform is as dangerous as it is vital.

Often influenced by their higher education in the West, the country's few liberals advocate greater personal freedoms from the Shari'a courts, and western-style liberties. Some concentrate on economic reforms, such as wider roles for private business and reduced regulation of them.

Others desire social changes, including fewer restrictions on women.

Daily events sometimes support arguments for greater liberalism. For example, 15 girls died in a school fire because the religious police refused to allow the pupils to escape without wearing their scarves and cloaks. Then, editors and authors who criticized the police actions too strongly found themselves dismissed or even arrested.

Opposition groups are illegal, and generally not tolerated. However, in 2003, several hundred Saudi intellectuals—dozens of women as well as men—signed a petition to the crown prince entitled "In Defense of the Nation." It presented the reformist argument that the lack of popular participation in government fostered extremism, and it warned that radical reforms were needed soon.

Soon afterwards, just as the government hosted the country's first human rights conference, a small but unprecedented rally in the center of Riyadh called for political reform. Although bearded men led the group in chanting "God is Great," the police broke up the demonstration and arrested many suspected participants, including some young women. The Grand Mufti condemned the gathering, claiming that "demonstrations are the behavior of non-Muslims." Perhaps this demonstration and several others elsewhere, shook the government's self-confidence.

When further petitions called for urgent reforms, the government arrested several leaders, carefully selecting members of both the liberal and the Islamic reform movements. More were arrested after the exiled *Movement for Islamic Reform in Arabia* called for demonstrations. The poet Ali al-Demaini and two other reformers who urged the government to hasten change and issue a constitution were punished by lengthy prison terms for "stirring up sedition."

Nevertheless, cabinet members discussed the possibility of electing, some years hence, some members of the Consultative Council. The first formal elections in the country's history were the municipal elections in 2004–05. However, with political parties banned, religious conservatives won most seats, and at least initially the councils accomplished little.

In 2003, simultaneous suicide car-bombers struck three residential complexes for foreigners in Riyadh, killing or wounding scores of Westerners and Saudis. The next year, terrorists struck repeatedly in Riyadh, in Yanbu, at the security forces headquarters in Riyadh, and at a luxury business and hotel complex in Khobar. Individual Westerners also became targets, a policy that could harm the oil industry.

Police launched hunts for militants in Mecca and fought several pitched battles elsewhere. Although the security forces killed a number of militants and seized large caches of weapons, at first the terrorists possessed the initiative. Their attacks, some involving the cold-blooded murder of non-Muslims, shook international confidence in the Saudi government's ability protect foreign workers. They also strengthened suspicions that Islamic fundamentalists—not alleged "alcohol wars" among foreigners—were responsible for a series of highly publicized murders of Westerners.

By 2005, terrorist attacks had diminished, and most militants wanted by the government were dead or in captivity. Nevertheless, the violence confirmed that Islamist groups drew strength and political allure from the country's economic and political malaise. Besides the young, often unemployable graduates of religious schools, hundreds of Saudi men a decade earlier had trained with Osama bin Laden in Afghanistan. These "Afghans" maintained loose ties, and spread their messages by fax as well as sermons. Their proclamations may be impractical, but they are appealing: the militants advocate replacing corruption with morality, repression with legitimate Islamic govrnment, and weakness with a strong military.

In fairness, it must be remembered that well before the 2003 attacks—in fact, even before 9-11—the regime had arrested militants, perhaps hundreds of them, for allegedly threatening national security. The Islamic courts declared some activities illegal. One critic, Muhammad al-Masari of the *Committee for the Defense of Legitimate Rights*, fled to London, and faded from public opinion. Others proved more derogatory and even violent. In response to the attacks, the government purged over 2,000 mosque imams of their positions, and instituted cultural education courses for hundreds who remained in office. In 2008, it announced that 40,000 clerics would be re-trained.

Abdullah Ascends the Throne

After years as an invalid in declining health, King Fahd died in 2005. Crown Prince Abdullah, his half-brother, smoothly took power, and confirmed Prince Sultan, his half-brother, as his heir and deputy. However, the position of the second deputy prime minister—the heir to the heir—was not filled. Speculation mounted that Abdullah, recognized as something of a reformer, lacked support within the royal family to appoint another reformer, Prince Salman, or more radically, a prince from the next generation.

Abdullah did act to create a new institution to guide the succession. The Alle-

Aboard spaceship *Discovery*: Prince Sultan bin Salman during an experiment.

Courtesy: NASA

Saudi Arabia

Mounted troops of the Saudi Arabian National Guard

giance Committee composed of sons and grandsons of Abd al-Aziz can reject the king's nominee and thereby force discussion of other potential heirs. The leading conservative candidate is probably Prince Nayef, the long-serving interior minister considered suspicious of foreign cultural and political influences. Regardless of family disputes, a decision will be made soon: Abdullah was born in 1924 and most surviving brothers a few years later.

Saudi government decisions are generally taken within a closed group. While the effective ruler for a decade, Abdullah encouraged several types of reform. He curbed privileges for members of the royal family (such as free water, free electricity, and free tickets on Saudia, the national airline). He also favored the country's successful application to the World Trade Organization, to raise the standard of competition generally and streamline the bureaucracy. In the political realm, he championed elections for half the city councilmen, although they were won by religious conservatives and had not met months later. In 2009 his gradual efforts at reform resulted in the dismissal of both the head of the religious police and the country's most senior judge, who had ear-

lier approved killing the owners of satellite TV channels that offered immoral content. He also appointed a woman as government minister, a first for the country. Her role as the sole high-ranking female official will certainly prove unique: within days of her appointment she announced that she would not be visiting male colleagues in their offices,

Culture: To understand the workings of Saudi Arabia, one must appreciate some aspects of its social structure, such as the unwritten laws relating to kinship. The most important unit is the extended family or clan: all people who are descended from a common ancestor carry responsibilities to one another. In past eras of desert raids, this system was necessary to protect individuals. Membership in the family system is based on male descent; a person belongs to the same clan as the father's family, but not necessarily the mother's family and clan. The House of Saud, the ruling family in Saudi Arabia, is just such a clan—these relatives have the duty of looking after their collective interests.

Groups of clans that allied together historically and believe they share descent

from a common ancestor form a tribe. Until the establishment of the Kingdom of Saudi Arabia there was no important group larger than the tribe. Though tribes often had temporary alliances, they often skirmished with each other.

As Saudis gain more wealth, travel abroad, and study in universities, the traditionally strong family bonds are weakening. Conservative Saudis associate these weaker bonds with lowered ethical and moral standards and even illegal drugs. Naturally, Saudi leaders seek to maintain the strong sense of family loyalty and discipline, considering them to be part of the Islamic religion.

Whatever one's family standing, *kabsa* is the main food. This Saudi national dish is a large tray of boiled meat and rice, usually covered with a tomato sauce seasoned with mild spices.

The Hajj and the Role of Islam

Hijaz, the western part of Saudi Arabia, is the holy land to all Muslims, and thus about one human in six. At least once in their lifetime, millions perform the pilgrimage to the cities of Mecca and Medina where the Prophet Muhammad lived and recited the words of the Qur'an, the Islamic scriptures. The Islamic creed, "There is no god but God (Arabic *Allah*) and Muhammad was the Apostle of God" is written on the flag of Saudi Arabia.

Now that inexpensive air travel has replaced camel caravans from Cairo or Damascus, over two million pilgrims annually perform the *Hajj*. All of them hope to spend the identical five days praying at the Grand Mosque, circling the Ka'aba with its black stone, and joining the final ceremonies on Mount Arafat, where Muhammad preached his last sermon. Transported by 10,000 buses from Jeddah to Mecca, most pilgrims sleep in a vast tent city, where they meet fellow-believers from across the globe. They slaughter half a million animals as sacrifices.

Given the size of the crowds, Saudi officials attempt to take careful precautions, screening for communicable diseases and providing the services of thousands of medical personnel, guards, food preparers and cleaners. After an inferno killed hundreds in the 1990s, the authorities supplied fireproof tents and carved large water storage tunnels in nearby mountains. They also widened passageways where a crowd might stampede. Nevertheless, disasters continue, including a stampede in 2004 that killed several hundred pilgrims.

The major teachings of Islam rest on belief in one God, the Creator and Sustainer of the world, who at the Day of Judgment will render justice to both the righteous and the evil. Knowledge of God comes through the prophets, especially Muhammad, whose Qur'an ("Recitation") is the literal Word of God. Supplemented by the Traditions (*Hadith*) of Muhammad, as well as limited reasoning, the Qur'an provides the basis for personal behavior, laws for the orderly society of the believers, and a guide to the treatment of non-believers (see Historical Background).

There are two principal holy days in Islam. The Day of Sacrifice falls on the tenth day of *Dhu-l-Hija*, the last month in the Islamic calendar and the month of pilgrimage. While celebrated by Muslims everywhere, it relates specifically to the lamb or goat sacrificed by each pilgrim in Mecca. The Festival of Breaking Fast is on the first day of *Shawwal*, the tenth month—it celebrates the ending of the fast during Ramadan, the ninth month.

The impact of a calendar with months rotating through the seasons can best be imagined by remembering that during Ramadan the faithful neither eat nor drink between sunrise and sunset. In some years Ramadan falls in the winter, with short days and cooler weather, but when it arrives in the summer the faithful endure a fast, without water, for 13 or 14 hours in maximum temperatures that often exceed 110 degrees F.

Time in Saudi Arabia is still commonly observed according to the traditional system where a day begins not at midnight, but at sunset. This means that in spring when the daylight gradually lengthens, a Saudi day takes slightly longer than 24 hours. In the fall, of course, it takes slightly less. For obvious reasons, this system of time is not suitable for international airline schedules and many business purposes, where Saudi Standard Time (GMT +3) is observed.

Although Islam teaches the brotherhood and equality of all believers, class distinctions have developed. In the old days, some tribes considered themselves more socially important than others, and would not intermarry with them. Some clans and tribes also had more prestige than others. Modernization reduces class distinctions of these traditional types, for wealth and education are becoming the tokens of status, but family prestige still matters.

Based on Islam and enforced in a traditional fashion, the legal system varies considerably from Western practices. A woman's testimony carries half the weight of a man's, the practice of non-Islamic religions is forbidden even to foreigners, and freedoms of speech and the press are extremely limited. The courts impose one of the highest execution rates in the world, for drug dealing, rape, murder, and witchcraft, though if the victim's family accepts blood money, the criminal may be released. Lesser crimes may be punished by beating;

for example, a passenger who persisted in using his cell phone during an airliner's takeoff received 70 lashes. However, the severity of Saudi sentences is sometimes offset by royal pardons, or by the substitution of payments to a victim's family.

Foreigners are sometimes surprised by the absolute ban on alcoholic beverages, in accordance with strict Islamic belief. A non-Saudi businessman found with any quantity of alcohol in his belongings is normally deported on the next available flight. Penalties for possession of narcotics are also strictly imposed, and importers of narcotics risk the death penalty. On the other hand, tobacco is allowed, and an education program warning against the health hazards of smoking is only now becoming significant.

In 2007, King Abdullah announced major reforms of the judicial system that will create a supreme court, a system of appeals courts, and courts for commercial and labor matters. Besides modernizing the system, the reforms apparently aim to reduce the wide discretion judges have had to impose their own, sometimes unique, interpretations of Shari'a law. Lacking an effective appeals process, it required King Abdullah to pardon "the Qatif girl," a victim of gang rape sentenced, on appeal, to 200 lashes and jail for being alone with a man when they were abducted and raped.

The modern side of Islam is reflected in the style and substance of the "satellite sheikhs," popular preachers like Ahmad al-Shugairi or Amr Khaled who expound religious perspectives over television and the internet, often working the emotions of crowds in ways similar to American televangelists. The emotional, joyful perspectives of such preachers attract the young and relatively secular who find traditional preaching quite boring.

Other signs of social modernization also suggest some relaxation from the strictest Wahhabi practices. Sheikh Muhammad al-Habadan, a judge, might still claim that a two-eyed veil offered too much opportunity for decadent sensuality, and an eight-year-old bride sought an annulment to her marriage to a man in his 50s. However, more concerts and other cultural activities are reported, and the first Saudi commercial film since at least the 1970s appeared recently. Movie theatres are still prohibited.

Education's Expansion and Reform

As suggested above, education very rapidly changed life in the kingdom. In 1953 only ten junior and senior high schools offered public instruction, with a total enrollment of 1,315. By 1973, there were 573 schools at these levels with 105,853 students. During the same 20 years the num-

ber of elementary pupils increased from 39,000 to more than half a million. Access to primary education is now virtually universal, with millions of children in gender-segregated schools.

Critics of the country's schools often focus on their educational style. Thanks in part to the country's heavy religious influence and resulting conservatism, student learning often becomes the memorization of facts, which is much safer for teachers than the development questioning minds that think critically. Both foreign commentators and some Saudi commentators have also faulted the sometimes reactionary comments and interpretations of Islam found in a number of textbooks.

The first full institution of higher education was Riyadh University, and the university system expanded in the 1970s with the rise in oil revenues. However, with the decline in oil prices in the mid-1980s, the expansion of higher education slowed. To avoid producing more highly educated young than the economy could absorb, university admissions were restricted. At the turn of the century, only eight public universities existed for a population that exceeded 20 million.

Since 2004, however, more than 100 new colleges and universities have opened, as the higher education budget tripled. The most impressive new institution is undoubtedly the graduate-level King Abdullah University of Science and Technology, which opened in 2009. Funded by $10 billion of the monarch's personal wealth, its research orientation and goal of educating women and men together are precedent-setting. It offers programs in fields like nanotechnology, water and conservation technology, the biosciences, energy and the environment, and applied computer science. This curricular emphasis is no accident. An estimated 80% of Saudi college students major in history, geography, Arabic literature and Islamic studies, but the economy generates fairly few jobs in these areas.

The Slowly Changing Status of Women

Aside from King Abdullah University, education carries the burden of separate schools and other facilities for girls and women. In the cause of maintaining sexual purity, Saudi women must be kept apart from men outside the family, and at least to the political and religious leadership of the country—which is exclusively male—this is a matter of modesty and separation rather than inequality. Demands from religious conservatives on occasion suggest minds possessed with a desire to root out any display of the feminine, for example by the argument that two-eyed veils promote immorality by leading women to adorn the eyes too greatly.

Saudi Arabia

To Western critics, though, regulations of the status of women extend beyond Islamic concerns of morality to a desire to keep women in a "perpetual childhood" that requires male relatives to exercise "guardianship" over them. Saudi women have to obtain permission from male relatives to work, travel, study, receive health care, or even open bank accounts for their children, matters sometimes removed from sexual morality, but key elements of the social order.

That order is the strictest in the world. Vice police ensure utmost modesty in dress and brevity in contact. Cinemas and theaters are all forbidden, let alone nightclubs, lest men and women meet. Naturally, unaccompanied women do not frequent shopping centers and malls. When several dozen Saudi women broke the tradition against driving and formed a procession of luxury cars in 1990, they were arrested, dismissed from their jobs, and condemned by the vice police as prostitutes. Thereafter, the law was officially changed to prohibit women from taking the wheel. In 2007–08, reform-minded women began petitioning the king to revise the law on economic and practical grounds (hiring a male driver is increasingly expensive).

For decades the vice police overlooked one peculiar mixing of men and women. Although regulations prohibited unrelated men and women from, for example, sitting in a restaurant, stores that carried intimate female apparel hired only male clerks. In 2006, finally, new regulations required such stores to hire female sales clerks, but enforcement was delayed. Religious conservatives disapprove, and so do the stores' owners, who fear financial loss when replacing cheap Indian and Pakistani clerks with higher-paid Saudi women. In 2010, some women demanded a boycott of stores using male clerks.

Reem Asaad, campaigner for women-staffed lingerie stores

Courtesy: Royal Embassy of Saudi Arabia

Though the pace is sometimes glacially slow, change is occurring. Additional economic sectors may also open up for women, partly because Ghazi al-Gosaibi, the minister of labor, recognizes the waste of talent and resources when women compose 55% of university graduates but only 5% of the workforce. What matters most, though, is culture—and the message is mixed. In 2007 a popular Saudi TV comedy portrayed an unaccompanied woman driving her children home from the movies. But as Valentines Day 2008 approached, the religious police banned the sale of red roses and other items that might reflect Western ideas of friendship between men and women.

Economy: Before the discovery of its oil, most inhabitants of the country's arid lands lived by herding flocks, or raised dates and a few other crops in an oasis. The yearly pilgrimage, or Hajj, to Mecca and Medina employed others, but the camel trade routes of ancient times could not compete with sea freight, especially after the introduction of steam and the construction of the Suez Canal. Then came oil.

It is difficult to over-estimate the impact of oil on Saudi Arabia. It typically funds about three-quarters of the government budget, directly contributes over 40% of GDP, and provides 95% of exports. In addition, rapid industrial development, centered on petrochemicals, depends on oil as a raw material.

Saudi Oil Policy

Having persuaded King Abd al-Aziz to grant a concession for drilling, prospectors for a group of American oil companies struck commercial quantities of oil in 1938. After World War II, oil production by the Arabian American Oil Company (Aramco) increased by nearly 20% a year, and soon Saudi Arabia ranked with Iran and Iraq as a leading Middle East producer. In the following decades, the search for oil, its production, and its export revenues completely transformed the Saudi economy.

Initially much income was squandered, but from the late 1950s economic development became a priority. This created a challenge, because the industry provided only a few thousand jobs. How could millions of people be transformed from a life of subsistence herding and agriculture to the levels of income and comfort enjoyed by advanced industrial nations? One answer came from Aramco, which built a hospital, clinics, schools and housing. It also provided assistance for agriculture, and lent advice for a variety of projects, including the kingdom's railroad.

The cooperation between Aramco and the government contrasted with usually bitter relations in other oil exporting nations. Nevertheless, Saudi Arabia became a founding member of the Organization of Petroleum Exporting Countries (OPEC), where it usually adopted a firm but moderate stance. Given the country's reserves and production, its opinion mattered.

By the early 1970s, with its oil sales rising at 25% per year, the country became the dominant Middle East producer, and Sheikh Ahmad Yamani, the Petroleum Minister, became a leading figure in the cartel. He played a major role in the 1973 oil embargo, and in later agreements that drove the price of oil from roughly $2.50 in 1970 to $32 in 1980. However, when high prices encouraged production elsewhere and reduced consumption through conservation, demand declined for OPEC's exports. Saudi production, prices, and oil revenues all plummeted.

Taken over by the Saudi government after the great 1970s increases in oil prices, Saudi Aramco invested in additional pipelines to carry crude to the Red Sea, closer to European customers and beyond the potential bottleneck of the Strait of Hormuz. Investment also increased oil production capacity to about 10 million barrels per day. During the Gulf Crisis of 1990–91, Saudi Aramco actually boosted production substantially above its quota, and it met world oil needs while exports from Iraq and Kuwait were halted. During the next era of tight oil supplies, 2005–08, Aramco initiated projects to raise output to over 12 million barrels per day, nearly a 25% increase.

The high crude oil prices of the mid-decade bring enormous wealth to the country, but might also harm Saudi Arabia's longer-term good. When money rolls in, the pain of economic reform seems less necessary. Prosperity makes it difficult to build a consensus supporting reasonable but unpopular measures like raising the prices of gasoline or electricity. For example, gasoline is cheap, and electricity virtually free.

Growth of the National Economy

From the late 1950s to the early 1970s, the government erected public buildings, paved roads and highways, and began to offer education and health services for its citizens. Oil revenues supplied foreign exchange to purchase all manner of imports from cars to cloth and even building materials. Money that found its way into private hands frequently went into large homes, as well as stores and office buildings. Reluctant to have a "Central Bank," with implications of interest payments, the nation established the Saudi Arabian Monetary Authority (SAMA) to provide modern control over national finances.

Following the 1973 spiraling of oil prices, the nation's economic development spurted to higher levels of growth. Recognizing dangers in depending only on oil, the government offered tax breaks and subsidies to attract firms in other industries. Factories began to appear, sometimes joint ventures with foreign firms. The early ones typically provided consumer goods or construction materials for the building boom, such as a mill for rolling steel rods. With the decline in oil prices in the mid-1980s, government subsidies diminished.

In general, Saudi industrial projects suffer from a number of common difficulties. Lucrative profits in trade and other services also discourage long-term investment in manufacturing. Once established, local entrepreneurs, managers, and skilled workers are scarce. Until recently, inadequate financial markets made it more convenient for Saudi capitalists to buy shares in foreign companies rather than take ownership of local factories. Finally, for all its famed wealth, the country represents a relatively small market, whose consumers are fewer than those of Belgium or Illinois, and until recently much poorer. Per capita income was less than $9,000 in 2002.

The most impressive industrialization effort is the petrochemical producer, SABIC. It rapidly grew to massive size, the only Arab industrial company on the international Fortune 500. By 1988, its major plants had been constructed, and profits soared as the company turned cheap petroleum raw materials into fertilizers, plastics and other products. By 2004, SABIC held 10% of world sales of petrochemicals. It also produced a much larger proportion of specialty products like MTBE (methyl tertiary butyl ether), a gasoline additive that reduces carbon monoxide emissions and replaces lead in enhancing octane. Profits exceeded $1 billion for the first time in 1994, and privatizing the government's 70% share of ownership could provide a windfall to cushion the budget deficit. In 2007, SABIC purchased the plastics subsidiary of General Electric.

Another success is the national airline, Saudia. True to national culture, its flights begin with Muhammad's prayer for travelers, and ceiling-mounted compasses indicate to passengers the direction of Mecca for prayer. Attention to religious details did not hamper its rise to the largest regional carrier, offering service between Western Europe and East Asia.

In one of the less predictable turns of fate, Saudi Arabia became a major exporter of grains by the end of the 1980s. Fearing a possible American food embargo to retaliate for the 1973 oil embargo, the government provided extensive subsidies for grain farmers, including costs for wells, fertilizers and other supplies. The money proved persuasive. Cultivated acreage increased tenfold, and giant green circles provided bumper crops of wheat. From a mere 3,000 tons in 1976, output climbed to 3 million tons in 1989, three times consumption. Other subsidies raised output of eggs, dairy products, and dates. These policies also spread national wealth and diminished migration to the cities by keeping a quarter of the population in agriculture.

Unfortunately, the successes came expensively, and did not last long. Annual wheat subsidies of $1 billion equaled *eight times* the cost of equivalent imported wheat. By 1996 price supports had been cut 25%, and production fell to half the record of 4 million tons. In 2004, they were slashed again, by 30%, and experts expected many small family farms to halt production. In 2008, the country again became a net importer of wheat.

Nature reinforced the financial austerity. About 90% of the water supplies come from "fossil" sources, trapped far below the soil during a much wetter climatic age. In the 1990s, the nation used 18 billion cubic meters of this fossil water annually. Given apparently reliable esti-

**The University of
Petroleum and Minerals, Dhahran**

Saudi Arabia

mates of only 500 billion cubic meters in the aquifers, that rate will exhaust the aquifers in less than 20 years. Desalinized water, while expensive for household use, becomes exorbitant for wheat farming, raising total costs 700%. Imaginative alternative supplies—from the Nile, Turkey, Iraq, or Antarctic icebergs—likewise appear prohibitively costly and uncertain. Thus, despite its policies, Saudi Arabia's future as a food producer seems limited to drought-tolerant crops, plus fish and shrimp from the sea.

Economic and Budget Policies

When oil prices fall, Saudi Arabia suffers financial distress. If they fall sufficiently, it will face a budget deficit as well. To cover such deficits, the government borrows money, while obeying the Islamic prohibition of the payment of interest. Thus it issues "development bonds," whose payment depends in theory on the success of the project. Total indebtedness by 2003 exceeded $130 billion, a much higher level than most developed countries, but with annual oil revenues of about the same amount, it was a trustworthy borrower. They hit $200 billion in 2007.

Other revenue sources are difficult to find. Only a few acceptable taxes exist, for the wealthy and commoners alike expect government services to be financed somehow by oil. An attempt to impose income taxes on foreign workers created such difficulties that it was withdrawn. Higher tariffs on imports largely breed domestic inflation, and are no longer an option since the country joined the World Trade Organization (WTO).

Despite the boom in oil prices, Saudi Arabia still requires foreign financing for major electric, water, and petrochemical projects. Estimates of the funds needed by 2025 are astounding. Development of natural gas reserves will probably cost even more than the $45 billion Aramco is spending, plus the $25 billion initially agreed by several major oil companies. To meet the estimated electricity needs in 2025 will require $120 billion in new generating plants and transmission facilities, and the water industry another $50 billion. The six new "economic cities" planned for 5 million inhabitants by 2020 will cost another $100 billion, perhaps achieving the goal of being steps towards a post-petroleum era.

Clearly unable to finance the required investment (at least before the recent rise in oil prices and possibly after their decline), the government promised larger roles for private companies. However, international firms capable of billion-dollar projects hesitate to become involved in supplying the Saudi market, with its unprofitable traditions of nearly-free water and electricity. They particularly desire to invest in oil production, but Aramco strongly opposes such involvement, and the petrochemical firm SABIC also remains off-limits to foreign companies.

After stock market prices fell by 60% in 2008, the Saudi Arabian Monetary Authority (the central bank) lowered interest rates and eased capital requirements for banks.

The Future: Optimism is tempting for a country that possesses 25% of global oil reserves, protects pilgrimage centers for one-sixth of the world population, and boasts a decades-old special relationship with the only superpower. Nevertheless, some sleepless nights should appear in the forecasts for the 7,000 Saudi princes who form the ruling elite.

In 1980, per capita incomes matched those of the U.S. The country's wells still produce nearly as much oil, and now at about the same inflation-adjusted prices. But the population has doubled, and per capita incomes have tumbled. Economic reforms to correct decades of paternalism and dependence on services provided by foreigners will not come easily. However, the economic difficulties may prove far easier to solve than the ideological and political.

The electronic revolution is now destroying the isolation of a younger generation of a vast size. Nearly half of the population is under the age of 17, and their videos, satellite TV, and internet sites typically portray the purpose of living to be pleasure, rather than worshipping Allah. Despite the kingdom's intense emphasis on the sanctity of women, some 70% of the cell phones of a sample of unruly male teenagers contained pornography. The world is getting through.

Equally threatening for the royal family and its religious establishment are Western intellectual influences emphasize that truth comes from testing conflicting ideas, and individuals make personal choices rather than accept writings from a book or pronouncements from a traditional authority figure.

It is impossible to know whether the real struggle will be that against al-Qaeda and its associated groups, or against officially correct but reactionary clerics. The royal family's great challenge is to move reforms quickly enough to satisfy those with modern inclinations, while avoiding changes that alienate the religious establishment and increase the allure of al-Qaeda among the devout. It will not be easy.

King Abdulaziz Al-Saud meets with President Franklin D. Roosevelt on board the USS Quincy in the Suez Canal's Great Bitter Lake, February 1945

The Syrian Arab Republic

Desert Protector: This little-known fortress towers about the ruins of Palmyra.

Area: 71,498 sq. mi. (185,180 sq. km.).
Population: 20.8 million.
Capital City: Damascus (pop. 2.5–3 million, estimated).
Climate: Summers are generally hot and dry; winters are mild in low areas, cooler with increasing elevation. Winter brings adequate rain in the western part of the country, but the remainder is arid.
Neighboring Countries: Turkey (North); Iraq (East); Jordan (South); Lebanon (West); Israel (Southwest).
Time Zone: GMT +2 (+3 in summer).
Official Language: Arabic.
Other Tongues: Kurdish and Armenian.
Ethnic Background: On the basis of language and culture, nearly all Syrians are identified as Arab.
Principal Religion: Islam (about 82%, mainly *Sunni*), Christianity; Druze and Alawi Islamic communities.
Chief Commercial Products: Petroleum and natural gas; textiles, cement, processed food, wheat, barley, cotton, grapes, olives, sheep, chicken and other farm products.
Major Trading Partners: Germany, France, Italy, Netherlands, Greece, Russia, Lebanon.
Currency: Lira (1 SL = 100 piasters).

Former Colonial Status: French mandate (1920–1946).
Independence Date: April 17, 1946, marking French evacuation.
Chief of State: Bashar al-Asad, President; new term, 2007.
Head of Government: Naji al-'Utri (or Otari), Prime Minister.
National Flag: The flag consists of three horizontal stripes of (top to bottom) red, white and black; two green, five-pointed stars are aligned on the central white stripe.
Gross Domestic Product: $61 billion (at current prices); $104 billion (Purchasing Power Parity), 2007.
GDP per capita: $5,000 (PPP), 2007.

Lying at the eastern end of the Mediterranean Sea, Syria consists of two main climate zones. The western region includes the coastal mountains, the Orontes River valley, and a range of interior hills or mountains. On its eastern limits, the western zone includes Damascus and Aleppo and it provides the home of four-fifths of the population.

The eastern zone takes the form of foothills descending from an average elevation of 3,000 feet to the vast, open desert cut by the Euphrates River as it flows across Syria from north to southeast. Its two main tributaries come from the north, and they also support agriculture along their banks. Arabs invading the region called the area north of the Euphrates *al-Jazira*, "The Island," a cultivated expanse of green surrounded by desert.

Most of Syria has an average rainfall of less than ten inches a year, but the western zone enjoys more. The seaward slopes of the coastal range may receive as much as 50 inches near the crest, which in some places is 5,000 feet high. Cities such as Damascus and Homs along the eastern base of the inland range are great oases watered by springs and streams fed by the mountain rains.

History: Human civilization extends back as far in time in Syria as anywhere else. Many of antiquity's great empires occupied the country, although no Syrian dynasty arose to conquer the region, a reflection perhaps of its diversity of geography and population. For the 2,700 years between Assyrian conquest and Ottoman expulsion, Syria's history is deeply intertwined with the events related in the **Historical Background** of this book.

Syria

In the 7th and 8th centuries, Syria became host to the world empire of the Arab Umayyads, a Meccan dynasty that ruled from Damascus. The region flourished, with the construction of new cities and palaces. However, the Abbasids overthrew the faltering Umayyad dynasty in 750, and the capital was moved to Iraq. As the united Muslim empire disintegrated in the following centuries, Syria's important geographical position attracted invasions from every side except the desert: Seljuk Turks, Egyptian caliphs, European Crusaders, Mongols, Mamluks, and finally, the Ottoman Turks.

By 1900, most of the territory now included in Syria formed the two major provinces of Aleppo and Damascus. The present international borders did not exist, even as provincial boundaries. Jordan and parts of Israel and Lebanon reported to Damascus, while Antakya and some smaller regions of southern Turkey near the city of Aleppo formed part of Aleppo province.

Before the outbreak of World War I, most inhabitants accepted Ottoman rule by officials of the Sultan in Istanbul, though the politically active upper class of landowners, officials and Muslim scholars increasingly demanded a greater degree of local self-government. The *Decentralization Party* reflected this desire, and most Syrian voters sympathized with its reformist goals. In the late 19th century,

greater education and economic development encouraged the rise of a consciousness of being Arab in language and culture. Just before World War I broke out, this cultural identity developed into small, secret societies, *al-Fatat* and *al-Ahd*, that demanded independence for the Arab lands of the Empire.

After the Ottoman Empire joined the Central Powers in 1914, the Arab nationalists plotted with Sharif Husayn of Mecca to gain independence. They provided the details for territorial demands he made from Britain in exchange for an uprising against the Ottoman Empire. After the outbreak of the Arab Revolt in June 1916, Syrian opinion increasingly favored the Allies.

The great British victory over the Ottoman army in Palestine opened the way to Damascus. British and Arab forces raced for the city—historians still debate who conquered it—and pressed on to capture Aleppo in the last weeks of the war. Initially the Arab army administered the interior of Syria, and French troops were limited to Mt. Lebanon and the coast northward into Turkey. However, as part of the peace settlement, Britain supported granting France the mandates for Syria and Lebanon.

In early 1920, nationalists in Damascus proclaimed Syria independent and united (including Jordan and Lebanon), with Emir Faisal as king. The son of Sharif Husayn, Faisal had led the Arab army into

Damascus, but his rule was brief. Threatened by a French invasion, he attempted to compromise; this only alienated many of his supporters. Syrian forces collapsed at the Battle of Maysalun in July 1920. France imposed its rule on Syria and proceeded to occupy it despite local nationalist revolts.

Although the French mandate provided some modernization and technical successes, it failed to convince Syrian public opinion. In the mid-1920s a revolt shook the entire eastern portion of the country. As fighting spread to Damascus itself, French artillery shelled sections of the capital sympathetic to the rebels. During the 1930s, protests and general strikes dominated political life, and when an agreement was reached between the Syrian nationalists and France, a change of government in Paris meant that it was not implemented.

Free to act without opposition from nationalist diplomacy, the French soon dismembered Syria into small regions that emphasized ethnic minorities, such as *Jabal Druze* in the southeast and an *Alawi* state based in Latakia. This weakened the overwhelming *Sunni* majority with its nationalist ideas, but it also blocked any cooperation between the nationalists and French officials. France also transferred to Lebanon the fertile Biqa' Valley and the western slopes of the Anti-Lebanon mountains. In 1939 it supervised the transfer of Antakya, a region in the far northwest, to Turkey. Syrians generally opposed these territorial losses, and even today many older Syrians argue that without imperialist interference, the territories of Palestine, Jordan, Lebanon and Antakya would naturally form parts of Syria.

After British-led troops expelled officials of the pro-Nazi French government from Syria during World War II, Free French forces took control. However, the joint efforts of the United States, the Soviet Union and Britain at the UN Security Council finally induced France to withdraw entirely. The last troops left on April 17, 1946, the day now celebrated as National Day.

Years of Political Instability

Syrian independence came to a country uncertain of its destiny. To the generation

Syria

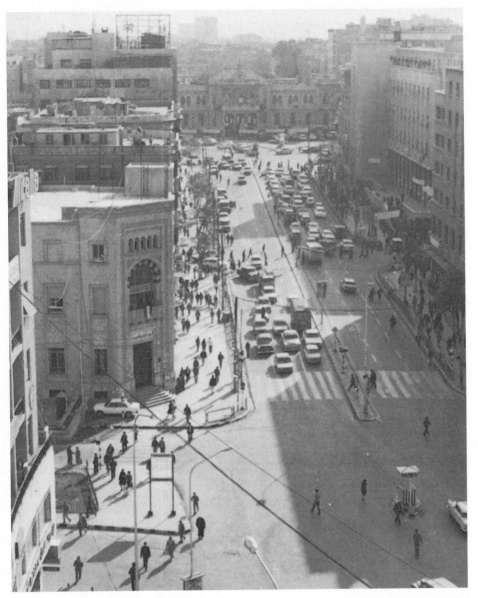

Downtown Damascus

Photo by Ray L. Cleveland

Elections generally showed popular support for pan-Arab and socialist politicians, whose rivals came from a small group of leading families who exercised great influence through their vast land holdings and wealth.

The *Ba'th Party* soon proved more influential than other radical ideologies such as the *Syrian Popular Party* and the communists. Founded in the early 1940s in Damascus by Michel Aflaq, a Christian, and Salah al-Din al-Bitar, a Sunni Muslim, the party took its name from the Arabic word for renaissance. Highly committed to a nation uniting all Arabs and thus bringing them self-respect instead of backwardness and defeat, its ideology naturally threatened Arab states created by European agreements rather than national identity. The party's socialist goals included the creation of a classless state, and its radicals threatened a government takeover of industry and trade as well. Though the party's legality was sometimes uncertain, it attracted disillusioned military officers in particular, and spread to Jordan, Lebanon and Iraq.

By the mid-1950s, the nationalist and anti-imperialist appeal of Gamal Abdul Nasser of Egypt reinforced the opinions of many Syrians suspicious of Western powers and their clients, the monarchies of Iraq and Jordan. As Syria lurched unsteadily leftward in its domestic politics, and received Soviet military equipment, several leading politicians sought a union with Egypt. In early 1958, the two countries officially formed the "United Arab Republic" with Nasser as president and ideological source of all authority. On paper, the merger replaced Syria's political parties with a *National Union* like that being organized in Egypt.

Economic problems aggravated by drought and friction between Egyptian and Syrian officials enabled conservative groups to organize a revolt which broke the union in 1961. Reformist politicians soon regained power, however, and in 1963, army officers favoring the *Ba'th Party* seized control in yet another coup d'etat and outlawed all rival political groups. Despite factional struggles within the *Ba'th Party*, it enacted many economic and social changes, such as the nationalization of petroleum and other major industries. The wealthy and tradition-minded complained in private about the transformation of the economy and society, but they could not successfully oppose the government as long as it had the support of the army.

Clashes with the militarily-powerful state of Israel across the demilitarized zone frequently broke out between 1949 and the 1960s. Occasionally they flared into serious incidents with artillery and

of nationalists who had opposed the French—and sometimes compromised with them—the opportunity to rule from Damascus was sufficient reward. One such politician, Shukri al-Quwatli, became the first president.

However, rival ideologies attracted support from students, army officers and even the army at large. Some sought the borders of geographical Syria; others, a merger with Iraq to counter the Jewish settlement of Palestine. Socialists hoped to weaken the power of the wealthy notable families who formed the top nationalist leadership in parliament. Increasingly these politicians appeared grasping for power. Corruption proved to be one cause among several for the Syrian army's conclusive defeat by Israel in 1948–49, when the army entered Palestine to attack the new Jewish state.

Against this background, Husni al-Za'im, the Chief of Staff, carried out Syria's first military coup d'etat in March 1949. He arrested leading politicians, arranged a cease-fire agreement with Israel, and reached a verbal alliance with Iraq. Al-Za'im offered to meet with Israeli Prime Minister Ben-Gurion for peace talks, but was rebuffed. After banning political parties, al-Za'im was elected president, but less than five months after seizing power, another military coup led to his execution. No Syrian leader ever again offered to meet Israel's prime minister.

By ending ineffective though constitutional government, al-Za'im ushered in a long era of instability. For the next twenty-one years, Syrian governments proved most unstable, suffering more than a dozen military coups, some quite bloody.

161

Syria

Young Syrians performing a traditional dance at a local festival

aircraft joining the battle. Several clashes followed Syria's attempts to divert headwaters of the Jordan River that had flowed to Israel.

Tensions along the Israeli border led to aircraft dogfights in May 1967, and full-scale war in June (see Israel: History). After quickly defeating Syria's Egyptian and Jordanian allies, Israeli forces stormed into Syria and up the slopes which rise to the fertile plateau known in Arabic as *Jawlan* (pronounced *Golan* by Israelis), occupying some 1,250 square miles. Israeli troops forced nearly all the remaining civilians to leave, and they destroyed or damaged public buildings and homes in the regional capital, Quneitra. Rather than permit the Syrian refugees to return to their farms and villages in accord with a UN resolution, Israel established its own settlements on the farmlands of the ousted Syrians.

Al-Asad Rises to Power; 1973 War

After an unsuccessful Syrian-Palestinian attempt to invade Jordan in 1970, General Hafiz al-Asad seized power from his fellow Ba'thist officers. Unlike its unstable predecessors, his regime succeeded in neutralizing all rivals, by crushing them or winning their support. It remained in

power longer than all other Syrian governments combined. Al-Asad ("The Lion") was elected president in 1971, as the only candidate on the ballot, and two years later a new constitution provided for an elected legislature, the People's Council. Power remains firmly with the president, who must be a Muslim. He appoints the vice president, prime minister, and cabinet.

Despairing of diplomatic efforts to recover their lost territory, Syria and Egypt began a surprise military offensive in 1973 in a desperate effort to drive out Israeli forces. Three weeks of intensive fighting again demonstrated Israeli military superiority, but with aid from Iraq and Jordan, the Syrian defenses did not break. U.S. mediation efforts led by Henry Kissinger in 1974 returned a small strip of territory to Syria and established a UN-patrolled buffer zone between the two armies.

Within the tightly-controlled country, al-Asad's government won broad public acceptance for its stability, reduced radicalism, and pragmatism. The relaxation of doctrinaire socialism encouraged economic growth. Syria was not a democracy, and al-Asad always won the referendum on the presidency with overwhelming majorities. Elections to the People's Council (parliament) always returned a Ba'th

Party majority, but some independents and minor leftist parties held a few seats.

By 1980, many Syrians desired fresh faces in government and the end of military rule. Like many other top officers, Hafiz al-Asad was a member of the Alawi community, an offshoot of Shi'a Islam that incorporates ideas from several other religions. Patronized by the French, but ignored in government spending after independence, the Alawis found few opportunities open to them. As a consequence, their young men tended to join the military. As Alawi soldiers moved up the ranks, military rule eventually meant an Alawi-dominated regime, although Sunnis always held important positions. By embracing *Ba'thist* socialism and linking with the *Communist Party*, the officers presented themselves as secular and modernizing.

Since Syria was a police state that prohibited all parties but the *Ba'th* and its allies, opposition to al-Asad's government came largely from the illegal Sunni *Ikhwan al Muslimin* (Muslim Brotherhood), which advocated an Islamic state. After several acts of violence, including the killing of nearly 50 Alawi military cadets in one incident, the *Ikhwan* launched a revolt in the conservative city of Hama in 1982. The military crushed the rebellion, but at the

162

The late President Hafiz al-Asad

cost of perhaps 20,000 lives and great damage to an old and picturesque city. The bloodshed ended most dreams of removing the regime by force.

When Israeli forces withdrew from most of Lebanon in 1985, most Syrian troops also departed. However, terrorism and anarchy prevailed in much of the country, and the troops returned two years later. Besides halting the fighting, Syria attempted to shape Lebanese politics. In 1988, heavy fighting broke out between units of the Lebanese army and Syrian forces they considered foreign occupiers (see Lebanon: History).

Responding to International Isolation

An important recurring theme in the country's recent history has been its isolation. Western nations often felt disturbed by terrorism allegedly masterminded in Damascus by Palestinian and other radical groups. The struggle to regain the Golan prohibited close friendship with Israel's fervent allies, but some Syrian intelligence services, perhaps but not necessarily following their own agendas, indulged in murderous exploits. Eventually, the Soviet Union, Syria's strongest ally, refused al-Asad's request for high-tech weapons because his government could not pay for them, nor his troops use them effectively, nor protect their secrets.

In 1975, Syrian attention turned to the civil war in Lebanon, where Al-Asad desired to maintain and if possible increase Syrian influence. To that end, Syria acted first as an ally of one side, then as a mediator, and finally as a military peacekeeper. Syria attempted to prevent any faction from becoming too powerful, first arming the Palestinians and leftists against the

Maronite militias, then attacking their former allies when they neared victory.

Al-Asad also desired to prevent pretexts for Israeli intervention in Lebanon, and the Syrian military valued defense positions in eastern Lebanon. Formal international approval for the Syrian occupation of Lebanon followed from the Arab League, but Syrian troops never ventured far into southern Lebanon, and they failed to oppose the Israeli invasion there in 1978, although they fought bitter artillery battles with Maronite militias around Beirut.

Other Middle Eastern disputes also cost Syria the international sympathy. Most Arab states feared the Iranian Islamic Revolution, and when Iraq in 1980 invaded Iran, they supported Iraq, but al-Asad uniquely allied with Iran. The next year, Israel recognized Syria's isolation as an opportune moment and annexed the occupied Golan Heights. When the few Syrian citizens there, mainly members of the *Druze* community, objected to their new Israeli identity cards, the Israeli army used stern methods to impose them.

Within the Middle East, the revolutionary *Ba'thist* vision of a single Arab state from the Atlantic to the Gulf naturally prohibited enduring alliances with monarchies. Al-Asad's uncompromising stand against the Camp David Agreement precluded friendship with Egypt or the U.S., and quarrels with Yasir Arafat isolated Syria when the Palestine National Council and the United Nations favored Arafat's diplomatic approach.

Diplomatically isolated in the late 1980s, al-Asad proved his dexterity and craftiness. He skillfully muted criticisms

of less vital issues like Egypt and the Palestinian peace efforts. On Lebanon, a strategic concern, he remained uncompromising, and won: the Arab League failed to demand Syria's withdrawal. Indeed, the revised Lebanese constitution (see Lebanon: Politics) preserved Syria's right to station troops in Lebanon indefinitely. Perhaps not coincidentally, Syria helped to gain the release of two American hostages from Lebanon in early 1990, a far cry from the suspected involvement of its intelligence agents in the bombing of the Marine barracks in Beirut a decade earlier.

Iraq's seizure of Kuwait in 1990 threatened to strengthen very greatly Syria's long-standing *Ba'thist* rival. Al-Asad therefore publicly supported the posting of American troops in Saudi Arabia, and even dispatched 20,000 men of his own armed forces. However, popular opinion accepted such behavior only reluctantly. Syrian troops played only a defensive role and did not invade Kuwait or Iraq. Thus, Syria became a member of the Coalition, but on its own terms.

Rewards followed nevertheless. Syria regained international standing, diplomatic ties with Britain resumed, and the European Community dropped sanctions imposed over an attempted airplane bombing by Syrian intelligence in 1986. President Bush met with President al-Asad, despite past terrorist links. Financial assistance from the Gulf states, Japan and Europe surpassed $2 billion. In Lebanon, Syrian troops crushed the forces of Michel Aoun, and the parliament in Beirut approved treaties granting Damascus wide pretexts for intervention.

A covered 17th century *souk* (shopping area) in the old part of Damascus

Syria

President al-Asad again surprised observers—and upstaged Israel—in 1991 when he accepted a U.S. invitation to a peace conference on the Middle East. The alternative, a military re-conquest of the (Syrian) Jawlan was clearly impossible, given the end of Soviet assistance and the destruction of Iraq (often a potential ally against Israel, though daily a bitter *Ba'thist* rival).

Negotiations with Israel proved surprisingly hopeful during the *Labor* government of Yitzhak Rabin. His negotiators conceded the possibility of withdrawing from the Golan; Damascus suggested that if Israel acknowledged Syrian sovereignty, demilitarized zones and agreement over water rights might form part of the peace settlement.

Neither the simplicity of the solution nor the advantages of peace brought agreement. Each side demanded conditions the other would obviously reject. Israel insisted on retaining observation posts, despite al-Asad's oft-repeated insistence that all territory be returned. In turn, that apparently simple phrase by Syria claimed the 1949 armistice lines rather than the international boundary. The crucial difference is a strip of land in places just over 11 yards wide along the shore of the Sea of Galilee. The mandate preserved the entire lake within Palestine (and therefore its successor, Israel), but the 1949–1967 armistice lines recognized a Syrian advance to the water's edge.

After the newly-elected Barak cabinet in Israel raised hopes for peace in 1999, negotiations again broke down. It is not clear that Israel was ever prepared to withdraw to either line in exchange for peace. Major parties like *Likud* oppose a withdrawal, and in 2009 officials emphasized the need to hold the Golan "in depth."

Under Hafiz al-Asad, Syria enjoyed official friendship with Lebanon, but relations with other Arab neighbors often seemed chilly. Muslim opposition groups sometimes operated from Jordan, and Iraq remained a bitter and sometimes deadly ideological rival. Not surprisingly, Syria followed an independent and sometimes lonely foreign policy, reflected in the virtual absence of ambassadors abroad.

Because of left-wing solidarity and as a reprisal to Turkish diversion of the Euphrates River, during most of the 1990s Syria permitted Abdullah Ocalan, the leader of the Marxist Kurdish workers party, the *PKK*, to direct its rebellion against Turkey from Syrian-occupied Lebanon. When faced with Turkish military threats in 1998, Syria expelled Ocalan, but significant tensions remained with Turkey, particularly over Antakya, the division of the Euphrates River waters, and its military links with Israel. The very first visit

Portrait of a Young Man **by noted Syrian artist Fateh Almudarres**

of a Syrian president to Turkey, in 2004, suggested that relations might improve.

In 2007 Israeli aircraft attacked a building near the eastern town of Dair al-Zor. The attack initiated claims that a nuclear reactor was being built with North Korean assistance. Despite denials of unapproved activities, the site was razed. Subsequently the International Atomic Energy Agency (IAEA) claimed uranium at the site differed from that used in Syria's recognized research.

Domestic Affairs and the Succession

Syrian domestic affairs traditionally receive little foreign attention, in part because the public rarely expresses itself, and the press, controlled, bland and propagandistic, questions little. The regime has not remained in power for three decades by fostering a variety of viewpoints, but rather by removing any possible alternative leaders from influential positions and independent wealth. Anyone expressing discontent was frequently arrested and detained indefinitely. In 1992 Syria still held an estimated 5,000 political prisoners. A few hundred probably remain today, the numbers rising or falling depending on the regime's sense of security. Many political activists seek exile abroad.

164

The village of Ma'aloula where the Aramaic language of Christ is still spoken

Because opposition parties have been illegal for decades, the legislature remains a forum for the non-political discussion of non-partisan matters. Under Hafiz al-Asad, most Syrians accepted the reality of an authoritarian regime and set aside political ideologies. Typically, one-third of the seats in the legislature were contested by approved independents; the remaining seats belonged to the *Ba'th* party's *National Progressive Front*. The latest election, in 2007, not only drew little public interest, but Syrians actually felt free enough to comment about it. In the presidential contest, a 99.9% "yes" vote is standard for al-Asad, whether Hafiz or Bashar.

Two widely-shared public concerns have been corruption and a stagnant economy. In contrast to the simple living conditions of most people, the politically influential sometimes obtained luxury goods as a result of the Syrian involvement in Lebanon and its drug trade.

During the 1990s, oil production climbed to nearly 600,000 barrels per day. The additional exports, plus some reduction in the myriad economic regulations, led to increased prosperity for the middle and upper classes. However, poverty remains obvious and the infrastructure totters, with frequent rationing of electricity.

A car crash in 1994 killed Basil al-Asad, the elder son of Hafiz, an air force officer with a reputation as clean-living and athletic. Basil's younger brother, Bashar, subsequently emerged from a low-profile, non-political role. He supervised the country's initial computerization, and a crackdown on corruption.

After Hafiz al-Asad died in 2000, the legislature nominated Bashar for the presidency although constitutionally he was six years too young. He won overwhelming (and probably genuine) support in the popular vote that followed.

In his inauguration speech, Bashar called for openness and reform. Hundreds of political prisoners were released, and the special security courts were abolished. The infamous Mezze prison was closed, along with the special security courts. Internet access greatly increased. On the foreign scene, relations improved with Jordan, with Yasir Arafat, and even with Iraq, which began exporting oil to Syria after Syria reopened the long-sealed border to trade. This broke UN trade sanctions, but the import of perhaps 250,000 b/d of Iraqi oil permitted a similar increase in Syrian petroleum exports.

Progress towards democracy and individual freedom encouraged Riad Seif, a member of parliament to form the Friends of Civic Society. The first independent newspapers appeared since the 1960s, a satirical paper followed by a business journal. The arts, reflected the greater openness, and actors enjoyed the new freedom to express on stage sentiments often felt by people on the street.

The "Damascus Spring" proved brief. Just one year into Bashar's era, in 2001, Seif was arrested, charged with trying to change Syria's constitution by illegal means, and sentenced to years in prison. Dozens more activists were arrested but mostly released a few days later. Apparently the most sensitive topics were corruption and the wide activities of the intelligence services and secret police. Attacks on them threaten the old guard, and thus the very foundations of the regime. The Bashar administration feels far more comfortable with private banks than with free speech.

The president seems to value reform, and replaced his prime minister in 2003 with Naji al-'Utri, apparently to push for faster change. However, the regime plays games with activists, arresting those who press too hard in sensitive areas, and releasing some prisoners to win public support. Both patterns were illustrated in 2005–07, when several leading dissidents and critics were sentenced to long terms.

Given its own bloody conflict with Islamic groups in the 1980s, Syria's leadership privately offered important intelligence cooperation with the U.S. in the aftermath of September 11. However, with its own Golan Heights occupied, Damascus naturally proclaims some of the most virulent anti-Israeli propaganda of any Arab state, and considers national resistance against Israel "a social, religious, and legal right." Syria openly supported *Hizbullah's* struggle to free South Lebanon in the 1990s, and it provided the supply route for its missiles used against Israel during the war in 2006. With lesser justification, Damascus hosts a variety of groups whose violent acts proved useful in the past.

Faced with President Bush's demand that Damascus "choose the right side in the war on terror," Syria voted for UN Security Council Resolution 1441, which demanded new inspections and threatened severe consequences if Iraq did not cooperate. However, Syria strongly condemned the U.S. invasion that followed. It quietly allowed Arab volunteers to pass through Damascus en route to battle. Militants continued to do so even after the fall of Saddam's regime, though a border barrier was erected and some Iraqis were arrested and turned over to Baghdad.

The U.S. occupation of Iraq threatened the near-encirclement of Syria by rival or

Syria

President Bashar al-Asad

enemy states. Moreover, U.S. critics also attacked Damascus for supporting anti-Israeli groups and its occupation of Lebanon. Congress passed sanctions that prohibited U.S. companies from trading with Syria. In response, Bashar al-Asad undertook to strengthen relations with Turkey, Europe, and other possible moderating influences on Washington. The election of Barack Obama, and his appointment of George Mitchell as Middle East envoy, sparked a thaw in U.S.-Syrian relations at a time when the botched Iranian elections weakened Syria's most significant ally. However, no significant progress was evident, and the U.S. Congress even blocked the appointment of an ambassador to Damascus.

Hariri's Murder Threatens the Regime

Nevertheless, al-Asad played directly into his critics hands, when in 2004 Syria—apparently Bashar himself—attempted to extend Lebanese President Lahoud's term of office, contrary to that country's constitution.

International condemnation rose rapidly against the obvious manipulation of Lebanese politics. The Security Council unanimously voted for a free election and the withdrawal of Syrian troops and intelligence agents. Syria's international position worsened greatly in 2005, when an expertly executed explosion killed Rafiq Hariri, the leading Lebanese politician. Lebanon's official investigation seemed so incompetent as to suggest complicity, but massive demonstrations in Beirut called for Syria's complete withdrawal. Entirely isolated diplomatically, Damascus withdrew its troops and known intelligence offices to the eastern Biqa' valley, and then ended 29 years of occupation with a complete military withdrawal from Lebanon.

Despite patriotic celebrations for the returning troops, Bashar al-Asad's regime had clearly suffered serious setbacks. Worse followed. The Syrian interior minister and former chief in Lebanon, Ghazi Kanaan, committed suicide in mysterious circumstances. Days later, the interim UN investigation into Hariri's murder named as suspects both the commander of the Syrian Presidential Guard, Maher al-Asad (Bashar's brother), and the head of military intelligence, Asaf Shawkat, Bashar's brother-in-law. One witness even reported that planning for the assassination took place in Shawkat's home.

Admittedly, suspicion is not conviction. Syria alternately cooperated with the UN investigation and hampered it, by creating its own investigation that kept witnesses from appearing in Beirut. In 2007 the UN approved an international tribunal to deal with the murder.

After forty years of *Ba'thist* dictatorship, many Syrian opponents of the regime viewed the withdrawal from Lebanon and the UN investigation as signs of an eventually fatal weakness. A long-time vice president, Abd al-Halim Khaddam, fled the country and publicly accused Bashar of having threatened Hariri and intelligence officials of involvement in the murder. Khaddam formed, with leaders of the *Muslim Brotherhood*, an umbrella opposition alliance, the *National Salvation Front*.

Threatened internally and externally, the regime asserted its strength partly by cracking down on intellectuals and critics, such as those who had issued the "Damascus Declaration for Democratic and National Change" in 2005. It called for an end to emergency laws, political repression, and a national conference to move the country from a security state to a civil state. More significant than the actual de-

Modern Syria

mands, the Declaration united secular intellectuals, Kurdish parties, and even the *Muslim Brotherhood*.

Culture: Over half of Syria's population lives in cities or towns. The others mostly live in villages or farm communities, and a few nomads now form under 1% of the total population. The two principal cities are Damascus and Aleppo (Halab); the latter is smaller than the capital, but each exceeds one million residents. Most industry is concentrated around those cities and at Homs. City populations are currently boosted by over one million Iraqi refugees fleeing the carnage in their homeland.

A majority of Syrians are Sunni Muslims. The Arab Christian minority is mainly Greek Orthodox; the once-sizable Armenian community is in decline due to emigration. Several other groups merit mention, including *Druze* (see Lebanon: Culture) in the southeast and *Alawis* along

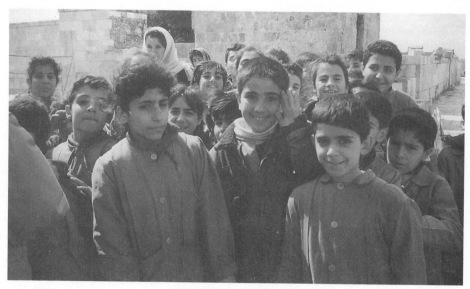

School kids at Citadel

the Mediterranean coast and nearby mountains. Together these groups form about 16% of the population.

Developing their beliefs and ritual secretly in the rugged mountains, the impoverished and disadvantaged *Alawis* for centuries remained something of a mystery. Modern scholars, little better informed, find major *Shi'a* influences, especially the *Ismaili* variant. The Imam Ali, for example, is revered as the incarnation of God. Other beliefs and the liturgy suggest Christian and other religious influences.

Though they do not form as great a community as in Turkey, Iraq, or Iran, several hundred thousand Kurds live in the northern and eastern border areas. Though Syria provided sanctuary for Turkey's Kurdish rebels, its own Kurds enjoy no legal rights to organize. They appeared restive in 2004, rioting after a soccer match. Further riots followed the kidnapping and murder of a religious leader in 2005, this time with hints at Kurdish demands for independence rather than simply fair treatment.

The Jewish community of Damascus faces extinction. After thousands of years of vibrant life and two generations of experience surviving the Arab-Israeli dispute, by 2002 it had dwindled to about 50 members worshipping in one surviving synagogue. The demise did not result from direct persecution. Rather, legal changes permitted families to emigrate together to the West, and as the community dwindled, the U.S. seemed more appealing to the few who remained.

In spite of the religious differences, there has been little strife between communities. Sectarian differences are not recognized in the government structure as they are in Lebanon, and legal political parties were not formed along religious lines. The *Ba'th Party* has no formal religious element to it, and was founded by both Christians and Muslims. For decades, it favored a distinctly secular society, forbidding head scarves in schools or soldiers worshipping in mosques.

However, growing allegiance to Islam, evident in women's dress and men's beards, suggests that the ideologies of secularism and pan-Arabism are being replaced by faith in Allah. The variety of expression is broad, ranging from students in Islamic schools to women's Qur'anic discussion groups and then members of the outlawed *Muslim Brotherhood*. Little is known of the militant Islamist group, *Tanzim Jund al-Sham,* (Organization of the Soldiers of Damascus) except that the government has reported gunfights with it.

Like Egypt and Iraq, Syria contains numerous archaeological sites of great historical importance, stretching from recent times back to the earliest village life. The spectacular ruins of the caravan city of Palmyra lie in the middle of the desert beside the modern oasis village of Tadmor. Queen Zenobia once ruled there until defeated by the Romans and carried off to Rome as a royal prisoner.

At Aleppo, in the northern part of Syria, a great citadel of bygone days arises on a high mound in the middle of a modern city. Damascus boasts it is the oldest continuously-inhabited city, anywhere. The National Museum contains one of the finest displays of Islamic art to be found anywhere. In the city center, adjacent to the covered market known as the *Souk al-Hamidiya,* the Umayyad Mosque preserves gold leaf from the 7th century. Other museums illustrate the lifestyle of wealthy families during the Ottoman period, while in small villages outside Damascus the inhabitants still speak Aramaic, the language used by the Jews of Palestine at the time of Jesus.

Economy: Syria has a more balanced economy than most nations of Southwest Asia. One-third of the population still depends directly on agriculture. Farmers raise cotton in irrigated fields along the Orontes and Euphrates rivers, wheat and other grains on the steppe, or fruits and vegetables in oases like the Ghuta outside Damascus.

In years of abundant rainfall, Syria's farms produce grain for export, but usually the country imports food. There is great scope for improved farming methods, and experimental programs are carried on with the United Nations. Given the high cost of importing food, agricultural development is vitally important. Increases in the area of irrigated land resulting from the Euphrates dam proved much lower than expected.

The largest single industry is still textiles. Domestic cotton from the Euphrates Valley, the Aleppo Plain and elsewhere supply the mills. Raw cotton is also exported, but in lesser quantities as more and more is woven into textiles in Syria. Because of its socialist regulations, the country receives little foreign investment outside tourist projects. Because government funds rarely allow any large new development projects, emphasis is being placed on improving production levels in existing projects.

An oil pipeline from the modest deposits in the northeast to a refinery in Homs and the port of Tartus has operated since 1968. Syria's oil exports were a major earner of foreign exchange during the 1970s, but declining exports and lower prices brought a drop in this income. Promising deposits of oil east of Dair al-Zor reached commercial production in 1989, but whether because geology or a lack of reinvestment, they have since declined. The search for oil and its production continues, as production declines in

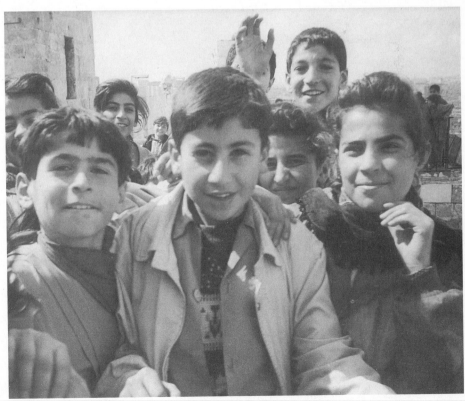

School outing to the Citadel in Aleppo

Syria

existing oilfields. However, the country has failed to attract steady exploration activities by foreign firms, and several majors have left the country in recent years. In the near future, it could become a net importer of oil, as local consumption exceeds production.

The Future: An ophthalmologist by trade, Bashar al-Asad specialized in correcting the sight of others before his brother's fatal accident set him on the path to power. During his first eight years as president, Bashar failed to act decisively on the big issues and allegedly involved himself in some nasty ones, like the murder of Lebanon's Rafiq Hariri that threatened the regime. His allies must have hoped that his own foresight would improve sufficiently to steer Syria through crisis.

Like his father, however, Bashar outlasted two simultaneous crises, an international investigation that he could not control, and the defection of long-time aides. Four years later, his regime seems more stable, his international acceptability has increased, and some dissidents have been released.

Fear of "Another Iraq," of anarchy or sectarian violence, is perhaps the major reason that domestic and foreign demands for change did not become a flood. Expect opposition groups to seize every opportunity to show their good will to each other and promise to share power, should opportunity come their way. Also expect Bashar al-Asad to manipulate circumstances, particularly relations with the U.S. and the conflict with Israel, so that power remains within his small circle, even as the economy continues to liberalize at glacial speed.

Vendor selling nuts and spices in a traditional market

The Republic of Turkey

Near the mouth of the Bosporus in Istanbul survive old residences and, looming above them, the Sultan Ahmet I Mosque—the "blue mosque." Photo: Miller B. Spangler

National Day: October 23 (Proclamation of the Republic, 1923).

Head of State: Abdullah Gül, President (2007)

Head of Government: Recep Tayyip Erdoğan, Prime Minister.

National Flag: Red field containing a large white crescent with a smaller five-pointed star between its points.

Gross Domestic Product: $590 billion (at current prices); $915 (Purchasing Power Parity), 2008

GDP per capita: $12,900 (PPP), 2008.

During the early 1920s, a new nation arose on the historical peninsula of Asia Minor and the adjacent tip of Europe. The Ottoman Empire had ruled a mosaic of Greeks, Armenians, Kurds, and Turks in the territory before World War I, but faced dismemberment after its defeat. A former Ottoman general, Kemal Atatürk, led the Turkish community to seize its independence and establish a national state. Although the Turkish tribes originated in Central Asia and only 5% of the new country lay in Europe, Atatürk strove to create a modern, secular and European country to replace the religiously-inspired empire.

Geography: Besides a small European portion around the historic city of Istanbul, modern Turkey covers Asia Minor, known as Anatolia, and the mountainous region to its east. Although the nation enjoys a long coastline on the Aegean Sea, almost none of the major islands are Turkish. Instead, though often located only a few miles from Asia Minor, they belong to Greece.

Two long, narrow straits divide European from Asian Turkey. The Dardanelles leads from the Aegean Sea into the small Sea of Marmara. Vessels continuing to the Black Sea then sail up the Bosporus. For centuries, authority over the straits between the Black Sea and the Mediterranean has been important, for whatever power rules the straits influences the commercial and strategic well-being of other Black Sea states.

Apart from its long seacoasts, Turkey is a country of high elevations, and averages more than 3,500 feet above sea level. Asia Minor forms a plateau surrounded, except on the west, by mountain ranges. The highest mountains are in the eastern part of the country. A spectacular peak on the Iranian border, called *Ağri Daği* in Turkish and Mt. Ararat in English, reaches 16,945 feet. Many other mountains exceed 10,000 feet, and the plateau itself varies in elevation from 2,500 to 7,000 feet.

The heart of Asia Minor is largely desert, because mountains to the north and south block out rain-bearing clouds.

Area: 300,948 sq. miles (779,452 sq. km.).

Population: 71.2 million (2008).

Capital City: Ankara (pop. 3.5 million, est.).

Climate: Mostly hot and dry in the summer, though humid along the coasts; winters generally are wet and mild on the coasts, cooler inland and very cold in the eastern mountains.

Neighboring Countries: Greece (West); Bulgaria (Northwest); Georgia, Armenia (Northeast); Azerbaijan (East); Iran (East); Iraq (Southeast); Syria (South).

Time Zone: GMT +2 (+3 in summer).

Official Language: Turkish.

Other Principal Tongues: Kurdish; far fewer speak Arabic, Greek or Armenian.

Ethnic Background: Turkish linguistically and culturally, but physical characteristics vary. European features predominate rather than Central Asian.

Principal Religion: Islam (about 98%).

Chief Commercial Products: Cotton and textiles, mohair, tobacco, hazelnuts, raisins, sorghum, grains, meat, iron and steel, chromite, petroleum products, manufactures, including televisions, refrigerators, automobiles, and textiles.

Major Trading Partners: Germany, U.S., Libya, Russia, Iran, Switzerland and the U.K.

Currency: New Turkish Lira.

Former Political Status: Heart of the Ottoman Empire; independent.

Turkey

In this region Lake Tuz has one of the highest concentrations of salt and minerals of any lake or sea. To the east, Lake Van also contains high levels of salt, and no visible outlet, although underground channels may connect it to the Tigris or Euphrates. All together, many lakes comprise 3,256 square miles of the total area of the country.

Two traditionally useful rivers are the Kizil Irmak and the Sakarya, both draining into the Black Sea. The Seyhan and Ceyhan empty into the Mediterranean, after running through the fertile plain around Adana, where much of Turkey's cotton is grown. The mighty Tigris and Euphrates both originate in Turkey, but they pass through steep mountain gorges, so their usefulness was originally irrigation of the plains of Syria and Iraq. Now they serve as the basis for GAP, the Southeast Anatolia Project for agricultural and industrial development, a massive power and irrigation scheme.

Western Asia Minor generally enjoys good winter rains, as do the southern Taurus Mountains. The Pontus Mountains along the north coast have moderate rains throughout the year, especially in the spring. The eastern highlands receive abundant precipitation, but the elevation and rugged terrain makes them often not suitable for agriculture. Forests grow in these mountains and those of the north, but few trees grow elsewhere.

History: The modern Republic of Turkey rose from the ruins of the Ottoman Empire, which was defeated and dismembered at the close of World War I. Secret agreements during the war divided many areas with little regard for national feeling, and left only a very small Turkish-ruled area in northern Asia Minor. At the Paris Peace Conference, the Arab parts of the empire fell as prey to Britain and France, and Turkish-speaking provinces seemed destined for partition among Italy, Greece and Armenia as well.

To enforce their colonial claims, Greek troops occupied Izmir and moved inland, while the French, despite some resistance, sought the region around Adana. Pending a peace treaty, British forces occupied the Sultan's capital, Istanbul, while Armenians and Kurds both appealed to the Peace Conference for their own states. However, in 1920 an energetic and determined army officer, Mustafa Kemal, summoned delegates to Ankara, to save the nation. Calling themselves the Grand National Assembly, the delegates elected Kemal as its president; he later adopted the surname Atatürk. In the next months, they established an independent Turkish nation with the small railroad town deep in Anatolia as the capital.

To the astonishment of the allied victors, Atatürk molded Ottoman troops and volunteers into a fervent and disciplined force. It pushed the French back to Aleppo, and retook provinces claimed by Armenia. The Italians withdrew from southwest Asia Minor, and France recognized the new Turkish regime quickly, hoping to gain national advantage. Disagreements and rivalries had split the victors into national camps.

Peace with Greece only followed a bitter war, worsened because in retreat the Greek troops destroyed everything and committed outrages upon Turkish vil-

Kemal Atatürk

lagers. The small British force left alone to defend Istanbul, was finally withdrawn. Reflecting these military successes, the Treaty of Lausanne gave Turkey full sovereignty over most of the territory it now possesses.

Stone heads of gods built for King Antiochus I in southwestern Turkey over 2,000 years ago

In 1923, the Grand National Assembly proclaimed Turkey a republic, and under Atatürk's leadership, deep changes shook Turkish society. The office of Caliph was abolished in 1924, along with religious law courts. The 1924 constitution made Ankara the capital, designated the National Assembly as the center of authority and guaranteed freedom of speech, press and travel. While the document provided for a democratic form of government, in fact Kemal Atatürk ruled as a dictator. Opposition was ruthlessly crushed, particularly that by Kurds in the southeast.

The new government determined to rush Turks towards modernity. It forbad men to wear Muslim-style hats without brims. It forced people to dress like Europeans, and as far as possible, to think and act like them. The government replaced the Arabic script with the Latin alphabet, making every book and sign in the country obsolete, a process that helped purify Turkish of many Arabic and Persian loanwords. Even names changed, as Mustafa Kemal and the rest of the nation adopted the use of family names. Kemal himself became "Atatürk," Father of the Turks. The policy of secularization closed religious schools, abolished the dervish brotherhoods, and eliminated many other aspects of Ottoman culture. The Western calendar replaced the Muslim, polygamy was ended, and women received a new status. Codes of law based on European models replaced Ottoman procedures influenced by the Islamic *Shari'a*. The day of rest was moved from Friday to Sunday.

The pace of change moved rapidly in other social and economic spheres. Universal primary education was proclaimed, corruption attacked, and Atatürk committed the military to continuing reform. In subduing the Christian Armenians and Greeks, the Turkish army was ruthless (although most of the 1.5 million Armenians perished during World War I). This caused almost all members of these minorities to emigrate, leaving Turkey short of managerial talent and entrepreneurs.

Economically, Atatürk favored a program of industrialization behind high tariff barriers. When private industry failed to expand sufficiently during the Great Depression of the 1930s, the government created State Economic Enterprises to operate in textiles, metals, banking and other areas.

Kemal Atatürk died in 1938, recognized as the hero of his nation in his own lifetime. The National Assembly elected a close associate of Atatürk, Ismet Inonu, as the second president of the Republic. He soon faced the difficult task of guiding the nation through World War II. Turkey remained neutral, but at the end of the war threats from the Soviet Union forced it to seek allies in the West. Beginning in 1947, Turkey received massive U.S. economic and military aid, given to help resist Soviet pressure. To help defend itself against the Soviet Union, Turkey joined the North Atlantic Treaty Organization in 1951.

After becoming a member of the United Nations (1945), Turkey moved cautiously toward democracy at home. The *Republican People's Party* treasured Atatürk's legacy, but in 1950 the *Democratic Party*, which appealed to the conservatism of old-fashioned landlords and little-educated peasants, won a landslide.

During the 1950s the *Democratic Party* became authoritarian, banned all political activity by the opposition, and plunged the country seriously into debt. With the country slipping badly, since the military considers itself the heir of Atatürk's reforms, in 1960 officers seized power and arrested high officials and *Democratic Party* politicians. Then the military oversaw the creation of a new constitution, and after elections handed power back to the politicians.

Though it returned Turkey to formal democracy and set a precedent for a watchdog role, the military intervention did not solve the underlying political and economic problems. Indeed, some of its drastic measures created bitterness for a whole generation. Throughout the 1960s, the *Justice Party* led by Suleyman Demirel controlled parliament, but it foundered in 1971 and Turkey fell into serious unrest. Student protests, unemployment and violence by extremist groups shook public confidence. The army forced Demirel's resignation and took strong measures to restore law and order.

In 1974, Prime Minister Bulent Ecevit seized the opportunity to invade Cyprus

Turkey

(see Cyprus: History, in Wayne Thompson's *Nordic, Central and Southeastern Europe*). Despite international condemnation, the move won emotional support from a public concerned over previous mistreatment of the Turkish minority.

Nevertheless, by the late 1970s, protests and assassinations shook the country. Extremists on both the Marxist left and Islamic right reinforced old communal rivalries and in 1978 unrest erupted into mob fighting in Marash, east of Adana. The Shi'a and Alevite communities, generally poorer than the majority Sunni Muslims, suffered more than 100 dead and several hundred injured. Since the Shi'a and Alevite supported the *Republican People's Party*, and the Sunnis backed the conservative *Justice Party*, the conflict reflected socio-economic, political, and religious divisions. Despite the imposition of martial law in many regions, the toll from the violence exceeded 5,000.

Finally, in 1980, the military seized power and installed a governing Council that took vigorous steps against terrorism, arresting more than 10,000 suspects during the first month. Strict controls were imposed on the press, hundreds of mayors were dismissed, and taxi drivers were ordered to shave daily. Within months, violence declined and the country even looked cleaner. However, many innocent people languished in prison.

The Return to Democracy

Criticizing the 1961 constitution as unworkable, the military leaders drafted a new one. To encourage new leadership, it banned the previous political parties and

Austere, cold and imposing, the Ataturk Mausoleum in Ankara reflects the character of modern Turkey's founder.
Photo by Wayne Thompson

about 100 leading politicians, including Ecevit and Demirel, from political activity for ten years. Meanwhile, martial law courts punished participants in the violence, sentencing tens of thousands to prison, sometimes for lengthy terms. To little surprise, many prisoners were tortured and mistreated in ways common to Turkish prisons, such as corporal punishment, solitary confinement in a small, dark cell, or bread-and-water diets.

Two issues dominated Turkish political life during the 1990s, challenging both the

military and political elite. Throughout the Southeast, a major rebellion by disaffected Kurds led to the deaths of perhaps 30,000 civilians and the evictions of hundreds of thousands of others from their villages. Meanwhile, against a background of political and economic stagnation, the Islamic-influenced *Welfare Party* won local elections and finally came to govern Turkey.

The Kurdish Insurrection

For millennia, tough mountain tribesmen have inhabited the heights and valleys where the borders of Iraq, Iran and Turkey converge. Outside East and South Asia, these Kurds form the largest ethnic group lacking independence. Kurds have rebelled against each state where they form sizable local majorities.

Today's political problems result directly from the breakup of the Ottoman Empire after World War I, when Armenians, Kurds and Turks all claimed eastern Anatolia as their national land. However, the Armenians were defeated, and the Kurds failed to influence the peace settlement. The Treaty of Lausanne brushed aside Kurdish desires for independence, and divided them mostly between Turkey, Iran, and Iraq (see Iraq: History).

For decades, Turkey officially classified Kurds as "Mountain Turks," and manipulated their dialectic differences to avoid recognizing a separate national group. Kemal Atatürk and his successors rigorously crushed Kurdish revolts and suppressed any evidence of Kurdish identity. Regulations prohibited the language from use in personal names, public speeches, and at weddings and social occasions. Until 1991,

The old Galata Bridge, Istanbul, stretching across the Golden Horn

Turkey

no books, papers, street signs or pamphlets legally appeared in the language. Legalizing Kurdish TV broadcasts took another decade. However, the dialects remained alive, even when illegal. Cassettes in Kurdish circulated widely, and in recent years satellite broadcasts enabled programs from Europe to reach viewers.

Traditionally most Kurds lived in mountain villages, divided from others across the mountains by dialect and tribal loyalties. They received little formal education and that in Turkish, so for many reasons most Kurds tended to ignore politics. However, some became successful politicians, like Ismet Inonu, and advanced to the top of national politics. Indeed, usually one-quarter of all members of parliament claimed some Kurdish ancestry, but such politicians frequently became assimilated, a threat that television and modernization bring to members of the middle classes. At the other extreme, many Kurds desire their own schools and autonomy, or even independence.

In the 1980s, violence spread across the southeast and east, fomented by the *Kurdish Workers Party (PKK)*, a Marxist group led by Abdullah Ocalan (pronounced O-ja-lan). Financed and supported by Syria and by Kurds working in Europe, *PKK* fighters infiltrated into Turkey. The military, a largely conscript army, responded roughly to attacks by the *PKK*. On occasion it used heavy weapons within towns, and its brutal treatment of civilians often alienated the local population. To cut off guerrillas from food and shelter, civilian supplies were often tightly controlled, and by the mid-1990s over 800 villages had been forcibly evacuated.

Despite a heavy rebel death toll and innovations like winter operations, the military proved unable to crush the insurgency. In 1992 and again in 1995, it mounted large-scale invasions of alleged *PKK* bases in Iraqi Kurdistan and reported hundreds killed. In fact, alerted by the massive military buildup, most guerrillas had slipped away.

For its part, the *PKK* massacred civilians, especially Kurds who cooperated with the government. The annual toll of violence rose sharply in the 1990s. Foreign travelers became targets, even in Istanbul, as the *PKK* threatened the important tourist industry.

Turkey's laws and methods often aroused resentment even by Kurds unsympathetic to the *PKK*. For example, Article 8 of the constitution prohibited separatist propaganda in any form, including calls for ethnic autonomy. It was used to convict dozens of journalists, politicians, and labor unionists on charges of sedition.

Though some Turkish intellectuals reasoned that greater Kurdish freedoms might

Turkish Republic of Northern Cyprus
Area: About 1,350 square miles.
Population: About 200,000.
Capital City: Turkish sector of Nicosia.
Location: 40 miles from the Turkish coast.
Ethnic Background: Turkish Cypriot, with immigrant mainland Turks.
Chief Commercial Products: Citrus fruits, grain, light manufactures
Trading Partner: Turkey.
Former Status: Part of the Republic of Cyprus (1960–1974)
National Day: November 15.
Chief of State: Dervis Eroglu (2010).
National Flag: A red crescent on a white field between two horizontal red bars.
GDP per capita: About $4,000.

Ethnic violence between its Greek and Turkish communities during the early 1960s marred the independence of the small island of Cyprus. A 1974 coup against the Greek Cypriot president enabled Turkey to invade and protect Turkish-inhabited villages and towns, as well as seize Greek ones in the north. The assault captured 38% of the island and divided it along the "Attila Line," to protect the Turkish 18% of the population. The two communities periodically bowed to international pressure and held talks on a settlement, but neither proved willing to compromise.

The Turkish-Cypriot Legislative Assembly proclaimed the independence of the "Turkish Republic of Northern Cyprus" in 1983. Only Turkey recognized this new state, and thus virtually all trade and travel must take place through Turkey. Rauf Denktash, formerly vice president of the entire island, became its president until retirement in 2005.

Living in Northern Cyprus has imposed great sacrifices in return for freedom from Greek control. Turkish Nicosia initially possessed no cinema or commercial art gallery and only five public telephones for its 40,000 people. Until recently, per capita incomes averaged about one-third the Greek level ($4,500 to over $13,000). Foreign investment is negligible, especially since European Union courts have allowed Greek owners to sue for their property sold to Europeans. Mainland Turkey provides almost half the zone's budget and funds all major public works. This requires use of the Turkish Lira, one of the least valued European currencies. Military forces from mainland Turkey control the local police, and journalists who question such links have been arrested on dubious charges. Moreover, immigrants from Turkey may now outnumber the Turkish Cypriots in their own territory.

During three decades of sporadic peace talks, Turkish Cypriots consistently demanded most territory north of the Attila Line, desiring to keep about 30% of the island and a form of federalism that would provide virtual independence. Greek leaders seemed somewhat more willing to compromise. However, in a bizarre turn of events, in 2003, many Turkish Cypriots rejected President Denktash's hardline voted to accept the UN proposals, while the newly-elected Greek Cypriot president opposed the compromise for granting the Turks too much. Thus Greek Cyprus joined the EU on terms constructed to encourage the Turks to compromise, while the Greeks refused the UN compromise themselves. Recognizing the considerable injustice of events, the European Union began to consider trade and economic benefits for Turkish Cyprus.

Mehmet Ali Talat won the 2005 presidential election. He desired reunification and EU membership for the entire island. In 2008, Demetris Christofias of the AKEL Communist Party won the Cypriot presidential election, campaigning on a broadly similar viewpoint. The two agreed to reopen Ledra Street—the traditional shopping closed since the 1964 communal troubles—and undertake talks on the many unresolved issues. The two leaders expressed a sense of urgency in striving for a federal republic of two zones and two communities, granting the smaller Turkish community political equality with the Greek Cypriots.

Time solved some problems—Cyprus uses the Euro, so control of the central bank makes little difference. However, grave problems remained, like the return of refugees, restitution of property, the Turkish settlers and troops, security, and the constitution. The lack of progress contributed to loses by Talat's party in the 2009 legislative elections, and his defeat by Dervis Eroglu, a separatist, in 2010.

173

Turkey

reduce the appeal of revolution, Turkish courts and the military allowed scant room for peaceful criticism. Kurdish parties faced frequent attempts to ban them from elections. Human rights activists suffered at the hands of the police, who arrested even minor employees and seized files. Yasar Kemal, one of Turkey's greatest living writers and the author of *Memed, My Hawk*, received a 20-month suspended jail term just for questioning policy toward the Kurds. Outside the law, a series of unsolved murders decimated journalists and leaders sympathetic to Kurdish hopes.

With the war against the *PKK* yielding only modest gains, Turkey strengthened its links with Israel and in 1998 forced Syria to crack down on *PKK* activities and expel its leader, Ocalan. This eventually led to his capture in Kenya by Turkish commandos, a tremendous boost to Turkish pride. Britain also closed down a Kurdish satellite channel, Med-TV. Broadcasting across Europe and the Middle East, it had advocating killings in reprisal for the capture of Ocalan.

On trial for his life, Ocalan called the *PKK* rebellion a "mistake," and ordered his followers to exchange violence for a peaceful political struggle. In 2000, a party congress formally adopted Ocalan's political strategy of peacefully improving the Kurdish community within Turkey. This formally implied the end of the independence struggle, and most *PKK* fighters withdrew to Iraq.

Two years later, the PKK disbanded, presumably to avoid the "terrorist" label and resulting international limitations after the September 11 attacks. It returned to low-scale warfare in 2003, and demanded an amnesty for all PKK prisoners, including Ocalan, as a condition for a renewed truce. By 2010 the revived attacks on the Turkish military, *PKK* threats to take the war to Turkish cities, halted the modest conciliation attempted by the government. In addition, the Constitutional Court dissolved the *Democratic Society Party (DTP)* because of alleged links with the rebels. The party had publicly feted *PKK* fighters and civilians who had returned to Turkey, thus antagonizing most Turks.

One great obstacle to peace remains the uncompromising attitude common among Turkish officers and officials, a reflection of their strident nationalism. Arbitrary arrest, torture, and bureaucratic heavy-handedness long remained the ways of life in the Southeast. For example, arrests followed a soccer game when one team wore the red, yellow and green stripes of the Kurdish colors. For these reasons and for better economic opportunity, about 500,000 Kurds migrate to western Turkey annually.

To comply with the human rights provisions of the European Union, Parliament voted major reforms by 2004, including permission for Kurdish schools and radio broadcasts. However, changed attitudes in the military and government bureaucracy came grudgingly and slowly. For example, applicants for licenses to teach Kurdish found themselves blocked by repeated technicalities, and Kurdish broadcasting by the state-owned radio and TV service only began after transmissions of such locally-insignificant languages as Bosnian. Indeed, the 30-minute weekly programs in two Kurdish dialects were not even described as Kurdish.

Such obstructionism may seriously harm Turkey in the long run. In northern Iraq, Kurds have enjoyed autonomy since 1991. United after the fall of Saddam, they hold

Only the patient and brave (with good lateral vision and quick reflexes) dare to drive Istanbul's Tanlabas Boulevard.

Photo: Miller B. Spangler

174

elections, govern provinces, run universities, and broadcast in Kurdish dialects. Their fighters form distinct units in the Iraqi military. These moves pointed towards eventual statehood—or at least a very loose federalism—and thus threaten the very concept of a unitary Turkish state.

Stagnation and the Rise of AK Party

The second great theme of the 1990s was the country's stagnation, both economic and political. Rampant inflation, a by-product of the government's printing easy money to win elections, eroded workers' wages. In response, unions demanded pay increases as high as 300%, and strikes spread in government-owned industries. Accepting the workers' pay demands, and those of farmers and civil servants, guaranteed even higher inflation. However, given the growing numbers of Islamic radicals and Kurdish separatists, rejecting their claims might bring about disorders and provoke a military takeover. In 1960, 1970–1971, and 1980 the military had dismissed the government. With conditions worsening, many expected another intervention in 1990–1991.

Fortunately for democracy, in 1991 the prime minister called early elections. With inflation high (about 70%), the veteran politician Suleyman Demirel, leader of the winning *True Path Party*, formed a coalition and installed his seventh cabinet. Demirel promised to achieve many of the perpetual goals in Turkish politics—including the privatization of state-owned factories and better human rights. Though threatened by inflation, a large budget deficit, and terrorism from left-wing radicals and the *PKK*, the cabinet enjoyed broad public support. However, the president's unexpected death in 1993 dramatically shifted Turkish politics, because parliament elected Demirel president, and then selected an American-educated economist, Tansu Ciller, as prime minister.

The first Turkish woman to hold the office, Ciller faced formidable difficulties. In a few months, the lira lost 50% of its value against the dollar, and several banks failed. The root of the crisis concerned money: the government could not collect enough taxes to pay its normal expenses, aid inefficient state industries, and finance the war against the *PKK*. Since the government covered the gap by printing money, inevitably, inflation rose.

With annual interest rates of 140% and people fearing an economic collapse, Ciller instituted a temporary "inflation tax," sold bits of state-owned industry, closed unprofitable coal mines and steel plants, and raised prices on goods sold by state monopolies. These measures caused a severe recession and failed to eliminate the structural difficulties, but they also cut inflation in half and stabilized the lira. Public opinion splintered, and during the mid-1990s, burdened by their ideological differences and personal rivalries, political leaders found it impossible to form a stable ruling majority. Six cabinets took and left office in just three years.

One particular challenge was the rise of the Islamic *Welfare (Refah) Party*, which came first, though with only 21% of the vote, in the 1996 elections. Civilian and military secularists attempted to keep the *Welfare Party* from office. Over several years they had watched Islamic militancy threaten Atatürk's legacy, as *Welfare* won mayors' races in Istanbul and Ankara and swept the southeast.

Though Ciller had attacked the *Welfare Party* for "sinking the country into darkness," she feared that parliamentary investigations of corruption might implicate her. Ciller therefore sought the safety of office through an alliance with her ideological enemy, the *Welfare Party*. Thus petty and corrupt squabbles among mainstream parties enabled an Islamic party to take office, despite military misgivings and the country's tradition of secularism. *Welfare's* leader, Necmettin Erbakan, became the country's first Islamist prime minister.

Erbakan clearly sought to reorient foreign policy away from the West and toward the Islamic world. He visited Iran to sign a major gas deal, and toured Libya. When some local officials of the *Welfare Party* openly contradicted the secularist tradition, the military quietly encouraged parliamentary maneuvering that collapsed the coalition in 1997. For good measure, the Constitutional Court later banned the party because it had permitted women to wear head-scarves in public buildings, encouraged Islamic schools, and kept (unproven) links with secret societies. The courts also convicted Erbakan and several other party officials, including the mayor of Istanbul, of making statements deemed too Islamist.

Hoping to form a stable government, Turkey held early elections in 1999. Bulent Ecevit's left-wing but nationalistic *Democratic Left Party* swept to first place. Though Ecevit "won" the election when his party received the most votes and seats, the old bonus for being the largest party no longer applied. Nevertheless, Ecevit succeeded in forming an unusual alliance with the right-wing *Nationalist Action Party*.

The decade had witnessed nine governments in as many years, but Ecevit now provided stable leadership, waging a war on corruption that landed "big fish" (particularly bankers) as well as petty criminals. The police discovered that the Turkish paramilitary group *Hizbullah* (no direct

American style still sells in Turkey
Photo by Wayne Thompson

relation to the Lebanese group) had murdered more than 100 secular intellectuals, Marxist Kurds, and other victims. Control over spending brought the rate of inflation below 40%. In 1999 the European Union at last accepted Turkey as a candidate for membership.

In 1999 an earthquake devastated seven western provinces—the country's industrial heartland. The civil administration and the military both proved inept at rescue efforts, though better at feeding and sheltering hundreds of thousands left homeless. Despite its location on a major geological fault, Turkey had not developed specialized rescue teams. Television pictures that showed a centuries-old mosque and its slender minaret standing intact beside collapsed apartment buildings illustrated an equally serious failing: for decades, officials had failed to issue and enforce appropriate building codes.

As President Demirel's term expired in 2000, parliament elected Ahmet Necdet Sezer, chairman of the Constitutional Court, as his successor. A legal scholar rather than a politician, Sezer strongly emphasized the rule of law. The changes that Sezer advocated became the more powerful because he desired reform not so much to please Europe but to benefit Turks.

The strong personalities of President Sezer and Prime Minister Ecevit clashed seriously in 2001. Ecevit claimed that he had been insulted; stock market investors took flight. Those with money (including, allegedly, the governor of the Central Bank!) speculated against the Turkish lira, draining $7 billion from the Central

Turkey

President Abdullah Gul

Bank's reserves within hours. Overnight interest rates reached an annual level of 5000%, and the country plunged into its worst economic recession since World War II.

While devaluation and massive loans from the IMF did calm the markets, the GDP fell by almost 10%, and nearly a million workers lost their jobs. The rates of suicide, theft, prostitution and stress-related illness all climbed, and media experts warned of a "social explosion." Another symptom of the misery came from the 1.5 million people who canceled their cell phones.

Besides the government's deficit, the banking system lay at the heart of the trouble. Many banks had borrowed funds abroad and lent them for politically-important projects with little chance of business success. Saving such banks required billions of dollars, much of it from the IMF. Turkey became its largest debtor.

In 2002, Ecevit's coalition fragmented. The *Nationalist Action Party* opposed human rights proposals like banning capital punishment and allowing Kurdish-language TV broadcasting. Finally, members of Ecevit's own party forced early elections.

The proponents of early elections had hoped to catch the Islamist political forces disorganized. After the *Welfare Party* had been declared illegal, Islamist deputies failed to unite. However, the *Justice and Development Party* (known by its initials as *AK Party*), was led by the country's most popular individual politician, Recep Tayyip Erdoğan, a former mayor of Istanbul previously convicted of inciting religious hatred by publicly quoting from a poem. Banned by the Supreme Court from running for parliament, he remained party leader, claiming that *AK Party* was not Islamist, but merely Islamic-rooted.

Voting day transformed Turkish politics. Not a single party from the previous parliament managed to win 10% of the national vote, and therefore, all of them, both government and opposition, failed to enter the new parliament. The victor was *AK Party*, with 34% of the popular vote and nearly two-thirds of the seats. The *Republican People's Party* captured most of the rest and formed the opposition. Coalition politics had ended. The large *AK Party* majority soon overturned the law that Erdoğan had broken, rendering him eligible to run for parliament. After a by-election victory, he took office in early 2003.

The initial challenge was the U.S. desire to attack Iraq. The U.S. had long regarded Turkey as a special ally, the overwhelmingly Muslim and staunchly anti-Communist member of NATO. American strategists now sought permission to launch an invasion from Turkey into northern Iraq.

However, the Turkish constitution requires parliamentary approval of any foreign troops stationed in the country, and public opinion polls showed that about 90% of the population opposed an unprovoked attack on a fellow Muslim country. Business leaders feared the loss of markets and another recession. Strategists and the military worried that Iraqi Kurds might declare independence or seize Kirkuk. Despite promises of substantial U.S. aid, parliament narrowly rejected the U.S. plan.

A visionary with a proven record as an administrator, Erdoğan took office with both goals and energy. He traveled abroad—to Greece—to convince European leaders of his reformist ideas and to

**Prime Minister
Recep Tayyip Erdoğan**

reassure Greek politicians of his peaceful intensions. He pressured Rauf Denktash, the obstinate Turkish-Cypriot leader, to accept the UN plan for peace on the island (see box).

In his first two years of office, Erdoğan guided a legal revolution in human rights through parliament. After a decade of immobilized coalitions, the *AK Party's* majority enabled it to abolish the death penalty, restrict torture by the police, and increase the media's freedom of expression. A major reform of the penal code protected women, established life sentences for perpetrators of "honor killings,"

In the political domain, parliament curbed the military by making the National Security Council advisory, under civilian rather than military leadership. Military spending was even placed under parliamentary control. Political detainees, including some Kurdish militants, were amnestied.

Recognizing these long-delayed improvements in human rights, as well as Erdoğan's moderate stand over Cyprus, the EU opened talks on Turkey's admission in 2005. The talks proved difficult, as predicted, both for objective reasons like the culture, size, and poverty of Turkey, and cultural fears about the arrival of 70 million Muslim Turks as Europeans. One particular stumbling block is the requirement that Turkey open its ports and airports to all EU members—including Cyprus—but its Greek government refuses trade with the Turkish north.

One unsettled issue—at least for conservative police and prosecutors—is the prohibition on statements that "insult" the nation. For Orhan Pamuk, the words "One million Armenians and 30,000 Kurds were killed in these lands" sufficed to bring criminal charges in 2005. The charges were dismissed, fortunately so, because the next year Pamuk won the Nobel Prize for literature. Three of his novels have been published in English, *The White Castle, My Name is Red,* and *Snow*.

Orhan Pamuk escaped the state prosecutors, but the deeper intolerance, plus a payment, motivated a teenager to assassinate the country's leading Armenian journalist, Hrant Dink. Although Dink had been convicted of claiming that Armenians had suffered genocide during World War I, his murder evoked a surprising outpouring of regret and sympathy from liberal-minded Turks.

Crises over Presidential Elections, 2007

Political tensions inevitably rose in 2007, when the five-year election cycle of the Grand National Assembly coincided with the seven-year term of the presidency, set to expire in May. Massive demonstrations by secularists reflected fears that the *AK Party* majority in the Assembly would enable it to select the next president. Two pillars of the state predictably supported the secularists. President Sezer warned that the danger of Islamic radicalism was greater than ever. The military chief bluntly stated that a committed secularist was needed in the presidential palace. Symbols matter, and many secularists abhor the thought of a president's wife wearing a headscarf while hosting a reception in the Çankaya Palace.

Very carefully, *AK Party* leaders announced their candidate just before the filing deadline, reducing time for public protests. Rather than Prime Minister Erdoğan, with the past conviction for reciting an Islamist poem, the party selected Abdullah Gül, the Foreign Minister. His nomination lacked a two-thirds majority by a few votes on the initial ballot, but victory seemed assured with the third ballot, when a simple majority would suffice. However, the Constitutional Court insisted, on dubious legal grounds, on a two-thirds quorum for a presidential election. The ballot therefore did not take place, and without a first ballot there could not be a third.

In response, Erdoğan sought to demonstrate the nation's will. He called early parliamentary elections for July 2007, and he and his party won by a landslide. He proposed, among other reforms, amending the constitutional to elect the president by the people rather than by members of the Assembly. Vetoed once by President Sezer on grounds that a popularly elected president might conflict with a popularly elected parliament, the proposal passed parliament a second time. Sezer, unable to veto the same bill twice, duly called a referendum on the proposal.

Despite the determined opposition of staunch secularists, Erdoğan's *AK Party* won an overwhelming triumph in the 2007 parliamentary elections. Capturing nearly half (48%) of all votes, it gained a majority of seats that enabled it to rule without a coalition partner. The victory also eliminated any legitimacy of a military intervention pretending to "preserve democracy."

Two issues dominated Turkish political life during the following year. First, the *AK Party* nominated Abdullah Gül as president, rather than a less partisan individual. His election by the Assembly meant that the first lady attended receptions wearing a headscarf.

Second, the *AK Party* formed a tactical alliance with the ultra-nationalists and passed a constitutional amendment banning the exclusion of students from universities except for reasons stipulated by law. This met the aspirations of millions

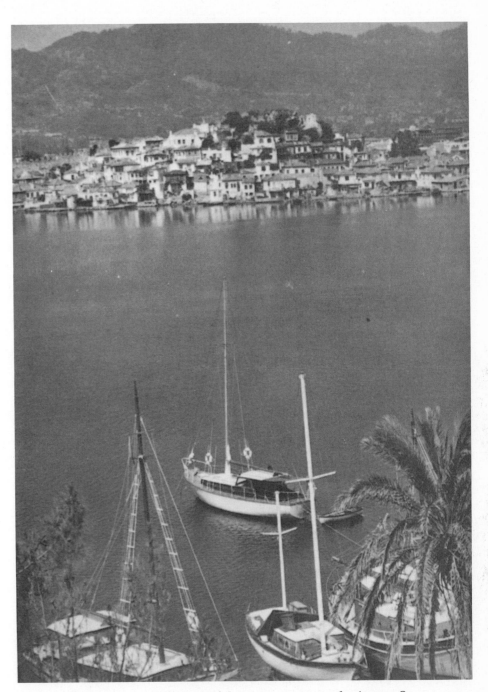

Mararias, one of the beautiful summer resorts on the Aegean Sea

of party supporters, but infuriated secularists, who hold the principles of Kemalism above the constitution. The Constitutional Court soon struck down the amendment.

Turkish democracy faced serious threat in 2008 when prosecutors brought charges that the *AK Party* had sought to undermine secularism and should be banned. Clearly, Prime Minister Erdoğan and the party had attempted to abolish the ban on wearing headscarves at universities and had strengthened religious education. Many commentators expected the Con-

stitutional Court to rule in favor of the prosecutors, but it decided that since the party had raised human rights standards and had not acted violently, its punishment was the loss of half its government subsidy.

The long-running investigation of alleged secularist plots may also shake state institutions. According to the government, a shadowy group of secular extremists named Ergenekon unleashed violence against secular targets like an attack on a newspaper and a court in 2006 in order to stoke unrest and provoke an army coup.

Turkey

Dozens of prominent secularists, ranging from university professors, prominent journalists, two retired generals, other former army officers, and members a police special operations unit were arrested in 2008 and 2009. To place retired military officers on trial in civilian court for the first time should test Turkish democracy, especially when so many of the alleged conspirators were prominent critics of the *AK Party*. By 2010 two further groups of alleged military and civilian plotters had been arrested. least a very loose federalism—and thus threaten the very concept of a unitary Turkish state.

Foreign Relations: A New Regional Role

After serving as the eastern bulwark of NATO for decades as a valued Cold War ally of the U.S., military partner of Israel, and (unsuccessful) applicant to join the European Union, in the first decade of the 21st century, foreign policy increasingly set an independent course. With the economy developing rapidly, Prime Minister Erdoğan desired to win new markets for the country's industries, as well as to play a much greater role in regional relations. He attempted unsuccessfully to mediate between Israel and Syria, then sought an arrangement with Iran for Turkey to process its partially-enriched uranium for research and medical purposes. The government also supported Turkish Islamist groups participating in the flotilla of vessels challenging the Israeli blockade of Gaza. Vociferous criticism followed the 2010 Israeli commando raid on the Turkish vessel *Merve Marmara* in international waters that killed nine Turkish citizens.

The special relationship between the two non-Arab but Middle Eastern states seemed at an end. Indeed, within days the cabinet agreed to establish a free trade zone with Syria, Lebanon and Jordan.

Culture: One cannot think of Turkey without thinking of Istanbul—one of the great historic cities of the world. The ancient Greek colony of Byzantium later became Constantinople, capital of the Eastern Roman Empire. It evolved into the capital and center of the Byzantine world, where ancient Hellenistic culture persisted until its capture in 1453 by the Ottomans under Sultan Mehmet II. The Ottomans renamed it Istanbul and installed their sultan in the Topkapi Saray, the Great Palace overlooking the Bosporus and Golden Horn. The spectacular mosques of Istanbul still remain places of deep reverence.

Although Ankara, located near the nation's center, is the political capital, Istanbul is the modern cultural and economic heart of Turkey. Europe's largest city, with a population approaching 12 million, it extends for miles along both sides of the Bosporus. Its great variety of people and different ways of living make it one of the world's most interesting cities.

By contrast, Ankara is a very modern city, but has the unhappy distinction of possessing some of the worst air pollution of any city anywhere. This is not the result of heavy industry, but of geography—the city lies in a natural bowl, trapping smoke and fumes.

Turkish culture today blends strong pride in ethnic heritage with a culture influence by religion from Arabia and modern arts and ideas from Europe and North America.

The tradition of Kemal Atatürk decrees secularism, and successive cabinets—if necessary prodded by the military-remained aloof or even hostile to religion. Nevertheless, today Islam lives as a vital part of the beliefs of most Turks. Religious classes returned to schools after the 1980 military coup, as part of the cultural heritage of the country. Instruction about religion was not intended as indoctrination, though sometimes it had that effect. During the 1980s the Kemalist ban on words of Arabic origin and Islamic connotation was removed, and terms and phrases last used by educated people of the Ottoman Empire now reappear in writing and on radio and television.

In many ways, Turkey is a land of two cultures. From a country long considered overwhelmingly agricultural and rural, between 1970 and 1990 Turkey rapidly changed into a nation of city dwellers. In the cities one hears Western music and modern young women can meet male friends in a restaurant or dance in nightclubs.

The Battle over Headscarves

In a decision hinting that Prime Minister Erdoğan and his *AK Party* may shortly be banned from politics, in June 2008 Turkey's Constitutional Court ruled that parliament's constitutional amendment to permit women to wear headscarves in universities conflicted with the principle of secularism. Why so great a concern over such modest pieces of fabric?

From one perspective, it is a clear issue of conscience and human rights. If a devout Muslim girl or woman wishes to enhance her modesty by wearing a scarf over her hair, should government interfere? There are more pressing national problems to address.

Opponents, some of them practicing Muslims, provide a very different perspective: the scarf announces a woman's religious persuasion, a view that a woman's attire in the 14th (Muslim) century should be based on customs from the 1st century. By a small extension, the scarf also proclaims a woman's loyalty to Islamist political parties. Political insignia do not belong in public places such as universities. Even in the individualistic West, American schools ban gang-related insignia.

Proponents of headscarves respond that women in scarves intend no criminal conduct. They may vote for any party they please: it is not a return to the brownshirts worn by Hitler's followers in Germany. Furthermore, the ban causes unnecessary grief. For example, when the mother of a wounded soldier visits him in a military hospital, she must remove her scarf.

After the prime minister approved their use in 1998, the courts and military overruled. The election of two scarf-wearing parliamentarians, one from the Islamist *Virtue Party*, sharpened the issue. Parliamentary regulations did not explicitly prohibit the scarf, and some reasoned that elected representatives should be entitled to wear whatever they deemed appropriate. However, traditional secularists regarded parliament as the heart of Atatürk's legacy and argued that it would be difficult to prohibit elsewhere what was acceptable in the legislature.

Virtue's Merve Kavakci disrupted parliament's opening session in 1999, when she appeared wearing a scarf. Accused of violating the republic's basic secular principles, she refused to remove the offending cloth, or leave the chamber. Parliament was forced to adjourn; literally as well as symbolically, government came to a halt, even before the president had designated the new prime minister. As critics noted, the legislature did not need this distraction from its most serious business of forming a government. Stripped of her Turkish citizenship, Ms. Kavakci now wears her scarf in peace, in U.S. exile.

By some estimates, the country's secular universities—there are no others—have dismissed a quarter-million scarf-wearing women this decade, some because of excessive absences. Because their convictions of modesty conflicted with Kemalist conceptions of secularism, these women lost the opportunity for intellectual development and career options. In 2005, the European Court of Human Rights sided with the ban, justifying it as "protecting the rights and freedoms of others and maintaining public order."

A combine harvesting wheat in southern Turkey

Old ways die hard in rural areas, however. In many villages for both cultural and Islamic reasons the feeling is still strong that women should not attend public events with men. Women and girls do not attend the *halkevi*, "people's house," which is the center of social life in most villages. Likewise, in remote villages the visitor may rarely see a woman's face, but in Istanbul, Izmir, and Ankara women work in most positions they hold in Europe or America.

Since the founding of the Republic, educated Turks have deliberately tried to imitate the literature and drama of Europe. There is a state theater performing Western plays or plays following Western forms, but the typical Turk finds this alien. Karagoz, the shadow puppet and his friends and enemies are more to Turkish taste; both fantasy and real-life situations appear in the puppet shows. Likewise, the great majority of Turks love their own music. To the accompaniment of three or four instruments, including a lute (bazouki), a drum and perhaps a violin, one person will sing folk songs telling of love, war, heartbreak or death—often in long, drawn-out and high-pitched quavering tones, using minor toned scales.

Education has been a primary concern of the government for decades. Elementary education is completely free, and nearly universal. The "middle schools"

are similar to three-year junior high schools, while the lycée corresponds to an academic high school and is primarily intended to prepare students for university study. Only higher-ranked graduates of middle schools are able to enter the lycées.

Turkey now has dozens of universities. The oldest is Istanbul University, which traces its founding to Mehmet the Conqueror in 1453. It now enrolls over 30,000 students; the next largest is Ankara University. Another institution in Ankara offers instruction in English rather than Turkish, Middle East Technical University. Expanded with assistance from the UN, and several foreign nations, it serves other countries of the Middle East as well as Turkey. To attend any government-run institution, a Muslim woman must give up her head-scarf, a firmly-held principal of the secularists that the European Court of Human Rights justified in 2005 as maintaining order (see box).

Economy: Long famous for carpets, mohair and dried fruits, Turkey remained a land of relatively poor and traditional farmers who struggled for a living in remote villages. As recently as the 1970s agricultural products amounted to half the nation's exports.

Industry developed slowly, partly because local handicrafts suffered competition from European manufactured goods.

The first major thrust of industrialization occurred only in the 1930s, sponsored by the government for political and social reasons as well as economic ones. Protected by high tariffs, regulation and other trade barriers, the factories of the State Economic Enterprises (SEEs) failed to become efficient competitors. High inflation and shortages of foreign exchange frequently halted periods of strong economic growth.

In the 1980s, Prime Minister Turgot Özal launched reforms to transform the economy. He freed markets, reduced tariffs, eliminated exchange controls, and removed the heavy hand of government trade restrictions. This encouraged investment by both domestic and foreign firms. Industry seized the opportunity to expand, and the resulting export-led growth transformed the stagnant economy of the late 1970s into one enjoying rapid rates of real GNP growth. Exports rose by 400% between 1980 and 1987.

Özal's free market policies alleviated but failed to eliminate many traditional economic problems. Population growth at 2.5% per year absorbs a major portion of national income growth. Consequently, although many Turks work abroad, unemployment often hovers around 20%, and incomes reach just 34% of the European Union's average. Public education lags greatly, and social security is minimal

Turkey

(though government employees like teachers retire young). Tax revenues fall far short of requirements, creating a budget deficit regularly exceeding 10% of GNP, and the foreign debt of about $65 billion requires large payments for interest and principal. Monopolies exist in tobacco, sugar, and alcohol, while regulations elsewhere discourage entrepreneurs.

Nevertheless, profitable opportunities abound in many fields. Tourism climbed rapidly in recent years, hampered by insufficient infrastructure and sanitary facilities as well as fears of terrorism. Given beautiful scenery, a warm climate, exotic customs, and a wealth of historic locations, the nation attracts some 14 million visitors annually, and tourism constitutes a multi-billion dollar industry.

A world apart from luxury tourist hotels, the Southeast Anatolia Project (GAP) offers the possibility of improving some of the country's most impoverished areas. A complex of 20 dams, 19 hydroelectric plants, tunnels and irrigation canals, the project's expected cost will exceed $32 billion. Besides generating large amounts of electricity from the Atatürk Dam, initially the world's sixth largest, and others on the Euphrates and Tigris Rivers, the project is planned to divert enough water to irrigate some four million acres.

Several problems threaten completion of the project. The combined plans for water use by Turkey, Syria, and Iraq may drain the Euphrates dry, so armed conflict remains possible if unlikely (see "When Will the Taps Go Dry?" p. 2). Declining

Designing a carpet pattern, Istanbul WORLD BANK Photo

The Keban Dam on the Euphrates River WORLD BANK Photo

economic benefits, combined with rising costs, make some dams less profitable than alternative ways of generating electricity, and concerns over soil salinity, chemical pollution and water quality may limit irrigation.

The start of the Ilisu Dam near Hasankeyf on the Tigris in 2006 aroused concerns as well over the eventual flooding of an archaeological marvel, a city left undestroyed throughout the Middle Ages. Although insurers later brought construction to at temporary halt, critics argue that villagers displaced by the reservoirs are often not compensated significantly, because the land may be owned by rich landlords, and the villagers are conveniently removed for their protection from the *PKK*. Thus GAP's electrification, roads and farming services may never reach the average farmer in the style of America's TVA, and the local Kurds may lose their heritage without economic gain.

In 2005, the country celebrated the opening of another pipeline, this one nearly 1,200 miles long from Baku, Azerbaijan. It is valuable to consumers in Eu-

Turkey

rope because it avoids two important difficulties: Russian control (like the other routes out of the Caspian basin), and shipping through the crowded Bosporus.

The Future: After taking office in 2002, Recep Tayyip Erdoğan brought Turkey economic prosperity. He transformed its human rights laws by distinguishing clearly between Islamic roots—a philosophical orientation—and Islamic subservience—submission to traditional practices. Voters returned the *AK Party* to office in 2007 in the greatest electoral triumph of modern Turkish history.

Both Turkish secularists and Israeli sympathizers depict Erdoğan and the *AK Party* as strongly Islamist and unbalanced in decisions. Certainly, they walk a fine line between the expectations of the lower- and middle-class majority, and the aspirations of the secularists who traditionally rule. If the Ergenekon trials appear to result in a miscarriage of justice or if the cabinet carries through with proposals to try the military involved in

the 1980 coup, expect serious attempts at another softly orchestrated change of government.

In the meantime, Prime Minister Erdoğan will continue to win political points at home by vigorous foreign policy statements, such as denouncing Israel's attack on the aid flotilla attempting to break the Gaza blockade, or condemning China's clampdown on the Turkic-speaking Uyghurs after rioting in Urumqi. The direction Turkey's future movement appears east, not west.

On the Bosporus near the Black Sea

Photo: Miller B. Spangler

181

The United Arab Emirates

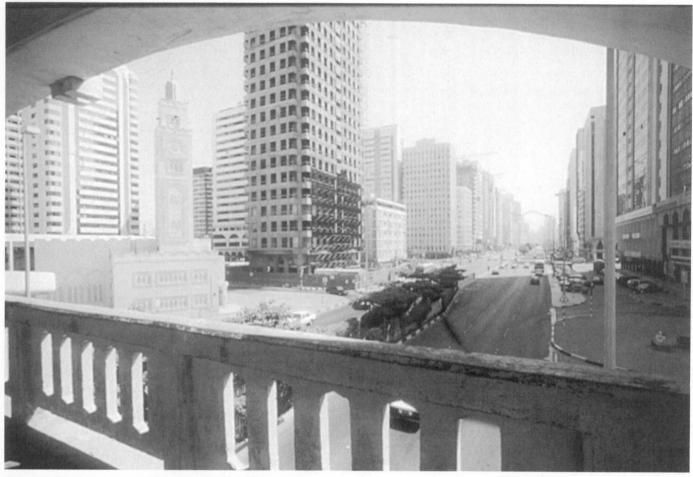

The Abu Dhabi business district from a pedestrian crossover

Courtesy: Caltex Petroleum Corp. (Joe Brignolo '95)

Area: 30,000 square miles (77,700 sq. km.).

Population: 5 million (about 3 million of them foreigners.)

Capital City: Abu Dhabi (pop. 580,000, estimated).

Climate: Extremely hot except for moderate winters. Precipitation is rare, though some rain falls in the highlands between Ras al-Khayma and Fujayra.

Neighboring Countries: Oman (Northeast and Southeast); Saudi Arabia (South and West).

Time Zone: GMT +4.

Official Language: Arabic.

Other Principal Tongues: English (widely used), Hindi, Urdu and Farsi (Persian).

Ethnic Background: Arab-speaking citizens comprise about 20% of the population, while expatriate workers from Pakistan, India and Iran compose a majority.

Principal Religion: Islam (92%; mostly Sunni).

Chief Commercial Products: Petroleum, liquefied natural gas (LNG), petrochemicals, including plastic and paint, food processing, dates, machinery, boat repair and aluminum.

Major Trading Partners: Japan, Germany, U.K., U.S., Singapore, South Korea.

Currency: Dirham (= 100 fils).

Former Colonial Status: Each sheikhdom accepted British protection and control of foreign affairs, but enjoyed domestic autonomy (1892–1971).

National Day: December 2, 1971 (Independence Day).

Chief of State: Sheikh Khalifa bin Zayed Al Nahyan (Ruler of Abu Dhabi), President of the Supreme Council of Rulers.

Head of Government: Sheikh Muhammad bin Rashid Al Maktoum (Ruler of Dubai), Vice-President and Prime Minister.

National Flag: Three equal bands of green, white and black (top to bottom) are flanked at the pole by a vertical red band of the same width.

Gross Domestic Product: $256 billion (at current prices); $195 (Purchasing Power Parity), 2008

GDP per capita: $38,000 (PPP), 2008

Abu Dhabi and five smaller states along the southern limit of the Arab Gulf, plus one on the Gulf of Oman, comprise the federation known as the United Arab Emirates. Most of the land is desert and the climate hot and humid. For centuries, the inhabitants farmed or herded sheep and goats in the interior, or sought a living from fishing and pearling. A further career was piracy, especially in the extremely shallow Gulf whose sandbanks and coral reefs protected locals from strangers.

Most of Abu Dhabi (pronounced ah-bu za-bi) is low coastal plain and flat desert. In the south, imperceptibly, they become the Empty Quarter of Saudi Arabia. Their topography contrasts greatly with the rugged slopes of the Hajar mountain range that marks the border between Abu Dhabi and Oman and continues to the tip of the "Horn of Arabia." Scattered rainfall in the mountains provides several oases with water for irrigation; the largest is *Al-'Ain* in eastern Abu Dhabi. While there are no permanent rivers, several dozen dams trap runoff for irrigation or to recharge aquifers.

Each of the seven states bears the name of its capital city, and is headed by an *Emir* ("Prince"), who uses the traditional title

United Arab Emirates

of *Sheikh*. The territory of Abu Dhabi is about three times as large as the other six states combined. Each state maintains considerable internal autonomy under its hereditary ruler:

Abu Dhabi (pop. 1.9 million, estimated). Sheikh Zayed bin Sultan Al Nahyan

Dubai (pop. 1.5–1.7 million, estimated). Sheikh Muhammad bin Rashid Al Maktoum; Sheikh Hamdan bin Muhammad, crown prince

Sharja (pop. 350,000 estimated) Sheikh Sultan bin Muhammad al-Qasimi

Ajman (pop. 50,000, estimated). Sheikh Humaid bin Rashid al-Nuaimi

Umm al-Qaywayn (pop. 30,000, estimated). Sheikh Rashid bin Ahmad al-Mualla

Ras al-Khayma (pop. 120,000, estimated). Sheikh Saqr bin Muhammad al-Qasimi

Fujayra (pop. 50,000, estimated). Sheikh Hamad bin Muhammad al-Sharqi

In a society developing as rapidly as this, population figures are very rough estimates at best, and the division of the population is a somewhat delicate issue. From the 180,000 inhabitants at independence in 1971, in twenty-five years the total reached *12 times* as large. (Had the U.S. population then grown that rapidly, it would now surpass China and India combined.)

Overlapping territorial claims by the various states produced a number of neutral zones, some involving more than two Emirates. They are shown darkly shaded on the accompanying map, the lack of clarity reflecting the actual identity of the territories.

History: Recent archeological discoveries show continuous habitation of the coast for the past 7,000 years, and scattered settlements in the *wadis* (desert valleys) for much of the period. One graveyard excavated in Sharja that dated about 200 B.C. included two horses and 13 camels apparently sacrificed during burial ceremonies. By 2,000 years ago, ports in the region traded as far away as India and China. Perhaps linked to trade, Christianity spread widely, attested by burials, churches, and even a monastery.

The Islamic conquest apparently brought years of substantial prosperity during the Umayyad and early Abbasid dynasties. Later constructions, however, seem mostly fortifications. After centuries of Muslim Arab settlement and sporadic Iranian incursions, in the 1500s the Portuguese seized the dominant role in the Gulf. They soon lost it to the Dutch and British, who sought freedom of commerce rather than colonies.

At the turn of the 19th century, *Wahhabi* envoys from Central Arabia incited some local sailors to attack Western commerce, hence its reputation in Europe as the Pirate Coast. Britain then intervened in local fighting, and beginning in 1820, forced treaties on the states to suppress piracy and prohibit warfare at sea. Thus the terms Trucial States or Trucial Oman came into use, though Arabs generally called it the Oman Coast.

According to treaties signed at mid-century Britain controlled foreign affairs and defense. Internal matters remained under the rulers, and little development took place. Indeed, the major events of world history had little impact, although competition from cultured pearls drove down profits from pearling and reduced the standard of living. As late as the 1950s disputes over borders or pearling rights led to skirmishes between desperately poor emirates. One continuing dispute in the 1940s and 1950s concerned rival claims by Saudi Arabia, Oman and Abu Dhabi to the Buraimi oasis.

The search for petroleum in the emirates began in the 1930s, and the later president of the U.A.E., Sheikh Zayed bin Sultan, served as a guide to one of the first exploration teams. Twenty years later, in 1958, commercial deposits were discovered, and oil production began in Abu Dhabi in 1962. Its revenues rapidly transformed the economy and society. Dubai also discovered oil, though relatively small amounts, and it deliberately developed into the region's chief trading center.

Faced with rising anti-colonialism and the high military costs of maintaining the protectorate, Britain withdrew from the Gulf in 1971. It encouraged the emirates to unite. Six formed the U.A.E., and Ras al-Khayma joined later, but Qatar and Bahrain opted for independence. The federal constitution adopted in 1971 divided responsibility for governance between federal institutions and the individual emirates. The seven sheikhs rule some internal affairs of their own states; they determine oil policy and may even possess their own military. However, responsibility for education, public health and currency belongs to the federation. Given the imposing wealth of Abu Dhabi, other states have tended to cooperate.

At the federal level, authority lies with the Supreme Council of Rulers. It chose as

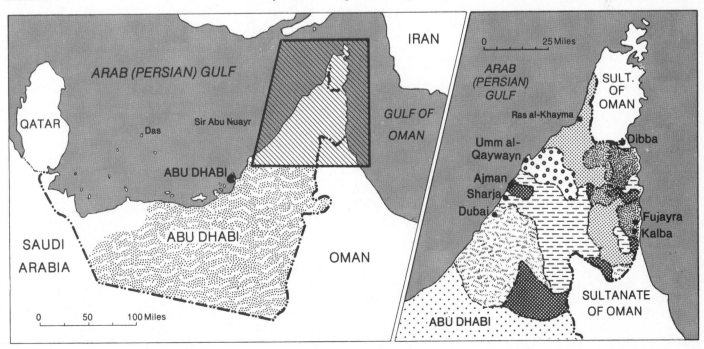

183

United Arab Emirates

H.H. Sheikh Zayed bin Sultan Al-Nahyan, Ruler of Abu Dhabi and President, UAE

H. H. Sheikh Maktoum bin Rashid Al-Maktoum, Ruler of Dubai and Vice President, UAE

H. H. Sheikh Sultan bin Muhammad al-Qasimi Ruler of Sharja

H. H. Sheikh Humaid bin Rashid al-Nuaimi, Ruler of Ajman

H. H. Sheikh Rashid bin Ahmad al-Mualla, Ruler of Umm al-Qaywayn

H.H. Sheikh Saqr bin Muhammad Al-Qasimi, Ruler of Ras al-Khayma

H. H. Sheikh Hamad bin Muhammad Al-Sharqi, Ruler of Fujayra

its first president Sheikh Zayed, and re-elected him for seven consecutive five-year terms. The president appoints the prime minister, typically the ruler of Dubai. Something akin to a legislature exists, the Federal National Council, whose 40 members represent individual emirates. Abu Dhabi contains the largest population, 95% of the oil deposits, and contributes the overwhelming portion of the national budget. It finances development in all states and plays the major role in the federation.

The 1980s brought two difficulties. Some off-shore oil platforms were attacked during the Iran-Iraq War, disturbing commerce. After the collapse of OPEC's price structure in the mid-1980s, oil revenues fell 40%, and an economic recession struck. By 1990, however, construction cranes again sprouted across the major cities, signaling a return to economic growth. New tourist hotels, shopping centers, commercial buildings and factories suggested that while oil continued to provide the mainstay of the economy, diversification will play an important role in the future. Currently only 70% of GDP comes from the oil sector.

To pay for the growth, the country allegedly sold more oil than its OPEC quota (see Economy). Iraq condemned the Emirates as well as Kuwait, and in 1990 the U.A.E. quickly joined the Gulf War coalition to liberate Kuwait. The conflict emphasized the presence of foreign workers in the Emirates, where a law demanding the replacement of all foreign employees of the federal civil service proved impossible to implement.

In 1992 Iran reopened an old dispute over three small but strategic islands in the Gulf, Abu Musa and the two Tunbs. Iran had contested their ownership with Sharja after Britain's withdrawal in 1971, but for two decades a working compromise allowed both countries a role. Iran's unilateral action in 1992, perhaps the hasty result of Tehran politics, aroused Arab fears. While the U.A.E. desires to settle the matter through the International Court of Justice, Iran has refused and continues to develop the islands. However, Iran is a major trading partner of Dubai, and as long as Iran seeks friendly relations with Arab states, the issue lies dormant. Meanwhile, Abu Dhabi remains a major purchaser of modern weaponry and the country hosts a major arms exposition.

As the twentieth century closed, a number of signs suggested that the seven emirates were gradually strengthening their sense of unity. In 1996 a national law replaced individual emirate rules on traffic offenses, and the next year a federal environmental law took effect. Although probably dwarfed by the (undisclosed) Abu Dhabi budget, the federal budget continued to provide funds for the economic and social development of the poorer emirates, and the rivalries of Dubai and Abu Dhabi remained friendly rather than contentious. The sense of unity seems likely to increase: younger inhabitants reportedly feel a greater loyalty to the U.A.E. than do their parents.

After several years of declining health, Sheikh Zayed of Abu Dhabi, died in 2004 at the age of 86. People from all the emirates mourned the passing of a leader they considered the generous and wise founder of the country. The succession proved swift and smooth, as Zayed's eldest son Khalifa had been appointed crown prince 35 years earlier.

Dubai's economy suffered particularly hard from the world economic recession of 2008–09, even though the emirate only indirectly depends on oil income. Wealthy expatriates found themselves unable to purchase new properties, speculators pulled out of the market, and real estate prices fell by perhaps 40%. The decline in world trade hurt trans-shipment and aluminum demand fell 30%. As local firms ran short of cash, a massive loan of $10 billion from the UAE central bank cushioned the downturn and provided cash to pay some building costs. Nevertheless, construction on many projects came to a halt. Tens of thousands of expatriates, thrown out of work with construction companies, financial firms, and elsewhere, left for home.

Culture: The culture of the United Arab Emirates is not essentially different from that found in neighboring countries. The majority of the native Arabs, who are *Sunni*, retain a sense of their tribal backgrounds and traditions.

Women in the U.A.E. play a greater role in society than in many conservative Muslim countries. Not only are girls educated, but the government fosters adult education programs that have reduced the female illiteracy rate to around 20%. While women hold a few significant positions in the private sector, the government employs large numbers, especially in education and health care. By the 1990s, women comprised 16% of the workforce.

Modern education arrived relatively recently. In 1968, the adult literacy rate was only 21%. At independence, a decade after oil exports began, only 30,000 children attended school. By the mid-1990s, the figure had climbed to 400,000, and enrollments rose even more rapidly in high school. The construction of schools in even the most remote hamlets provides all children with the opportunity to learn; education is compulsory from the age of six.

Long a particular concern of Sheikh Zayed, who grew up when the emirates lacked a single modern school, adult education programs have proved so successful that the literacy rate reached 85% in the mid-1990s. Government policies indicate a concern with the quality of education as well as its extent.

Higher education was traditionally represented by technical colleges, several private institutions, and the Emirates University located in al-'Ain. Founded in 1978, by the early 1990s it graduated its first classes of physicians. Women comprise about two-thirds of the roughly 13,000 students, reflecting the greater likelihood that young men will study abroad.

In 2007, Dubai created International Academic City, incorporating Knowledge Village and its 20 foreign higher-education institutions, now including Michigan State University, or one university for every 20,000 inhabitants.

The Federation's Marriage Fund ranks as one of the most unusual features of a society where the state takes responsibility for the welfare of its citizens between the cradle and the grave. Realizing that marriage to a woman from the country had become prohibitively expensive for many of its young men, in 1994 the Federation created the Marriage Fund. The fund built special "Wedding Halls" where receptions cost far less than at hotels. The government also urged fathers to accept lower dowries, a major expense for many. It provides up to $19,000 to couples of limited income who wish to marry. In its first

Neat as an architect's model: housing in Dubai   Courtesy: Royal Embassy of Saudi Arabia

United Arab Emirates

year the fund gave or lent nearly $100 million to 3,000 couples. By 2000 this had grown to 44,000 couples, and marriages to foreign women had fallen from 64% of total weddings to 26%.

A major purpose for the Marriage Fund is the need to increase the indigenous population. Nationals are outnumbered about four to one by foreign residents who have found work in the country. Native and immigrant Arabs together constitute no more than 40% of the population, with Indians (30%) and Pakistanis (25%) comprising major communities. Nearly 90% of the officers and men of the federation army of 40,000 are not native Arabs.

In a society with many single men, but few amusements and limited (legal) alcoholic beverages, sports attract great attention. Thoroughbred racing arouses particular passion, and the Dubai World Cup has become the world's richest horserace ($21 million in prizes, 2007), and the stable of Sheikh Muhammad, Dubai's ruler, often leads the world in victories. Further down the social scale, one finds auto racing and even camel races, held on a special track. The Emirate's powerboat racing team led the world championship in 1995 until an accident killed its most talented driver.

Economy: Despite the relatively late development of its petroleum deposits (exports began in 1962), the oil reserves of the U.A.E. now exceed 97 billion barrels, and rank the fifth largest in the world. So vast are the deposits that with present discoveries alone, the U.A.E. can maintain its present level of exports until about the year 2099. Most deposits lie in Abu Dhabi, whose production exceeds 90% of the national total, with very modest output from Dubai and Sharja. Thus it was Abu Dhabi's oil revenues that transformed much of the country. The U.A.E. also possesses the world's fourth largest reserves of natural gas.

Historically, the U.A.E. received a fairly small OPEC quota (e.g., 1.1 million barrels per day, 1989), but partly because of agreements with oil companies, it overproduced. The collapse of Iraqi and Kuwaiti exports in 1990 provided opportunity for increased exports, and U.A.E. experts correctly predicted that increasing world demand for oil, plus declining reserves in several OPEC nations, would reduce excess supplies and render quotas relatively unimportant.

Outside the petroleum industry, the inhabitants find a variety of ways to earn a living. Agriculture remains an important source of employment, with over 20,000 farms. Currently the Emirates produce roughly half the vegetables that the population consumes—and all the dates. In fact, with over 20 million date palms—approximately five per person, yielding nearly 20 lbs. each—the country is one of the world's most important growers.

The Hajar mountain range provides Ras al-Khayma and Fujayra with water for irrigation. Besides dates and other traditional fruits and vegetables, these areas export strawberries, chrysanthemum, tomatoes and other high-value winter crops to Europe. Agricultural research stations attempt to adapt plants and animals to the demanding climate conditions, and seek plants that tolerate saline ground-water.

Rain falls infrequently in the Emirates, and several dams store the natural flow of the seasonal *wadis* for agricultural use and to recharge aquifers. By contrast, the population depends on desalinized water, and the al-Taweela plant gives Abu Dhabi the world's largest single unit in the world.

All the Emirates possess stretches of beach, some quite lengthy. Fujayra also enjoys a flourishing tourist trade based on trips to the mountains, including picturesque waterfalls. Sharja and other Emirates issue their own stamps, including some of the world's most eye-catching commemorative issues for sale to collectors.

The Amazing Success of Dubai, Inc.

Dubai ranks as the undisputed commercial center of the nation as well as the region, and symbols of its brash confidence abound. Its World Trade Center already ranked among the tallest buildings in the Middle East, but the Burj Khalifa, opened in 2010 become the world's tallest at 2,716 feet, a half-mile high, twice the Empire State Building. The city claims the world's most luxurious hotel, the Burj al-Arab; some consider it 7-Star, and rumors suggest some suites may cost $25,000 per night. Still under construction, Dubailand will become the largest entertainment complex in the Middle East—a family-style Vegas the size of Manhattan with complete theme parks, but no gambling, alcohol, or evident illicit sex.

The government aims for 15 million tourists a year by 2015. Many facilities already exist, including the Gulf's busiest airport, and a $3.7 billion subway system under construction. In 2001 the government-owned airline, Emirates, announced it would spend $15 billion on passenger jets, the largest order ever announced.

Aiming to become the home of international jet-setters, but limited by its relatively short (40-mile) waterfront, Dubai has constructed a series of artificial islands. Seen from the air, several take the shape of a palm tree, and their fronds, each over a mile long, extend the emirate's shoreline and provide the setting for planned communities of luxury homes, each with a view of the beach. Another project created islands in the shape of the world. However, the really grandiose multi-billion project, known as Dubai Waterfront, was planned to house 400,000 people on an area nearly three times the size of Washington, D.C. The coastlines of the various islands will stretch 500 miles, and feature more exclusive hotels (one, the Atlantis, underwater), more shops, and other entertainment centers. The world's largest mall, incorporating 31 hotels, will be across town.

Dubai's business model is free-trade zones in the desert, where firms with similar interest cluster together and take advantage of capitalism at its least regulated: no taxes, no tariffs, no limits on transferring funds, no visa difficulties for professionals. Media City, Internet City, several villages and parks, and recently Healthcare City often bring millions of feet of square feet of space devoted to state-of-the-art in the industry.

Obviously these projects greatly exceed the needs of Dubai's inhabitants. When planned, they made sense only because the emirate aimed for millions of visitors, and expected the population to reach two million by 2010, as wealthy retirees and business tycoons moved to a land of perpetual sunshine, negligible income taxes and unsurpassed internet service. One challenge in the future may be a struggle against drug use and other forms of hedonism, among the support staff if not the wealthy themselves. Already, gambling, alcoholic drinks and prostitution are becoming less discrete.

Old-fashioned work also exists. The Jebel Ali Free Trade zone provides warehousing for transshipping goods through the world's largest man-made port. Over 1,000 companies use the zone, including Dubai Aluminum's smelter, one of the largest in the world, with a capacity of

Courtesy: Caltex Petroleum Corp. (Joe Brignolo '95)

Renamed in 2010 after the UAE president, at 2,716 feet Burj Khalifa is the tallest building in the world, an amazing challenge to desert wind and heat.

about 1,000,000 tons in 2009. Its accompanying electric generating plant provides almost half the city's drinking water through desalination.

Given Dubai's trade, construction almost everywhere, and growth industries like aluminum and liquefied natural gas (LNG), the Emirates enjoy increasing economic diversity. In 2006, petroleum accounted for only about one-third of the economy, an exceptionally low proportion given the high per capita incomes. The country constantly expands its infrastructure—by some estimates, in 2007 about 20,000 building cranes were in service in Dubai, alone—and its military acquisi-

tions provide a competitive battleground for defense contractors throughout the world, especially for big-ticket items like tanks and jet fighters.

During the years of rapid income growth, the U.A.E. gained the distinction of providing a greater percentage of national income to foreign aid than any country. Much of the funding comes from the Abu Dhabi Fund for Development. Originally established in 1971 to help poorer Arab states, the Fund by 1995 had aided some 44 countries in Asia and Africa with loans and grants surpassing $3 billion.

One distinct shadow hanging over the entire construction boom is the treatment

of manual workers. Eager to work hard for a few years, then return home able to purchase a home and small farm, manual laborers from the Indian subcontinent and China often find themselves working in health-threatening heat (over 100° Fahrenheit), at dangerous jobs without insurance or healthcare. Pay checks sometimes come months late, and living conditions may mean 10 men to a room. However, Dubai's rulers showed some concern: after unofficial demonstrations at the Burj Dubai (renamed Burj Khalifa) project involved 3,000 workers and some violence, in 2006 the government announced that a labor union would be permitted—and even granted a right to strike. In addition, afternoon construction work was banned in the summer.

Another fundamental challenge to the business model is the 2008-09 world recession. It depressed housing prices in Dubai by about 60% as jobs disappeared and thousands of foreign professionals left. There was room to fall: apartments in Burj Khalifa had reportedly sold for $2,700 per square foot. Dubai World, the emirate's investment arm, found itself unable to pay billions of dollars of debt to its banks, and attempted to restructure $23 billion of debt after being rescued by the government. In the process, banks may lose up to 50% of the value of their loans. Dubai's total debt in mid-2010 was estimated at over $100 billion.

The Future: At its birth, the United Arab Emirates seemed just another alliance of traditional rulers whom departing colonial officials hurriedly patched together. Thanks to oil, the pragmatism of Sheikh Zayed, and the dynamic entrepreneurial spirit of Sheikh Maktoum bin Rashid, the U.A.E. enjoyed growth and prosperity. The recent passing of both those admired rulers failed to dent the high level of economic confidence.

The astounding scale of Dubai's business model made it the Hong Kong of this decade (indeed, it reportedly used more cranes than anywhere else but China). Its culture of business initiative, prosperity, and cultural tolerance—and the insignificance of politics—is exactly the opposite of most Middle Eastern countries. Then, just as commercial rents became among the most expensive in the world, the world recession hit and the property bubble burst.

While the worst may be over, expect major bankruptcies, handled quietly where possible, and efforts to clean up signs of corruption. For the moment, though, Dubai is over-built. When the world recession ends, there should be more cutting edge projects—but they will involve buildings in Abu Dhabi, and from Pakistan to Turkey rather than Dubai.

A view of Dubai City. The building in the foreground with the ball on top is the headquarters of the Emirates Telecommunications Corporation.
Courtesy: Caltex Petroleum Corporation
Photo by Marina Volochine

The Republic of Yemen

The old walled city of San'a. "San'a' must be seen, however long the journey, though the hardy camel droop, leg-worn on the way" Traditional Arab poem

Courtesy: Caltex Petroleum Corporation

Area: 207,286 square miles (536,869 sq. km.).

Population: 24.4 million.

Capital City: San'a (pop. 1.5 million, est.).

Climate: Extremely hot and humid on the coastal plain, cooler in the mountains, often cold at night. Rainfall is moderate on the western slopes of the mountains and the highest peaks sometimes have snow.

Neighboring Countries: Saudi Arabia (North); Oman (East).

Time Zone: GMT +3.

Official Language: Arabic.

Other Principle Tongues: Mahri; English in school and international business.

Ethnic Background: Arab, with varying physical appearances; short and olive-skinned people in the mountains; heavy African admixture along the coast.

Principal Religion: Islam. The *Zaidi* sect of *Shi'a* Islam dominates the northern mountains; most other Yemenis are *Sunnis* of the *Shafi'i* legal school.

Chief Commercial Products: Crude oil, cotton, coffee, qat, livestock and hides, tobacco, vegetables, dried and salted fish.

Major Trading Partners: U.S., Japan, France, Germany, Saudi Arabia.

Currency: Yemeni Rial (= 100 fils).

Former Colonial Status: Ottoman Rule sporadic after the 16th century; British in the South (1839–1967).

National Day: May 22 (Union Day).

Chief of State: Ali Abdullah Salih, President (elections due September 2006).

Head of Government: Abd al-Qadir Ba-Jammal, Prime Minister.

National Flag: Three horizontal stripes of red, white and black.

Gross Domestic Product: $32 billion (at current prices); $62 billion (Purchasing Power Parity), 2008.

GDP per capita: $2,600 (PPP), 2008.

In 1990, the Yemen Arab Republic (North Yemen) and the People's Democratic Republic of Yemen (South Yemen, or Aden) merged to form the Republic of Yemen. Although the area had never formed a unified state, the population widely felt itself "Yemeni." While the merger of traditional and marxist political cultures proved uneasy, the union continues.

Located in the southwestern corner of the Arabian Peninsula, Yemen's varied topography contrasts greatly with the flat, stony plains and sand dunes of central and eastern Arabia. In western Yemen, the geography takes the form of zones running from north to south. The first zone, the Tihama plain, lies along the coast of the Red Sea. Level, hot, and arid, the Tihama also inflicts high humidity on its inhabitants.

Some 30 miles inland steeply rising slopes mark a scenic mountain range and plateau that run from the Saudi border in the north to the Gulf of Aden. Peaks in the range reach 10,000–12,000 feet. By blocking air currents from the sea, they cause summer rains that make the western slopes the wettest region of Arabia, with precipitation averaging 15 inches yearly, and as much as 30 inches in a good year. However, there are no year-round rivers, but rather seasonal streams in the valleys, known as *wadis*.

San'a (Sanaa), the capital, lies in the interior plateau; its elevation of 6,500 feet is one of the highest of any national capital. East of the mountains, the high plateau gradually slopes down to the desert, eventually joining the *Rub al-Khali* or Empty Quarter of Saudi Arabia.

Southern and southeastern Yemen, bordering the Gulf of Aden, endures a harsher geography. Its lonely, barren landscape of desert plateaus and jagged mountains is broken by two important valleys. In the southwest, the oases around Lahj provide much of the region's limited produce. In the east, the Wadi Hadhramut forms a narrow strip of green. Yemen also rules several islands, including the strategically important Perim Island in the Bab al-Mandab, the strait between Arabia and Africa.

History: Ancient and civilized kingdoms existed in what is now Yemen long before the time of Christ. One of the most famous was Saba, or Sheba. Near its capital, Marib, a great stone dam captured the runoff from summer rains. Honored in literature and legend, the dam contributed to the reputation of this region as *Arabia Felix* (Fertile Arabia), famous in Roman times for its trade in frankincense and myrrh. However, during the early Christian centuries rival Jewish and Christian chiefs sought to conquer the region. Foreign armies invaded, the dam failed, and its irrigation system deteriorated. Islam arrived towards the end of Muhammad's lifetime, during the seventh (Christian) century, and spread partly as a reaction against religions linked to foreign powers.

The *Zaidi* sect of Shi'a Islam (see Iran: Culture) became dominant in mountain regions during the ninth century, and its leader, styled an Imam, became the traditional ruler. The early Islamic period provided security and prosperity. The population increased greatly, and many terraces on the steep, rain-fed slopes date from that era.

In the 16th century the Ottoman Sultans lay claim to Yemen, but its remoteness and terrain ensured that it was never completely subjugated. Indeed, the Ottomans withdrew in the 17th century and the British gained influence at Mukha (Mocha) where they established a trading station, while the interior remained under the *Zaidi* Imams. The Ottomans attempted to regain the coast and more accessible regions after 1849, with limited success, and their rule ended in 1918.

The southern and eastern regions were variously held by feuding tribal chieftains for untold centuries. Britain seized the port of Aden in 1839. It became a valuable coaling station for ships plying the Egypt-India route, but Britain took minimal interest in the interior. Between 1882 and 1914, its sheikhs and other local leaders signed treaties that ceded authority over foreign affairs to Britain in exchange for protection.

After the Ottoman Empire collapsed in 1918, the *Zaidi* ruler, Imam Yahya, tried to expand Yemen's boundaries. In the south, his expansion was stopped by Britain's defense of Aden and its hinterland. Yahya also claimed sovereignty over Asir, the

coastal region to the north. Its ruler then allied with the powerful Saudi monarch, King Abd al-Aziz. After Yahya's forces attacked pro-Saudi tribes, war followed. Saudi forces routed Yahya's poorly equipped tribesmen and captured Hudaida. By the 1934 Taif Agreement, Yahya ceded Asir, although its eastern border remained unsettled and subject to temporary agreements.

Yahya was assassinated in 1948, and the rule of his son and successor, Ahmad, followed the familiar pattern: severe and ill-informed. Few foreign "infidels" (unbelievers) were permitted to enter the country; Yemen was as isolated from the world as Tibet. The inhabitants lived much as their ancestors had a thousand years previously.

Soon after Ahmad's death in 1962, army officers inspired by Egypt's revolution against King Farouk seized control of San'a. They declared Yemen a republic, headed by Colonel Abdullah Sallal. Ahmad's son, the Imam, attempted to return to power, but even with support from mountain tribesmen, he failed, and ultimately fled Yemen. The U.S. and the UN recognized the new republic in 1962.

Civil war followed, with the bitterest fighting in the winter of 1963–1964. The Imam was supported by the Saudis, the Republic by Egyptian troops and money. Many Yemenis desired modernization and

progress under a republic, but disliked Abdullah Sallal. After Egyptian troops began withdrawing during the Arab-Israeli war of 1967, Sallal the republicans replaced Sallal with a *Zaidi* religious leader, Abd al-Rahman Iryani. He sought to unite the various republican factions while warding off armed royalists who again threatened the capital. This danger ebbed by 1969, because Iryani won the respect of royalist tribes by his religious prestige and political moderation. In addition, Saudi Arabia cut off most of its aid to the royalists.

The civil war ended in 1970 and full attention turned to developing a country ravaged by a near-decade's fighting. In 1971 a Consultative Assembly was established, under Iryani.

Aden Colony Becomes South Yemen

Events moved quite differently in the south. In 1937 Britain created a crown colony of the city of Aden, while loosely supervising the local rulers of the interior as long as they refrained from violence. After decades of little political development, in 1958 British officials sought to unite the various tribal leaders as a counter to growing Arab nationalism. By 1966, all the local sheikhdoms had joined the Federation of South Arabia.

Following the rise of political consciousness in Aden, spurred by the expansion of British bases, unrest and terrorism grew. Urban nationalists sensed a British design to govern them through the two dozen tribal rulers of the Federation. Local troops mutinied in 1967, and nationalists seized several of the states. Despite conflict between rival rebel groups, one Egyptian-influenced, the other the marxist *National Liberation Front (NLF)*, the federation collapsed.

In 1967 Britain withdrew from Aden, permitting the *NLF* to take control. Adopt-

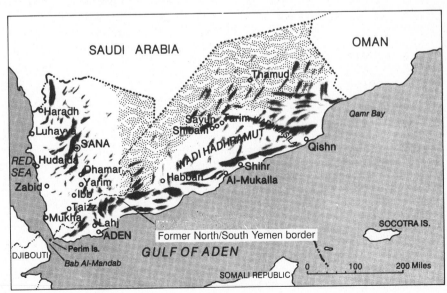

Yemen

ing the title People's Republic of South Yemen, the *NLF* divided the country into six states to replace the traditional principalities. But the *NLF* proved incapable of stable government. For the first three years, the political pot boiled, as alliances shifted almost continuously. In 1969, a strongly communist clique came to power, added "Democratic" to the country's title, and promised an elected People's Supreme Council. However, elections never occurred.

Political turmoil erupted again in 1978, when the president was overthrown and executed. Thereafter the *NLF* joined the local communist and *Ba'th* parties to form the *Yemen Socialist Party (YSP)*. Its factions plunged into open civil war in 1986. Thousands died before the defeated president fled to North Yemen with thousands of armed followers.

Largely unnoticed by the outside world, in the late 1980s considerable social and political change took place in South Yemen. Though marxist and Soviet-influenced, it permitted non-party candidates in local elections and then allowed opposition parties. Women's rights were among the most advanced in the entire Arab world. In foreign affairs, with the Soviet Union collapsing and the economy in shambles, the regime mended links with Arab states and sought closer relations, even unity, with Northern Yemen.

These were dramatic changes indeed. From its start, most Arab governments felt concern, or even hostility, about the regime in Aden, because of the country's radical policies and its sponsorship of Omani rebels of the threateningly-named *People's Front for the Liberation of the Occupied Arabian Gulf*. In 1972 a serious border war broke out with North Yemen, a conflict temporarily resolved with promises to unite the two Yemeni states. Border clashes again flared fiercely in 1979 and 1981, and in Yemeni fashion resulted in further unfulfilled agreements to unite.

The North Achieves Stability under Salih

Struggles for power also persisted in San'a. A Military Command Council took control of North Yemen in 1975. It established a degree of unity between the various factions and maintained firm central control. More important, it developed good relations with Saudi Arabia, which lent financial assistance. But both the first two rulers were assassinated, the latter by a bomb from Aden's communists. Stability only came, unexpectedly, when Colonel Ali Abdullah Salih became president (1978).

Despite political unrest, assassination attempts, two border wars, and a major earthquake that destroyed 200 villages, in

the 1980s Salih established stable government and added democratic elements to the military dictatorship. The first general election for the *Majlis al-Shura* ("Consultative Council") took place in 1988. It was widely contested, but President Salih's *General People's Congress* won the most seats. The *Muslim Brotherhood* and tribal independents also acquired significant representation.

In 1989, the leaders of the two countries again proclaimed plans for a merger. This seemed merely another ritual, but the next year public opinion in both North and South Yemen surged in favor of rapid union. Long divided by conflicting domestic and foreign policies, the two states showed signs of increasing similarity. They both held elections, a rarity for the Arabian Peninsula. Trade increased between them, a consequence of greater freedom for private farmers and businessmen in the South.

President Ali Abdullah Salih
Photo courtesy of the White House

Surprising almost everyone, the two states merged ahead of schedule in 1990, perhaps to out-maneuver domestic and foreign opponents. Approved unanimously by Aden's government, the merger faced opposition in San'a from members of the *Majlis al-Shura* linked to the *Muslim Brotherhood*, who feared irreligious influences from Aden. President al-Attas of the South became Prime Minister of united Yemen, and a 302-member Council of Deputies included a variety of parties.

Merged, but not United

United Yemen faced grave difficulties, including the legacy of a history littered with failed merger attempts. The South's

economy lay in tatters; its adjustment to greater competition and imports remained uncertain. The North's relative economic success, combined with a population four times that of the South, created fears it would dominate any union. Perhaps surprising to Americans, the North's social development lagged significantly behind that of communist-influenced Aden.

Exceptional challenges arose during the first year of union. Linked to Iraq by trade and Kuwait by aid, Yemen attempted to maintain neutrality after Iraq invaded Kuwait. As the only Arab member of the UN Security Council, however, this was impossible. Yemen's demands for an Iraqi withdrawal received less publicity than its uncertainty about the Kuwaiti ruling family's legitimacy. Greater domestic freedom permitted an outpouring of protest after Western forces arrived in Saudi Arabia.

The neutrality and protests threatened economic ruin. Saudi Arabia, already uneasy about sharing miles of unsettled frontier with a united Yemen equal in national population, cut all financial aid and expelled roughly one million Yemenis. They returned to face unemployment. Other nations cut development aid, so the central bank printed money and inflation climbed. However, a referendum approved unity by a large majority, and oil discoveries suggested reserves to support greater production.

As parliamentary elections approached in 1992, a series of murders swept the country. They claimed some 30 members of the *Yemen Socialist Party*, and led Prime Minister al-Attas to threaten to resign. In response, elections were postponed. Then food riots broke out in major cities, as inflation surpassed 100% and unemployment rose higher.

Despite a background of high inflation and food riots, in 1993 Yemen held the first free multi-party elections of the entire Arabian Peninsula, with some 5,000 candidates for the Council of Deputies. Allegations of vote-buying and favoritism in television coverage aside, the elections were considered broadly accurate. However, the results reflected strong regional differences. Salih's *General People's Congress* led the Islamic *Islah* in the north, while the *YSP* won every southern seat but few elsewhere. Nevertheless, the three parties formed a coalition government.

Personal rivalries and budget conflicts soon led to increasing hostility between President Salih and Vice President Ali Salem al-Baidh, a southerner. Al-Baidh left San'a for Aden, charging that the president sought a dictatorship and paralyzing government. As tensions mounted, clashes broke out between military units and then, in 1994, full-scale civil war. Northern troops attempted to capture Aden against determined resistance. Aided by water shortages in besieged Aden and tribal resentments against the *YSP,* they crushed the rebellion, whose leaders fled.

Despite their formal unity, the two Yemens had clearly not merged their governments in practice. The two armies had remained separate. Both currencies had remained in circulation, and disputes paralyzed even the adoption of annual government budgets.

In victory, Salih released southern prisoners of war and proclaimed a general amnesty. He permitted the *YSP* to exist, under new leaders who had opposed the rebellion. He also won re-appointment as president after parliament approved a new, more Islamic constitution that gave the president greater powers.

The war damaged further an already precarious economy. The budget deficit soared, and to meet its bills, the state turned to printing money. Inflation became so great that the government refused to release the figures, though it did devalue the *rial* by a factor of 10. Salaried professionals found their standard of living destroyed, and Yemeni university professors struck because their monthly pay of $140 equaled less than 10% of foreigners' salaries. Subsidies for wheat, flour, and oil products became unbearable burdens, but their reductions doubled prices and triggered riots. Unemployment reached 30%. Further cuts in government subsidies occurred according to the IMF-approved plan in 1996. However, some foreign aid was received as a reward.

Yemen held the first contested presidential election in the history of all Arabia in 1999. Salih won a landslide victory, in formally free voting. However, the electoral manipulation had occurred earlier. Parliament rejected all opposition nominees as candidates, so the *YSP* again boycotted the campaign, *Islah* nominated Salih as its candidate, and to meet the constitution's requirement of two candidates, one of Salih's supporters ran against him.

The country boasts some 60 million firearms, three times its population. Very few of them are hunting rifles: given their tumultuous history, men expect they will be called to fight. Law and order therefore remain sporadic. In the 1990s, tribesmen in remote areas discovered a new form of pressure politics: kidnapping foreigners to gain government projects. Tourists, petroleum workers, and even diplomats found themselves seized as bargaining chips for schools, roads, water projects and other aid. To protect the oil and tourist industries, officials typically promised to meet some demands, and gained the release of the hostages. Eventually, however, to maintain its authority, the government imposed the death penalty for kidnapping.

In 2000, suicide bombers unexpectedly maneuvered a small boat filled with explosives alongside the destroyer *U.S.S. Cole* as it refueled in Aden harbor. The subsequent explosion pierced the side of the vessel and killed nearly two dozen sailors. Yemeni authorities worked closely with U.S. officials to discover those responsible, though they limited American access to interrogations.

Though eventually blamed on Yemenis connected with *al-Qaeda,* the attack on the *Cole* raised questions about the nature of the growing Islamic fervency. Most Yemenis are poor or even impoverished. They usually hold very traditional values, and regard Western ways with suspicion. The wave of popular Islamic devotion—though not violence—is fostered by the separate system of religious schools created by the Islamist *Islah* party when it ran the education ministry during the 1990s. The party also changed the public schools' curriculum to include a large dose of religious studies, based on books *Islah* selected. President Salih broke with *Islah* in 2001, and modified some such policies.

Rumors that the U.S. might avenge the 9/11 attacks with assaults on Yemen's Islamic extremists apparently prompted an unusually strong crackdown on Islamic militants. Scores of foreign students at Islamic study centers were expelled, and others arrested. Republican Guard and Special Forces units, commanded by the president's son, Ahmad, also attempted to extend government authority over tribal areas.

Nevertheless, popular sympathies lie with those who preach Islam rather than with the West. Tens of thousands of Yemeni veterans of the Afghan war against the Soviets sympathize with *al-Qaeda.* So do many foreign students attracted to study Islam in the religious seminaries. Anti-western bomb attacks occasionally take place in the capital and other cities, and in 2008 the U.S. embassy ordered out all non-essential staff.

Most militant Islamists come from the country's Sunni majority. However, in the distant northern province of Saada a *Zaidi* preacher, Hussein al-Huthi (or Houthi), defied the government, in the *Zaidi* tradition that permits rebellion against an unjust regime. When the army attempted to enforce its control, open warfare broke out involving heavy weapons. Al-Huthi died in the fighting, but his followers continued to resist. These rebels, conservative and Shi'a rather than linked to Sunni *al-Qaeda,* may really desire to restore rule by the imams. In 2007 their new leader, Hussein's brother Abd al-Malik al-Huthi, promised to halt the violence, but occasional attacks on the army and police continued.

After 27 years in power, in 2005 Salih ruled himself out of the 2006 presidential elections just when a financial crisis threatened. Heavy subsidies had kept gasoline and diesel fuel cheap for trucks, buses, and irrigation pumps. However, perhaps one-third of the subsidized fuel was actually smuggled out of the country, mostly to Somalia. The subsidy became unaffordable, and aid-giving agencies considered it a source of corruption.

To escape popular blame for the higher prices, two days before the cabinet cut the subsidies and tripled the price of diesel Salih announced that he would not run again. After the price increases, violent riots shook the country, killing dozens; the army had to patrol the streets. Salih then intervened, to raise salaries, cut sales taxes, and order a small cut in fuel prices. Thus, Salih struck the pose of a caring father of the nation, in contrast to the cabinet. A carefully stage-managed convention of the *General People's Congress* nominated him for re-election, while other parties pondered their options.

In contrast to the staged election of 1999, in 2006 opposition parties ranging from the secular *YSP* to the religious *Islah* set aside other rivalries and united behind the nomination of Faisal Bin Shamlan. A retired economist with an unmatched reputation for honesty, he attacked the country's high level of corruption and attracted wide attention. Though the battle was uneven—government officialdom knew whom to support and discretely did so—Shamlan won over 20% of the vote in the first genuinely contested presidential election in the Arab Middle East. His level of support suggested that Ali Abdullah Salih would face popular opposition to his son's automatic succession to the presidency.

Man on the streets of San'a

Yemen

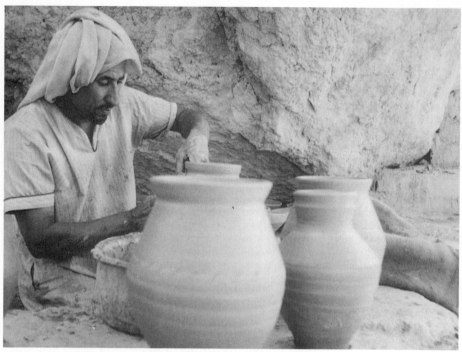

A potter works his trade near Aden

Tipping Towards a Failed State

By 2009, multiple crises challenged the government. The northern Huthi rebellion blazed again into the open when the military launched Operation Scorched Earth, eventually using air raids and heavy weapons on rebels in the provincial capital, Saada, and elsewhere. The rebellion reflected Shi'a dissatisfaction, and when fighting spread into Saudi Arabia, the crisis invited Iranian interference as well. When a truce was finally reached in 2010, photographic evidence showed attacks on markets, mosques, and residential areas, evidence substantiating claims that hundreds or even thousands of unarmed civilians had died.

To fight the Huthi rebellion, the military mobilized extremist Sunni groups influenced by Osama bin Laden. Indeed, apparent toleration of Sunni extremists enabled some of those convicted of extremist violence such as the attack on the *U.S.S. Cole* to escape prison, then to receive pardons for both the escape and the original crimes. However, the local cell apparently strengthened and launched attacks on Korean tourists, other foreigners and the U.S. embassy. It also renamed itself *al-Qaeda in the Arabian Peninsula*, suggesting threats to neighboring countries. The organization took credit for the attempt by a Nigerian to blow up a U.S. airliner landing in Detroit.

Meanwhile, protests by retired southern army officers over pensions fanned perceptions of discrimination and the corrupt acquisition of land and property by northerners. A loosely organized *Southern*

Movement emerged, including both former socialists and Islamic militants. Some sympathizers openly demand succession and independence. It required a full military operation to crush the militants who seized one town, and protests led to fatalities in several southern locations.

President Salih traditionally responds to such crises by forging alliances with some rivals against others, while using predictions of disaster to frighten sympathetic countries into increasing foreign aid. However, the failure to keep *al-Qaeda* followers in prison poisoned relations with the U.S., whose human rights concerns differ substantially from those of Saudi Arabia and other oil states who might prefer to fight *al-Qaeda* abroad.

The underlying socio-economic crisis simultaneously deprives Salih and his government of Yemeni resources. Income from oil exports fell 75% in 2009, and output is expected to fall further, so subsidies are not available to offset unpopular rises in imported food prices. The budget deficit prevents large-scale attempts to reduce unemployment, estimated at 30%. For the longer term, a population growing at 3.7% per year needs social services, but widespread corruption erodes good intentions, and much of the population lacks access to medical care. The growing population requires access to water, but the limits of sustainable pumping have been exceeded, and the water table is dropping rapidly around many cities.

In response, the government postponed parliamentary elections, imprisoned an investigative journalist for reporting on

the Huthi rebellion, closed several newspapers, and bombed a southern town. Although Yemenis denied the warnings of American and European experts that a failed state was possible—that Yemen might become another Somalia—a hasty international conference met in early 2010 to focus attention on the multiple crises and encourage the government to reform.

Culture: About 70% of the population lives in the traditional style in small towns, villages or isolated clusters of houses. Until recently, most loyalties were local, mainly to the family, clan, and tribe. Devotion to the nation—as distinct from rejection of other nations—has been a rather new feeling which spreads slowly. A few people are nomads, mainly in the eastern and southern part of the country, while considerably more live in the growing cities, where the alien architecture of new buildings often clashes with the greater dignity and appeal of traditional designs.

Unfortunately many of the mud-brick skyscrapers are in danger of collapse, threatened particularly by running water and burst pipes. Foreign governments have funded a UNESCO campaign to restore San'a, paving streets and restoring portions of the *souk* (market place). However, the walled cities of Hadhramut, east of Aden and far off tourist routes despite their beauty, face the danger of buildings 500 years old collapsing.

While virtually all Yemenis are Muslims, they form two major sects. In the coastal plain and much of the settled south, inhabitants profess *Sunni* Islam and provide a center for the *Shafi'i* school. In the North, the conservative *Zaidi* sect of *Shi'a* Islam prevails, and for a thousand years until the 1962 revolution, the Imams ruled the country from the mountains.

In a uniquely Yemeni custom, every afternoon, most Yemeni men and many women gather in small social groups to chew leaves of *qat*, a tree cultivated on the terraced mountainsides. Large globs of leaves, when chewed for hours, reportedly produce a mildly narcotic effect that relaxes a person and gives a sense of contentment.

The cultivation and use of *qat* brings undesirable effects to a country seeking development. It consumes vast amounts of time, occupying most of the afternoon (the workday obligingly ends at 2 p.m.). Producing all the *qat* consumed by Yemenis provides employment for hundreds of thousands of farmers, and it is a far more profitable crop than coffee or grains. Much of the nation's limited supply of agricultural water goes to the crop.

Qat consumption is expensive, and some families spend one-fifth their incomes to enjoy it (and to escape giving the impres-

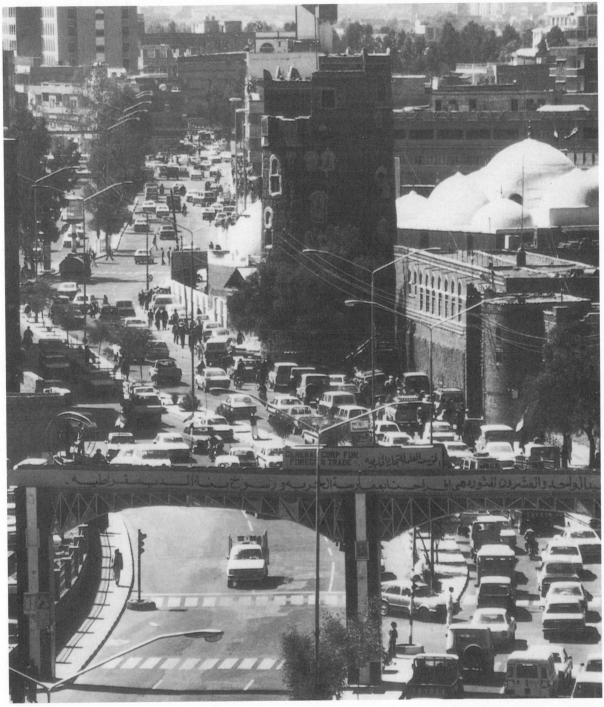

Busy downtown San'a

Courtesy: Caltex Petroleum Corporation

sion they are too poor to afford it). Though not physically addictive, it leads to a state of relaxation that discourages hard work. It may cause serious illness, and at least one study of heavy users shows a greatly increased risk of heart attacks. In 1999 President Salih announced that he was giving up the leaves, and he urged the nation to follow his example. Presumably when Yemeni adults chew the leaves, they find greater enjoyment than from any other use of their money, but given Yemen's pitiful

levels of nutrition, health and education, the habit casts a long shadow over social and economic development.

Throughout Yemen, since the fall of the monarchy and the arrival of freedom from colonialism, education has taken great strides among men, though only 7% of adult women read. There are universities at San'a and Aden, and competition to enroll is fierce. The use of English in education is becoming widespread, since one of Yemen's most valuable assets is the workers

which it sends abroad. In turn, they have sent badly needed money back home.

In their struggle for water, roads, schools and other projects for a better standard of living, Yemenis often formed "development associations," to pool resources for their goals. Relatively rare elsewhere in the Middle East, these community action groups involve both traditional and modern interests, and reflect a Yemeni sense that the poverty requires cooperation rather than simple competition. Unfortunately, the

Yemen

cooperative movement has on several occasions suffered from government attempts to take it over or politicize it.

Economy: Although agriculture is still at the center of the economy, it is fast being overtaken by petroleum. On the coast, one finds date palms and grains suitable to the hot climate. The upper slopes of the mountains, which receive good rainfall, are among the most intensively cultivated in the world. Over the centuries, farmers have built elaborate terraces with stone walls—at some places right up to the crests of the mountains.

Coffee was traditionally the important cash crop. Shipped from the old port of Mukha, it became renowned as "Mocha coffee." In recent decades, lower world coffee prices reduced production in Yemen, because the production of *qat* became more profitable.

Animal herding plays an important role in the economy. Millions of sheep, goats and humped cattle are raised for milk, meat and hides. Donkeys and mules are still the most common beasts of burden as camels are not suitable in the rugged mountains, though they are far from unknown in Yemen.

It is possible that mineral deposits in commercial quantities exist in the country, but little surveying has been done thus far. Manufacturing remains in the handicraft stage; while it exhibits a high degree of skill and artistic merit, handmade products cannot supply a comfortable standard of living like machine-factory production.

Yemen is the poorest country in the Middle East, and one of the poorest in the world. Ever since the 1960s, foreign nations have provided important assistance for development, including roads, health projects and farm programs. Northern Yemen in particular proved adept at soliciting funds from rival nations, including the Soviet Union, China, the United States, West Germany and several Arab oil exporters. By contrast, its communist ties prevented South Yemen from receiving Western and Arab aid.

After oil exports commenced in 1988, the importance of foreign aid declined somewhat. By 1995 total production reached 400,000 barrels per day, and the country approved a $3 billion project to liquefy natural gas for export. However, only modest quantities of oil have been discovered, and the volume of exports is small, about 5% that of Saudi Arabia. Consequently, Yemen did not join OPEC.

Rising oil prices at mid-decade disguised the diminishing oil output, but the 75% decline in government oil revenues in 2009 reinforced fears of a possible economic collapse. Unless new discoveries are made, exports will plummet rapidly beginning this year, and end in 2017. However, many promising geological formations have failed to yield oil, and the growing violence from *al-Qaeda* discourages foreign companies Earnings from exports of liquefied natural gas will only partially replace oil revenues.

The Future: Almost every indicator of national success recently turned dangerous. Three insurgencies—the *Huthi* rebellion among Zaydis in the north, the *Southern Movement*, and *al-Qaeda in the Arabian Peninsula*—simultaneously challenge the state. Though they are unlikely to unite, their separate actions would challenge a solid, well-financed government. Splintered by sect, tribe, region, ideology and *Salafi* extremists who oppose links with the U.S., Salih's regime is far from solid.

Its finances are likewise crumbling. Oil exports are falling to insignificance. Once expected to last until 2020, they may cease by 2015, and they provide over 75% of all government revenue. Donors have cut foreign aid, because corruption climbed so far, so quickly. However, the growing young population desperately requires a growing economy to produce jobs. Ecologically, water will run short, as aquifers are over-pumped.

President Salih's accommodation with the opposition *Islah* party and the dominant Hashid tribal confederation appears frayed. His term ends in 2013. It is as difficult to predict his successor as to see why Yemen will not suffer more characteristics of a failed state before then.

Girl with her father

Courtesy: World Bank Photo by Tomas Sennett

The Middle East and South Asia 1910

BURMA

BAY OF BENGAL

CHINA

Tibet

BHUTAN

NEPAL

CEYLON

BRITISH INDIAN EMPIRE

RUSSIAN EMPIRE

MALDIVE ISLANDS

INDIAN OCEAN

AFGHANISTAN BRITISH SPHERE

RUSSIAN SPHERE

BRITISH SPHERE

ARABIAN SEA

GULF OF OMAN

CASPIAN SEA

OMAN BRITISH SPHERE

P E R S I A

SOCOTRA

PERSIAN GULF

TRUCIAL OMAN

KUWAIT

BAHRAIN

QATAR

[Tribal Rule]

ADEN PROTECTORATES

GULF OF ADEN

ADEN

BRITISH SOMALILAND

OTTOMAN EMPIRE

BLACK SEA

ERITREA

FRENCH SOMALILAND

ITALIAN SOMALILAND

RED SEA

CYPRUS

MEDITERRANEAN SEA

EGYPT

SUDAN

ABYSSINIA

ESTABLISHED BOUNDARIES
APPROXIMATE EXTENT OF JURISDICTION

MILES

0 100 200 300 400 600

DEPENDENT

BRITISH

Islamic Republic of Afghanistan

Afghan and international security forces protected voters from _Taliban_ threats during the presidential election

Major Trading Partners: Pakistan, Iran, Uzbekistan, Japan, Pakistan, India, and the U.S.

Currency: 1 New Afghani = 100 puls.

Former Political Status: Under British influence (1837–1919).

National Day: August 19 (traditional); May 5 (liberation of Kabul from communist rule).

Chief of State and Head of Government: President Hamid Karzai.

National Flag: Black, red, and green vertical stripes with a white emblem centered in the red containing a mosque, two flags, and sheaves of wheat (horizontally striped flags are also used).

Gross Domestic Product (GDP): $15 billion (at current prices); $27 billion (PPP), 2008

GDP per capita: $900 (PPP), 2008.

Afghanistan means "Land of the Afghans." Afghan in a strict sense means Pashtun or Pathan, that is, a member of any tribe speaking Pashtu, but now Afghan is applied to any citizen of this nation sometimes described as the "Turnstile of Asia."

A treeless, wind-swept land, Afghanistan's environment is hostile to human comfort and even survival, except for the short spring season when moderate temperatures and green vegetation follow winter rain and snow. Summer temperatures in the low valley of the Amu Darya (Oxus River to the ancient Greeks) often hover at 110°F. In the winter, blizzards rage in the high mountains and even at the medium elevations where most people live, temperatures may drop below zero for a few weeks. However, in the low valleys agriculture is intensively pursued, and native poplar trees abound to provide wood for rough houses.

The most striking geographical feature of the country is the complex series of mountains extending from the eastern tip for some 600 miles southwest before leveling out in the plateau near the border with Iran. Majestic peaks of the central Hindu Kush Mountains tower more than 20,000 feet above sea level, inspiring visitors, but the rugged terrain makes transportation difficult.

As a landlocked country, Afghanistan depends on transit through neighboring countries for its external trade. Most imports and exports traditionally passed through Pakistan, utilizing the railroad between Karachi and Peshawar, but depending on trucks between Peshawar and points inside the country. Another important trade route runs from Iran to Herat in the northwest, and the country's most valuable export, heroin, apparently reaches world markets through Central Asia.

Area: 251,773 square miles (652,225 sq. km.).

Population: Uncounted; 29.6 million (2007).

Capital City: Kabul (pop. 3.1 million).

Climate: Extremely dry, hot summers (but with cool nights); cold winters with moderate rain and snow in the mountains, scanty rain on the plain. Strong winds and dust storms are common.

Neighboring Countries: Pakistan (South and East); Iran (West); Turkmenistan, Uzbekistan, Tajikistan (formerly USSR; North); China (Northeast).

Time Zone: GMT + 4½ hours. When it is noon in Denver, it is 11:30 P.M. in Kabul.

Official Languages: Pashtu and Dari (Persian).

Other Principal Tongues: Uzbek, Turkmen, and Baluchi.

Ethnic Background: The varied facial features reflect the characteristics of the country's invaders. Ethnic membership is mainly by language and family culture. The Dari-speaking Hazaras are distinguished from Tajiks by descent, geography, and Shi'ism.

Principal Religion: Sunni (87%) and Shi'a Islam (12%).

Main Exports: Agricultural products (dried fruit, nuts, lambskins, raw cotton, wool, grain), carpets and textiles. Opium production ranks largest in the world, with 75% of total output.

Afghanistan

History: The mountains of Afghanistan form a natural divide that separates the Indian Subcontinent from Central Asia to the northwest, and Iran to the west. Until modern times, the territory did not form a separate political unit. Indeed, its steep mountains and remote valleys usually felt the impact of formal government only lightly. Nevertheless, the land and its people suffered migrations, raids and conquests as a consequence of its position as the "turnstile of Asia's fate." (see Historical Background). Iranian languages were established in the region more than 3,000 years ago, and related languages have been used ever since by the majority of the population. Islam entered what had been a Buddhist land during the seventh century, and became dominant by the tenth century.

From the 14th to the 19th centuries, invaders swept across the mountains and valleys: the Mongols, followed by the plundering hordes of Timur Lang (Tamerlane), and then Babur, a Turkish chief from Central Asia who claimed descent from Timur. Babur established his capital at Kabul in the 16th century; his warriors conquered the Indus and Ganges Valleys, founding the great Mogul Empire. Meanwhile, the Safavid Empire in Iran ruled Herat and sometimes Kandahar.

After two centuries of Mogul and Safavid rule, Pashtu-speaking tribes began to exercise greater local authority, though they often feuded with one another. These tribes referred to themselves as Pashtun (*Pakhtun* was a dialectic variation), but the Persians called them Afghans, a name of unknown origin. When Safavid rule proved particularly severe and rapacious, the Afghans of Kandahar revolted and defeated the Persian army in 1711. By mid-century, Ahmad Khan Durani had proclaimed himself king (shah) in Kandahar and seized the eastern part of the Persian empire, but his successors proved unable to create an Afghan state.

In the early 19th century, chiefs of a rival family, the *Mohammedzai,* consolidated their control over the principal centers of the country. Dost Mohammed eventually proclaimed himself Amir of Kabul and ruled as king, though it was decades later

before any of his line assumed the title of shah. Dost Mohammed concentrated on controlling a smaller territory rather than overextending his forces as the previous dynasty had done. His last achievement was to drive Persian forces out of Herat.

For the next century, the two main themes in Afghan political history were the struggles between rival leaders and the interference of British Indian officials. Direct descendants of Dost Mohammed remained in power until 1978, but only by repeatedly defeating rivals—often brothers and other close relatives. Most rulers died violent deaths; power passed to brothers or cousins as often as to sons.

Between 1839 and 1919, British Indian troops periodically intervened in Afghanistan, usually in support of a rival claimant to the throne who appeared to be more agreeable to policy in Delhi. They did not always win: the First Afghan War in 1841 ended with some 4,500 British and 10,000 Indian troops massacred in the rugged mountain gorges while retreating between Kabul and the Khyber Pass.

The major motive for Britain's intervention was the desire to block Russian influence. After a century of expansion toward the Hindu Kush Mountains, by 1875 the Russian Empire nearly reached the Amu Darya—the later border of the Soviet Union. As Russian expansion continued, a new British invasion in 1878 began two years of fighting with the Afghan tribes. In the end, the new ruler, Abdurrahman, was required to put foreign relations in

the hands of British authorities. Anglo-Russian rivalry in Afghanistan continued until the Tsar's government acknowledged the country to be an area of British influence.

Although the country remained neutral during World War I despite the opportunity to strike at British positions in India, in 1919 Amir Amanullah sought to gain popularity by a half-hearted attack on British India. This war lasted only a month, but ended with Britain recognizing the independence of Afghanistan in foreign as well as internal affairs.

Modernization came very slowly to the country during the first half of the 20th century, and its geographical remoteness and rigid Islam kept foreign influence to a minimum. Amanullah was forced from power after returning from an extended foreign trip and proposing reforms. His successor was assassinated in a blood feud. Family and palace intrigues dominated the first three decades of King Zahir's rule (1933-mid-1960s). However, in 1964 the king granted a new constitution that expanded the legal system beyond Islamic religious law and prohibited the king's relatives from serving as minister, chief justice or as a member of the legislature.

As a concession to an educated minority, the king allowed elections for the legislature in 1965. Political parties were not allowed, however, and the king did not permit the elected representatives to assume real law-making power, though the wealthy landowners who dominated the legislature and were able protect their interests and block progressive tax laws.

Before the scheduled 1973 elections, an army coup d'etat deposed the king and abolished the constitution. It was led by Mohammed Daud Khan, the king's cousin and brother-in-law who had previously served as prime minister. He immediately proclaimed the country a republic and named himself both president and prime minister. Thus, the overthrow of the monarchy actually concentrated power in the ruling member of the Mohammedzai family.

President Daud's dictatorial rule failed to satisfy many people, and there were at least three attempts to overthrow him. To legitimize his rule, he managed his election as president in 1977 by a National Assembly (loya jirga), but in 1978 a day-long battle in Kabul between communist sympathizers and loyalists ended with the deaths of thousands, including President Daud. The Communist army officers who led the coup had studied in the Soviet Union and learned the arts of political subversion along with the art of war.

Under Communist Rule, 1978–89

The victors acted in typical Communist fashion. They set up a Revolutionary Council and appointed an elderly poet and journalist as a figurehead president. The new regime rapidly formed close ties with the Soviet Union. Domestically, it adopted a red flag, and radical social and economic measures. A drastic land reform law limited an individual's maximum holding to 15 acres, Islamic schools were closed, and changes in family law conflicted with traditional Islam.

Not surprisingly, opposition surfaced, and perhaps 50,000 to 100,000 people perished during the land reforms. Resistance turned to rebellion, inspired by Islam and its religious teachers. The government sought Soviet aid to crush the widespread rebellion of the mujahidin (meaning "those who undertake jihad"), but the Soviet presence probably inflamed nationalist and Muslim opposition.

Further complicating matters, the Afghan communists were divided into two often hostile factions, Khalq ("Masses") and Parcham ("Banner"). To avert a likely defeat of communism, in late 1979 a Soviet invasion force suddenly attacked Kabul, attacking and killing the (communist) president before installing Babrak Karmal of Parcham as president.

Some 90,000 Soviet troops entered the struggle to defeat the mujahidin. They successfully occupied most of northern Afghanistan and the major cities of Kabul, Herat, and Kandahar, as well as the roads connecting them. However, the mujahi-din, although poorly armed and divided into rival groups, operated across much of the country's rugged terrain, and won many small victories. In response, the Soviets adopted a policy of ruthless air and artillery attacks on towns and villages.

The invasion and its indiscriminate bombing and shelling turned the population into refugees. Nearly five million civilians fled the fighting, some to Iran but most to Pakistan. Their giant refugee camps, funded by Saudi Arabia, other Arab nations, and the United States, became staging bases for the mujahidin.

The Islamic resistance operated most successfully in the mountains near its supply centers in Pakistan. Another stronghold was the Panjsher Valley north of Kabul, not far from the strategic Salang highway linking the capital to northern Afghanistan. There, under the most highly regarded mujahidin commander, Ahmad Shah Masoud, the rebels withstood repeated Soviet attacks. In the west and south, other mujahidin groups fought for Herat and Kandahar, and the fighting destroyed large portions of these two historic cities.

Cruelty and inhumanity accompanied much of the fighting. Soviet forces bombed villages and dropped explosives disguised as toys in rebel areas. Soviet and Afghan troops killed hundreds of civilians in reprisal raids and tortured captured mujahidin before executing. On the other hand, some western journalists reported that rebel groups often preferred to take no prisoners and executed government supporters in newly-captured towns.

The mid-1980s Soviet policies suffered strong condemnation in the world press, even in many "non-aligned nations" that the U.S.S.R. had courted carefully for years. Moscow began to recognize that the Kabul regime remained entirely dependent on Soviet support. The military situation worsened after the United States finally provided some mujahidin with Stinger anti-aircraft missiles and other modern weapons that threatened to neutralize Soviet air power and render very difficult the supply of remote outposts.

Recognizing that Babrak Karmal had proved ineffective, in 1986 the Soviet Union forced his resignation "for health reasons." Najib Ahmadzai, then head of security in Kabul and a leading figure in Parcham, took control of government as the General Secretary of the Communist party. In 1987 he was elected president by a loya jirga (national assembly) dominated by Communists but given a smattering of legitimacy by a few tribal leaders and others.

A more flexible politician than his predecessors, Najib restored the Islamic form of his name, Najibullah, and offered polit-ical concessions, including a coalition government. However, he won over only a few inconsequential groups. By 1988, after Afghan casualties surpassed one million dead plus many millions more wounded or exiled, the Soviet leader, Mikhail Gorbachev, promised to withdraw Soviet troops and let the Afghans decide their future government.

The last Soviet troops departed in 1989 against a background of rocket attacks on Kabul and fierce fighting for several provincial cities. In the capital, crowded by over two million inhabitants, siege conditions appeared, for rebel activity often closed the Salang highway to the north and a Soviet airlift of supplies proved insufficient. Food prices rose sharply, so that the price of a large family's monthly flour—the staple food—exceeded two months' average pay. Malnutrition threatened. However, by summer the guerrillas abandoned their use of mass hunger against the regime and allowed food trucks through. Nevertheless, rocket attacks continued from the surrounding mountains and killed hundreds of people, nearly all of them Muslims and many of them children.

The stalemate at the capital reflected the country at large. The mujahidin fiercely assaulted Jalalabad, between Kabul and the Khyber Pass, but failed despite the highest casualties of the war. Similarly, in Herat, Kandahar and elsewhere the government continued to govern essentially the same cities and territory. Some officials and soldiers defected, but others fought with greater determination, fearing that capture meant death.

Victory eluded the guerrillas largely because they could not unite. Military coordination often proved weak, and separate groups made uncoordinated attacks. Personal antagonisms, ethnic rivalries, and traditional blood-feuds often overshadowed the struggle against the communist regime. In particular, the Pashtun Hizb-i Islami, dominant along the Pakistani border, hijacked supplies intended for its northeastern rival, Masoud's largely Tajik Jamiat-i Islami. Ambushes and battles broke out between them. Shi'a and Sunni mujahidin differed over their concepts of the state. Moreover the majority Sunni fractured between moderate conservatives and fundamentalists, who tended to follow Gulbuddin Hikmatyar of the Hizb-i Islami. In contrast, only a few mujahidin attacked the departing Soviet troops, and several groups arranged informal cease-fires with Kabul.

The disintegration of the Soviet Union in 1991 disrupted food and fuel supplies for Kabul, and the new Russian leaders desired to end an adventure that had cost more than $110 billion. The Kabul government tottered, then collapsed when Gen-

Afghanistan

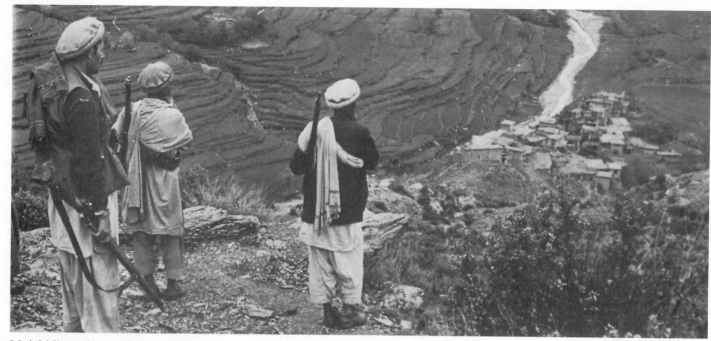

Mujahidin resistance fighters look down on a village after a Soviet aerial attack. At left are terraced crop fields.

eral Abdul Rashid Dostam and his tough, Uzbek militia at Mazar-i-Sharif switched sides and formed an alliance with Ahmad Shah Masoud, the Tajik leader who had captured much of the northeast for the mujahidin. Moving quickly southwards, General Dostam's militia and Masoud's *Jamiat-i Islami* mujahidin cut the Salang highway and captured the Bagram airbase near Kabul. When Gulbuddin Hikmatyar of the *Hizb-i Islami* sent his forces to infiltrate Kabul, Dostam's militia and Masoud's guerrillas then rushed for the city, some flown by air force helicopters. Najibullah attempted to flee, but was captured, and the communist regime formally transferred power to an Islamic Afghan regime in April 1992.

Deprived of their prize, Hikmatyar's forces rocketed the city, killing and maiming the first of tens of thousands of Muslim dead by Muslim hands in the Islamic Republic. However, conditions in the capital did not reflect the country. Some areas enjoyed relative calm under the control of local warlords, and several million refugees returned from Pakistan to their often-destroyed towns and villages.

Kabul changed perceptibly under Islamic rule. Women who previously dressed in jeans and T-shirts now covered their hair and wore long black robes, some perhaps for piety; others to avoid molestation. Alcoholic beverages vanished from stores and hotel bars closed. Former officials and agents of Khad, the secret police, disappeared to avoid reprisals; some executions occurred.

Despite the creation of a Leadership Council to guide the country, politics remained confused. Amid accusations of bribery and pressure, a large council elected Burhanuddin Rabbani of the *Jamiat-i Islami* as president. However, Rabbani failed to win recognition from Hikmatyar and the *Hizb-i-Islami*, and later attempts to bring Hikmatyar into the government also failed, ushering in a four-year struggle to rule Kabul. Rival mujahidin leaders made and broke alliances, all apparently to ensure that no one leader became powerful enough to rule the nation. The most cynical alliance joined Dostam and Hikmatyar, longstanding ideological and ethnic rivals, now united by resentment of Rabbani's rule over Kabul. Blockades on roads ended most travel, and the airport closed. Hundreds of thousands fled.

The Rise of the Taliban

As the nation collapsed into anarchy, a new political force inspired hope. A protest movement of religious scholars, the *Taliban* ("Students") emerged in the southern Pashtun city of Kandahar against the violence, sexual immorality and corruption of local mujahidin. Desiring to establish Islamic government under the leadership of the reclusive Mullah Omar, *Taliban* fighters ended thievery on the roads and established order.

Most *Taliban* conquests were relatively bloodless in a nation suffering great war fatigue. The *Taliban*'s superior firepower was reinforced by the mobility of their four-wheel drive pickups and the obvious faults of many corrupt mujahidin. With little fighting, the *Taliban* quickly conquered much of the Pashtu-speaking south and advanced on the capital. Briefly repulsed by Rabbani's forces, the *Taliban* rapidly conquered Herat in 1995, then launched air and missile attacks against residential areas of Kabul. In 1996 the capital fell, and Najibullah was quickly executed. Aided by Pakistani volunteers and defections among Dostam's officers, in 1998 the *Taliban* conquered the second largest city, Mazar-i Sharif, and much of the north. The opposition *Northern Alliance* led by Dostam and Masoud controlled only the Pan-

Najibullah

A windstorm sweeps down upon an Afghani sheep and camel market

Photo by Jon Markham Morrow

jsher Valley and the far northeast, a region lacking significant cities, plus Shi'a areas in the central mountains.

Taliban rule shocked the world. It banned television and required beards on all men, offenders who trimmed their beards too much risking their noses being cut off. To Western and even much Muslim opinion, the treatment of women defied human dignity and extended far beyond female modesty in dress. Although several hundred thousand war widows struggled to provide for their families, the *Taliban* ordered women not to work outside their homes. Later it relented for necessary tasks like nursing (for female patients only), but it demanded extreme measures to keep men from seeing women even at a distance. Even after such precautions were observed, it closed down UN-sponsored bakeries run by women. After closing universities, the *Taliban* proposed opening them for men only. It apparently desired education for girls to stop at the age of eight, and teachers caught schooling girls in homes were arrested and probably tortured.

Only three countries, most prominently Pakistan and Saudi Arabia, ever extended diplomatic recognition. Russia, India, and several Central Asian republics remained critics, sustaining the *Northern Alliance* and other opposition groups in a bleak existence.

Sanctuary for Osama bin Laden and September 11

The son of a leading Saudi construction magnate from Yemen, Osama bin Laden accepted militant Islamist ideas and joined the Afghan mujahidin to fight the Soviets. He established a loosely-organized society called *al-Qaeda* ("The Base"), and became known for criticizing Arab and Western governments. Pressured by Saudi Arabia and the U.S., he moved to Sudan in the early 1990s, where his violent diatribes against the U.S. led Sudan to ask him to leave. He returned to rural southern Afghanistan, where he established training camps.

In 1998 truck bombs at two American embassies in Africa killed hundreds. Evidence pointed to *al-Qaeda*, but Mullah

Omar refused U.S. demands to hand over Osama, a "guest." UN sanctions followed in 1999 that banned most flights to the country and grounded the national airline. *Al-Qaeda* followers attacked the *U.S.S. Cole* in 2000 in Yemen. After the infamous September 11 attacks, evidence again quickly implicated bin Laden and *al-Qaeda*, and again the *Taliban* refused to hand over Osama, perhaps because on September 9, 2001 Arab suicide bombers assassinated Ahmad Shah Masoud.

On October 6, the U.S. aerial offensive began, with the usual attacks on air defenses, command centers, and communications facilities. U.S. Special Forces infiltrated Afghanistan to strengthen the *Northern Alliance* and to mark targets for smart weapons. Fearing that the U.S. would assist a *Northern Alliance* attack along the front lines, the *Taliban* had moved its troops and many Arab and Pakistani volunteers to the northern city of Kunduz before the bombing began. This left the other major cities lightly defended.

General Dostam recognized that the capture of Mazar-i Sharif would break the

Afghanistan

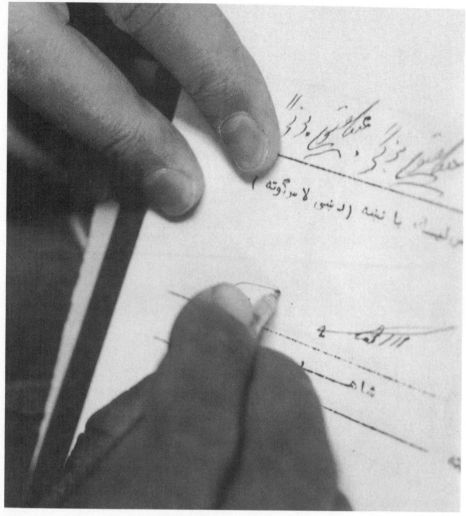

An Afghani farmer signs an application for a tractor

Taliban's supply line and prevent a retreat by the troops concentrated in the north. With U.S. air support, Dostam's forces fought bitterly for the city and won. Days later, airpower enabled the largely Tajik forces of the *Northern Alliance* to break through the *Taliban* defenses outside Kabul and enter the city, almost unopposed. Despite fears that the city might again become a battlefield between rival mujahidin, the population celebrated the *Taliban's* collapse and the legalization of music, kite flying, and education for girls.

In the south, particularly around Mullah Omar's home town of Kandahar, the *Taliban* faded more slowly. The Pashtun heartland could not be captured by the *Northern Alliance*. However, local anti-*Taliban* rivals emerged to provide the soldiers for the conquest. In the eastern mountains of Paktia province U.S. troops and Afghan militiamen fought mopping-up operations near Gardez. Large caves in the rugged terrain had provided refuge for the mujahidin fighting the Soviets. The

vast weapons stockpiles had passed to the *Taliban*, and Osama bin Laden himself had frequented the area. However, though possibly wounded, he eluded his pursuers.

Karzai, Warlords, and Elections

Hamid Karzai, a Pashtun of notable family, was selected by representatives of several factions at a council in Germany to serve as the provisional national leader. Civilized, thoughtful, and distinguished, Karzai persuaded wealthier nations to donate nearly $5 billion in aid. The money was critical: civil servants had not been paid in seven months, and the treasury was bare.

Hundreds of delegates, from all significant population groups and even some (appointed) women, formed a much-anticipated *loya jirga* in 2002 to select an interim ruler pending a new constitution and elections. After the aged ex-King Zahir Shah, who came to the throne in 1933, withdrew from consideration, the *loya jirga* selected Hamid Karzai as president.

Forming his cabinet proved difficult. Tajiks from the *Northern Alliance* and other militia leaders demanded significant roles, disproportionate to their ethnic groups' shares of the population. Personal rivalries and conflicting political ideologies also complicated matters. The *Northern Alliance* eventually received the ministries of defense, finance, and foreign affairs, although gradually its members would be forced from office.

His cabinet formed, Karzai faced significant problems in actually ruling. Rather than disarm after victory, the militias remained, and their leaders often controlled their home districts. U.S. forces, disinterested in nation-building, worsened the problem by hiring sometimes unsavory warlords as mercenaries against suspected *Taliban* and *al-Qaeda* hideouts. For practical reasons—there were fewer American soldiers in Afghanistan than police in New York—the U.S. could not disarm the militias. In 2003 the UN-sponsored Disarmament, Demobilization and Reintegration Program at last offered militiamen money, clothes and food vouchers in exchange for weapons.

Lacking supreme authority, Karzai risked becoming little more powerful than the mayor of Kabul, protected by American bodyguards and an international security force. However, militia warlords were not all petty thugs who seized provincial capitals and forced Karzai's governors to flee. In Herat, Ismail Khan ignored Kabul's regulations and appropriated customs revenues locally, depriving Kabul of tax revenues. But he ran a fairly effective though authoritarian mini-state. Its streets were clean and paved, and opium production was minimal.

Several achievements marked Karzai's early years in office. Three million children entered school, and two million refugees returned. Aid organizations began widespread humanitarian relief. Committees drafted a new constitution that delicately managed the role of Islam. Business flourished as refugees invested funds held abroad, and the economy grew rapidly. The central bank issued a new currency, also called the Afghani, worth 100 times the value of the old one. The new bills conveniently ended the ability of some local rulers to print their own. Reconstruction projects repaired the Salang tunnel and the Kabul-Kandahar highway. Entrepreneurs established mobile phone systems in several cities.

The 2004 presidential election allowed the nation to render its verdict on Hamid Karzai. Karzai picked a Tajik—the brother of Ahmad Shah Masoud—to share the ticket. The voters proved highly enthusiastic about the first free election, and more of them registered to vote than the probable

President Hamid Karzai flanked by his two vice presidents, Mohammed Fahim, a Tajik, and Karim Khalili, a Hazara.

adult population. Despite *Taliban* threats, little violence occurred, and Karzai won 55% of the vote. Significantly, Karzai's share of the vote usually reflected the Pashtun share of the provincial population, from about 90% near Kandahar in the south to only 10% in the Tajik northeast. In effect, the vote became an ethnic census.

Uniquely for the Southern Asia, the constitution reserves 25% of the seats in parliament for women. While some very traditional relatives of warlords were elected, even a woman as outspoken as Malalai Joya won a seat. True to her reputation, she addressed the opening session of parliament and attacked the warlords among its members as criminals "with hands stained by the blood of the people."

The *Taliban* Return

In early 2005 the top U.S. general proclaimed security "exceptionally good." However, when spring returned the *Taliban* and foreign volunteers launched attacks on isolated troops, murdered aid workers, assassinated officials, harassed candidates, and destroyed schools. Techniques from the Iraqi insurgency, particularly roadside bombs and even suicide bombings, made their appearance. Anti-American activists seized on an alleged desecration of the Qur'an to stir up deadly riots. Progress in creating a national army, meanwhile, was hampered by low literacy levels, poor pay, and low compensation for soldiers killed in battle.

Trusting local intelligence sources, American forces sometimes struck hard at innocent civilians. An important convoy and

several wedding celebrations were bombed, killing dozens of civilians and wounding scores. Informants wishing to settle old scores had suggested that *Taliban* suspects might be in the area, and Afghans celebrating the joyful occasion by firing into the air became the targets of missiles. By 2006, the *Taliban* cynically adopted the tactic of entering a village, attracting U.S. attention, and then withdrawing before the air strikes, which inevitably killed innocent civilians. President Karzai later protested the policy to the U.S., complaints that were repeated with increasing forcefulness. More than once, the U.S. forces denied causing civilian deaths, only later to admit some casualties.

Why, years after the ouster of the *Taliban*, have casualties climbed to hundreds per month in the summer? Why do they operate on such a scale that they dominate parts of Helmand, Zabul, Uruzgan and Kandahar provinces in the south, while enforcing rules as far north as Kunduz? In one dramatic weekend in 2008, they freed all the inmates of Kandahar prison and took over villages just a few miles outside of the city. According to U.S. intelligence estimates, they control 10% of the countryside to the government's 30%, with the remaining territory tribal.

Analysts suggest that a number of factors encouraged the resurgence. Most of all, the U.S. and its NATO allies initially failed to occupy the south, but left the region's pacification to traditional warlords who failed to impose decisions from Kabul. Over time, these warlords became corrupt as well as inefficient, so much so

that NATO commanders successfully demanded the replacement of several governors before agreeing to replace U.S. forces there.

Second, the government proved fairly ineffective even in relatively safe cities. Cities desperately needed new housing, streets repaired, and sewers that worked. An army of the unemployed could have provided the labor for much of the work. But between a penniless state and lavish foreign aid spent on experts' salaries and other priorities, reconstruction proved slow. Polls indicated that a majority felt that foreign aid had not benefitted them. The police proved both corrupt and inefficient, and violence increased in Kandahar, the capital, and elsewhere, particularly in the form of crime and suicide bombings. Though a presidential election campaign was approaching, the NATO secretary general publicly blasted "corrupt and inefficient" government, and demanded government action, after the blood shed and money donated by NATO members.

President Karzai stresses two additional causes. U.S. and allied air attacks killed somewhere between 200 (U.S. estimates) and 600 (UN) civilians in 2008. Popular dissatisfaction with the high casualty rate became a national issue, with 77% of respondents in a national poll condemning them. Finally, *Taliban* fighters enjoyed sanctuary across the border in Pakistan. Nevertheless, according to survey results, a majority of Afghans still support the international troops and Karzai himself—though the levels fell between 2007 and 2009.

Afghanistan

Finally, the *Taliban* movement itself proved remarkably resilient, spreading quietly across the rural countryside, collecting taxes and attacking girls schools when powerful enough to do so. Joining nationalist slogans to the religious, it depicted Karzi as a foreign agent and sought to create a sense of inevitable victory after the foreigners' inevitable departure. Throughout, both the *Taliban* and warlords enjoyed great profits from the opium trade.

The Challenge of Opium

For the long run, the greatest challenge to a democratic administration will be the production and trade of opium, because it funds warlords, strengthens the *Taliban*, and corrupts the government. In 2001 the *Taliban* had prohibited growing opium poppies, but under Karzai the absence of authority encouraged many impoverished farmers to resume opium cultivation *because opium provides between 40 and 200 times the income of wheat* per acre. Local Muslim theologians agree that Muslims should not consume it, though they differ as to whether growing opium for use by non-Muslims really conflicts with Islam.

To avoid arousing anti-American feelings, U.S. forces initially did not attack opium fields or refining facilities. After rising ten-fold in 2002, opium production doubled again in 2003. Presently, production totals about 8,000 tons from 13 of the 34 provinces. The industry's value is worth over half the GDP, and the *Taliban* stronghold of Helmand province produces more opium than the second-largest producing nation, Myanmar. Total world output had reached only 600 tons in 1999.

The opium trade weakens Karzai's government in many ways. It strengthens many warlords, who tax or even trade the drug. Corruption flourishes, as payoffs protect certain fields and smugglers. An internationally-funded program to pay farmers to destroy their opium crops ended up in many cases paying the warlords' supporters instead. Aerial spraying to destroy the crops upsets aid agencies, who reason that farmers would be driven to desperation if no alternative income was provided. Though costing about $1 billion annually, the eradication effort is considered a failure in many provinces. The combination of broader economic development and stricter enforcement of laws may prove the key, but achieving either, let alone both, remains beyond the reach of the Karzai administration in many southern areas.

Election Fraud Weakens Government

As presidential elections approached in 2009, President Karzai's popularity reached new lows, and American support for him wavered. His 40 election rivals included candidates of many viewpoints, some with ability and close contact with the U.S., a sign of increasing distrust between Kabul and Washington. However, Karzai deftly played several issues, standing up to Washington over casualties from air attacks and demanding Supreme Court approval for the postponement of the elections from April to August, a delay necessary for both security and administrative reasons.

Few of Karzai's rivals enjoyed national stature of any significance, and polls indicated that two of his most serious rivals enjoyed limited support. Moreover, Pashtun voters would not likely support a Tajik or other minority candidate, and Karzai reached out to that community by carefully selecting General Mohammed Fahim, a former Tajik militia commander, as a vice presidential nominee. The president's campaign also enlisted the support of tribal leaders, officials, and others.

Although the election passed off peacefully, allegations of mass fraud quickly overwhelmed initial claims of an impressive Karzai victory (55% to 30% for Dr. Abdullah Abdullah). Fraud apparently touched the entire process, beginning with voter registration in the absence of an identification system and continuing through bribery and falsified ballots. The results plunged the country into a political and constitutional crisis, and the election commission stripped Karzai of sufficient votes to force a run-off vote. However, Dr. Abdullah conceded, claiming that the run-off could not be free and fair.

Despite waning popularity after years in office, President Karzai would likely have won a fair contest against a non-Pashtun. Instead his triumph in a corrupt election left him weakened internationally and domestically. When he attempted to repay political allies by appointing them to the cabinet, parliament rejected nearly 75% of his nominees. Relations with the U.S. and other nations declined, as donors threatened to halt aid to ministries run by corrupt politicians. However, corruption seems almost universal, with a UN estimate that bribe payments totalled about 25% of legal GDP, and half the population bribing at least one official annually.

To no surprise, administrative failures handicapped the struggle against the *Taliban*. Some estimates suggested that in 2010, only 25% of the most important regions of the country were secure and supporting the government. The arrival of 30,000 additional U.S. troops provided increased firepower, especially in the south.

However, the Afghan military is underpaid, largely illiterate, and poorly trained. While the troops are considered a vital partner to U.S. and NATO forces, they had difficulty in maintaining security in towns and villages after *Taliban* fighters had been defeated. As a consequence, the much-publicized U.S. offensive to bring security to Kandahar, the second largest city, was delayed.

Against indications of a military stalemate, both Afghan officials and Western diplomats sought a compromise with the *Taliban*, and the president summoned delegates to a loya jirga to discuss options for peace. However, at least publicly, the *Taliban* refuse to negotiate as long as foreign troops remain.

Political Institutions: The constitution created in 2003 by a *loya jirga* (national assembly) reflects the Pashtun preference for a presidential form of government. The more-powerful of the two houses is popularly-elected lower house, the *Wolesi Jirga*. Another contentious issue, the status of minority languages, was settled by granting minority languages legal status in districts where their speakers are a majority. The constitution does not explicitly base legislation on Muslim law, the *Sharia*. However, by demanding that legislation conform to Islam, it allows courts to impose the *Sharia* in practice.

During the war against the Soviets, a number of political parties existed in name, most of them the political expression of mujahidin leaders. Most of these parties no longer exist. New laws attempt to break the links between militias and politicians, by prohibiting formal links between parties and fighters.

Culture: Like many other nations of the modern world, Afghanistan does not possess a culture which is entirely distinct from that of nearby lands. This is true not only of the folkways of a mainly pastoral and agricultural society, but also of religion, art and political organization.

The ties of blood and tribe are strong. Loyalty to the extended family, clan and ethnic group often exceeds nationalism. It is considered not only a duty, but the normal way of doing things to side with cousins and other relatives or to aid them in time of need, as well as to share in the happy times of weddings, births (especially of sons) and the celebration of holidays. The most firmly implanted of all secular holidays is *No Ruz*, in honor of the first day of spring—March 21st or 22nd.

Most Afghans farm. They live in small villages, typically located on a slope at the edge of a cultivated valley. Until the civil war, many people had never traveled any distance from their birthplace, and most villages are still fairly isolated. A few nomads move frequently in search of pasturage for their sheep, goats, cattle and (in the case of a few tribes), camels.

Religion is as natural to the people of Afghanistan as the air they breathe. The name of God is invoked on every possible occasion, and political leaders can oppose the dominance of religious practices only at their peril. Though many people speak Dari, a form of Persian, most Afghans feel a general distinctness because they are Sunni Muslims, while most Iranians are Shi'a.

Literary expression largely takes the form of poetry, ranging from the intricate, elegant poems of professionals to the more direct, forceful and colorful folk poetry which displays the soul of the people. Poetry often expressed and preserved Pashtun identity and cultural values of Pashtuns, and the works of two 17th century poets, the warrior Khushhal Khan Khattak and the mystic Rahman Baba are still popular in a country where only 7% of the population enjoys electricity and poetry readings are large public events.

Especially in Pashtun areas, fundamentalist objections and suspicions often extend to all Western ideas, a view that limits education. The UN Development Report for 2005 ranked the educational system as the worst in the world. In some areas, it has not progressed since then. As few as 14% of the adult population can read and write, while until recently a high school diploma was almost unknown outside the cities and larger towns. Although the new constitution enshrines the right of education for girls, only a very few girls' high schools exist, and those who attend them often suffer threats and harassment.

Higher education, backed by the communists, suffered during the civil wars of the 1990s and essentially collapsed under the *Taliban*. During the first five years of Karzai's rule, the number of public universities and teacher-training institutes tripled, to 19, and enrollment climbed rapidly to 40,000 students—nearly ten-fold. But since 50,000 high school students took university entrance exams in 2005, admission is highly competitive, despite often-dilapidated facilities, shortages of faculty, and poor security.

Religion and local traditions combine with poverty and illiteracy to continue to create great hardship for women even though the worst fundamentalist regulations have been removed and women are permitted to seek employment. According to the UN, women are often condemned to lives of malnutrition, exclusion from public life, rape, violence and forced marriage. Amnesty International blames feudal customs for women being treated like property—and men suffering no consequences for abusing them. Among the most unfortunate are the tens of thousands of war widows, and young women forced into arranged marriage. Many of these girls are married before the legal age of 18, and many find their conditions desperate. Suicide attempts are on the rise. Cultural change will take longer than a new series of legal edicts.

Despite its poverty, and current cultural attitudes against the visual arts and public presentations by women, as the turnstile of Asia Afghanistan historically produced masterworks of art and decoration, variously showing Islamic, Chinese, Indian, and Hellenistic influences. Many such *objets d'art* were already gathered in Kabul's National Museum when the Soviet invasion took place in the 1970s. The Bactrian Hoard, some 22,000 pieces dating back 2,000 years and considered the "most important gold treasure ever found in Asia," was discovered about the same time.

One of the most remarkable if unlikely band of heroes during the country's 30 years of conflict were a small group of museum guards and curators who hid and protected the most valuable objects in the National Museum. Some objects were apparently stored in the presidential palace, in a safe that even a notable militia leader could not blast open. Artifacts left in the National Museum suffered rocket attacks, looting, and finally the deliberate destruction of art by *Taliban* activists. De-

A young Afghan farmer

Afghanistan

spite suffering unemployment and cases of torture, those who hid the precious objects succeeded in saving them.

The museum curators could not save from the *Taliban* two outdoor statues of the Buddha near Bamian. Carved into a cliff over 1,300 years ago, before the Muslim conquest of Afghanistan, the larger of the two statues measured about 150 feet high and ranked as the tallest standing Buddha in the world. Despite an international outcry, troops used artillery to demolish these unique relics.

Economy: The civil war inflicted suffering on some of the world's poorest people and postponed badly-needed reconstruction. Poverty stalks the land, and only a few African countries suffer worse conditions; indeed, since the ouster of the *Taliban* in 2001, the country has slipped from 117 to 181 in the UN rankings, the second lowest. The child mortality rate exceeds that of every other country. Millions of land mines still threaten. Over 100,000 Afghans, many of them children, have lost limbs; in 2005 the casualty rate averaged 100 dead or wounded per month.

Agriculture is the livelihood of the country. Yet, only 20% of the country at most can be irrigated, and less than half of that potential farm land is actually cultivated. In good years the country is self-sufficient in cereal grains, but frequent droughts require grain imports. The high price of cotton on world markets has encouraged increased its production, though of course present profits lie in opium.

The skins and wool of the Karakul sheep remain important exports in keeping with long tradition. The United States has been one of the principal purchasers, particularly of the skins of the Karakul lambs. While the wool of the mature sheep is coarse, stringy and brown, that of the newborn lambs is tightly curled and a glossy black, highly prized as a material for fur coats.

The northern part of the country has significant deposits of natural gas and a little oil. Natural gas exports to the Soviet Union were halted when the withdrawing Soviets capped the wells, but may eventually supply Uzbekistan as well as the area around Mazar-i Sharif. Mineral resources, such as iron ore and coal in the Hindu Kush Mountains, have not yet been exploited. Perhaps these and other mineral resources contributed to Soviet desires to control the country. Soviet data led American geologists to survey the country much more intensively, leading to the discovery of the largest known lithium deposits and huge veins of iron, copper, cobalt, gold and other minerals that could make Afghanistan a world mining center.

Developing such resources will prove difficult in a country with minimal roads and railroads. Given these conditions, despite the U.S. military involvement and discovery of the resources, western companies often fail to invest. A Chinese company is developing one of the world's largest copper mines in Logar province at a cost of $3 billion, and other Chinese investment seems likely.

The Future: Insecurity nourishes fundamentalism, feuds, and opium production. Given its international backing, Hamid Karzai's government must support a) the fight against the *Taliban* and b) the war against opium. Waging these struggles simultaneously is difficult: some allies against the *Taliban* can only earn a decent living from the opium trade. Many war-

Afghan vegetable vendor, Kabul
Photo by Jon Markham Morrow

lords will oppose effective central government, recognizing that opium production and heroin refining provide the profits to pay their fighters, who lack alternative employment. Facing all this, by 2009 a national poll suggested only 40% of Afghans considered the country headed in the right direction, compared to 75% in 2005.

On the surface, change seems on the way. In response to rising anti-American, anti-NATO, and general anti-foreign feelings, the Obama administration replaced the U.S. commander for the country; his successor proclaimed the importance of avoiding civilian casualties. More troops will enable rural areas to be held, not simply swept of *Taliban* suspects then left uncontrolled for their return. The *Taliban* sanctuary in Pakistan may fall to military occupation, thus weakening the movement.

Given President Karzai's flawed reelection victory, no dramatic changes in the level of corruption or the effectiveness of government seem likely, and the *Taliban* have few incentives for a national deal. So behind the more vigorous military campaign, expect lower American goals for the war. Informal compromises may even occur that leave some areas with a strong *Taliban* presence under an Afghan truce.

Ahmad Shah Masoud, Tajik Mujahidin Leader

The People's Republic of Bangladesh

Passengers disembark from a ferry boat at Narayanganj, Bangladesh

WORLD BANK Photo

Area: 55,598 square miles (143,998 sq. km.). Land appears and disappears from the rivers and Bay of Bengal.

Population: 167 million.

Capital City: Dhaka (pop. 6.8 million, plus suburbs).

Climate: Tropical and rain soaked; the country is subject to destructive hurricanes.

Neighboring Countries: Surrounded by India on three sides; a short border with Burma lies on the southeast.

Time Zone: GMT +6. When it is midnight in Bangladesh, it is noon in Chicago.

Official Language: Bengali.

Other Principal Tongues: English (in schools and commerce).

Ethnic Background: Over 98% Bengali, except small tribal groups in the Chittagong hills.

Principal Religion: Islam (87%) and Hinduism (11%).

Chief Commercial Products: Garments, textiles, jute, tea, rice, wheat, sugar, hides.

Major Trading Partners: U.S., India, China, U.K., Japan, United Arab Emirates.

Currency: 1 Taka = 100 paisa

Former Colonial Status: Part of British India (1765–1947) then a province of Pakistan under the name *East Pakistan* (1947–1971).

Independence Date: Proclaimed independent in March 1971; achieved in December.

National Day: December 16.

Chief of State: President Zillur Rahman (2009).

Head of Government: Hasina Wajed, Prime Minister (2009).

National Flag: A green field with a large red circle in the middle.

Gross Domestic Product: $99 billion (at current prices); $259 billion (PPP), 2008.

GDP per capita: about $1500 (PPP), but 30% the population lives on less than one dollar per day.

Most of the land of Bangladesh is flat, wet alluvial plain, formed over scores of centuries by three great river systems depositing their silt as they near the Bay of Bengal. Indeed these rivers, the Ganges, the Brahmaputra and the Meghna, lose their identities as their waters become mingled in a maze of waterways and swamps along the southern coast. Much of the country is less than 30 feet above sea level.

Four traditional scourges annually threaten life and property in Bangladesh. The rivers flood during the summer monsoons, covering half or more of the land. Tropical storms like Cyclone Sidr (2007)—equivalent to hurricanes—sweep in from

208

the Bay of Bengal, strengthened by a funnel effect of the shoreline that creates high tides of salt water. Disease spread by polluted waters, and famine resulting from destroyed crops, complete the list.

Of all the countries in Asia, nature threatens humans most in Bangladesh. Bacteria flourish in the tropical climate, and the frequent floods multiply the consequences of inadequate sanitation. Dense population in a country with little industry forces landless farmers onto silt islands barely above high tide. Then floods, or even shifting river channels, destroy land and crops, threatening famine for those who can not afford to buy food. Beyond individual and local tragedies, the statistics of overpopulation paint a grim picture for the future. Although roughly three-quarters of its people live by farming and less than 20% in urban areas, the country's population density exceeds 1,800 per square mile—far higher than the Netherlands in Europe with its employment concentrated in commerce, industry, and services.

The 1998 monsoon floods illustrated the harshness of life. As rivers overflowed their banks, the deluge submerged two-thirds of the country, and destroyed one home in five. It stranded millions of people on roofs, trees and small areas of high ground where they were threatened by disease and poisonous snakes. Unofficial estimates by relief workers placed the death toll at around 800. The economic impact appeared equally severe: thousands of miles of roads destroyed, bridges swept away and half the season's rice seedlings lost. The depth of the water surpassed even the 1988 flood (the previous "worst in memory"), but better precautions reduced the death toll. Ironically, within a few months the northeast faced drought.

Although foreign aid arrived as soon as Dhaka airport reopened, the long-term future appears grim. Ecologists blame the worsening floods on the deforestation of the Himalaya Mountains in India and Nepal, where the great rivers of Bangladesh originate. The loss of forest increases flooding for two reasons. First, the soil retains less water, causing faster runoff. Second, the rapid runoff carries deposits of silt downstream, raising the level of river beds and diverting them. Former president Ershad declared the floods a "man-made curse," and proposed regional cooperation to end them, as well as better control of the rivers in Bangladesh. However, geologists also suspect the river delta is simply sinking into the ocean.

Where family farms measure a few acres at best, only rice provides subsistence. Two or even three crops per year, tended with much labor and scarcely any

machinery, enable the country in a good year almost to feed itself.

Unfortunately, another consequence of the same deforestation of mountain forests is seasonal drought in the west of the country. Essentially, by late winter and spring too little water flows through the region's many rivers. Shipping becomes dangerous, and irrigation canals dry up just when water is vital for young crops. One solution, the construction of dams to regulate water flow, will require years of study before construction begins, and the estimated cost exceeds $1 billion.

Geography forces the use of boat and barge for most travel and transportation. There are 3,000 miles of navigable rivers, but only about 10,000 miles of surfaced roads. The marshy ground and many rivers render road building difficult and costly. Many streams of the delta are not bridged, and ferry service causes many delays.

A small region southeast of Chittagong is located above the deltas and flood plains of the rivers. Its hills, valleys and forests make this region, known as the Chittagong Hill Tracts, the only one in the nation where virtually all the land is not used for agriculture.

History: Bangladesh and territory to the west for many centuries bore the native name *Bangla*. The region was designated by English officials as the presidency, or state, of Bengal in 1699. With the partitioning of British India and independence of India and Pakistan in 1947, the territory became East Pakistan. Although united by the bond of a common religion, the Bengalis of East Pakistan were often unhappy with government dominated by men from West Pakistan.

Dissatisfaction grew rapidly in the late 1960s, with resentment over attempts to promote Urdu, the major language of West Pakistan, and the award most foreign aid and development projects to West Pakistan. In 1970 the *Awami League* of Sheikh Mujibur Rahman pledged autonomy for East Pakistan, and won a majority of seats in elections for the National Assembly of Pakistan. However, General Yahya Khan, the president, prevented the National Assembly from meeting, and hence the *Awami League* from taking power. Sheikh Mujib was arrested. Uprisings then broke out in the East.

In March, 1971 Bangladesh ("The Bengal Nation") proclaimed its independence. A popular rebellion broke out, but for nine months the Pakistani occupation army repressed it, reportedly with three million Bengali deaths (a figure disputed by Pakistan). Millions more sought refuge across the border, and in December 1971 India attacked the Pakistani occupiers. Two weeks later they surrendered.

During 1972 the new nation and its government took form. The Indian army withdrew and massive international aid arrived for the great tasks of aiding the refugees and restoring an economy devastated by war. Months were required for the nearly 10 million Bengalis who had fled to India in 1971 to return to their homeland—often to find that their homes had been destroyed.

Sheikh Mujibur Rahman dominated political life during these years. Still imprisoned in West Pakistan when independence was won, he was immediately declared president of the new nation. Freed in 1972, he received a hero's welcome in Dhaka. His first official acts were to resign as president and take the office of prime minister.

During the first years of independence, political power lay fully in the hands of Sheikh Mujib and loyal members of his *Awami League*, especially after the 1973 elections gave the party almost all the 300 seats in the National Assembly. However, those in power frequently sought personal gain. Much of the international relief sent to alleviate starvation and suffering was used by government officials and army officers to enrich themselves.

Bangladesh

Public feeling eventually turned strongly against the authorities over their failure to improve the lot of the poverty-stricken masses. Even Sheikh Mujib's personal popularity melted away amidst the corruption, banditry and violent disorders. He made himself a virtual dictator. He used emergency regulations to censor the press rigorously and he jailed critics of the administration without trial.

In 1975, a group of military officers murdered Mujib and overthrew his government. They ruled only briefly, however, for soon General Ziaur Rahman seized power. No relation to Mujib, Zia at first placed a retired Supreme Court justice as president, and then assumed the title himself in 1977.

Although initially a military dictator, President Zia moved toward allowing political activity by organizing his own *Bangladesh National Party (BNP)*. Zia won the 1978 presidential election that year, but his assassination during an unsuccessful military coup in 1981 ended an era of relative stability.

Severe political difficulties filled the entire following decade. Civilian government faltered, and in 1982 General Hussain Mohammad Ershad led a bloodless coup, pledging to purge the country of corruption, then to return power to civilians. However, Ershad soon proclaimed himself president, and later postponed the promised elections indefinitely. Stability eluded his dictatorship despite his imposition of martial law and banning political activities.

Remarkably for a Muslim country, the two largest parties have been led by women. Sheikh Hasina Wajed, the daughter of Sheikh Mujibur Rahman, inherited his title, a rare occurrence in the Islamic world, and has led the *Awami League*. Her rival, Khaleda Zia, adopted the Hindu royal title of begum after the death of her husband, Ziaur Rahman. She has headed the more conservative *BNP* that her husband founded. Both women cooperated in strikes, protests and boycotts against President Ershad.

Demonstrations and riots in 1990 followed the familiar strike patterns, but this time the opposition groups jointly demanded Ershad's immediate resignation and free elections. Riots followed the reported arrests of opposition leaders, and troops fired on crowds killing dozens. When members of Ershad's own *Jatiya Party* left parliament and senior army officers refused to take control, Ershad resigned.

The parliamentary election campaign of 1991, like every election since, seemed an often bitter competition between two dead men. The *Awami League* extolled Mujibur Rahman, while the *BNP* praised Ziaur Rahman. The results brought Khaleda Zia and the *BNP* an eventual majority in the 300 elected seats. She took office as prime minister; the *Awami League*, more socialist and pro-Indian, led the opposition.

The two women alternated in power for nearly all the next 15 years, the periods of exception being the months immediately preceding an election, when a nonpartisan interim administration was appointed. Typically, the economy did well at mid-term, but as parliamentary elections approached, there were usually strident accusations of corruption, parliamentary walkouts, frequent general strikes, demonstrations, riots, and travel blockades organized by the opposition party. These often brought the economy to a halt.

One major change during the 1990s was investment by foreign firms. In over 1,000 clothing factories, a million women stitched garments for U.S. firms, producing about 60% of the country's exports. By

Sheikh Hasina Wajed, Prime Minister

attracting women out of their homes, and placing even modest earnings in their hands, the factories encouraged social liberalization as well as economic growth.

For Sheikh Hasina, one contentious issue remained bringing to justice the plotters who overthrew and murdered Sheikh Mujib and nearly his entire family. Sheikh Hasina herself escaped death only because she was abroad; two decades later as prime minister she ordered the arrest of surviving suspects, despite a promise of immunity issued by military rulers. General Ziaur Rahman apparently did not participate in the plot, but after he took power he sent some of the plotters abroad, and the *BNP* considered him the real hero of independence. Symbolically, Sheikh Hasina's government dismantled the pontoon bridge to Ziaur Rahman's island grave, removed his name from the airport, and closed exhibits in the national museum. Finally, in 2010, five convicted plotters were hanged for the murders.

In the 2001 general elections, the less-secular *BNP* won an overwhelming victory at the polls. With its allies (including the *Jamaat-i Islami*) it captured two-thirds of the seats in parliament. The overwhelming majority provided Khaleda Zia the ability to move quickly against the public's two greatest concerns: corruption and crime. However, she failed with the first. Repeatedly ranked the most corrupt nation on earth by Transparency International, Bangladesh proved particularly unable to punish high-level bribe-takers. The anti-corruption bureau operated out of the prime minister's office, and never charged prominent members of a ruling party.

Popular discontent with crime became so great that mobs lynched nearly a dozen suspected criminals in the capital during broad daylight. Unfortunately, immediate reductions in the crime rate were unlikely,

Fishing for shrimp and rock lobster

Country boats on a Bangladesh river

because the police were considered the most corrupt institution in the country. Crimes with particularly low rates of punishment include throwing acid at women's faces and attacks on the Hindu minority. Recognizing that she had failed to keep her election promise to reduce violent crime, in 2003 the prime minister ordered 40,000 troops into the cities to help police in a massive roundup of suspected criminals. However, crime levels fell only modestly, and public lynching continued despite the military's involvement.

Political violence was disproportionately aimed at the *Awami League*. The nation was shocked by a grenade and shooting attack on Sheikh Hasina during a political rally in

Begum Khaleda Zia

the capital city that killed nearly twenty people, some of them prominent party leaders. Usually, the assailants in political violence escaped capture and trial, but *Awami League* claims that the *BNP* was behind some killings proved justified by the murder conviction of some party members.

Numbering dozens of publicly identified groups, the extreme Islamist movement includes both peaceful and violent activists. Secular politicians are not their only victims: movie theaters, circuses, and other entertainments have been attacked. Possibly because the *BNP* governed in coalition with the fundamentalist *Jamaat-i Islam*, the government only really cracked down after the extremist *Jamaat-ul-Mujahideen* exploded 500 bombs across the country timed to the same hour. The same group attacked several courts and assassinated two judges—since the *Jamaat* desires to impose Shari'a Islamic law, courts are a particular target. After they were captured and tried, six *Jamaat* leaders were executed in 2007.

Demonstrations and general strikes began in 2006 months before the appointment of an interim administration to replace the *BNP* cabinet during the last months before elections. Faulting the outdated and allegedly falsified electoral register, the *Awami League* determined to boycott the elections, and plunged the country into chaos with violence, strikes, and transport blockades. Finally, with the *BNP* already claiming victory in uncontested races, in 2007 the president declared a state of emergency and appointed Dr. Fakhruddin Ahmad to head an interim government supervised by the military.

A former central banker, Dr. Ahmad determined create a voting system worthy of the public's faith. A massive new electoral register was ordered, complete with digital photographs and fingerprints of perhaps 90 million adults, to deter anyone from voting several times. To provide time for the registration, the election was postponed for nearly two years, and the names of 12 million fake voters were removed from the rolls.

In common with his military backers, Dr. Ahmad also sought to punish corrupt politicians and halt the destructive rivalry between the two major parties. All political activity was banned. Dozens of former cabinet members and leaders both parties found themselves under arrest, as did Khaleda Zia's son, Tarique Rahman and eventually Khaleda herself, charged with corruption. Sheikh Hasina, who was initially abroad, was arrested after her return and charged with extortion.

After considerable political jostling, in December 2008 campaigning began for parliamentary elections, again with the same two parties headed by the same two women, both out on bail for corruption charges they considered politically motivated, making the same promises of cheaper food and tackling corruption and crime. Sheikh Hasina's *Awami League* and its allies won an overwhelming victory, gaining 250 of the 300 seats.

The month following her swearing-in as prime minister, Sheikh Hasina faced a brutal revolt by troops of the paramilitary border guards, the Bangladesh Rifles over low pay and the appointment of army of-

Bangladesh

The bicycle-rickshaws of bustling Dhaka.

ficers as their commanders. Scores of officers and civilians were murdered, but the revolt failed, and an investigation into its causes was promptly released publicly.

Political Parties: Four major political groups represent most political aspirations within the country. The *Bangladesh National Party* favors economic liberalization and a conservative Muslim orientation, in contrast to the traditionally socialist and pro-Indian leanings of the *Awami League*. Although discredited by revelations of corruption during Ershad's years, his *Jatiya Party* retains seats in parliament, more a collection of aspiring politicians than an ideological force.

Fundamentalist Muslims form the *Jamaat-i Islami*, which elected Golam Azam as its leader in 1991. However, in 1971 he had opposed Bangladesh's independence, and for years lived in Dhaka as a Pakistani. His selection as a party leader has led to strikes demanding his trial for treason. Mock trials indicated he should hang; nevertheless, the party joined the *BNP* coalition in 2001. Its current leader, Motiur Rahman Nizami, was arrested on corruption charges in 2008.

One particularly unfortunate side effect of the political strife takes place on university campuses. Well over 100 students have died in political clashes. Arsonists burned dormitories and other facilities as the students became players—merely pawns—in the struggle to topple one regime or another. The strife worsened in the late 1980s, when Dhaka University canceled classes for 120 of 150 working days. In recent times, pitched political battles became rare, but women students, frequently harassed and even raped, demonstrated for better security.

After independence, the structure of government alternated between presidential and parliamentary styles. However, in 1991 the newly-elected parliament restored its prime minister to supremacy and rendered the president a figurehead.

Culture: For the three-quarters of the population directly involved in farming, plus the small-town merchants, craftsmen and officials, life revolves around the agricultural seasons. The typical farmer lives with his large family in a simple hut of thatch and mud built on a low mound of earth for protection against monsoon floods. Since the land is extremely fertile, a very small plot can be one man's farm. He sells the produce from his little farm at one of the small towns located on the intersections of waterways. He can afford no modern luxuries; his main entertainment is sitting with his family and friends, talking about the day's events and problems.

Reflecting the poverty of the country, only 40% of the population is literate, with the rate for women half that for men. Fortunately, widespread primary education is increasing the rate for each: roughly 75% of all children receive some formal education.

Besides vocational and professional institutes, there are several universities, the largest of them the University of Dhaka. Students clashed with police in 1992, after the government approved a law to punish those caught cheating on final exams with five to ten years in prison. Although other students recognize that widespread cheating diminishes the respectability of their degrees, 4,000 students were expelled in 2000 for cheating on the English exam required for university graduation.

Despite Bangladesh's staggering population, it has only a handful of large cities. With the allure of a capital city's opportunities, Metropolitan Dhaka's population has passed the ten million mark, and it consumes about half the electricity produced in the country. Ringed by rivers, the city was forced to expand upwards rather than outwards and recently experienced a building boom. Inadequate control of building permits and the illegal construction of high rises near the airport have led international aviation authorities to demand their removal. The second largest city is Chittagong, the nation's main port, with more than a million.

The country's 135 million Muslims form the world's fourth largest Muslim community, following those of Indonesia, Pakistan and India. Nevertheless, the Provisional Constitution made the nation a secular state that provides all religions with equal legal standing. Public holidays include Muslim holy days, Christmas, and various Hindu and Buddhist festivals. Islam itself shows a national coloring here, influenced by some Hindu and other ideas.

The recent rise of fundamentalist Islamic groups has coincided with increasing intolerance. Often those who suffered were women. For example, Dhaka University reimposed the "Sunset Law," a 1922 regulation requiring women students to return to their dormitories before darkness. The restriction, said one faculty member, was "a shield to protect the women's chastity." Outside the university, women's participation in sport has been condemned, and women swimmers were excluded from a swim meet after threats of violence.

Other women suffered much worse harm. A few hundred women (and men) annually suffer acid attacks that disfigure their faces, usually because of land disputes against their families or by rejected suitors. Fortunately, after special fast-track courts were established to impose the death penalty on offenders quickly, the number of these assaults has fallen.

Society victimizes women in other ways. Composed of village elders and clerics,

Children fortunate enough to attend school

**Thousands of children work
as domestic help**

village arbitration councils designed to settle property disputes illegally ordered whippings or even stoning for several girls and women charged with sexual immorality. Other women and young girls are victimized into debauchery: according to police reports, kidnappers annually sell some 10,000 into brothels, some abroad.

Death by hanging is the sentence commonly demanded by Islamic militants for both Taslima Nasreen and Farida Rahman. The latter, a Member of Parliament, aroused the ire of fundamentalist Muslims when she noted that there would be no harm in allowing women to inherit more than the small percentage set by the Qur'an. Nasreen, a feminist whose novel of the plight of Hindus in Bangladesh became a bestseller, denied that she had proposed that the Qur'an be revised to fit the modern world. Charged with blasphemy, she overcame her legal problems, but fled the country because of threats on her life.

There are two principal dialects of the Bangla language. The old literary one is much admired but not understood by ordinary Bengalis, while the modern colloquial, understood and used by both the educated and uneducated is the country's language. It is written in a form of the *Nagari* alphabet, widely used for the languages of India.

The earliest preserved literature in Bangla dates to the 14th century. Until two centuries ago, it was only verse, intended to be recited or sung. Bangla prose began in 1800 when a missionary, with the help of native assistants, translated the Bible into that language. The vast literary outpouring of the 19th and 20th centuries included novels and drama. The short stories and poems of Rabindranath Tagore received the Nobel Prize for literature in 1913, one of the first awards for a non-European language. Besides modern approaches such as this, there remain the traditional poetry and other aspects of the rich culture of Bengal.

However flourishing, the Bangla culture is not the culture of all inhabitants. During the partition of India in 1947, thousands of Muslims from Bihar and elsewhere moved to East Bengal. Loyal to a Muslim state rather than a Bengali one, they tended to support Pakistan during the conflict in 1971. With Pakistan unable, or perhaps unwilling, to bear the cost of these two-time refugees, about 300,000 of them live destitute in camps in Bangladesh, awaiting some distant solution to their lives of desperation. A high court decision in 2008 granted citizenship to those born in the country after 1950, an important step towards greater rights and economic opportunity.

Other non-Bengalis live in the Chittagong Hills, where some local tribes practice Buddhism, Christianity or Hinduism. Violence flared in the 1970s after Bengalis moved into the area seeking land. By the mid 1990s, the scattered violence of 20 years had caused over 8,000 deaths, and thousands of tribesmen fled to India and Burma. Following a peace treaty in 1997, some 35,000 refugees returned from India, but slow implementation of the accord leaves some observers fearing renewed violence.

Economy: Even today, most Bangladeshis live on farms. Across most of the country, the climate and soil combine to produce good yields of rice, and in years without catastrophes more than 10 million tons are harvested. However, this is not enough to feed the large population, and output falls after devastating floods or cyclones. The government has made valiant efforts to increase food production—for instance by digging irrigation canals to water an extra crop in the dry season. Much food still must be imported, and paid for partly by foreign aid.

The country's traditional export crop was jute, the tough plant fiber used to make burlap and rope. When industrial nations turned increasingly to synthetic fibers, world demand for jute declined, and Bangladesh suffered falling profits and cuts in wages and employment. For decades the leading source of jobs and exports, the jute industry now employs only a few thousand workers. Their conditions are pitiful: when strikers in 1995 demanded raising the minimum wage of less than $40 per month, the privatized mills paid sub-minimum wages and cut their workforces further. After continuing losses, in 2002 the government closed the Adamjee Jute Mills, at one stroke putting 19,000 workers out of work.

The poverty results partly from misguided economic policies, past and present. Seeking to raise the standard of living by encouraging industry, early in 1972 the new country took over the businesses, banks and industries owned by West Pakistanis. It then nationalized most other foreign trade, banks and basic industry, leaving only some British tea and jute interests privately owned.

During two decades of mismanagement, few government-owned businesses ever earned a profit. Sectors like telecommunications, electricity and banking still remain inefficient under government ownership. The nationally-owned Biman Bangladesh Airlines managed its fleet of aging aircraft so poorly that it reportedly lost $80,000 on each flight to New York, owed millions of dollars for jet fuel, and could not pay for repairs on several aircraft. The airline cut jobs severely in 2007, both to reduce payroll and attract a foreign partner.

Privatization and large-scale investment by Japanese and Korean firms seemed the best hope for economic expansion in the early 1990s, but instead, employment grew in an unexpected way. Hundreds of small clothing factories sprang up to employ growing numbers of workers to produce coats, dresses and other garments for export. More than one million women in cities and in towns found jobs in the industry, despite low safety standards and appalling wages of roughly $1 a day, about half that of men.

Thanks to the previously insignificant level of exports, Bangladeshi garments were not subject to international quotas, and output often rose at 10%–20% per year. Besides earning important foreign exchange—by 2006, 80% of all export earn-

Water, water, everywhere . . . river traffic

Bangladesh

ings—the industry may improve social conditions by providing vital income for women. However, wages remain abysmal, in some cases less than $20 per month. Touched off by dismissals at one factory, strikes over wages and safety issues broke out in 2006, and some 80 factories were set ablaze, before promises were made of higher pay. Workers demanded higher wages again in 2010, to $72 per month, still among the lowest in the world, and about one-sixth the amount necessary to house and feed nutritiously a family of four.

For men born to poor families—the vast majority in the country—the route to prosperity often involved working abroad, particularly in the oil states around the Persian Gulf. Some six million held jobs abroad in 2008, mostly as laborers in construction and domestic service. Unfortunately, the world recession left tens of thousands of the migrant workers without jobs, and often still owing substantial debts to the middlemen who had arranged their overseas employment

Recent discoveries of natural gas, both onshore and offshore, offer potential economic benefits, if appropriate policies can be created. The greatest dispute involves whether the gas should be exported to India, where a ready market exists in Calcutta. The foreign companies involved in discovering and developing the fields desire to do so, partly to sell in a more prosperous market. However, nationalists strongly oppose such sales, arguing that in a country where only 18% of the population is connected to electricity, there is a huge market for the gas in power plants as well as in producing fertilizer and re-

placing gasoline in buses and trucks. Following the unwillingness of the government to permit exports, Shell and Unocal, the largest companies involved, sold their interests to smaller companies more willing to make risky investments. The lack of investment now threatens to reduce supplies below national needs by 2015.

One major nonpolitical issue facing the government is arsenic poison that threatens the water supply of nearly half the population. The arsenic occurs naturally in the soil, and water from deep wells drilled to deliver water with lower bacteria levels frequently carries traces of arsenic. Though not immediately fatal, the arsenic levels often cause scattered tumors and may lead to cancer; some two million people suffer from arsenic poisoning. In 2006 scientists at Rice University in the U.S. discovered that the arsenic would attach to particles of iron oxide (i.e., rust) about 1/5,000 the width of a human hair. In turn, a simple magnet could then remove the iron oxide, but it will take years to provide filters to the 25 million people who knowingly poison themselves by drinking impure water.

Roughly 50 million Bangladeshis exist below the poverty line, and their daily incomes of $1 mean they often survive on only one meal a day. As always, the poorest are usually women and children; these paid a large price when political chaos interrupted work and deterred investment. By any standard, Bangladesh remains one of the poorest nations in the world, and public health statistics illustrate the poverty. A majority of children are malnourished and stunted. Sixty percent of the

population lacks access to even simple health clinics, and about 80% of homes have no electricity.

Nevertheless, there are some success stories. In the mid-1980s, children composed 40% of the workforce, a rate that officially fell below 10% by the end of the decade. In 2009, estimates suggested that about half of all children aged 6–10 attended school, though only 10% of teenagers enrolled in high school.

One reason that some families could afford to have their children studying rather than working was the Grameen Bank. Founded by Muhammad Yunus in 1976, the bank specializes in making small loans to poor individuals who have productive ideas but lack property to use as security for a loan. In 2006, when he and the bank received the Nobel Peace Prize, Yunus's microcredit program had nearly 7 million customers, the vast majority of them women who repaid their loans on time. Microcredit thus empowered those at the bottom of the social scale and stimulated a revolution of sorts.

The Future: To the surprise of many, Bangladesh enjoyed a relatively clean election that provided a clear majority in parliament. Stable government appears likely in the short run under Sheikh Hasina and the *Awami League* while the *Bangladesh National Party* attempts to regroup.

The challenges remain enormous, from rising river levels (which the prime minister desires to tame) to poverty so vast that many families depend on child labor for regular meals and two-thirds of the population lacks access to electricity.

"Two women in Maijpara"

Taktsang ("The Tiger's Nest") Monastery, situated high in a cliff near Paro in western Bhutan, was destroyed by fire in April 1998. The King has called the incident a national disaster and promised to rebuild it. According to legend, Padma Sambhava—or Guru Rinpoche, as he is also known—flew here on a tiger to meditate when he was introducing Buddhism into Tibet and Bhutan from India in the 8th century A.D. The monastery was built on the site at a later date.

Photo by Edwin Bernbaum

Bhutan

Area: 14,812 square miles (38,364 sq. km.).

Population: 670,000 (2005 census; IMF); 2.3 million (UN, 2007).

Capital City: Thimphu (pop. 100,000, estimated).

Climate: Frigid in the high mountains, temperate with good rainfall in the central valley and extremely hot and humid with torrential rains on the south.

Neighboring Countries: India (South and East); China (North).

Time Zone: GMT +6.

Official Language: Dzongkha (Tibetan dialect), with English the language of schooling.

Other Principal Tongues: Sarchopkha, a Tibetan dialect, and Nepalese in the south.

Ethnic Background: Ngalop or Bhutanese (60%), Sharchops of Indo-Mongolian origin in the East (20%), Nepalese in the southwest (15%), and smaller aboriginal groups.

Principal Religions: Mahayana Buddhism (about 80%) and Hinduism.

Chief Commercial Products: Hydroelectric power, lumber and wood products, cement, fruit, rice, yaks and other livestock, woven textiles and other handicrafts.

Major Trading Partner: India.

Currency: 1 Ngultrum = 100 chetrum.

Historical Status: Independent, though subject to guidance from Britain and then India.

Date of U.N. Membership: 1971.

National Day: December 17, honoring the first king (1907).

Chief of State: Jigme Khesar Namgyal Wangchuck, the *Druk Gyalpo* ("Dragon King").

Prime Minister: Jigmi Y. Thinley.

National Flag: A rectangular field of yellow and vermillion, divided diagonally with a large white serpent-like dragon in the center.

Gross Domestic Product: $1.5 billion (at current prices); $4.1 billion (Purchasing Power Parity), 2008.

GDP per capita: $6,100 (PPP, 2007).

A small nation squeezed between two giants, Bhutan shares the cultural of Tibet across its Chinese border, while its trade and political alignment lie with India to the south.

Geographically, Bhutan resembles Nepal—both are located on the southern slopes of the Himalayan Mountains. Bhutan's rivers rise in the Great Himalayas in the north and flow southward through intensively-cultivated valleys. The rivers all flow into India and empty into the Brahmaputra River.

This land of rugged natural beauty presents a striking contrast between the snow-clad northern peaks, the lower mountain

slopes covered with woods, and the dense, lush undergrowth of the southern foothills. Deer, tigers, elephants and other wildlife live mostly in the foothills.

History: Few documentary sources provide details of the early history of this land. In the 9th century, Tibetan-speaking peoples entered the rugged mountain valleys. Followers of Mahayana Buddhism, by the 15th century they structured their society around fortified monasteries known as dzongs, and maintained links with Tibet. However, there was limited central authority the leading lama, the Dharma Raja, and raids against the expanding British East India Company ended with a treaty in 1865 that cost Bhutan territory, but gained recognition of its autonomy and a British subsidy.

After defeating his rivals in a series of civil wars, Ugyen Wangchuck, Penlop (governor) of Tongsa, became the dominant power, and in 1907 an assembly of lamas, chiefs and officials elected him the country's first hereditary *Druk Gyalpo*, or Dragon King. Authority since then has passed from father to son.

Britain recognized Bhutan by the 1910 Treaty of Punakha, and gained authority over its foreign affairs. Bhutan signed the treaty partly in fear of Chinese claims to its territory, based on alleged Chinese con-

trol from Tibet in the 18th century. A new treaty in 1949 with India recognized Bhutan's independence and provided free trade; it was revised in 2007 to provide Bhutan more freedom in military and diplomatic matters. India provides an annual subsidy that accounts for much government revenue.

After China claimed parts of the country in the 1950s, defense relations were strengthened with India. The border with China is not demarcated and remains closed, but Chinese troops allegedly crossed it in 2005 and built roads. Bhutan's joining the United Nations marked the nation's full independence (1971).

Until the mid-20th century, Bhutan imposed a rigid isolation upon itself, so that it remained as closed to the world as Tibet. However, when Jigme Dorji Wangchuck became Druk Gyalpo in 1952, he introduced changes. He freed slaves, ended the custom of making his subjects bow down before him with their faces on the floor, set up schools, restricted land ownership, modernized the system of land taxes and established the Tsongdu, or National Assembly.

When Jigme Dorji Wangchuck died in 1972, his 17-year-old son, Jigme Singye Wangchuck, ascended the throne. Under the new ruler the country continued its slow awakening to the modern world. In

216

1988, responding to public worries about the succession, the king married publicly the four sisters he previously had wed privately. The celebration distinctly echoed the king's desire to preserve Bhutan's society from outside influences: foreign diplomats were not invited.

Two changes in 1999 brought the population into direct contact with the world outside when Bhutan inaugurated internet service and lifted its ban on the corrupting influence of television. The government intended the single channel to present national arts and culture, rather than rebroadcast Hollywood or Indian programs. However, many viewers preferred to connect to cable, so when a wrestling channel and American music channels enticed too many Bhutanese, the government blocked them.

Ethnic tensions represent a continuing challenge to the country. Many ethnic Bhutanese have feared that the Nepalese minority in the lowlands, boosted by illegal Indian and Nepali migrants across poorly guarded frontiers, threatened to become a majority. In response, the monarchy classified them as aliens and vastly reduced the official estimate of population. As part of educational reforms, the required teaching of Nepali in schools was dropped.

In 1990 riots and demonstrations broke out in southern Bhutan, apparently organized by the (illegal) *Bhutan People's Party* and other Nepali groups. Police and troops repressed the disturbances, and some 100,000 people sought refuge in Nepal. The king took steps to reduce tensions, including reopening schools and reappointing some officials of Nepali origin. The U.S. has offered to accept over half of the refugees, whose camps have been infiltrated by Maoists and other extremists.

In 2004 Bhutan became the only country to ban the sale of cigarettes and chewing tobacco, though smoking itself is not yet illegal. Bhutan's first ruler banned the

Jigme Khesar Namgyal Wangchuck, the Druk Gyalpo or "Dragon King"

use of tobacco in government buildings, but modern arguments for the ban revolved around economics: the government pays medical care, and can ill-afford to subsidize unhealthy habits. Health authorities also fear another social danger. The stresses and opportunities of modernization have encouraged abuse of alcohol. By one estimate 30% of hospital deaths are due to alcoholism.

King Jigme Singye Wangchuck unexpectedly abdicated in 2006 in favor of his eldest son, Jigme Khesar Namgyal Wangchuck. Young and single, educated in the U.S. and Britain, he had won respect in the kingdom and popularity on official trips abroad. His coronation in 2008 proved a lavish affair by local standards, with thousands of foreign dignitaries and media personality.

Politics: Though by tradition an absolute ruler, King Jigme Singye Wangchuck yielded additional powers in 1998 and then extended democracy with the 2005 constitution. It retains the monarch as the

symbol of the state—but he or she must retire at age 65.

A fascinating mixture of tradition and modernity, the constitution was released on the web to facilitate discussion. It stresses the spiritual heritage as well as the government's responsibility to protect biodiversity and maintain a minimum forest cover of 60%. Legislative authority resides in a parliament of two houses, the elected National Assembly and the non-partisan National Council. To answer the vexing question of political parties, the National Assembly includes two, and only two, political parties. The leader of the larger serves as prime minister.

Elections in 2007–08 determined the members of first the National Council and then the National Assembly. Because candidates must hold a university degree, the victors were young, some aged in their 20s. Two parties contested the National Assembly elections, the *People's Democratic Party (PDP)* closely linked to the queen mother, and the *Bhutan Harmony Party*, headed by a commoner, Jigmi Thinley. He claimed to represent ordinary Bhutanese, and became prime minister after his party won 44 of the 47 seats.

Culture: The population is comprised mostly of hardy tillers of the soil and herders. They live in small communities scattered in the fertile valleys cut deeply into the rugged mountains of the central and southern part of the country. No one lives permanently in the high mountains of the north, while those who live in the narrow tropical fringe along the southern border lead a way of life quite different from the rest of Bhutan. Citizens are required by law to wear traditional dress; a quick trip to the pharmacy in jeans and T-shirt may result in arrest.

No real urban centers exist yet. Communities tend to cluster around a dzong, found in every major valley and settled region. A dzong was originally a great fort built on a strategic spot commanding a river. In times of war, people from the surrounding area sought refuge there. After warlords passed from the scene, dzongs came to serve as administrative centers, monasteries, or even warehouses. Many of them have prayer halls with elaborately carved interiors, walls covered with religious paintings, statues of Buddha and quarters for officials, lamas and guilds.

The new national capital of Thimphu has been constructed beside the great Tashi Chho Dzong, once the headquarters of powerful penlops. Thimphu reflects the country's determination to modernize in its own fashion. All buildings must be constructed in the traditional style, and the only traffic light was removed. However, the government provides TV broadcasts,

Capital with a difference: Thimphu has no traffic lights.

Bhutan

and the newspaper, originally a public relations sheet, appears in Dzongkha, English, and Nepali.

Economy: Unlike most of the world, where the economy as measured by the Gross Domestic Product (GDP) is considered the chief measure of well-being, Bhutan values an even less precise measure, the Gross National Happiness (GNH). Given the prevailing Buddhist philosophy, this stresses inner peace and satisfaction, rather than material wealth, and a rise in the suicide rate is therefore a matter of serious concern.

Government policy encourages people to remain on the land, essentially as small-scale farmers and herdsmen who nevertheless enjoy access to electricity, simple medical care, and education. While this preserves the culture and therefore GNH, the small, inefficient farms can not compete in price with imported grains and meat. To protect its small farmers, Bhutan has not joined the World Trade Organization.

Given the topography, the small country produces a wide range of foods, ranging from rice and tropical fruits through citrus and temperate-climate vegetables. The mountain slopes provide abundant pasturage for livestock. Cattle are common up to more than 12,000 feet above sea level in summer, and yaks are grazed at even higher elevations.

Since 1961 a series of five-year plans have encouraged development, and usually stressed investment in roads, education, agriculture, health, minerals and hydroelectric power. Exports of electricity to India now provide government revenues and foreign exchange. Recent policy favored privatizing the ownership of several corporations, including the cement and insurance companies. The goal of privatization was to encourage a modern middle class, because unlike government-run corporations in most countries, these were profitable monopolies.

After building two hotels to provide lodging for foreign dignitaries attending the King's coronation in 1974, Bhutan cautiously permitted a small tourist industry to develop, and two five-star hotels were opened in 2005. Travelers may enter by one of only two ways: a difficult land route, or by regularly scheduled air service to Paro by Druk Air.

In deference to local sensitivities, temples and other holy places were closed to tourists in 1988, but the Dzongs are still accessible. In addition to cultural tours through Dzongs, town and villages, there are also organized treks along steep mountain trails to isolated mountain valleys. Added to concern about tourism's sometimes corrosive effects on culture, traditions, and values, environmentalists worry about its pollution.

To preserve its natural resources, Bhutan has banned hunting wildlife, prohibited lumbering, and provided a special route for migrating elephants. The government even warned against the cutting of young trees for use as poles for Buddhist prayer flags believed to guide the dead. However, reports of erosion and polluted water in some locations suggest that population pressure may degrade Bhutan just as it does India and Nepal.

The Future: Bhutan features one of the last races between preservation of a culture and the modern culture of materialism and personal pleasure. Television, videos, and even education corrode the personal inner peace so important to the philosophy of the country.

Most societies lose this race. But the calm determination of Bhutan's monarchs offers the hope that this small country might succeed in preserving, happily, its uniqueness.

Farm buildings in Bhutan

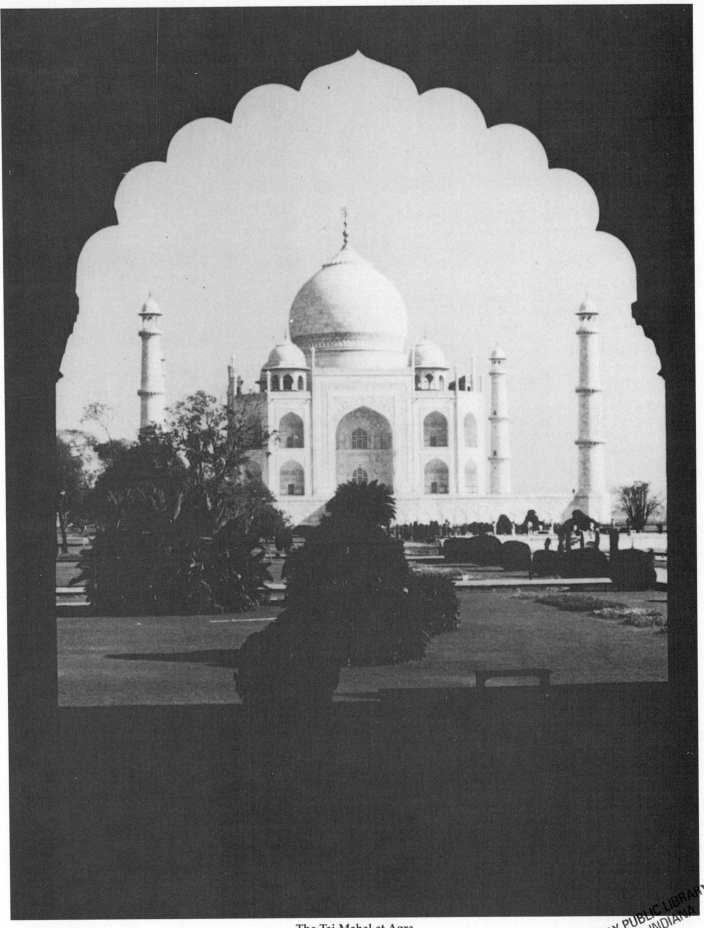

The Taj Mahal at Agra

The Republic of India

Area: 1,210,700 square miles (3,136,500 sq. km.), including Indian sector of Jammu and Kashmir.

Population: 1.220 billion.

Capital City: New Delhi (pop. 3 million; with Delhi, 14 million).

Climate: Tropical except for the northern mountains. The three seasons are rainy (June to October), cool (November to February), and hot (March to May).

Neighboring Countries: Pakistan (Northwest); China, Nepal, Bhutan (North); Burma, Bangladesh (East); Sri Lanka (off southern coast).

Time Zone: GMT + 5 hours. At noon, in New York, it is 10:30 P.M. in India.

Official Languages: Hindi and English. Seventeen languages have regional status, including Assamese, Bengali, Gujarati, Kannada, Kashmiri, Malayalam, Marathi, Oriya, Punjabi, Sanskrit, Tamil, Telugu and Urdu.

Other Principal Tongues: Newspapers within India are reportedly published in at least 49 languages.

Ethnic Background: Communities are differentiated primarily on the basis of language and religion; differences in physical characteristics do not generally correspond with these communal distinctions.

Principal Religions: Hinduism (84%), Islam (11%), Christianity (2%), Sikhism (0.7%) Buddhism (0.7%), other.

Chief Commercial Products: Textiles, clothing, gems and jewelry, steel, cement, automobiles, machinery, computer software, motorcycles, processed food, consumer appliances, coal, chemicals, and various metals.

Main Agricultural Produce and Livestock: Rice, wheat, barley, potatoes, corn (maize), cassava, bananas, coconuts, beans, mangoes, tea, coffee, tobacco, pepper, sugar cane, cattle, goats, buffalo, sheep, pigs and poultry.

Major Trading Partners: U.S., Japan, U.K., Germany, Russia, Iraq (pre-war).

Currency: Rupee (= 100 paisa).

Former Colonial Status: British Indian Empire (1858–1947).

National Day: January 26, Republic Day.

Chief of State: Pratibha Patil, President (2007).

Head of Government: Manmohan Singh, Prime Minister (2004)

National Flag: A tricolor with equal horizontal bands of deep saffron, white and dark green. Centered on the white stripe is the wheel of Asoka in navy blue.

Gross Domestic Product: $1,340 billion (at current prices); $3,800 billion (Purchasing Power Parity), 2008.

GDP per capita: $3,125 (PPP), 2008.

Second only to China in population, India occupies most of the South Asian subcontinent and ranks seventh among the world's nations in area. The size of its population, combined with its historical and cultural heritage developed over thousands of years, often overwhelm the imagination and make comparisons difficult. For example, India's population exceeds that of all Africa south of the Sahara, or more than the population of all the other countries in this volume combined. Indeed, the annual growth in the number of India's citizens exceeds the population of most countries in this volume. A land of stunning contrasts in geography as well as the

quality of human life, India represents a major cultural force in the modern world. In areas as diverse as religion, food, and computer software engineering, India's influence greatly exceeds its boundaries.

Three major topographical regions divide the subcontinent. On the northern borderlands tower the Himalayas, the perpetual snow and ice of their summits overlooking lesser peaks and foothills at their base. Rivers and streams from the mountains flow south to the great plain that provides a home for much of the country's population. Centered on the Ganges River, the plain is also watered by the Indus on the west and the Brahmaputra on the east. The third region is the peninsula that juts out into the ocean, a triangle of plateaus, valleys and mountains. The coastal plains around this region are moist and tropical, particularly in the narrow plain between the Arabian Sea and the Western Ghat Mountains, and densely populated.

Extreme variations in rainfall and temperatures produced great variations in vegetation. On average only a few inches

India

BRITISH INDIA

them. Land reform was set aside, and the upper classes conciliated.

The Mutiny encouraged Britain to abandon the goal of Europeanizing Indians, and the emphasis turned instead to public works to make the land more productive within the empire. The spirit of imperial grandeur led, in 1877, the government to proclaim Queen Victoria Empress of India.

Two trends in India during imperial rule deserve mention. First, colonial laws and officials provided unity for a vast region previously divided by ethnic and religious groups. A single administrative and judicial system, roads, railways and postal communications aided the physical unification. Western-style education provided a new professional class with a common language, English, and greatly contributed to a sense of unity.

Second, a national consciousness distinct from religious or social feelings arose against foreign rule. Its first outward sign was the formation in 1885 of the *Indian National Congress,* which reflected the aspirations of the new professional class. In its early years, it failed to persuade the colonial rulers to recognize its demands, and it also proved unable to incite the illiterate masses, especially villagers, to any kind of action.

Though it continued to develop among the tiny minority of Indians educated in English, nationalism had no visible effect otherwise until World War I. Then a man with rare gifts of leadership, Mohandas Karamchand Gandhi, later called *Mahatma* ("Great Soul"), returned to India as an attorney experienced as a political activist in South Africa. Unrest and occasional outbursts of violence were already beginning when his public work in India began. His insight and an ability to translate nationalist ideas into terms that had meaning for the uneducated masses of Hindus enabled him to capture the leadership of the *Indian National Congress* by 1920.

Gandhi's methods appealed to the religious nature of Hindus. Rejecting violence, the weapon he used was passive resistance, a policy of non-cooperation with colonial rule. After he imposed the necessary discipline on his followers, non-cooperation became a weapon that the British could not effectively oppose. Slowly, the *Congress* demands won concessions. Indians were allowed into the Indian civil service and were granted limited local self-government.

Although *Congress* was not intended as a Hindu party, Gandhi was not able to bridge the gap between Hindus and Muslims in India, and tensions between the two communities increased. The leading Islamic party was the *All-Muslim League* led by Muhammad Ali Jinnah. Strongly

fall annually in the western desert of Rajasthan, but the record in one village of Assam approached *40 feet* of rainfall in a year. The northeast is typically the wettest region; it and the ocean side of the Western Ghats generally receive more than 100 inches of precipitation annually. Most of the rain falls during the summer, brought by the southwest monsoon. The Ganges Plain, the northwest and the coast of Tamil Nadu also receive varying amounts of winter rainfall.

The land and the climate show great contrasts—and so do the people. Religious practices vary greatly within the Hindu majority and there are also followers of a multitude of other religions. Folkways differ considerably in various parts of the country, or even between communities in the same city. Sometime allegiances to language, religion, and ethnic group threaten the unity of India. However, a functioning democracy and economic integration reinforce the national unity forged in the independence struggle against the British.

History: While India possesses a cultural tradition that extends back for several thousand years, the formation of the present nation began only with the British conquest (see Historical Background) some 250 years ago. By bringing many small states and petty princes under its

rule, Britain laid the foundation for both the Republic of India and other nations in the region.

As regions fell under East India Company rule, they desperately needed reform. India was overtaxed and undereducated, with crime rampant and the arts in decay. Several Indian practices offended British opinion, from the several hundred annual burnings of widows and other ritual murders to values expressed by idol worship. However, British reforms and the seizure of several Indian states aroused both Muslim and Hindu opinion by the 1850s, especially in the north, and led directly to the so-called Indian Mutiny of 1857 (see Historical Background). Surprising the British by both its extent and its ferocity, the Mutiny drew strength from traditional groups outside the army as well as native troops from both Hindu and Muslim backgrounds. Although the rebellion was crushed, Parliament ended the East India Company's rule and replaced it with British colonial administration.

The Mutiny produced major changes. Loyal ethnic groups thereafter played greater roles in the army, and the close contact between British officers and Indian troops built traditions that remain today. Because the princes had generally remained loyal, the policy of replacing their rule in conquered territories was abandoned in favor of close contacts with

221

India

focused on the interests of the Muslim community, Jinnah and his party led the move to partition India, although recent scholarship shows the crucial role played in this decision by rebuffs from Jawaharlal Nehru, president of the *Congress Party,* in 1946.

Independence and Partition

India gained independence as a dominion in August, 1947, after British officials gained agreement for a partition plan creating a separate Muslim nation (see Pakistan). The precise borders between India and Pakistan remained a British secret, lest the inevitable violence following their announcement spoil the festivities. Jawaharlal Nehru, Gandhi's chief lieutenant in the *Congress Party,* became the country's first prime minister.

Strife between Hindus and Muslims plagued the partition. In many frontier areas the population was mixed, making it impossible to divide Muslims from Hindus and others. In the end, the British chairman of the boundary commission had to rule on the borders. The most dangerous regions were the Punjab in the northwest and Bengal in the east.

In the Punjab, savage fighting erupted between the two religious communities. Fearful of strife and of becoming a minority, Hindus on the Pakistani side of the border fled toward India while Muslims on the Indian side fled toward Pakistan. Nearly four million people took part in this two-way flight. Many thousands of them were massacred on both sides. To avert further bloodshed, Gandhi toured the country, preaching peace and cooperation between the two religious groups, an activity credited with averting massacres in Bengal. However, Hindu extremists hostile to his moderation assassinated Gandhi in 1948.

Government and Politics

A new constitution in 1950 made India a fully independent republic and broke the last formal ties to Britain. The presidency is a largely ceremonial post; real power lies with the prime minister and the lower house of the legislature, known as the *Lok Sabha* or "House of the People." In contrast, the relatively powerless members of the upper house (*Rajya Sabha* or "Council of States") reflect the state governments that select them. The Prime Minister governs with the support of Parliament, and maintaining a majority in the *Lok Sabha* regularly proved difficult after the rise of regional parties prevented any party from winning a majority.

A major challenge at independence was the formation of a modern administration. Britain had often maintained the existing rulers' authority as dependents of the British Crown, and in 1947 Britain restored the rights that the rulers had lost generations earlier. Thus, the Indian government faced some 562 "princely states" ranging in size from Hyderabad (82,000 square miles, 16 million subjects) to tiny states of a few square miles.

To retain the rights of all these rulers meant chaos. By 1949, through persuasion, threats, and promises of pensions (withdrawn some 20 years later), India had been reorganized into 30 states and territories. Two cases proved especially difficult. The Muslim ruler of Hyderabad, which had a large Hindu majority, sought independence, but unrest and the alleged abuse of Hindus provided an opportunity for the central government to send in troops. His authority thus undermined, the ruler ceded Hyderabad to the central government in 1949.

The other case was a dispute with tribesmen and Pakistan over the princely state of Jammu and Kashmir, where the population was largely Muslim but the ruling family was Hindu. Kashmir remains unresolved after a half century (see Disputed Territory: Kashmir).

Boundaries in British India, often drawn by historical circumstances, frequently separated people speaking the same language. Despite occasional ethnic violence, the government altered the political map of India. Many states disappeared, and new states were created out of parts of the old. For example, Andhra Pradesh, largely Telugu-speaking, emerged from what had been Hyderabad and Madras despite desires of some for a separate Telangana state in the interior.

Though generally successful, the creation of ethnic states faced difficulties in the northeast and in Punjab. Near the borders of Tibet and Burma, many tribes in remote areas of what had been called Assam speak their own languages and are less influenced by Hindu culture. Several small ethnic groups there desired their own states, or even independence, and sometimes adopted guerrilla warfare to achieve it. The first ethnic state, Nagaland, was created in 1961. In the 1970s and 1980s, more states followed, all among India's smallest in population. Political instability has been frequent, whether the consequence of independence movements or an influx of others wishing to settle there.

Arunachal Pradesh faces an unusual difficulty: China claimed almost the entire state, based on an interpretation of Tibet's one-time borders. Chinese claims also threatened Sikkim, squeezed between Nepal and Bhutan. Sikkim gained statehood in 1975, following an Indian protectorate established in 1950 and intervention at the request of the Maharajah in 1974.

Ethnic tensions also arose over the state of Punjab, the country's breadbasket, with its south strongly Hindu but the rest largely Sikh, a separate religious group whose members desired their own state. Punjab was divided in 1966, right down to the capital, Chandigarh, between the Sikh Punjab and a Hindi-speaking state of Hariana. Nevertheless, Sikh militants demanded the creation of an independent "Khalistan." In 1983 they occupied the Golden Temple in Amritsar, the focus of Sikh religious life. Faced with outright insurrection, Indira Gandhi ordered the army to assault the temple. Many Sikhs, not all of them militants, resisted the invasion of their shrine, and heavy casualties resulted. Sikh separatism remained acute for a decade complicated by Sikh rivalries, government repression, and unfulfilled promises of justice. Only after the return of civilian rule in the 1990s did violence subside in a conflict that claimed about 20,000 lives.

Three distinctive regions received statehood in 2000, each one reflecting separate cultures or local resentments. Mineral-rich Jharkhand, formed from districts of Bihar, holds major deposits of mica, coal, iron and copper. However, after decades of Bihar's corrupt politics and exploitation by government-owned mining and steel companies, the region is littered with the remains of dying industries. Like the tribal state of Chhattisgarh created at the same time, Jharkhand faces rebellions and violence from radical groups. Lying just west of Nepal, Uttaranchal shares with it

Mahatma **Gandhi**

India

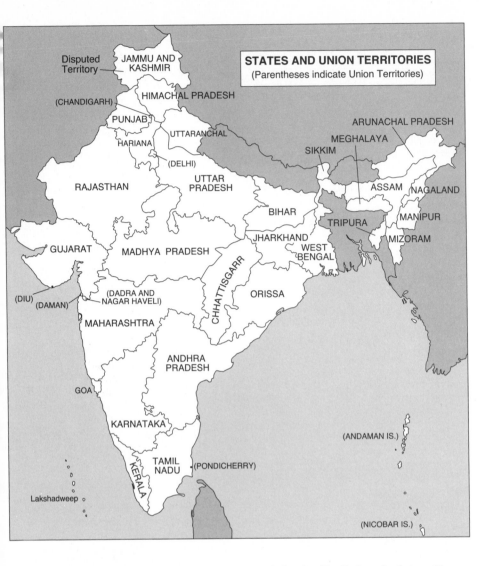

STATES AND UNION TERRITORIES
(Parentheses indicate Union Territories)

Disputed Territory

JAMMU AND KASHMIR

HIMACHAL PRADESH

(CHANDIGARH)

PUNJAB

UTTARANCHAL

HARIANA

(DELHI)

RAJASTHAN

UTTAR PRADESH

ARUNACHAL PRADESH

MEGHALAYA

SIKKIM

ASSAM

NAGALAND

BIHAR

TRIPURA

MANIPUR

(DIU)

JHARKHAND

WEST BENGAL

MIZORAM

GUJARAT

MADHYA PRADESH

(DAMAN)

(DADRA AND NAGAR HAVELI)

CHHATTISGARR

ORISSA

MAHARASHTRA

ANDHRA PRADESH

GOA

KARNATAKA

(ANDAMAN IS.)

TAMIL NADU

(PONDICHERRY)

KERALA

Lakshadweep

(NICOBAR IS.)

the Himalayan foothills and mountains. Its population desired statehood to address their particular problems, including land prices forced up when rich city folk purchased vacation homes in the cooler mountains.

State governments are sometimes vast, matching their populations. The people of Uttar Pradesh, for example, outnumber any two countries of the European Union. In each state, the chief minister runs the executive and is responsible to the state legislature. When a state lacks a stable government or fails to maintain calm, the president may place the state under presidential rule, usually until order is restored. Presidential rule occasionally serves to the benefit of the party ruling in New Delhi.

Nehru Sets the Country's Directions

Well before Gandhi's death, Jawaharlal Nehru had emerged as a national figure in his own right and Gandhi's successor to lead the *Congress Party* from the 1940s to the 1960s. Though an aristocrat, Nehru appeared the modern, secular socialist

needed to lead India into the future. Young leftists idolized him, and by his patriotism, his integrity, and he won the hearts of the masses by his sympathy with even women

and the lowest castes. Energetic, and determined, he emerged victorious from three general elections. In the words of one historian, he had a freer hand in molding policy than anyone since the Great Moguls (see Historical Background).

In domestic matters, Nehru focused on economic and social improvements, and he set the broad outlines of national policy for the next forty years. He created an Indian socialism that allowed some private enterprise but kept government ownership of heavy industry, transport, and other key sectors. A series of five-year economic plans attempted to focus on national goals; with foreign assistance, personal incomes rose despite rapid population growth. However, the richest 10% of the country enjoyed most of the benefits of economic growth; they received 40% of personal income, and enjoyed a comfortable standard of living. In contrast, most Indians remained desperately poor, some only employed at planting and harvest.

Social policy stressed equality. The constitution of the Republic abolished untouchability, and prohibited its practice. Caste distinctions in general were discouraged, and the privileged of all types—from the former princes of Indian states to rural tax collectors—came under attack. Landlords, especially powerful in an overpopulated agricultural society, found their lands distributed to the farmers by land reform. New laws provided women with equal property inheritance and alimony for divorce. Education expanded considerably, but as in many other developing countries, it grew too much at the top (university) and too little at the bottom (mass literacy and skills).

Nehru created an international reputation as a prominent leader of the nonaligned nations neutral in the Cold War

Prime Minister Nehru with Lord Mountbatten

Courtesy: Government of India

India

who sought independence for European colonies. Nehru often suspected the motives of Western nations and sympathized with the Soviet Union. Such sympathy, however, carried practical benefits, because the rivalry of both communist and Western nations for influence in India meant that both sides provided economic aid.

India's major foreign policy concern, then as now, was Pakistan. Deep suspicions remained after the 1949 war over Kashmir, and an arms race began, Soviet weapons for India, American jets and tanks to Pakistan. Relations also worsened when Indian irrigation projects threatened to divert rivers flowing into Pakistan and used for irrigation there. The international community solved this problem by a technical solution, for the World Bank provided funds to Pakistan so it could utilize other rivers instead (see **When will the Taps Go Dry,** p. 2). Tension flared over Kashmir in 1965. Pakistan infiltrated irregulars first, then plunged into conventional war by an armored attack (see Disputed Territory: Kashmir). Indian forces halted the invaders, and the Soviet Union sponsored negotiations that ended the fighting. Each side withdrew to the 1949 boundaries.

India initially welcomed the Chinese communist revolution, but the Chinese conquest of Tibet in 1950 brought together the two most populated nations along a lengthy border. After the Dalai Lama fled to India to lead a moral struggle for his people, his supporters sought supplies and weapons to continue the fight. Tension increased when China constructed a road across the desolate, but strategic, Aksai Chin Plateau that India claimed as part of Kashmir. In 1962 a border war broke out, and Chinese troops defeated Indian units before withdrawing. The border dispute soured relations between the two countries for 25 years, and it encouraged China to ally with Pakistan, India's arch-enemy. Before his death in 1964, Nehru was faulted for the failure of his policy toward China, but the nation deeply mourned his passing.

Indira: Emergency Rule

In 1966 *Congress Party* leaders selected Indira Gandhi as party leader and prime minister. Nehru's daughter and thus long acquainted with political issues, she inherited a stumbling economy and a weak party. Mrs. Gandhi increasingly adopted socialist policies, and she nationalized the banks in 1969. The masses adored her, and provided a landslide victory in 1971. Further nationalizations followed. Mrs. Gandhi also led India into a successful war with Pakistan in 1971 that created Bangladesh, and the country conducted its first nuclear test in 1974.

Mrs. Gandhi signs the Visitor's Book at the White House, July 1982

By the mid-1970s, Mrs. Gandhi's programs proved less popular, and after a state court found Mrs. Gandhi guilty of election violations in 1971, she declared a "National Emergency" that invoked extraordinary powers to jail several thousand opposition leaders, censor the press, and announce drastic economic reforms. Indira's Emergency was India's closest brush with dictatorship, and the voters disapproved. *Congress* lost the next election, but in another major feature of Indian politics, a coalition of small parties failed to rule successfully. Elections returned Gandhi to power and the challenge of communal unrest. She was assassinated by bodyguards angered by the military attack on Sikh insurgents in the Golden Temple at Amritsar in 1984.

Disaster of a different sort struck Bhopal, the capital of Madhya Pradesh, that same year. Poisonous gas used to make the agricultural pesticide Sevin leaked into the atmosphere from a chemical plant owned by the Indian subsidiary of Union Carbide. The gas killed more than 6,500 people, and injured perhaps 200,000,

many of them doomed to early deaths. Legal wrangles delayed settlement until 1989, when Union Carbide agreed to an Indian court's settlement of $470 million. In 1990 the government began paying the minimal compensation of $12 per month to each of the injured, and in 2004 the courts ordered payment of all remaining funds.

Religious Tensions and Economic Reform

Immediately after Indira's death, key cabinet members selected her second son, Rajiv, as prime minister, Heir to the Nehru tradition of leadership, yet in many ways a fresh face, Rajiv seized the moment of sympathy over his mother's death and called fresh elections. *Congress* emerged triumphant, winning the largest margin of victory since independence, more than 50% of the popular vote and 400 of the 542 seats in the *Lok Sabha*.

As prime minister, Rajiv began reducing the vast web of government regulations and encouraged international trade. However, Rajiv had been Indira's "non-political" son, a pilot who enjoyed a lavish lifestyle, and found government details boring. Two failures marked his rule. First, his attempt to bring peace to Sri Lanka's Tamil rebellion failed when the leading rebel force, the *Tamil Tigers,* turned against Indian troops sent to maintain peace. Second, Swedish investigators discovered secret payments to Rajiv's friends linked to the sale of Bofors field artillery to India. "Bofors" became synonymous with corruption, and the scandal brought down his government and initiated a brief period of rule by a coalition of other parties. A *Tamil Tiger* suicide bomber assassinated Rajiv during the 1991 elections.

Destruction of the Ayodhya Mosque

Controversy over the Babri mosque at Ayodhya in Uttar Pradesh dominated Indian politics in the early 1990s. Built by the Mogul emperor Babur, the Babri mosque was holy to Muslims, but Hindus regarded it as the sacred birthplace of their god *Ram* and sought to rebuild the Hindu temple they believe preceded the mosque. Militant Hindu revival groups such as the *Vishwa Hindu Parishad* and its political ally, the *Bharatiya Janata Party*

(BJP), sought to destroy the mosque and rebuild the temple. Initially, national and state governments took extraordinary precautions to prevent violence, arresting the *BJP* leader, Lal Krishan Advani, and some 100,000 others. However, in late 1992, political maneuvering gave way to direct action. Under cover of ceremonies to construct a Hindu temple, well-organized militants attacked the dome and walls of the mosque. Ordered by the state's *BJP* government not to fire, the police stood by, and in a few hours the mosque lay destroyed, replaced by a makeshift temple.

Within hours, fighting between Muslims and Hindus spread from Ayodhya across India in the worst communal strife since independence. Days of violence claimed some 1,200 lives; thousands more were injured, most of them Muslim, and many the result of police bullets. The violence and curfews halted normal business, and losses amounted to billions of rupees. The *BJP's* parliamentary leader, L. K. Advani, was arrested, and the government banned several militant Hindu organizations, including the *Rashtriya Swayam Sevak Sangh* (the *RSS*) and the *Vishwa Hindu Parishad,* as well as two Muslim groups. Calm returned, but only slowly. Further

anti-Muslim rioting in Bombay, the commercial capital, cost hundreds more lives.

After 400 sittings, 48 extensions, and 17 years in preparation, in 2009 the report of the Liberhan Commission on events at Ayodhya confirmed that the destruction of the mosque involved painstaking, premeditated preparations, and blamed both *BJP* leaders and local officials.

Violence in Kashmir and Bihar

Sectarian violence flared for different reasons in Kashmir. It enjoyed a special status, with separate laws and land ownership restricted to Kashmiris, but years of political manipulation and election-rigging—most notably in 1987—destroyed any legitimacy of the state government. Its overwhelming Muslim majority probably desired an end to Indian rule, though it was divided between favoring independence or unity with Pakistan. Only force and direct control from New Delhi retained Kashmir within India. Economic development languished, and a state with some of the greatest potential for hydroelectric power actually imported most of its electricity.

In the early 1990s, Muslim protests demanded freedom from India. Armed militants took and occasionally murdered hostages, while the often non-Kashmiri police killed dozens of protestors and militants. The leading Muslim activist, Maulvi Mohammad Farooq, was assassinated, and by 1996 the death toll had reached about 20,000.

The violence was often financed and supplied by Pakistan. In 1999 Islamic fighters and Pakistani troops secretly crossed the Line of Control dividing Kashmir and established positions high on peaks overlooking Kargil on the vital highway to Leh, near the Tibetan border. To repulse the invaders, Indian troops advanced up steep slopes with little cover. It took ten weeks of determined battle, significant casualties, and world opinion to persuade Pakistan to withdraw the remaining infiltrators. Two nuclear powers had fought significant land battles without going to war, but the results might not prove as fortunate next time.

Jammu and Kashmir held state elections in 2002. This was not the exercise of civic responsibilities. Pakistani-based militants murdered moderates, and the *All-Party Hurriyat Conference,* a loose confederation of 23 separatist groups, boycotted the vote. But, the elections were sufficiently free and honest to defeat the *National Conference,* the pro-Indian party that traditionally won corrupt elections. A new coalition government released some militants, and promised to relieve the harsher regulations and police actions. It has not been entirely successful, and Human Rights Watch has

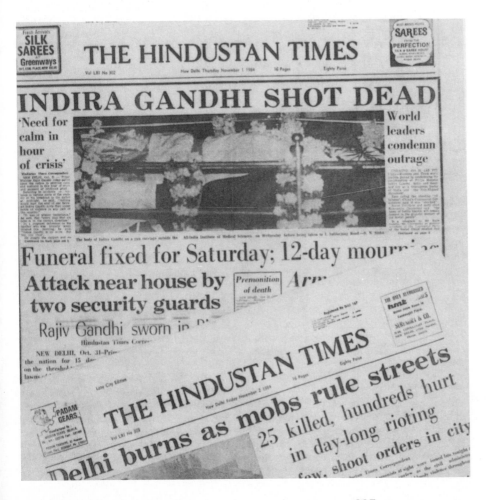

India

faulted the Indian military for killings of suspects without trial, and Pakistan for backing the armed militants.

Confidence-building progress between Pakistan and India at mid-decade brought further hopes for improvements in Kashmir, even if its broad solution remains distant. Bus service between Srinagar, the capital of India's portion, and Muzaffarabad permitted relatives to see each other after nearly sixty years. Moreover, Kashmiris on each side of the Line of Control began to visualize new types of solutions. Moderate opposition groups even traveled the bus, and held a conference that increased the popularity of non-violent solutions. Though a settlement eluded Kashmir, the level of violence declined.

Violence of a different nature swept portions of rural Bihar during the 1990s. Again the initial causes were political, social, and economic. The Bihar state government had failed to provide security—or schools, clinics, roads, and electricity. The chief minister, Laloo Prasad Yadav, of a low-ranking, cow-herding caste, used state jobs and contracts as sources of patronage for his supporters. Corruption charges finally forced him from office in 1997, but his illiterate wife replaced him when their party won state elections. Without economic reform and foreign investment, the level of poverty increased yearly. Signs of improvement only followed the election of a new state government in 2006, whose policies and spending on infrastructure brought signs of growth through road construction and other projects.

Political Corruption and BJP Victories

At the Supreme Court's prodding, not long before the 1996 elections investigators revealed an immense scandal involving illegal payments to many prominent politicians and officials. Public uproar forced the resignation of *Congress* cabinet members and the *BJP* leader, L. K. Advani. Suspicion of corruption generally discredited politicians and government.

The venality seemed high by any standards. Prime Minister Narasimha Rao had apparently accepted a bribe from an industrialist, but then bestowed the favor elsewhere—and he failed to return the money. Police seized 10,500 saris and over 60 pounds of gold from Jayalalitha Jayaram, a former movie star from Tamil Nadu. The home of the previous minister of communications yielded over *36 million rupees in cash.*

The 1996 elections finally ended *Congress's* role as the natural ruling party. Without a champion from the Nehru-Gandhi family, it turned for leadership to elderly men suspected of corruption. Among the upper castes, its secular plat-

Rajiv Gandhi

form was gravely threatened by the *BJP's* vision of a Hindu nation. Regional loyalties, the defection of many Muslims, and caste-based ideologies likewise cost *Congress* support, as voters selected new groups like the caste-based *Samajwadi* and *Bahujan Samaj* parties or leftist alliances ranging from *Janata Dal* to the *Communist Party-Marxist.* The electorate resoundingly rejected *Congress.*

In 1998 the *BJP's* moderate leader, Atal Bihari Vajpayee successfully formed a coalition, but the other parties forced him to drop the most extreme planks of his party's platform, such as building a temple at Ayodhya or laws to prohibit Muslims from practicing polygamy. His coalition's moderate goals, however, were soon forgotten when a series of nuclear explosions in Rajasthan stunned the world and delighted most Indians. The tests changed India's rank from "nuclear-capable" to "nuclear power."

Vajpayee argued that improved weapons elsewhere (apparently Chinese and Pakistani missiles and nuclear abilities) threatened India, so the bomb was needed for its security. While the U.S. and Japan immediately halted aid, the European nations did not. Pious platitudes proved inconsequential. The blasts heightened the government's popularity despite Pakistani counter-blasts, and India outlasted U.S. sanctions.

For a year, Vajpayee played an artful game of foreign policy, to divert attention from a fracturing coalition. He authorized highly symbolic missile tests that threatened Pakistan and China, but pursued equally publicized acts of friendship. He

rode the first bus scheduled between Delhi and Lahore in decades, and the Pakistani cricket team played a series of matches across the country. In 1999, Vajpayee's coalition won a modest victory (300 of 534 constituencies) in the third general election in three years and he gained a reasonable chance of a working government. *Congress* had its worst parliamentary showing. However, the vital difference proved to be the success of regional, often caste-based allies.

With a majority so large that no particular ally's defection could destroy the coalition's majority, Vajpayee's cabinet concentrated on economic and defense issues. It raised prices of diesel fuel and kerosene (used for cooking); the federal budget could ill afford subsidies that kept imported fuel far cheaper than elsewhere. Most additional spending went for defense, for the battle against the infiltrators in Kashmir stirred military desires for expensive weaponry. This included T-90 tanks, an aircraft carrier, and jet fighters from Russia; jet trainers from Britain; perhaps a submarine or two from France; and locally-produced missiles and nuclear weapons.

Considering the country's size, India's spending on the military had been modest, but unfortunately, New Delhi delayed creating a coherent nuclear policy. Pakistan lacked one entirely, simply threatening first-use in case of an Indian conventional victory. Both countries face the challenge of developing effective policies when their capitals are just five minutes apart by ballistic missile.

Closer Relations with the U.S.

The September 11 attacks deepened the growing friendship between the U.S. and India. Officially and popularly, India sympathized with any victim of Islamic extremists—India also was a victim, in Kashmir. However, because Pakistan shared information with the U.S. and allowed U.S. access to Afghanistan, India did not win conclusive American support. Most countries still consider Kashmir a disputed territory.

Kashmiri guerrillas launched a deadly attack on the Indian Parliament in late 2001. Prime Minister Vajpayee responded by demanding that Pakistan ban the two groups allegedly involved, *Jaish-i Muhammad* and *Laskar-i Toiba*, and generally clamp down on extremists. The army prepared for battle, and moved to the border. Fearful of the first real war between nuclear-armed antagonists, the U.S. and other nations counseled Pakistan to yield, and it did. However, brutal attacks again took place on the Indian military and non-Muslim civilians of Kashmir.

Conflict between religious communities broke out again in 2002, when a trainload of Hindu militants returning to Gujarat from Ayodhya was allegedly attacked by Muslim extremists, leaving nearly 60 dead. (A later inquiry blamed the deaths on disputes and a riot, not a terrorist attack). For days thereafter, well-organized Hindu mobs conducted a pogrom of the Muslim districts of Ahmedabad, the state capital. The mobs slaughtered about 1,500, vandalized businesses and homes, and caused many thousands to flee to refugee camps. The police failed to protect them even there.

Significantly, Gujarat was one of the few states ruled by the *BJP*. Horror at the violence led coalition parties in the national government to demand the dismissal of Gujarat's chief minister. However, nothing happened, and none bolted the coalition. Moreover, the *BJP* easily returned to power in Gujarat's state elections. Hindu militants therefore saw the religious-nationalist ideology of "Hindutva" as the key to power.

Hoping instead for victory based on the country's prosperity, Prime Minister Vajpayee called elections for 2004. A moderate, he adopted the electoral slogan "Shining India," a vague or even meaningless phrase intended to tap "feel good" sentiments after several years of rapid economic growth. *BJP* advertising showed smiling children at school, and well-dressed families relaxing. Sophisticated technology showed in campaign methods, too, with recordings from the prime minister sent to all cell-phones.

By contrast, *Congress* failed to present a slick message, and its leader, Sonia Gandhi, found herself targeted as a foreigner. However, she traveled tirelessly to speak to crowds about the many who had been left behind by "Shining India," including women, youth, and farmers.

The nation was stunned by an upset victory for *Congress*. It replaced the *BJP* as the largest party in parliament, and its alliance gained 217 seats to the *BJP's* 185. Both alliances fell well short of a majority in the 545-seat *Lok Sabha*, and *Congress* sought a common understanding with communist and left-wing parties. Sonia Gandhi surprised the country, again, by refusing to become prime minister. Her party then nominated Manmohan Singh, the "father of economic reforms" responsible for India's rapid growth back in the 1990s. The stock market rebounded and he formed a coalition with minor parties. The *Left Front* supported *Congress* in parliament but did not participate in governing.

A fitting, if unintended symbol of *Congress's* greater toleration for non-Hindus, Singh became the first Sikh prime minister just before the twentieth anniversary of the battle for the Golden Temple in Amritsar. By coincidence, the president was

The World's Sixth Nuclear Power

Indian interest in atomic power began before independence, when the industrial Tata Company set up a research program. In the 1950s, the U.S., Canada and Britain all provided nuclear facilities, hoping to encourage research and generate cheap electricity. However, despite its public stand against nuclear weapons, India never signed the Comprehensive Test Ban Treaty, and its Atomic Energy Commission undertook the design and construction of nuclear reactors free from inspection by the International Atomic Energy Agency.

After China exploded its first atomic bomb in 1965, the scientists at the Atomic Energy Commission secretly began accumulating the enriched uranium from those reactors for possible atomic bombs. In 1974, an explosion in Rajasthan proclaimed that the country was the world's sixth nuclear power, but New Delhi confirmed that its program was peaceful, though it now had the ability to explode weapons.

By the 1990s, politicians desired further nuclear tests, to illustrate the country's ability, and no doubt to enhance their own reputation. Reportedly Prime Minister Rao ordered tests in 1995, but the U.S. discovered the plans, and threatened to publicize them. In response, Rao called off the tests. By contrast, in 1998 Prime Minister Vajpayee publicly promised that India would not test weapons, while secretly authorizing the five explosions that set off the South Asian nuclear arms race with Pakistan.

Even military strategists who accepted the legitimacy of some nuclear weapons frequently condemn India's acquisition of them. Very predictably, the 1974 explosion led Pakistan to create its own bomb. Within both countries, the creation of weapons raced far ahead of designing strategies for their use, and possibly control over them. Thus, serious consideration of a hot line between the two countries only surfaced in 2004. Far from enhancing India's security, the explosions may actually make South Asia more likely to suffer conventional wars. The resulting arms races for both nuclear and conventional weapons impose unnecessary suffering on populations whose average incomes reach only $400–$600 per year, but no doubt the satisfaction of citizenship in a nation armed with atomic weapons removes the pangs of hunger and stills the sorrows resulting from some of the highest infant death rates in the world.

not a Hindu either, but a Muslim who won fame as a rocket scientist linked with the nuclear weapons program.

Hampered by the demands of 24 coalition parties plus those of the supporting *Left Front*, Singh's accomplishments proved modest. He failed to reform labor laws or to privatize poorly-run government companies. One very significant achievement was the institution of Value Added Tax (VAT), which should reduce corruption and spread the tax burden. It also should reduce the deficits of state governments, a serious concern.

Determined to spread the nation's prosperity to rural areas, Singh's alliance created the National Rural Employment Guarantee Scheme. Rather than cash welfare payments, it promotes "Growth with a Human Face" through providing a minimum of 100 days employment per unemployed household per year, often in local self-help projects that pay little over $1 per day. The scheme achieved modest results in its first year, but the cabinet deemed it effective enough, and it was extended to the entire country in 2008. Its advocates see the project providing many good things: increased economic security through higher farm wages, slower migration to the overcrowded cities, the creation of productive infrastructure, and greater independence of women.

Less successfully, the government proposed to raise the quotas in higher education for the socially disadvantaged castes from 22.5% to 49.5%. The better Indian universities already turn away many applicants, and extending the quota would exclude many middle-class students. Demonstrations against the proposal spread across the country, and even doctors and medical students went on strike against it. Nevertheless, the ruling coalition remained stable, partly because there was no alternative majority. The proposal was soon delayed by the courts.

With national elections approaching, Singh's Communist allies in the *Left Front* deserted the alliance over a nuclear technology deal with the U.S. To help develop India's energy resources, Singh won an agreement from the U.S. that separated India's military and civilian nuclear programs and then granted India access to civilian nuclear technology and fuel—both previously denied because India had developed its own nuclear weapons. The proposal provided significant benefits, but for ideological reasons the *CPI (Marxist)* and its allies launched popular protests against it and attempted to bring down the government with a vote of no confidence. Singh won, with the assistance of a smaller party.

In late 2008 a group of gunmen came ashore in Mumbai and launched attacks

India

The "cold shower"   WORLD BANK photo by Ray Witlin

on the Taj Mahal and Oberoi luxury hotels, a popular restaurant, a Jewish center, a hospital and a train station, shocking the nation and the world. Anti-terrorism police responded slowly, and nearly 200 civilians died in the suicide raid. Evidence, partly from a surviving attacker, quickly implicated the Pakistani extremist group *Laskar-i Toiba* in the attack, a group long suspected of working closely with Pakistani military intelligence. India demanded that Pakistan ban the group and arrest its leaders and other terrorists; the new civilian government moved slowly in that direction.

The Mumbai attacks apparently did not influence the 2009 *Lok Sabha* election campaign, though the *BJP* attempted to cast Prime Minister Singh as weak and ineffective, controlled by Sonia Gandhi. Abandoned by its former leftist allies, *Congress* promised to spread prosperity to the poor, and ran on a record of economic growth and domestic peace. It nominated Singh (age 78) for another term, against the *BJP's* equally aged Lal Krishna Advani (81). Analysts widely predicted that neither major party would emerge with enough seats to create a strong coalition; some believed a

third group of leftist and caste-based parties might even emerge strongest. Given the massive electorate of 714 million voters and over 800,000 voting centers, voting took place regionally, spread over four weeks.

Congress emerged with a remarkable win, the greatest by a single party in two decades. Its *United Progressive Alliance* gained over 50 seats, and needed only a few additional votes for a majority in parliament. By contrast, each rival group suffered defeat, the *BJP* signaling a lack of direction, the leftist parties collapsing in their traditional power centers, and regional or caste-based parties losing ground:

United Progressive Alliance	262
National Democratic Alliance	158
Third Front (Leftist alliance)	76
Fourth Front (regional)	27
Other Parties	20

In one respect, the gods indeed favored Singh and *Congress*. After years of prosperity, the world recession left the economy growing almost as fast as China. Indians also voted after five years of good monsoons, two months before the 2009

rains came late and sparse to the western regions of the country, but flooded the east.

The Maoist threat

In the words of the newly-elected prime minister, the Maoist insurgency had become India's greatest internal security threat. Since the 1960s, Maoist revolutionaries have considered rural India's strong caste divisions, tribal populations and great inequality of wealth fertile conditions for class warfare. Operating across state borders, they organized bands comprised of tribal peoples and Dalits for actions against the police and landowners.

Active particularly in forested rural districts of West Bengal, Chattisgarh, Bihar and Jharkand, and Orissa, the Maoists provided a voice to tribal complaints that their lands were sold to outsiders for development projects such as bauxite and iron mines while they remained landless and poor, lacking in the schools, roads, and investment essential for prosperity. As violence escalated in 2009–10, the Maoists hijacked one train and derailed an intercity express. For its part, the government launched a massive paramilitary operation to clear large sections of forest of the Maoist threat, only for the troops to suffer a major ambush. The struggle has claimed over 6,000 lives.

Culture: India does not have an official religion; it is a land of many religions. Yet it is a Hindu nation, and that fact is in part responsible for the toleration of other religions. About 80% of the population is Hindu, but there are 140 million Muslims (over 13%) and about 20 million Christians, the third largest group. There are also many Buddhists in this land where Buddha lived in the sixth century B.C. and preached a message which emphasized the sanctity of life in all forms.

Hinduism is not merely part of a culture, it *is* a culture—not simply a religion in the normal Western sense. One example of its all-embracing nature is its rigid social order dominated by the concept of caste. Hundreds of castes exist; all Hindus belong to one of them. Caste membership comes by birth, and remains for life. Social contacts overwhelmingly occur within the caste, and marriages rarely cross caste boundaries or take place within the same sub-caste.

Each caste traditionally involved a particular occupation, and with some exceptions members of the upper castes also represented the upper economic classes. The distinctions are far more than economic, and include dietary restrictions on the higher castes as well as social discrimination against members of lower castes. For example, many Brahmins will not eat

Tibetian woman sells her wares in Kalimpong Photo courtesy of Karla Allen

food if the shadow of an "untouchable" has passed over it.

Traditionally castes fell into four broad groups. At the top, the Brahmins (priest-intellectuals), kshatriyas (warrior-nobles) and vaishyas (businessmen) compose over one-sixth of India's population. The shudras (peasants and laborers), now politically described as the backward castes, amount to 44%.

Below all of these ranks are the "scheduled Castes," now called Dalits. Comprising over 15% of the population, before independence they faced the discrimination their title "untouchable" proclaimed, while carrying out essential but dirty and dangerous occupations like street sweeping, slaughtering animals, and disposing corpses and human wastes. The Indian constitution removed legal discrimination against these unfortunates, and government programs have provided assistance. Nevertheless, upper class Hindus will not drink from a Dalit's glass, or patronize the same barbershop. Despite the constitutional protection, in practice Dalits are often banned from temples, cremation grounds, and bathing spots along riverbanks. Dalits who converted to some Christian churches found that they faced similar obstacles: they were shunned from particular pews or even churches by other Christians.

Rituals and ceremonies are prominent in Hinduism, and these are closely related to the family, for the rites are often performed at home. The major rituals relate to birth, marriage and death. The dead are cremated with as much decorum as the family can afford in keeping with its position on the social scale. Other features of Hinduism include the rejection of worldly

pleasure, belief in the soul's transmigration after death to another form of life, the sanctity of the cow and the belief in many gods.

One Hindu celebration, the Kumbh Mela, brings together more people than any other single religious event worldwide. The "pitcher fair" is named after drops of the elixir of immortality that fell to earth during a struggle between gods and demons. Every few years, the alignment of the stars makes washing away the sins of the body particularly effective at the city of Allahabad, the confluence of the Ganges, the Yamuna, and the mythical (but sacred) Sasaswathi. Millions converge on Allahabad, often taking weeks to walk there, carrying everything needed on their heads. About 80 million attended the 2001 ceremony.

Holidays and festivals are associated with each cultural community. There are three important Hindu holidays. *Diwali*, the festival of lights, is a happy celebration commemorating the homecoming of the legendary hero Rama after he defeated the demon king Ravana. The family performs special ritual prayers in the home on this occasion. *Dussehra* has varied meanings in different parts of the country and is celebrated in various ways; in some places with great happiness, in others with more religious ritual, while for some it ends with carefree folk dancing. *Holi* is an occasion in March for noise and fun, and usually folk songs are sung at gatherings around bonfires.

Muslims celebrate the same holidays as in other countries (see Saudi Arabia: Culture) but with local variations. In addition to the religious holidays, three secular festivals are being promoted. Republic Day

is celebrated on January 26, Independence Day on August 15, and *Gandhi Jayanti* (Gandhi's birthday) on October 2.

Hindi and certain other Indian languages are descended from ancient Sanskrit. Most of the ancient literature of India was written in that language, including the early religious text *Rigveda*. Slightly later, several dramas appeared in Sanskrit; the playwright Kalidasa is the most famous. That was the beginning of a long literary history enriched by contributions from Persia and finally Western ideas and forms. Literature flourishes in contemporary India in a number of the native languages, but there are also poems, novels and other works in English.

It is only natural when one thinks of the culture of India to think of the Taj Mahal at Agra—and this is not an isolated example of architectural opulence in this land. There are rock-cut temples and architectural monuments from as early as the time of the Emperor Asoka in the third century B.C. The most admired buildings come from the era of the Hindu-Islamic synthesis beginning in the eighth century A.D. and continuing up until a few centuries ago. The Kurb Minar at Delhi and the Adina Masjid at Ahmedabad come from early in this period; the Taj Mahal, Agra Fort and Akbar's Mausoleum, the latter at Sikandra, come from later during the rule of the Moguls (15th–16th centuries). After independence, conscious attempts to create a new national architectural style achieved success in combining elements of the past and present, particularly at Chandigarh.

Painting and sculpture, especially the latter, have an ancient history in India. The stone model for the lion of the State Seal, for instance, dates from the third century B.C. But the new generation of artists is not being limited to any tradition or

Former Prime Minister A. B. Vajpayee

India

A stroll through the market

time; it is boldly experimenting with great freedom.

Dancing, music and drama are three arts that in India belong together. Traditionally, plays are acted in dance to the accompaniment of music. Dancing also exists separately and is a very highly developed art with elaborate symbolism.

Modern cultural forms play an important role. The movie industry produces more full length films every year (about 800) than does any other country. Because studios in Bombay traditionally dominated the industry, it became known as "Bollywood," but most movies today come from producers in southern India, in languages like Telegu and Tamil. Most Indian movies attract the entire family: they feature little violence, frequent music and dance, and exaggerated emotional attractions. But there is no obvious sexual activity, and the finish is always "happily ever-after." Stars in the industry draw huge followings, and some transfer their talents to the political stage, on occasion becoming a state's chief minister.

Exported for many years across Asia and Africa as an alternative to the culture of Hollywood, the movie industry drew additional strength from the rapid growth of cable TV in India and satellite TV around the world. Because costs of production are relatively low, foreign distribution rights alone can sometimes meet the cost of production. However, until Indian movies are filmed in English, their audience in North America will typically be limited to expatriate Indians. The 2009 best-picture winner *Slumdog Millionaire* gave many Americans their first taste of Bollywood.

Television, long stagnant under a government monopoly, broke wide open with the growth of (unregulated) cable TV. Now both Indian and Western programs reach the remotest villages, brought by some 30,000–70,000 cable companies to 30 million customers, who pay modestly ($2.50–$4.00 per month) for up to 75 channels.

Independence in 1947 is a dividing line in the history of education in India. Before independence there was no mass education. Since then, the government has tried to provide free and universal education through eight years of "basic school." These eight elementary years provide instruction in crafts along with reading and writing. After a rapid increase in education during the 1990s, over 80% of children now complete elementary school, and two-thirds enter high school. Nevertheless, some 70 million children are not in school, and nearly 30% of the population remains illiterate, and half of women. About half the world's illiterates are Indian.

Secondary schools also expanded rapidly in both technical fields and preparation for university study, though India's poverty prohibits universal high school

Dalits "untouchables" polishing shoes

studies. There were 17 universities in 1947; by 2006 there were some 350 universities and over 7,000 colleges. A panel of experts has called for 1,500 universities by 2015, to educate 15% of young adults rather than the 7% who study today.

While the Indian Institutes of Technology rank with the world's best in computer sciences, elsewhere the system of education requires reform. In 2007 Prime Minister Singh claimed that two thirds of the universities and 90% of the colleges were rated "below average" (by "average" he apparently meant "reasonable quality" rather than the mathematical mean). In Singh's words, "We need better facilities, more and better teachers, a flexible approach to curriculum development to

Prime Minister Manmohan Singh

From 12th century bronze . . .

widowhood on occasion ends in pressures to commit suicide.

Economy: With 650,000 villages and scores of bustling cities, the economy of India is marked by contrasts greater than any other nation. It is home to humanity's greatest collection of the poor—some 300 million people, one-third of all those world-wide who are so impoverished that they subsist on less than $25 per month. Nevertheless, the middle class numbers about 200 million, and the number of very wealthy may exceed the number of millionaires in the United States. The rapid economic growth of this decade may transform at least parts of the country.

Poverty Partly from Choice

The poverty is not inevitable: the land possesses good soil that is easily irrigated and large deposits of coal, iron ore, and other minerals, though insufficient oil. The conditions that produced modern poverty lay first in human reactions to the natural conditions.

Culture and regulation have kept poverty in place when economic growth could have alleviated it. Regular rainfall, good soil and tropical warmth encouraged a very large and dense population in the plains and river valleys. Society then forced the lower strata of society into poverty while some members of the nobility enjoyed vast riches. In the traditional world of religious belief and caste divisions, the mixture of poverty and riches seemed natural and inevitable. Fate, or *karma*, dictated life's difficulties. Accepting it might lead to rebirth in better circumstances.

make it more relevant, more-effective pedagogical and learning methods, and more-meaningful evaluation systems." Nevertheless, it takes an act of parliament to create a university, and the lack of an accreditation process means that quality often remains murky. For example, over half of all college teachers lack a graduate degree, and 25% of university positions are vacant. Salaries are far too low to attract the vast numbers of Indian academics working abroad.

Even as it educates only 7% of its young adults, India has the largest number of unemployed graduates in the world, as well as the largest number of illiterates. The unemployed often studied in the wrong disciplines, but desire the high salaries of computer scientists, engineers, and finance majors.

Widespread condemnation of the Miss World contest held in Bangalore in 1996 drew attention to the position of Indian women. Traditionalists condemned beauty contests for degrading women, while feminists pointed out serious problems that women face. These begin before birth, with the (illegal) abortion of unwanted girls, and continue through childhood, when more than half of all children are malnourished. Girls typically study for fewer years than boys, and as they mature, the need to provide funds for a dowry sometimes leads to prostitution. Girls also marry young: though the legal age is 18, nearly half (44%) of all brides wed before that. Women rarely enjoy a healthy diet: in poor families mothers and sisters often forego food to give husbands and sons more, and 60% of women are anemic. While successful marriage may lead to joy,

The British conquest meant some public works, along with tariff-free imports. Factory-made textiles, machinery, and consumer goods flooded India, undercutting local craftsmen and hindering attempts to industrialize. At the same time, fewer famines and better medical knowledge helped the population grow rapidly. At independence, roughly 200 million people, half the population, lived below the poverty line.

In the first 40 years of independence, the number of impoverished grew to exceed 300 million, and economists applied the term "Hindu Rate of Growth" to the

. . . to the most advanced rocketry. India's spacecraft reached the moon in 2008.

India

Praying in the Ganges at Varanassi, one of Hinduism's holiest spots

Photo courtesy of Karla Allen

economy's performance. However, the relatively slow growth resulted not from religious culture, but from regulation, planning, and high tariffs rather than free enterprise.

Public health and other statistics give some sense of the desperate poverty of many inhabitants. Both bubonic and pneumonic plague broke out in 1994, striking initially at slums on the outskirts of cities like Surat and Bombay, where crowded immigrants live without clean water or sanitation. By official estimates, some 30,000 tons of waste remain uncollected daily, and in rural areas only 10% of homes have a toilet or outhouse and over 600 million people lack access to a latrine. Government efforts for better sanitation have had little impact, but the recent publicity campaign "No Toilet, No Bride" links toilets to courtship and thus may bring comfort and sanitation to those above abject poverty.

Surveys in the 1990s revealed that over 300 million people lived in households so poor no one could afford a watch, and utter poverty condemned 30% of the population to fewer than two meals per day. Very few adults will escape from that poverty except through death, and by 2010 the number in poverty had climbed to 400 million. There have been hundreds of suicides by hopelessly indebted farmers, but sales of laundry detergents and cosmetics seem to be rising among those just above the poverty line.

After drastic food shortages in the 1960s, great efforts were made to increase the country's grain production. The Green Revolution—selecting strains of rice and wheat that produce well with fertilizers and irrigation—enabled the country to feed itself in 1971 for the first time since independence. In the contest between better farming and more mouths, freeing markets in the 1990s led to still greater harvests. This progress could be halted or reverse if reports of falling water tables prove correct, or if climate change reduces the extent and reliability of rainfall.

For years, the seas around India abounded in fish that an efficient industry could exploit, but the lack of processing and storage facilities, as well as poor transportation, allowed the fish to swim unmolested. By the late 1980s, however, India had improved the industry, and ranked eighth in the world in annual fishing catch. Now the Indian Ocean may be over-fished, particularly near the shores.

A diamond-finishing industry began in India in the 1960s when it was discovered that low wages made it profitable to work imported diamonds that were discarded by the South African syndicate. An estimated 350,000 craftsmen in India now work in tiny sweatshops where they are paid by the piece. A socio-religious group, the *Palanpuri Jains* (from the former princely state of Palanpur), have established a worldwide network to market gems cut in India. India has become the leading exporter of cut and polished diamonds.

Seeking Rapid Economic Growth

The modern Indian economy finally "took off" in the 1990s, when Manmohan Singh, the finance minister, reduced regulation, encouraged investment by foreigners, and ended most of the industrial licensing that had handicapped Indian industry. Singh also attempted to sell state businesses, simplify taxes, and reduce them for the rich. The opposition charged that the International Monetary Fund wrote the budget, but India started, somewhat timidly, to follow the East Asian models of export-led economic prosperity.

With lower inflation, higher exports, and lower tax rates, Indian and foreign companies expanded. By mid-decade, newly-permitted foreign companies ex-

Shanty town on a Calcutta street

panded telephone links and constructed power plants. Spurred partly by advertising on many new TV channels, consumers sought appliances and household items. Investment by foreign companies soared, freeing Indian funds for other purposes. Exports doubled. As the growth rate of GDP reached 7%, some commentators considered India the next Asian Tiger.

The years of rapid economic growth produced two Indias, one sometimes quite rich, the other usually oppressively poor. Economic growth failed to bring much relief to those living in poverty, especially the rural poor. Over 80% of the population continued to live on less than $2.00 (U.S.) per day, at the same time as the middle and upper classes bought flashy consumer goods and speculated in India's own hi-tech stocks.

Certain states managed to capture most of the economic prosperity, particularly Gujarat, Maharashtra, and Karnataka in the west and south. By contrast, the vast Ganges plain across Uttar Pradesh, Bihar and West Bengal experienced virtually no improvement in personal incomes. Relatively rapid population growth also reduced the growth rate per capita.

Virtually all state governments operate in deficit, and even the best may fail to provide the necessary infrastructure or enable private firms to do so. India's airports are often a horror story. Until its recent modernization and massive new terminals, one among the world's largest, New Delhi's Gandhi International Airport had only one runway .

The country lags far behind most other Asian nations in telephone lines (about three per 100 inhabitants) and internet use (just five users per 100,000 inhabitants). To provide just six telephones per 100 inhabitants will cost $60 billion; to saturate the country with lines for faxes and computers required by the flourishing software industry, far more. Although the necessary funds could come from foreign investment, after a decade of encouraging foreign firms to undertake projects, their annual investment totaled only about $5 billion in 2004, far short of government plans, and a stark contrast with China's level of $50 billion.

Much of the investment in the 1990s took the form of large, headline-grabbing projects to meet the tremendous electricity shortages. However, political interference and red tape deterred many investors from completing their projects. Indians still suffer frequent power cuts and voltage fluctuations that wear out motors, but foreign investors deserted the electricity industry after the Maharashtra failed to pay the agreed price for electricity from an American company's project. In response to widespread shortages,

The Indian Institute of Science symbolizes Bangalore's long tradition of excellence in science, technology, and the arts. Today, the city's industrial skills have earned it a reputation as the Silicon Valley of India.   Photo by Miller B. Spangler

many software firms and factories generate their own power.

Other problems in the electricity sector typify the challenges facing the country as it moves from socialism to greater free markets. State-owned utilities generally produce and distribute electricity. Their operations are among the least efficient in the world and they frequently suffer power "losses" (mostly theft) of 30%. In

Making friends in an Indian Village

India

the capital, New Delhi, losses amount to 55% of production. By contrast, the world standard is just 10%. Other challenges to an effective system include many non-metered users who pay a flat rate (perhaps 60% of all use), and politicians who promise free electricity for farmers and other special-interest groups.

In electricity and telephones, as in much else except cable TV, government control and ownership lie at the heart of most problems. Privatization efforts suffer because the law prohibits closing factories employing over 100 people, and labor unions protested a proposal to raise the limit to 1,000. States like Kerala have such reputations for leftist policies and militant trade unions that neither foreign nor Indian investment has been significant.

Subsidies for water, electricity and cheap food consume large portions of most state budgets, and reached 10% of GDP in 2000. Moves to slash them meet intense political opposition, but they devour so many resources that little is left for education, public health (800 million people do not have access to clean water), roads, or housing.

Twenty-seven government-owned state banks dominate the banking industry, thanks to regulations that kept out private firms until the 1990s and still limit foreign banks to a minority (49%) stake. The state banks' profits have been hampered by bad loans to failing government enterprises and regulations that allow bankrupt manufacturing firms to continue operating.

Political pressures mandate, loans at low interest rates to farmers and other special interests. Reform of the financial sector is a major challenge to any government.

Success in Computer Services and Autos

The success of Indian-owned firms in the computer software industry, such as Hotmail in the U.S. and Infosys Technologies of India, illustrate the potential of the country's millions of engineers, scientists and other well-trained professionals. Software exports grew at the astounding rate of 40%–50% *per year* in the late 1990s. The industry employed over 2 million people by 2008, and exported products worth $50 billion, more than the country's entire exports in 2000. As many (sometimes-frustrated) American consumers know, India also became the world center for call centers and other back-office procedures like the transcription of medical records. In 2006, IBM announced plans for investment worth $6 billion, so growth of these sectors seems limited mostly by the numbers of qualified employees and the infrastructure.

Until the 1980s, policy favored public transportation over private, with so few cars produced annually that prospective customers had to sign up, and then wait years for delivery of a locally-made copy of a 1950s-era European car. A joint venture with Suzuki began to produce the Maruti in the 1980s. After Asian, European and U.S. firms set up production in the 1990s; car sales climbed 20–50% per

year and by 2005 reached one million, growing at 10–12% per year.

Automobile production in India mixes modern engineering and traditional construction. Among the 10 million employees in the industry there is more unskilled labor, because low labor costs make it profitable to do by hand what elsewhere is done by machine. The product mix, too, reflects the mixture of wealth and modest incomes. BMW and Mercedes now produce expensive luxury autos, while Tata Motors, a local firm, unveiled its rear-engined 33-horsepower Nano in 2008, the world's least expensive car. It costs under $2,500.

As the number of cars on the roads doubled, they quickly overwhelmed the streets and highways. Even national highways are often pot-holed, crowded, and narrow, so that aside from toll roads, few truckers can drive more than 250 miles per day while an estimated 40% of fruits and vegetables rot before reaching market. The ambitious target for new roads announced in 2010 is to complete 12 miles of road per day, 4,200 miles per year, an enormous task priced at $50 billion, with urban streets costing even more. Again, besides success in software, the dominant theme in the Indian economy for the next decade will be "Infrastructure Development," with projected spending of at lest $200 billion per year.

The Future: Untouched by the world recession, the prosperity unleashed by software companies and other exporters is spreading across the economy. In 2001, there were no shopping malls. Now there may be 360. Though it is subtle and often ignored, perhaps the most important long-term result of the prosperity is to attract India's best and brightest students into productive employment, rather than into the often-sterile realm of politics. Manmohan Singh and Sonia Gandhi enjoy an unrivaled opportunity to remake India.

Formidable challenges lie ahead: new roads, power plants and other infrastructure are essential. The school system needs reform, and the university system is too small. Public health services are insufficient, and there are *400 million people* below the poverty line, living in absolute need.

Manmohan Singh has been described as a steel fist in a velvet glove. Expect gentle action on each of these fronts, but a brutal, multi-year campaign against the Maoist uprising now present in almost one-third of the country's districts. However, rather than force it is gentle action to remedy injustices felt by tribal peoples that will prove most effective in reducing sympathy for the Maoists.

A dairy farmer in Rajasthan

Source: World Bank photo by Ray Witlin

The Republic of the Maldives

Typical Maldivian boats known as Dhonis wait for passengers, Malé

Major Trading Partners: Japan, Sri Lanka, India and U.K.
Currency: Rufiaa (1 rufiaa = 100 laari).
Former Colonial Status: Controlled by Britain (1796–1965).
Independence Day: July 26, 1965. March 29th is celebrated, as it marks the final surrender of rights by Britain in 1976.
Chief of State: Mohammed "Anni" Nasheed, President (2008).
National Flag: A green rectangle bearing a white crescent is centered on a red field.
Gross Domestic Product: $1.4 billion (at current prices); $1.75 billion (Purchasing Power Parity), 2008.
GDP per capita: $5,100 (PPP, 2008).

Long known to Arab seamen as "Islands of the Moon," the Maldives are a string of 26 coral atolls scattered 550 miles along the top of a submarine ridge in the Indian Ocean. These atolls contain altogether almost 2,000 picturesque islets. About 200 of the larger ones are inhabited, but few of them extend even a mile in any direction. Islands rarely reach more than six feet above high tide; neither hills nor rivers exist. However, there are abundant coconut palms, white sandy beaches, and crystal clear lagoons formed by coral reefs. With hundreds of species of tropical fish and many varieties of shells and corals, the islands rank as a diver's paradise.

Located close to the equator, the Maldives experience two monsoons each year, and average about 75 inches of rain annually. Between April and October the southwest monsoon brings rain, but the dry winds of the northeast monsoon of "winter" originate in Asia and bring fair weather from December to March.

Area: 115 sq. mi. (298 sq. km) of land, amid 34,500 sq. mi. (90,000 sq. km.) of water.
Population: 350,000.
Capital City: Malé (population 100,000, estimated).
Climate: Warm and humid. The annual rainfall is about 75 inches, mostly from May to October.
Neighboring Countries: India and Sri Lanka are located northeast of the Maldives.
Time Zone: GMT +5.

Official Language: Dhivehi (or Divehi; similar to Sinhala of Sri Lanka).
Other Principal Tongues: Arabic and English.
Ethnic Background: A mixture of Sinhalese, Indo-European, Arab and Negro.
Principal Religion: Islam. All citizens must be Muslim.
Chief Commercial Products: Fish (canned, dried and frozen); garments, boats, handicrafts. The export of many types of live fish and shells is prohibited.

History: Straddling the sailing route between the Red Sea and East Asia, the islands were mentioned by voyagers from Rome, Egypt and China, but scholars dispute when the first settlers arrived in the islands. Discoveries by the explorer Thor Heyerdahl suggest that early inhabitants traded with ancient Egypt and Mesopotamia. Nearly nothing is known of those inhabitants, but about 2,500 years ago settlers arrived from Sri Lanka and India. Buddhism came to dominate religious life, and over the centuries sailors from Africa and Arabia joined the ethnic mix. Besides supplying vessels

235

Maldives

**Former President
Maumoon Abdul Gayoom**

passing through, the Maldives exported vast quantities of cowrie shells, which became the currency in parts of Africa. From this trade, the islands earned the title "the money islands." In 1153 King Dovemi Kalaminja adopted Islam, a crucial event in the island's culture, and thereafter the kings became known as sultans.

During the following centuries, the islanders developed a unique unwritten constitution. It balanced the powers of monarchs with councils of nobles, and although a dynasty might last more than 150 years, a son rarely followed his father on the throne. One of the most important tasks of most sultans was defense—chroniclers recorded 13 wars against invaders.

Portugal captured the Maldives in 1558. However, 15 years later Muhammad Thakurufaanu led a revolt against the Portuguese. In the brutal conflict that followed the occupiers were exterminated, and Muhammad Thakurufaanu won recognition as "The Great" for liberating his country, for improving the administration, and for introducing the Thaana script to write Dhivehi. Nevertheless, under most sultans the islands remained relatively weak. Pirates from South India often threatened during the northeast monsoon, and in 1752 one expedition abducted the sultan and briefly ruled the islands.

After Britain gained control of India and then Sri Lanka (1796), the dangers of pirate invasion receded. Britain itself seemed uninterested in the remote, malaria-infested islands whose chief product was dried fish. However, fearing the growing power of Indian merchants, in 1887 the Sultan sought British protection. Aside from control over foreign affairs and defense, Britain left the islanders largely to their own ways, not even posting a resident in Malé. In 1932 a committee appointed by the sultan drafted the first written constitution. Based on both local and British traditions, it proved the first of 14 constitutions.

With the proclamation of a republic in 1953, the Maldivians symbolically entered their modern era. Although this First Republic lasted only one year, its president, Muhammad Ameen Didi, won respect for reviving Dhivehi and its literature. He reformed the system of education, improved the position of women, opened government stores to undercut foreign merchants, and also introduced strict Islamic laws. Partly to reduce the drain on foreign exchange, he banned the importation and smoking of cigarettes. Thus the Maldives became the first country to ban tobacco in the modern era, but popular dislike of such laws, as well as Didi's increasingly autocratic rule, led to his ouster and the collapse of the republic.

In 1965 a treaty with Britain provided full independence, though Britain retained—and paid for—use of an airfield and a radio communications station on Gan Island in the southernmost atoll. That same year, the Maldives became the smallest nation then received into full membership of the UN. Britain formally returned Gan Island in 1976.

A constitutional change in 1968 again established a republic. The sultan retired; his prime minister, Amir Ibrahim Nasir, won the presidency. Nasir encouraged modernization and tourism, but dissatisfaction over rising prices of fuel and other goods encouraged two unsuccessful uprisings. Sensing deep popular dissatisfaction, Nasir resigned in 1978.

Popular opinion favored Maumoon Abdul Gayoom, a previous cabinet minister, and a referendum approved him as president after the *Majlis*—the parliament—nominated him. The president serves a five-year term, and Gayoom's policies of harbor development, women's rights, and limited high-end tourism helped him win reelection every five years, as the only candidate proposed by the *Majlis*.

Tamil mercenaries hired by disaffected Maldivians attempted a military takeover in late 1988, the first invasion in four centuries. The Maldives has no army or navy, but the small National Security Service offered sufficient resistance for President Gayoom to escape his palace and request aid from friendly countries. Within hours, Indian paratroops landed; outgunned, the mercenaries eventually surrendered. The fighting left more than two dozen dead, some of them hostages, and awoke the nation aware to the need for modern defense, from radar and a trained fighting force to patrol vessels.

A prison riot of uncertain causes in 2003—torture was claimed, but denied—led to apparently spontaneous mob attacks on the parliament, the election commission, and other official buildings. More than a case of idle youths letting off steam, the riots did follow Amnesty International's accusations that the government imprisoned critics for political reasons and sometimes resorted to torture. They also preceded by just days parliament's selection of the nominee for the presidential referendum. Despite the mob's furor, the unanimous choice was a sixth term for President Gayoom, then Asia's longest-serving ruler.

Tasteful but too ostentatious for Nasheed: the presidential home in Malé

No mountains, no traffic, and short distances: no wonder they ride bicycles in Malé.

In the aftermath of the violence, security forces arrested hundreds, including anyone who had been identified in pictures of the rioters. The firm hand of government blocked access to the web site of the only opposition, the *Maldivian Democratic Party (MLD)*. Two cabinet members considered sympathetic with political activists lost their jobs. Although Gayoom publicly accepted reforms, the special assembly he created to consider constitutional revision made little progress—it was twice the size of the parliament. In 2004, another demonstration turned violent.

The 2004 tsunami centered off Indonesia wreaked vast damage to the small country: its capital city, Airport Island, and 47 other inhabited islets were flooded, and over 20 of the 87 resort islands were put out of operation. However, the loss of life reached only about 100, surprisingly low compared to seacoasts with higher land. Apparently the reefs around the islands absorbed much of the waves' power and the sea wall around Malé broke their force there. The consequence was flooding, rather than catastrophic destruction.

With world attention focused on the tsunami and its aftermath, the government had little alternative but reform. It released prisoners, and held elections for the *Majlis*. While not exactly fair—rallies, speeches and political parties were still prohibited, while the media directly or indirectly remained in government hands—the elections were free enough for candidates supported by the *MLD* (from exile) to win 18 of the 42 seats. In fairness to Gayoom, he congratulated even the *MLD* victors, and encouraged the new *Majlis* to enact reforms. It established, at least on paper, multi-party democracy, and widened press freedoms; eventually it produced a democratic constitution that Gayoom ratified in 2008.

Presidential elections fell due in 2008, and Gayoom sought a seventh term, promising the voters "dynamic years" under his trustworthy leadership. Arrayed against him, four rivals attacked his lavish lifestyle and nepotism. Strongly supported in the more traditional outer islands, Gayoom won 50% more votes than his nearest challenger, but was forced to a run-off. Supporters of the losing candidates then switched to Mohamed Nasheed of the *MDP*, and the former prisoner won the presidency.

With a flair for communication, Nasheed expressed a desire to buy a new Maldivian homeland should global warming flood the islands. He also promised carbon neutrality by 2020, with electricity from solar power and virtually no use of fossil fuel. Domestically, Nasheed moved out of the presidential mansion, and planned to sell the multi-million dollar presidential yacht. He also planned to privatize the government-owned media, reform education, and restructure government.

President Nasheed conducted the world's first underwater cabinet meeting in 2009, with 11 colleagues who dove to their chairs set about 12 feet below the surface in a publicity stunt. The wider purpose, the threat of rising sea levels, did receive attention in the world's press.

Culture: All Maldivians are at least nominally Muslim, and often bear Arab names as a result. Their lives center around fishing, agriculture and a few light handicrafts. To a large extent the islanders follow strict Islamic standards of behavior, and laws prohibit drinking alcohol, Western-style dancing, possessing pornography and extra-marital sex.

Despite its geographical remoteness, few resources and relative poverty, the Maldives boast the highest literacy rate for women aged 10–45 in the Muslim world: 98%. This achievement becomes even greater considering that the English-language and modern Maldivian school systems date only to the 1960s and 1970s respectively. Not until 1979 did the government establish primary schools in every atoll, but by the late 1990s it had achieved virtually universal primary education.

For older generations, basic education took place not in a formal school, but in a Kiyavaage, a private home where children studied Dhivehi, a little arithmetic, and the Qur'an. Thereafter they could enter a Makthab or Madhurasaa, schools adapted from Islamic models. To date there is no institution of higher education in the country, though Islamic, teacher-training, and health institutes exist.

Strengthened by their education, women occupy a distinctive role in Maldivian society. Important even as rulers before Islam, in law and apparently in practice they enjoy equal opportunities in employment, remuneration, and cultural activities. Though respecting the stipulations of Islamic law regarding inheritance, Maldivian practice allows a woman to apply for a divorce even against her husband's desires.

Girls do marry—the minimum age is 15, and most women who do not study abroad marry as teenagers. Negotiations establish the "bride price" the groom must pay, and this is retained by the woman if the marriage breaks up. Nevertheless, the divorce rate of 70% is among the highest anywhere.

In recent decades, competition from foreign goods and modern factories closed some employment opportunities in traditional women's crafts (mat weaving and rope making, plus agriculture and fish processing). Today, women make important contributions in tourism, business and light industry. They manage companies, and practice law.

Though modernized and expanded upwards and outwards onto reclaimed land, the capital city of Malé retains a number of unusual features. Its population of about 80,000 has no buses, no dogs, and

President Mohamed Nasheed

Maldives

not a single traffic light. With almost no crime and little entertainment over the single local TV channel, its people enjoy socializing outdoors in the evening and weekends at the beach, where the women retain their modesty fully clothed. The relatively few tourists who actually linger enjoy the absence of hassle and a pleasant, laid-back atmosphere with the ocean always a few blocks away.

Economy: Lacking agricultural land, for centuries Maldivians turned to the ocean for fish and commerce. Until very recently, fishing was the principal livelihood for men, and shipments of dried and smoked tuna ("Maldive Fish") accounted for more than 90% of exports. Until the 1970s, fishing craft were small sailing boats, but a

government program aided the fleet's conversion to diesel power. Modernization also took place in fish processing, with frozen and canned exports now accounting for over four-fifths of the total.

Many coconut palms and a few species of other fruit trees dot the islands, but agriculture is limited by the few areas of fertile soil on the tiny coral islets. The government is eager to encourage light industry, but there are few natural resources. Saudi Arabia, Japan and China have provided some foreign assistance.

Tourists began arriving in significant numbers in the 1970s, attracted by the natural beauty and cheap living. However, the islanders gained little economic benefit, and the spread of drugs, nudity and alcohol offended local society.

After President Gayoom took office in 1978, the country radically changed its approach to tourism. The jet airport opened in 1981, bringing tourists on package tours seeking relaxation, sunshine and water sports. Far different from the backpacking crowd of the 1970s, these visitors stayed at self-contained resorts on "uninhabited islands" that were taxed significantly and required to provide increasing levels of luxury. Other regulations reduced pollution, protected reefs and marine animals, and generally preserved the pristine underwater beauty for those willing to pay for it. Foreigners wishing to visit inhabited islands except the capital or a few villages on escorted trips require special permits.

Before the 2004 tsunami, resorts of varying levels of luxury operated on about 90 islands. Spending by the 500,000 annual visitors from Europe and East Asia provided about one-quarter of GDP and a much larger proportion of government revenue. The waves destroyed about 20 of the resorts, and tourist bookings fell by 50%. The government estimates that recovery will take years, especially at remote islands, and cost more than $1 billion.

One difficulty facing the Maldives is an adequate supply of clean fresh water despite the heavy annual rainfall. The rains do soak to fresh water aquifers underlying most islands, but unfortunately improper sewage facilities often pollute them. The islands' geography offers no convenient reservoirs or storage areas for potable water, and Malé uses reverse osmosis from sea water.

The Future: The unique culture of the Maldives, the often unspoiled beauty of its atolls, and wise decisions in Gayoom's early years combined to foster commendable achievements in education, opportunities for women, and economic growth. The policy of isolating tourists on their own islands limits their influence on the population, but the images and music of satellite TV bring socially divisive consequences as well as benefits. Fortunately, the islanders seem more likely than most to preserve important values.

President Nasheed has a flair for spotting good issues for the media, but he also recognizes serious challenges to society, including Islamic fundamentalism and growing heroin use among the young. After decades of sleepy politics, expect energetic leadership from the president and more contention in parliament.

Because the Maldives lies along East Asia's maritime trade routes to the Middle East and Europe, the strategic importance of the islands is increasing. Expect India to desire much closer military links, probably including basing radar on remote atolls.

A Maldivian newspaper in Dhivehi

Federal Democratic Republic of Nepal

Downtown Kathmandu

Area: 56,827 square miles (147,181 sq. km.).
Population: 28.2 million (2005)
Capital City: Kathmandu (pop. about 1 million).
Climate: Very hot on the southern plains; cooler in the hills, and frigid in the high mountains on the northern border. The plains and lower slopes have heavy rainfall during the summer monsoon.
Neighboring Countries: China (North); India (East, South, West).
Time Zone: GMT +5 hours 40 minutes. When it is 1:00 o'clock in India, it is 1:10 o'clock in Nepal.
Official Language: Nepali (also called Gurkhali).
Other Principal Tongues: Gubhajius (Newari), Gurungkura, Hindi, Kiranti, Limbukura (Limbuani), Magarkura and Tibetan.
Ethnic Background: A mixture of Mongolian, Indian and Tibetan, who identify themselves as distinct communities based on language and traditions.
Principal Religions: Hinduism (about 85%) and Buddhism.
Chief Commercial Products: Woven carpets, textiles, rice, wheat, corn, millet, jute, oilseeds, cane, sugar, timber and hides.
Major Trading Partners: India (more than 50%), Japan, Germany, U.S. and Bangladesh.
Currency: Nepali Rupee (= 100 paisa).
Former Colonial Status: Limited British control, 1816–1923.
Independence Date: December 21, 1923.
Chief of State: Ram Baran Yadav, President (July 2008).
Head of Government: Prime Minister Madhav Kumar Nepal (caretaker, 2010).

National Flag: Unusually, it consists of two red triangular pennants, one above the other, each bordered in blue. In the field of the upper is a symbolic moon, while the lower bears a symbolic sun.
Gross Domestic Product: $15 billion (at current prices); $35 billion (Purchasing Power Parity).
GDP per capita: $1,250 (PPP, 2008).

Because its northern border runs along the crest of the Himalayas and its southern frontier lies on the tropical Ganges Plain, Nepal enjoys as great a geographical diversity as can be found in any small country. From an elevation of about 600 feet in the southeast to majestic Mt. Everest's 29,028 feet is a distance of little more than 100 miles by air. The entire length of Nepal from east to west is about 500 miles; at no point is it wider than 140 miles.

The strip of hot, marshy plain, averaging 30 miles wide along the southern border is called the *Tarai*. It is famed for its jungles and wildlife, though parts have been cleared. Its population and agriculture reflect those found in adjacent areas of India. While the least typical of Nepal, its agriculture is the most productive.

The slopes north of the *Tarai*, known as the *Hills*, are inhabited to an elevation of about 8,000 feet and in summer used for grazing herds to about 13,000 feet. The *Hills*, in turn, become the high mountains called the *Snows*. Some parcels of Nepali territory lie on the northern side of the crest of the Himalayas. Tibetans live there with their yaks and dzos (hybrids of yaks and ordinary cattle).

Another notable characteristic of the land is the pattern of rivers and streams flowing south from the High Himalayas to the Ganges Plain. These rivers carved out valleys with strips of relatively flat land. Surrounded by high mountains, the capital, Kathmandu, lies in the Valley of Nepal, the intensively cultivated bed of an old lake lying at an elevation of 4,500 feet and occupying about 300 square miles. The Valley of Nepal gives its name to the whole country.

History: Until the 18th century, individual cities and towns formed the basic political units. Their ruling families often descended from Hindu aristocrats who had fled from Muslim rule in India during the 14th Century. They and their retainers subjugated the mainly Mongol-Tibetan population and subsequently mixed with it.

Nepal's unity began when Prithwi Narayan rose to power in the town of Gurkha and in the 1760s completed conquest of the Valley of Nepal. Prithwi Narayan's successors, the kings of the Shah dynasty, attempted to expanded their rule, but were blocked by a large Chinese army in Tibet and defeated by the British (1815), who then controlled most of the Ganges Plain. A British resident was posted in Kathmandu, and only gradually did Nepal win recognition as lying outside India rather than forming an Indian kingdom.

After a period of instability, factional strife, and massacre under weak kings, a capable noble, Jang Bahadur, seized effective control. He retained the king—many Hindus revered him as a god—but kept him as a symbol while ruling in his name. His family, the Rana, became hereditary possessors of the office of prime minister. The Rana remained in power until the revolution of 1950–51.

An astute manipulator, Jang Bahadur balanced China and British India against each other for the benefit of Nepal. During the Indian Mutiny of 1857, he supplied Gurkha troops to fight against the rebels. The Gurkhas' courage and loyalty won British respect, and the tradition of recruiting Gurkhas for the British Empire began. Britain henceforth considered Nepal as a friendly ally and favored protected state and granted it formal independence in 1923.

India's independence in 1947 spread new ideas of nationalism and liberalism. Politically sophisticated activists from leading families who detested the Ranas' dictatorial methods formed the *Nepali Congress Party*. Influenced by the Indian party of the same name, they advocated democracy under the king.

As political tensions rose, King Tribhuvan was dismissed by the Rana prime minister and fled to India. Supporting the king, the *Nepali Congress* launched a revolution and gained control of parts of the

239

Nepal

country. In 1951 the alliance between King and *Congress* successfully removed the Rana family from the government, and the party leader became prime minister. India and Nepal formed a special relationship that granted their citizens common rights of residence and land ownership, and promised military cooperation against any external threat.

In 1959, the *Nepali Congress* won absolute control of parliament and Bishweshwar Prasad Koirala became prime minister of Nepal's first elected government. However, King Tribhuvan had died; his son, King Mahendra quickly moved to rule rather than reign. He dismissed Koirala, arrested him, suspended parliament, and charged *Congress* politicians with corruption. All political activity was banned and the king became supreme.

For the next 30 years, Nepal's kings attempted autocratic rule, sometimes with non-political elections of local councilors. This suited traditionalists, who regarded the king as the incarnation of the Hindu god Vishnu.

In 1989 India blocked most trade across the border, on the pretext of fighting smuggling, but probably to punish Nepal's purchase of Chinese weapons. The Nepalese suffered greatly, finding themselves desperately short of gasoline, cooking fuel, medicine and other essentials. The weakness displayed by the royal government encouraged the *Congress Party* to join the communist-influenced *United Left Front* in protest movement.

When the police violently repressed the demonstrators, killing many, the shocked nation responded strikes by almost all groups, even newspaper hawkers and health workers. Unsupported even by the elite, King Birendra called for a new constitution and appointed a coalition cabinet of the *Congress Party*, the *United Left Front* and royal nominees took power. The constitution of 1990 established multiparty democracy and an independent judiciary. It thus ended absolute rule by the Shah dynasty.

Congress won an absolute majority in the subsequent elections. The party dominated politics for the next 12 years, but it failed to maintain internal discipline. Two aging veterans of the struggle for democracy in 1950, Girija Prasad Koirala and Sher Bahadur Deuba, manipulated party rules and alliances to gain office or oust each other. Certainly, *Congress* could win elections—it came second only once, defeated by the *Communist Party (United Marxist-Leninist)* of Man Mohan Adhikari in 1995. However, it could not provide stable government. Cabinets changed about yearly; politics centered on chasing office.

The parliamentary leftists failed to provide a viable alternative. A social democrat rather than a communist (despite the party's name) their leader, Man Mohan Adhikari, sought free elementary education, more funds for local governments, and tax reforms. However, his party never won a majority in parliament, and in opposition it suffered defections.

In such circumstances, politics became the rapid search for the rewards of office rather than an opportunity to serve the public good. Corruption was so rampant that cynics claimed "Governing Nepal is the art of appropriating foreign aid for personal use without getting caught." One cabinet included 37 members, one-third of the ruling *Congress Party*'s members of parliament. International aid agencies and donor nations became disillusioned.

Throughout the 1990s, economic growth often stagnated, and the distribution of income became more unequal. For example, the poorest 20% of the population received less than 4% of national income, while the top 12% owned 70% of the wealth. Disillusionment with democracy spread widely.

A stubborn *Maoist* rebellion broke out in poor western districts in 1996. Partly because politicians failed to address the causes of popular distress, and partly because the police lacked the training, resources, and ideas to combat a guerrilla movement, the *Communist Party of Nepal (Maoist)* gradually grew in power and destructiveness. It proved particularly adept

Prachanda, Maoist leader

at interfering with schools and colleges, whether by presenting programs, holding students for indoctrination sessions, or closing campuses during political strikes.

Last Years of the Monarchy

In 2001 the murders of King Birendra, his wife, and several relatives shook the nation. Crown Prince Dipendra, surviving in a coma, was declared king, but died within hours. Prince Gyanendra, Birendra's brother and perhaps the country's richest industrialist, then assumed the throne, the third king in four days. Official accounts blamed a drunken Prince Dipendra for the murders, but many blamed conspiracies, and the nation hesitantly accepted King Gyanendra.

Gyanendra soon dissolved parliament and appointed his prime minister. Democracy formally ended in 2002. Few Nepalis except the politicians themselves initially seemed to care, and the king promised elections after defeating the *Maoists*. To crush the rebellion, he declared a state of emergency and ordered the army into combat. However, the rebellion spread, and sympathetic strikes shut down the capital itself. Negotiations between the monarchy and the *Maoists* failed, because the latter desired a new, republican, constitution, a demand the king totally rejected.

The *Maoists* seemed particularly inept at public relations—even China condemned them. Bombing the Coca Cola plant in Kathmandu won grudging support from nationalists who criticized expensive foreign drinks, but discouraged foreign investment. Needing money, the *Maoists* extorted it from virtually every possible source, including tourist backpackers (asking modest amounts) and hotel owners (demanding much more). Unable to sustain their military units with volunteers, they turned to conscription, seizing several thousand children for indoctrination and military service. In response, hundreds of schools closed, and thousands of teenagers fled to India.

However, Chairman Prachanda ("majestically terrible," the adopted name of Pushpa Kamal Dahal) and his party stood for more than brutalities and bloodshed. In a country with high illiteracy and 50% of the population below the poverty line, they demanded education for all children (girls included) and an end to feudal land holding. Many of the fighters were female, and their women's organization pressed for greater rights. They also demanded a ban on alcohol, which they considered a serious social problem leading to violence within the home.

Failing to appoint a prime minister acceptable to the political parties, in 2005 the king dismissed the cabinet and took direct power. He ended freedom of the press, arrested many politicians, and tried those alleged of corruption without normal court procedures. Like the Maoists, the military and its vigilante groups committed more human rights abuses. International donors withheld aid, and demanded the restoration of democracy.

As public resentment rose, the *Maoists* declared a unilateral ceasefire and agreed to cooperate with the two major political parties, *Congress* and the *Communist Party (UML),* for an end to "tyrannical monarchy." The political parties then initiated nationwide protests against the king's direct rule.

While the king, apparently on his astrologer's advice, enjoyed his lakeside retreat near Pokhara, demands for a repub-

A solitary spot to pray at Boudnath Temple, Kathmandu. Photo courtesy of Karla Allan

lic strengthened. Thousands of demonstrators defied prohibitions on public meetings, and attempted to march on Kathmandu. Royal officials failed to halt the protests and strikes, even with the bloodshed of shoot-on-sight curfews. After losing support among the military and even within his cabinet, Gyanendra capitulated. He recalled parliament, but the political parties, not the king, named Girija Prasad Koirala as prime minister. At Koirala's request, the *Maoists* lifted their blockade of Kathmandu.

Parliament moved rapidly to eradicate the political roles of the king. It abolished the title "His Majesty's Government," and removed his title as commander-in-chief. It stripped his image from the designs for coins and paper money, ended his freedom from taxation, and took away his power of veto. Nepal had been a Hindu kingdom. With the fate of the monarchy unresolved, the state was declared secular.

The *Maoist* cease-fire had made the protests possible, and large *Maoist* demonstrations in Kathmandu prompted the cabinet to negotiate. Prachanda and Prime Minister Koirala agreed to major changes in a Comprehensive Peace Accord in 2006. The *Maoists* entered parliament (mostly represented by women and minorities) and joined the cabinet. To reduce the danger of violent confrontation, the army was ordered to barracks, and the rebels to camps, where the UN monitored their surrender of weapons. After perhaps 13,000 deaths from the rebellion, peaceful change seemed possible, but not certain.

Ethnic conflicts rapidly replaced warfare over ideology. Speaking Indian lan-

guages rather than Gurkhali, many Madhesis of the southeastern plains felt distressed by their low level of government employment and virtual absence from the army. Protests led to riots against *Maoist* activists, killing many; the police seemed to disappear.

As expected, elections to the vital constitutional assembly involved some intimidation and even violence. The Maoist *Young Communist League (YCL)* received particular condemnation. Its 300,000 members, led by former fighters, were accused of threatening rivals, demanding payments from businesses, and forming a sort of parallel police force. The danger seemed real that Prachanda and his party leaders had unleashed a force they could not control.

Nevertheless, imperfect elections were widely preferred to strife in determining the country's future. Sensing this, the *Maoists* left the cabinet and threatened an election boycott if their two key demands were not met—proportional representation with quotas for women and underrepresented groups, and the abolition of the monarchy before the elections, rather than afterwards. The other major parties eventually yielded, and parliament approved a "federal democratic republican state" by an overwhelming majority.

The 2008 elections passed remarkably peacefully. The shock came with the results. The *Maoists* captured 220 of the 601 seats, more than the combined totals of *Congress* (110) and the *UML* (103). The monarchy's doom was certified by the near-total defeat of royalists, and ex-king Gyanendra left the palace. Until recently a *Maoist* rebel, Prachanda became prime minister.

Nepal

The late King Birendra,
much loved and revered

Ex-King Gynendra, deposed in 2008

gress. With the *Maoists* in opposition and boycotting the Constituent Assembly, it still failed to meet its 2010 deadline to complete a constitution. Its authority was extended, but a fundamental gap remains between most politicians, who value law and government institutions, and the *Maoists* who see the military as an instrument. In May 2010 the party declared an indefinite general strike to force the cabinet's resignation, but popular criticism of the economic shut-down forced an end to the strike. The next month Prime Minister Nepal resigned anyway.

He recognized that he faced three particular tasks, the first to guide the Constituent Assembly in drafting a new constitution due by 2010. Second, the economy needed relief. Most pressing of all, the 20,000 *Maoist* fighters idling in their special camps needed to be integrated into the National (formerly Royal) Army. This the military command fiercely opposed, even threatening to boycott athletic events that mixed soldiers and former rebels. When the president vetoed his removal of the army chief, Prachanda resigned, before completing his first year of office.

Madhav Kumar Nepal of the *UML* subsequently became the prime minister with a coalition of 22 parties, including *Con-*

Culture: Though considering themselves Nepalese, most inhabitants retain a strong loyalty to their tribe. Groups such as the Magars, Newars or Gurkhas have distinctive languages and customs; little social contact or intermarriage takes place between them. The Gurkha have enjoyed the most prestige, forming the military caste. During the political ferment in 2005–07, minority groups, whether the indigenous Janjatis or the Madhesis of the southeastern plains, pressed for greater rights.

Although in the hills and mountains the predominant physical characteristic is Mongolian, suggesting the population's origins from the north and east, religion and customs often belong to the south and west. Hinduism (see India: Culture) has been the official religion, followed by most Nepalis, though some Buddhists claim under-representation. The constitution required that the king be a Hindu and "Aryan," but in 2006 parliament declared the state to be secular.

Dancing and singing are the principal folk entertainment. Men and women usu-

ally hold such celebrations separately; it is not uncommon for young men to dress in women's clothing for the performance of certain dances. Except for simple flutes played by herdsmen, Nepalis of noble tribes will not touch musical instruments; the lowly Damais provide musicians for celebrations.

Most Nepalis are very superstitious. Women are commonly confinement away from the house and others for 10 days after the birth of a child, and exorcising evil spirits is still practiced. After a person has died, various rites are used to drive his spirit out of the house. Many superstitions relate to animals, such as the belief that keeping three cows is unlucky. If a farmer has four cows and one dies, he must either sell one or obtain another. Nepalis take astrology so seriously that astrologists were jailed for suggesting that the king's fate was "under bad stars."

Isolated and impoverished by its mountains, Nepal only slowly developed modern health and educational systems. Although most boys and half the girls

Nepali school boys meet at Hindu Temple

receive a primary education, only about 40% of adults are literate. The leading center of higher education is Tribhuvan University, established in 1959.

Economy: An agricultural country whose inhabitants live close to the subsistence level, Nepal is one of the 10 poorest countries in the world. Its per capita income of about $300 per year reflects low levels of agricultural productivity and little industry. Manufacturing concentrates on processing local produce and simple consumer goods. The leading sectors are cotton textiles, pulp and paper, and construction.

The most productive farming region is the low-lying *Tarai*, where farmers raise two successive crops in a year. Rice is grown in the wet monsoon, other grains in the drier seasons. Level land in valleys as high as 5,000 feet above sea level are also farmed with the help of irrigation. The uplands are used extensively for grazing livestock.

A series of plans beginning in 1956 aimed to improve farm output, expand public services and generate electricity. India financed projects such as important roads, as did the U.S., the Soviet Union, Britain, and China. Beset by corruption and political turmoil, recent plans failed to reach their targets, and the economy has stagnated. Moreover, one of the major employers, the garment industry, suffered severe competition from India in its export markets after the end of the international quota system in 2005.

Nepal's new highways, sometimes blocked by landslides as they run through the mountainous terrain, have attracted concentrations of population along them. As the main source of energy for cooking and heating is firewood, the mountains have become denuded of trees several miles on either side of these roads. The result is massive erosion, and more landslides. At the same time the women who carry the firewood in heavy baskets must climb higher and higher on the slopes to obtain their fuel.

Tourism developed at a modest rate in the 1980s but surged in the 1990s, partly because of lower airfares for European and American visitors. Before the Maoist rebellion and political upheavals, the income from tourism exceeded twice the amount earned from the traditional, but declining service of Gurkhas in the British army.

The next order of business is development of Nepal's hydroelectric power potential, optimistically estimated to exceed 83,000 megawatts. Less than 1% has been exploited, insufficient to supply the present needs of industry and homes. The government has proposed projects worth billions of dollars to foreign firms, but funding proved relatively difficult to obtain, not only because of environmental concerns. The electricity would be needed: in Nepal itself 85% of the population lack access to it, and neighboring India has tens of millions of potential consumers, though its states may be unable to pay.

The Future: The nationwide protests of 2006 swept away the stagnant equilibrium of the three major opposing forces: the palace, the political parties, and the *Maoist* rebels. The 2008 elections of April 2008 granted primacy to the former rebels, but their leader, Prachanda, resigned after failing to dismiss the army chief. Expect the *Maoists* to seek a better balanced coalition after Prime Minister Madhav Nepal's resignation.

Nepal stands mid-way through a revolution. Fierce disputes seem inevitable as the Constitutional Assembly drafts a constitution that replaces monarchy with republic, centralism with federalism, and an insurgency with routine politics. The massive protests that ousted Gyanendra unleashed ethnic, linguistic, caste, and sectarian passions that may prove difficult to conciliate. Nepal's next years are therefore particularly difficult to predict. Will 2010–2011 witness a new constitution, or will cabinet instability prove the incompetence of politicians even without the king?

For the longer run, Prachanda covets the presidency and a form of socialism that involves drastic changes. He has the agenda and the determination to get there—if he can accept the grind of daily politics, elude the plots of his many enemies, and build a broad enough alliance to take power peacefully. The antics of the Maoist youth leagues threaten any such alliance.

"Elderly postal delivery man in Kathmandu"   Source: Mary M. Hill Forida

The Islamic Republic of Pakistan

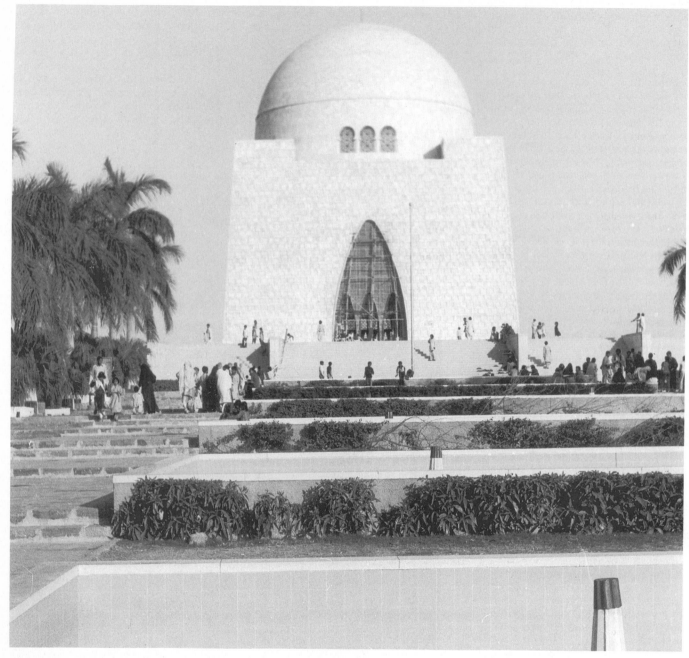

Monumental shrine in Karachi dedicated to Mohammad Ali Jinnah, regarded as the founder of Pakistan   Photo by Ray L. Cleveland

Area: Some 307,374 square miles (796,095 sq. km.), plus 32,323 square miles—83,716 sq. km.—of Kashmir.

Population: 167 million.

Capital City: Islamabad (pop. 960,000).

Climate: Generally dry, except for the mountains of the northeast; very hot except for mountainous areas.

Neighboring Countries: India (Southeast), Iran (West); Afghanistan (North); China (Northeast).

Time Zone: GMT +5.

Official Language: Urdu.

Other Principal Tongues: Panjabi, Sindhi, Pashtu, Baluchi, Jatki, Kashmiri, and English (as nationwide language of the educated).

Ethnic Background: Communities are distinguished by language and religion, but these divisions do not correspond to physical features. More than half the people are identified as Punjabis on the basis of language.

Principal Religion: Islam (about 95%), principally *Sunni.*

Chief Commercial Products: Textiles, rice, leather products, cotton products, tobacco, sugar.

Major Trading Partners: Japan, U.S., Germany, Saudi Arabia, China.

Currency: Pakistani Rupee (= 100 paisa)

Former Colonial Status: Part of British India (to 1947).

Independence Date: August 14, 1947.

National Day: March 23, "Pakistan Day."

Chief of State: Asif Ali Zardari, President.

Head of Government: Yusuf Raza Gillani, Prime Minister (2008).

National Flag: A large Islamic crescent and a five-pointed star in white lie within a field of green; at the pole there is a broad, vertical white stripe.

Pakistan

Gross Domestic Product: $178 billion (at current prices); $457 (Purchasing Power Parity), 2008.
GDP per capita: $2,750 (PPP), 2008.

Geographically, the heart of Pakistan is the Indus River. Tumbling from the Himalayas, the river and its tributaries traverse a vast plain stretching from the Punjab to the coast near Karachi. Irrigation from the rivers and the system of connecting canals supports intensive farming.

Southeast of the Indus Valley, the Thar Desert extends into India. This arid waste of sand and gravel receives less than 10 inches of rain per year, and supports scattered camel-breeding tribes. West of the Indus Valley, desert conditions prevail in Baluchistan, a dry mountainous region with elevations up to 11,000 feet. This thinly populated area has some irrigation and farming, but most inhabitants are Baluchi nomads who call the region Makran. The north and northwest are mountainous, including the world's second-highest peak, K-2.

History: Before British rule in the 19th century, the territory that now comprises Pakistan had never formed a distinct political unit. Instead, various states and kingdoms ruled parts of it (see Historical Background and India: History). However, when the Indian independence movement raised the possibility of the end of British rule, Muslim leaders like Muhammad Ali Jinnah dreaded the prospect of becoming a religious minority in an India dominated by its Hindu majority. The *Muslim League of India* publicly endorsed the goal of establishing a separate state for the subcontinent's Muslims in 1940. Staunchly opposed to Hindu rule and inclined to exaggerate its potential difficulties, separatist Muslims did not foresee the problems that partition would create.

In 1947 Britain approved partition: the creation of two dominions, Hindu and Muslim. However, many Muslims lived in Hindu areas outside any possible Muslim state. Moreover, while Britain administered areas like Punjab and Bengal, and could divide them on the basis of religion, it granted the rulers of the princely states the choice of which nation to join—if either. From the partition emerged the new nation of Pakistan, the "Land of the Pure," composed of West Pakistan and East Pakistan—two areas separated physically by India (see map of India; Bangladesh was formerly East Pakistan). Ethnically fractured, and held together only by religion, Pakistan would rarely achieve national consensus over any significant secular issue.

With the British withdrawal rapidly nearing, Muslim leaders hastily improvised a government in Karachi, a port city

near the mouth of the Indus River. Muslims elected in 1946 to the Indian constitutional convention now sat in Karachi as the Constituent Assembly and legislature for Pakistan. Government offices had to be built from practically nothing. Civil servants proved scarce, though soldiers were plentiful, for Hindus had dominated the bureaucracy under British rule, just as Muslims had often led in the army.

Unfortunately, the new state soon lost its guiding personalities. Muhammad Ali Jinnah, the *Muslim League* leader who so strongly demanded partition based on religion, became the first governor-general, but died shortly after independence. Liaqat Ali Khan, the first prime minister and thus chief executive, was assassinated by a fanatic in 1951. Political instability became the normal course of life in Pakistan.

A massive two-way flight of Hindus and Muslims marked the actual partition.

Pakistan lost many merchants and clerks while gaining large numbers of poor peasants. While Mohandas Gandhi almost miraculously averted strife in Bengal, in the Punjab militants on each side massacred hundreds of thousands. A dispute over Kashmir led to conventional war (see Disputed Territory: Kashmir), because the Hindu prince of a Muslim-majority state cast its lot with India. About 1.5 million Hindus fled East Pakistan (now Bangladesh) in 1950 for West Bengal in India, while some one million Muslims went in the opposite direction. A total of eight million people moved from one country to another.

Many Indian politicians resented the separation of Pakistan, and strained relations between the two nations proved a recurring feature until the present. A dispute over currency exchange (1949–1951) disrupted trade. Conflicts also arose over three eastern tributaries of the Indus used for irrigation in India. In a rare diplomatic achievement, this dispute was settled by treaty in 1961 (see When Will the Taps Go Dry?).

Pakistan gained United States military aid in 1954, though for much different reasons than Washington recognized. While the U.S. sought to recruit and strengthen an ally against world communism, Paki-

Pakistan

stan (which had dismissed its civilian government not long before) valued arms for possible war with its closer neighbors. Pakistan became a member first of the Southeast Asia Treaty Organization and then also of the Baghdad Pact.

From independence to the 1990s, constitutional disputes regularly marked politics. Pakistan produced few political geniuses, but many bitter rivals. The Constituent Assembly failed to determine such practical matters as whether Urdu or Bengali should be the official language. The voting strength of the Bengali—East Pakistani—members of the Assembly countered the governor-general who was from West Pakistan. After the *Muslim League* lost public support in East Pakistan in 1954, the governor-general dissolved the Assembly. Pakistani politicians and military rulers adopted many devices to manipulate the electorate and avoid the simple will of the people, as they continued to do up to the present. Simultaneously, economic problems continued to mount, causing widespread dissatisfaction with the government.

A constitution instituted in 1956 established the Islamic Republic of Pakistan. However, elections were never held under that constitution: after just two years, a military coup d'etat ended the flawed attempt at democracy. The army commander, General Ayub Khan, took the presidency himself, for a decade during which Pakistan began an inconclusive conventional war with India over Kashmir (1965).

Pakistan Falls Apart

Riots and political unrest in the late 1960s led Ayub Khan to resign, but the same political and economic problems festered under his successor, General Yahya Khan. In 1970 voters for yet another constituent assembly gave the *Awami League* of East Pakistan an absolute majority. Bengalis sensed a legal means to correct the economic and political discrimination that they believed Pakistani governments had practiced against them. However, Yahya Khan postponed the assembly and arrested Mujibur Rahman, the *Awami League's* leader. This triggered an outpouring of long-suppressed feeling in East Pakistan and resulted in its declaration of independence in 1971 as Bangladesh.

Yahya Khan's attempt to use the army to hold the two Pakistans together resulted in the destruction of whole villages and the massacre of their inhabitants. India intervened, and its army defeated the Pakistani forces and secured the independence of Bangladesh.

Alternate Military and Civilian Rule

Discredited by the defeat, Yahya Khan resigned. Zulfikar Ali Bhutto, an experienced opposition leader, became president and like nearly every Pakistani leader, he won wide initial popularity. This disappeared, however, when economic decisions and ideological differences alienated significant groups. Business leaders particularly disliked Bhutto's socialist seizure of private businesses.

Despite his socialism, Bhutto came from the landowning aristocracy of Sindh, and he dominated the Sindhi-based *Pakistan People's Party (PPP)*. The *PPP* won the 1977 elections, but the opposition accused Bhutto's government of fraud in counting votes. Riots and demonstrations led to martial law, and within weeks General Muhammad Zia ul-Haq led a military coup. He arrested Bhutto and other politicians "to save democracy for the nation."

Despite the promise of democracy, Zia canceled promised elections and banned political activity. His military regime ruled firmly, controlled the press tightly, and executed Bhutto. To foster his regime's popularity, in 1984 Zia proposed further Islamic features to the constitution and a ban on political parties. A national referendum endorsed the changes.

The Soviet Union's military occupation of neighboring Afghanistan rescued Zia's regime politically and internationally. Refugees from the brutal fighting flooded into Pakistan's border areas, burdening local society, and sometimes disturbing the peace. However, the U.S. and conservative Arab regimes, considering Pakistan a bulwark between Soviet troops and the Indian Ocean, provided weapons and funds to both the refugees and Zia's military regime.

After President Zia was killed in a plane crash in 1988, military rule collapsed. Benazir Bhutto, daughter of the executed Zulfikar, had already led agitation for democracy. Now the *PPP* quickly became the major national party, and it struck alliances with several regional parties. By contrast, the conservative *Muslim League* dominated the heavily-populated Punjab. Led by Nawaz Sharif, an industrialist, it became the fierce rival of the *PPP*.

Alternating Rule by Bhutto & Sharif

For the next 11 years, power alternated between Bhutto and Sharif. Three years in office proved long enough for each to commit enough mistakes to justify dismissal. Both Bhutto and Sharif won elections to come to power, but neither ever completed a term.

To generalize, Bhutto won fame and good relations in the West, but proved ineffective in domestic politics and her husband, Asif Ali Zardari, allegedly amassed wealth from corrupt dealings. He certainly amassed a reputation as "Mr. 10%." Open disputes flared between Bhutto, various presidents, and leading generals.

By contrast, Nawaz Sharif broke the tradition that reserved the office for wealthy landowners from Sindh. Sympathetic with economic freedoms, he attempted to establish the Islamic Shari'a as the highest law and adopted the death penalty for blasphemy against the Prophet Muhammad. Under the guise of fighting corruption, political opponents were arrested, most prominently Benazir Bhutto's husband.

Neither Bhutto nor Sharif brought peace of Karachi, the largest city if no longer the capital. Violence escalated there between the native Sindhis and the Muhajirs; it became an urban battle zone. The police acted brutally, but failed to contain the violence, and fatalities reached 800 in 1994 alone as factions of the splintered *MQM* attacked each others supporters. When Karachi's spiraling political violence claimed 600 lives in 1998, Sharif ordered military courts to render swift justice (three days maximum for trial, another three days for appeal, then execution). The carnage did decline, but civilian courts declared the special courts unconstitutional.

After India's nuclear tests in 1998, intense domestic pressure built up to display Pakistan's atomic weaponry. Despite strong foreign warnings and threats of sanctions, Sharif ordered tests in response. Their success propelled Pakistan into the small group of nuclear powers and won him great public applause. However, the blasts also deepened the discord with India, and brought economic punishment by foreign nations.

Perhaps reasoning they possessed an "atomic shield" against a conventional Indian attack, in 1999 Sharif and the military secretly sent Pakistani troops into Indian Kashmir to occupy and fortify positions at Kargil, overlooking India's vital road to Leh. The invaders inflicted heavy casualties on the first Indian troops sent to evict them. However, the invasion turned to fiasco when Indian success on the battlefield and public condemnation by world leaders forced Sharif to withdraw the troops without even a face-saving gesture.

Following the humiliating withdrawal from Kashmir, Sharif proved particularly incapable. Rampant corruption flourished, and insensitive appointments antagonized public opinion. To intimidate the press, a respected journalist was beaten up. It was, after all, the third year of Sharif's term.

When Sharif attempted to dismiss the chief of staff in 1999, General Pervez Musharraf managed a bloodless *coup d'etat*. He proclaimed a state of emergency, suspended the constitution, dissolved parliament and became chief executive. He promised to attack corrupt officials and make wealthy defaulters repay their loans. The public cheered, and the courts granted him three years to reform society.

Though powerful, Musharraf faced opposition. The attack on corruption moved very slowly, appeared mainly designed to control politicians and snared only a few. Conservative Islamists halted a proposal to reform the blasphemy law, and a strike against the new sales tax by shopkeepers weakened the new tax (they paid no direct taxes, either). Suspicions mounted that the military intelligence service (the *ISI*) really ran the country.

Joining the War on Terror

After the September 11 attacks, the government faced a dilemma. The *Taliban* regime that hosted Osama bin Laden in Afghanistan was in part a Pakistani creation. Musharraf could either acquiesce in an American attack on Islamic Afghanistan, or defy those U.S. efforts and lose any remaining international standing.

Risking assassination, Musharraf joined the war on terrorism. He granted permission for U.S. flights across the country, and allowed U.S. troops to cross the border in hot pursuit. However, many Pakistanis opposed U.S. policies, and therefore Musharraf. The leaders of two Muslim parties, the *Jaamat-i Islami* and the *Jamiat-ul Ulema Islam*, called the regime illegal. Two assassination attempts in 2003 narrowly missed him, and fearing a coup d'etat, he reshuffled the high command and retired the *ISI* director sympathetic to the *Taliban*. The government ordered the 20,000 Islamic schools to stop all military training.

Yielding to U.S. pressure, the government moved the military to root out *Taliban* and *al-Qaeda* fighters along the border with Afghanistan, a region suspected as the hiding place for Osama bin Laden. However, the critical border regions had long enjoyed autonomy as tribal agencies. In the South and North Waziristan regions of the North West Frontier Province, attempts to establish military authority resulted in bitter skirmishes costing hundreds of soldiers their lives in battle against fighters who knew the terrain and enjoyed local support. It may be worth noting that the most prominent *al-Qaeda* operatives were arrested in the cities, not the border areas.

After years of skirmishes with local militants and tribesmen, in 2007 the military adopted a different strategy. It agreed to withdraw the border regions of North and South Waziristan if the pro-Taliban tribesmen living there expelled foreign militants and ended cross-border attacks. Fighting between Uzbek militants and local tribesmen did follow the agreement, perhaps evidence of the strategy's success. However, one agreement established a peace committee headed by a Pakistani *Taliban* commander.

The struggle against America's terrorist enemies proved difficult because of deep popular passions about injustice to Muslims in Kashmir, Palestine, and elsewhere. For years, military agencies had stirred up these passions and supported the militants. Popular magazines extolled the virtues of jihad. Groups outlawed because of foreign pressure often reorganized quickly under new names. For example, the leader of the banned *Sipah-i Sahaba*, bailed from jail, successfully stood for parliament—and supported Musharraf's prime minister.

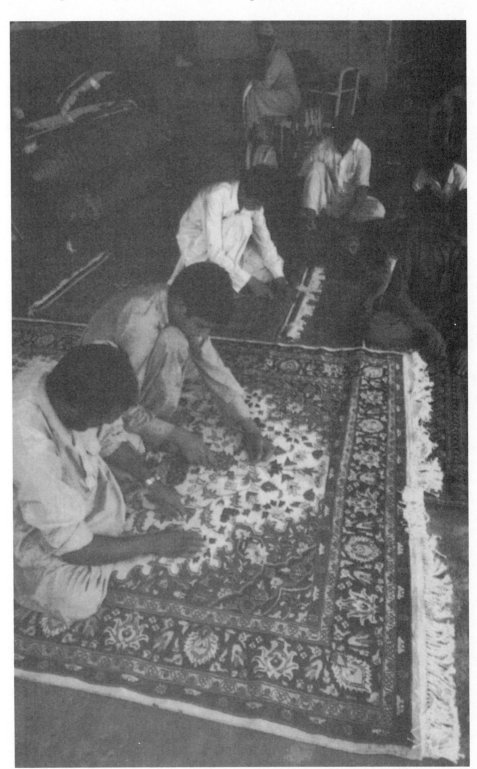

Quality control workers inspect carpets when they come off the looms and trim excess wool
Courtesy: Caltex Petroleum Corporation

247

Pakistan

General Muhammad Zia ul-Haq

The war against terrorism brought benefits. Musharraf's role led many in the West to forget that he overthrew an elected government. The U.S. dropped the sanctions imposed after the nuclear tests and provided new aid. Both the Karachi stock exchange and the Pakistani rupee surged in value.

Searching for Political Stability

Though perhaps hidden at the time by the needs of government, Musharraf's later years in office became a dominated by desires to ensure control of politics. To overcome the Supreme Court's three-year limit for military rule, a 2002 referendum was held to extend his presidential term by five years. Lavishly-funded propaganda favored the proposal, and despite a boycott by the major political parties, the result was 97.5% "Yes." This was discredited by low turnout and allegations of irregularities. The manipulation was probably unnecessary: the poor often liked the general, while the middle classes and more secular-minded citizens despaired of politicians and desired an end to the violence.

Musharraf then restored the president's power to dismiss parliament (but not directly the prime minister). He established a National Security Council of elected politicians and top military officers to review government actions. By involving the military in government, he argued, it would render the army less likely to overthrow democracy.

Before the 2002 National Assembly elections, the regime weakened opposition political parties when it banned anyone who had served two terms from taking office again. Threats of prosecution kept Benazir Bhutto and Nawaz Sharif, the most famous politicians, out of the country. While the *PPP* remained loyal to Bhutto, the *Pakistan Muslim League* split. Most of its supporters formed the *PML Quaid-i Azam (PML-Q)* that accepted General Musharraf's plans. Several Islamic parties united to form the *Muttahida Majlis-i Amal (MMA)* and concentrated their campaign against Pakistan's anti-terrorist alliance with the U.S.

No party won a majority of the assembly's 342 seats, but the greatest surprise was the third-place showing of the *MMA*. It also gained control of Baluchistan and the North West Frontier Province, the two regions where the war on terrorism was most concentrated. The latter province soon passed laws limiting contact between men and women, for example, banning male physicians from examining female patients. It also gave the Shari'a precedence over other laws, thus prohibiting the payment of interest and changing the nature of education. These moves reflected *Taliban* ideology across the Afghan border.

Open fighting in Baluchistan in 2005 drew attention to that poverty- and drought-stricken province. Less than 5% of the population enjoys running water, and society retains many traditional values. Baluchis list many grievances, including the exploitation of the region's natural gas and other resources with few benefits for the locals. They also fear an influx of non-Baluchis and dislike the military presence. Nawab Akbar Bugti, the rebel leader, died fighting in 2006, reducing the organization behind the revolt but not its basic causes.

Despite its sometimes inept politics, the Musharraf administration earned respect for improved relations with India and for policies that provided faster economic growth. An attack by Kashmiri militants on India's parliament in 2001 brought the two nations close to war. However, Musharraf proved much more flexible than elected politicians. He yielded to New Delhi's demands and promised to halt infiltration across the Line of Control. He banned two extremist groups and the police arrested thousands of militants (though many soon reappeared on the streets). The *ISI* had sponsored the militants; now it encouraged them to disband.

With relations warming, despite extremists' threats a bus service began between Srinagar in Indian Kashmir and Muzaffarabad, the capital of Pakistan's portion, in 2005. Train travel followed, to Lahore.

Economic success resulted from capable appointees and wise policies. To head the finance ministry, Musharraf picked a Citibank executive with international experience, Shaukat Aziz. With no political debts, Aziz gained business confidence and encouraged investment in industry. The rate of economic growth then doubled to 6%–8%. Aziz was appointed prime minister in 2004.

A higher standard of living will require much greater spending for social goods like roads, electricity, and water. Musharraf set the goal of water purification plants for every urban area by 2008; meanwhile, polluted water killed several in the second largest city, Lahore. The 2005 UN human development index assessed socio-economic living conditions in 177 countries, and placed Pakistan in 135th place. Only three non-African countries ranked lower. Another ranking in 2006, by the U.S. magazine *Foreign Policy*, listed Pakistan as one of the top ten "failed states."

Years of Challenge, 2007–10

Both parliamentary elections and the presidential selection fell due in 2007, so political tensions rose dramatically. At least in retrospect, Musharraf repeatedly took decisions that cost him good will among the public. After ruling for eight years, he still desired a new term as president, and he wished the outgoing parliament to vote for the president because his supporters formed majority. To overcome the legal roadblocks to this unusual approach, the president dismissed Chief Justice Iftikhar Muhammad Chaudhry for abuse of office.

A visionary for constitutional rule, Chaudhry turned the dismissal into a campaign for an independent judiciary. Thousands of lawyers and judges demonstrated in his support, but in Karachi dozens were killed when his supporters were attacked after the police vanished. These events weakened Musharraf's support among the modernized middle classes.

At the Lal Masjid, the Red Mosque of Islamabad just blocks from the intelligence headquarters, Islamic extremists seized the

General Pervez Musharraf

Pakistan

opportunity to demand Shari'a law for the capital city. After attacking brothels and burning disapproved music and videos, they kidnapped a group of Chinese workers, creating international complications.

Police then surrounded the mosque. While some militant leaders surrendered, only a direct assault restored authority, at the cost of 100 lives. Musharraf's support plummeted among conservative Muslims.

Women in Pakistan

Although Pakistan elected the first Muslim female prime minister, its women rarely escape from the restrictions traditional in Iran and the Arab world. Women play so small a role in public life that some are literally invisible, uncounted even by the national census.

National statistics portray them confined to very traditional roles. Only 10% of adult women are "economically active" or employed outside the home. Over 80% of adult women are illiterate, and in rural areas the figure exceeds 90%. Male life expectancy (52 years) exceeds that for females. Only three other countries, all in the Indian subcontinent, have shared that distinction. The ratio of women to men, the lowest in the world and dropping, is 91:100. A figure this depressed suggests that the practice of purdah, or seclusion, renders some females non-persons. It also reflects high female death rates, including at childbirth. More sinisterly, an estimated 1,000 women are murdered annually for allegedly bringing dishonor on their families.

Other evidence reinforces the statistical conclusions. During Zia's rule, television and the media blamed working women for defiling society. It became questionable for women to vote, study in classes with men, and even drive. Striking deep roots in the country, such ideas remained even when a woman became prime minister. Benazir's cabinet proposed requiring women TV announcers to cover their hair.

The 1973 constitution bans discrimination, but the adoption of the Islamic Hudud Ordinance in 1979 turned legal practices strongly against female equality, especially in areas of sexuality. The maximum penalty for an adulterous spouse became death, though more commonly prison sentences were imposed, which accounted for over three-quarters of the country's female inmates. The pregnancy of an unmarried woman provided sufficient proof of her illegal sexual intercourse; no trial was necessary for a prison term. Her male partner must be identified, charged, and tried.

The law placed rape victims with a dilemma. Failure to report the rape left free the assailant—or assailants, as gang rape is not rare. However, a woman's report of rape provided evidence that intercourse took place. Conviction of rape requited the testimony of four male witnesses, usually an impossibility, but the rape victim's report to police provided evidence of her illegal sexual activity. Despite strong opposition by religious conservatives, parliament replaced these portions of the Hudud Ordinance with the Women's Protection Bill in 2006.

One recent rape case portrays the terrible plight some women face. To punish her brother for a romantic interest across tribal lines, a rural council ordered Mukhtaran Mai to be gang-raped. Fortunate to survive the experience, she related her experience to the world press. International contributions enabled this brave woman to found two schools in her village and a trauma center for women. However, when she was invited to address a human rights conference in New York in 2005, the government blocked her trip. Another rape victim, a physician whose assault led to open fighting in Baluchistan, took her place.

The 1984 Law of Evidence states that in financial matters, the evidence required of two men may be provided by one man and two women, thus establishing the principle of one man's testimony legally equal to that of two women. Such restrictions reflect both Islamic values and the even older customs of the sub-continent. For conservative Muslims, the Qur'an is the literal word of God, and a country's laws must fit its prescriptions, regardless of secular values or economic harm.

The greatest challenge to such a worldview comes from secular education, but Pakistan ranks among the lowest in the world in the percentage of girls in elementary school. Thus the next generation's women, like those of the present, will largely define themselves in the traditional roles of housewife and mother with little freedom outside the house.

Unable to find support for his desire to remain military commander as well as president, Musharraf promised to resign from the military if he were elected president. He also restored the Chief Justice, and in October 2007, he won parliament's presidential poll. However, the Supreme Court delayed recognizing the decision, on grounds that it had not yet ruled on the eligibility of a presidential candidacy by the military commander.

To offset the strength of Nawaz Sharif in the approaching parliamentary elections, and seeking a natural ally opposed to the militants and religious parties, Musharraf sought an accommodation with Benazir Bhutto, the *PPP* leader. Like Sharif, she had been exiled over corruption charges, so the president granted amnesty to leading politicians with pending corruption cases. She, her husband, and Sharif soon returned from exile. Bhutto's triumphal tour of the country drew large crowds, but was marred by bombings in Karachi that killed scores of *PPP* supporters.

In the name of fighting terrorism, but actually to prevent the Supreme Court from voiding his presidential election while still military commander, Musharraf declared a state of emergency in late 2007. He suspended the constitution, banned political rallies, curbed the media, and dismissed the Supreme Court justices. Subsequently, his newly-appointed judges approved his election, and Musharraf handed over command of the army to General Ashfaq Kayani, a widely respected career soldier. Musharraf had attempted an orderly transition to civilian president, and he ended emergency rule. Nevertheless, he was widely disliked.

Benazir Bhutto was assassinated as she left a political rally in Lahore in December 2007. Many suspected a branch of military intelligence of complicity and blamed the government for negligence, partly because Bhutto had earlier written Musharraf that both extremist suicide squads and a group of senior politicians and intelligence officials were plotting to kill her. Though officially the attack was blamed on Islamic militants, her security was clearly inadequate, and shoddy police investigation of the crime—for example, the scene was hosed down immediately—also pointed to failure by the government.

Responding quickly to the death of its leader, the *PPP* transferred power to her husband, Asif Zardari. The *PPP* triumphed in the subsequent parliamentary elections, winning the most seats of any party (87), while the pro-Musharraf *Pakistan Muslim League-Q* retained only 40.

Though the largest party, the *PPP* had not won a majority. Its leaders formed a coalition with Nawaz Sharif, whose *PML-N* emerged the second largest party

Pakistan

In the name of Allah, Most Gracious, Most Merciful

FOUNDED BY QUAID-I-AZAM MOHAMMAD ALI JINNAH

THE
PAKISTAN TIMES

National English Daily with the largest circulation — Published simultaneously from Islamabad & Lahore

Regd. No. R-1 Vol. XLVII No. 108   Islamabad, Thursday, May 27, 1993 — Zilhaj 4, 1413 A.H.   Tele: No. 825893, 825766, Reporters 829297; Telex 54672 44811 (Times PK). Fax: 823467. Price Rs. 4.00

Pakistanis abroad hail SC verdict

NEW YORK, May 26: Pakistani immigrants hailed as historic the Supreme Court judgment reinstating the National Assembly and Prime Minister Nawaz Sharif, saying they were proud of the contribution of the country's judiciary to strengthening the democratic process, reports APP's special correspondent.

They said that the Nawaz Sharif government had worked for the betterment of the country and that it had achieved definite progress.

PM lauds role of Press

ISLAMABAD, May 26: Prime Minister Muhammad Nawaz Sharif has lauded Press for its outstanding commitment to democracy from the day of dissolution of the National Assembly till its restoration.

He was addressing a news conference at the Prime Minister Secretariat this evening.

Muhammad Nawaz Sharif thanked the Press for making his (Nawaz) cause its own cause.—PPI.

Supreme Court declares Presidential Order as *ultra vires* in a historic verdict

National Assembly, Nawaz Govt. restored

Court also dismisses review petition

By Muhammad Ilyas

ISLAMABAD, May 26: The Supreme Court of Pakistan, in a historic decision, today restored the National Assembly, the Prime Minister and his Cabinet with immediate effect.

The Court also outrightly dismissed the request on behalf of the President for suspension of the restoration order pending decision on the Review Petition which would be filed against the Court's order on Mr. Nawaz Sharif's constitutional petition.

As soon as the Court's decision became known, the corridors and vaults of the under-construction building of Supreme Court resounded with slogans of "Nawaz Sharif Zindabad" which were chanted by a large number of his supporters thronging the premises. Mr. Shahbaz Sharif MNA, younger brother of Prime Minister Nawaz Sharif was among those present in the Courtroom when Chief Justice Dr. Nasim Hassan Shah announced the keenly awaited judgement.

(Text of SC verdict)

(See Page 5)

The National Assembly, elected in October 1990, is the 7th Assembly of Pakistan and, thanks to the Supreme Court's verdict, is the first one to be revived. Only two other Assemblies — one elected in 1962 and the other in 1970 — had their culmination under constitutional dispensation. Six Assemblies met with unnatural demise unsung and unredeemed.

Chief Justice Mr. Justice Nasim Hasan Shah at the Supreme Court along with 10 other judges in Islamabad on Wednesday. (More pictures on Pages 3,5,12)

Pledge to work within legal framework: Cooperation of political forces sought

Nawaz vows to pursue policies with new vigour

By Maqbool Malik

ISLAMABAD, May 26: Describing the decision of the Supreme Court as historic, Prime Minister Muhammad Nawaz Sharif has vowed to work within the legal and constitutional framework and pursue his programmes with renewed vigour to propel the country out of the setbacks it had suffered in the wake of the dissolution of the National Assembly.

Addressing a crowded press conference at the Prime Minister Secretariat here Wednesday evening after the restoration of the National Assembly and his government by the Supreme Court, he observed that Pakistan suffered heavily in terms of rapid progress, foreign investment and its international image.

He asserted that his government would endeavour to bring about a new political order in the country which would be free of hypocrisy, unscrupulousness and blackmail tronic media.

The Prime Minister went on to say that the character assassination campaign unleashed against him by the caretaker government died down in the eyes of the public as the caretaker government could not find any valid material against his government. "Had they any valid material against us, why did they not go to the courts to prove it, he questioned.

He asserted that masses did not heed the character assassination campaign launched against "me and my friends, rather they were depressed and unhappy, mourning the dissolution of the National Assembly and dismissal of my government.

Continued on page 5 col. 2

Gen. Waheed, Admiral Saeed meet Nawaz

ISLAMABAD, May 26: Chief

---

after campaigning about inflation, unemployment, and the Supreme Court justices. The *PPP*'s Yusuf Raza Gillani, a man of character who had served five years in jail on possibly trumped-up charges, became prime minister.

The new cabinet addressed many issues. It revised education policy, published the military budget, and righted past wrongs. The most compelling demands for change involved the fight with militants, and the restoration of the Supreme Court judges.

Because both the *PPP* and the *PML-N* had supported restoration of the Supreme Court judges, an agreement on doing so seemed within reach. However, the two parties failed to settle the matter, probably because their goals differed. Nawaz Sharif clearly desired Musharraf's ouster, so he hoped a restored Supreme Court would void the presidential election. By contrast, Asif Zardari apparently preferred that Musharraf remain president, because a Supreme Court decision dismissing the presidential election might also void his own pardon from corruption charges.

The crisis over the Supreme Court judges reached its conclusion in 2008. Just days before his impeachment on charges of violating the constitution, Pervez Musharraf resigned the presidency. It was, many felt, a landmark moment for Pakistan, the ouster of a former military ruler by orderly political process. Parliament subsequently elected Asif Ali Zardari president.

Multiple crises soon tested the new regime. The alliance with Nawaz Sharif became a bitter dispute over demands to reinstate the Supreme Court Chief Justice. In response to forceful demonstrations and a threatened march on Islamabad, Zardari's government arrested hundreds of opposition activitist, but eventually gave way and reinstated the full Supreme Court.

Predictably, the court addressed the pardon that Musharraf had granted Zardari. Originally designed to free Benezir Bhutto and top *PPP* leaders from the threat of politically-motivated charges, the pardon was expanded by Musharraf's legal team to benefit his allies and others of influence. As a result, when the court proclaimed the

legislation illegal, it plunged some 8,000 politicians, administrators and other members of the country's elite into legal limbo. While as president Zardari enjoyed immunity from prosecution, the opposition demanded his resignation. His popularity slumped as the nation's media became consumed with one topic: how Zardari would be replaced or sacked.

While clinging to office, Zardari did accept major changes that weakened the role of the president. He turned over control of the nuclear weaponry to the prime minister, and signed major constitutional changes that also ceded the power to appoint the military chiefs, judges, and the chief election commissioner. Most significant, he lost the power to dissolve parliament and to impose emergency rule on a province. In effect, the presidency became largely symbolic.

In an unrelated matter, the bill revising the constitution also renamed the North West Frontier Province Khyber Pakhtunkhwa, "the Pakhtun land on the Khyber side." The government separately changed the administration of its seven semi-autonomous Federally Administered Tribal Areas that occupy the most rugged and remote parts of the province. Pakistan had continued the British practice of granting these areas separate legal status with limited government under tribal leaders and officials posted as political agents. As a result, human rights were ignored by practices such as collective punishment and detention without trial. While retaining tribal law, the changes will allow the areas to elect members of parliament who belong to national political parties, a further step towards democracy and likely a moderation of the local culture that enabled terrorism to flourish.

President Asif Ali Zardari

Still Struggling against Terrorism

In 2007, suicide bombers killed nearly 1,000 Pakistanis. Soldiers had also died while fighting the "War on Terror" in border regions where the *Afghan Taliban* had gained local support. Additional casualties, militants as well as unfortunate civilians, resulted from American missile strikes in those regions. Tired of the struggle, many politicians argued in favor of negotiations with the militants rather than their conquest. For its part, the *Pakistan Taliban Movement (Tehrek-i Taliban Pakistan)* argued that its struggle was with America.

The government of the North West Frontier Province approved talks with various militant groups, and in 2009 negotiated a truce for Swat, a beautiful, rugged region not far from Islamabad, where a few thousand insurgents had

fought the military to a standstill. In return for a cease-fire, the agreement released militant leaders and imposed Sharia law in Swat and adjoining regions. Human rights organizations and the international community were horrified at the victory for militancy, and the possibility of punishments such as the amputation of limbs, whipping and execution for adultery by stoning. Politicians, however, hoped that concessions over Swat and other regions would halt the extremist violence. No doubt some intelligence and military officers preferred to see the army defend Kashmir rather than attack tribal areas.

The truce quickly failed, for militant fighters soon appeared in Buner, a district only 60 miles from the capital. Open warfare resumed between the military and

Taliban fighters. Hundreds of thousands fled the conflict, but at least in Swat and Buner the army regained formal control, and refugees began to return to their homes.

Terrorist strikes continued across the country, including an attack on the visiting Sri Lankan cricket team, and a massive bombing of the police emergency response headquarters in Lahore. Furthermore, the insurgency threatened to spread. Impoverished areas of southern Punjab seem likely to support the *Taliban* and other groups committed to violent jihad. The region's poverty, high illiteracy, and feudal system provide the conditions where such militancy often flourishes.

Recognizing the need to destroy *Taliban* rule over border areas, in 2009 the military launched a relatively successful offensive in South Waziristan and attempted to secure most other tribal areas. However, the army and civilian government have not yet formulated a complete counter-insurgency strategy. The army has acted to achieve the first two steps—to "clear and hold" an area. However, the government has failed both to reconstruct the thousands of homes, businesses, schools and offices destroyed in the conflict, and to develop civil society, the final two steps implied by the "build and transfer" elements of modern strategy. Consequently, militancy and terrorism seem likely to reappear given the opportunity. Beheaded bodies dumped in South Waziristan carry the label of "ISI" or "CIA" spy, and such killings are spreading to Peshawar.

To date, the military has largely ignored the North Waziristan tribal area, despite the presence of thousands of fighters. Perhaps the military is really stretched too thin by conflicts in other areas, but the reluctance to occupy the area is likely because Gul Bahadur, the autonomous local *Taliban* leader, has proclaimed that his focus is liberating Afghanistan, not Pakistan. He provides a sanctuary for Jalaluddin Haqqani, the Afghan militant, Central Asian exiles, Chechens, Arabs, and Kashmiris. Given this coalition of al-Qaeda allies, and because the Times Square bomber trained in explosives there, the vast majority of recent drone missile strikes by U.S. forces have been aimed at North Waziristan.

In times of crisis, the deciding element is often an unplanned event. Pakistani public opinion about militant Islam apparently changed perceptibly after a two-minute video showed militants flogging a screaming young girl. Interviewed later on television, *Taliban* leaders awoke national concern by condemning schools, music, most entertainments, alcohol, democracy, and much else, not just in Swat, but anywhere in the country.

Prime Minister Yusuf Raza Gillani

Pakistan

Culture: Pakistan is a land of villages, and traditional landowners dominate society and government. The two cities of Karachi and Lahore best represent urban society. With nearly 12 million inhabitants, Karachi dominates the nation's business as the major port and industrial center. Karachi is hot, noisy, crowded and dusty; the poor are seen everywhere. Lahore is a more traditional city of about three million. Like most urban areas, both cities are crowded with picturesque but tiny stores and workshops, where handicrafts are sold directly by the artists. By contrast, Islamabad, the newly-constructed capital, was planned along modern lines.

Life in the irrigated valley of the Indus and its tributaries differs greatly that in the Thar Desert or the mountains to the northwest. In the deserts and near-deserts, camel and goatherds move continuously in search of sparse vegetation.

Though the teachings of Islam minimize class distinctions, society in Pakistan is deeply divided between a small class of wealthy landowners and millions of impoverished farm workers, some of them bonded laborers who will never escape their debts until death passes them to their children. Though the laws do not recognize a special status for the landowners, thanks to their political influence the landowners pay almost no taxes, while the urban middle classes are taxed heavily to compensate. Land reforms and the spread of education are very slowly reducing these distinctions.

For those with leisure time, soccer and cricket are popular sports. One unique local festival is Basant, the spring kite-flying festival in Lahore. Though a picturesque sight, Basant's kite-flying is sometimes dangerous because the fliers' goal is to cut the string of rival kites. To that end, they coated strings with glass particles, creating a sometimes lethal hazard to unfortunate motorcyclists and bicyclists who caught the strings of falling kites around their necks. Banned for safety reasons in recent years, it was revived in 2007 with glass strings prohibited.

Female participation in outdoor sports has been targeted by Islamic militants, and sometimes prohibited. When women were suddenly permitted to participate in a recent one kilometer road race in Lahore, some wore the long, traditional salwar kameez (shirt plus pants), and even high heels.

The Role of Islam and Human Rights

Although it was created as a state for India's Muslims, Pakistan's early leaders avoided direct involvement in religion. However, in the mid-1970s a trend began toward enforcing Islamic practices, possibly to gain political support. Zulfikar Ali Bhutto banned alcohol and replaced Sunday (a tradition brought by Britain) with Friday as the weekly day of rest (Sunday regained its status in 1997). For his part, General Zia ordered Islamic punishments: flogging criminals in public, and amputating the right hands of convicted thieves.

The lives of two boys in the mid-1990s illustrate the complicated nature of human rights. Sold by his parents at the age of four to serve as a bonded carpet weaver, Iqbal Masih worked in a factory, often shackled to a loom, until he was ten. His detailed accounts of life as a child slave brought international recognition. Reebok awarded him a "Youth in Action" tribute. However, he was shot dead while delivering food to a relative. Pakistan prohibited the employment of children in 1991, when some eight to ten million children worked in carpet factories, small industries, domestic service and agriculture. Not all are slaves, and the numbers are falling. Given family poverty, some must work to survive.

At the age of 14, Salamat Masih, was sentenced to death because he allegedly wrote irreverent remarks on paper thrown into a mosque. Convicted under the blasphemy laws, he and his uncle fortunately gained asylum in Germany. A third defendant was murdered, allegedly by the same imam who brought the charge of blasphemy.

Both boys were Christians, but human rights abuses are not primarily a Christian issue. Individual abuses are sometimes deadly: a mob burned alive a Muslim cleric who accidentally set a copy of the Qur'an on fire. Communal violence sheds much more blood. Hundreds of *Shi'a* worshippers have been gunned down in mosques, and a reprisal suicide double-bombing killed dozens of Sunnis at a ceremony in Karachi.

The Ahmadiyya offshoot of Islam, considered heretical because it regards its 19th century founder as a prophet, face particular animosity. In the 1970s they were declared non-Muslims, and in the 1980s they were banned from calling their places of worship mosques and from preaching their faith. Many members of the community fled the country, but a number of worshippers were massacred in an attack in 2005.

Several factors enhance popular concern over morality and a desire to uphold an Islamic (and therefore "just") society. Widespread corruption intensifies the appeal of fundamentalist demands for Islamic purity and justice. The struggle against Indian rule in Kashmir also strengthens the appeal of political Islam. However, rival Islamic groups also manipulate the sympathies of the population. Iran and Saudi Arabia apparently subsidize *Shi'a* and *Sunni* schools that sometimes become centers for violence within Pakistan as well as across its borders.

Ignorance strengthens the appeal of groups that preach hatred based on ethnic and religious differences. Only a minority of adults can read even the simplest documents, and given the size of its population, Pakistan spends very little on education. Some ten million children never attend school; many others make only a brief acquaintance with book learning. Children average only 1.9 years of schooling, com-

Busy intersection in Karachi

Photo by Ray L. Cleveland

Mangla Dam powerhouse　　　　　WORLD BANK Photo by Tomas Sennett

pared with 2.4 in India. As always, boys attend rather more; girls, much less.

In 1998, soldiers visited every government school in Punjab. They discovered that many schools existed only on paper. Everything from teachers to exams, even repairs and sports results, had been faked. Nearly half (40%) of all teachers turned up at work only once per month, to collect their pay. To be fair, the pay hardly provided subsistence living.

The most important private system begins with rural schools and culminates in the Aga Khan University hospital and medical school. The spiritual leader of millions of *Ismaili* Muslims scattered through some 25 countries of Asia and Africa, the Aga Khan sponsors a variety of charitable works. The *Ismailis* form one Shi'a portion of Islam and accept Ismail, an eighth-century descendant of the prophet, as the seventh and last *Imam* (see Iran: Culture).

Higher education replicates the pattern, with some private colleges and universities earning excellent reputations. By contrast, the many state institutions face budgetary problems and their graduates lack respect because of widespread cheating scandals.

Economy: After its creation in 1947, Pakistan made progress from an exclusively agricultural economy, but farm products still account for most of the national income. Besides the fertile soil of the Indus basin, few natural resources exist. Only minor oil reserves have been found, though substantial natural gas deposits

exist in Baluchistan. Industrialization developed around local farm products, particularly cotton textiles.

In recent decades many engineers, technicians and skilled labor found employment in the prosperous states of the Arab Gulf. They sent home valuable foreign exchange, but also created severe shortages of qualified personnel in public services. The same factor has slowed the development of industry. Many lost their jobs dur-

ing the 2008–09 world recession, and their return home heightened already-severe unemployment.

The valley of the Indus forms the largest canal-irrigated area in the world. Further development is being carried forward by the Indus Basin Development Fund Agreement, supported by the World Bank and several western nations. The largest irrigation projects have been the huge Mangla Dam on the Jhelum tributary and the even larger Tarbela Dam. These dams greatly increased the land under irrigation, and they supply large amounts of electricity. However, because forests in the watersheds above the dams are being stripped away, the water in the rivers has become very muddy. At the present rate of silting, the Tarbela Dam will be useful for only about 50 years.

Reacting against the dominance of industry by an alleged elite of "22 Families," Zulfikar Ali Bhutto—himself a wealthy landlord—nationalized most large private firms. By 1990 the government owned some 80% of industry. Ironically, when she won power, his daughter, Benazir Bhutto, attempted to privatize some of the same firms. The process proved both difficult and slow. Pakistani businessmen know the virtue of keeping wealth hidden, and the stock market is too small and erratic to absorb large blocks of shares. Sales to foreign investors can provide foreign exchange and managerial skills, but they risk political condemnation. Most of all, though, corruption plagues all privatization attempts.

The Bhuttos owned land. By contrast, as a businessman, Nawaz Sharif favored a

A rural scene in the Sindh area, Pakistan　　　　　WORLD BANK Photo

Pakistan

flourishing private economy. His government sold a few inefficient firms, opened the stock markets to foreign capital, and loosened restrictions on foreign exchange. It reduced regulations over new machinery and factories to encourage private companies to invest. Nevertheless, the country presents many obstacles to business. The costs of borrowing are very high, and the local market frequently proves too small for an efficient scale of production. Heavy indirect taxation of industry, to compensate for the almost complete absence of taxes on the farming sector, means high-priced supplies, and the low level of education accounts for much of the low productivity per worker.

To provide the two or three million additional jobs annually for new workers requires steady economic growth. In Pakistan's case, this is threatened by poor educational achievements, a decrepit infrastructure, growing pollution and an investment climate marred by ethnic violence. On the other hand, massive investments in banking and Karachi real estate by companies in Dubai offers some hope that foreign funds may spark faster economic growth.

For years, under Dr. Abdul Qadeer Khan, Pakistan's nuclear industry secretly worked hard, with stolen plans, to construct the centrifuges necessary to enrich uranium for nuclear weapons. The broad outlines of the industry were suspected well before the first test explosions in 1997. However, six years later the discovery of tubes for centrifuges on a vessel bound for Libya enabled investigators from the U.S. and other countries to sketch the outline of a Pakistani "cash for bombs" network. Plans, supplies, and perhaps vital materials were shipped to Libya, Iran, and North Korea. For the moment, at least, world attention has halted that export business.

The Future: Pakistan remains a feudal society where most adults cannot read and write, and women matter so little that men officially outnumber them (a rarity, given the average female lifespan). However, in the past two years, it has experienced dramatic changes. A president was forced to resign because he sacked judges, and the reinstated judges restored corruption charges against his elected successor. The government admitted that an extremist group within the country launched a terrorist attack on Mumbai, and switched from a policy of concessions to the local *Taliban* to direct attacks on areas the extremists controlled.

The events of 2008–10 may well benefit Pakistan in the long run. However, prosperity and public satisfaction require effective government as well as democracy. The crucial challenge in the near term is to direct politics to the construction of a better society and economy, in one of the most corrupt nations.

Because border regions offer hospitality to the Afghan *Taliban* and their supporters, the U.S. conducts raids of border region with Predator aircraft that kill civilians as well as militants. One result is a country full of latent anti-Americanism—an additional challenge for moderate leaders like the president and prime minister.

Farmer inspecting a new tractor

WORLD BANK Photo

The Democratic Socialist Republic of Sri Lanka

The way home from school on a rainy afternoon

WORLD BANK photo

Area: 25,332 square miles (65,610 sq. km.).

Population: 20.4 million.

Capital City: Colombo (pop. 1 million, estimated); Parliament meets in Sri Jayawardenapura.

Climate: Uniformly warm throughout the year, except for comfortably cool temperatures in the higher mountains. It rains almost continuously from May to August in the Wet Zone of the southwest; elsewhere rainfall varies unpredictably.

Neighboring Countries: At its closest, India lies some 33 miles away across the Palk Strait.

Time Zone: GMT + 6.

Official Languages: Sinhala; Tamil (majority in the north).

Other Principal Tongue: English (among the educated).

Ethnic Background: The main communities identified by language and tradition are Sinhalese (73%), Tamil (19%), Moor (7%), Eurasian Burgher, and Malay.

Principal Religions: Buddhism (70%), Hinduism, Christianity, Islam.

Chief Commercial Products: Textiles and clothing, tea, rubber, rice, consumer goods, petroleum products, spices, coconuts, sugarcane, manioc and gemstones.

Major Trading Partners: U.S., U.K., Germany, Japan, India, Iraq—prewar.

Currency: Rupee (= 100 cents).

Former Colonial Status: British Crown Colony (1802–1928); self-governing British Colony (1928–1948).

Independence Date: February 4, 1948.

Chief of State: Mahinda Rajapakse, President.

Head of Government: Disanayaka Mudiyanselage "D.M." Jayaratne, Prime Minister.

National Flag: Centered on a dark crimson field with gold borders is a large gold lion in profile facing the pole and holding a sword in its right paw; at the pole are two vertical stripes, one of green and one of saffron, framed together in a gold border.

Gross Domestic Product: $38 billion (at current prices); $103 billion (Purchasing Power Parity), 2008.

GDP per capita: $5,000 (PPP), 2008.

The pear-shaped island of Sri Lanka, or Ceylon as it was first known in English, lies at the southeastern tip of India. Its climate and people resemble those of the nearby regions of India, but under the influence of Buddhism it developed a distinctive culture. Until weakened by civil war in the past two decades, Sri Lanka offered the possibility of social development—good health and education—despite relatively low incomes.

Most of Sri Lanka, including all the northern half of the island and a coastal belt around the south end, is low, flat country. The remaining one-fifth, lies above 2,000 feet in elevation, with mountains rising to peaks above 8,000 feet. These highlands force the humid summer monsoon winds from the southwest to rise, producing heavy rainfall in the southwestern quarter of the island and earning it the title "the wet zone" in recognition of its annual precipitation of 100–200 inches.

The rest of the island forms the dry zone, although its rainfall would be considered sufficient in cooler climates. Rain in the dry zone is unpredictable; it may be quite sudden and heavy, causing damaging floods that dump precious water into the ocean. Precipitation in the dry zone also comes from the northeast winter monsoon. Ground water can be raised for irrigation in most of the dry zone, from

255

Sri Lanka

**Former Prime Minister
Ratnasiri Wickremanayake**

Jaffne to Batticaloa. Given the tropical climate, agriculture revolves around the patterns of rainfall rather than temperature. Wet and dry seasons replace the familiar summer and winter of temperate climates.

The two major population groups inhabit distinctly different climate zones. The Sinhalese majority is concentrated in the wet zone, while the Sri Lankan Tamils live almost exclusively in the northern and northeastern limits of the dry zone—principally on or near the Jaffne (Jaffna) Peninsula.

History: Civilization, cities, and governments began in the dry zone of the island's north, and early ethnic conflicts remain today. Sinhalese kings had already established their capital at Anuradhapura in the third century B.C. when Buddhism gradually spread over the island and absorbed many existing religious practices. Sinhalese society skillfully designed irrigation systems and storage reservoirs to make maximum use of the dry zone's scarce water, and an impressive civilization developed.

Attracted by the prosperity of the kingdom, adventurers from India occasionally tried to seize the island, but they never succeeded in retaining it. With some interruptions, Anuradhapura remained the capital for over 1,300 years. In the 14th century a Dravidian ruler from South India succeeded in establishing a Tamil

kingdom on the northern end of the island. Meanwhile, aided by improved technology, Sinhalese society had moved south into the wet zone, which had apparently remained dense jungle. By the 16th century, the Sinhalese kings ruled from Kotte, near modern Colombo.

The first European sailing vessels came from Portugal and reached Colombo Harbor in 1505. Searching for spices, the Portuguese soon built forts and by the end of the 16th century laid claim to all Ceylon. However, the highland kingdom of Kandy maintained its independence.

Superior in both business and warfare, the Dutch East India Company contested the Portuguese domination of Ceylon's trade in the 17th century. The Dutch captured Colombo in 1656, and soon controlled Ceylon's trade by holding all the ports. The Kandyan kings, who had hoped the Dutch would recognize them as rulers of the entire island, remained in control of only the interior. The last Sinhalese king of Kandy was captured and exiled in 1815, by the British.

Dutch domination noticeably influenced the island's communities. Many settlers arrived from Holland and other European countries; their descendants became known as Burghers. From their Indonesian colonies the Dutch brought soldiers and workers. Their descendants remained Muslim—the Malay are still distinct from the earlier Muslim communities who are known as Moors, using the Portuguese term for them. In a few cases the Dutch rulers moved either Tamil or Sinhalese communities to other parts of the island.

When Holland allied with France during the Napoleonic wars in the 1790s, British forces captured Ceylon and declared it a Crown Colony in 1802. It proved a success. Plantations to raise coconuts, cotton, coffee, sugar, indigo and opium flourished by the mid-19th century. When a plant disease ruined the coffee industry, tea began to replace the coffee bean. When a shortage of plantation workers developed, laborers were imported from southern India, most of them Tamils. Their descendants now form a separate community known as the Indian Tamils, and they made a strong impact on the wet zone Sinhalese regions where the tea plantations were located.

In the late 19th century a cultural reaction developed against European culture and rule. Interest in Buddhism and Hinduism revived, and strengthened in the 20th century. Renewed interest also arose in the ancient arts and literature. These movements all encouraged national feeling by restoring attachment to the period before European domination.

British officials very slowly permitted representative government on the island. In 1931 all adults received voting rights, within British rule. The constitution of

256

Fishermen at sea with their catamarans

1946, with provisions to protect the Tamils and other minorities, established the legislative system. Independence came peacefully in 1948. Two political parties have dominated Sinhalese politics ever since.

Representing the Sinhala elite, the *United National Party (UNP)* formed the first post-independence government. Its great rival, the more nationalistic *Sri Lanka (Holy Ceylon) Freedom Party* led by Solomon Bandaranaike took power in 1956 and enacted a number of reforms. However, it blundered by stripping English of its official status and adopting Sinhala as the only official language. Tamil was permitted "reasonable use." Violence immediately broke out in many Tamil areas. After the murder of Mr. Bandaranaike in 1959, the party was held together by his widow. She led the party to victory at the polls and became the first woman prime minister in any country.

Besides differing over Tamil rights, the two major parties clashed over economic issues, with the *Freedom Party* typically seeking a more socialist solution. Mrs. Bandaranaike again won power in 1970, but soon faced a guerrilla uprising led by the *People's Liberation Front,* known by its Sinhala initials *JVP.* At the time a communist group whose doctrines attracted many educated but unemployed young people, the *JVP* capitalized on the lack of economic development, and its Maoist-influenced uprising became violent. With foreign military aid, Mrs. Bandaranaike's government suppressed the *JVP.*

She also undertook several radical changes. Although a member of a high-caste and influential family, she adopted socialist policies like supplying free rice, but this led to economic recession and shortages. Symbolically, a 1972 Constitution ended the nation's ties to the British Crown and changed Ceylon's name to the Socialist Republic of Sri Lanka. The presidency became largely ceremonial, while Mrs. Bandaranaike continued as prime minister.

These decisions and her style of ruling provoked opposition. Continued high unemployment and a declining economy, coupled with charges of mismanagement and corruption, led to her electoral defeat by the *UNP* in 1977.

From Ethnic Strife to War

The worst communal violence since independence swept the country in 1983, after rebels of the *Liberation Tigers of Tamil Eelam* ambushed troops near Jaffne. Seeking revenge, Sinhalese mobs (and sometimes security forces) attacked Tamils in Colombo, Kandy and elsewhere. Altogether perhaps 2,000 Tamils died, while arson left some 50,000 homeless, mainly in Colombo. Calm was not restored for more than a week. Most Tamils suspected that the country's leadership was behind the riots, and this strengthened the appeal of the *Tamil Tigers.*

Parliament then catered to Sinhalese nationalism by banning any party that advocated separatism or even autonomy.

This move ended any effective Tamil representation in parliament. While Sinhalese leaders did attempt to reduce tensions and violence when convenient, the ethnic rift had become too wide to bridge with minor reforms.

As Tamil guerrilla activity increased, their terrorist acts were matched by massacres by undisciplined units of the largely Sinhalese army. By 1985 the dispute had plunged Sri Lanka into open civil war. Sinhalese leaders intended to reassert the (Sinhalese) government's rule over a united country. But to protect their cultural identity, many Tamils demanded an independent state of their own.

During the first stage of the war, Tamil guerrillas attacked the police, army units, and Sinhalese civilians in the north and east. Headed by Velupillai Prabhakaran, the *Tiger* leadership developed a disciplined ferocity among their followers, including a willingness to die for the cause. Their fanaticism, plus refuge, training and arms from the Indian state of Tamil Nadu, enabled the *Tamil Tigers* to defeat other Tamil militias and take control of the Jaffne Peninsula. In response, the (Sinhala) army and police tended to treat all Tamils as rebels, thus extinguishing moderate political viewpoints.

In 1987, Prime Minister Rajiv Gandhi of India sought to intervene, and pressured the two sides to accept a ceasefire and a small force of Indian peacekeepers to maintain order while disarming the Tamil militias. After peace was achieved, Sri Lanka would unite the northern (undoubtedly Tamil) province with the Eastern province, where Tamils, Muslims, and Sinhalese had lived in approximately equal numbers.

The agreement aroused wide Sinhalese hostility. Moreover, the *Tigers* soon stopped surrendering heavy weapons, apparently never intending to keep Gandhi's agreement. They attacked other Tamil groups and massacred hundreds of Sinhalese civilians living in the east. Facing Sinhalese accusations that India failed to defend innocent civilians, the Indian military mounted a major invasion of the *Tigers* in Jaffne. Although the Indian force rose to 50,000 troops, far outnumbering the entire Sri Lankan army of 32,000, victory proved elusive. The second stage of the war ended inconclusively, but the army replaced Indian troops in Jaffne.

The *Tamil Tigers* launched another offensive in 1990 that forced the army to abandon Jaffne fort and most of the peninsula. The *Tigers* attempted to offset the military's superior numbers and equipment with daring attacks, and increasingly depended on teenagers who entered battle with cyanide capsules, ready to prevent capture by committing suicide. In the Sinhalese heartland, the *Tigers* assassinated

Sri Lanka

military commanders and politicians. A suicide bomber on a bicycle even killed President Premadasa. Although the assassin carried the cyanide capsule trademark of the *Tigers*, many suspected retaliation for the death of a Sinhalese political rival.

After elections in 1994 brought Chandrika Kumaratunga of the *Freedom Party* to power, she achieved an extended cease-fire with the *Tigers*. However, Mrs. Kumaratunga refused the *Tigers'* demand that the army evacuate its major military base in the north. During the cease-fire, in 1995 the *Tigers* suddenly shot down a military transport aircraft and sank most of the small navy. The war resumed, and clashes revealed that the *Tigers* had again used a cease-fire for military purposes, this time infiltrating the east coast as far south as Batticaloa.

To avert defeat, the government purchased jets, patrol craft, and artillery from Israel, China and elsewhere. The better-equipped troops recaptured Jaffne city and much of the peninsula, while the *Tigers* responded with human wave attacks and truck bombs that devastated economic targets in Colombo, including the Central Bank and the port. Another bomb exploded in Kandy, at the venerated shrine housing the Buddha's tooth. It missed the precious relic but disrupted celebrations of the island's 50 years of independence.

Anticipating a truce, in 2000 the military relaxed. Again, the *Tamil Tigers* struck, concentrating on the southern tip of the Jaffne peninsula. The army's large base at Elephant Pass dominated the causeway linking the peninsula with the mainland. Using long-range artillery, the *Tigers* shelled the camp, and then advanced to capture its water supply. When the direct assault came, the garrison vastly outnumbered the attackers, but the fort fell quickly, the greatest battlefield victory of the war until 2008–09. At the height of their power, the *Tigers* controlled about one-third of the country.

With secure access to the peninsula, the *Tigers* moved steadily towards Jaffne city and the vital airstrip nearby. Sri Lanka appealed to India, Israel and other nations for immediate military assistance to avert the city's fall and the complete defeat of 35,000 troops. Reinforced and rearmed with advanced weapons, the military halted the *Tigers'* advance just outside Jaffne city. Late in 2000 and 2001 the army undertook the slow task of regaining lost territory, against a background of cease-fires proclaimed by the *Tigers*. These probably reflected the *Tigers'* weakness in sustained conventional warfare; once again, they used draftees in their early teens.

A dramatic suicide raid on Colombo's international airport and military airbase in 2001 significantly changed the military, economic, and political realities. The loss of eight military aircraft gutted the air force, and the army proved unable to reply with a similarly devastating attack on the *Tigers*.

By wiping out half the country's Air Lanka passenger jets, the *Tigers* also created international fears about the safety of commercial property. Tourists canceled plans to visit, and some airlines halted flights to the island. Marine insurance companies imposed an expensive war zone surcharge on vessels entering Colombo port. Local companies suffered directly: exporters had to absorb the extra freight costs, while importers had to add the extra freight charges. Inflation rose, and many employees lost their jobs in the airline, port, and tourist industries. The economy slumped into a severe recession.

Under the impact, President Kumaratunga's coalition disintegrated. The opposition *UNP* won the elections that followed, and formed a cabinet under Ranil Wickremesinghe. Taking the initiative, Wickremesinghe quickly met many *Tiger* demands. After the *Tigers* announced a cease-fire, he restored trade with the north and ended an embargo that had kept even food and medicine out of the area. Norwegian mediation arranged a "permanent" cease-fire, with detailed agreements to treat many expected problems. Then the government lifted restrictions on travel that had long been used to harass

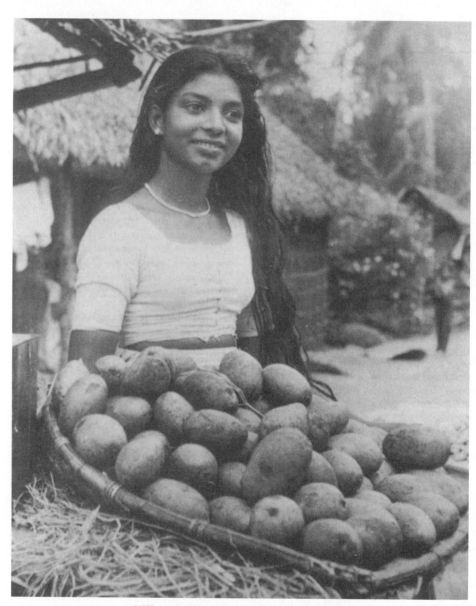

Village belle with a basket of mangoes

258

Tamil civilians The *Tigers* in turn opened highway A9, the route north to Jaffne, for the first time in a decade.

The "Permanent" Cease-fire

The cease-fire was only possible because the *Tigers* also desired a respite from warfare. Besides the evident difficulties drafting additional troops (increasingly, they were young teenagers), concern over public relations also played a role. Britain and Canada had declared them a terrorist organization and, like the U.S., froze billions of dollars of the group's funds. In response, talk of self-determination and a Tamil homeland began to replace calls for independence. Velupillai Prabhakaran apologized for mistreating Muslims and expelling them from Jaffne.

Another incentive peace was the harsh living conditions within the *Tigers'* zone. Although perhaps 200,000 civilians emigrated, similar numbers remained as impoverished refugees. Mines often littered roads and abandoned farmland. Many buildings damaged in the fighting had not been repaired and some schools, for example, lacked roofs, windows, and books. Lighting usually came from kerosene lamps: an entire generation grew up without electricity, never using a computer or surfing the web. Unfortunately, the *Tigers* themselves inflicted further suffering after the cease-fire, particularly by abducting children to serve in their military.

The rapid progress of negotiations noticeably improved the living conditions of ordinary people. However, the *Tigers* refused to disarm, and demanded the immediate creation of an autonomous zone in the north and east. The *Sea Tigers* broke the terms of the cease-fire, while forced enlistment of children did the same on land. In 2003, negotiations collapsed, though fighting did not resume.

Matters became even more complicated in 2004 when Colonel Karuna, the *Tiger's* top commander in the east, denounced the movement's leadership. In response, troops loyal to the *Tiger* leader, Velupillai Prabhakaran, crushed Karuna's forces. He escaped to government-controlled areas, and despite the murder of several of his associates, Karuna proved an irritant to the *Tiger's* leadership.

The Indonesian tsunami of 2004 hit both Tamil and Sinhalese coastal areas hard, killing thousands and destroying homes, government buildings, and businesses. International aid poured into the island, but a critical question arose of who would distribute it. The *Tigers* desired to distribute relief supplies themselves in Tamil areas, rather than permit aid agencies to operate, presumably to avert any other focus of popular loyalty. However, without government approval, the agencies could not turn over supplies to a rebel movement labeled as terrorist. Negotiations failed over this, too.

Sinhalese Politics and Strife

In amazing feats for a nation drenched in ethnic bloodshed and sometimes facing terrorist campaigns, Sri Lanka held provincial, presidential, and parliamentary elections throughout the civil war era. The two major parties, the *United National Party* and the *Freedom Party* alternated in office, but they rarely won an absolute majority in parliament. This frequently forced unstable coalitions.

National reconciliation proved elusive even within the Sinhalese community. In the late 1980s and early 1990s violence

Former President Chandrika Kumaratunga

struck within the majority community. The communist *JVP* that had launched a guerrilla war in the 1970s now adopted the cause of militant Sinhalese nationalism, and launched a bloody revolt in the south. It especially assassinated members of the ruling *United National Party*.

When President Premadasa sought an all-party conference to address the problems, the *JVP* opposed talks. Soon after this public relations blunder, several *JVP* leaders were killed. These losses weakened the intra-Sinhalese violence, but the cost of victory had been high. Possibly 60,000 people had died, many at the hands of death squads. Most victims were innocent, secretly denounced by rivals or opponents.

Elections in 1994 confirmed that after 17 years of *UNP* rule, the voters desired a change from its authoritarian style and increasing corruption. The left-leaning *People's Alliance* that included the *Freedom Party* won the parliamentary elections, and Chandrika Kumaratunga became prime minister. A few months later, she won a smashing victory for the presidency. Mrs. Kumaratunga did not exactly come from nowhere. Her mother, the elderly Sirimavo Bandaranaike, had been the first woman prime minister. She now regained the office she had first held in 1959.

Mrs. Kumaratunga had promised to investigate corruption, negotiate peace, and reform the economy. As president, she did suspend suspicious contracts, cut taxes on imports, and attempt to defeat the *Tigers* on the battlefield. She narrowly escaped death in an assassination attempt during her campaign for a second term in 1999, and won re-election.

Her second term proved difficult. Her injuries from the assassination attempt required treatment abroad, and her aging mother's health failed. At times neither the president nor prime minister could fulfill the duties of their offices.

After a vicious parliamentary campaign, in 2001 the *UNP* won an unexpectedly decisive victory on its platform of seeking peace and prosperity. After a brief constitutional crisis, the *UNP* and its allies formed a cabinet under Ranil Wickremesinghe, "cohabiting" with President Kumaratunga whose party formed the parliamentary opposition.

Although Prime Minister Wickremesinghe showed notable sympathy with many of the Tamil demands, President Kumaratunga proved far more suspicious of the *Tigers*. Other groups wary of Tamil separatism, even within a federal Sri Lanka, included the often-mistreated Muslims, Buddhist clergy, and the militantly nationalist *JVP*. In 2004, Kumaratunga called early elections.

Capable though not charismatic, Wickremesinghe took credit for the cease-fire and promised voters that the emerging prosperity was the first reward of the peace. However, crucial groups of Sinhalese voters felt that prosperity had reached only the rich, and that the *Tigers* had gained too much. They also considered the *UNP* corrupt. A plurality favored the president's *Freedom Party/JVP* alliance, and gave 105 the parliament's 225 seats. Tamil voters chose the *Tamil National Alliance*, a front for the *Tigers*. Another party led by militant Buddhist clergy opposed concessions to the Tamils. It gained seats.

Months later, the 2004 tsunami that originated off Indonesia hit Sri Lanka with great force. It killed over 30,000 and rendered hundreds of thousands homeless and jobless. The fishing and tourist industries suffered severe damage, even on the southwestern coast.

Sri Lanka

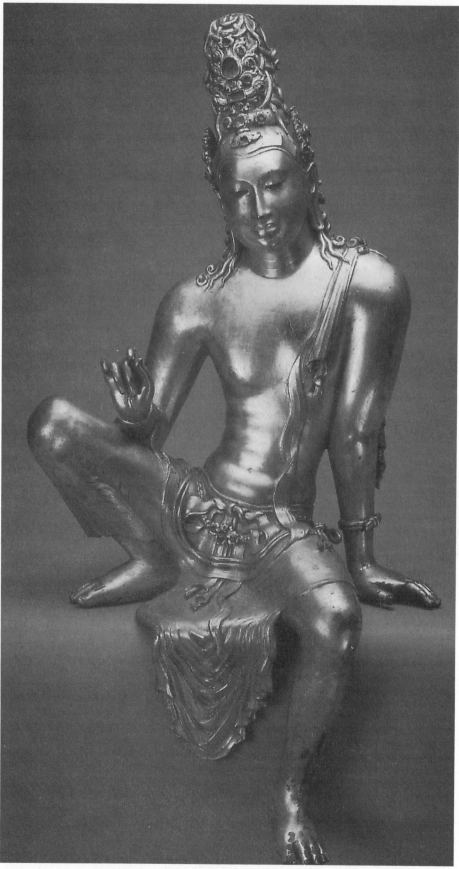

Bodhisattva Avalokiteshvara, 8th–9th century A.D.,
gilt, bronze and crystal in the National Museum, Colombo

President Kumaratunga's successor as *Freedom Party* leader, Mahinda Rajapakse, won a narrow victory in the 2005 presidential elections, partly because Tamils had to vote outside *Tiger*-controlled areas. On the crucial issue of the day, the civil war, Rajapakse represented the uncompromising wing of the party and the Sinhala community. He allied with the *JVP* and the Buddhist monks' party and rejected even a federal state as a compromise solution. The president and the defense minister, his brother Gotabaya Rajapakse, determined to crush the *Tigers* rather than compromise over their demands.

The *Tigers'* leader, Velupillai Prabhakaran, played into their hands. In 2006 hundreds of civilians and military died, because the *Tigers* deliberately broke the ceasefire with assassinations and attacks. The *Tigers* even created a small air force of prop-driven planes and bombed the country's major airbase.

Strengthened by arms from China, Pakistan and Russia, the hard-line military commander, General Sarath Fonseka, doubled the size of the army. He adopted aggressive tactics at sea, destroying the *Tigers'* supply vessels far offshore. With new jets and helicopters, the air force attacked suspected *Tiger* positions with some ruthlessness, and on land commandos struck key defensive points.

Then the army took advantage of its much larger forces to launch multiple attacks from different directions to squeeze the *Tamil Tigers* out of the northern third of the island. From the northwestern coast and from the south, troops advanced on Kilinochchi, the *Tiger's* administrative center. It fell at the end of 2008; days later Elephant Pass did as well. For the first time in decades, the government controlled the entire length of the A-9 highway up the center of the island to Jaffne. Unable to obtain a ceasefire, and determined not to surrender, the *Tigers* made their last stand north of Mullaitivu on the northeast coast.

It seems clear that Prabhakaran considered Tamil civilians as his ultimate trump card. Throughout the fighting in 2008 and 2009, the quarter-million civilians under his control were forced to retreat with rebel units; those seeking to flee were often shot. Hoping to win international pressure for a ceasefire, *Tiger* propaganda claimed large numbers of civilian casualties, many from heavy artillery even in a "No Fire" zone the army had pledged to honor. However, the military denied the claims—and both sides kept away independent reporters, so the truth is not yet known.

In May 2009, the *Tigers* collapsed, with most of their leadership killed in the final days. Very possibly some 10,000 Tamils,

President Mahinda Rajapakse

most of them civilians, had died during the desperate final weeks of a battle where defeat was clearly certain. Victory left the Sri Lankan government with countless refugees, most of them ill-fed and ill-housed in strictly-controlled camps, the largest at Menik Farm with 300,000 displaced people. The crucial challenge facing the government is to free and rehabilitate the refugees without providing new opportunities for any revived *Tiger* activities. A year after victory, most had returned to their often-destroyed homes and farms, but some 80,000 still remained incarcerated.

Translating military victory into political dominance, in 2010 President Rajapakse called presidential elections nearly two years early. Campaigning as the architect of a rare national victory over an insurgency, he solidly defeated the opposition candidate, Sarath Fonseka. The general who led the military through the final assault, Fonseka then fell out with the president and accused his brother, Defense Minister Gotabhaya Rajapaksa, of ordering the execution of *Tiger* leaders as they surrendered. Weeks later, the Rajapaksas' *Sri Landa Freedom Alliance* achieved an overwhelming victory in parliamentary elections, gaining nearly two-thirds of all seats. Human rights observers noted, however, that the media had been intimidated, and taht government resources had assisted *Freedom Alliance* candidates.

Culture: Culturally, modern Sri Lanka looks in two directions for its inspiration. Extremists may try to exclude one or the other of the two elements, but most people look both to the ancient culture and

also to the technical advantages of modern industrial civilization. For example, some contemporary Sri Lankan artists reflect the influence of the European masters, but their works still convey the uniqueness of a native tradition.

The oldest and most famous paintings in Sri Lanka are wall frescoes of maidens at Sigiriya, the palace of a fifth-century king, Kasyapa I. The palace itself lies below a rock summit, and for decades served as a monument to Sinhalese achievements. In the 1990s, archeologists discovered the full extent of the palace gardens, the largest and most complex in Asia. Given the dry climate, the gardens required a complex system of cisterns and irrigation tunnels to maintain fountains, streams and a water garden some 300 feet long.

Much earlier architectural monuments from the past impress the visitor at Anuradhapura, for a millennium the Buddhist capital in the dry zone. Enormous domes known as stupas preserved relics, while temples and shrines were filled with stone carvings. The city's skillful engineers were masters of designing complexes of buildings complete with large bathing pools. To provide water in the dry zone, the planners laid out a series of reservoirs and aqueducts to supply not only the capital but also villages along the way. In recent years some of these water systems have been restored and put back into service with new irrigation and hydro-electric projects belonging fully to the 20th century.

Sculpture was another ancient means of artistic expression of beauty and religious feeling, as was also the ancient Sinhala poetry. Literature also took the form of grammatical studies and philosophy. Ancient literary pieces were all written in the Sinhala language, but modern literature appears in Tamil as well, as do newspapers in both languages and English.

Economy: During British rule, Ceylon tea became world-famous, and other plantations produced crops like rubber for export. These provided the income and foreign exchange to pay for imports of rice, other foods and manufactured goods. After independence, socialist politicians who distrusted international markets attempted to make the economy less dependent on foreign sales of tea and rubber. Farmers were encouraged to raise food crops for the local market, especially rice, which for some years was distributed free to all.

Today the country remains the world's largest exporter of tea. Hit by competition from East African producers, its share of the world market has fallen from about one-half to one-fifth. Many of the Indian Tamils who formed the industry's workforce were gradually repatriated, and by the late 1990s plantations provided only one-third of the crop. The rest came from 500,000 small farms that sold the green leaves to processors. In the 1990s, difficulties in two large export markets, Iraq and Russia, reduced sales and profits. Al-

Tea pickers on a plantation near Colombo

261

Sri Lanka

though the government removed the tea export tax in 1993, it appears that many processors and farmers face serious losses, given low world prices.

Replacing tea as the greatest export are garments and other textiles. Beginning with an investment promotion zone established beside the international airport in 1978, textile manufacturing has spread across the southern part of the country. Low wages and a literate, mostly female workforce have attracted foreign firms and joint ventures to the industry. Other factories now manufacture electronics components for export as well. However, in the mid-1990s workers demanded higher pay and better conditions, and struck a number of firms. Militants even held a manager hostage. This apparently surprised companies that expected little union activity. In the words of one foreign owner, "We want the government to keep industrial peace and discipline."

Hundreds of thousands of Sri Lankan women also work abroad, chiefly as maids in Kuwait and the United Arab Emirates. When Iraq invaded Kuwait, some 100,000 Sri Lankans, the vast majority of them women, lost their employment and returned home penniless. A decade later, a limited restitution should be reaching these victims of aggression, financed by the Iraqi export of crude oil.

Sri Lanka's largest single development project, in the northeast, consisted of a series of dams on the Mahaweli River, the country's largest. However, the project has become widely criticized, for a design that produced hydroelectric power instead of irrigation for the (Tamil-populated) countryside, and for construction flaws may reduce the long-term potential of the project.

With natural beauty, a warm climate and a variety of appealing sights for visitors, tourism developed rapidly in the early 1980s, bringing in about 15% of foreign earnings. However, attracting foreigners has proved difficult: the *JVP* attacked tourist centers, wiping out profits in the industry, and then the *Tigers* destroyed the airline. The 2002 ceasefire boosted the number of visitors to about 500,000 per year, before the tsunami destroyed many hotels.

Before the current ethnic and political violence, Sri Lanka showed one way to a relatively advanced quality of life without high incomes or large per-capita use of energy and natural resources. Compared to surrounding countries, the nation is well educated (85% adult literacy, twice the rate in much richer Saudi Arabia), and its citizens enjoy average life expectancy rates of over 65 years. They also enjoy 174 non-working days a year, the likely world record. Birth rates and death rates both

rank low, the courts and democracy muddle through, and the potential seems to exist for a quality of life which, though not rich, allowed the simple pleasures to be enjoyed in relative security.

Ethnic violence threatened to destroy this potential on the narrowly economic as well as the broader human level. Besides its gruesome toll of dead and injured, the war cost 6% of GDP even without expensive arms purchases. Despite modest foreign assistance, the budget deficit tempted the government to print money to pay its debts. It neglected improvements to roads, electricity and other utilities, leaving the country one of the very few of its size without a single expressway.

The Future: As President Rajapakse rightly claims, Sri Lanka is one of the very few nations to defeat a well-armed, long-established insurgency that had held extensive territory. With the end of the war, he enjoys a hard-earned opportunity to shape a magnanimous peace with moderate Tamil support. Similarly, peace offers the possibility of rapid economic growth for all areas, with large projects built by foreign governments..

Given their great success, the Rajapakse brothers (president, defense minister, and presidential aide) risk over-reaching themselves. Hugely popular with the Sinhalese masses, who feel secure in the streets for the first time in decades, they seem little concerned with media freedom or incorporating the Tamils into Sri Lankan civil society. Relations will be uneasy with external groups that value democracy and human rights, and the UN seems unlikely to lay to rest questions about the fate of Tamil civilians caught in the final battles.

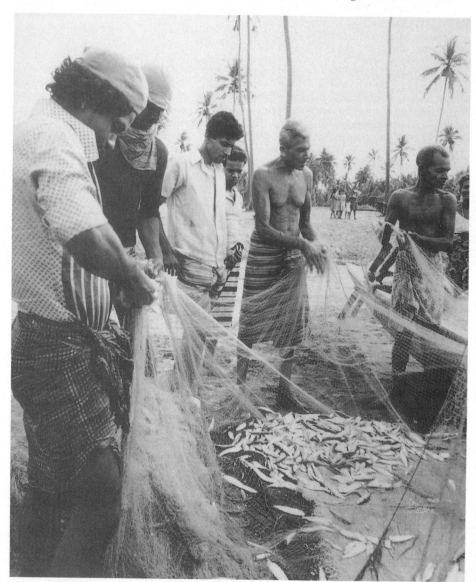

A fisherman's catch

Dependency of Britain

British Indian Ocean Territory

Area: About 22 square miles (57 sq. km.).
Population: Only military and support personnel.

The British Indian Ocean Territory (BIOT) consists solely of the Chagos Archipelago situated midway between East Africa and Indonesia. These wettest coral isles in the Indian Ocean, with some 145 inches of rain a year, share the same underwater ridge as the Maldives and lie 200 miles south of Gan. The BIOT was created to provide sites for British and American military installations safe from the nationalistic sentiments of independent states.

Until the BIOT was organized in 1965, the Chagos Group was a dependency of Mauritius, which received some $8.5 million in compensation for the loss. At the same time, three other island groups far to the west with little or no population—Aldabra Islands, Farquhar Group and Iles Desroches—were separated from the administration of the Seychelles and put in the BIOT.

Britain first considered the use of Aldabra for a military base, but these islands, among the last places on earth almost entirely unaffected by human settlement, contain rare birds and giant tortoises, as well as unique species of invertebrates. A determined "Save Aldabra" campaign led by the Royal Society of Britain, the U.S. National Academy of Sciences, and the Smithsonian Institution resulted rather in the leasing of Aldabra to the Royal Society as a wildlife sanctuary. Control of these three island groups was returned to the Seychelles at its independence in 1976.

In 1966 the U.S. and Britain signed a 50-year agreement for the use of Diego Garcia, the largest atoll in the Chagos group, as a joint base. The 1,800 inhabitants of this archipelago were removed by Britain to Mauritius and the Seychelles. In 1971 the U.S. Navy constructed a jet landing strip and a communications center. Later, the lagoon was dredged for use as an anchorage and the runway was lengthened. By 1988 Diego Garcia had become a major permanent U.S. base, the only one between Italy and the Philippines. Nuclear submarines can be supplied there, while warehouse ships moored in the lagoon stock enough weapons and provisions for an amphibious Marine brigade. Transient Filipino workers have been imported, because Mauritius, which claims sovereignty, withdrew its nationals working there in 1983 in support of the idea of making the Indian Ocean a "zone of peace" and keeping big-power military rivalry out.

After three decades of life in Mauritius and elsewhere, in 2000 the Chagos islanders won an appeal to the High Court in Britain that restored the islands to them. Arguing that they have not adapted successfully to living in other locations and suffer widespread poverty and distress, the islanders insisted on the right of return to Diego Garcia itself. Mauritius likewise demands sovereignty over the islands. However, returning the island to its inhabitants would violate the treaty between Great Britain and the U.S. Diego Garcia proved vital for B-52 bombers during the 1991 Gulf War, and later during fighting in Afghanistan and Iraq. In 2008 the Law Lords, Britain's highest court, blocked the islanders' return.

In 2010 the British government announced the establishment of the world's largest marine reserve, a 210,000 square mile area twice the size of Britain. One of the world's richest marine ecosystems, it hosts the Great Chagos Bank, the largest living coral and home to more than 220 coral species and 1,000 species of reef fish. The reserve further complicates the fate of the islanders because it was created without their consent it will limit commercial fishing, their traditional livelihood.

Occupied Territories

Quneitra District "Golan Heights"

Area: About 450 square miles (1,165 sq. km.)
Population: 10,000 Syrians, most of them Druze, plus 12,000 Israeli settlers (estimated).

During the 1967 Arab-Israeli War, Israel seized the southwestern portion of Syria, including its administrative center, Quneitra (or Qunaytra). For two decades the plateau provided tactical military advantages for the Syrian military, who had on occasion shelled Israeli settlements from the heights overlooking the Jordan Valley and Lake Tiberias. As Syrian troops retreated, Israeli forces rapidly occupied Quneitra district, which became known as the Golan Heights, the Hebrew term similar to the Arabic "Jolan" or "Jawlan."

Jolan has good rainfall, especially in the northern part, near the high mountains. Much of it is satisfactory agricultural land, though broken and stony, especially to the north, where the terrain is suitable for little more than pasturage. In addition to the Semitic tribes which had grazed their flocks in Jolan since late Roman Empire times, Shi'a and Druze villagers had established themselves on the flanks of Jabal as-Shaykh (Mount Hermon) by modern times. The main town of Quneitra was largely deserted through the first part of the 19th century, but was revived, beginning in 1873, by Chechen and Circassian refugees from the Caucasus Mountains after the Russian Empire imposed its rule on their homeland.

In the population mosaic of the Golan—typical of many parts of Syria in 1967—there were besides the Druze, Shi'a, Circassian and Arab tribes, also some Turkomans and a sprinkling of Kurds and other scattered minorities. All used Arabic in education and outside their own communities. In the fury of the Israeli invasion, thousands of these peaceful Syrian citizens fled battle scenes, while others were expelled by Israeli troops.

For reasons presumably related to Druze loyalty in Israel, the Israelis permitted only Druze villagers to resume life in the occupied zone; the Circassian, Arab and other inhabitants of the district became displaced persons, mostly around Damascus. During the 1973 October War, Syrian tank and infantry units pushed into the zone, but were eventually thrown back, and Israeli forces advanced close to Damascus. However, the greatest destruction to the town of Quneitra occurred not during warfare, but when the Israel military deliberately ransacked and destroyed buildings, including mosques and a church, before returning them to Syria according to ceasefire agreements.

By 1988 more than a score of Israeli settlements, most of them kibbutzim, had been founded in Jolan on lands owned by displaced Syrians. Some settlements are right on the narrow buffer zone, patrolled by UN observers, separating Israeli and Syrian troops. This location within easy range of Syrian guns is curious, because one of the excuses for invading and holding Jolan was to prevent Syrian artillery from shelling Israeli settlements to the southwest.

Disputed Territories

The Israeli officials who allowed the Druze to remain in Jolan may have been surprised to discover that many Druze identified themselves as Syrian Arabs and would not docilely cooperate with Israeli policies. They have protested Israeli economic measures affecting them, including high taxation without corresponding benefits. They have protested restrictions on their freedom of movement from village to village. In an attempt to disrupt them, the Israeli army has at times imposed long curfews to prevent them from carrying out their work; at other times demonstrations were forcefully broken up in confrontations where some were shot to death. When they were told they must have Israeli identity cards in order to leave their villages for any purpose, as this would have been recognition of the permanency of the occupation, they refused. After long curfews and other measures they succeeded in having the regulation relaxed.

These Druze are in a difficult position. They are obliged to cooperate to some extent with the occupation in order to survive, but not too much, lest if returned to Syrian control they might be considered collaborators.

In 1981 Israeli law was extended over occupied Jolan, and the area was added as a subdistrict to the Northern District, one of the six administrative units into which the State of Israel is divided. This act, tantamount to an annexation, was denounced by the UN. Successive attempts to negotiate peace between Israel and Syria have floundered over Syria's demand for a complete Israeli withdrawal and Israel's refusal to do so.

East Jerusalem

Area: 68 square miles (175 sq. km.) form the proposed international zone recommended by the U.N. in 1947.

Population: Nearly 140,000 Muslim and Christian Palestinians, as well as a varying number of foreign residents, mostly associated with church institutions. The number of Israelis living in East Jerusalem is small but growing.

The status of the city of Jerusalem has become a signal part of the strife in the Holy Land. Old Jerusalem, with its numerous shrines, archaic buildings, narrow streets and picturesque walls (last rebuilt in the Ottoman Period), has special significance to Jews, Christians and Muslims. Because of the city's sanctity, observers sometimes overlook the non-religious factors, such as political and economic considerations involved in the present contest for control of the city.

After many generations of relatively little alteration, the 20th century brought massive changes to the city. As the British administrative center of Palestine under a League of Nations Mandate, Jerusalem saw a new city growing up to the west and north of the walled city. The new city, mostly developed for Jewish immigrants, also had modern Arab areas. Then in the plan for partition of Palestine recommended by the General Assembly of the UN in November 1947, Jerusalem was given a separate status. The plan proposed an internationally administered zone of 68 square miles, including all of Jerusalem, the town of Bethlehem to the south, and a number of nearby Arab villages. This plan, however, was not implemented by the UN Security Council and the issue was the subject of an armed contest in 1948.

When an armistice agreement was signed in 1949, the new State of Israel held the western part of the city, from which thousands of Muslim and Christian Palestinians had been forced to flee, while the Kingdom of Jordan held the remainder, including Old Jerusalem, from which several hundred Jews had been safely removed under the auspices of the International Red Cross. The proposed Jerusalem International Zone was ignored in fact—except by foreign governments, as a diplomatic nicety.

Besides forcing both Jews and Arabs from their homes, the armistice divided the city and deprived Jews of all nationalities visiting privileges to their holy places in the Jordanian sector. Two separate cities in fact came into existence, each with its own character and economy, sharing nothing except a name. Jordanian-ruled Jerusalem (Arabic "al-Quds") was conservative and native Arab in character; Israeli Jerusalem was essentially modern European. Psychologically and socially the two cities could have been more than a thousand miles apart.

As a result of the war between Israel and neighboring Arab states in 1967, Israeli military occupation was imposed on Arab Jerusalem. East Jerusalem, as it came to be known, was joined to the municipality of the Israeli city. Israeli authorities then worked systematically to absorb the former Jordanian sector into the large Israeli city, disregarding entirely UN demands that Israel refrain from annexation of East Jerusalem.

Since its conquest of East Jerusalem, Israel has rapidly moved ahead to develop the city as part of its national territory. Homes for Israelis have been built on land seized for development, private buildings have been torn down to make way for public projects and Arab Jerusalemites who fled in 1967 have not been permitted to return to their homes. A number of prominent Arabs accused of resisting the Israeli administration have been deported to Jordan, including the former mayor of Arab Jerusalem.

Israeli spokesmen have declared emphatically that the "reunification" of Jerusalem will never be reversed and that the unified city will remain the capital of the State of Israel. Against considerable resistance, officials have encouraged the Christian and Muslim Arabs to vote in municipal elections, but have not given them Israeli citizenship (technically, they remain Jordanian citizens). They hope, in general, for deliverance from the present situation, while many Arabs and some Muslims elsewhere are determined that Old Jerusalem will be restored to Arab control.

Palestinian uprisings in the occupied territories which began at the end of 1987 magnified the division between Israeli Jerusalem and East Jerusalem. In spirit they had never been united. There have been separate areas of residence, social life and work, exemplified in the two downtowns. Christian Arabs in Jerusalem, as elsewhere in the occupied territories, have joined their Muslim fellow Palestinians as never before, having learned that the Israelis will not show them preference as the British administration did prior to 1948. Many Arab residents of Jerusalem have torn up their Israeli identity cards, which symbolize their inferior status in the Israeli scheme. Teddy Kollak, defeated

after 20 years as mayor, recognized that municipal attempts to unify the two populations failed. "Co-existence in Jerusalem," he said, "is dead."

Tensions over East Jerusalem arise almost annually, often when Jewish settlers

attempt to establish or expand residences in Christian or Muslim quarters. Projects as seemingly innocuous as an archaeological park also lead to disputes when they remove Arab homes.

Kashmir

Area: 84,471 square miles (218,670 sq. km.). Of this area, 53,665 square miles (138,992 sq. km.) are controlled by India; 32,358 square miles (83,806 sq. km.) are under the control of Pakistan.

Population: About 4.8 million in the Indian zone; 1.4 million in the Pakistani zone.

The disputed territory of Kashmir, or more properly, Jammu and Kashmir, was ruled by a Hindu Maharaja, Sir Hari Singh, at the time of the partition of British India in 1947 (see India: History). The territory consisted of the districts of Jammu, Kashmir, Ladakh, Gilgit and several smaller areas, all in the northernmost part of British India. The Valley of Kashmir is one of the most pleasant parts of the entire region geographically; Ladakh, the largest district, is in the Himalayas and is mostly ice-bound.

Unrest invaded the region when British India was partitioned and the nation of Pakistan was created. The Maharaja suppressed his Muslim subjects in one area, and soon bands of plundering Muslim tribesmen were streaming toward his capital of Srinagar in Kashmir province. He fled to the city of Jammu and there signed a document on October 26, 1947 incorporating his domains into the Republic of India, although about 75% of the population was Muslim.

Indian troops were flown to Srinagar to save it from the tribesmen and to take control. Troops from Pakistan were drawn into the war which took place in the winter of 1947–48. Under United Nations auspices an agreement to stop shooting was negotiated; it became effective on January 1, 1949. The cease-fire line, which ran through the provinces of Jammu and Kashmir and then into the icy wastes of Ladakh, left India in occupation of about three-fifths of the entire disputed area.

Although the cease-fire halted open warfare, it did not bring peace, and the future of Kashmir remained undecided. Pakistan

demanded a plebiscite carried out by the United Nations, but India held local elections and claimed that they served the purpose of a plebiscite—although the future of the territory was not on the ballot, and many Muslims boycotted the elections.

Kashmir remained a subject of great emotion on both sides. But outright violence was not serious until August, 1965, when Pakistan sent armed infiltrators across the Line of Control (LOC) to commit acts of sabotage and terrorism. Indian troops later crossed the LOC in three places, ostensibly to halt infiltration. Since Pakistani public opinion strongly supported fighting, its military launched a conventional invasion of Jammu with tanks and other heavy equipment in September. India responded by invading West Pakistan, near Lahore, and then farther south with a drive aimed at Karachi. Pakistan struck at India itself with attacks into Punjab and Rajasthan.

After the fighting reached a stalemate, the UN Security Council demanded a cease-fire, a decision simplified because both the Soviet Union and the United States opposed the war. The combatants complied, partly because they could not replenish their military supplies from the major powers. However, each side suspected the other of seeking further advantage, and refused to withdraw their forces from positions captured during the fighting.

In 1966 the Soviet Union invited Pakistani President Ayub Khan and Prime Minister Shastri of India to Tashkent, in the southern Soviet Union. There they were persuaded to sign an agreement for complete withdrawal behind their own borders and the 1949 LOC. Despite the withdrawal, the causes of the dispute remained. In 1999 Pakistani forces and irregulars secretly crossed the LOC and seized several peaks before being dislodged by Indian forces (see India: History). Feelings run strong in both nations, but India shows little desire to seize Paki-

stani Kashmir, and Pakistan's military recognizes that Indian forces are superior.

A further complication to the Kashmiri problem came when China, to facilitate road links, occupied desolate mountainous regions mapped as part of British India. One disputed zone lay in Pakistani Kashmir, but the larger occupied area, the Aksai Chin plateau, borders the Ladakh region of India. Since the 1962 India-China War, it has been occupied by China.

In the 1970s, Pakistan and China constructed the Karakoram highway to join their countries across some of the world's highest mountain ranges. The highway is 537 miles long and runs from Kashgar in China's Xinjiang province through Mintaka Pass, at an elevation of 15,000 feet in the Karakoram Range. It then continues south to Gilgit in Kashmir. At the time of its construction, the highway raised concerns not only in India, but also in the U.S. and the Soviet Union. These worries have slowly faded.

After several months of bombings and killings by a small group of Kashmiri secessionists, in 1990 police fired on a demonstration in Srinagar, killing about 50 people and marking the beginning of a popular uprising. As "freedom fighters" ambushed police, and civilians endured almost continuous curfews, talk of war mounted in New Delhi and Islamabad. Pakistan again demanded a plebiscite to allow Kashmiris to determine their own fate.

India naturally opposes any possible dismemberment, and the coalition governments in New Delhi often lack the power to make changes. Nevertheless, compromise may prove the only remaining alternative to brute force to retain Kashmir. Though the two nations negotiated a cease-fire in the Himalayan heights of Ladakh, where artillery battles had raged at a record 18,000 feet, some observers caution that popular feelings, aroused by revolt and repression, could force one weak government or the other into starting a war. The dispute promises to continue.

Regional Organizations

Gulf Cooperation Council

The rulers of Saudi Arabia, Kuwait, Qatar, the United Arab Emirates, Bahrain and Oman agreed in 1981 to form the Gulf Cooperation Council to further their common interests, especially security and defense. Apprehensive of republican sentiments generally, and alarmed by the violent revolution in Iran, the six autocracies sought to protect themselves by cooperation. In 1982, under the leadership of Saudi Arabia, an Arab Consortium of Defense Industries was planned with an initial investment of $10 billion. This faced numerous obstacles, for most member countries lacked any significant manufacturing ability.

The GCC's first practical step was the formation of an Arabian free trade area through elimination of customs barriers between member states. In 1983 they abolished tariffs on agricultural, manufactured and animal products originating in member states. Professional people were also to be allowed freedom to move between member states to work. Other joint projects related to uniformity of educational systems and expansion of educational opportunities such as the Gulf University at Bahrain.

By 1990, the GCC showed some signs of achievement and maturity. It shifted its attention from the distant problems of Israel and Lebanon to areas closer to the GCC, including peace between Iran and Iraq. The organization also formed a brigade-strength joint defense force, stationed in Saudi Arabia.

Although the GCC failed to deter Iraqi aggression against Kuwait, all its members supported the international Coalition in the Second Gulf War. Following the conflict, they formed, with Syria and Egypt, the Arab Mutual Defense Organization, offering those countries substantial assistance in return for a military alliance, but no force was set up.

Economic issues now appear most prominent. The members are divided about relations with the European Community, for some suffer discriminatory tariffs on petrochemical exports. The GCC countries would benefit from a common industrial policy (to avoid duplicating expensive projects), a unified external tariff, and a similarity of subsidies and other benefits to businesses. Upset by the decision to locate the central bank in Saudi Arabia, the UAE withdrew from the proposed monetary union in 2009, and Kuwait later delayed the issuance of a euro-style single currency by the remaining members.

The South Asian Association for Regional Co-operation (SAARC)

In 1985, the heads of government from seven regional nations met in conference in Dhaka and voted to establish the South Asian Association for Regional Co-operation (SAARC). Influenced by the success of alliances like the European Union and ASEAN, the founders hoped to promote economic cooperation (meaning fewer restrictions on trade), and thus reduce poverty and raise standards of living. Other objectives included better relations between countries and the creation of institutions like weather offices that could serve the entire region.

In a series of summits in the early years, SAARC's members agreed to conventions on narcotics and establishing food reserves. They adopted measures to simplify visas and travel between member nations. The Southern Asia Preferential Trading Arrangement adopted at the seventh SAARC Summit in 1993 looked forward to a regional free trade zone by 2001. Little happened immediately, but a new decision in 2005 called for the first steps in 2006, with the more developed economies of India, Pakistan and Sri Lanka abolishing all tariffs on imports from member nations by 2013.

Despite these signs of progress, trade remains limited between the seven member nations—Bangladesh, Bhutan, India, the Maldives, Nepal, Pakistan and Sri Lanka. Regulations often mean that many products are smuggled between members or shipped via other nations. In political matters, disputes between India and Pakistan often immobilized the organization. The Dhaka Declaration of 1985 forbad official discussions on contentious or bilateral issues, so SAARC is unlikely to address the most significant problems of the region. Afghanistan is expected to become a full member in 2007.

The League of Arab States

Representatives of all independent or self-governing Arab countries in the heart of the Arab world met to form the League of Arab States in 1945. The League initially included seven members, aside from Egypt all of them in Southwest Asia:

1. Egypt
2. Iraq
3. Jordan (then Transjordan)
4. Lebanon
5. Saudi Arabia
6. Syria
7. Yemen (Republic of Yemen, 1990)

Later, other nations which considered themselves to possess Arab character joined the League upon attaining political independence or soon thereafter (listed with year of adherence and, for those countries not described in this book, location):

8. Libya (1953), North Africa
9. Sudan (1956), Northeast Africa.
10. Morocco (1958), Northwest Africa.
11. Tunisia (1958), North Africa.
12. Kuwait (1961).
13. Algeria (1962), North Africa.
14. Peoples Democratic Republic of Yemen (1967–1990).
15. Bahrain (1971).
16. Oman (1971).
17. Qatar (1971).
18. United Arab Emirates (1971).
19. Mauritania (1973), Northwest Africa.
20. Somali Republic (1974), East Africa.
21. Palestine (1976).
22. Djibouti (1977), East Africa.

Djibouti, Mauritania and the Somali Republic are the only member nations in which Arabic is not the principal spoken language, though it is the main language used in schools and mosques. Djibouti has indicated its intention of making Arabic the official language and retaining French as a second language.

"Palestine" was admitted to membership by a unanimous vote in September 1976, although the Palestinian Liberation Organization then controlled no territory.

Until 1979, the League's was headquartered in Cairo on the east bank of the Nile. When Egypt signed a peace treaty with Israel considered unsatisfactory by other members, Egypt was expelled from the organization and the headquarters was moved to Tunis. Egypt rejoined the League in 1989. The League's majority condemned the invasion of Kuwait, but the sharply divided organization lost its Secretary General and returned its headquarters to Cairo thereafter. An Egyptian diplomat, Ismat Abd al-Majid became Secretary General.

Through efforts of the League, Arabic became the sixth official and working language of the UN beginning January 1, 1983. This decision was reached by the Security Council and followed a practice already common in the General Assembly. League members pay the extra expenses of the use of the additional language by the UN.

Selected Bibliography of Key English Language Sources

WEB SITES
Useful General Sites:
www.un.org (Web site for United Nations. Many links.)

www.unsystem.or (Official UN website)

http://europa.eu.int (EU server site)

www.oecd.org/daf/cmis/fdi/statist.htm (OECD site)

www.osce.org (Site of OSCE)

www.wto.org (World Trade Organization site)

www.worldbank.org/html/Welcome.html (World Bank news, publications with links to other financial institutions)

www.ceip.org (Carnegie Endowment for International Peace, using a fully integrated Web-database system)

www.cia.gov/index.html (Central Intelligence Agency)

www.odci.gov/cia (Includes useful CIA publications, such as *The World Factbook* and maps)

www.state.gov/www/ind.html (U.S. Department of State, including country reports)

http://usinfo.state.gov (U.S. Department of State)

lcweb2.loc.gov/frd/cs/cshome.html (Library of Congress with coverage of over 100 countries)

www.embassy.org/embassies (A site with links to all embassy web sites in Washington D.C.)

www.psr.keele.ac.uk\official.htm (Collective site for governments and international organizations)

http://mideastweb.org (Middle East Web Gateway resource)

http://www.palestinemonitor.org (The Palestine Monitor)

http://mfa.gov.il (Israeli Ministry of Foreign Affairs)

http://usembassy-israel.org.il (U.S. Embassy, Israel)

http://www.us-israel.org (The Jewish Virtual Library)

http://www.jpost.com (The Jerusalem Post, internet edition)

Newspapers, Journals and Television with good coverage on international affairs:
www.chicagotribune.com (Named best overall US newspaper online service for newspapers with circulation over 100,000.)

www.csmonitor.com (Respected U.S. newspaper, *Christian Science Monitor*. Named best overall US newspaper online service for newspapers with circulation under 100,000.)

www.economist.com (British weekly news magazine)

www.nytimes.com (Respected U.S. newspaper, *The New York Times*)

www.washingtonpost.com (Good international coverage)

www.foreignaffairs.org (One of best-known international affairs journal)

www.cnn.com (Latest news with external links)

www.news.BBC.co.uk (British Broadcasting Corporation site)

www.c-span.org (Includes C-SPAN International)

BOOKS
Middle East—general
Abi-Aad, Naji and Michel Grenon. *Instability and Conflict in the Middle East: People, Petroleum, and Security Threats.* New York: Saint Martin's Press, 1997.

Aburish, Said K. *A Brutal Friendship: the West and the Arab Elite.* New York: Saint Martin's Press, 1998.

Andersen, Roy R., et al. *Politics and Change in the Middle East: Sources of Conflict and Accommodation.* Upper Saddle River, NJ: Prentice Hall, 5th ed. 1997.

Anderson, Ewan E., et al. *The Middle East: Geography and Geopolitics.* 8th ed. New York: Routledge, 2000.

Bates, Daniel G., et al. *Peoples and Cultures of the Middle East.* Upper Saddle River, NJ: Prentice Hall, 2001.

Bensahel, Nora and Daniel L. Byman, eds. *The Future Security Environment in the Middle East.* Santa Monica, CA: Rand, 2003.

Choueiri, Youseff. *Arab Nationalism.* Malden, MA: Blackwell Publishers, 2001.

Cleveland, William L. and Martin Burton. *A History of the Modern Middle East.* Boulder, CO: Westview Press, 2008.

Dalrymple, William. *From the Holy Mountain: Journey among the Christians of the Middle East.* New York: Henry Holt & Company, 1998.

Deshen, Shlomo and Walter P. Zenner, eds. *Jews among Muslims: Communities in the Precolonial Middle East.* New York: New York University Press, 1996.

Dorraj, Manochehr, ed. *Middle East at the Crossroads: the Changing Political Dynamics and the Foreign Policy.* Lanham, MD: University Press of America, 1999.

Doubato, Eleanor A. and Marsha Posusney, eds. *Women and Globalization in the Arab Middle East: Gender, Economy, and Society.* Boulder, CO: Lynne Reinner, 2003.

Eickelman, Dale F. *Middle East and Central Asia.* Upper Saddle River, NJ: Prentice Hall, 1997.

Feldman, Shai. *Nuclear Weapons and Arms Control in the Middle East.* Cambridge, MA: MIT Press, 1997.

Fernea, Elizabeth W. and Robert A. Fernea. *The Arab World: Forty Years of Change.* New York: Doubleday, rev. ed. 1997.

Fisk, Robert. *The Great War for Civilisation: The Conquest of the Middle East.* New York: Vintage, 2007.

Freeman-Grenville, G.S. *Historical Atlas of the Middle East.* New York: Simon & Schuster, 1993.

Gerner, Deborah J., ed. *Understanding the Contemporary Middle East.* Boulder, CO: Lynne Reiner, 2000.

Gher, Leo A. *Civic Discourse and Digital Age Communications in the Middle East.* Westport, CT: Greenwood Publishing Group, 2000.

Gilbar, Gad G. *The Middle East Oil Decade and Beyond.* Portland, OR: International Specialized Book Services, 1997.

Gilbar, Gad G. *Population Dilemmas in the Middle East.* Portland, OR: International Specialized Book Services, 1997.

Gilsenan, Michael. *Recognizing Islam: Religion and Society in the Modern Middle East.* New York: I.B. Tauris & Company, 2000.

Glasser, Bradley L. *Economic Development and Political Reform: the Impact of External Capital on the Middle East.* Northampton, MA: Edward Elgar Publishing, 2000.

Guazzone, Laura. *Middle East Global Change: the Politics and Economics of Interdependence Versus Fragmentation.* New York: Saint Martin's Press, 1997.

Halliday, Fred. *Nation and Religion in the Middle East.* Boulder, CO: Lynne Rienner Publishers, 2000.

Hansen, Birthe. *Unipolarity and the Middle East.* New York: Saint Martin's Press, 2001.

Hawthorne, Amy W. *Democracy Deficit. U.S. Democracy Promotion Efforts in the Arab World.* Washington D.C.: Brookings, 2003.

Herb, Michael. *All in the Family: Absolutism, Revolution, and Democratic Prospects in the Middle Eastern Monarchies.* Albany, NY: State University of New York Press, 1999.

Hess, Andrew C. *Oil and Money: a Global Study of the Middle East in the Oil Era.* Chicago: Firtzroy Dearborn Publishers, 1999.

Hinnebusch, Raymond and A. Ehteshami, eds. *The Foreign Policies of the Middle East States.* Boulder, CO: Lynne Rienner, 2002.

Hiro, Dilip. *A Dictionary of the Middle East.* New York: Saint Martin's Press, 1996.

Hiro, Dilip. *The Middle East.* Phoenix, AZ: Oryx Press, 1996.

Issawi, Charles P. *The Middle East Economy: Decline and Recovery.* Princeton, NJ: Markus Wiener Publishers, rev. ed. 1996.

Jabar, Faleh A., ed. *Post-Marxism and the Middle East.* Portland, OR: International Specialized Book Services, 1997.

Kamalipour, Yahya R. *The U.S. Media and the Middle East: Image and Perception.* Westport, CT: Greenwood Publishing, 1995.

Kaufman, Burton I. *Arab Middle East and the United States.* Old Tappan, NJ: Macmillan Library Reference, 1996.

Kemp, Geoffrey and Robert E. Harkavy. *Strategic Geography and the Changing Middle East.* Washington, DC: Carnegie Endowment for International Peace, 1997.

Lewis, Bernard. *The Middle East: a Brief History of the Last 2,000 Years.* New York: Simon & Schuster, 1996.

Lewis, Bernard. *Multiple Identities of the Middle East.* New York: Schocken Books, 1999.

Lindholm, Charles. *The Islamic Middle East: an Historical Anthropology.* Malden, MA: Blackwell Publishers, 1996.

Link, P.S., ed. *Middle East Imbroglio: Status and Prospects.* Commack, NY: Nova Science Publishers, 1996.

Long, David E. and Bernard Reich. *The Government and Politics of the Middle East and North Africa.* 4th ed. Boulder, CO: Westview, 2002.

Maddy-Weitzman, Bruce, ed. *Middle East Contemporary Survey.* Boulder, CO: Westview Press, 2000.

Maoz, Moshe and Ilan Pappe, eds. *Middle Eastern Politics and Ideas: a History from Within.* New York: Saint Martin's Press, 1998.

Maoz, Zeev. *Regional Security in the Middle East: Past, Present, Future.* Portland, OR: International Specialized Book Services, 1997.

McKale, Donald M. *War by Revolution: Germany and Great Britain in the Middle East in the Era of World War I.* Kent, OH: Kent State University Press, 1998.

Moghadam, Valentine M. *Modernization Women: Gender and Social change in the Middle East,* 2d ed. Boulder, CO: Lynne Reinner, 2003.

Murden, Simon W. *Islam, The Middle East, and the New Global Hegemony.* Boulder, CO: Lynne Reinner, 2002.

Nawawy, Mohammed el and Adel Iskandar. *Al-Jazeera. How the Free Arab News Network Scooped the World and Changed the Middle East.* Boulder, CO: Westview, 2003.

Niblock, Tim. *"Pariah States" and Sanctions in the Middle East: Iraq, Libya, Sudan.* Boulder, CO: Lynne Rienner, 2002.

Norton, Augustus R. *Civil Society in the Middle East.* Boston, MA: Brill Academic Publishers, 1994.

Ochsenwald, William L. and Sydney Nettleton Fisher. *The Middle East: a History.* New York: McGraw-Hill, 7th. ed. 2010.

Ovendale, Ritchie. *Britain, the U.S., and the Transfer of Power in the Middle East 1945–1962.* Herndon, VA: Books International, 1996.

Owen, Edward R. *A History of Middle East Economies in the Twentieth Century.* Cambridge, MA: Harvard University Press, 1999.

Owen, Roger. *State Power and Politics in Making of the Modern Middle East.* New York: Routledge, 2000.

Peleg, Ilan, ed. *The Middle East Peace Process: Interdisciplinary Perspectives.* Albany, NY: State University of New York Press, 1997.

Pervin, David J. and Steven L. Spiegel. *Practical Peacemaking in the Middle East, Vol. 1: Arms Control and Regional Security.* New York: Garland Publishing, 1995.

Pervin, David J. and Steven L. Spiegel. *Practical Peacemaking in the Middle East, Vol 2: The Environment, Water, Refugees, and Economic Cooperation and Development.* New York: Garland Publishing, 1995.

Richards, Alan and John Waterbury. *A Political Economy of the Middle East.* Boulder, CO: Westview Press, 1996.

Rogan, Eugene. *The Arabs: A History.* New York: Basic Books, 2009.

Rubin, Barry, et al., eds. *From War to Peace: Arab-Israeli Relations, 1973–1993.* New York: New York University Press, 1994.

Saikal, Amin and Albrecht Schnabel, eds. *Democratization in the Middle East.* Washington D.C.: Brookings, 2003.

Savir, Uri. *The Process: 1,100 Days That Changed the Middle East.* New York: Random House, 1998.

Schwedler, Jillian and Deborah J. Gerner. *Understanding the Contemporary Middle East.* Boulder, CO: Lynne Rienner Publishers, 2008.

Soffer, Arnon. Translated by Mory Rosovesky. *Rivers of Fire: the Conflict over Water in the Middle East.* Lanham, MD: Rowman & Littlefield Publishers, 1999.

Tal, David, ed. *The 1956 War: Collusion and Rivalry in the Middle East.* Portland, OR: Frank Cass Publishers, 2000.

Tamini, Sargon. *Islam and Secularism in the Middle East.* New York: New York University Press, 2000.

Vatikiotis, P.J. *Middle East: from the End of Empire to the End of the Cold War.* New York: Routledge, 1997.

Viorst, Milton. *Sandcastles: the Arabs in Search of the Modern World.* New York: Random House, 1994.

Williams, Mary E. *The Middle East: Opposing Viewpoints.* San Diego, CA: Greenhaven Press, 2000.

Islam

Allison, Robert J. *The Crescent Obscured: the United States and Muslim World, 1776–1815.* New York: Oxford University Press, 1995.

Arkoun, Mohammed. *Rethinking Islam: Common Questions, Uncommon Answers.* Boulder, CO: Westview Press, 1994.

Armstrong, Karen. *Islam: a Short History.* New York: Modern Library, 2000.

Braswell, George W. Jr. *Islam: Its Prophet, Peoples, Politics, and Power.* Nashville, TN: Broadman & Holman, 1996.

Brown, L. Carl. *Religion and State: the Muslim Approach to Politics.* New York: Columbia University Press, 2000.

Butterworth, Charles E. and I. William Zartman, eds. *Between the State and Islam.* New York: Cambridge University Press, 2000.

Chebel, Malek. *Symbols of Islam.* New York: Saint Martin's Press, 1997.

Davidson, Lawrence. *Islamic Fundamentalism.* Westport, CT: Greenwood Publishing Group, 1998.

_____ . *Encyclopedia of Islam.* Boston, MA: Brill Academic Publishers, 1997.

Esposito, John L., ed. *The Oxford History of Islam.* New York: Oxford University Press, 2000.

Esposito, John L. *Political Islam: Revolution, Radicalism, or Reform.* Boulder, CO: Lynne Reinner, 1997.

Feldman, Noah. *The Fall and Rise of the Islamic State.* Princeton, NJ: Princeton University Press, 2008

Halliday, Fred. *Nation and Religion in the Middle East.* Boulder, CO: Lynne Reinner, 2000.

Hathout, Hassan. *Reading the Muslim Mind.* Plainfield, IN: American Trust Publications, 1994.

Hawting, G.R. *The Idea of Idolatry and the Emergence of Islam: from Polemic to History.* New York: Cambridge University Press, 2000.

Huband, Mark. *Warriors of the Prophet: the Struggle for Islam.* Boulder, CO: Westview Press, 1999.

Khan, Muhammad Z., translator. *The Quran.* Northampton, MA: Interlink Publishing Group, 1997.

Kramer, Martin, ed. *The Islamic Debate.* Syracuse, NY: Syracuse University Press, 1997.

Memon, Ali N. *The Islamic Nation: Status and Future of Muslims in the New World Order.* Beltsville, MD: Writer's, Inc., 1995.

Moussalli, Amhad. *Historical Dictionary of Islamic Fundamentalist Movements in the Arab World, Iran and Turkey.* Lanham, MD: Scarecrow Press, 1999.

Nagel, Tilman and Bernard Lewis, eds. *The History of Islamic Theology: from Muhammad to the Present.* Princeton, NJ: Markus Weiner Publishers, 1999.

Nomani, Asra Q. *Tantrika: Traveling the Road of Divine Love.* San Francisco: Harpers, 2003. (Explores women's boundaries within Islam)

Noreng, Ystein. *Oil and Islam: Social and Economic Issues.* New York: John Wiley & Sons, 1997.

Palmer, Monte and Princess Palmer. *Islamic Extremism: Causes, Diversity, and Challenges.* Lanham, MD: Rowman & Littlefield, 2007

Renard, John. *Seven Doors to Islam: Spirituality and the Religious Life Of Muslims.* Berkeley, CA: University of California Press, 1996.

Roy, Olivier. *Globalized Islam: The Search for a New Ummah.* New York: Columbia University Press, 2006.

Van Donzel, E.J., ed. *Islamic Desk Reference.* Boston, MA: Brill Academic Publishers, 1994.

Viorst, Milton. *In the Shadow of the Prophet: the Struggle for the Soul of Islam.* Boulder, CO: Westview Press, 2001.

Zepp, Ira G., Jr. *A Muslim Primer: Beginner's Guide to Islam.* Fayetteville, AR: University of Arkansas Press, 2000.

Palestinians

Abu-Nimer, Mohammed. *Dialogue, Conflict Resolution, and Change: Arab-Jewish Encounters in Israel.* Albany, NY: State University of New York Press, 1999.

Arnon, Arie and Jimmy Weinblatt. *The Palestinian Economy: between Imposed Integration and Voluntary Separation.* Boston, MA: Brill Academic Publishers, 1997.

Ciment, James. *Palestine Israel: the Long Conflict.* New York: Facts on File, 1997.

Cragg, Kenneth. *Palestine: the Prize and Price of Zion.* Herndon, VA: Cassell Academic, 1997.

Dannreuther, Roland. *Soviet Union and Palestine Resistance.* New York: Saint Martin's Press, 1998.

Diwan, Ishac and Radwan A. Shaban. *Development under Adversity: the Palestinian Economy in Transition.* Washington, DC: The World Bank, 1999.

Farsoun, Samih K. and Christina E. Zacharia. *Palestine and the Palestinians: a Stateless Nation.* Boulder, CO: Westview Press, 1997.

Holliday, Laurel. *Children of Israel, Children of Palestine.* New York: Pocket Books, 1998.

Inbari, Pinhas. *The Palestinians between Terrorism and Statehood.* Portland, OR: International Specialized Book Services, 1998.

Jabar, Hala. *Hezbollah: Born with a Vengeance.* New York: Columbia University Press, 1997.

Kass, Ilana and Bard O'Neill. *The Deadly Embrace: the Impact of Israel and Palestinian Rejectionism on the Peace Process.* Lanham, MD: University Press of America, 1996.

Khalidi, Rashid. *Palestinian Identity.* New York: Columbia University Press, 1997.

Kimmerling, Baruch. *Palestinians: the Making of a People.* New York: The Free Press, 1993.

Mattar, Philip. *Encyclopedia of the Palestinians.* New York: Facts on File, 1999.

Nazzal, Nafez and Laila A. Nazzal. *Historical Dictionary of Palestine.* Lanham, MD: Scarecrow Press, 1997.

Peleg, Ilan. *Human Rights in the West Band and Gaza.* Syracuse, NY: Syracuse University Press, 1995.

Robinson, Glenn E. *Building a Palestinian State: the Incomplete Revolution.* Bloomington, IN: Indiana University Press, 1997.

Rouhana, Nadim N. *Palestinians in an Ethnic Jewish State: Identities in Conflict.* New Haven, CT: Yale University Press, 1997.

Shemesh, Moshe. *The Palestinian Entity, 1959–1974: Arab Politics and the PLO.* Portland, OR: International Specialized Book Services, rev. ed. 1996.

Swedenburg, Ted. *Memories of Revolt: the 1936–39 Rebellion and the Palestinian National Past.* Minneapolis, MN: University of Minnesota Press, 1995.

Toubbeh, Jamil I. *Day of the Long Night: a Palestinian Refugee Remembers the "Nabka."* Jefferson, NC: McFarland & Company, 1997.

Persian Gulf

Abdelkarim, Abbas. *Change and Development in the Gulf.* New York: Saint Martin's Press, 1999.

Baldwin, Sherman. *Ironclaw: a Navy Carrier Pilot's Gulf War Experience.* New York: William Morrow & Company, 1996.

Coughlin, Sean T. *Storming the Desert: a Marine Lieutenant's Day-by-Day Chronicle of the Persian Gulf.* Jefferson, NC: McFarland & Company, 1996.

Donnelly, Michael and Denise Donnelly. *Falcon's Cry: a Desert Storm Memoir.* Westport, CT: Greenwood Publishing Group, 1998.

Edington, L. Benjamin and Michael J. Mazarr, eds. *Turning Point: the Gulf War.* Boulder, CO: Westview Press, 1995.

El-Shazly, Nadia El-Sayed. *Gulf Tanker War.* New York: Saint Martin's Press, 1998.

Grossman, Mark, ed. *Encyclopedia of the Persian Gulf War.* Santa Barbara, CA: ABC-CLIO, 1995.

Head, William Jr. and Earl Tilford. *The Eagle in the Desert: Looking Back on the United States Involvement in the Persian Gulf.* Westport, CT: Greenwood Publishing Group, 1996.

Hutchinson, Kevin D. *Operation Desert Shield-Desert Storm: Chronology and Fact Book.* Westport, CT: Greenwood Publishing Group, 1995.

Khadduri, Majid and Edmund Ghareeb. *War in the Gulf, 1990–91: the Iraq-Kuwait Conflict and Its Implications: Views from the Other Side.* New York: Oxford University Press, 1997.

Metz, Helen Chapin, ed. *Persian Gulf State: Country Studies.* Washington, DC: U.S. GPO, 3rd ed. 1994.

Mohamedou, Mohammad-Mahmoud. *Iraq and the Second Gulf War: State Building and Regime Security.* Bethesda, MD: Austin & Winfield Publishers, 1997.

Murray, Williamson and Wayne W. Thompson. *Air War in the Persian Gulf.* Mount Pleasant, SC: Nautical & Aviation Publishing Company, 1995.

Newell, Clayton R. *Historical Dictionary of the Persian Gulf War, 1990–1991.* Lanham, MD: Scarecrow Press, 1998.

Orgill, Andrew. *The 1990–91 Gulf War: Crisis, Conflict, Aftermath: an Annotated Bibliography.* Herndon, VA: Cassell Academic, 1995.

Schwartz, Richard A. *Encyclopedia of the Persian Gulf War.* Jefferson, NC: McFarland & Company, 1998.

Summers, Harry G., Jr. *The Persian Gulf War Almanac.* New York: Facts on File, 1995.

Yetiv, Steve A. *The Persian Gulf Crisis.* Westport, CT: Greenwood Publishing Group, 1997.

Zahlan, Rosemarie Said. *The Making of the Modern Gulf States: Kuwait, Bahrain, Qatar, the United Arab Emirates, and Oman.* Reading, England: Ithaca Press, 1998.

Terrorism

Anderson, Sean and Stephen Sloan. *Historical Dictionary of Terrorism.* Lanham, MD: Scarecrow Press, 1995.

Combs, Cindy C. *Terrorism in the 21st Century.* Upper Saddle River, NJ: Prentice-Hall, 1999.

Crenshaw, Martha and John Pimlott, eds. *Encyclopedia of World Terrorism.* Armonk, NY: M.E. Sharpe, 1996.

Egendorf, Laura K. *Terrorism: Opposing Viewpoints.* San Diego, CA: Greenhaven Press, 2000.

Gearty, Conor. *Terrorism.* Brookfield, VT: Ashgate Publishing Company, 1996.

Grosscup, Beau. *The Newest Explosions of Terrorism: Latest Sites of Terrorism in the 1990's and Beyond.* Far Hills, NJ: New Horizon Press, 1998.

Gurr, Nadine. *The New Face of Terrorism: Threats from Weapons of Mass Destruction.* New York: I.B. Tauris & Company, 2000.

Harmon, Christopher C. *Terrorism Today.* Portland, OR: Frank Cass Publishers, 1999.

Higgins, Rosalyn and Maurice Flory, eds. *Terrorism and International Law.* New York: Routledge, 1997.

Hunter, Thomas B. *The A to Z of International Terrorist and Counterterrorist Organizations.* Lanham, MD Scarecrow Press, 1999.

Kressel, Neil J. *Mass Hate: the Global Rise of Genocide and Terror.* New York: Plenum Publishing, 1996.

Laqueur, Walter. *The New Terrorism: Fanaticism and the Arms of Mass Destruction.* New York: Oxford University Press, 1999.

LeMesurier, Charles and Marc Arnold. *Terrorism.* London: Jane's Information Group, 1997.

Mickolus, Edward F. and Susan L. Simmons. *Terrorism, 1992–1995: a Chronology of Events and a Selectively Annotated Bibliography.* Westport, CT: Greenwood Publishing Group, 1997.

Nasr, Kameel B. *Arab and Israeli Terrorism: the Causes and Effects of Political Violence,*

1936–1993. Jefferson, NC: McFarland & Company, 1996.

Netanyahu, Binyamin. *Fighting Terrorism: How Democracies Can Defeat Domestic and International Terrorists.* New York: Farrar, Straus & Giroux, 1995.

O'Ballance, Edgar. *Islamic Fundamentalist Terrorism, 1979–95: the Iranian Connection.* New York: New York University Press, 1996.

Prunckun, Henry W., Jr. *Shadow of Death: an Analytic Bibliography on Political Violence, Terrorism, and Low-Intensity Conflict.* Lanham, MD: Scarecrow Press, 1995.

Stern, Jessica. *The Ultimate Terrorists.* Cambridge, MA: Harvard University Press, 1999.

Tanter, Raymond. *Rogue Regimes: Terrorism and Proliferation.* New York: Saint Martin's Press, 1997.

Taylor, Max and John Horgan, eds. *The Future of Terrorism.* Portland, OR: Frank Cass Publishers, 2000.

Tucker, David. *Skirmishes at the Edge of the Empire: the United States and International Terrorism.* Westport, CT: Greenwood Publishing Group, 1997.

Tucker, Jonathan B., ed. *Toxic Terror.* Cambridge, MA: MIT Press, 2000.

White, Jonathan R. *Terrorism: an Introduction.* Belmont, CA: Wadsworth Publishing Company, 1997.

Wieviorka, Michel. Translated by David G. White. *The Making of Terrorism.* Chicago: University of Chicago Press, 1993.

Water

Pachova, Nevelina I., Mikiyasu Nakayama and Libor Jansky, eds. *International Water Security: Domestic Threats and Opportunities.*

South Asia—general

Babb, Lawrence A. and Susan S. Wadley, eds. *Media and the Transformation of Religion in South Asia.* Philadelphia, PA: University of Pennsylvania Press, 1995.

Bahri, Deepika and Mary Vasudeva, eds. *Between the Lines: South Asians and Postcoloniality.* Philadelphia, PA: Temple University Press, 1996.

Baxter, Craig, et al. *Government and Politics in South Asia.* 5th ed. Boulder, CO: Westview, 2001.

Bose, Sugata and Ayesha Jalal. *Modern South Asia: History, Culture and Political Economy.* New York: Routledge, 1998.

Breton, Roland J. *Atlas of the Languages and Ethnic Communities of South Asia.* Thousand Oaks, CA: Sage Publications, 1997.

Chadda, Maya. *Building Democracy in South Asia: India, Nepal, Pakistan.* Boulder, CO: Lynne Reinner, 2000.

Dixit, J.N. *India-Pakistan in War and Peace.* NY: Routledge, 2002.

Ganguly, Sumit and Ted Greenwood, eds. *Mending Fences: Confidence and Security-Building Measures in South Asia.* Boulder, CO: Westview Press, 1996.

Hewitt, Vernon. *The New International Politics of South Asia.* New York: Saint Martin's Press, 1997.

Hossain, Moazzem. *South Asian Economic Development: Transformation, Opportunities and Challenges.* New York: Routledge, 1999.

Jalel, Ayesha. *Democracy and Authoritarianism in South Asia: a Comparative and Historical Perspective.* New York: Cambridge University Press, 1995.

Krepan, Michael L., ed. *Conflict Prevention, Confidence Building, and Reconciliation in South Asia.* New York: Saint Martin's Press, 1995.

Ludden, David. *An Agrarian History of South Asia.* New York: Cambridge University Press, 1999.

Mitra, Subrata K. And R. Alison Lewis, eds. *Subnational Movements in South Asia.* Boulder, CO: Westview Press, 1996.

Pasha, Mustapha K. *South Asia: Civil Society, State, and Politics.* Boulder, CO: Westview Press, 1999.

Peimani, Hooman. *Nuclear Proliferation in the Indian Subcontinent: the Self-Exhausting "Superpowers" and Emerging Alliances:* Westport, CT: Greenwood Publishing Group, 2000.

Schmidt, Karl J. *An Atlas and Survey of South Asian History.* Armonk, NY: M.E. Sharpe, 1995.

Schwartzberg, Joseph E. *A Historical Atlas of South Asia, 2nd Impression with Additional Material.* New York: Oxford University Press, 1993.

Synnott, Hilary. *The Causes and Consequences of South Asia's Nuclear Tests.* New York: Oxford University Press, 1999.

Tambiah, Stanely J. *Leveling Crowds: Ethno-Nationalist Conflicts and Collective Violence in South Asia.* Berkeley, CA: University of California Press, 1997.

Indian Ocean

Metz, Helen C., ed. *Indian Ocean: Five Island Countries.* Washington, DC: U.S. GPO, 3rd. ed. 1995.

Afghanistan

Adamec, Ludwig W. *Dictionary of Afghan Wars, Revolutions, and Insurgencies.* Lanham, MD: Scarecrow Press, 1996.

Adamec, Ludwig W. *Historical Dictionary of Afghanistan.* Lanham, MD: Scarecrow Press, 1997.

Cordovez, Diego. *Out of Afghanistan: the Inside Story of the Soviet Withdrawal.* New York: Oxford University Press, 1995.

Galeotti, Mark. *Afghanistan: the Soviet Union's Last War.* Portland, OR: Frank Cass & Company, 1995.

Glatzer, Bernt. *Afghanistan.* NY: Routledge, 2002.

Grasselli, Gabriella. *British and American Responses to the Soviet Invasion of Afghanistan.* Brookfield, VT: Ashgate Publishing Company, 1996.

Kakar, M. Hassan. *Afghanistan: the Soviet Invasion and the Afghan Response.* Berkeley, CA: University of California Press, 1995.

Magnus, Ralph H. and Eden Naby. *Afghanistan: Marx, Mullah and Mujahid.* rev. ed. Boulder, CO: Westview Press, 2002.

Margolis, Eric. *War at the Top of the World: the Struggle for Afghanistan, Kashmir and Tibet.* New York: Routledge, 2000.

Olesen, Asta. *Islam and Politics in Afghanistan.* Concord, MA: Paul & Company Publishers Consortium, 1995.

Pedersen, Gorm. *Afghan Nomads in Transition.* New York: Thames & Hudson, 1995.

Rais, Rasul Bakhsh. *Recovering the Frontier State: War, Ethnicity, and the State in Afghanistan.* Lanham, MD: Rowman & Littlefield, 2009

Rubin, Barnett R. *The Fragmentation of Afghanistan: State Formation and Collapse in the International System.* New Haven, CT: Yale University Press, 1994.

Rubin, Barnett, R. *The Search for Peace in Afghanistan: from Buffer State to Failed State.* New Haven, CT: Yale University Press, 1996.

Schuyler, Jones. *Afghanistan.* Santa Barbara, CA: ABC-CLIO, 1992.

Weinbaum, Marvin G. *Pakistan and Afghanistan: Resistance and Reconstruction.* Boulder, CO: Westview Press, 1994.

Bahrain

Khuri, Fuad Ishaq. *Tribe and State in Bahrain: the Transformation of Social and Political Authority in an Arab State.* Chicago: University of Chicago Press, 1980.

Lawson, Fred Haley. *Bahrain: the Modernization of Autocracy.* Boulder, CO: Westview Press, 1989.

Bangladesh

Baxter, Craig. *Historical Dictionary of Bangladesh.* Lanham, MD: Scarecrow Press, 1996.

Choudhury, Dilara. *Constitutional Development in Bangladesh: Stresses and Strains.* New York: Oxford University Press, 1997.

Dayal, Edison. *Food, Nutrition and Hunger in Bangladesh.* Brookfield, VT: Ashgate Publishing Company, 1997.

Heitzman, James and Robert L. Worden, eds. *Bangladesh: a Country Study.* Washington, DC: U.S. GPO, 2nd ed. 1989.

Hossain, Akhtar. *Macroeconomic Issues and Policies: the Case for Bangladesh.* Thousand Oaks, CA: Sage Publications, 1996.

Mohsin, Amena. *The Chittagong Hill Tracts, Bangladesh: On the Difficult Road to Peace.* Boulder, CO: Lynne Reinner, 2003.

Pokrant, Bob. *Bangladesh*. Santa Barbara, CA: ABC-CLIO, 2000.

Sisson, Richard. *War and Secession: Pakistan, India, and the Creation of Bangladesh*. Berkeley, CA: University of California Press, 1990.

Wahid, Abu N. and Charles E. Weis, eds. *The Economy of Bangladesh: Problems and Prospects*. Westport, CA: Greenwood Publishing Group, 1996.

Warrick, Richard A. and Q. K. Ahmad, eds. *The Implications of Climate and Sea-Level Change for Bangladesh*. Norwell, MA: Kluwer Academic Publishers, 1996.

Wood, Geoffrey D. and Iffath A. Shariff. *Who Needs Credit? Poverty and Finance in Bangladesh*. New York: Saint Martin's Press, 1998.

Bhutan

Apte, Robert Z. *Three Kingdoms on the Roof of the World: Bhutan, Nepal, and Ladakh*. Berkeley, CA: Parallax Press, 1990.

Savada, Andrea Matles, ed. *Nepal and Bhutan: Country Studies*. Washington, DC: U.S. GPO, 1993.

Zeppa, Jamie. *Beyond the Sky and the Earth: a Journey into Bhutan*. New York: Putnam Publishing Group, 1999.

Egypt

Beattie, Kirk J. *Egyptian Politics during Sadat's Presidency*. New York: Saint Martin's Press, 2000.

Boutros-Ghali, Boutros. *Egypt's Road to Jerusalem: a Diplomat's Story of the Struggle for Peace in the Middle East*. New York: Random House, 1997.

Cromer, Evelyn Baring. *Modern Egypt*. New York: Routledge, 2000.

Elkhafif, Mahmoud A. *The Egyptian Economy: a Modeling Approach*. Westport, CT: Greenwood Publishing Group, 1996.

Gershoni, Israel. *Redefining the Egyptian Nation, 1930–1945*. New York: Cambridge University Press, 1995.

Gorst, Anthony and Lewis Johnman. *The Suez Crisis*. New York: Routledge, 1997.

Harik, Iliya F. *Economic Policy Reform in Egypt*. Gainesville, FL: University Press of Florida, 1997.

Holland, Matthew F. *America and Egypt: from Roosevelt to Eisenhower*. Westport, CT: Greenwood Publishing Group, 1996.

Lucas, Scott. *Britain and the Suez Crisis: the Lion's Last Roar*. New York: Saint Martin's Press, 1996.

Meital, Yoram. *Egypt's Last Struggle for Peace: Continuity and Change, 1967–1971*. Gainesville, FL: University Press of Florida, 1997.

Metz, Helen Chapin, ed. *Egypt: a Country Study*. Washington, DC: U.S. GPO, 5th ed. 1991.

Nagi, Saad Z. *Poverty in Egypt: Human Needs and Institutional Capacities*. Lanham, MD: Lexington Books, 2000.

Sullivan, Denis J. and Sana Abed-Kotob. *Islam in Contemporary Egypt: Civil Society vs. the State*. Boulder, CO: Lynne Rienner Publishers, 1999.

Weaver, Mary Anne. *A Portrait of Egypt: a Journey through the World of Militant Islam*. New York: Farrar, Straus & Giroux, 2000.

Woodward, Peter N. *Nasser*. White Plains, NY: Longman Publishing Group, 1991.

India

Bayly, Susan. *Caste, Society and Politics in India from the 18th Century to the Modern Age*. New York: Cambridge University Press, 2001.

Bouton, Marshall M. and Philip Oldenburg, eds. *India Briefing: a Transformative 50 Years*. Armonk, NY: M.E. Sharpe, 1999.

Burke, Samuel M. and Salim Al-Din Quraishi. *The British Raj in India: an Historical Review*. New York: Oxford University Press, 1995.

Chadda, Maya. *Ethnicity, Security and Separatism in India*. New York: Columbia University Press, 1997.

Chary, M. Srinivas. *The Eagle and the Peacock: U.S. Foreign Policy toward India since Independence*. Westport, CT: Greenwood Publishing Group, 1995.

Chatterjee, Partha, ed. *State and Politics in India*. New York: Oxford University Press, 2000.

Cohen, Stephen P. *India. Emerging Power*. Washington, DC: Brookings, 2002.

Cohn, Bernard S. *Colonialism and Its Forms of Knowledge: the British in India*. Princeton, NJ: Princeton University Press, 1996.

Currie, Bob. *The Politics of Hunger in India: a Study of Democracy, Governance and Kalahandi's Poverty*. New York: Saint Martin's Press, 2000.

Dandekar, Vinayak M. *The Indian Economy, 1947–92: Population, Poverty and Employment*. Thousand Oaks, CA: Sage Publications, 1996.

Dantwala, M.L., et al., eds. *Dilemmas of Growth: the Indian Experience*. Thousand Oaks, CA: Sage Publications, 1996.

Derbyshire, Ian D. *India*. Santa Barbara, CA: ABC-CLIO, rev. ed. 1995.

Edney, Matthew H. *Mapping the Empire: the Geographical Construction of British India*. Chicago: University of Chicago Press, 1997.

Frankel, Francine R., et al., eds. *Transforming India: Social and Political Dynamics of Democracy*. New York: Oxford University Press, 2000.

Ganguly, Sumit, ed. *Understanding Contemporary India*. Boulder, CO: Lynne Rienner Publishers, 2001.

Hansen, Thomas Blom. *Saffron Wave: Democracy and Hindu Nationalism in Modern India*. Princeton, NJ: Princeton University Press, 1999.

Harrison, Selig S., et al., eds. *India and Pakistan: the First Fifty Years*. New York: Cambridge University Press, 1998

Heitzman, James and Robert L. Worden, eds. *India: a Country Study*. Washington, DC: U.S. GPO, 5th ed. 1996.

James, Lawrence. *RAJ: the Making and Unmaking of British India*. New York: Thomas Dunne Books, 1998.

Jayal, Niraja G. *Democracy and the State: Welfare, Secularism, and Development in Contemporary India*. New York: Oxford University Press, 1999.

Jenkins, Rob. *Democratic Politics and Economic Reform in India*. New York: Cambridge University Press, 1999.

Johnson, Gordon. *Cultural Atlas of India*. New York: Facts on File, 1996.

Keay, John. *India: a History*. New York: Grove/Atlantic, 2000.

Khan, Yasmin. *The Great Partition: The Making of India and Pakistan*. New Haven: Yale University Press, 2007.

Kulke, Herman and Dietmar Rothermund. *History of India*. New York: Routledge, 1998.

Maitra, Priyatosh. *The Globalization of Capitalism and Its Impact on Third World Countries: India as a Case Study*. Westport, CT: Greenwood Publishing Group, 1996.

Mansingh, Surjit. *Historical Dictionary of India*. Lanham, MD: Scarecrow Press, 1996.

Mehta, Gita. *Snakes and Ladders: Glimpses of Modern India*. New York: Doubleday, 1997.

Moorhouse, Geoffrey. *India Britannica: a Vivid Introduction to the History of British India*. Chicago: Academy Chicago Publishers, 1999.

Paz, Octavio. *In Light of India: Essays*. San Diego, CA: Harcourt Brace & Company, 1997.

Rao, C. Hanumantha and Hans Linnemann, eds. *Economic Reforms and Poverty Alleviation in India*. Thousand Oaks, CA: Sage Publications, 1996.

Read, Anthony. *The Proudest Day: Indian's Long Road to Independence*. New York: W.W. Norton & Company, 1998.

Royle, Trevor. *The Last Days of the Raj*. North Pomfret, VT: Trafalgar Square, 1998.

Saberwal, Satish. *Roots of Crisis: Interpreting Contemporary Indian Society*. Thousand Oaks, CA: Sage Publications, s1996.

Sachs, Jeffrey D., et al., eds. *India in the Era of Economic Reforms*. New York: Oxford University Press, 2000.

Sanguly, Sumit and Neil DeVotta, eds. *Understanding Contemporary India*. Boulder, CO: Lynne Reinner, 2003.

Sekhon, Joti. *Modern India*. New York: McGraw-Hill, 1999.

Sidhu, Waheguru and Jing-dong Yuan. *China and India: Cooperation or Conflict?* Boulder, CO: Lynne Reinner, 2003.

Sridharan, Kripa. *The ASEAN Region in India's Foreign Policy*. Brookfield, VT: Ashgate Publishing Company, 1996.

271

Srinivasan, T.N. and Suresh D. Tendulkar. *India in the World Economy*. Washington, DC: Institute for International Economics, 2001.

Sugata, Bose. *Nationalism, Democracy, and Development: State and Politics in India*. New York: Oxford University Press, 1999.

Tharoor, Shashi. *India: from Midnight to the Millennium*. New York: Arcade Publishing, 1997.

Thomas, Raju G. *Democracy, Security, and Development in India*. New York: Saint Martin's Press, 1996.

Tomlinson, B.R. *The Economy of Modern India, 1860–1970*. New York: Cambridge University Press, 1993.

Vanaik, Achin. *The Furies of Indian Communalism: Religion, Modernity and Secularization*. New York: Verso, 1997.

Vohra, Ranbir. *The Making of India: a Historical Survey*. Armonk, NY: M.E. Sharpe, 2000.

Wolpert, Stanley A. *A New History of India*. New York: Oxford University Press, 3rd ed. 1989.

Wolpert, Stanley A. *Nehru: a Tryst with Destiny*. New York: Oxford University Press, 1996.

Iran

Abrahamian, Ervand. *Khomeinism: Essays on the Islamic Republic*. Berkeley, CA: University of California Press, 1993.

Abrahamian, Ervand. *A History of Modern Iran*. New York: Cambridge University Press, 2008 (paper).

Adelkhah, Fariba. *Being Modern in Iran*. New York: Columbia University Press, 2000.

Amuzegar, Jahangir. *Iran's Economy under the Islamic Republic*. New York: Saint Martin's Press, 1994.

Azimi, Fakhreddin. *The Quest for Democracy in Iran: A Century of Struggle against Authoritarian Rule*. Cambridge: Harvard University Press, 2008.

Baktiari, Bahman. *Parliamentary Politics in Revolutionary Iran: the Institutionalization of Factional Politics*. Gainesville, FL: University Press of Florida, 1996.

Bayandor, Darioush. *Iran and the CIA: The Fall of Mossadeq Revisited*. New York: Palgrave Macmillan, 2010.

Cordesman, Anthony H. and Ahmed S. Hashim. *Iran: Dilemmas of Dual Containment*. Boulder, CO: Westview Press, 1997.

Cordesman, Anthony H. *Iran's Military Forces in Transition*. Westport, CT: Greenwood Publishing Group, 1999.

Daneshar, Parviz. *Revolution in Iran*. New York: Saint Martin's Press, 1996.

Farmanfarmaian, Manucher and Roxane Farmanfarmaian. *Blood and Oil: Memoirs of a Persian Prince*. New York: Random House, 1997.

Gheissari, Ali. *Contemporary Iran: Economy, Society, Politics*. New York: Oxford University Press, 2009.

Gieling, Saskia M. *Religion and War in Revolutionary Iran*. London: I.B. Tauris, 1999.

Goode, James F. *United States and Iran: in the Shadow of Musaddiq*. New York: Saint Martin's Press, 1997.

Heiss, Mary Ann. *Empire and Nationhood: the United States, Great Britain, and Iranian Oil, 1950–1954*. New York: Columbia University Press, 1997.

Keddie, Nikki R. *Iran and Muslim World: Resistance and Revolution*. New York: New York University Press, 1995.

Mackey, Sandra. *The Iranians*. New York: NAL/Dutton, 1998.

Metz, Helen Chapin, ed. *Iran: a Country Study*. Washington, DC: U.S. GPO, 4th ed. 1989.

Moses, Russell L. *Freeing the Hostages: Reexamining U.S.-Iranian Negotiations and Soviet Policy*. Pittsburgh, PA: University of Pittsburgh Press, 1996.

Nafisi, Azar, *Reading Lolita in Tehran*. New York: Random House, 2003.

Peimani, Hooman. *Iran and the United States: the Rise of the West Asian Regional Grouping*. Westport, CT: Greenwood Publishing Group, 1999.

Riesebrodt, Martin. *Pious Passion: the Emergence of Modern Fundamentalism in the United States and Iran*. Berkeley, CA: University of California Press, 1993.

Sciolino, Elaine. *Persian Mirrors: the Elusive Face of Iran*. New York: The Free Press, 2000.

Walsh, Lawrence E. *Firewall: the Iran-Contra Conspiracy and Cover-Up*. New York: W.W. Norton & Company, 1997.

Wright, Robin B. *The Last Great Revolution: Turmoil and Transformation in Iran*. New York: Alfred A. Knopf, 2000.

Iraq

Al-Hawaheri, Yasmin Husein. *Women in Iraq: The Gender Impact of International Sanctions*. Boulder, CO: Lynne Rienner Publishers, 2008.

Al-Khalil, Samir. *Republic of Fear: the Inside Story of Saddam's Iraq*. Collingdale, PA: DIANE Publishing Company, 2000.

Arnove, Anthony, ed. *Iraq under Siege: the Deadly Impact of Sanctions and War*. Cambridge, MA: South End Press, 2000.

Baram, Amatzia and Barry Rubin, eds. *Iraq's Road to War*. New York: Saint Martin's Press, 1994.

Bhatia, Shyam and Dan McGrory. *Brighter Than the Baghdad Sun: Saddam Hussein's Nuclear Threat to the United States*. Washington, DC: Regnery Publishing, 2000.

Braude, Joseph. *The New Iraq*. Boulder, CO: Westview, 2003.

Butler, Richard. *The Greatest Threat: Iraq, Weapons of Mass Destruction and the Crisis of Global Security*. New York: Public Affairs, 2000.

Clawson, Patrick, ed. *How to Build a New Iraq after Saddam*. Washington D.C.: Brookings, 2002.

Cockburn, Andrew. *Out of the Ashes: the Resurrection of Saddam Hussein*. New York: HarperCollins, 2000.

Cordesman, Anthony H. and Ahmed S. Hashim. *Iraq: Sanctions and Beyond*. Boulder, CO: Westview Press, 1997.

Danspeckgruber, Wolfgang F. and Charles R. Tripp, eds. *The Iraqi Aggression against Kuwait: Strategic Lessons and Implications for Europe*. Boulder, CO: Westview Press, 1996.

Elliot, Matthew. *Independent Iraq: British Influence from 1941–1958*. New York: Saint Martin's Press, 1996.

Fawn, Rick and Raymond Hinnebusch, eds. *The Iraq War: Causes and Consequences*. Boulder, CO: Lynne Rienner Publishers, 2006.

Grossman, Mark, ed. *Encyclopedia of the Persian Gulf War*. Santa Barbara, CA: ABC-CLIO, 1995.

Haj, Samira. *The Making of Iraq, 1900–1963: Capital, Power and Ideology*. Albany, NY: State University of New York Press, 1997.

Haselkorn, Avigdor. *The Continuing Storm: Iraq, Poisonous Weapons, and Deterrence*. New Haven, CT: Yale University Press, 1998.

Lukitz, Liora. *Iraq: the Search for National Identity*. Portland, OR: Frank Cass & Company, 1995.

Marr, Phebe. *Modern History of Iraq*. 2d ed. Boulder, CO: Westview, 2003.

Metz, Helen Chapin, ed. *Iraq: a Country Study*. Washington, DC: U.S. GPO, 4th ed. 1990.

Mohamedou, Mohammad-Mahmoud. *Iraq and the Second Gulf War: State Building and Regime Security*. Bethesda, MD: Austin & Winfield Publishers, 1997.

Musallam, Musallam A. *Iraqi Invasion of Kuwait: Saddam Hussein, His State and International Power Politics*. New York: Saint Martin's Press, 1996.

Nakash, Yitzhak. *The Shiis of Iraq*. Princeton, NJ: Princeton University Press, 1994.

Rahaee, Farhang, ed. *The Iran-Iraq War: the Politics of Aggression*. Gainesville, FL: University Press of Florida, 1993.

Shadid, Anthony. *Night Draws Near: Iraq's People in the Shadow of America's War*. New York: Henry Holt and Company, 2006

Simons, G.L. *Iraq: from Sumer to Saddam*. New York: Saint Martin's Press, 1994.

Stansfield, Gareth and Robert Lowe, eds. *The Kurdish Policy Imperative*. Washington: Brookings, 2009

Stiglitz, Joseph E. and Linda J. Bilmes. *The Three Trillion Dollar War: The True Cost of the Iraq Conflict*. New York: W.W. Norton, 2008

Israel

Arain, Asher. *The Second Republic: Politics in Israel*. Chatham, NJ: Chatham House Publishers, 1997.

Avruch, Kevin and Walter P. Zenner, eds. *Critical Essays on Israeli Society, Religion, and Government: Books on Israel.* Albany, NY: State University of New York Press, 1996.

Barkai, Haim. *The Lessons of Israel's Great Inflation.* Westport, CT: Greenwood Publishing Group, 1995.

Barnett, Michael N., ed. *Israel in Comparative Perspective: Challenging the Conventional Wisdom.* Albany, NY: State University of New York Press, 1996.

Bar-On, Mordechai. *In Pursuit of Peace: a History of the Israeli Peace Movement.* Washington, DC: United States Institute of Peace Press, 1996.

Barzilai, Gad. *Wars, Internal Conflicts, and Political Order: a Jewish Democracy in the Middle East.* Albany, NY: State University of New York Press, 1996.

Ben-Ari, Eyal, ed. *Grasping Land: Space and Place in Contemporary Israeli Discourse and Experience.* State University of New York Press, 1997.

Ben Meir, Yehuda. *Civil-Military Relations in Israel.* New York: Columbia University Press, 1995.

Benson, Michael T. *Harry S. Truman and the Founding of Israel.* Westport, CT: Greenwood Publishing Group, 1997.

Bickerton, Ian J. and Carla L. Klausner. *A Concise History of the Arab-Israeli Conflict.* Upper Saddle River, NJ: Prentice Hall, 1997.

Boyarin, Jonathan. *Palestine and Jewish History: Criticism at the Borders of Ethnography.* Minneapolis, MN: University of Minnesota Press, 1996.

Bregman, Ahron. *Israel's Wars, 1947–1993.* New York: Routledge, 2000.

Buchanan, Andrew S. *Peace with Justice: a History of the Israeli-Palestinian Declaration.* New York: Saint Martin's Press, 2000.

Chesin, Amir S., et al. *Separate but Unequal.* Cambridge, MA: Harvard University Press, 1999.

Cohen, Asher. *Israel and the Politics of Jewish Identity: the Secular-Religious Impasse.* Baltimore, MD: Johns Hopkins University Press, 2000.

Cohen, Avner. *Israel and the Bomb.* New York: Columbia University Press, 1998.

Cohen, Stuart A. *Democratic Societies and Their Armed Forces: Israel in Comparative Context.* Portland, OR: Frank Cass Publishers, 2000.

Cordesman, Anthony H. *Perilous Prospects: the Peace Process and the Arab-Israeli Military Balance.* Portland, OR: Frank Cass & Company, 1996.

Corzine, Phyllis. *The Palestinian-Israeli Accord.* San Diego, CA: Lucent Books, 1996.

Dumper, Michael. *The Politics of Jerusalem since 1967.* New York: Columbia University Press, 1996.

Eban, Abba S. *Diplomacy for the Next Century.* New Haven, CT: Yale University Press, 1998.

Edelheit, Hershel and Abraham J. Edelheit. *Israel and the Jewish World, 1948–1993: a Chronology.* Westport, CT: Greenwood Publishing Group, 1995.

Evron, Boas. *Jewish State or Israeli Nation?* Bloomington, IN: Indiana University Press, 1995.

Ezrahi, Yaron. *Rubber Bullets: Power and Conscience in Modern Israel.* New York: Farrar, Straus & Giroux, 1996.

Freeman, Robert Owen, ed. *Israel's First Fifty Years.* Gainesville, FL: University Press of Florida, 2000.

Garfinkle, Adam. *Politics and Society in Modern Israel: Myths and Realities.* Armonk, NY: M.E. Sharpe, 1997.

Gilbert, Martin. *Israel: a History.* New York: William Morrow & Company, 1998.

Gilbert, Martin. *Jerusalem in the Twentieth Century.* New York: John Wiley & Sons, 1996.

Goldscheider, Calvin. *Israel's Changing Society. Population, Ethnicity, and Development.* 2d. ed. Boulder, CO: Westview, 2002.

Gordon, Haim. *Quicksand: Israel, the Intifada, and the Rise of Political Evil.* East Lansing, MI: Michigan State University, 1995.

Hartman, David. *Israelis and the Jewish Tradition: an Ancient People Debating Its Future.* New Haven, CT: Yale University Press, 2000.

Hazony, Yoram. *Jewish State.* New York: Basic Books, 2000.

Hohenberg, John. *Israel at 50.* Syracuse, NY: Syracuse University Press, 1998.

Horovitz, David, ed. *Shalom, Friend: the Life and Legacy of Yitzhak Rabin.* New York: Newmarket Press, 1996.

Ilan, Amitzur. *The Origin of the Arab-Israeli Arms Race: Arms, Embargo, Military Power and Decision in the 1948 Palestine War.* Albany, NY: New York University Press, 1996.

Indyk, Martin. *Innocent Abroad: An Intimate History of American Peace Diplomacy in the Middle East.* New York: Simon & Schuster, 2009

Isserlin, Ben. *The Israelites.* New York: Thames & Hudson, 1998.

Karpin, Michael and Ina Friedman. *Murder in the Name of God: the Plot to Kill Yitzhak Rabin.* New York: Henry Holt & Company, 1998.

Karsh, Efraim, ed. *Between War and Peace: Dilemmas of Israeli Security.* Portland, OR: Frank Cass & Company, 1996.

Karsh, Efraim, ed. *From Rabin to Netanyahu: Israel's Troubled Agenda.* Portland, OR: Frank Cass & Company, 1997.

Khatchadourian, Haig. *The Quest for Peace between Israel and the Palestinians.* New York: Peter Lang Publishing, 2000.

HH Sheikh Rashid Bin Humaid al-Nuaimi, the deceased Ruler of Ajman

273

Kop, Yaakov and Robert E. Litan. *Sticking Together. The Israeli Experiment in Pluralism*. Washington D.C.: Brookings, 2002.

Lawless, Richard I. *The Arab-Israeli Conflict: an Encyclopedia*. Santa Barbara, CA: ABC-CLIO, 2001.

Lazin, Frederick A. and Gregory S. Mahler, eds. *Israel in the Nineties: Development and Conflict*. Gainesville, FL: University Press of Florida, 1996.

Levey, Zach. *Israel and the Western Powers, 1952–1960*. Chapel Hill, NC: University Press of North Carolina, 1997.

Levran, Aharon. *Israel after the Storm: Strategic Lessons from the Second Gulf War*. Portland, OR: Frank Cass & Company, 1997.

Levy, Yagil. *Trial and Error: Israel's Route from War to De-Escalation*. Albany, NY: State University of New York Press, 1997.

Linn, Ruth. *Conscience at War: the Israeli Soldier As a Moral Critic*. Albany, NY: State University of New York Press, 1996.

Litwin, Howard. *Uprooted in Old Age: Russian Jews and Their Social Networks in Israel*. Westport, CT: Greenwood Publishing Group, 1995.

Lomsky-Feder, Edna and Eyal Ben-Ari, eds. *The Military and Militarism in Israeli Society*. Albany, NY: State University of New York Press, 2000.

Makovsky, David. *Making Peace with the PLO: the Rabin Government's Road to the Oslo Accord*. Boulder, CO: Westview Press, 1995.

Metz, Helen Chapin, ed. *Israel: a Country Study*. Washington, DC: U.S. GPO, 3rd ed. 1990.

Netanyahu, Benjamin. *A Place among the Nations: Israel and the World*. New York: Bantam Books, 1993.

Peres, Shimon. *Battling for Peace: a Memoir*. New York: Random House, 1995.

Peres, Shimon. *For the Future of Israel*. Baltimore, MD: Johns Hopkins University Press, 1998.

Peretz, Don. *The Arab-Israeli Dispute*. New York: Facts on File, 1996.

Peri, Yoram, ed. *The Assassination of Yitzhak Rabin*. Stanford, CA: Stanford University Press, 2000.

Plessner, Yakir. *The Political Economy of Israel: from Ideology to Stagnation*. Albany, NY: State University of New York Press, 1993.

Quandt, William B. *Peace Process: American Diplomacy and the Arab-Israeli Conflict since 1967*. Washington D.C.: Brookings, 2005.

Rabin, Leah. *Rabin: Our Life, His Legacy*. New York: The Putnam Publishing Group, 1997.

Rabinovich, Itamar. *The Brink of Peace: the Israeli-Syrian Negotiations*. Princeton, NJ: Princeton University Press, 1998.

Reich, Bernard. *Historical Dictionary of Israel*. Lanham, MD: Scarecrow Press, 1992.

Reich, Bernard and David H. Goldberg. *Political Dictionary of Israel*. Lanham, MD: Scarecrow Press, 2000.

Reich, Bernard. *Securing the Covenant: United States-Israeli Relations after the Cold War*. Westport, CT: Greenwood Publishing Group, 1995.

Reinharz, Jehuda. *Chaim Weizmann: the Making of a Statesman*. New York: Oxford University Press, 1993.

Rouhana, Nadim W. *Palestinian Citizens in an Ethnic Jewish State: Identities in Conflict*. New Haven, CT: Yale University Press, 1997.

Rubin, Barry, et al., eds. *From War to Peace: Arab-Israeli Relations, 1973–1993*. New York: New York University Press, 1994.

Said, Edward W. *The End of the Peace Process; Oslo and After*. New York: Pantheon Books, 2000.

Sela, Avraham. *The Decline of the Arab-Israeli Conflict: Middle East Politics and the Quest for Regional Order*. Albany, NY: State University of New York Press, 1997.

Shafir, Gershon, ed. *New Israel*. New York: HarperCollins, 2000.

Sharkansky, Ira. *Policy Making in Israel: Routines for Simple Problems and Coping with the Complex*. Pittsburgh, PA: University of Pittsburgh Press, 1997.

Sheffer, Gabriel, ed. *U.S.-Israeli Relations at the Crossroads*. Portland, OR: Frank Cass & Company, 1997.

Shindler, Colin. *Israel, Likud, and the Zionist Dream: Power, Politics, and Ideology from Begin to Netanyahu*. New York: Saint Martin's Press, 1995.

Shlain, Avi. *The Iron Wall: Israel and the Arab World*. New York: W.W. Norton & Company, 2000.

Sternhell, Zeev. Translated by David Maisel. *The Founding Myths of Israel: Nationalism, Socialism and the Making of the Jewish State*. Princeton, NJ: Princeton University Press, 1998.

Thomas, Baylis. *The Dark Side of Zionism: The Quest for Security through Dominance*. Lanham, MD: Rowan & Littlefield, 2009

Troen, S. Ilan and Noah Lucas, eds. *Israel: the First Decade of Independence*. Albany, NY: State University of New York Press, 1995.

Van Creveld, Martin. *The Sword and the Olive: a Critical History of the Israeli Defense Force*. New York: Public Affairs, 1998.

Wheatcroft, Geoffrey. *The Controversy of Zion: Jewish Nationalism, the Jewish State, and the Unresolved Jewish Dilemma*. Reading, MA: Addison Wesley Longman, 1996.

Yiftachel, Oren, ed. *Ethnic Frontiers and Peripheries: Perspectives on Development and Inequality in Israel*. Boulder, CO: Westview Press, 1998.

Jordan

Brand, Laurie A. *Jordan's Inter-Arab Relations: the Political Economy of Alliance Making*. New York: Columbia University Press, 1995.

Fischbach, Michael R. *State, Society and Land in Jordan*. Boston, MA: Brill Academic Publishers, 2000.

Lukacs, Yehuda. *Israel, Jordan, and the Peace Process*. Syracuse, NY: Syracuse University Press, 1996.

Metz, Helen Chapin, ed. *Jordan: a Country Study*. Washington, DC: U.S. GPO, 4th ed. 1991.

Piro, Timothy J. *The Political Economy of Market Reform in Jordan*. Lanham, MD: Rowman & Littlefield, 1998.

Salibi, Kamal. *A Modern History of Jordan*. New York: Saint Martin's Press, 1998.

Satloff, Robert B. *From Abdullah to Hussein: Jordan in Transition*. New York: Oxford University Press, 1994.

Kuwait

Anscombe, Frederick F. *The Ottoman Gulf: the Creation of Kuwait, Saudi Arabia, and Qatar, 1870–1914*. New York: Columbia University Press, 1997.

Clements, Frank A. *Kuwait*. Santa Barbara, CA: ABC-CLIO, rev. ed. 1996.

Cordesman, Anthony H. *Kuwait: Recovery and Security after the Gulf War*. Boulder, CO: Westview Press, 1997.

Crystal, Jill. *Oil and Politics in the Gulf: Rulers and Merchants in Kuwait and Qatar*. New York: Cambridge University Press, 1995.

Longva, Anh Nga. *Walls Built in Sand: Migration, Exclusion and Society in Kuwait*. Boulder, CO: Westview Press, 1997.

Smith, Simon C. *Kuwait, 1950–1965: Britain, the Al-Sabah, and Oil*. New York: Oxford University Press, 1999.

Tetreault, Mary Ann. *Stories of Democracy: Politics and Society in contemporary Kuwait*. New York: Columbia University Press, 1999.

Lebanon

Abraham, A.J. *The Lebanon War*. Westport, CT: Greenwood Publishing Group, 1996.

Abukhalil, Asad. *Historical Dictionary of Lebanon*. Lanham, MD: Scarecrow Press, 1998.

Bleaney, C.H. *Lebanon*. Santa Barbara, CA: ABC-CLIO, 1992.

Colello, Thomas, ed. *Lebanon: a Country Study*. Washington, DC: U.S. GPO, 3rd ed. 1989.

El-Solh, Raghid. *Lebanon and Arabism*. New York: Saint Martin's Press, 1999.

Harris, William. *Faces of Lebanon: Sects, Wars and Global Expansion*. Princeton, NJ: Markus Wiener Publishers, 1997.

Kalawoun, Nasser M. *The Struggle for Lebanon: a Modern History of Lebanese-Egyptian Relations*. New York: I.B. Tauris & Company, 2000.

Maasri, Zeina. *Off the Wall–Political Posters of the Lebanese Civil War*. London: I.B. Tauris,

Malik, Habib C. *Between Damascus and Jerusalem: Lebanon and the Middle East Peace Process.* Washington, DC: The Washington Institute for Near East Policy, 2000.

Phares, Walid. *Lebanese Christian Nationalism: the Rise and Fall of an Ethnic Resistance.* Boulder, CO: Lynne Rienner Publishers, 1994.

Picard, Elizabeth. Translated by Franklin Philip. *Lebanon: a Shattered Country* New York: Holmes & Meier Publishers, 2001.

Ranstorp, Magnus. *Hizb'allah in Lebanon: the Politics of the Western Hostage Crisis.* New York: Saint Martin's Press, 1997.

Schulze, Kirsten E. *Intervention, Israeli Covert Diplomacy and the Maronites.* New York: Saint Martin's Press, 1997.

Shehadi, Nadim and Dana Haffar-Mills, eds. *Lebanon: a History of Conflict and Consensus.* New York: Saint Martin's Press, 1993.

Winslow, Charles. *Lebanon.* New York: Routledge, 1996.

Zamir, Meir. *Lebanon's Quest, 1929–1939.* New York: Saint Martin's Press, 1998.

Zisser, Eyal. *Lebanon: the Challenge of Independence.* New York: I.B. Tauris & Company, 2000.

The Maldives

Metz, Helen Chapin, ed. *Indian Ocean: Five Island Countries.* Washington, DC: U.S. GPO, 3rd ed. 1995.

Nepal

Cameron, Mary M. *On the Edge of the Auspicious: Gender and Caste in Nepal.* Champaign, IL: University of Illinois Press, 1998.

Gellner, David, et al., eds. *Nationalism and Ethnicity in a Hindu Kingdom: the Politics and Culture of Contemporary Nepal.* Newark, NJ: Gordon & Breach Publishing Group, 1997.

Savada, Andrea Matles, ed. *Nepal and Bhutan: Country Studies.* Washington, DC: U.S. GPO, 3rd ed. 1993.

Oman

El-Solh, Rahbih, ed. *Oman and the South-Eastern Shore of Arabia.* Milford, CT: LPC/InBook, 1997.

Joyce, Miriam. *The Sultanate of Oman a Twentieth Century History.* Westport, CT: Greenwood Publishing Group, 1995.

Kechichian, Joseph A. *Oman and the World: the Emergence of an Independent Foreign Policy.* Santa Monica, CA: The Rand Corporation, 1995.

Pakistan

Ahmed, Samania and David Cortright, eds. *Pakistan and the Bomb: Public Opinion and Nuclear Options.* Notre Dame, IN: University of Notre Dame Press, 1998.

Blood, Peter R., ed. *Pakistan: a Country Study.* Washington, DC: U.S. GPO, 6th ed. 1995.

Burki, Shahid Javed. *Historical Dictionary of Pakistan.* Lanham, MD: Scarecrow Press, 1999.

Fair, C. Christine. *The Madrassah Challenge: Militancy and Religious Education in Pakistan.* Washington: US Institute of Peace Press, 2008

Haqqani, Husain. *Pakistan: Between Mosque and Military.* Washington: Carnegie Endowment for International Peace, 2005

Harrison, Selig S., et al., eds. *India and Pakistan: the First Fifty Years.* New York: Cambridge University Press, 1998.

Husain, Ishrat. *Pakistan: the Economy of an Elitist State.* New York: Oxford University Press, 1999.

Hussain, Jane. *A History of the People of Pakistan: toward Independence.* New York: Oxford University Press, 1998.

Looney, Robert E. *The Pakistani Economy: Economic Growth and Structural Reform.* Westport, CT: Greenwood Publishing Group, 1997.

McGrath, Allen. *The Destruction of Pakistan's Democracy.* New York: Oxford University Press, 1999.

Raza, Rafi, ed. *Pakistan in Perspective, 1947–1997.* New York: Oxford University Press, 1998.

Raza, Rafi. *Zulfikar Ali Bhutto and Pakistan 1967–1977.* New York: Oxford University Press, 1997.

Rizvi, Hasan Askari. *Military, State and Society in Pakistan.* New York: Saint Martin's Press, 2000.

Samad, Yunas. *A Nation in Turmoil: Nationalism and Ethnicity in Pakistan, 1937–1958.* Thousand Oaks, CA: Sage Publications, 1995.

Sattar, Babar. *The Non-Proliferation Regime and Pakistan: the Comprehensive Test Ban Treaty as a Case Study.* New York: Oxford University Press, 2000.

Shafqat, Saeed. *Civil-Military Relations in Pakistan: from Zulfikar Ali Bhutto to Benazir Bhutto.* Westport, CT: Westview Press, 1997.

Shah, Mehtab A. *The Foreign Policy of Pakistan: Ethnic Impacts on Diplomacy, 1971–1994.* New York: Saint Martin's Press, 1997.

Siddiqa, Ayesha. *Military Inc.: Inside Pakistan's Military Economy.* London: Pluto Press, 2007.

Talbot, Ian. *Pakistan: a Modern History.* New York: Saint Martin's Press, 1999.

Wirsing, Robert G. *India, Pakistan and the Kashmir Dispute: on Regional Conflict and Its Resolution.* New York: Saint Martin's Press, 1994.

Zaidi, S. Akbar. *Issues in Pakistan's Economy.* New York: Oxford University Press, 2000.

Ziring, Lawrence. *Pakistan in the Twentieth Century: a Political History.* New York: Oxford University Press, 1998.

Palestine National Authority

Diwan, Ishac and Radwan A. Shaban. *Development under Adversity: the Palestinian Economy in Transition.* Washington, DC: The World Bank, 1999.

Klieman, Aharon. *Compromising Palestine: a Guide to Final Status Negotiations.* New York: Columbia University Press, 1999.

Mattar, Philip, ed. *Encyclopedia of the Palestinians.* New York: Facts on File, 2000.

Qatar

Anscombe, Frederick F. *The Ottoman Gulf: the Creation of Kuwait, Saudi Arabia, and Qatar, 1870–1914.* New York: Columbia University Press, 1997.

Reich, Bernard and Steven Dorr. *Qatar.* Westport, CT: Westview Press, 1996.

Saudi Arabia

Cordesman, Anthony H. *Saudi Arabia: Guarding the Desert Kingdom.* Westport, CT: Westview Press, 1997.

Fancy, Mamoun. *Saudi Arabia and the Politics of Dissent.* New York: Saint Martin's Press, 1999.

Hart, Parker T. *Saudi Arabia and the United Stated: Birth of a Security Partnership.* Bloomington, IN: Indiana University Press, 1998.

Kostiner, Joseph. *The Making of Saudi Arabia, 1916–1936: from Chieftaincy to Monarchical State.* New York: Oxford University Press, 1993.

Long, David E. *The Kingdom of Saudi Arabia.* Gainesville, FL: University Press of Florida, 1997.

Metz, Helen Chapin, ed. *Saudi Arabia: a Country Study.* Washington, DC: U.S. GPO, 5th ed. 1993.

Pampanini, Andrea H. *Cities from the Arabian Desert: the Building of Jubail and Yanbu in Saudi Arabia.* Westport, CT: Greenwood Publishing Group, 1997.

Peterson, J.E. *Historical Dictionary of Saudi Arabia.* Lanham, MD: Scarecrow Press, 1993.

Vassiliev, Alexei. *The History of Saudi Arabia.* New York: New York University Press, 2000.

Wilson, Peter W. and Douglas F. Graham. *Saudi Arabia: the Coming Storm.* Armonk, NY: M.E. Sharpe, 1994.

Yizraeli, Sarah. *The Remaking of Saudi Arabia: the Struggle between King Sa'ud and Crown Prince Faysal, 1953–1962.* Syracuse, NY: Syracuse University Press, 1998.

Sri Lanka

Athukorala, Prema-Chandra and Sarath Rajapatirana. *Liberalization and Industrial Transformation: Sri Lanka in International Perspective.* New York: Oxford University Press, 2000.

Bartholomeusz, Tessa J. and Chandra R. De Silva, eds. *Buddhist Fundamentalism and Minority Identities in Sri Lanka.* Albany, NY: State University Press of New York Press, 1998.

De Silva, K.M. *Regional Powers and Small State Security: India and Sri Lanka, 1977–1990.* Baltimore, MD: Johns Hopkins University Press, 1995.

Perera, Nihal. *Society and Space: Colonialism, Nationalism and Postcolonial Identity in Sri Lanka.* Boulder, CO: Westview Press, 1998.

Ross, Russell R. and Andrea Matles Savada, eds. *Sri Lanka: a Country Study.* Washington, DC: U.S. GPO, 2nd ed. 1990.

Rotberg, Robert I. *Creating Peace in Sri Lanka: Civil War and Reconciliation.* Washington, DC: Brookings Institution Press, 1999.

Samarasinghe, S.W. and Vidyamali Samarasinghe. *Historical Dictionary of Sri Lanka.* Lanham, MD: Scarecrow Press, 1997.

Wignaraja, Ganeshan. *Trade Liberalization in Sri Lanka: Exports, Technology and Industrial Policy.* New York: Saint Martin's Press, 1998.

Wilson, A. Jeyaratnam. *Sri Lankan Tamil Nationalism: Its Origins and Development in the Nineteenth and Twentieth Centuries.* Vancouver, BC: UBC Press, 1999.

Syria

Agha, Hussein J. and Ahmad S. Khalidi. *Syria and Iran: Rivalry and Co-Operation.* New York: Council on Foreign Relations, 1995.

Commins, David. *Historical Dictionary of Syria.* Lanham, MD: Scarecrow Press, 1996.

Gelvin, James L. *Divided Loyalties: Nationalism and Mass Politics in Syria at the Close of Empire.* Berkeley, CA: University of California Press, 1998.

Hinnebusch, Raymond. *The State and the Political Economy of Reform in Syria.* Boulder, CO: Lynne Rienner Publishers, 2008.

Kienle, Eberhard, ed. *Contemporary Syria: Liberalization between Cold War and Peace.* New York: Saint Martin's Press, 1997.

Lawson, Fred H. *Why Syria Goes to War: Thirty Years of Confrontation.* New York: Cornell University Press, 1996.

Perthes, Volker. *Political Economy of Syria under Asad.* New York: Saint Martin's Press, 1997.

Quilliam, Neil. *Syria and the New World Order.* Lowell, MA: Ithaca Press, 1999.

Rabinovich, Itamar. *The Brink of Peace: the Israel-Syrian Negotiations.* Princeton, NJ: Princeton University Press, 1998.

Saunders, Bonnie F. *The United States and Arab Nationalism: the Syrian Case.* Westport, CT: Greenwood Publishing Group, 1996.

Seale, Patrick. *Asad: The Struggle for the Middle East.* Berkeley, CA: University of California Press, 1988.

Turkey

Ahmad, Feroz. *The Making of Modern Turkey.* New York: Routledge, 1993.

Abramowitz, Morton, ed. *The United States and Turkey. Allies in Need.* Washington, D.C.: Brookings, 2003.

Altunisik, Meliha Benli and Ozlem Tur Kavli. *Turkey.* NY: Routledge, 2002.

Balim, Cigdem, et al., eds. *Turkey: Political, Social and Economic Challenges in the 1990s.* Boston, MA: Brill Academic Publishers, 1995.

Balkir, Canan and Allan M. Williams, eds. *Turkey and Europe.* New York: Saint Martin's Press, 1993.

Barkey, Henri J. and Graham E. Fuller. *Turkey's Kurdish Question.* Lanham, MD: Rowman & Littlefield, 1997.

Bugra, Ayse. *State and Business in Modern Turkey: a Comparative Study.* Albany, NY: State University of New York Press, 1994.

Dadrian, Vahakn N. *Warrant for Genocide: Key Elements of Turko-Armenian Conflict.* Piscataway, NJ: Transaction Publishers, 1998.

Davison, Andrew. *Secularism and Revivalism in Turkey: a Hermeneutic Reconsideration.* New Haven, CT: Yale University Press, 1998.

Fuller, Graham E. and Ian O. Fuller. *Turkey's New Geopolitics: from the Balkans to Western China.* Boulder, CO: Westview Press, 1993.

Fuller, Graham E. *Turkey as a Pivotal State in the Muslim World.* Washington: U.S. Institute for Peace Press, 2007.

Gunter, Michael M. *Kurds and Future of Turkey.* New York: Saint Martin's Press, 1997.

Heper, Metin, et al., eds. *Turkey and the West: Images of a New Political Culture.* New York: New York: Saint Martin's Press, 1993.

Howe, Marvine. *Turkey Today. A National Divided over Islam's Revival.* Boulder, CO: Westview, 2000.

Kahveci, Erol, et al., eds. *Work and Occupation in Modern Turkey.* Herndon, VA: Cassell Academic, 1996.

Kasaba, Resat and Sibel Bozdogan, eds. *Rethinking Modernity and National Identity in Turkey.* Seattle, WA: University of Washington Press, 1997.

Kedourie, Sylvia. *Seventy-Five Years of the Turkish Republic.* Portland, OR: Frank Cass & Company, 2000.

Kedourie, Sylvia, ed. *Turkey: Identity, Democracy, Politics.* Portland, OR: Frank Cass & Company, 1998.

Kramer, Heinz. *Changing Turkey: Challenges to Europe and the United States.* Washington, DC: Brookings Institution Press, 1999.

Larrabee, F. Stephen and Ian O. Lesser. *Turkish Foreign Policy in an Age of Uncertainty.* Santa Monica, CA: Rand, 2002.

Mango, Andrew. *Turkey: the Challenge of a New Role.* Westport, CT: Greenwood Publishing Group, 1994.

Mastny, Vojtech and Craig Nation, eds. *Turkey between East and West: New Challenges for a Rising Regional Power.* Boulder, CO: Westview Press, 1997.

McDonagh, Bernard. *Turkey.* New York: W.W. Norton & Company, 2000.

Muftuler-Bac, Meltem. *Turkey's Relations with a Changing Europe.* New York: Saint Martin's Press, 1997.

Olsen, Robert, ed. *The Kurdish Nationalist Movement and Its Impact on Turkey in the 1990's.* Lexington, KY: University Press of Kentucky, 1996.

Pitman, Paul M., III, ed. *Turkey: a Country Study.* Washington, DC: U.S. GPO, 4th ed. 1988.

Pope, Hugh and Nicole Pope. *Turkey Unveiled: a History of Modern Turkey.* New York: Overlook Press, 1998.

Rittenberg, Libby, ed. *The Political Economy of Turkey in the Post-Soviet Era: Going West and Looking East?* Westport, CT: Greenwood Publishing Group, 1998.

Togan, S. and V.N. Balasubramanyam, eds. *The Economy of Turkey since Liberalization.* New York: Saint Martin's Press, 1996.

Yilmaz, Bahri. *Challenges to Turkey: the New Role of Turkey in International Politics since the Dissolution of the Soviet Union.* New York: Saint Martin's Press, 1999.

Zürcher, Erik J. *Turkey: a Modern History.* London: I.B. Tauris, 1994.

United Arab Emirates

Al-Fahim, Mohammed. *From Rags to Riches: a Story of Abu Dhabi.* New York: Saint Martin's Press, 1998.

Camarapix Staff. *Spectrum Guide to the United Arab Emirates.* Northampton, MA: Interlink Publishing Group, 1998.

Clements, Frank A. *United Arab Emirates.* Santa Barbara, CA: ABC-CLIO, rev. ed. 1998.

Yemen

Al-Madhaqi, Ahmed Nomen. *Yemen and the U.S.A.: a Super-Power and a Small-State Relationship.* New York: Saint Martin's Press, 1996.

Auchterlonie, Paul. *Yemen.* Santa Barbara, CA: ABC-CLIO, rev. ed, 1998.

Burrowes, Robert D. *Historical Dictionary of Yemen.* Lanham, MD: Scarecrow Press, 1995.

Dresch, Paul. *Tribes, Government, and History in Yemen.* New York: Oxford University Press, 1994.